NEW TOPICS IN THEORETICAL COMPUTER SCIENCE

NEW TOPICS IN THEORETICAL COMPUTER SCIENCE

OLEG N. TERIKHOVSKY
AND
WILLIAM N. BURTON
EDITORS

Nova Science Publishers, Inc.
New York

For permission to use material from this book please contact us:
Telephone 631-231-7269; Fax 631-231-8175
Web Site: http://www.novapublishers.com

Library of Congress Cataloging-in-Publication Data

New topics in theoretical computer science / Oleg N. Terikhovsky and William N. Burton (editors).
p. cm.
ISBN 978-1-60456-100-5 (hardcover)
1. Computer science. 2. Machine theory. I. Terikhovsky, Oleg N. II. Burton, William N.
QA76.N482 2008
004--dc22

2007049416

Published by Nova Science Publishers, Inc. ✦ New York

CONTENTS

PREFACE

Theoretical computer science focuses on the more abstract, logical and mathematical aspects of computing, such as the theory of computation, analysis of algorithms and semantics of programming languages. This new book presents the latest research in the field from around the globe.

Chapter 1 – Contextual grammars were introduced by S. Marcus in 1969 with a deep linguistic motivation. In contrast to the standard rewriting grammars, these grammars generate languages by adjoining contexts in each sentencial form, according to a selector present in the string and the grammars have no distinction between terminal and non-terminal. In this chapter, the authors present a few results which are of interest to the domain of mildly context sensitive (MCS) formalisms. With this aim, they discuss two new classes of contextual grammars, namely *end-marked maximal depth-first* (*emdf*) and *inner end-marked maximal depth-first* (*iemdf*) contextual grammars and raise arguments that the grammars can be considered as generative models for natural languages. These variants are obtained by imposing special conditions in *selectors* and *contexts* of *maximal depth-first* grammars. The authors prove that the three basic *non-context-free constructions* in natural languages can be realized upon using these variants with regular selectors, and the *membership problem* for these families of languages is decidable in polynomial time. The family of languages generated by *iemdf* grammars with regular selectors contains semilinear languages only, but however, the family of languages generated by *emdf* grammars with regular selectors contains non-semilinear languages also. The authors also solve the semilinear issue for the family of languages generated by *maximal depth-first* (*mdf*), *maximal lengthwise depth-first* (*mldf*) and *maximal local* (*mloc*) contextual grammars. Consequently, it is shown that the family of languages generated by *iemdf* grammars possess the MCS formalism. Further, the authors show that any recursive enumerable language can be obtained from the languages generated by *emdf, mdf* and *mldf* grammars with regular selectors by taking appropriate morphisms, weak coding and left quotient.

Chapter 2 – Multialgebras are relational structures where selection of one argument as the "result" yields strong algebraic properties missing in the case of relations. However, such properties can be obtained only by choosing an appropriate definition of homomorphism and this question has been neglected or left implicit in most of the literature on power structures. The authors summarize their earlier results on the possible notions of compositional homomorphisms of multialgebras and investigate in detail one of them, the outer-tight homomorphisms which, unlike other alternatives, yield rich structural properties and interesting constructions. A series of classical algebraic properties is demonstrated for the resulting category and the notion of associated congruence -- bireachability -- is presented. It reflects the "observational" nature of multialgebras with the chosen homomorphisms in that it requires propagation of distinctions, the complement of the relation, dually to the traditional congruences and bisimulations, which require propagation of the relation.

The category is co-complete. Final objects have quite an interesting nature but, unfortunately, are not guaranteed to exist. To guarantee their existence, the category must be extended by admitting algebras over proper classes, in the same way as it has to be done for co-algebras involving power-set functor. The authors give an exact characterisation of the large objects as co-limits of small algebras or, equivalently, as algebras where each element is reachable from at most a set of other elements. Finally, a construction of products is given. A particular case gives a new construction of products for co-algebras over (bounded) power-set functor. The results (for the category of small algebras) extend to this category which is thus complete and co-complete. The category of small algebras may lack final objects and products, but possesses other limits and all co-limits. The authors characterize its subcategories, of κ-bounded multialgebras, which are complete and co-complete.

Examples and remarks illustrate relations to total and partial algebras, co-algebras, automata theory and topology.

Chapter 3 – Model transformation and refinement are playing a key role in Model Driven Development, or MDA. Although well-established standards for creating meta-models such as the Meta-Object Facility exist, there is currently no mature foundation for specifying transformation and refinement among models. Recently, the authors have developed a refinement calculus of object system rCOS which can support model translation and refinement. Mathematical characterization of object-oriented concepts is presented by defining observation oriented semantics of rCOS with a rich variety of features including subtypes, visibility, inheritance, type casting, dynamic binding and polymorphism.

rCOS is class-based and the refinement is about making correct changes to the structure, methods of classes and the main program. The logic of rCOS is a conservative extension of standard predicate logic. In their model, both commands and class declarations are identified as predicates whose alphabets include logic variables representing the initial and final values of program variables, as well as those variables representing the contextual information of classes and their links. A variable of a built-in primitive type, such as the type Int of integers, stores data of the corresponding type whereas a variable of an object type holds the identity or reference and the current type information of an object as its value. The authors define the traditional programming constructs, such as conditional, sequential composition and recursion, in exactly the same way as their counterparts in an imperative programming language without reference types. This makes the approach more accessible to users who are already familiar with the existing imperative languages. All the laws about imperative commands remain valid without the need of reproving. rCOS has been proven to provide formal support to software design and program re-factoring. All these features together show that rCOS can be used as a formal framework for the model based development. With rCOS, models can be constructed according to the object-orient design principles and use patterns as refinement laws.

As UML is now used as a standard modeling language, the authors reinforce the ability of UML in modeling software architecture by defining a generic model of component and software architecture, and integrate the model with UML class model and interaction model to unify software development process. In UML, software development is modeled in different views. With formal semantics, designer can keep consistency among these views. The authors demonstrate how to use the method to construct software and how to keep the consistency among different models.

Chapter 4 – Given a set $\mathcal{N}$ of phylogenetic networks, the maximum agreement phylogenetic subnetwork problem (MASN) asks for a subnetwork embedded in every $N_i \in \mathcal{N}$ with as many leaves as possible. MASN can be used to identify shared branching structure among phylogenetic networks or to measure their similarity. In this chapter, the authors prove that the general case of MASN is NP-hard already for two phylogenetic networks (in fact, even if one of the two input networks is a binary tree), but that the problem can be solved efficiently if each of the two input phylogenetic networks exhibits a nested structure. For this purpose, the authors introduce the concept of a nested phylogenetic network and study some of its underlying fundamental combinatorial properties. They first show that the total number of nodes $|V(N)|$ in any nested phylogenetic network N with n leaves and nesting depth d is $O(n\ (d+1))$. They then describe a simple algorithm for testing if a given phylogenetic network is nested, and if so, determining its nesting depth in $O(|V(N)| \cdot (d+1))$ time. Next, they present a polynomial-time algorithm for MASN for two nested phylogenetic networks N_1, N_2. Its running time is $O(|V(N_1)| \cdot |V(N_2)| \cdot (d_1+1) \cdot (d_2+1))$, where d_1 and d_2 denote the nesting depths of N_1 and N_2, respectively. In contrast, the previously fastest algorithm for this problem runs in $O(|V(N_1)| \cdot |V(N_2)| \cdot 2^{f1+f2})$ time, where $f_1 \geq d_1$ and $f_2 \geq d_2$. Finally, the authors prove that if the nodes are allowed to have outdegree greater than~\$2\$ then the problem becomes NP-hard even if restricted to two phylogenetic networks with nesting depth 1.

Chapter 5 – Hierarchical bit vectors represent sets of integers using a collection of bit vectors. At the top level, a single bit is set if the set is non-empty. The bits of this next level summarize ranges of the elements. In the case of a binary hierarchical bit vector the two bits of the next level summarize two ranges: the lower half and the upper half of the possible elements. At the lowest level each bit records the membership of a particular integer.

Hierarchical bit vectors find application in information retrieval, bioinformatics, non-averaging sets, and the conversion of *NFA*s to *DFA*s. Competing data structures for such applications include simple bit vectors and tree-based structures such as skip-lists. A comparison of hierarchical bit vectors with two other representations (simple bit vectors and binary search trees) is presented. The comparison includes both analytical and empirical analysis of the hierarchical bit vectors.

The analytical results show that as the size of the set used increases, hierarchical bit vectors enjoy an advantage over tree-based structures and that as the sets used become sparser, hierarchical bit vectors perform better than standard bit vectors. The empirical results confirm that hierarchical bit vectors sit in between the other two. The empirical investigation also highlights the impact that the processor cache has on the break-even points.

Chapter 6 – In this chapter, the authors propose a methodology based on genetic programming to automatically generate data-flow based specifications for hardware designs of combinational digital circuits. The authors aim at allowing automatic generation of balanced hardware specifications for a given input/output behaviour. It minimises space while maintaining reasonable response time. The authors show that the evolved designs are efficient and creative. They do so comparing the obtained circuits of some benchmarks against those that were produced by human designers as well as to other evolutionary ones.

To emphasize the applicability of the methodology to real-world problems, the authors use genetic programming as an alternative methodology to automatically generate secure and minimal hardware designs of public-key cryptosystems such as RSA encryption system. They evolve optimal hardware circuits for modular exponentiation, which a cornerstone operation in almost every cryptographic system. The evolved circuits minimize both space (i.e. required gate number) and time (i.e. encryption and decryption time). The evolved designs are shielded against side-channel leakage and hence secure. The structure of the cryptographic circuit is random and so the private key cannot be deduced using known attacks. The authors compare their results against existing well-known designs, which were produced by human designers based on the binary method.

Chapter 7 – This chapter analyzes the performance of directional collision avoidance schemes, in which antenna systems are used to direct the transmission and reception of control and data packets in channel access protocols based on four-way handshakes to try to avoid collisions. The first analytical model to consider directional reception and the possible difference in gain between omni-directional and directional transmissions is presented. Analytical results show that, when the directional collision avoidance scheme in which all transmissions are directional is augmented with directional receiving, one-hop throughput does not decrease due to the increased spatial reuse, even when the number of competing nodes within a region increases. It is also shown that, as expected, the performance of directional collision avoidance schemes degrades when directional transmissions have much higher gain than omni-directional transmissions. However, this degradation is relatively small. Simulations of the IEEE 802.11 protocol and its directional variants validate the results predicted in the analysis. The simulation results also show that the presence of broadcast traffic does not degrade the performance of the all-directional collision avoidance scheme significantly, even for relatively large percentages of broadcast traffic. The performance results of this study indicate that the most attractive collision avoidance approach consists of using directional transmissions of control and data packets, together with the directional reception of packets whenever a node is expecting a particular packet. Given the high tolerance to broadcast traffic of directional collision avoidance schemes, it is argued that the periodic transmission of beacons omni-directionally suffices to provide such schemes with the relative location of neighbouring nodes.

Chapter 8 – Radio networks are widely used today. People access voice and data services via mobile phones, Bluetooth technology replaces unhandy cables by wireless links, and wireless networking is possible via IEEE 802.11 compatible network equipment. Nodes in such networks exchange their data packets usually with fixed base stations that connect them with a wired backbone. However, in applications such as search and rescue missions or environmental monitoring, no explicit communication infrastructure may be available. In this case, the wireless hosts have to organize in a so-called wireless ad hoc network. As long as all of the hosts are within transmission range of each other, the problem of exchanging information in such a network basically boils down to designing suitable medium access control protocols, but if not all hosts can directly communicate with each other, suitable routing algorithms are also needed. Designing routing algorithms for wireless ad hoc networks is an extremely challenging task and still research in progress. In this chapter, the authors mostly focus on the simpler question of how to maintain an overlay network of wireless links between the hosts so that, as long as this is in principle possible,

1. every node is reachable from every other node, i.e. the graph formed by the links is connected,
2. or better, for every pair of nodes (v,w) there is a route from v to w with a close to minimum possible hop distance or energy consumption,
3. and ideally, good routes to any destination can be discovered locally (i.e., without involving a global search operation), as long as the position of the destination is known.

The graph formed by the wireless links should also have a low degree to ensure a low maintenance cost, it should allow to find routes for the messages that have a low congestion, and it should be easy to update in case of arrivals or departures of nodes or changes in their positions. This chapter will present various local-control algorithms for reaching these goals.

Chapter 9 – Bluetooth is a promising technology which enables the design of low-power, small-sized, low-cost radios that can be embedded in existing portable devices. Due to the limitation of a single channel capacity, scatternet techniques are proposed to increase the communication bandwidth. However, since a bridge may be shared by several piconets, simultaneously polling the bridge may result in bridge conflicts, and then seriously degrade the system performance. Thus, the potential of the scatternet may not be realized without a good scatternet-wide scheduling algorithm. In this chapter, the authors propose a dynamic scatternet-wide scheduling (DSS) scheme to address the problems associated with scatternet-wide traffic scheduling. The proposed scheme is based on a switch-table concept to avoid bridge conflicts. Further, the switch-table can be dynamically adjusted based on the traffic load to improve the system performance. Simulation results demonstrate that the DSS algorithm can significantly reduce the packet dropping rate and the transmission delay.

Chapter 10 – The motivation of this text is to provide a set of research work that discusses the above mentioned fundamental issues in the context of mobile ad hoc networks. The authors have been trying to include chapters that address those issues by way of mathematical analysis because they can give us the insights into the system internals and reveal tradeoffs. At the same time, we're interested in providing systematic way of performance analysis by asking questions like: What to measure, how to design experiments, how to model the network, traffic and mobility and how to summarize the results? The authors hope that the collection of research works presented in this chapter provide a groundwork for future research in the area of ad hoc networking. Before presenting summary in Section 4, the authors overview IEEE 802.11 MAC and ad hoc routing algorithms in Sections 2 and 3, respectively, as they are basic building blocks that the text tries to measure up to or improve upon.

Chapter 11 – Ad hoc networks are dynamically created and maintained by the individual nodes comprising the networks. They do not require a pre-existing architecture for communication and do not rely on any type of wired infrastructure. Thus, ad hoc networks have great flexibility and low cost of operation, which make them play an important role in future life. In recent years, many research works have been done to design and develop ad hoc networks, such as mobility modeling, MAC and routing protocol design and analysis, etc. The research works on mobility is one of the most important research works in ad hoc networks. In this chapter, the authors summarize recent research works of mobility in ad hoc networks. Firstly, they summarize the mobility models used in ad hoc networks. Secondly, the detailed impact of mobility on the link and path BER, link and path stabilities, network capacity,

MAC performance, and routing performance are provided. These summaries are very useful for researchers in ad hoc networks for reference.

In: New Topics in Theoretical Computer Science
Editor: Oleg N. Terikhovsky et al, pp. 1-25
ISBN 978-1-60456-100-5

Chapter 1

NEW CLASSES OF CONTEXTUAL GRAMMARS FOR MILDLY CONTEXT SENSITIVE FORMALISMS*

Lakshmanan Kuppusamy†
School of Computing Sciences
VIT University
Vellore - 632 014, India

Abstract

Contextual grammars were introduced by S. Marcus in 1969 with a deep linguistic motivation. In contrast to the standard rewriting grammars, these grammars generate languages by adjoining contexts in each sentencial form, according to a selector present in the string and the grammars have no distinction between terminal and non-terminal. In this chapter, we present a few results which are of interest to the domain of mildly context sensitive (MCS) formalisms. With this aim, we discuss two new classes of contextual grammars, namely *end-marked maximal depth-first* ($emdf$) and *inner end-marked maximal depth-first* ($iemdf$) contextual grammars and raise arguments that the grammars can be considered as generative models for natural languages. These variants are obtained by imposing special conditions in *selectors* and *contexts* of *maximal depth-first* grammars. We prove that the three basic *non-context-free constructions* in natural languages can be realized upon using these variants with regular selectors, and the *membership problem* for these families of languages is decidable in polynomial time. The family of languages generated by $iemdf$ grammars with regular selectors contains semilinear languages only, but however, the family of languages generated by $emdf$ grammars with regular selectors contains non-semilinear languages also. We also solve the semilinear issue for the family of languages generated by maximal depth-first (mdf), *maximal lengthwise depth-first* ($mldf$) and *maximal local* ($mloc$) contextual grammars. Consequently, we see that the family of languages generated by $iemdf$ grammars possess the MCS formalism. Further, we show that any recursive enumerable language can be obtained from the languages generated by $emdf, mdf$ and $mldf$ grammars with regular selectors by taking appropriate morphisms, weak coding and left quotient.

---

*This chapter is the extended and revised version of the paper that appeared in the proceedings of *Development in Language Theory 2006* (DLT'06), Lecture Notes in Computer Science, 4036, 339–350, 2006.

†E-mail address: klachu@gmail.com

Keywords: contextual grammars, mildly context sensitive formalisms, non-context-free languages, membership problem, semilinearity, recursive enumerable languages.

1. Introduction

After a long debate started in the sixties, linguists seem to finally agree that natural languages are not context-free and probably most natural languages contain non-context-free constructions [1], [4]. Similar non-context-free features were discovered in programming languages [6] as well as in many other areas where formal grammars were used as a modeling tool. Thus, the need of a class of grammars extending beyond the family of context-free languages is apparent. The next higher class family of languages in Chomsky hierarchy is context-sensitive, but they are considered to be very powerful for modeling natural languages as they contain languages which have no connection with natural languages. Besides, the membership problem for these family is too tough to handle.

In these circumstances, one natural idea is to consider grammars based on context-free rules used in a non-context-free manner. The goal is to generate a strict super family of the context-free languages but preserving as many context-free properties (like membership, decidability, semilinearity) as possible. The above idea of keeping the generative power under the control has led to the concept of *regulated rewriting* in formal languages and *mildly context-sensitive* (MCS) family of languages and formalisms [10] in natural language processing. The properties that characterize such MCS families are

1. The class should contain the following three basic non-context-free constructions:
   - *multiple agreements:* $L_1 = \{a^n b^n c^n | n \geq 1\}$,
   - *crossed dependencies:* $L_2 = \{a^n b^m c^n d^m | n, m \geq 1\}$, and
   - *marked duplication:* $L_3 = \{wcw | w \in \{a, b\}^*\}$.
2. All the languages are *parsable in polynomial time*.
3. The class contains *semilinear* languages only.

Sometimes the third property is considered to be strong and is replaced by the following weaker property.

$3'$. All the languages in the class have the *bounded growth property*. That is, for any infinite languages L, there is a constant k_L such that, for any $n \geq 1$, if L contains words of length n, then it also contains words of some length between $n+1$ and $n+k_L$. In other words, there should not be arbitrarily large gap between two consecutive words present in the language.

One of the important problems in the area of formal language theory and natural language processing is to obtain certain classes of languages that provide an appropriate description for natural languages. In fact, the classes of languages searched for should have the above said MCS property. These classes of languages are considered to be a good model for the syntactical description of natural languages [10], [18]. One such example is Tree Adjoining Grammar (TAG) [11]. It was shown that the class of languages generated by TAG has the MCS formalism. We make a clear note here that so far no unanimously agreed definition for mildly context sensitive formalism is available, but we stick to the above specified conditions for mildly context sensitive formalism.

Contextual grammars were introduced as "intrinsic grammars", without auxiliary symbols, based only on the fundamental linguistic operation of inserting words (of the type (u, v)) in given phrases, according to certain contextual dependencies [14]. More precisely, contextual grammars produce languages starting from a finite set of *axioms* and adjoining *contexts*, iteratively, according to the *selector* present in the current sentential form. As introduced in [15], if adjoining the contexts is done at the ends of the strings, the grammar is called *external*. *Internal* contextual grammars were introduced by Păun and Nguyen in [23], where the contexts are adjoined to the selector strings appearing as substrings of the derived string. Later on, many variants of contextual grammars were introduced. For further details on variants of contextual grammars, we refer to the survey article by Păun [21].

Even though contextual grammars were introduced to give an appropriate model description for natural languages, the basic class, internal contextual languages itself failed to contain non-context-free constructions and also they contain non-semilinear languages [5], [7]. Further, the membership problem for the above families of languages still remains open [9], or is solvable only with exponential time [3].

In the last decade or so, some attempts have been made to introduce some variants of contextual grammars by restricting the selector chosen in the derivation to obtain certain specific classes of contextual languages. The first such main variant was *depth-first* contextual grammars [19]. In this mode, at each derivation step, the selector for the next derivation contains one of the contexts u or v, which was adjoined in the previous derivation. *Length-wise depth-first* grammars, a variant of depth-first contextual grammars were introduced in [12], in which, at each derivation step, the selector for the next derivation contains one of the contexts u or v whichever is of maximal length. Since in these variants, the current selector contains the previous adjoined context, they seem to be promising for back-tracking which may be helpful for solving the membership problem. But, however, these grammars were failed to generate the multiple dependency language $\{a^n b^n c^n \mid n \geq 1\}$ itself. So, further new classes of grammars were introduced, for instance, *global maximal* and *local maximal* [16]. In these modes, at each derivation step, a selector having maximal length than the other (either with respect to all selectors or with respect to the local selector) is chosen for the next derivation. Though these variants generate non-context-free languages, they still allow non-semilinear languages [17], [18]. Besides, in [3], it was proved that these maximal and internal contextual grammars can be transformed into equivalent *dynamic range concatenation grammars* [2]), can thus be parsed with exponential time complexity.

In [8], Ilie considered a new variant called *local* contextual grammars, in which, at each derivation, the contexts for the further derivations are adjoined inside or nearer to the contexts adjoined in the previous derivation. When the maximal restriction is included with this variant, the grammar is said to be *maximal local*. Ilie showed that the languages generated by maximal local grammars with regular selectors contain basic non-context-free languages and the membership problem for the family of these languages was solvable in polynomial time. But the question of semilinearity was left open for these languages and it was conjectured that they contain semilinear languages only, thus if the conjecture is proved affirmatively, we can say that the class of grammars are of MCS formalism.

In [13], a variant motivated by local (and so to maximal local) contextual grammars, called *absorbing right context grammars* (denoted by arc) was introduced in order to solve the semilinear problem for the restricted version of maximal local variant. In this arc mode, every time, the selector absorbs the first half of the right context v (which we call as v') adjoined in the previous derivation, where $v = v'v''$ and $|v'| = \lceil \frac{|v|}{2} \rceil$, $|v''| = \lfloor \frac{|v|}{2} \rfloor$. The class of languages generated by arc grammars with regular selectors was shown to possess all the properties that needed for MCS formalism and thus this is the first family in internal contextual languages proved to have the MCS formalism. Also, in [13], two more new variants of internal contextual grammars, namely *maximal depth-first* grammars (denoted by mdf), and *maximal lengthwise depth-first* grammars (denoted by $mldf$) were introduced, by combining the maximal, depth-first modes and maximal, lengthwise depth-first modes respectively. Like maximal grammars, the family of languages generated by these variants contain non-context-free languages, but the membership and semilinear problems were left open for these languages.

In this chapter, we continue the work of the last mentioned two papers [8], [13], in the sense that here we attempt to solve the problems which were left unsolved for the variants maximal local, maximal depth-first and maximal lengthwise depth-first. More specifically, for maximal local languages, we solve the semilinear problem in an affirmative way that the grammars generate semilinear languages only, but for maximal depth-first and maximal lengthwise depth-first contextual languages, we show that non-semilinear languages exist for them. Though, we are still unable to solve the membership problem for the languages generated by mdf and $mldf$ grammars, when further conditions are added to maximal depth-first grammars it is found that the membership problem is solvable in polynomial time, but at the same time, the capability of the generating non-context-free languages is also maintained. In the restricted versions, we impose the following *end-marked* condition to maximal depth-first grammars. Whenever, some contexts u and v are introduced in a derivation, the selector for the next derivation should either begin or end with one of the contexts u or v, and the context (u or v) which begins or ends with the selector for the next derivation is specified while defining the grammar itself. We call these variants as *end-marked maximal depth-first* and *inner end-marked maximal depth-first* contextual grammars. We analyze the new classes of grammars with respect to the properties of mildly context sensitive languages. We prove that, the class of languages generated by inner end-marked maximal depth-first grammars satisfies all the properties needed for MCS formalism and thus they may be treated as one of the MCS formalisms. Besides analyzing the properties of MCS formalism for the above mentioned variants, we also analyze the generative power of the new variants, especially, we provide an interesting characterizations of recursive enumerable languages by means of the mdf, $mldf$ and $emdf$ grammars with regular selectors using the operations of morphism, weak coding and left quotient. The interest comes from the fact that the respective grammars do not look powerful from themselves.

This chapter is organized as follows. Section 2 deals with preliminaries in formal language theory and contextual grammars; Section 3 describes the definition and functionality of the variants introduced in this chapter; Section 4 analyzes the mildly context sensitiveness property for the introduced variants and it contains three subsections - the first one deals with the generation of basic non-context-free languages with $emdf$ and $iemdf$ grammars, the second one discusses the membership problem for the introduced variants, and the third subsection deals with semilinear property for the variants discussed in this chapter; Section 5 offers the representation of recursive enumerable languages in terms of *mdf*, *mldf*, and *emdf* grammars; and Section 6 concludes the chapter with some possible future work.

2. Preliminaries

In this section, we introduce some formal language theory notions and notations which are used in the chapter. A finite non-empty set V is called an *alphabet*. We denote by V^* the free monoid generated by V, by λ its identity or the *empty string*, and by V^+ the set $V^* - \{\lambda\}$. The elements of V^* are called *words*. For any word $x \in V^*$, we denote by $|x|$ the *length of* x. $|x|_a$ is the number of occurrences of the symbol a in the word x. For a word $x \in V^*$, we denote by $Sub(x)$, $Pref(x)$, $Suf(x)$, the set of *subwords, prefixes*, and *suffixes* of x, respectively. The families of *finite* and *regular* languages are denoted by FIN, REG, respectively.

Assume that $V = \{a_1, \ldots, a_k\}$. The *Parikh mapping* of V is given by $\Psi : V^* \longrightarrow \mathbb{N}^k$,

$$\Psi(w) = (|w|_{a_1}, \ldots, |w|_{a_k}).$$

If L is a language, then its *Parikh set* is defined by $\Psi(L) = \{\Psi(w) \mid w \in L\}$. Two languages L_1 and L_2 are said to be *letter equivalent* iff $\Psi(L_1) = \Psi(L_2)$. A *linear* set is a set $M \subseteq \mathbb{N}^k$ such that

$$M = \{v_0 + \sum_{i=1}^{m} v_i x_i \mid x_i \in \mathbb{N}\},$$

for some $v_0, v_1, \ldots, v_m$ in $\mathbb{N}^k$. A *semilinear set* is a finite union of linear sets and a *semilinear language* is a language L such that $\Psi(L)$ is a semilinear set. We have a result from [25] that context-free languages are semilinear.

Consider now two alphabet sets V and U, and a mapping $h : V \longrightarrow 2^{U^*}$, which is extended to V^* by $h(\lambda) = \{\lambda\} = \lambda$, $h(xy) = h(x)h(y)$, $x, y \in V^*$. If $card(h(a)) = 1$ for each $a \in V$, then h is a *morphism* and we write $h(a) = x$ instead of $h(a) = \{x\}$. A morphism $h : V^* \longrightarrow U^*$ such that $|h(a)| \leq 1$, for all $a \in V$ is called a *weak coding*. If $h : V^* \longrightarrow U^*$ is a morphism, then the mapping $h^{-1} : U^* \longrightarrow 2^{V^*}$ defined by $h^{-1}(x) = \{y \in V^* \mid h(y) = x\}$, $x \in U^*$, is called the *inverse morphism* associated to h.

The left quotient of a language L_1 with respect to a language L_2 is defined as

$$L_2 \backslash L_1 = \{x \mid yx \in L_1,\ y \in L_2\}.$$

For more details on formal language theory, we refer to [24], [25].

Now we shall present some basic definitions of contextual grammars. An *internal contextual grammar* is a construct

$$G = (V, A, (S_1, C_1), ..., (S_m, C_m)),\ m \geq 1,\ \text{where}$$

- V is an alphabet,
- $A \subseteq V^*$ is a finite set called the set of *axioms*,

- $S_i \subseteq V^*$, $1 \leq i \leq m$, are the sets of *selectors*,
- $C_i \subseteq V^* \times V^*$, C_i finite, $1 \leq i \leq m$, are the sets of *contexts*.

The *modular presentation* [22] of a contextual grammar is given as $G = (V, A, P)$ where V, A are as defined above and P is the finite set of selector-context rules of the form $(S_1, C_1), \ldots, (S_m, C_m)$. The usual derivation in the *internal mode* is defined as

$$x \Longrightarrow_{in} y \text{ iff } x = x_1 x_2 x_3,\ y = x_1 u x_2 v x_3,\ \text{for } x_1, x_2, x_3 \in V^*,$$
$$x_2 \in S_i, (u, v) \in C_i,\ \text{for some } 1 \leq i \leq m.$$

Given a contextual grammar G, the derivation δ is given by

$$\begin{aligned} \delta &= w_1 \Longrightarrow_{in} w_2 \Longrightarrow_{in} \cdots \Longrightarrow_{in} w_n = z,\ n \geq 1,\ \text{such that} \\ w_1 &\in A, \\ w_j &= x_{1,j} x_{2,j} x_{3,j},\ x_{1,j}, x_{2,j}, x_{3,j} \in V^*, \\ w_{j+1} &= x_{1,j} u_j x_{2,j} v_j x_{3,j},\ x_{2,j} \in S_j,\ (S_j, (u_j, v_j)) \in P,\ 1 \leq j \leq n-1, \end{aligned}$$

where each (w_j, w_{j+1}) defines a *derivation step*.

Depth-first contextual grammars were introduced in [19]. In depth-first contextual grammars, at each derivation step (except the first one), at least one of the words of the context u or v introduced in the previous derivation step must be a subword of the currently used selector. The restricted version of depth-first contextual grammars called *lengthwise depth-first* contextual grammars were introduced in [12], where at each derivation step (except the first one), the selector must contain the context u or v (introduced in the previous derivation step) whichever is of maximal length. When the lengths of u and v are of equal length, the selector is chosen non-deterministically which contains u or v. Next, we define *local maximal* grammars [16] which we refer simply as *maximal* grammars throughout this chapter since we are not considering the *global maximal* here and also to avoid the confusion between the terms local maximal and *maximal local*, which is another variant of contextual grammars, introduced shortly in the following paragraphs.

Consider a contextual grammar $G = (V, A, (S_1, C_1), \ldots, (S_m, C_m))$. We define the *maximal use of selectors* in the following way.

$$\begin{aligned} x \Longrightarrow_m y \ \text{iff}\ & x = x_1 x_2 x_3,\ y = x_1 u x_2 v x_3, \\ & \text{for } x_2 \in S_i,\ (u_i, v_i) \in C_i,\ 1 \leq i \leq m, \\ & \text{and there are } \mathbf{no}\ x_1', x_2', x_3' \in V^*,\ \text{such that} \\ & x = x_1' x_2' x_3',\ x_2' \in S_i,\ \text{and } x_2' \text{ contains } x_2 \text{ (i.e. } |x_2'| > |x_2|). \end{aligned}$$

We say that $\Longrightarrow_m$ is a derivation in the *maximal* mode (ie., no strict superword of the *selector* can be used by the same production). Such grammars are called *maximal* contextual grammars.

Now, we define maximal depth-first grammars. Given a contextual grammar G as above, a *maximal depth-first derivation* (denoted by *mdf*) in G is a derivation

$$w_1 \Longrightarrow_{mdf} w_2 \Longrightarrow_{mdf} \cdots \Longrightarrow_{mdf} w_n,\ n \geq 1,\ \text{where}$$

(i) $w_1 \in A,\ w_1 \Longrightarrow w_2$ in the maximal way,

(ii) For each $i = 2, 3, \ldots, n-1$, if $w_{i-1} = z_1 z_2 z_3,\ w_i = z_1 u z_2 v z_3$ ((u, v) is the context adjoined to w_{i-1} in order to get w_i), then $w_i = x_1 x_2 x_3,\ w_{i+1} = x_1 s x_2 t x_3$, such that $x_2 \in S_j,\ (s, t) \in C_j$, for some $j,\ 1 \leq j \leq m$, and x_2 contains one of the contexts u or v as a substring (satisfying the depth-first condition). That is, at every derivation, the selector $x_2 \in S_j$ contains one of the contexts u or v which was adjoined in the previous derivation

(iii) For each $i = 2, 3, \ldots, n-1$, if $w_i \Longrightarrow_{df} w_{i+1}$ then there will be no other derivation in G with $w_i \Longrightarrow_{df} w'_{i+1}$ such that $w_i = x'_1 x'_2 x'_3,\ x'_2 \in S_j$ and $|x'_2| > |x_2|$ where $x_2 \in S_j$ (satisfying the maximal condition). That is, at every derivation, w_i should have no other subword x'_2 with $x'_2 \in S_j$ of greater length than $x_2 \in S_j$.

Lengthwise depth-first grammars, are the restricted versions of depth-first grammars, introduced in [12], where at each derivation, the selector for the next derivation must contain the context u or v (introduced in the previous derivation) whichever is of maximal length. When the lengths of u and v are equal, the selector is chosen non-deterministically (which contains u or v). In a similar way like maximal depth-first grammars, we can define *maximal lengthwise depth-first* grammars (denoted by $mldf$), where, at each derivation, the selector contains one of the contexts u or v whichever is of maximum length and the selector is of maximal.

The next variant we define is local contextual grammars. Given a contextual grammar G, we define the *local* mode in the following way. For $z \in A,\ z \Longrightarrow_{in} x$ such that $z = z_1 z_2 z_3,\ x = z_1 u z_2 v z_3,\ z_2 \in S_k, (u, v) \in C_k$, for $z_1, z_2, z_3 \in V^*,\ 1 \leq k \leq m$, then $x \Longrightarrow_{loc} y$ is called local with respect to $z \Longrightarrow x$, iff we have $u = u'u'',\ v = v'v'',\ u', u'', v', v'' \in V^*,\ y = z_1 u' s u'' z_2 v' t v'' z_3$ for $u'' z_2 v' \in S_j,\ (s, t) \in C_j, 1 \leq j \leq m$. When the maximal restriction is included with this local variant, the grammar is said to be *maximal local* (denoted by $mloc$).

The language generated by a grammar G in the mode β, $\beta \in \{in, mdf, mldf, loc, mloc\}$ is given by $L_\beta(G) = \{w \in V^* \mid x \Longrightarrow^*_\beta w,\ x \in A\}$, where $\Longrightarrow^*_\beta$ is the reflexive transitive closure of the relation $\Longrightarrow_\beta$. If all the sets of selectors $S_1, \ldots, S_m$ are in a family F of languages, then we say that the grammar G is with F selection (or F selectors). As usual, the family of languages $L_\beta(G)$, for G working in $\beta \in \{in, mdf, mldf, loc, mloc\}$ mode with F selection is given as $ICC(F), ICC_{mdf}(F), ICC_{mldf}(F), ICC_{loc}(F)$, and $ICC_{mloc}(F)$, respectively. For more technical details and for formal definition of basic classes of contextual grammars, we refer to the monograph on contextual grammars by Păun [22].

3. End-marked Maximal Depth-first Contextual Grammars

We start this section by introducing two new classes of contextual grammars, which are obtained by imposing certain conditions to maximal depth-first grammars. We add the end-marked condition as the selector for the next derivation should either begin or end with one of the contexts introduced in the previous derivation. We name this variant as end-marked maximal depth-first contextual grammars. The second variant is obtained by adding one more extra condition to the end-marked maximal depth-first grammars that the selector for the next derivation should be inside the contexts introduced in the previous derivation. We shall now introduce the new classes of grammars formally.

An *end-marked maximal depth-first* contextual grammars is a construct $G = (V, A, (S_1, C_1), \ldots, (S_m, C_m)), m \geq 1$, where $V, A, S_1, \ldots S_m$, are as mentioned in the definition of internal contextual grammar and $C_j \subseteq (V^+_{\{L,R\}} \times V^*) \cup (V^* \times V^+_{\{L,R\}})$, C_j finite, $1 \leq j \leq m$, are the set of contexts. The elements of C_j's are of the form $(u_L, v), (u_R, v), (u, v_L)$, and (u, v_R), $u, v \in V^*$. The suffix L (for left) and R (for right) represent the end marker (left end or right end) for the selector of the next derivation. u_L (or v_L) indicates the selector for the next derivation should start with u (or v). In other words, u (or v) is the left end of the selector for the next derivation. Similarly, u_R (or v_R) indicates the selector for the next derivation should end with the context u (or v). In other words, u (or v) is the right end of the selector for the next derivation. Given such a grammar G, an end-marked maximal depth-first derivation (denoted by *emdf*) in G is a derivation $w_1 \Longrightarrow_{emdf} w_2 \Longrightarrow_{emdf} \cdots \Longrightarrow_{emdf} w_n$, $n \geq 1$, where

- $w_1 \in A$, $w_1 \Longrightarrow w_2$ in the maximal way,
- For each $i = 2, 3, \ldots, n-1$, if $w_{i-1} = z_1 z_2 z_3$, $w_i = z_1 u z_2 v z_3$, such that $z_2 \in S_k$, $1 \leq k \leq m$, then $w_i = x_1 x_2 x_3$, $w_{i+1} = x_1 s x_2 t x_3$, such that $x_2 \in S_j$, $1 \leq j \leq m$, and x_2 will be of one of the following four cases:

  (i) $x_2 = u z_2'$, if $(u_L, v) \in C_k$, with $z_2' \in V^*$ is of maximal (i.e., there exists no $z_2'' \in V^*$, such that $u z_2'' \in S_j$, with $|z_2''| > |z_2'|$).

  (ii) $x_2 = z_1' u$, if $(u_R, v) \in C_k$, with $z_1' \in V^*$ is of maximal (i.e., there exists no $z_1'' \in V^*$, such that $z_1'' u \in S_j$, with $|z_1''| > |z_1'|$).

  (iii) $x_2 = z_2' v$, if $(u, v_R) \in C_k$, with $z_2' \in V^*$ is of maximal (i.e., there exists no $z_2'' \in V^*$, such that $z_2'' v \in S_j$, with $|z_2''| > |z_2'|$).

  (iv) $x_2 = v z_3'$, if $(u, v_L) \in C_k$, with $z_3' \in V^*$ is of maximal (i.e., there exists no $z_3'' \in V^*$, such that $v z_3'' \in S_j$, with $|z_2''| > |z_2'|$).

Now, we introduce the second variant which is a restricted version of the above introduced grammar. Given a *emdf* grammar G, we can define the *inner end-marked maximal depth-first grammar* (denoted by *iemdf*) by imposing the following changes in the grammar and in the derivations:

- $C_j \subseteq (V_L^* \times V^*) \cup (V^* \times V_R^*)$.
- As the elements of C_j's are of the form (u_L, v) and (u, v_R), the cases (ii) and (iv) discussed above will become void and only the cases (i) and (iii) will be valid. That is, the next selector should neither end with the left context u nor should start with the right context v, where u and v are adjoined in the previous derivation.
- The selector for the next derivation should be strictly inside the subword that starts with u and ends with v, where u and v are the contexts adjoined in the previous derivation. More precisely, if u and v are the contexts adjoined to a selector, say z_2, then the next selector, say x_2, will be a strict subword of $u z_2 v$ and x_2 should either begin with u or end with v in order to satisfy the end-marked condition.

The language generated by a grammar G in the mode $\beta,\ \beta \in \{emdf, iemdf\}$ is given by

$$L_\beta(G) = \{w \in V^* \mid x \Longrightarrow_\beta^* w,\ x \in A\},$$

where $\Longrightarrow_\beta^*$ is the reflexive transitive closure of the relation $\Longrightarrow_\beta$.

As usual, the family of languages $L_\beta(G)$, for G working in $\beta \in \{emdf, iemdf\}$ mode with F selection is given as $ICC_{emdf}(F)$, and $ICC_{iemdf}(F)$, respectively.

The following assumption is made throughout this chapter. As we do not discuss external contextual grammars or any other grammars in this chapter, we simply refer internal contextual grammars as grammars in many occurrences. We also call maximal length as maximal and the selector for the next derivation as next selector in many places for the sake of brevity. We do not consider (λ, λ) contexts, but one sided contexts of the form (λ, v) or (u, λ) are considered in many occasions.

4. Analyzing MCS Properties

In this section, we investigate whether the families of languages generated by the grammars introduced in the previous section are meeting the properties that define the mildly context sensitive formalisms and languages.

4.1. Non Context-free Constructions in Natural Languages

Here, we show that all the three basic non-context-free constructions in natural languages, that is, *multiple agreements*, *crossed dependencies* and *duplication* can be realized using *emdf*, *iemdf* grammars with regular selection.

Lemma 1 *(multiple agreements)*
$L_1 = \{a^n b^n c^n | n \geq 1\} \in ICC_\alpha(REG),\ \alpha \in \{emdf, iemdf\}$.

Proof. Consider the following grammar

$$G_1 = (\{a, b, c\}, abc, \{(ab^+, (a, bc_R)), (b^+c, (ab_L, c))\}).$$

Any derivation in $\alpha \in \{emdf, iemdf\}$ mode of G_1 is as follows:

$$^{\downarrow}ab^{\downarrow}c \Longrightarrow_\alpha \underline{a}a^{\downarrow}b\underline{bc}^{\downarrow}c \Longrightarrow_\alpha aa^{\downarrow}\underline{ab}bb^{\downarrow}c\underline{c}c \Longrightarrow_\alpha aa\underline{a}a^{\downarrow}bbb\underline{bc}^{\downarrow}ccc \Longrightarrow_\alpha^* a^n b^n c^n.$$

The underlined symbols are the newly inserted contexts in the derivation. The word between the two down arrows indicates the selector for the next derivation. Starting from the axiom abc, ab is considered as the selector for the first derivation and (a, bc) is adjoined. As bc is the right end-marker, the selector for the next derivation should end with bc and of maximal. Therefore, b^2c is the selector. Now (ab, c) is adjoined and ab is the left end marker. Therefore, the selector for the next derivation is ab^3 and (a, bc) is adjoined to $aabbcc$. Continuing the derivation in this fashion, we can see that $L_\alpha(G_1) = L_1,\ \alpha \in \{emdf, iemdf\}$. □

Lemma 2 *(crossed agreements)*
$L_2 = \{a^n b^m c^n d^m | n, m \geq 1\} \in ICC_\alpha(REG),\ \alpha \in \{emdf, iemdf\}$.

Proof. Consider the grammar

$$G_2 = (\{a,b,c,d\}, abcd, (b^+c^+, \{(b_L, d), (a, c_R)\})).$$

Any derivation in the mode $\alpha \in \{emdf, iemdf\}$ in G_2 is as follows:

$$a^{\downarrow}bc^{\downarrow}d \Longrightarrow_{\alpha} a\underline{a}^{\downarrow}bc\underline{c}^{\downarrow}d \Longrightarrow_{\alpha} aa^{\downarrow}\underline{b}bcc^{\downarrow}\underline{d}d \Longrightarrow_{\alpha} aa^{\downarrow}\underline{b}bbcc^{\downarrow}\underline{d}dd \Longrightarrow_{\alpha}^{*} a^n b^m c^n d^m.$$

$$\text{or} \quad a^{\downarrow}bc^{\downarrow}d \Longrightarrow_{\alpha} a^{\downarrow}\underline{b}bc^{\downarrow}\underline{d}d \Longrightarrow_{\alpha} a^{\downarrow}\underline{b}bbc^{\downarrow}\underline{d}dd \Longrightarrow_{\alpha} a\underline{a}^{\downarrow}bbbc\underline{c}^{\downarrow}ddd \Longrightarrow_{\alpha}^{*} a^n b^m c^n d^m.$$

Starting from the axiom $abcd$, bc is considered as the selector for the first derivation and (a, c) is adjoined (one can also adjoin (b, d) instead of (a, c) and continue the derivation accordingly). As c is the right end marker, the selector for the next derivation should end with c and of maximal. Therefore, bc^2 is the selector. Now, (b, d) is adjoined and b is the left end marker, the selector for the next derivation should begin with b. Therefore, b^2c^2 is the selector and (b, d) is adjoined to the word $aabbccdd$. Continuing the derivation, we can see that $L_\alpha(G_2) = L_2$, $\alpha \in \{emdf, iemdf\}$. □

Lemma 3 *(marked duplication)*
$L_3 = \{wcw \mid w \in \{a,b\}^*\} \in ICC_\alpha(REG)$, $\alpha \in \{emdf, iemdf\}$.

Proof. Consider the following grammar

$$G_3 = (\{a,b,c\}, c, (\{cx \mid x \in \{a,b\}^*\}, \{(a, a_R), (b, b_R)\})).$$

Any derivation in $\alpha \in \{emdf, iemdf\}$ mode in G_3 is as follows:

$$^{\downarrow}c^{\downarrow} \Longrightarrow_{\alpha} \underline{w_1}^{\downarrow}c\underline{w_1}^{\downarrow} \Longrightarrow_{\alpha} w_1\underline{w_2}^{\downarrow}cw_1\underline{w_2}^{\downarrow} \Longrightarrow_{\alpha} w_1w_2\underline{w_3}^{\downarrow}cw_1w_2\underline{w_3}^{\downarrow} \Longrightarrow_{\alpha}^{*} wcw,$$

where $w_i \in \{a,b\}$, $1 \le i \le |w|$, $w \in \{a,b\}^*$. The reader can easily verify that, $L_\alpha(G_3) = L_3, \alpha \in \{emdf, iemdf\}$. □

Remark. Take $c = \lambda$ in the above grammar G_3, then the derivation in the *iemdf* mode will be given as $\lambda \Longrightarrow_{iemdf} \underline{w_1}^{\downarrow}\underline{w_1}^{\downarrow} \Longrightarrow_{iemdf} w_1\underline{w_2}^{\downarrow}w_1\underline{w_2}^{\downarrow} \Longrightarrow_{iemdf}^{*} ww$. Note that in *iemdf* mode, every time, the selector for the next derivation is chosen inside the contexts adjoined in the previous derivation and of maximal. It is easy to see that $L_{iemdf}(G_3) = \{ww \mid w \in \{a,b\}^*\}$. This language is known as *non-marked duplication*. This result is important from contextual grammars point of view since no other existing contextual grammar is capable of generating this language except absorbing right context (arc) grammars [13].

From the previous three lemmas, we have the following theorem.

Theorem 1 *The families of languages $ICC_{emdf}(REG)$ and $ICC_{iemdf}(REG)$ contain all the three basic non- context-free constructions in natural languages.*

4.2. Computational Complexity

In this section, we show that the families of languages $ICC_\alpha(F)$, for $\alpha \in \{emdf, iemdf\}$, $F \in \{FIN, REG\}$ are parsable in polynomial time. That is, given a *emdf* or *iemdf* grammar G and a string $w \in V^*$ of length n, there exists a Turing machine M which accepts or rejects w in polynomial time.

Theorem 2 *For any end-marked maximal depth-first and inner end-marked maximal depth-first contextual grammar G with F selection, $F \in \{FIN, REG\}$, there is a polynomial time algorithm which accepts $L_\alpha(G)$, $\alpha \in \{emdf, iemdf\}$ on any input w of length n. In other words, $ICC_\alpha(F) \subseteq \mathcal{P}$ for $\alpha \in \{emdf, iemdf\}$, $F \in \{FIN, REG\}$*

Proof. We will prove the result for the case $\alpha = emdf$ and $F = REG$. The other case $\alpha = iemdf$ follows automatically.

Consider a *emdf* grammar $G = (V, A, (S_1, C_1), \ldots, (S_m, C_m))$, where $S_j \in REG$, $1 \leq j \leq m$. Given a input w of length $n, n \geq 1$, we denote the ith letter of w by w_i, $1 \leq i \leq n$. When $w = \lambda$ (i.e., $|w| = 0$), it can be easily verified by checking the axiom of G. For $x \in A$, any derivation in *emdf* mode can be given as $x = y_0 \Longrightarrow y_1 \Longrightarrow \ldots y_{k-1} \Longrightarrow y_k = w,\ k \geq 0$.

Construct a two tape non-deterministic Turing machine M which accepts the language $L_{emdf}(F)$ as follows:

- On the first tape, w is written as input and is never changed.
- On the second tape, M copies the input w from tape 1. During a computation on w, M works on tape 2 as follows:

  1. Check whether $w \in A$. If $w \in A$, then M accepts w; else, go to next step.
  2. M non-deterministically identifies four indices $p, q, r, s \in \{1, \ldots, n\}, p \leq q \leq r \leq s$ with the following property: $u_k = w_p \ldots w_{q-1},\ x_k = w_q \ldots w_r$, $v_k = w_{r+1} \ldots w_s$, where $x_k \in S_{j_k},\ (u_k, v_k) \in C_{j_k},\ 1 \leq j_k \leq m$.
     Also, whenever, M tries new combination of values to identify the indices p, q, r, s (with the above said property), M rewrites the input w on tape 2 and continues the computation.
  3. If there is no such four indices with the above property, then M rejects w. Otherwise, M goes to next step.
  4. At each time, M tries to back track the derivation by deleting the contexts u_h and v_h from y_h, $k \geq h \geq 1$ (initially, $h = k$). Let the modified resultant string be y_{h-1}. By definition of the grammar, the selector at any derivation (except the first derivation) should begin or end with the contexts which were adjoined in the previous derivation. Therefore, once the selector (say x_h which is $w_q \ldots w_r$) is identified, according to the definition of the grammar, one of the following cases is possible.

  case i: The selector x_h begins with the left context u_{h-1} introduced in the previous derivation.

  $x_h = u_{h-1} z_2,\ z_2 \in V^*,\ \exists$ three indices $q_1, r_1, s_1 \geq 0,$ where $q \leq q_1 \leq$

$r_1 \leq s_1$, such that $u_{h-1} = w_p \ldots w_{q_1-1}$, $x_{h-1} = w_{q_1} \ldots w_{r_1}$, $v_{h-1} = w_{r_1+1} \ldots w_{s_1}$, $x_{h-1} \in S_{j_{h-1}}$, $(u_{h-1}, v_{h-1}) \in C_{j_{h-1}}$, $1 \leq j_{h-1} \leq m$.

case ii: The selector x_h ends with the left context u_{h-1} introduced in the previous derivation.
$x_h = z_1 u_{h-1}, z_1 \in V^*$, $\exists$ three indices $q_2, r_2, s_2 \geq 0$, where $q_2 \leq r \leq r_2 \leq s_2$, such that $u_{h-1} = w_{q_2} \ldots w_r$, $x_{h-1} = w_{r+1} \ldots w_{r_2}$, $v_{h-1} = w_{r_2+1} \ldots w_{s_2}$, $x_{h-1} \in S_{j_{h-1}}$, $(u_{h-1}, v_{h-1}) \in C_{j_{h-1}}$, $1 \leq j_{h-1} \leq m$.

case iii: The selector x_h begins with the right context v_{h-1} introduced in the previous derivation.
$x_h = v_{h-1} z_3, z_3 \in V^*$, $\exists$ three indices $q'_3, q_3, r_3 \geq 0$, where $q'_3 \leq q_3 \leq q \leq r_3 \leq r$, such that $u_{h-1} = w_{q'_3} \ldots w_{q_3-1}$, $x_{h-1} = w_{q_3} \ldots w_{q-1}$, $v_{h-1} = w_q \ldots w_{r_3}$, $x_{h-1} \in S_{j_{h-1}}$, $(u_{h-1}, v_{h-1}) \in C_{j_{h-1}}$, $1 \leq j_{h-1} \leq m$.

case iv: The selector x_h ends with the right context v_{h-1} introduced in the previous derivation.
$x_h = z'_2 v_{h-1}, z'_2 \in V^*$, $\exists$ three indices $q'_4, q_4, r_4 \geq 0$, where $q'_4 \leq q_4 \leq r_4 \leq r$, such that $u_{h-1} = w_{q'_4} \ldots w_{q_4-1}$, $x_{h-1} = w_{q_4} \ldots w_{r_4-1}$, $v_{h-1} = w_{r_4} \ldots w_r$, $x_{h-1} \in S_{j_{h-1}}$, $(u_{h-1}, v_{h-1}) \in C_{j_{h-1}}$, $1 \leq j_{h-1} \leq m$.

5. M tries to identify three indices q_i, r_i, s_i, $i = 1, 2$, or q_l, q'_l, r_l, $l = 3, 4$, with the above mentioned property. If there exists three such indices, then M goes to next step. Else, M rejects w.

6. Check $y_{h-1} \in A$. If yes, then M accepts w. Else, M replaces the variables simultaneously as given below and goes to Step 4 for further back tracking. $(u_h, y_h, v_h \leftarrow u_{h-1}, y_{h-1}, v_{h-1})$ and one of the following.
(i) $(p, q, r, s \leftarrow p, q_1, r_1, s_1)$, (ii) $(p, q, r, s \leftarrow q_2, r+1, r_2, s_2)$, (iii) $(p, q, r, s \leftarrow q'_3, q_3, q-1, r_3)$, (iv) $(p, q, r, s \leftarrow q'_4, q_4, r_4, r)$.

Since M tries correct derivations only (with respect to G), it cannot accept a word not in the language generated by G, and so $L(M) \subseteq L_{emdf}(G)$. Conversely, if $w \in L_{emdf}(G)$, then there is a derivation in G yielding w from the axiom, and M guesses the right choices of the added contexts (in the reverse order) in step 4, thus M accepts w in step 6. Consequently, $L(M) = L_{emdf}(G)$.

The space required by M is the space needed to remember the four indices p, q, r, s, and three more indices during the computation and therefore M needed to store 7 indices all the time which is $\mathcal{O}(7log(|w|))$. Since the selectors are regular type and the contexts are finite, verifying the membership and the four cases require only finite amount of space. This follows, M operates in space $\mathcal{O}(logn)$. The remaining proof of the result follows from the well known result $NSPACE\ (log(n)) \subseteq \mathcal{P}$ [20]. □

4.3. Semilinear Property

In this section, we analyze the semilinear property for $ICC_{\alpha}(F)$, $\alpha \in \{emdf, iemdf, mloc, mdf, mldf\}$, $F \in \{FIN, REG\}$. For the families of languages generated by $emdf, mdf, mldf$ grammars we prove that they contain non- semilinear languages too, and for the families of languages generated by $iemdf, mloc$ grammars, we show that they contain semilinear languages only.

Theorem 3 *The family of languages $ICC_{emdf}(REG)$ contains non-semilinear languages.*

Proof. Consider the $emdf$ grammar $G = (\{a, b, c, d\}, cababc, P)$ with P consisting the following production rules:

$$1.\ (ca, (\lambda, b_L)),\ 2.\ (bba, (\lambda, b_L)),\ 3.\ (bbc, (\lambda, c_R)),\ 4.\ (bcc, (a_R, \lambda)),$$
$$5.\ ((ba)^+, (a_R, \lambda)),\ 6.\ (caba, (c_L, \lambda)),\ 7.\ (cca, (\lambda, b_L)),\ 8.\ (caba, (cd_L, \lambda)),$$
$$9.\ (aa, (cd_L, \lambda)),\ 10.\ (cdaa, (\lambda, d_R)),\ 11.\ (cdc(ab)^+c, (\lambda, d_R)).$$

The intuition behind the construction of the above rules is the following. Between every a and b, one b is introduced from left to right of the word by rules 1 and 2. Therefore, the number of b's are doubled when scanning from left to right of the word is finished. Now, between every two b, one a is introduced from right to left of the word by rules 4 and 5. Therefore, the number of a's are doubled when the scanning from right to left is finished. c is the terminal identifier of the word. Whenever, the scanning of the word is over (from left to right or right to left), c is incremented to one time (by rules 3 and 6), and the selector for further derivations move right or left in order to double the occurrences of b's or a's respectively. Rules 6 and 7 are applied to continue the derivations for further steps. To terminate the derivation the rules 8 followed by 11 or 9 followed by 10 are applied. Once, the context (λ, d_R) is introduced, no further derivation can be performed, as there is no selector ends with d. In below, we present a sample derivation in $emdf$ mode as below. The number in suffix of each derivation indicates the rule which is being applied. Initially, ca is assumed to be the selector for the axiom. One can also assume $caba$ as the selector for the axiom and can proceed the derivation accordingly.

$$\begin{gathered}{}^{\downarrow}ca^{\downarrow}babc \Longrightarrow_1 ca^{\downarrow}\underline{b}ba^{\downarrow}bc \Longrightarrow_2 cabba^{\downarrow}\underline{b}bc^{\downarrow} \Longrightarrow_3 cabbab^{\downarrow}bc\underline{c}^{\downarrow} \Longrightarrow_4 cab^{\downarrow}bab\underline{a}^{\downarrow}bc^2 \\ \Longrightarrow_5 ca^{\downarrow}b\underline{a}^{\downarrow}(ba)^2bc^2 \Longrightarrow_5 c^{\downarrow}a\underline{a}^{\downarrow}(ba)^3bc^2 \Longrightarrow_9 c^{\downarrow}\underline{cd}aa^{\downarrow}(ba)^3bc^2 \Longrightarrow_{10} \\ ccdaa\underline{d}(ba)^3bc^2.\end{gathered}$$

Now, consider the words containing two d's. One can also terminate the derivation at any time without doubling the occurrences of a's and b's and not introducing any d's. But, we do not bother for such words as our claim is that the generated language contains non-semilinear also. Now, intersect $\Phi_{\{a,b,c,d\}}(L_{emdf}(G))$ with the semilinear set

$$R = \{(n_1, n_2, n_3, 2) \mid n_1, n_2, n_3 \geq 1\},$$

we obtain

$$R' = \{|a| = 2^i + 1, |b| = 2^i, |c| = 2i, |d| = 2 \mid i \geq 1\},$$

which is not semilinear as the family of semilinear sets is closed under intersection. This proves that $L_{emdf}(G)$ is not semilinear. □

Though, *emdf* and *iemdf* grammars work in a very similar way, we prove a contrasting result for $ICC_{iemdf}(REG)$. Note that the proof of Theorem 3 does not hold for $ICC_{iemdf}(REG)$ for obvious reasons that the rules 1,2,4,5 and 7 are not of the form mentioned in the definition of *iemdf* grammars. Before, solving the semilinear problem for the family $ICC_{iemdf}(F)$, we solve an important open problem in the following theorem, which was addressed by Ilie in 1997 [8].

Theorem 4 *The family of languages generated by maximal local grammars with F selection $F \in \{FIN, REG\}$ is semilinear.*

Proof. We prove the result for local grammars and the proof can be easily extended to maximal local grammars. Let L be the language generated by the local grammar $G = (V, A, P)$ with finite or regular selectors, where P is the set of production rules are of the form $(S_1, C_1), \ldots, (S_m, C_m)), m \geq 1$.

For all $1 \leq j, f, r, s, t \leq m$, $u_f = u'_f u''_f, v_f = v'_f v''_f$ such that $u'_f \in Pref(u_f)$, $u''_f \in Suf(u_f)$, and $v'_f \in Pref(v_f)$, $v''_f \in Suf(v_f)$. As the contexts are finite languages, any u_f will be of finite length, say n. Then there will be only $(n+1)$ possible u'_f (since $u'_f = Pref(u_f)$) and u''_f (since $u''_f = Suf(u_f)$) exist. Similar statement holds true for v_f also. Also, as $x \in A$ is a finite language, $x_2 \in Sub(x)$ will also be finite. Therefore, once $x_2 \in S_f$ is known, checking $u''_f x_2 v'_f \in S_r$ will only be of finite combination (in fact, $(n+1)(k+1)$ possible combinations, if we assume $|v_f| = k$).

Now, construct a context-free grammar G' as follows:

$$G' = (\{S, S_{r,s} \mid 1 \leq r, s \leq m\}, V, \{S\}, P')$$

where P' consists of the following production rules:

$$\begin{aligned}
&(1)\ \{S \to x_1 x_2 x_3 \mid x = x_1 x_2 x_3 \in A\}\\
&(2)\ \{S \to x_1 x_2 x_3 u_j v_j \mid x_2 \in S_j,\ (u_j, v_j) \in C_j\}\\
&(3)\ \{S \to x_1 x_2 x_3 u''_j S_{j,r} v'_j \mid\ u''_j x_2 v'_j \in S_r,\ (u_r, v_r) \in C_r\}\\
&(4)\ \{S_{r,s} \to u'_r v''_r u''_s S_{s,t} v'_s \mid u'_r \ldots u'_j x_2 v'_j \ldots v'_s \in S_t,\ (u_t, v_t) \in C_t\}\\
&(5)\ \{S_{r,s} \to u'_r v''_r u_s v_s \mid u'_r \ldots u'_j x_2 v'_j \ldots v'_s \in S_t,\ (u_t, v_t) \in C_t\}.
\end{aligned}$$

Rules 1,2,5 are terminal rules which can be used to stop the derivation whenever necessary. The non-terminals in rule 3,4 will be used to simulate the derivations for further steps. It is easy to verify from the structure of P' that $L_{loc}(G)$ and $L(G')$ are letter equivalent. Since $L(G')$ is a context-free language, $L(G)$ is also semilinear. □

Theorem 5 *The family of languages generated by inner end-marked maximal depth-first grammars with F selection $F \in \{FIN, REG\}$ is semilinear.*

Proof. Let L be the language generated by the *iemdf* grammar $G = (V, A, P)$ with finite or regular selectors, where P is the set of production rules are of the form $(S_1, C_1), \ldots, (S_m, C_m)), m \geq 1$.

For all $1 \leq i, j, k \leq m$, we construct a context-free grammar G' as follows:

$$G' = (\{B, B_0, B^L_{i,j}, B^R_{i,j} \mid 1 \leq i, j \leq m\}, V, \{B\}, P')$$

where P' consists of the following production rules:

(1) $\{B \rightarrow x_1x_2x_3 \mid x = x_1x_2x_3 \in A \text{ of } G\}$
This is equivalent to start and end with the axiom.

(2) $\{B \rightarrow B_0\}$

(3) $\{B_0 \rightarrow x_1x_2x_3u_iB^R_{i,j} \mid x_2 \in S_i,\ (u_i, v_i) \in C_i, \text{ and } v_i \in Suf(S_j)\}$

(4) $\{B_0 \rightarrow x_1x_2x_3v_iB^L_{i,j} \mid x_2 \in S_i,\ (u_i, v_i) \in C_i \text{ and } u_i \in Pref(S_j)\}$

The rules (3), (4) are equivalent to start with a rule of the form $(S_i, (u_i, v_i))$, where $x_2 \in S_i$ and continue the derivation further.

(5) $\{B^R_{i,j} \rightarrow v_iB^L_{j,k}v_j \mid (u_j, v_j) \in C_j \text{ and } u_j \in Pref(S_k)\}$
This is equivalent to continue the derivation with a rule of the form $(S_j, (u_j, v_j))$ with $u_j \in Pref(S_k)$ and continue the derivation further.

(6) $\{B^R_{i,j} \rightarrow v_iB^R_{j,k}u_j \mid (u_j, v_j) \in C_j \text{ and } v_j \in Suf(S_k)\}$
This is equivalent to continue the derivation with a rule of the form $(S_j, (u_j, v_j))$ with $v_j \in Suf(S_k)$ and continue the derivation further.

(7) $\{B^L_{i,j} \rightarrow u_iB^L_{j,k}v_j \mid (u_j, v_j) \in C_j \text{ and } u_j \in Pref(S_k)\}$
This is equivalent to continue the derivation with a rule of the form $(S_j, (u_j, v_j))$ with $u_j \in Pref(S_k)$ and continue the derivation further.

(8) $\{B^L_{i,j} \rightarrow u_iB^R_{j,k}u_j \mid (u_j, v_j) \in C_j \text{ and } v_j \in Suf(S_k)\}$
This is equivalent to continue the derivation with a rule of the form $(S_j, (u_j, v_j))$ with $v_j \in Suf(S_k)$ and continue the derivation further.

(9) $\{B^L_{i,j} \rightarrow u_i\}$

(10) $\{B^R_{i,j} \rightarrow v_i\}$

(9) and (10) are equivalent to terminate the derivation at any time.

Rules 1,9, and 10 are terminal rules which can be used to stop the derivation whenever necessary. The rest of the rules are non-terminals which will be used to simulate the derivations to further steps. Note that, though the selectors are of regular type, thus having infinite length, exercising $u_i \in Pref(S_j)$ or $v_i \in Suf(S_j)$ takes only a finite number of steps, since to find the prefixes and suffixes, we just have to rewrite the selector S_j either till the length of u_i as of the form $u_iS'_j$ or till the length of v_i as of the form s'_jv_i. It is easy to verify from the structure of P' that $L_{iemdf}(G)$ and $L(G')$ are letter equivalent. Since $L(G')$ is a context-free language, $L(G)$ is also semilinear. □

Next, we shall discuss the problem of semilinear property for *mdf* and *mldf* families of languages which are left open in [13]. The proof given for $ICC_{emdf}(REG)$ does not hold to $ICC_{mdf}(F)$ languages, since in the production set P of *emdf* grammar, many one sided contexts of the form (u, λ) or (λ, v) were used. These contexts will create a problem if we directly apply them in *mdf* mode (to show non-semilinear result), since the selectors associated with the one-sided contexts can be used to any number of times and so the necessary language cannot be generated and will be different from the expected language. For example, consider the rule 3. $(bbc, (\lambda, c))$, which was used in *emdf* grammar of Theorem 3. If we apply the same rule in *mdf* mode, then, the same selector bbc can be used again and again (since bbc can be written as $\underline{\lambda}bbc$), thus the occurrences of c will be increased to arbitrarily large, and so the growth of occurrences of c will be definitely different from what was shown in the proof. Therefore, we need to prove the non-semilinear result for $ICC_{mdf}(F)$ separately.

However, the production rules considered in *emdf* grammars in theorem 2 hold well for *mldf* grammar also and they generate the same non-semilinear language. Note that the λ context cannot be used by the next selector in *mldf* mode, since the other corresponding context is of larger length than λ. Therefore, $ICC_{mldf}(REG)$ contains non-semilinear languages. However, in the following proof, since the length of the left context is equal to the length of the right context in all rules, the result will also hold true for *mldf* grammars.

Theorem 6 *The family of languages $ICC_\alpha(REG)$, $\alpha \in \{mdf, mldf\}$ contains non-semilinear languages.*

Proof. Consider the grammar $G = (\{a, b, c, d, e, f\}, dcababcd, P)$ with P consisting the following production rules:

$$1.\ (caba, (c, b)),\ 2.\ (cc^+a, (d, b)),\ 3.\ (c^+a(bba)^+, (d, b)),\ 4. (c^+a(bba)^+bbc, (d, c)),$$
$$5.\ (bcc^+, (a, d)),\ 6.\ ((ba)^+bcc^+, (a, d)),\ 7.\ (caa, (f, e)),\ 8.\ (cfc, (e, f)).$$

The intuition behind the construction of the above rules is the following. Initially, when we start reading the word from left to right we increase one c on the left of $caba$. Then, between every a and b, one b is introduced from left to right by rules 1,2 and 3. Therefore, the number of b's are doubled when we finish the reading from left to right of the word. When we end the reading (from left to right), we increase one c after bbc (by rule 4). Then, we start scanning the word from right to left in order to double the occurrences of a. Now, between every two b, one a is introduced in the word by the rules 5 and 6. Therefore, the number of a's are doubled when we finish the reading from right to left. Whenever, we finish the reading from right to left or from left to right, c is incremented to one time. Now, we can repeat the above process by using the rule 1 again, or we can start terminating the derivation by applying the rules 7 and 8. Once, the context (e, f) is introduced, no further derivation is performed, since the contexts are not covered by any of the selectors. The symbol d is considered to be end of the string, but however c is the terminal identifier whenever we scan the symbols from right to left and from left to right. Though, the symbol d is used as context in many rules, it is considered to be a dummy symbol, since no selector is having the symbol d and therefore we have to forcibly use the other context in the next selector. In fact, the rules are constructed in such a way that only one context is covered by the other selectors. We present a sample derivation in $mdf, mldf$ modes as below.

$$
\begin{aligned}
&d^{\downarrow}caba^{\downarrow}bcd \Longrightarrow_1 d^{\downarrow}\underline{c}ca^{\downarrow}ba\underline{b}bcd \Longrightarrow_2 d\underline{d}^{\downarrow}cca\underline{b}babbc^{\downarrow}d \Longrightarrow_4 dd\underline{d}^{\downarrow}ccabbab^{\downarrow}bc\underline{c}^{\downarrow}d \\
&\Longrightarrow_5 d^3ccab^{\downarrow}bab\underline{a}bcc^{\downarrow}\underline{d}d \Longrightarrow_6 d^3ccab\underline{a}bababcc\underline{d}dd \Longrightarrow_6 d^3c^{\downarrow}ca\underline{a}(ba)^3bcc\underline{d}d^3 \\
&\Longrightarrow_7 d^{3\downarrow}c\underline{f}caa\underline{e}(ba)^3bc^2d^4 \Longrightarrow_8 d^3\underline{e}cfc\underline{f}aae(ba)^3bc^2d^4.
\end{aligned}
$$

One can also stop the derivation at any time without doubling the occurrences of a's and b's and not introducing any e and f. But, we do not bother such words as our claim is that the generated language contains non-semilinear also. Therefore, we consider only the words containing two e and two f (this means that the occurrences of a and b are already doubled for necessary times).

Now, intersect $\Phi_{\{a,b,c,d,e,f\}}(L_{emdf}(G))$ with the semilinear set

$$R = \{(n_1, n_2, n_3, n_4, 2, 2) \mid n_1, n_2, n_3, n_4 \geq 1\},$$

we obtain

$$R' = \{|a| = 2^i + 1, |b| = 2^i, |c| = 2i, |d| = 2^{i+1} - 1, |e| = 2, |f| = 2 \mid i \geq 2\},$$

which is not semilinear as the family of semilinear sets is closed under intersection. This proves that $L_{mdf}(G)$ is not semilinear. □

5. Generative Power

In this section, we characterize recursive enumerable languages by means of $emdf$, mdf and $mldf$ grammars with regular selection. As we just proved that these languages contain non-semilinear languages, it is necessary to analyze their power in representing the recursive enumerable languages. The characterization of recursive enumerable languages in terms of internal and global maximal grammars with finite selectors is discussed in [22] and the following theorems use the proof technique of these results.

Theorem 7 *Every recursive enumerable language* $L \subseteq T^*$ *can be written in the form* $L = (R \backslash L') \cap T^*$ *where* $L' \in ICC_{emdf}(REG)$ *and* $R \in REG$.

Proof. Take $L \subseteq T^*$, $L \in RE$, and a type-0 grammar $G = (N, T, S, P)$ for L, where P consists the rules of the form $u \to v$. Consider the new symbols $\#, \$,], \dagger, \vdash$ and construct a contextual grammar $G' = (V', A, P')$ with

$$
\begin{aligned}
V' &= N \cup T \cup \{\#, \$,]^v, \dagger^{\alpha}, \dagger^{\#}, \vdash \mid \alpha \in (N \cup T), u \to v \in P\}, \\
A &= \{S\}
\end{aligned}
$$

and the set P' consists of the following productions:

1. $(S, (\#_L, \lambda))$
2. $\{(\#\alpha^* u, (\lambda, \$_R)) \mid u \to v \in P\}$
3. $\{(u\$, (\$,]^v_R)) \mid u \to v \in P,\ u \in (N \cup T)^+, v \in (N \cup T)^*\}$
4. $\{(\alpha\$u\$]^v, (\vdash_R, \alpha v)) \mid u \to v \in P, \alpha \in (N \cup T)\}$
5. $\{(\alpha \vdash (\beta \vdash)^* \vdash^*, (\vdash, \dagger^\alpha_L)) \mid \alpha, \beta \in (N \cup T)$
6. $(\dagger^\alpha (\dagger^\beta)^* \beta\$u\$]^v, (\vdash_R, \alpha))$
7. $(\# \vdash (\beta \vdash)^* \vdash^*, (\lambda, \dagger^\#_L))$
8. $(\dagger^\# (\dagger^\beta)^* \beta\$u\$]^v, (\lambda, \#_L))$
9. $\{(\#\$u\$]^v, (\vdash_L, v)) \mid u \to v \in P\}$
10. $\{(\vdash \#\$u\$]^v, (\lambda, \#_L))\}$.

Consider the regular language R over the set

$$U = \{\$u\$]^v\#, \#\$u\$]^v, \dagger^\alpha, \vdash, \vdash \dagger^\#, \vdash \alpha, \# \vdash \mid u \to v \in P,\ \alpha \in (N \cup T)\}.$$

Then, we can see that $L = (R \backslash L_{emdf}(G')) \cap T^*$. The intuition behind the construction of G' is as follows.

The symbols $\vdash, \dagger^\#, \dagger^\alpha$ are called markers which marks the symbols to be killed while the symbols $]^v$ and $\$$ are called killers. The symbols in between $\$$ and $]^v$ and the symbol immediately right of $\vdash$ are considered as dead symbols. The symbols on the right of $]^v$ other than $\#$ are called alive symbols, and $\#$ denotes the left end of the alive symbols. In the production rules P', β denotes the symbols which have already been transported to the right of $]^v$ and α denotes the symbol which is to be transported to the immediate right of $]^v$.

To begin with, $\#$ is introduced on the left of the starting symbol S by rule 1. As $\#$ is left end-marker, any next selector suppose to begin with the symbol $\#$. Rule 2 is used to identify the string u which has the rewriting rule $u \to v$ in P. Rule 3 is used to simulate the rules in P. Rules 4-8 are used to move the (alive) symbols appeared on the left of $\$u$, to the right of $\$]^v$. Note that since the chosen selector is of maximal in every derivation, the selector for rules 4-8 covers all the transmitted symbols β present on the left of $\$u$. Rule 9 and 10 are used when we have the strings of the form $\#u$ where $u \to v$ in P (i.e., when the symbol α to be transmitted to the right of $]^v$ is empty, for instance, $\#\$S\$]^v$ at the starting stage). When the rule 8 or 10 is applied in a derivation, it means, one production rule of G is simulated and the alive symbols in a string $x \in ICC_{emdf}(REG)$ correspond to a sentential form produced by G. Using the above production rules of P', we can now exemplify a sample derivation for better understanding of the formation of rules. Assume that we obtain a word $AabBcDF$ after some derivations by using the rules in P and there is a production rule $cD \to Ee$ in P which is to be applied in the next derivation. Then, we obtain $AabBEeF$ in the next derivation. Let us see how we can achieve this word by using the rules in P'. With out loss of generality, we can assume that starting from S of G', we can end up in a word $w\#AabBcDF$ where $w \in U$. Then,

$$
\begin{aligned}
& w^{\downarrow}\#AabBcD^{\downarrow}F \Longrightarrow_2 w\underline{\lambda}\#AabB^{\downarrow}cD\underline{\$}^{\downarrow}F \Longrightarrow_3 w\#Aab\vdash^{\downarrow}B\underline{\$}cD\$\underline{]^{Ee\downarrow}}F \Longrightarrow_4 \\
& w\#Aa^{\downarrow}b\underline{\vdash}^{\downarrow}B\$cD\$]^{Ee}\underline{BEe}F \Longrightarrow_5 w\#Aa\underline{\vdash}b\vdash^{\downarrow}\ \underline{\dagger}^{b}B\$cD\$]^{Ee\downarrow}BEeF \Longrightarrow_6 \\
& w\#A^{\downarrow}a\vdash b\vdash \underline{\vdash}^{\downarrow}\dagger^{b}B\$cD\$]^{Ee}\underline{b}BEeF \Longrightarrow_5 \\
& w\#A\underline{\vdash}a\vdash b\vdash\vdash^{\downarrow}\ \underline{\dagger}^{a}\dagger^{b}B\$cD\$]^{Ee\downarrow}bBEeF \Longrightarrow_6 \\
& w\#^{\downarrow}A\vdash a\vdash b\vdash\vdash \underline{\vdash}^{\downarrow}\dagger^{a}\dagger^{b}B\$cD\$]^{Ee}\underline{a}bBEeF \Longrightarrow_5 \\
& w\#\underline{\vdash}A\vdash a\vdash b\vdash\vdash\vdash^{\downarrow}\ \underline{\dagger}^{A}\dagger^{a}\dagger^{b}B\$cD\$]^{Ee\downarrow}abBEeF \Longrightarrow_6 \\
& w^{\downarrow}\#\vdash A\vdash a\vdash b\vdash\vdash\vdash \underline{\vdash}^{\downarrow}\dagger^{A}\dagger^{a}\dagger^{b}B\$cD\$]^{Ee}\underline{A}abBEeF \Longrightarrow_7 \\
& w\underline{\lambda}\#\vdash A\vdash a\vdash b\vdash\vdash\vdash\vdash^{\downarrow}\ \underline{\dagger^{\#}}\dagger^{A}\dagger^{a}\dagger^{b}B\$cD\$]^{Ee\downarrow}AabBEeF \Longrightarrow_8 \\
& w\#\vdash A\vdash a\vdash b\vdash^{4}\ \underline{\lambda}\dagger^{\#}\dagger^{A}\dagger^{a}\dagger^{b}B\$cD\$]^{Ee\downarrow}\underline{\#}AabBEeF = w'\#AabBEeF, w' \in U.
\end{aligned}
$$

In above, the number suffix in each derivation symbol $\Longrightarrow$ indicates the rule from P' which is being applied. Once the necessary rules in P' are applied to alive symbols, a string over T^* is obtained on taking the left quotient. This proves that $(R \backslash L_{emdf}(G')) \cap T^* \subseteq L$. The reverse inclusion follows from Church-Turing thesis. □

The previous construction can be modified as below to represent the recursive enumerable languages using the operations morphism and weak coding.

Corrollary 1 *Every recursive enumerable language L can be written in the form $L = h_1(h_2^{-1}(L'))$ where $L' \in ICC_{emdf}(REG)$, h_1 is a weak coding, and h_2 is a morphism.*

Proof. Starting from a type-0 grammar $G = (N, T, S, P)$, we can construct the grammar G' as above, and then we proceed as below.
Consider a new symbol b_w, associated with each string w in the set

$$U = \{\$u\$]^v\#, \#\$u\$]^v, \dagger^{\alpha}, \vdash, \vdash \dagger^{\#}, \vdash \alpha, \# \vdash \mid u \to v \in P,\ \alpha \in (N \cup T)\}.$$

Let us denote by W the set of all such symbols b_w and define the weak coding $h_1 : (W \cup T)^* \longrightarrow T^*$ by

$$h_1(b_w) = \lambda,\ w \in U,\ h_1(a) = a,\ a \in T,$$

as well as the morphism $h_2 : (W \cup T)^* \longrightarrow V'^*$ by

$$h_2(b_w) = w,\ w \in U, \quad h_2(a) = a,\ a \in T.$$

The inverse morphism h_2^{-1} can be applied only when a string in $(U \cup T)^*$ is obtained. This implies that all non-terminals are dead and the corresponding derivation in G is a terminal one. The weak coding h_1 removes all symbols b_w, so we obtain a string in T^*. With this explanations, the reader can easily verify that $L = h_1(h_2^{-1}(L'))$. □

In the following theorem, we give a representation for recursive enumerable languages in terms of maximal depth-first grammars using the operation left quotient.

Theorem 8 *Every recursive enumerable language $L \subseteq T^*$ can be written in the form $L = (R\backslash L') \cap T^*$ where $L' \in ICC_{mdf}(REG)$ and $R \in REG$.*

Proof. Take $L \subseteq T^*$, $L \in RE$. Let $G = (N, T, S, P)$ be a type-0 grammar in *Kuroda normal form* for L, hence, the production rules are of the forms

1. $A \to BC, A \to a, A \to \lambda,\ A, B, C \in N,\ a \in T,$
2. $AB \to CD,\ A, B, C, D \in N.$

Consider the new symbols $\#, \$, [,], \vdash$ and construct a contextual grammar $G' = (V', A, P')$ with

$$V' = N \cup T \cup \{\#, \$, [,], \vdash\},$$
$$A = \{S\}$$

and the set P' consists of the following productions:

1. $(S, (\#, \lambda))$
2. $\{(\#\alpha^* A, (\#, \$)) \mid \alpha \in \{N \cup T\},\ A \to BC/a/\lambda \text{ in } P\}$
3. $\{(\#\alpha^* AB, (\#, \$)) \mid \alpha \in \{N \cup T\},\ AB \to CD \text{ in } P\}$
4. $\{(A\$, ([,]BC)) \mid A \to BC \in P,\ A, B, C \in N\}$
5. $\{(A\$, ([,]a)) \mid A \to a \in P,\ A \in N, a \in T\}$
6. $\{(A\$, ([,])) \mid A \to \lambda \in P,\ A \in N\}$
7. $\{(AB\$, ([,]CD)) \mid AB \to CD \in P,\ A, B, C, D \in N\}$
8. $\{(\alpha(\vdash \beta)^*[A\$], (\vdash, \alpha)) \mid \alpha, \beta \in \{N \cup T\}\}$
9. $\{(\alpha(\vdash \beta)^*[AB\$], (\vdash, \alpha)) \mid \alpha, \beta \in \{N \cup T\}\}$
10. $\{(\# \vdash \alpha(\vdash \beta)^*[A\$], (\#, \#)) \mid \beta \in \{N \cup T\}\}$
11. $\{(\# \vdash \alpha(\vdash \beta)^*[AB\$], (\#, \#)) \mid \beta \in \{N \cup T\}\}$
12. $(\#[A\$], (\#, \#))$
13. $(\#[AB\$], (\#, \#))$.

Consider the regular language R over the set

$$U = \{\#, A\$, AB\$, \vdash \alpha, [A\$], [AB\$] \mid A, B \in N,\ \alpha \in (N \cup T)\}.$$

Then we can see that $L = (R\backslash L_{mdf}(G')) \cap V^*$. The intuition behind the construction of G' is as follows.

The symbols $\$, \vdash$ are called markers which marks the symbols to be killed while the symbols $[$ and $]$ are called killers. The symbols in between $[$ and $\$]$, and the symbol immediately to the right of $\vdash$ are considered as dead symbols. The symbols on the right of $\$]$ other than $\#$ are called alive symbols, and $\#$ denotes the left end of the alive symbols. In the production rules P', β denotes the symbols which have already been transported to the right of $]$ and α denotes the symbol which is to be transported to the immediate right of $]$.

To begin with, $\#$ is introduced on the left of the starting symbol S by rule 1. As the system works in *mdf* mode, the selector for the next derivation should contain one of the previously introduced contexts and also of maximal length. As λ is one of the contexts in rule 1, the same rule can be applied to any number of times because, in every derivation, the selector S (which is actually $S\lambda$) contains the adjoined right context λ. This produces $\#^*$ on the left of the alive symbols. However, this does not create any problem to the result since $\#^*$ is covered by the regular set R. Now, the last introduced context $\#$ (by rule 1), will be present on the immediate left of S and is covered by the selectors of rule 2 and 3 and so they may be applied further. The rules 2 and 3 are used to identify the string u which has the rewriting rule in P (here u is either A or AB). Rules 4-7 are used to simulate the rules in P and also they separate the string which has the rewriting rule, by the symbols [and]. Rule 8 and 9 are used to move the symbols appeared on the left of $[u$, to the right of $\$]$. Note that since the chosen selector is of maximal in every derivation, the selector for rule 8 and 9 covers all the transmitted symbols β present on the left of $[u$ (where u is either A or AB). When the rule 10 or 11 is applied, it means one derivation of G is simulated and the alive symbols in a string $x \in L_{emdf}(G')$ correspond to a sentential form produced by G. Rules 12 and 13 are used when we have the strings of the form $\#u$ where $u \to v$ in P. Using the above production rules of P', we can now exemplify a sample derivation. Assume that we obtain a word $AabBcDE$ after some derivations by using the rules in P and there is a production rule $D \to d$ in P which is to be applied in the next derivation. Then, we obtain $AabBcdE$ in the next derivation. Let us see how we can achieve this word by using the rules in P'. With out loss of generality, we can assume that starting from S of G', we can end up with a word $w\#AabBcDE$ where $w \in U$. Then,

$$\begin{aligned}
&w^{\downarrow}\#AabBcD^{\downarrow}E \Longrightarrow_2 w\underline{\#}\#AabBc^{\downarrow}D\underline{\$}^{\downarrow}E \Longrightarrow_5 w\#\#AabB^{\downarrow}c\underline{[}D\$\underline{]^{\downarrow}d}E \Longrightarrow_8 \\
&w\#\#Aab^{\downarrow}B\underline{\vdash}c[D\$]^{\downarrow}\underline{c}dE \Longrightarrow_8 w\#\#Aa^{\downarrow}b\underline{\vdash}B\vdash c[D\$]^{da}\underline{B}cdE \Longrightarrow_8 \\
&w\#\#A^{\downarrow}a\underline{\vdash}b\vdash B\vdash c[D\$]^{\downarrow}\underline{b}BcdE \Longrightarrow_8 w\#\#^{\downarrow}A\underline{\vdash}a\vdash b\vdash B\vdash c[D\$]^{\downarrow}abBcdE \\
&\Longrightarrow_8 w\#^{\downarrow}\#\underline{\vdash}A\vdash a\vdash b\vdash B\vdash c[D\$]^{\downarrow}\underline{A}abBcdE \Longrightarrow_{10} \\
&w\#\underline{\#}\#\vdash A\vdash a\vdash b\vdash B\vdash c[D\$]^{\downarrow}\underline{\#}AabBcdE = w'\#AabBcdE,\ w' \in U.
\end{aligned}$$

Once the necessary rules in P' are applied to alive symbols, a string over T^* is obtained by taking the left quotient. This proves that $(R\backslash L_{mdf}(G'))\cap T^* \subseteq L$. The reverse inclusion follows from Church-Turing thesis. □

One can prove a similar result for *mldf* grammars also with some small modifications in the above proof. In the above production rules, other than the rules 1,4,5,7, in the remaining rules, the length of the left context is equal to the length of the right context. In rule 1, the lengthier context $\#$ is covered by the selectors of other rules and so those rules can be applied for further derivations. But, for rules 4,5,7, the lengthier context is not covered by any of the selectors and so if those rules are applied, the derivation cannot be proceeded further. However, we can modify the rules in order to proceed the derivation further. For example, rule 4 and 9 of above can be modified as below.

4. $\{(A\$, ([[[[,]BC)) \mid A \to BC \in P,\ A, B, C \in N\}$,
9. $\{(\alpha(\vdash \beta)^*[[[[AB\$], (\vdash, \alpha)) \mid \alpha, \beta \in \{N \cup T\}\}$.

Note that, now in rule 4, the lengthier context is left context and is covered by the selector of rule 9. A similar modification can be done for the rules 5,7 and 8 (we can keep

$[^4$ as fixed left context for rules 5 and 7). Also, in the regular set U, instead of $[$, $[^4$ may be replaced. So, the following result can easily be verified.

Corrollary 2 *Every recursive enumerable language $L \subseteq V^*$ can be written in the form $L = (R \backslash L') \cap V^*$ where $L' \in ICC_{mldf}(REG)$ and $R \in REG$.*

In the following result, we represent recursive enumerable languages by means of mdf and $mldf$ grammars using the operations morphism and weak coding.

Corrollary 3 *Every recursive enumerable language L can be written in the form $L = h_1(h_2^{-1}(L'))$ where $L' \in ICC_\alpha(REG)$, $\alpha \in \{mdf, mldf\}$, h_1 is a weak coding, and h_2 is a morphism.*

Proof. We prove the result only for mdf grammars. For $mldf$ grammars, the proof is similar, but we use the above modified rules. Starting from a type-0 grammar $G = (N, T, S, P)$, we can construct the grammar G' as in the above theorem, and then we proceed as below. Consider a new symbol b_w, associated with each string w in the set

$$U = \{\#, A\$, AB\$, \vdash \alpha, [A\$], [AB\$] \mid A, B \in N, \ \alpha \in (N \cup T)\}.$$

Let us denote by W the set of all such symbols b_w and define the weak coding $h_1 : (W \cup T)^* \longrightarrow T^*$ by

$$h_1(b_w) = \lambda, \ w \in U, \ h_1(a) = a, \ a \in T,$$

as well as the morphism $h_2 : (W \cup T)^* \longrightarrow V'^*$ by

$$h_2(b_w) = w, \ w \in U, \quad h_2(a) = a, \ a \in T.$$

The inverse morphism h_2^{-1} can be applied only when a string in $(U \cup T)^*$ is obtained. This implies that all non-terminals are dead and the corresponding derivation in G is a terminal one. The weak coding h_1 removes all symbols b_w, so we obtain a string in T^*. With this explanations, the reader can easily verify that $L = h_1(h_2^{-1}(L'))$. □

6. Conclusion

In this chapter, we have introduced two new classes of contextual grammars and investigated their feasibility with respect to MCS formalism. Both the variants are capable of generating the non-context-free languages. The membership problem has been solved for these two new classes of languages. We have shown that the families of languages $ICC_{iemdf}(REG)$ and $ICC_{mloc}(REG)$ contain semilinear languages only and the families of languages $ICC_\alpha(REG)$, $\alpha \in \{mdf, mldf, emdf\}$ contain non-semilinear languages. Therefore, $iemdf$ and $mloc$ are the two variants in contextual grammars, whose languages satisfy the properties of MCS, thus, these two classes of grammars can be considered as generative model for natural languages. Though, the family of languages generated by $emdf$ grammars does not satisfy the semilinear property, it satisfies the bounded growth property since every derivation of a contextual grammar (of any mode) is obtained by adjoining the contexts of finite length and as each sentential form is included in the language, any two consecutive derivations can be easily bounded by a constant whose length is greater than $|u| + |v|$. Thus, we obtain one more new family of contextual languages which was shown to have the MCS formalism if we take the condition for MCS formalism as properties 1,2 and $3'$ mentioned in the introduction. Note that the membership problem for mdf, $mldf$ variants are still left open. We have also given representation for recursive enumerable languages in terms of $mdf, mldf, emdf$ grammars using the operations of morphism, weak coding and left quotient. We do not attempt to give such a recursive enumerable language representation for $iemdf, mloc$ grammars as we have shown that their power is very limited in the sense that they cannot produce non-semilinear languages. The future work of this chapter is mentioned below.

From the definition, it is understood that $iemdf$ grammars are a variant of $emdf$ grammars. We have also seen that the non-marked duplication language $\{ww \mid w \in \{a,b\}^*\}$ can be generated by $iemdf$ grammars, but not by $emdf$ grammars. Further, we have shown that $ICC_{emdf}(REG)$ contains non-semilinear languages which are not in $ICC_{iemdf}(REG)$, as we have seen that $ICC_{iemdf}(REG)$ contains semilinear languages only. This leads to the conclusion that the generative power for each variant is distinct and therefore the family of languages generated by $emdf$ and $iemdf$ grammars are *incomparable*. This interesting observation creates the necessity for analyzing the limit of generative power and the hierarchial relations for the variants discussed in this chapter. In the Chomsky family of languages, when the restrictions are increased to the grammar (from type-0 grammar to type-3 grammars), the generative power is decreased. On the other hand, in regulated rewriting (for instance, consider matrix grammars with and without appearance checking), when the restrictions are increased to the grammar, the generative power of the grammar is increased. Therefore, it would be an interesting result in the field of formal languages to show that there are class of grammars whose generative power is neither increased nor decreased but they are incomparable, when the restrictions are increased to the grammars. That is, if we can show that the families of languages generated by mdf and $mldf$, $mloc$ and arc grammars are incomparable, then, we achieve an excellent result in contextual grammars since $mldf$ grammars are restricted versions of mdf grammars and arc grammars are restricted versions of $mloc$ grammars. We conjecture that such a nice result is possible.

References

[1] Bar-Hillel, Y.; Shamir, E. Finite state languages: Formal representations and adequacy problems. In *Language and Information*; Bar Hillel, Y.; Ed.; Addison-Wesley: Reading, MA, 1964; pp 87–98.

[2] Boullier, P. Range concatenation grammars. Proceedings of *Sixth International Workshop on Parsing Technologies (IWPT '00)*. 2000, 53–64.

[3] Boullier, P. (2001). From contextual grammars to range concatenation grammars. *Electronic Notes in Theoretical Computer Science,* **53**.

[4] Chomsky, N. Formal properties of grammars. In *Handbook of Mathematical Psychology*; Luce, R.D.; et al.; Eds.; John Wiley: New York, NY, 1963; pp 323–418.

[5] Ehrenfeucht, A., Ilie, L.; Păun, Gh.; Rozenberg, G.; Salomaa, A. On the generative capacity of certain classes of contextual grammars. In *Mathematical Linguistics and Related Topics*; Paun, Gh.; Ed.; The Publ. House of the Romanian Academy: Bucharest, 1995; pp 105–118.

[6] Floyd, R.W. On the non-existence of a phrase structure grammar for Algol-60. *Comm. of the ACM*. 1962, 5, 483–484.

[7] Ilie, L. A non-seminlinear language generated by an internal contextual grammar with finite selection. *Ann. Univ. Bucharest Math. Inform. Series*. 1996, 45/1, 63–70.

[8] Ilie, L. On computational complexity of contextual languages. *Theo. Comp. Science*. 1997, 183/1, 33–44.

[9] Ilie, L. Some recent results in contextual grammars. *Bull. EATCS*. 1997, 62, 172–194.

[10] Joshi, A.K. How much context-sensitivity is required to provide structural descriptions: Tree adjoining grammars. In *Natural Language Processing: Psycholinguistic, Computational, and Theoretical Perspectives*; David, D.; Lauri, K.; Arnold, Z.; Eds.; Cambridge University Press: New York, 1985; pp 206–250.

[11] Joshi, A.K. An introduction to tree adjoining grammars. In *Mathematics of Language*; Manaster, R.A.; Ed.; John Benjamins: Amsterdam, PH, 1987; pp 87–114.

[12] Krishna, S.N.; Lakshmanan, K.; Rama, R. On some classes of contextual grammars. *Intern. J. of Comp. Math*. 2003, 80/2, 151–164.

[13] Lakshmanan, K.; Krishna, S.N.; Rama, R.; Martin-Vide, C. Internal contextual grammars for mildly context sensitive languages, to appear in *Research on Language and Computation*. 2007.

[14] Marcus, S. *Algebraic Linguistics, Analytical Models*; Academic Press: New York, 1967.

[15] Marcus, S. Contextual grammars. *Rev. Roum. Pures. Appl*. 1969, 14, 1525–1534.

[16] Marcus, S.; Martin-Vide, C.; Păun, Gh. On internal contextual grammars with maximal use of selectors. Proc. of *8th Conf. Automata and Formal Languages*. Salgotarjan, 1996. Also in *Publ. Math. Debrecen*. 1999, 54, 933–947.

[17] Marcus, S.; Martin-Vide, C.; Păun, Gh. Contextual grammars versus natural languages. Proc. of *Speech and Computers Conf. SPECOM '96*. St. Petersburg, 1996, 28–33.

[18] Marcus, S.; Martin-vide, C.; Păun, Gh. Contextual grammars as generative models of natural languages. *Computational Linguistics*. 1998, 24/2, 245–274.

[19] Martin-Vide, C.; Miquel-Verges, J.; Păun, Gh. Contextual grammars with depth-first derivation. In *Tenth Twente Workshop on Language Tech*; Nijholt, A.; Scollo, G.; Steetskamp, R.; Eds.; Twente, 1995; pp 225–233.

[20] Papadimitriou, C.H. *Computational Complexity*. Addison-Wesley: Reading, MA, 1994.

[21] Păun, Gh. Marcus contextual grammars: After 25 years. *Bull. EATCS*. 1995, 52, 183–194.

[22] Păun, Gh. *Marcus Contextual Grammars*; Kluwer Academic Publishers: Dordrecht, The Netherland, 1997.

[23] Păun, Gh.; Nguyen, X.M. On the inner contextual grammars. *Rev. Roum. Pures. Appl.* 1980, 25, 641–651.

[24] Rozenberg, G.; Salomaa, A.; Eds.; *Handbook of Formal Languages*; Springer-Verlag: Berlin, Heidelberg, 1997.

[25] Salomaa, A. *Formal Languages*. Academic Press: New York, 1973.

In: New Topics in Theoretical Computer Science
Editors: Oleg N. Terikhovsky *et al.*, pp. 27-93
ISBN 978-1-60456-100-5

Chapter 2

UNIVERSAL MULTIALGEBRA

***Michał Walicki*[*] *and Uwe Wolter*[†]**
Department of Informatics University of Bergen, Norway

Abstract

Multialgebras are relational structures where selection of one argument as the "result" yields strong algebraic properties missing in the case of relations. However, such properties can be obtained only by choosing an appropriate definition of homomorphism and this question has been neglected or left implicit in most of the literature on power structures. We summarize our earlier results on the possible notions of compositional homomorphisms of multialgebras and investigate in detail one of them, the outer-tight homomorphisms which, unlike other alternatives, yield rich structural properties and interesting constructions. A series of classical algebraic properties is demonstrated for the resulting category and the notion of associated congruence – bireachability – is presented. It reflects the "observational" nature of multialgebras with the chosen homomorphisms in that it requires propagation of distinctions, the complement of the relation, dually to the traditional congruences and bisimulations, which require propagation of the relation.

The category is cocomplete. Final objects have quite interesting nature but, unfortunately, are not guaranteed to exist. To guarantee their existence, we have to extend the category by admitting algebras over proper classes, in the same way as it has to be done for coalgebras involving power-set functor. We give an exact characterisation of the large objects as colimits of small algebras or, equivalently, as algebras were each element is reachable from at most a set of other elements. Finally, we give a construction of products. A particular case gives a new construction of products for coalgebras over (bounded) power-set functor. The results (for the category of small algebras) extend to this category which is thus complete and cocomplete. The category of small algebras may lack final objects and products, but possesses other limits and all colimits. We characterize its subcategories, of κ-bounded multialgebras, which are complete and cocomplete.

Examples and remarks illustrate relations to total and partial algebras, coalgebras, automata theory and topology.

[*]E-mail address: michal@ii.uib.no
[†]E-mail address: uwe@ii.uib.no

1. Background

Multialgebras are algebras where operations can return not only single values but also sets thereof. Multialgebras, or variants of power-set structures, have been given some attention in the mathematical community, e.g., [36, 37, 14, 39, 7, 30], with [6] presenting a comprehensive overview. The seminal work here was [25, 26] which introduced multialgebras (algebras of complexes) for representation of relational structures and demonstrated general representability of Boolean algebras with operators by such algebras. As Kripke-frames are naturally represented by such algebras, their relevance for modal logic has also been acknowledged, e.g., [4], if not widely recognized. (The works of McKinsey and Tarski, [31, 32, 33], provided the semantics for S4 logic directly in terms of Boolean algebras with closure operator.) Likewise, automata can be modeled as multialgebras where the power-set operation allows for a natural inclusion of nondeterminism. In the tradition of algebraic specifications, multialgebras have been used as an extension of algebraic semantics precisely for the purpose of modelling nondeterminism, e.g., [20, 21, 23, 44, 46]. In this context, it is important to distinguish between arbitrary sets and one-element sets (nondeterministic operations vs. usual functions), as well as to pay attention to the distinction between sets being second-order or first-order objects – the former corresponds to multialgebras (application of operations to sets is obtained by pointwise extension and hence is monotone) and the latter to power-set algebras (where operation applied to a larger set may yield a smaller result) – the distinction was investigated and used in [45, 47]. Some variants of multialgebras disallow empty result-sets, e.g., [44, 14], but most do not. Then, applying the standard isomorphism

$$A_1 \times ... \times A_n \to \mathcal{P}(A) \;\simeq\; \mathcal{P}(A_1 \times ... \times A_n \times A), \tag{1.1}$$

one obtains another representation of relational structures, although with more algebraic properties, as will be shown in what follows. This is the variant of multialgebras we will be using.

Following [18] (definition 3.1.2), a one-sorted multialgebraic operation α over a set A can be seen as a dialgebra $\langle A, \alpha\rangle$, namely, a function $\alpha : F(A) \to \mathcal{P}(A)$, where the endofunctor $F : \mathsf{Set} \to \mathsf{Set}$ on the category of sets gives the source of the operation and $\mathcal{P} : \mathsf{Set} \to \mathsf{Set}$ is the covariant existential-image power-set functor, i.e., sending a function $f : A \to B$ onto $\mathcal{P}(f)(X) = \{f(x) \mid x \in X\}$, for $X \subseteq A$. Although we will not use this model of multialgebras, we may occasionally refer to it. [41] presents a series of basic facts about dialgebras (called "bialgebras") which can be instantiated to either algebraic or colagebraic version depending on the choice of the functors. In general, instead of $\mathcal{P}$ one can use any endofunctor $G : \mathsf{Set} \to \mathsf{Set}$ and a morphism $\langle A, \alpha\rangle \to \langle B, \beta\rangle$ in the category Set^F_G is a function $f : A \to B$, such that $F(f);\beta = \alpha; G(f)$. The variations in the definitions of homomorphisms to be encountered below could be then seen as variations over this notion of morphism (requiring, in addition, lax transformations). Less abstractly, we can use the isomorphism (1.1), and view a multialgebra as a relational structure where, for each relation, one argument is designated as its "result" and used for composing the relation with others. This composition is obtained by pointwise extension.

Definition 1.2. *For a signature $\Sigma = \langle S, \mathcal{F}\rangle$, a Σ-multialgebra M is given by:*

- *a (family of) carrier set(s)* $|M| = \{s^M \mid s \in \mathcal{S}\}$,
- *a function* $f^M : s_1^M \times ... \times s_n^M \to \mathcal{P}(s^M)$ *for each* $f : s_1 \times ... \times s_n \to s \in \mathcal{F}$, *with composition defined through additive extension to sets, i.e.* $f^M(X_1, ..., X_n) = \bigcup_{x_i \in X_i} f^M(x_1, ..., x_n)$.

We will not distinguish in the notation between an algebra A and its carrier. Expressions involving set operations, e.g., $x \in A$, $X \subseteq A$, suggest that the carrier of A is meant. The only structures addressed in the paper are multialgebras, so "multialgebra" and "algebra" will be used interchangeably. We assume a given signature with f/R ranging over all operation/relation symbols.

Selection of the "result" argument corresponds, in a sense, to turning our considerations to binary relations with the additional operation of tupling the arguments. Composition of relations $R_1 : X_{11}...X_{1n} \to X_1, ..., R_k : X_{k1}...X_{kn} \to X_k$ and $R : X_1...X_k \to X$, corresponds to application of R to the tupling $\langle R_1...R_k \rangle$. When using relational notation, we write composition in diagrammatic order, $R; \phi$, resp. $\phi; R$, assuming implicitly ϕ to be binary (in fact, homomorphism or, in the case of $\phi; R$, a tuple $(\phi_1 \times ... \times \phi_{n+1})$ of unary functions, for each relevant argument/sort i of R.) The composition is, as just explained, an abbreviation for the multialgebraic one, i.e.:

$$\begin{array}{rcl} \langle a_1...a_n, b \rangle \in R; \phi & \iff & \exists a : \langle a_1...a_n, a \rangle \in R \wedge \langle a, b \rangle \in \phi \\ resp. \quad \langle a_1...a_n, b \rangle \in (\phi_1 \times ... \times \phi_n); R & \iff & \exists b_1...b_n : \langle a_i, b_i \rangle \in \phi_i \wedge \langle b_1...b_n, b \rangle \in R \end{array} \tag{1.3}$$

The central definition of OT-homomorphisms involves the converse of a function $\phi : A \to B$ and this also makes the use of relational notation often more convenient. We will freely switch between two equivalent formulations, in the category Rel, of sets with binary relations, and in Set, of sets with functions, as illustrated by the following diagrams:

$$\begin{array}{ccc} & \mathsf{Rel} & \\ s^A & \xrightarrow{R^A} & t^A \\ \phi_t^- \uparrow & & \uparrow \phi_t^- \\ s^B & \xrightarrow{R^B} & t^B \end{array} \qquad \begin{array}{ccc} & \mathsf{Set} & \\ \mathcal{P}(s^A) & \xrightarrow{f^A} & \mathcal{P}(t^A) \\ \phi_t^- \uparrow & & \uparrow \mathcal{P}(\phi_t^-) \\ s^B & \xrightarrow{f^B} & \mathcal{P}(t^B) \end{array} \tag{1.4}$$

Having made these precautions, we will write things as if all relations were binary, (most) algebras were one-sorted and homomorpisms simple functions (and not their families), but all considerations apply to the general case. (Occasionally, we may write argument sequences explicitly.)

Selection of the "result" among the relational arguments leads to more algebraic structure reflected by homomorphisms. (In particular, derived operators of a multialgebra are analogous to those of classical algebra, so that for a given signature Σ, the term structure T_Σ is itself a Σ-algebra, and preservation/reflection of Σ operations leads to the corresponding behaviour of the derived operators. For relational structures (without specified composition argument), on the other hand, derived operators are just boolean operators which are only very weakly related to the actual signature and need not be preserved by homomorphisms preserving the basic relations. [11], V.3, p.203, considers this the reason for the subordinate role of homorphisms in the study of relational structures.) This, however, does not simplify the study of the resulting structure – the number of possible definitions of homomorphisms, congruences, etc. hardly diminishes.

As the first step towards a simplification of the rather complicated picture, we have earlier in [43] classified compositional homomorphisms of (relational structures modeled as) multialgebras. In order to motivate our choice of the outer-tight homomorphisms, we recall now these results and in 1.2. review finite (co)completeness of the respective categories. Section 2. studies the basic algebraic notions (congruences, subalgebras) in the category of multialgebras with outer-tight homomorphisms. Section 3. extends this category allowing algebras with proper classes as carriers and shows its cocompleteness and existence of equalizers and final objects. Section 4. demonstrates then the existence of products, thus finishing the proof of completeness of the category. All constructions can be performed also (for small diagrams) in the category of small algebras with the exception of the constructions of final objects and products. These need not exist in the category of small algebras, and in Section 5. we identify a wide class of its subcategories of κ-bounded multialgebras, which are complete and cocomplete. Section 6. contains a brief summary and suggestions for further development. The appendix summarizes the assumptions used in the treatement of classes.

1.1. Compositional Homomorphisms of Multialgebras

Besides some preservation properties, the first minimal requirement for a definition of homomorphism seems to be compositionality: composition of two homomorphisms should yield a homomorphism. In fact, various proposed definitions (used to obtain specific results) violate this requirement. We therefore start by inquiring into the possible compositional definitions.

Definition 1.5. *A definition $\Delta[\_]$ of a function $\phi : A \to B$ being a homomorphism of the multialgebraic structures $A \to B$ has the form:*

$$\Delta[\phi] \iff l_1[\phi]; R^A; r_1[\phi] \bowtie l_2[\phi]; R^B; r_2[\phi]$$

where $l[\_]$'s and $r[\_]$'s are relational expressions (using only relational composition and converse), and $\bowtie \in \{=, \subseteq, \supseteq\}$.

One can certainly consider other formats but most proposed definitions of homomorphisms conform to this one as do, in particular, all compositional definitions which we have encountered.[1]

Definition 1.6. *A definition is* compositional *iff for all $\phi : A \to B$, $\psi : B \to C$, we have $\Delta[\phi]$ & $\Delta[\psi] \Rightarrow \Delta[\phi; \psi]$, i.e.:*

$$\begin{aligned} l_1[\phi]; R^A; r_1[\phi] &\bowtie l_2[\phi]; R^B; r_2[\phi] \ \& \\ l_1[\psi]; R^B; r_1[\psi] &\bowtie l_2[\psi]; R^C; r_2[\psi] \\ &\Rightarrow l_1[\phi;\psi]; R^A; r_1[\phi;\psi] \bowtie l_2[\phi;\psi]; R^C; r_2[\phi;\psi] \end{aligned}$$

[1] Of course, one can consider homomorphisms which are themselves relations, but such a generalisation goes beyond the scope of the present investigation.

The number of syntactic expressions of the kind $l[\phi]$ is infinite, however, since homomorphisms are functions we have the simple fact:

Fact 1.7. *a)* $\phi^-;\phi;\phi^- = \phi^-$ *b)* $\phi;\phi^-;\phi = \phi$ *c)* $\phi^-;\phi = id_{\phi[A]}$

Thus the length of each of the expression $l[\phi]$, resp. $r[\phi]$ (measured by the number of occurring ϕ's or ϕ^-'s) can be limited to 2.

On the other hand, both sides of definition 1.5 must yield relational expressions of the same type, i.e., of one of the four types $A \times A, A \times B, \ldots$, which will be abbreviated as $AA, AB, \ldots$

For each choice of $\bowtie$, this leaves us with four possibilities for each type. For instance, for AB we have the following four possibilities:

$\top_{AB} : \phi;\phi^-;R^A;\phi \bowtie \phi;R^B;\phi^-;\phi$ $\quad \bot_{AB} : R^A;\phi \bowtie \phi;R^B$

$E_{AB} : \phi;\phi^-;R^A;\phi \bowtie \phi;R^B$ $\quad W_{AB} : R^A;\phi \bowtie \phi;R^B;\phi^-;\phi$

The symbols denoting the respective possibilities are chosen for the following reason. Relational composition preserves each of the relations $\bowtie$, i.e., given a particular choice of $\bowtie$ and any relations C, D (of appropriate type), we have: $R_1 \bowtie R_2 \Rightarrow C;R_1 \bowtie C;R_2$ and $R_1 \bowtie R_2 \Rightarrow R_1;D \bowtie R_2;D$. Starting with $\bot_{AB}$ and pre-composing (on the "East") both sides of $\bowtie$ with $\phi;\phi^-;(\_)$, we obtain E_{AB}; post-composing (on the "West") both sides of $\bowtie$ with $(\_);\phi^-;\phi$, we obtain W_{AB}. Dual compositions lead from there to $\top_{AB}$. Thus we have that $\bot_{AB} \Rightarrow E_{AB}, W_{AB} \Rightarrow \top_{AB}$ and the corresponding lattices are obtained for the other three types starting, respectively, with

$$\bot_{AA} : R^A \bowtie \phi;R^B;\phi^- \quad \bot_{BB} : \phi^-;R^A;\phi \bowtie R^B \quad \bot_{BA} : \phi^-;R^A \bowtie R^B;\phi^-$$

Figure 1.8 shows the four lattices for each type (the choice of $\bowtie$ is uniform for all four).

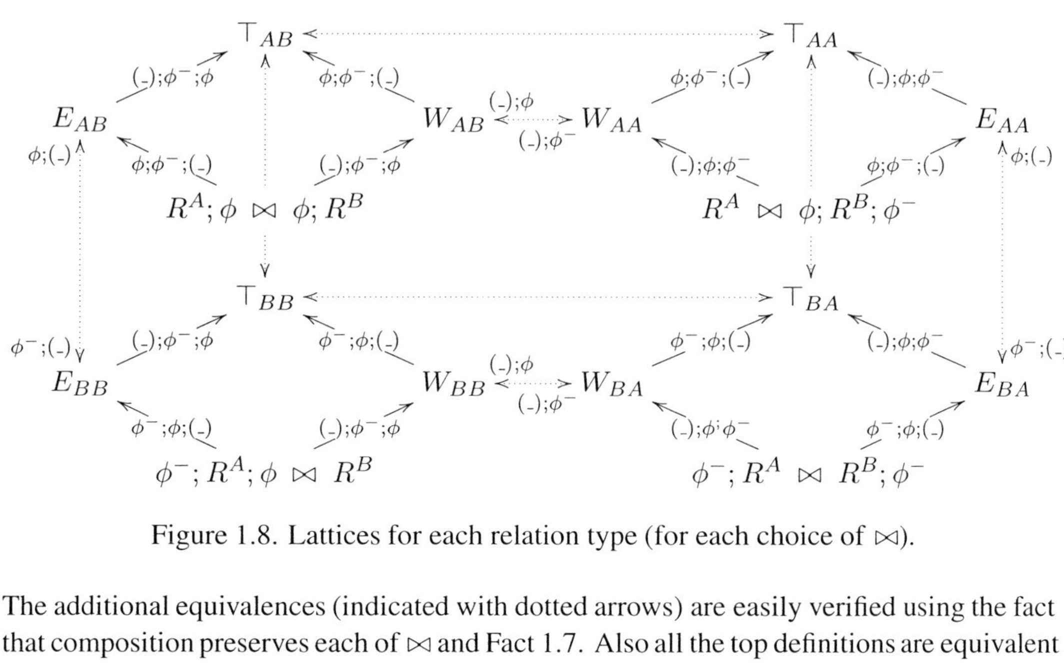

Figure 1.8. Lattices for each relation type (for each choice of $\bowtie$).

The additional equivalences (indicated with dotted arrows) are easily verified using the fact that composition preserves each of $\bowtie$ and Fact 1.7. Also all the top definitions are equivalent which follows by simple calculation.

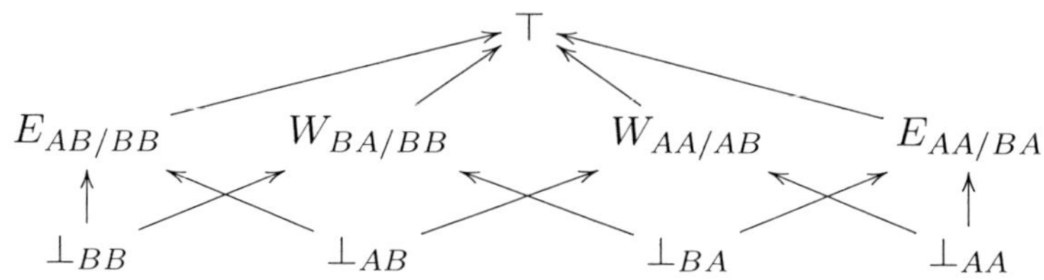

Figure 1.9. Possible definitions (for a given choice of $\bowtie$).

These observations simplify the picture a bit, leading, for each choice of $\bowtie$, to the order of 9 possible definitions shown in figure 1.9.

When the mappings between the structures are, as in our case, functions and not arbitrary relations, several elements of the ordering from 1.9 collapse.

Fact 1.10. *All definitions (of the form 1.5) involving $\subseteq$ are equivalent.*

We are thus left with one definition involving $\subseteq$ and 18 other definitions obtained from two instances (with $=$, resp. $\supseteq$ for $\bowtie$) of the orderings in figure 1.9. The following, main theorem shows that only the bottom elements of these orderings yield compositional definitions.

Theorem 1.11. *A definition is compositional iff it is equivalent to one of:*

$$1)\ R^A;\phi \bowtie \phi;R^B \qquad 2)\ \phi^-;R^A;\phi \rhd R^B \qquad 3)\ \phi^-;R^A \rhd R^B;\phi^- \qquad 4)\ R^A \rhd \phi;R^B;\phi^-$$

where $\bowtie \in \{=,\subseteq,\supseteq\}$ *and* $\rhd \in \{=,\supseteq\}$.

PROOF: For the "if" part, one easily checks that 1)–4) do yield compositional definitions. In fact, this part of the theorem holds for *any* transitive set-relation $\bowtie$. For instance, for 1) we verify:

$$\begin{array}{rcl@{\quad}c@{\quad}rcl} & \phi^-;R^A & \bowtie & R^B;\phi^- & \& & \psi^-;R^B & \bowtie & R^C;\psi^- \\ \Rightarrow & \psi\ ;\phi\ ;R^A & \bowtie & \psi^-;R^B;\phi^- & \& & \psi^-;R^B;\phi^- & \bowtie & R^C;\psi^-;\phi^- \\ & & & & \Rightarrow & (\phi;\psi)^-;R^A & \bowtie & R^C;(\phi;\psi)^- \end{array}$$

The "only if" part is shown providing counter-examples for the remaining possibilities. Although there are 10 cases left, they are easily shown by the following three counter-examples. In all cases, the given homomorphisms ϕ, ψ satisfy the respective definition with $=$ for $\rhd$ (hence, also for $\supseteq$), while their composition does not satisfy the respective definition with $\supseteq$ for $\rhd$. Thus we obtain immediately counter-examples for both $\rhd \in \{=,\supseteq\}$.

Vertical arrows represent the relation (R) in respective multialgebras; the dotted arrows illustrate the images under the respective homomorphisms:

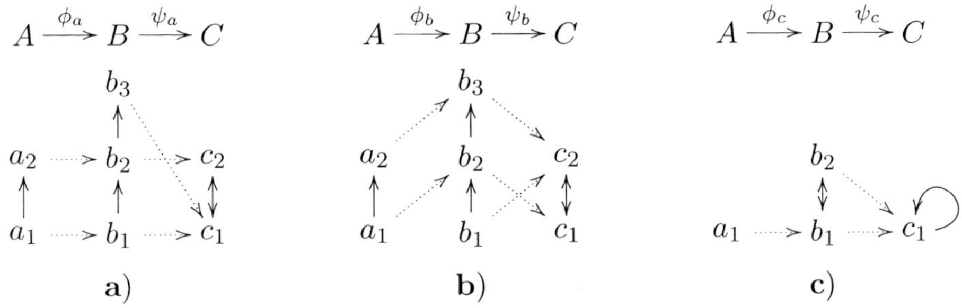

a) for W_{BB} : $\phi^-; R^A; \phi \;\triangleright\; R^B; \phi^-; \phi$. We have: $\phi_a^-; R^A; \phi_a = R^B; \phi_a^-; \phi_a$ and $\psi_a^-; R^B; \psi_a = R^C; \psi_a^-; \psi_a$. However, for the composition $\rho_a = \phi_a; \psi_a$, we have $\langle c_2, c_1\rangle \in R^C; \rho_a^-; \rho_a$ but $\langle c_2, c_1\rangle \notin \rho_a^-; R^A; \rho_a$, i.e., $\rho_a^-; R^A; \rho_a \not\supseteq R^C; \rho_a^-; \rho_a$.
b) for E_{BB} : $\phi^-; R^A; \phi \triangleright \phi^-; \phi; R^B$ is quite analogous. $\phi_b^-; R^A; \phi_b = R^B; \phi_b^-; \phi_b$ and $\psi_b^-; R^B; \psi_b = R^C; \psi_b^-; \psi_b$, but $\rho_b^-; R^A; \rho_b \not\supseteq \rho_b^-; \rho_b; R^C$ with $\langle c_2, c_1\rangle$ as a witness to this negation.
Both these examples can also be used as counter-examples for compositionality of $\top$, represented by $\top_{BB}$. For instance, in the first case, we have $R^B; \phi_a^-; \phi_a = \phi_a^-; \phi_a; R^B; \phi_a^-; \phi_a$ and the corresponding equality holds for ψ_a and R^C – so exactly the same argument yields a counter-example also for this case.
c) $W_{AA/AB}$ and $E_{AA/BA}$: ϕ_c and ψ_c are obviously W_{AB}: $R^A; \phi_c = \phi_c; R^B; \phi_c^-; \phi_c$ and $R^B; \psi_c = \psi_c; R^C; \psi_c^-; \psi_c$. But their composition gives: $\varnothing = R^A; \rho_c \not\supseteq \rho_c; R^C; \rho_c^-; \rho_c = \langle c_1, c_1\rangle$.
This gives also counter-example for $E_{BA} : \phi_c^-; R^A \triangleright \phi_c^-; \phi_c; R^B; \phi_c^-$. □

Table 1.11 summarises the naming conventions for the compositional cases. The name consists of two parts, the first (inner/left/...) indicating one of the four main cases in the theorem and the second (closed/tight/weak) the choice of the set relation.

Table 1.11. Compositional homomorphisms

	$R^A; \phi \bowtie \phi; R^B$	$\phi^-; R^A; \phi \triangleright R^B$	$\phi^-; R^A \triangleright R^B; \phi^-$	$R^A \triangleright \phi; R^B; \phi^-$
	inner	left	outer	right
closed	$\mathsf{MAlg}_{IC}(\Sigma)$: $R^A; \phi \supseteq \phi; R^B$	$\mathsf{MAlg}_{LC}(\Sigma)$: $\phi^-; R^A; \phi \supseteq R^B$	$\mathsf{MAlg}_{OC}(\Sigma)$: $\phi^-; R^A \supseteq R^B; \phi^-$	$\mathsf{MAlg}_{RC}(\Sigma)$: $R^A \supseteq \phi; R^B; \phi^-$
tight	$\mathsf{MAlg}_{IT}(\Sigma)$: $R^A; \phi = \phi; R^B$	$\mathsf{MAlg}_{LT}(\Sigma)$: $\phi^-; R^A; \phi = R^B$	$\mathsf{MAlg}_{OT}(\Sigma)$: $\phi^-; R^A = R^B; \phi^-$	$\mathsf{MAlg}_{RT}(\Sigma)$: $R^A = \phi; R^B; \phi^-$
weak	$\mathsf{MAlg}_W(\Sigma) : R^A; \phi \subseteq \phi; R^B$			

[12] studied in detail the four cases of weak morphisms as models of simulations between data types. However, as we observed in lemma 1.10, these four cases coincide when the morphisms are, as in our case, functions and not arbitrary relations, as in [12].

1.2. Finite Completeness and Cocompleteness

Earlier study of finite (co)completeness of the resulting categories, [43], is summarized in table 1.12.

Table 1.12. Finite limits and colimits in the categories of multialgebras

	initial	co-prod.	co-equal.	final	prod.	equal.
$\mathsf{MAlg}_W(\Sigma)$	$+$	$+$	$+$	$+$	$+$	$+$
$\mathsf{MAlg}_{IC}(\Sigma)$	$-$	$-$	$-$	$+$	$-$	$-$
$\mathsf{MAlg}_{IT}(\Sigma)$	$-$	$-$	$+$	$-$	$-$	$-$
$\mathsf{MAlg}_{LC}(\Sigma)$	$-$	$-$	$+$	$+$	$-$	$-$
$\mathsf{MAlg}_{LT}(\Sigma)$	$-$	$-$	$+$	$-$	$-$	$-$
$\mathsf{MAlg}_{OC}(\Sigma)$	$+$	$+$	$-$	$+$	$-$	$+$
$\mathsf{MAlg}_{OT}(\Sigma)$	$+$	$+$	$+$	$+/-$	?	$+$
$\mathsf{MAlg}_{RC}(\Sigma)$	$+$	$+$	$+$	$+$	$+$	$+$
$\mathsf{MAlg}_{RT}(\Sigma)$	$+$	$-$	$-$	$-$	$-$	$+$

The present paper addresses the category of outer-tight homomorphisms (the double row) and, in particular, provides the full answers to the places marked +/– and ?. In general, both are negative, but we will identify a wide range of subcategories of $\mathsf{MAlg}_{OT}(\Sigma)$ which are complete and cocomplete. First, however, a few words about the possible alternatives.

Remark 1.13. *Viewing (binary) relations as coalgebras for the existential image power-set functor ($\mathcal{P}(f)(X) = \bigcup_{x\in X} f(x)$), yields the homomorphism condition $R^A;\phi = \phi;R^B$, that is, the IT homomorphisms. As we see from the table, the category $\mathsf{MAlg}_{IT}(\Sigma)$ has rather few (co)limits. This, of course, looks suspicious, since we know from [38] that this category of coalgebras over sets will be, at least, cocomplete. The difference is, however, due to the fact that although the homomorphism conditions look the same, the respective representations of relations are not:*

The absence of final objects is here due to the fact that the table addresses only categories based on sets. The non-existence of colimits is due to the algebraic character of operations, in particular, constants which correspond to predicates. (Restriction to signatures containing only *binary relations would yield the same category as coalgebras mentioned in the first line of this remark.) For instance, for a signature with a single sort and constant $c :\to S$, the category $\mathsf{MAlg}_{IT}(\Sigma)$ has no intial multialgebra I. A multialgebraic constant is $c^I \subseteq S^I$, which corresponds to the arrow $c^I : \mathbf{1} \to \mathcal{P}(S^I)$, where $\mathbf{1}$ is a one-element set. Consequently, for any (in particular, empty) c^I there is no IT-homomorphism $\phi : I \to A$ making $\phi(c^I) = c^A$ when $|c^I| < |c^A|$. The desired equality $c^I;\phi = \phi;c^A$, for $I = \varnothing$, is achieved when constants are coalgebraic arrows, namely, $c^I : S^I \to \mathbf{2}$ (with $\mathbf{2}$ being, for* *instance, $\{\bot, \top\}$). The two diagrams illustrate the difference.*

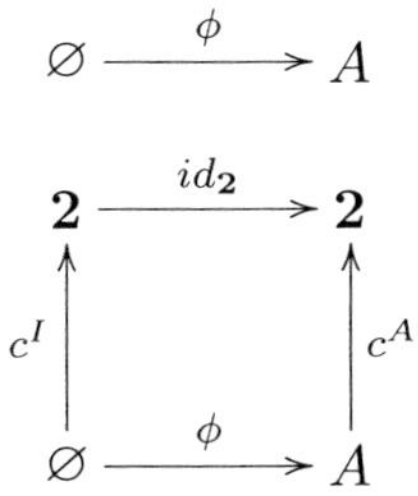

$c^I; id_\mathbf{2} = \varnothing = \phi; c^A$

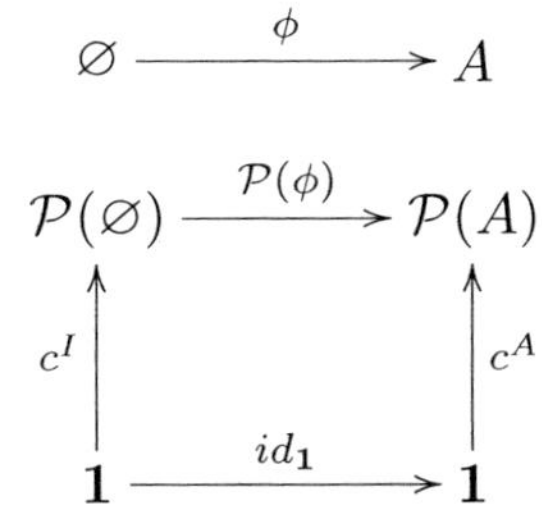

$c^I; \mathcal{P}(\phi) = \varnothing \neq c^A = id_\mathbf{1}; c^A$

The meaning of the condition is different in the two cases in that for coalgebras it requires equality of two functions while for multialgebras of two sets. As an example, take the carrier $X = \{1, 2\}$ and one constant c. Let, in a multilagebra M, $c^M = \{1, 2\}$, while in a coalgebra C, $c(1) = c(2) = \top$. Let $X' = \{1, 2, 3\}$ and $c^{M'} = \{1, 2, 3\}$ while in a coalgebra C', $c'(1) = c'(2) = c'(3) = \top$. Although both M and C, resp., M' and C' represent the same predicates, the inclusion $i : X \to X'$ is a coalgebraic homomorphism, since indeed $c; id_\mathbf{2} = i; c'$, but it is not a multialgebraic IT-homomorphism since $i(c^M) = i(\{1, 2\}) = \{1, 2\} \neq \{1, 2, 3\} = c^{M'}$.

This might be taken as a suggestion that the multialgebraic representation of relations is not the most sucessful one. However, using coalgebras as models of relations is by no means straightforward. For the first, one has to decide whether to use the functor $\mathcal{P}(X^n)$ or $\mathbf{2}^{(X^n)}$ – the difference in homomorphisms will be similar to that suggested in the above remark (between equality of sets and of functions). In either case one has to decide which power-set functor to use. Any choice involves sacrificing the pleasant and well understood behavior of polynomial functors. Additional complications arise if one wants to model many-sorted relations. (Although these are hardly theoretically demanding, they *are* complications, at least of the same order as in the case of many-sorted algebras.) Multialgebraic model, on the other hand, is in agreement with the traditional notion of relation/predicate as a subset. It deals with many-argument, as well as many-sorted, relations in the uniform and elementary way. In addition, one should also remark that multialgebras were introduced not merely as representations of relational structures but of Boolean algebras with operators and, on the other hand, as a generalisation of algebraic semantics to handle nondeterminism and partiality (most common institutions can be naturally embedded into the institution of multialgebras, with weak homomorphisms as morphisms in the model categories, [28]). The investigation of homomorphisms arises from this background and was motivated primarily by the search for the interesting canonical objects (initial or final) for algebraic specifications with nondeterminism.

Now, weak homomorphisms are those which are most commonly used. Unfortunately, this is an extremely weak notion which is also reflected in its name. Although the initial objects exist, they are of little interest having all predicates and relations empty. Lifiting existence of initial objects to the axiomatic classes depends, of course, on the language one wants to use, and this is by no means a clarified issue. Most approaches suggest, at least, the use of inclusions, but this again leads only to empty relations in the initial objects. Furthermore, even simplest formulae are not preserved. E.g., having two constants a, b interpreted in A as $\{1\}$, resp., $\{1, 2\}$ makes $A \models a \subseteq b$. But the inclusion, which is a weak homomorphism, into B with $a^B = \{1,3\}$ and $b^B = \{1,2\}$ does not preserve this formula. Counterexamples can be easily found also for preservation under homomorphic images. (Similar remarks apply to the other (co)complete category $\mathsf{MAlg}_{RC}(\Sigma)$.) One way would be to design a specific syntax ensuring adequate restrictions of the model classes, as was done, for instance, with membership alegbras, [35]. But this amounts to a specialisation of the problem motivated by particular applications which we are not addressing here. Perhaps even more serious shortcomming of the weak homomorphisms is that the associated congruence becomes simply equivalence.

The outer-tight homomorphisms seem to possess many desirable properties which are absent in the case of weak homomorphisms and vainly sought in other cases. (The condition $\phi^-; R^A = R^B; \phi^-$ is suggested as the definition of homomorphism between Boolean poly-algebras (yet another name for multialgebras) in [24], p.262 and p.264, def. 2.3.3. It is, however, not investigated there and seems to arise in order to preserve the Boolean structure which is not part of the definition of our multialgebras.) The objective of this paper is to substantiate the positive aspect of this claim: firstly, by showing the existence of several universal constructions in the category $\mathsf{MAlg}_{OT}(\Sigma)$ for an arbitrary signature Σ and, secondly, by observing how these constructions give rise to tight algebraic relationships missing in the case of weak homomorphism. The following section 2. summarizes some basic facts concerning the category $\mathsf{MAlg}_{OT}(\Sigma)$, discusses OT-congruences, subalgebras and illustrates the character of final objects. However, as the +/– in the table 1.12 indicates, such objects can be constructed only in special cases and, generally, do not exist due to the simple cardinality reasons. (The problem here is exactly the same as with coalgebras involving power-set functor.) Subsection 2.4. shows a special case when final objects exist by imposing some restrictions on the signature. The existence of final objects is shown in section 3. for the extended category $\mathsf{MAlg}^*_{OT}(\Sigma)$ where algebras may have carriers being proper classes. (The proof is analogous to that used for showing the corresponding fact for the categories of coalgebras for "set-based" functors in [2].) We show cocompleteness of this category (which result transfers easily to $\mathsf{MAlg}_{OT}(\Sigma)$). In section 4. we give a construction of products in $\mathsf{MAlg}^*_{OT}(\Sigma)$, which is entirely new result. The corresponding construction can fail in $\mathsf{MAlg}_{OT}(\Sigma)$, again due to cardinality reasons. Thus, for any signature Σ, we obtain a complete and cocomplete category of large algebras $\mathsf{MAlg}^*_{OT}(\Sigma)$, and a cocomplete category of small algebras $\mathsf{MAlg}_{OT}(\Sigma)$, with equalizers, but in general without final objects or products. We identify however a subcategory of κ-boundend multialgebras for any infinite cardinal κ, which is complete and cocomplete.

2. The Category Outer-Tight, $\mathsf{MAlg}_{OT}(\Sigma)$

The outer-tight homomorphism, OT-homomorphism, $\phi : A \to B$, is a function from the carrier of A to that of B, satisfying the condition that for every relation $R \in \Sigma$:

$$\phi^-; R^A = R^B; \phi^- \qquad \text{i.e., in the functional notation:} \qquad R^A(\phi^-(b)) = \phi^-(R^B(b))$$

which for constants specializes to $c^A = \phi^-(c^B)$.

The converse of the defining equation yields an equivalent definition: $(R^A)^-; \phi = \phi; (R^B)^-$, or functionally, $\phi((R^A)^-(a)) = (R^B)^-(\phi(a))$. This requirement of preser-

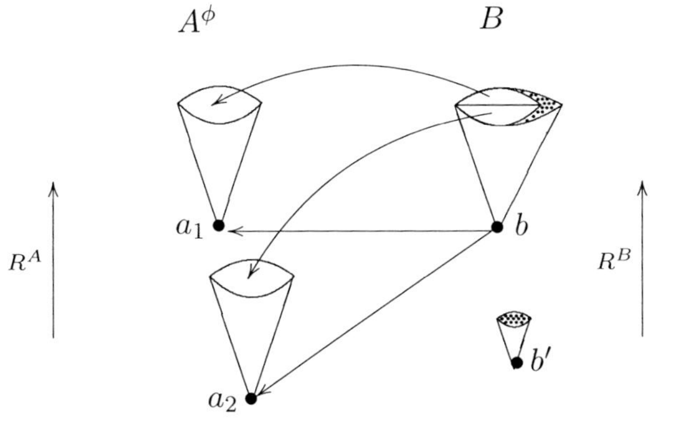

1) $b \in \phi[A] \Rightarrow$

$\bigcup_{a_i \in \phi^-(b)} R^A(a_i) = \phi^-(R^B(b))$

2) $b' \notin \phi[A] \Rightarrow R^B(b') \cap \phi[A] = \varnothing$

or, equivalently

$x \in \phi[A] \wedge x \in R^B(b) \Rightarrow b \in \phi[A]$

Figure 2.1. OT-homomorphisms.

vation and reflection of pre-image sets of the operations gives a simpler picture as shown in Figure 2.2.

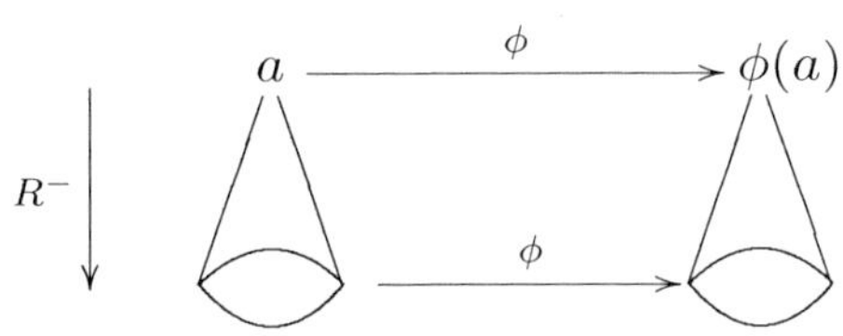

Figure 2.2. OT-homomorphisms.

The OT-requirement is strictly stronger than that of the weak homomorphism which requires merely preservation of images, i.e., $R^A; \phi \subseteq \phi; R^B$. In fact, $\phi^-; R^A = R^B; \phi^- \Rightarrow \phi; \phi^-; R^A; \phi = \phi; R^B; \phi^-; \phi$, and since $id_A \subseteq \phi; \phi^-$ and $\phi^-; \phi \subseteq id_B$, this equality yields $R^A; \phi \subseteq \phi; R^B$. Thus, every OT-homomorphism is also weak.

Remark 2.3. *As OT implies weakness and, in the special case when the involved multialgebras are classical (with all operations being total, deterministic functions), weakness implies classical homomorphism condition so, in this special case, the OT-homomorphisms become classical homomorphisms, i.e.,* $\phi^-; R^A = R^B; \phi^- \Rightarrow R^A; \phi = \phi; R^B$. *(For any* a*,* $R^B(\phi(a))$ *is then a unique value and so is* $R^A(a)$*; hence the inclusion* $R^A; \phi \subseteq \phi; R^B$ *becomes the equality* $\phi(R^A(a)) = R^B(\phi(a))$ *of single values.)*

However, not every classical homomorphism $\psi : A \to B$ *can be obtained as such a special case of an OT-homomorphism. E.g., for a signature with one operation* $R : s \to t$ *and the two algebras as shown below, the mapping* ψ *is a classical homomorphism satisfying* $\forall a : \psi(R^A(a)) = R^B(\psi(a))$*:*

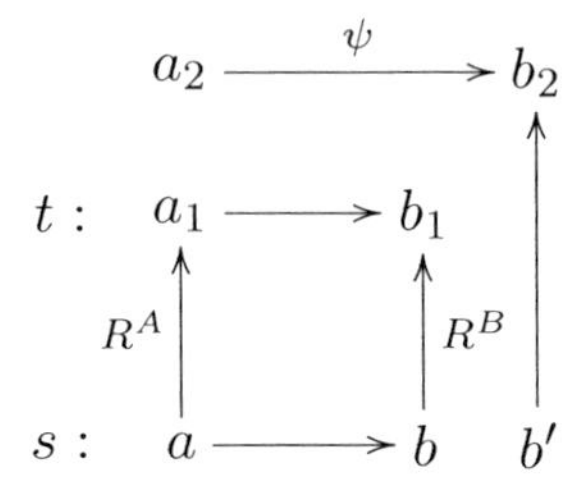

However, ψ *is not OT since* $R^A(\psi^-(b')) = \varnothing \neq \{a_2\} = \psi^-(R^B(b'))$*. In general, for classical algebras, we only have the implication* $R^A;\psi = \psi;R^B \Rightarrow \psi^-;R^A = \psi^-;\psi;R^B;\psi^- \subseteq R^B;\psi^-$ *and the above example shows that the inclusion can be proper. Thus, if we restrict the category* $\mathsf{MAlg}_{OT}(\Sigma)$ *to classical algebras only, we will obtain a wide – but not full – subcategory of the category* $\mathsf{Alg}(\Sigma)$ *of classical algebras and homomorphisms.*

Remark 2.4. *Partial algebras can be seen as deterministic multialgebras where operations return either 1-element sets or the empty set. OT-homomorphisms have here close associates, namely, the full homomorphisms. A mapping* $\phi : A \to B$ *is a full homomorphism iff*

1) $\phi(f^A(a)) \subseteq f^B(\phi(a))$
2) $\phi(a) \in (f^B)^- \wedge f^B(\phi(a)) \in \phi[A] \Longrightarrow \exists a' \in (f^A)^- : \phi(a) = \phi(a')$

where membership in the inverse image of an operation, $a \in f^-$*, is the same as membership in its definition domain,* $a \in dom(f)$*. OT implies fullness: the first condition is just the requirement of weak homomorphism, while the second follows since for OT homomorphism, the mere fact of* $f^B(b) \in \phi[A]$ *implies that* $b \in \phi[A]$ *and, moreover, that* $f^A(\phi^-(b)) = \phi^-(f^B(b)) \neq \varnothing$*, i.e.,* $\exists a' \in (f^A)^- : \phi(a') = b$*.*

Full surjective homomorphisms are quite central since they are exactly the quotient homomorphisms. Also full injective homomorphism are central since they provide the concept of a relative subalgebra: $A' \subseteq A$ *is a relative subalgebra of* A *if the inclusion is a full homomorphism. However, full homomorphisms without any additional (e.g., surjectivity) requirement are not compositional, as the following example from [8], 2.4.5, illustrates:*

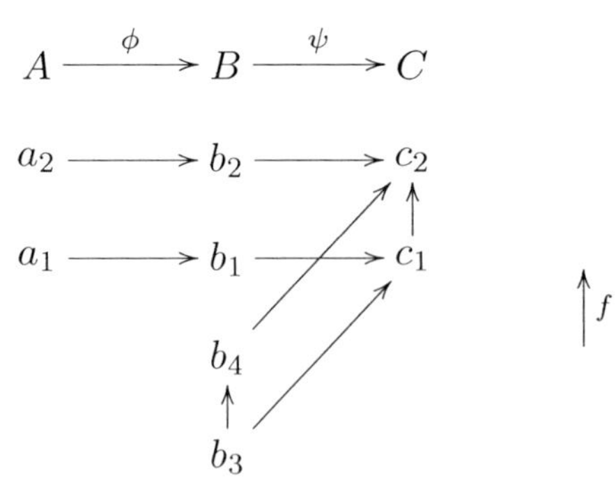

Both ϕ *and* ψ *are full, but* $\phi;\psi$ *is not.* ψ *is, of course, weak, but it is neither OT nor even OC, since* $f^B(\psi^-(c_1)) = \{b_4\} \not\supseteq \{b_2, b_4\} = \psi^-(f^C(c_1))$*.*

One considers a stronger notion (implying fullness) of closed homomorphisms, which are compositional. A mapping is a closed homomorphism iff it satisfies 1) and

3) $\phi(a) \in (f^B)^- \Longrightarrow a \in (f^A)^-$.

This notion appears rather strong, as it requires all ϕ*-preimages of a* $b \in (f^B)^-$ *to be in the domain of* f^A. *Thus, for instance,* ϕ *in the left diagram is OT (and hence full) but not closed:*

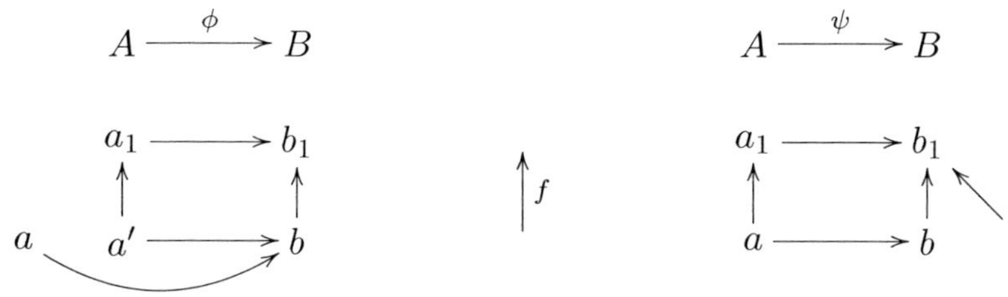

On the other hand, closedness does not imply OT, as shown by ψ *in the right diagram.*

As the OT-condition is expressible in terms of the inverse images of operations (cf. figure 2.2), that is, in terms of their definition domains, it might be a possible candidate for consideration in connection with partial algebras. Such considerations, however, fall outside the scope of this report.

We are dealing exclusively with the OT-homomorphisms, and so we will not qualify the name – saying "homomorphism" we will mean an OT-homomorphism unless qualified otherwise.

Remark 2.5. *One relational structure can be, in general, represented by various multialgebras depending on the choice of the result argument for each relation. This is reflected in the "essentially the same" mapping between structures qualifying or not qualifying as OT-homomorphism.*

The OT-homomorphism condition is, namely, sensitive to the chosen representation of a relation, i.e., it is not invariant under permutation of relational arguments. For instance, two relations $R^A = \{\langle a_1, a'_1\rangle, \langle a_2, a'_2\rangle\}$ *and* $R^B = \{\langle b, b'_1\rangle, \langle b, b'_2\rangle\}$, *can be represented as the multifunctions,* $f^{A1}(a_1) = a'_1, f^{A1}(a_2) = a'_2$ *or* $f^{A2}(a'_1) = a_1, f^{A2}(a'_2) = a_2$ *and, respectively,* $f^{B1}(b) = \{b'_1, b'_2\}$ *or* $f^{B2}(b'_1) = b = f^{B2}(b'_2)$.

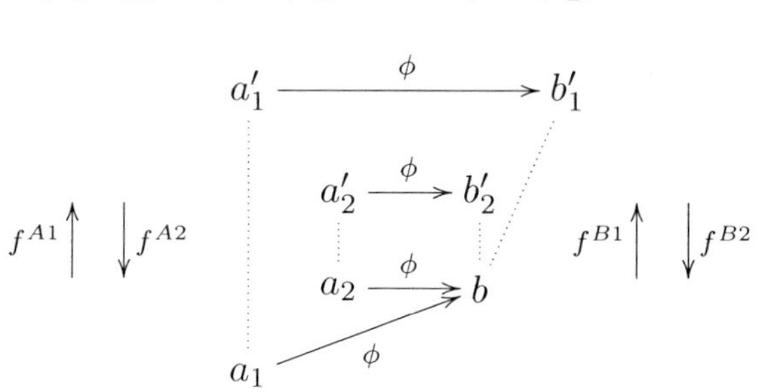

Now, the mapping $\phi(a_1) = \phi(a_2) = b$ *and* $\phi(a'_i) = b'_i$ *is OT homomorphism between* f^{A1} *and* f^{B1} *but not between* f^{A2} *and* f^{B2}. *(The example concerns, of course, not just the converse of a binary relation but the general situation, where the choice of the relational argument to function as the result of the multioperation can determine whether a given mapping is or is not an OT homomorphism.) Thus, although in the trivial sense of the*

isomorphism (1.1), multialgebras are only *representations of relational structures, so when homomorphisms are taken into consideration, the algebraic character of this representation becomes quite significant, as will become evident from the rest of this paper.*

As a possible example of OT-homomorphism consider the following.

Example 2.6. *Let the signature Θ have one sort and one unary operation $x \mapsto \overline{x}$. By the definition of multialgebra, we obtain that:*

1) $\overline{\varnothing} = \varnothing$

2) $\overline{X} = \bigcup_{x \in X} \overline{x}$*, for each subset* $X \subseteq M$*, in particular, 2.b)* $\overline{X \cup Y} = \overline{X} \cup \overline{Y}$

Let us restrict the class of Θ-multialgebras to those where the operation $\overline{x}$ satisfies two additional closure conditions, for every element $x \in M$:

3) $x \in \overline{x}$ *(and hence,* $X \subseteq \overline{X}$*, for all subsets* $X \subseteq M$*),*

4) $\overline{\overline{x}} = \overline{x}$ *(and hence,* $\overline{\overline{X}} = \overline{X}$ *for all* $X \subseteq M$*).*

In short, such a multialgebra is a topological space. The condition 2 is more general than that required for a topological closure operator, namely, 2.b). Consequently, the Θ-multialgebras will make closed not only finite but also arbitrary unions of closed sets. If, for instance, $\overline{x} = x$ for all $x \in M$, then M is a $\mathbf{T}_1$ space (where, by 2., $\overline{X} = X$ for every subset $X \subseteq M$, i.e., the topology with all subsets of M being clopen.)

The OT-homomorphism condition for $\phi : A \to B$ becomes now: $\forall y \in B : \overline{\phi^-(y)} = \phi^-(\overline{y})$ which yields, for every $Y \subseteq B$:

$$\phi^-(\overline{Y}) \stackrel{2}{=} \phi^-(\bigcup_{y \in Y} \overline{y}) = \bigcup_{y \in Y} \phi^-(\overline{y}) \stackrel{OT}{=} \bigcup_{y \in Y} \overline{\phi^-(y)} = \overline{\phi^-(Y)}$$

which implies, in particular, $\phi^-(\overline{Y}) \supseteq \overline{\phi^-(Y)}$, i.e., continuity of ϕ. If, in addition, we restrict ϕ to be injective, the above equality amounts to the requirement of ϕ being a homeomorphism between the spaces A and B.

The paranthetical "hence" phrase (in points 3-4 of Example 2.6) follows from the general fact:

Fact 2.7. *For any terms $t(x), s(x) \in \mathcal{T}(\Sigma, \{x\})$ and Σ-multialgebra M :*

$$\forall x \in M : s^M(x) = t^M(x) \iff \forall X \subseteq M : s^M(X) = t^M(X).$$

PROOF:$\Rightarrow$ follows directly from additivity of operations: $s^M(X) = \bigcup_{x \in X} s^M(x) = \bigcup_{x \in X} t^M(x) = t^M(X)$, while $\Leftarrow$ since $x \in M$ is but a special case of $X \subseteq M$, for $X = \{x\}$. □

Remark 2.8. *Alternatively to the above example, we can endow any multialgebra M over arbitray Σ with a topology by taking (for each sort s^M) as the subbasis, all the sets of the form $f^M(\overline{x})$, for $f \in \Sigma$ and $\overline{x} \in M$, together with s^M and $\varnothing$. (Opens will be the* *interpretations of all ground terms, as well as, all "reachable" sets, i.e., of the form* $t^M(\overline{x})$*, for some term* t *and all possible assignments to* $\overline{x}$*. The latter follows by induction on the depth of the term* t*:* $f^M(x)$ *is open and so is* $g^M(y)$ *for each* $y \in f^M(x)$*, hence also is* $\bigcup_{y \in f^M(x)} g^M(y) = g(f(x))^M$*.) Viewing opens as observations, [40], this amounts to viewing an operation* f *applied to an* x *as an* f*-observation, and the topology classifies all possible finitely verifiable observations.*

The OT-homomorphism condition implies then continuity, since $f^A(\phi^-(x)) \overset{OT}{=} \phi^-(f^B(x))$ *makes, for any open* $t^B(x)$*, its* ϕ*-preimage open in* A*, as a union of opens* $\bigcup_{a \in \phi^-(x)} t^A(a)$*. (Trivially, also,* $\phi^-(X \cap Y) = \phi^-(X) \cap \phi^-(Y)$ *and* $\phi^-(\bigcup_i X_i) = \bigcup_i \phi^-(X_i)$*, so that, e.g.,* $\phi^-(f^B(x) \cap g^B(y)) = \phi^-(f^B(x)) \cap \phi^-(g^B(y)) \overset{OT}{=} f^A(\phi^-(x)) \cap g^A(\phi^-(y))$*.)*

As in Example 2.6, the OT condition is stronger than continuity and falls between it and homeomorphism since, as observed in the example above, it is equivalent to homeomorphism provided that the mapping is injective. This topological aspect might merit closer study which, however, will not be undertaken here.

The following illustrates another way of arriving at OT-homomorphisms, establishing a tight connection between the category $\mathsf{MAlg}_{OT}(\Sigma)$ and the category of coalgebras for the corresponding Σ-functor.

Remark 2.9. *Consider, as an example, a functor* $\Sigma : \mathsf{Set} \to \mathsf{Set}$*, given by* $\Sigma(X) = X \times X$*. A* Σ*-coalgebra is then a function* $\alpha : A \to \Sigma(A)$*, i.e.,* $\alpha : A \to A \times A$*. The converse* $\alpha^- : A \times A \to A$ *is not, however, a function in case* α *is not injective: in general, it is a multifunction, i.e.,* $\alpha^- : A \times A \to \mathcal{P}(A)$*. Thus, a multialgebra can be seen as a converse of a coalgebra for an arbitrary polynomial functor* Σ*. There are, of course, multialgebras which can not be obtained in this way, namely, the ones whith* $f : S \to \mathcal{P}(S)$ *such that for two elements* $s_1 \neq s_2 \in S : f(s_1) \cap f(s_2) \neq \varnothing$ *(i.e., when the converse* $f^- : \mathcal{P}(S) \to \mathcal{P}(S)$ *is not determined by any function* $S \to S$*.) Thus, coalgebras (over polynomial functors) can be represented by multialgebras but not vice versa.*

A Σ*-coalgebra homomorphism* $\phi : \langle A, \alpha \rangle \to \langle B, \beta \rangle$ *is a function* $\phi : A \to B$ *such that the diagram to the left commutes:*

$$\begin{array}{ccc} A & \xrightarrow{\alpha} & A \times A \\ {\scriptstyle\phi}\downarrow & & \downarrow{\scriptstyle \phi\times\phi = \Sigma(\phi)} \\ B & \xrightarrow{\beta} & B \times B \end{array} \qquad\qquad \begin{array}{ccc} A & \xleftarrow{\alpha^-} & A \times A \\ {\scriptstyle\phi^-}\uparrow & & \uparrow{\scriptstyle (\phi\times\phi)^-} \\ B & \xleftarrow{\beta^-} & B \times B \end{array}$$

i.e., such that

$$\alpha; \Sigma(\phi) \quad = \quad \phi; \beta. \tag{2.10}$$

By taking the converse of both sides of this equation, we obtain $(\alpha; \Sigma(\phi))^- = (\phi; \beta)^-$*, i.e.,*

$$\Sigma(\phi)^-; \alpha^- \quad = \quad \beta^-; \phi^- \tag{2.11}$$

which is the OT condition on ϕ *for the multialgebras as shown in the diagram to the right. Thus, we not only obtain a pointwise representation of coalgebras, but also their morphisms are represented as the OT-morphisms between the corresponding multialgebras.*

Notice, however, that while the condition (2.10) involves only arrows in the category Set*, each of the arrows α^-, β^-, ϕ^- in the equation resulting in (2.11) can be a multifunction returning, for each argument, a subset of the target. The equality is thus not the equality of arrows in* Set *but in* Rel.

Remark 2.12. *As a special variation of the above remark, we can view coalgebras for the (direct image) power-set functor as multialgebras for the signature $f : S \to S$. (Recall the equivalence of the two diagrams from (1.4).)*

$$
\begin{array}{ccc}
A & \xrightarrow{\alpha} & \mathcal{P}(A) \\
{\scriptstyle\phi}\downarrow & & \downarrow{\scriptstyle\mathcal{P}(\phi)} \\
B & \xrightarrow{\beta} & \mathcal{P}(B)
\end{array}
\qquad\qquad
\begin{array}{ccc}
A & \xleftarrow{\alpha^-} & A \\
{\scriptstyle\phi^-}\uparrow & & \uparrow{\scriptstyle\phi^-} \\
B & \xleftarrow{\beta^-} & B
\end{array}
$$

$$\alpha;\mathcal{P}(\phi) = \phi;\beta \qquad\qquad \phi^-;\alpha^- = \beta^-;\phi^-$$

We represent any coalgebra $\alpha : A \to \mathcal{P}(A)$ by a multialgebra $\alpha^- : A \to \mathcal{P}(A)$ with $\alpha^-(x) = \{y \in A \mid x \in \alpha(y)\}$. Since $(\alpha^-)^- = \alpha$ we obtain the bijection between coalgebras and multialgebras. This bijection on objects extends to the isomorphism of the respective categories, since coalgebraic homomorphism condition is then equivalent to the OT-condition.

We can thus see multialgebras as both generalisation of algebras to handle partiality and nondeterminism and, on the other hand, as a possible representation of a large class of coalgebras. This representation is nevertheless to be studied from the algebraic perspective. It is mentioned primarily to emphasize again (in addition to the just mentioned topological aspect), that mutlialgebras capture also the notion of observability, which appears in a somehow dual form to the coalgebraic one. This duality will become well visible in considerations of bireachability, subsection 2.3. and later, as a converse of the coalgebraic bisimilarity: while coalgebraic bisimulations amount to compatibility/preservation of the results, i.e., future, the OT-congruences involve incompatibility/reflection of the arguments, i.e., history.

2.1. Some Preliminaries

Proposition 2.13. *An OT-homomorphism ϕ is*

1) *injective iff it is mono;*
2) *surjective iff it is epi; generally, a collection $\{\phi_i : A_i \to B \mid i \in I\}$ is jointly surjective iff it is epi-sink;*
3) *bijective iff it is iso.*

Proof: 1. $\Rightarrow$) Assume injectivity of ϕ and let (*) $\psi_1;\phi = \psi_2;\phi$ for two given homomorphisms $\psi_1, \psi_2 : X \to A$. All arrows can be seen as morphisms in Set, where injectivity of ϕ is equivalent to it being a monomorphism. But then (*) implies that $\psi_1 = \psi_2$ as Set-morphism, which implies their equality as OT-homomorphisms.

$\Leftarrow$) In section 2.3. we show that if ϕ is an OT-homomorphism then its kernel, $ker(\phi) = \phi;\phi^-$, is an OT-congruence (fact 2.40) which can be endowed with the algebraic structure (definition 2.54) such that the projections are homomorphisms (fact 2.55). Then, in the diagram $ker(\phi) \overset{\pi_1}{\underset{\pi_2}{\rightrightarrows}} A \xrightarrow{\phi} B$ we obtain $\pi_1; \phi = \pi_2; \phi$ and, assuming ϕ to be mono, $\pi_1 = \pi_2$. But this means that $ker(\phi) = id_A$, i.e., that ϕ is injective. Below, we spell out this proof in details without refering to the results to be introduced later on.

Assuming ϕ is not injective. Then there is at least one element $b \in B$ and a set of two or more elements $A_1 \subseteq A$ such that $a \in A_1 \Leftrightarrow \phi(a) = b$. Let a_i range over all elements in A_1. Since ϕ is OT: $\phi^-(f^B(b)) = \bigcup_{a_i \in A_1} f^A(a_i)$. We define an algebra X on the set $X = \{\langle x, y\rangle \mid x, y \in A \wedge \phi(x) = \phi(y)\}$ (in particular, $\forall x \in A : \langle x, x\rangle \in X$), by letting, for all constants, functions and arguments $\langle x_1, y_1\rangle \ldots \langle x_n, y_n\rangle \in X$:

$$\begin{aligned} c^X &= \{\langle x, y\rangle \in c^A \times c^A \mid \phi(x) = \phi(y)\} \\ f^X(\langle x_1, y_1\rangle \ldots \langle x_n, y_n\rangle) &= \{\langle x, y\rangle \in f^A(x_1 \ldots x_n) \times f^A(y_1 \ldots y_n) \mid \phi(x) = \phi(y)\} \end{aligned} \tag{2.14}$$

Let $\psi_1, \psi_2 : X \to A$ be projections. By (2.14) and the fact that $\forall x \in A : \langle x, x\rangle \in X$, we have:

$$\begin{aligned} \psi_1(c^X) &= c^A \\ \psi_1(f^X(\langle x_1, y_1\rangle \ldots \langle x_n, y_n\rangle)) &= f^A(x_1 \ldots x_n) \end{aligned}$$

and the corresponding equations hold for ψ_2. To prove that ψ_i are OT we have to show:

$$\psi_i^-(f^A(a_1 \ldots a_n)) = f^X(\psi_i^-(a_1) \ldots \psi_i^-(a_n))$$

for arbitrary $a_1 \ldots a_n \in A$. We show it for $i = 1$ as the proof for ψ_2 is entirely analogous. By definition of ψ_1 we obtain:

$$\psi_1^-(a) = \{\langle a, y\rangle \mid y \in [a]_\phi\} \tag{2.15}$$

where $[a]_\phi = \{a' \in A \mid \phi(a') = \phi(a)\}$. Furthermore, since ϕ is OT:

$$\forall \langle x, y\rangle \in X : \phi(x) = \phi(y) \wedge x \in f^A(a_1 \ldots a_n) \Rightarrow y \in f^A([a_1]_\phi \ldots [a_n]_\phi)$$

which means

$$\psi_1^-(f^A(a_1 \ldots a_n)) = \{\langle x, y\rangle \in f^A(a_1 \ldots a_n) \times f^A([a_1]_\phi \ldots [a_n]_\phi) \mid \phi(x) = \phi(y)\}$$

On the other hand

$$\begin{aligned} f^X(\psi_1^-(a_1) \ldots \psi_1^-(a_n)) &\overset{(2.15)}{=} f^X(\{\langle a_1, y_1\rangle \ldots \langle a_n, y_n\rangle \mid y_i \in [a_i]_\phi, 1 \leq i \leq n\}) \\ &\overset{(2.14)}{=} \{\langle x, y'\rangle \in f^A(a_1 \ldots a_n) \times f^A([a_1]_\phi \ldots [a_n]_\phi) \mid \phi(x) = \phi(y')\} \end{aligned}$$

Hence $\psi_1^-(f^A(a_1 \ldots a_n)) = f^X(\psi_1^-(a_1) \ldots \psi_1^-(a_n))$ and thus ψ_1 is OT.

By assumption we have at least two $a_1, a_2 \in A_1$, i.e., $\phi(a_1) = \phi(a_2) \wedge a_1 \neq a_2$. This means that $\langle a_1, a_2\rangle \in X$, and since $\psi_1(\langle a_1, a_2\rangle) = a_1$ while $\psi_2(\langle a_1, a_2\rangle) = a_2$, $\psi_1 \neq \psi_2$. But $\psi_1; \phi = \psi_2; \phi$, and thus ϕ is not mono.

2. We show the general statement for epi-sinks, from which the result for epis follows as a special case.

$\Rightarrow$) Assume joint surjectivity of ϕ_i and (*) $\phi_i; \psi_1 = \phi_i; \psi_2$ for all i and some $\psi_1, \psi_2 : B \to X$. Then $\forall b \in B\, \exists i\, \exists a \in A_i : b = \phi_i(a)$ and so $\psi_1(b) = \psi_1(\phi_i(a)) \stackrel{(*)}{=} \psi_2(\phi_i(a)) = \psi_2(b)$.

$\Leftarrow$) Assume that ϕ_i are not jointly surjective. Writing $\phi[A] = \bigcup_i \phi_i[A_i]$, we then have that $B_1 = B \setminus \phi[A]$ is non-empty. Since every ϕ_i is OT so for any $b_1 \dots b_n \in B$:

$$f(b_1 \dots b_n) \cap \phi_i[A_i] \neq \varnothing \Rightarrow b_1 \dots b_n \in \phi_i[A_i]$$

and, furthermore

$$\{b_1, \dots, b_n\} \cap B_1 \neq \varnothing \Rightarrow f^B(b_1 \dots b_n) \subseteq B_1 \tag{2.16}$$

We let $B_2 \simeq B_1$ be disjoint from B, and denote the bijections

$$\iota_{21} : (B_2 \cup \phi[A]) \longleftrightarrow (B_1 \cup \phi[A]) : \iota_{12}. \tag{2.17}$$

which are identities on the elements in $\phi[A]$.

We define an algebra structure on the set $X = B_1 \cup \phi[A] \cup B_2$ as follows:

$$\begin{aligned} c^X &= c^B \cup \iota_{12}(c^B \cap B_1) \\ f^X(x_1 \dots x_n) &= \begin{cases} f^B(x_1 \dots x_n) \cup \iota_{12}(f^B(x_1 \dots x_n)) & iff \mathrm{x}_1 \dots x_n \in \phi[A] \\ f^B(x_1 \dots x_n) & iff \mathrm{x}_1 \dots x_n \in B_1 \cup \phi[A] = B \\ \iota_{12}(f^B(\iota_{21}(x_1) \dots \iota_{21}(x_n))) & iff \mathrm{x}_1 \dots x_n \in B_2 \cup \phi[A] \\ \varnothing & otherwise \end{cases} \end{aligned} \tag{2.18}$$

The four disjuncts of the above definition are to be understood exclusively, i.e., the second case applies only when the first does not, etc.

We define two mappings $\psi_1, \psi_2 : B \to X$, as follows: $\psi_1(b) = b$ for all $b \in B$, while $\psi_2(b) = b$ for all $b \in \phi[A]$ and $\psi_2(b) = \iota_{12}(b)$ for all $b \in B_1$.

To prove that ψ_1 and ψ_2 are OT we observe first that both are injective, and so:

$$\psi_1^-(x) = \begin{cases} x & if \mathrm{x} \in \phi[A] \\ x & if \mathrm{x} \in B_1 \\ \varnothing & otherwise; \mathrm{x} \in B_2 \end{cases} \qquad \psi_2^-(x) = \begin{cases} x & if \mathrm{x} \in \phi[A] \\ \iota_{21}(x) & if \mathrm{x} \in B_2 \\ \varnothing & otherwise; \mathrm{x} \in B_1 \end{cases} \tag{2.19}$$

We consider four (disjoint) cases, corresponding to those in (2.18):

1) If $x_1 \dots x_n \in \phi[A]$:

$$\begin{aligned} \psi_1^-(f^X(x_1 \dots x_n)) &\stackrel{(2.18)}{=} \psi_1^-(f^B(x_1 \dots x_n) \cup \iota_{12}(f^B(x_1 \dots x_n))) \\ &\stackrel{(2.19)}{=} \psi_1^-(f^B(x_1 \dots x_n)) \\ &\stackrel{(2.19)}{=} f^B(\psi_1^-(x_1) \dots \psi_1^-(x_n)) \end{aligned}$$

2) If $x_1 \dots x_n \in B$:

$$\begin{aligned} \psi_1^-(f^X(x_1 \dots x_n)) &\stackrel{(2.18)}{=} \psi_1^-(f^B(x_1 \dots x_n)) \\ &\stackrel{(2.19)}{=} f^B(\psi_1^-(x_1) \dots \psi_1^-(x_n)) \end{aligned}$$

3) If $x_1 \dots x_n \in B_2 \cup \phi[A]$, with at least one $x_i \in B_2$:

$$\begin{aligned}
\psi_1^-(f^X(x_1 \dots x_n)) &\overset{(2.18)}{=} \psi_1^-(\iota_{12}(f^B(\iota_{21}(x_1) \dots \iota_{21}(x_n)))) \\
&\overset{(2.17)}{=} \psi_1^-(\iota_{12}(f^B(b_1 \dots b_n))), b_1 \dots b_n \in B, b_i \in B_1 \\
&\overset{(2.16)}{=} \psi_1^-(\iota_{12}(B_1')), \quad B_1' = \{b \in f^B(b_1 \dots b_n)\} \subseteq B_1 \\
&\overset{(2.17)}{=} \psi_1^-(B_2'), \quad B_2' = \{b \in \iota_{12}(B_1')\} \subseteq B_2 \\
&\overset{(2.19)}{=} \varnothing
\end{aligned}$$

$$f^B(\psi_1^-(x_1) \dots \psi_1^-(x_n)) \overset{(2.19)}{=} \varnothing, \text{ since for at least one } x_i \in B_2 : \psi_1^-(x_i) = \varnothing$$

4) Otherwise (there are at least two elements x_i and x_j such that $x_i \in B_1$ and $x_j \in B_2$):

$$\begin{aligned}
\psi_1^-(f^X(x_1 \dots x_n)) &\overset{(2.18)}{=} \psi_1^-(\varnothing) = \varnothing \\
f^B(\psi_1^-(x_1) \dots \psi_1^-(x_n)) &\overset{(2.19)}{=} \varnothing, \text{ since for } x_i \in B_2, x_j \in B_1 : \psi_1^-(x_j) = \varnothing = \psi_2^-(x_i)
\end{aligned}$$

Thus, for all $x_1 \dots x_n \in X : \psi_1^-(f^X(x_1 \dots x_n)) = f^B(\psi_1^-(x_1) \dots \psi_1^-(x_n))$, i.e., ψ_1 is OT. We defined the algebraic structure on $B_2 \simeq B_1$ and the proof for ψ_2 is entirely analogous.

Now, $\psi_1(b) \neq \psi_2(b)$ for any $b \in B_1$, while for all $b \in \phi[A] : \psi_1(b) = \psi_2(b)$. Hence for all $i : \phi_i; \psi_1 = \phi_i; \psi_2$, while $\psi_1 \neq \psi_2$, i.e., $\{\phi_i \mid i \in I\}$ is not en epi-sink.

3. If ϕ is not bijective, there can be no inverse. If it is, then ϕ^- is easily verified to be OT. □

Remark 2.20. *The general fact about dialgebras (e.g., proposition 18 in [41]) is that for a function $f : A \to B$ which is a dialgebra morphism in Set_G^F:*

1) if F preserves weak pushouts, then f is epi iff it is surjective, and

2) if G preserves weak pullbacks, then f is mono iff it is injective.

In our case, both these conditions are satisfied, since F is the polynomial functor (coproduct of products) while $G = \mathcal{P}$ which does preserve weak pullbacks. However, the proposition cannot be applied since our OT-homomorphisms are not the same as the morphisms in $\mathsf{Set}_{\mathcal{P}}^F$.

2.2. Subalgebras

We say that A' is a subalgebra of A, $A' \sqsubseteq A$, if A' is an algebra with $A' \subseteq A$ and such that the inclusion is a homomorphism. (The following considerations would not be significantly affected, if we adopted the categorical definition, according to which subobject is an equivalence class of monomorphisms.) If $A, A' \in \mathsf{MAlg}_{OT}(\Sigma)$ and $A' \subset A$, this does not mean that the inclusion is an OT-homomorphism, i.e., it may still happen that A' is not a subalgebra of A, $A' \not\sqsubseteq A$. E.g., $A' : \begin{array}{c} b \\ \uparrow \\ a_1 \end{array}$ is not a subalgebra of $A : \begin{array}{ccc} & & b \\ & \nearrow & \uparrow \\ a_1 & & a_2 \end{array}$. If b is in the carrier of a subalgebra, then so must be all its pre-images: all the elements of the argument-sorts, from which b is reachable by some operations (cf. condition 2 in figure 2.1.) Hence, the only subalgebra of A containing b is A itself. This closure condition is – by requiring the presence of all elements from which a present element is reachable – converse of the classical one which requires closure under the results of the operations. Notice the equivalence of the two following closure conditions, for a subset $A \subseteq B$, with $\overline{A} = B \setminus A$:

$$\begin{aligned} &1)\ x \in A \Longrightarrow f(x) \subseteq A \text{ and} \\ &2)\ y \in \overline{A} \wedge y \in f(x) \Longrightarrow x \in \overline{A} \end{aligned} \tag{2.21}$$

(The equivalence for the classical/deterministic algebras is obtained by taking $f(x) \in A$ and $y = f(x)$, respectively.) That is, closure of a subset A under images (of operations) is equivalent to closure of its complement under pre-images. What happens in our case of OT-homomorphisms, is that the latter is taken as the closure condition on the subset A and not on its complement (cf. condition 2. in Figure 2.1). It reflects the similarly converse character of the OT-congruences to be studied shortly.

Inclusion is not necessarily a homomorphism, but it is when restricted to subalgebras of the same algebra.

Fact 2.22. *Inclusions between subalgebras of the same algebra are OT homomorphisms. I.e., if $A_1 \sqsubseteq A$ and $A_2 \sqsubseteq A$ and $A_2 \subseteq A_1$, then also $A_2 \sqsubseteq A_1$.*

PROOF: We have two inclusion homomorphisms $\iota_k : A_k \to A$, $k = 1, 2$, and inclusion $i : A_2 \to A_1$ which we want to show is a homomorphism. We thus have: 1) $\iota_1^-; R^{A_1} = R^A; \iota_1^-$, 2) $\iota_2^-; R^{A_2} = R^A; \iota_2^-$ and 3) $i; \iota_1 = \iota_2$. 2,3) $\Rightarrow \iota_1^-; i^-; R^{A_2} = R^A; \iota_1^-; i^- \overset{1)}{\Rightarrow} \iota_1^-; i^-; R^{A_2} = \iota_1^-; R^{A_1}; i^- \Rightarrow \iota_1; \iota_1^-; i^-; R^{A_2} = \iota_1; \iota_1^-; R^{A_1}; i^-$. Since ι_1 is inclusion, we have that $\iota_1; \iota_1^- = id_{A_1}$ and so we obtain $i^-; R^{A_2} = R^{A_1}; i^-$. □

Taking into account the equivalence (2.21), we also have the following characterisation of subalgebras:

Fact 2.23. *Given $A, A' \in \mathsf{MAlg}_{OT}(\Sigma)$ with $A' \subseteq A$, the following conditions are equivalent:*

1) *$A' \sqsubseteq A$, i.e., inclusion $i : A' \to A$ is OT*
2) *A' is closed under pre-images of A-operations (i.e., $a' \in A' \wedge a' \in f^A(a) \Longrightarrow a \in A'$)*
3) *$A \setminus A'$ is closed under images of operations*

Remark 2.24. *Consider for the moment only classical, i.e., deterministic algebras. As observed in remark 2.3, OT-homomorphism becomes then a special case of IT, i.e., the classical homomorphism. (Similarly, LT and RT will be special cases of IT, and the observation below applies also to these alternatives.) One can then define a more specific concept of an OT-subalgebra by requiring that the inclusion is not only a homomorphism but an OT-homomorphism. In view of the above fact, such a subalgebra $A' \sqsubseteq A$ would be closed under pre-images (inclusion being OT) but also under images (OT being IT). Thus also the complement $A'' = A \setminus A'$ would be closed under images and pre-images, i.e., would* *be a subalgebra of A. In other words, an OT-subalgebra would amount to partioning the algebra A into two disjoint subalgebras.*

Given a collection of subalgebras, $A_k \sqsubseteq A$, their intersection C is obtained as $C = \bigcap_{k \in K} A_k$, with $f^C(a) = f^A(a) \cap C$ for all $a \in C$. The drawing below gives one example with two subalgebras $A_1, A_2 \sqsubseteq A$, and their intersection C :

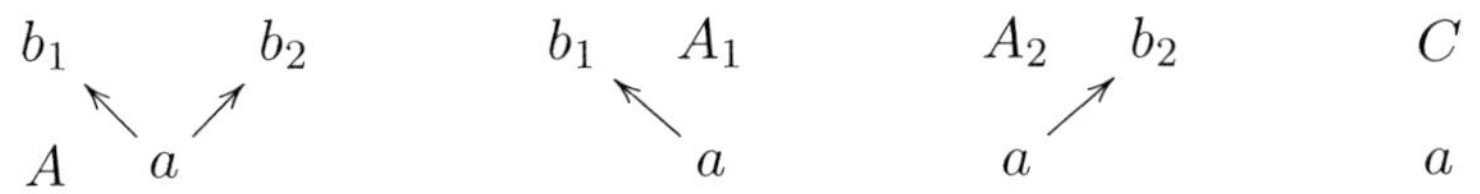

We do have the counterpart of the classical result that intersection of subalgebras yields a subalgebra.

Fact 2.25. *Given a collection $\{A_k \mid k \in K, A_k \sqsubseteq A\}$, then also $\bigcap_{k \in K} A_k = C \sqsubseteq A$.*

PROOF: For each $k \in K$ we have the inclusion homomorphism $i_k : A_k \hookrightarrow A$ and also the inclusion $c_k : C \subseteq A_k$. If at least for one such k, c_k is a homomorphism, the claim follows. We will show it for an arbitrary (and hence every) k.
Since we consider only inclusions, for every k, l we have that $c_k; i_k = c_l; i_l$ and hence also

$$i_k^-; c_k^- = i_l^-; c_l^- . \tag{2.26}$$

Moreover, just like for an $X \subseteq A : i_k^-(X) = X \cap A_k$, so for $Y \subseteq A_k$:

$$c_k^-(Y) = Y \bigcap_{l \neq k} A_l. \tag{2.27}$$

Let $k \in K$ be arbitrary, and consider two cases for the expression $R^C(c_k^-(a))$, where $a \in A_k$.
1) $c_k^-(a) = \varnothing$ (for at least one argument a, which we simplify in notation by ignoring other arguments), and thus also $R^C(c_k^-(a)) = \varnothing$ but, in particular,

$$\begin{array}{llll}
a \in A_k \ \&\ a \notin C & \Rightarrow & \exists A_l : a \notin A_l,\ i.e.,\ i_l^-(a) = \varnothing & (2.27) \\
& \Rightarrow & R^{A_l}(i_l^-(a)) = \varnothing & R(\varnothing) = \varnothing \\
& \Rightarrow & i_l^-(R^A(a)) = \varnothing & i_l\ is\ OT \\
& \Rightarrow & c_l^-(i_l^-(R^A(a))) = \varnothing & c_l^-(\varnothing) = \varnothing \\
& \Rightarrow & c_k^-(i_k^-(R^A(a))) = \varnothing & (2.26) \\
& \Rightarrow & c_k^-(R^{A_k}(i_k^-(a))) = \varnothing & since\ i_k\ is\ OT \\
& \Rightarrow & c_k^-(R^{A_k}(a)) = \varnothing & since\ i_k(a) = a
\end{array}$$

Thus, if $c_k^-(a) = \varnothing$ then the condition $R^C(c_k^-(a)) = c_k^-(R^{A_k}(a))$ is satisfied.
2) The second case assumes $c_k^-(a) \neq \varnothing$. Then $c_k^-(a) = a \in C$.
a) $R^C(c_k^-(a)) = R^C(a) \stackrel{def.\ of\ C}{=} R^A(a) \cap \bigcap_{l \in K} A_l$.
b) $c_k^-(R^{A_k}(a)) \stackrel{(2.27)}{=} R^{A_k}(a) \cap \bigcap_{k \neq l \in K} A_l$.
c) $R^{A_k}(a) = R^{A_k}(i_k^-(a)) = i_k^-(R^A(a)) = R^A(a) \cap A_k$ and substituting this into b) gives equality with a). □

Hence, given an algebra A, the collection of its subalgebras, $\downarrow(A)$, with the subalgebra relation, $\langle \downarrow(A), \sqsubseteq \rangle$ is a lower semilattice with the greatest element A, and so:

Fact 2.28. *For an algebra A, $\langle \downarrow (A), \sqsubseteq \rangle$ is a complete lattice with meets given by intersection.*

In view of the equivalences from fact 2.23, we obtain thus also a "complementary" lattice of subsets of A closed under images, since every $A' \sqsubseteq A$ determines such a closed subset $A \setminus A'$ and vice versa.

The above verifies also the following fact – according to which the diagram of subalgebras is directed – which, however, we also prove separately providing the explicit construction.

Fact 2.29. *For every set $X \subseteq A$, there is a smallest subalgebra $A_X \sqsubseteq A$ with $X \subseteq A_X$.*

PROOF: The construction extends the given set X to obtain a subalgebra. X is sorted, and the construction extends in each step each sort (if at all):

1) $X_0 = X$

2) For all $x \in A$, if $f^A(x) \cap X_i \neq \varnothing$ then include into X_{i+1} also all such x.

3) $X_\omega = \bigcup_{i \in \omega} X_i$

We define Σ structure A_X on X_ω by letting, for all $x \in X_\omega$ and every operation f from the signature: $f^{A_X}(x) = f^A(x) \cap X_\omega$. This makes A_X obviously closed under pre-images of all operations.
The inclusion $\iota : X_\omega \hookrightarrow A$ is OT. We have $\iota^-(Y) = Y \cap X_\omega$, and have to check that $f^{A_X}(\iota^-(a)) = \iota^-(f^A(a)) = f^A(a) \cap X_\omega$. Now if $f^A(a) \cap X_\omega \neq \varnothing$ then, by 2., $a \in X_\omega$ and we have $f^{A_X}(\iota^-(a)) = f^A(a) \cap X_\omega$, i.e., the required equality holds.
If, on the other hand, $f^A(a) \cap X_\omega = \varnothing$, then either $a \notin X_\omega$ and so $f^{A_X}(\iota^-(a)) = \varnothing$, or else $a \in X_\omega$ and then $f^{A_X}(a) = f^A(a) \cap X_\omega = \varnothing$. So the equality holds also in this case.
A_X is in fact smallest subalgebra of A containing X. For removing any element from its carrier, would require removing it either from X or else from among elements added in step 2). In the former case, the result would not contain X, while in the latter would not be a subalgebra of A (inclusion would not be an OT-homomorphism). □

Thus, if $A_1, A_2 \sqsubseteq A$, then there is also (a smallest) $A_3 \sqsubseteq A$, with $A_1 \cup A_2 \subseteq A_3$.

Example 2.30. *Given an alphabet, all its symbols can be viewed as operations acting on the single sort of states. A given set of states and definition of these functions determine then a possibly nondeterministic automaton. For instance, the automaton (multialgebra) A has 8 elements in the sort of states and, e.g., $a^A(1) = \{2, 3\}$ while $b^A(1) = \varnothing$, $c^A(2) = \{5\}$ and $d^A(6) = \{5, 8\}$. The subalgebras generated by the state 3, resp. 7 are shown to the right:*

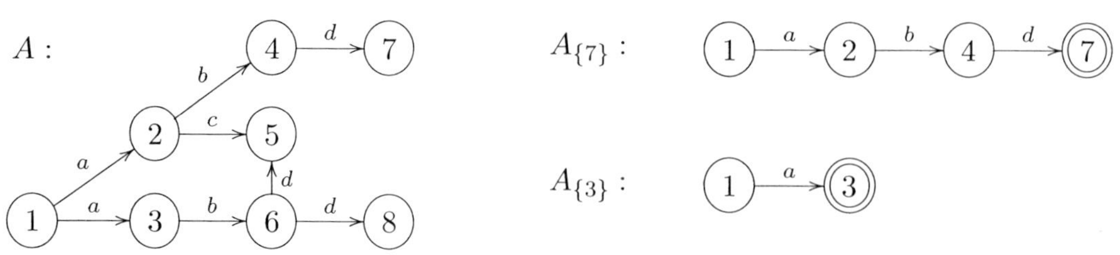

The subalgebra generated by $X \subseteq A$ is thus, in this example, the maximal set of states A_X all reaching X (with the Σ-structure inherited from A), i.e., such that $s \in A_X$ iff there exists a path (derived operator) p for which $p^A(s) \cap X \neq \varnothing$. If we think of multialgebra as a (possibly action-labeled) OR *search (or game, like minimax) graph, the subalgebra generated by X will thus pick up the paths/strategies leading to the goals in X.*

We also have a dual construction of a largest subalgebra $A^X \sqsubseteq A$ with $A^X \subseteq X$.

Fact 2.31. *For every set $X \subseteq A$, there exists a largest subalgebra $A^X \sqsubseteq A$ with $A^X \subseteq X$.*

PROOF: The construction is, in a sense, dual to that from the previous fact and it removes now, from the given set X, elements to obtain a subalgebra.

1) $X^0 = X$
2) If $\exists x \in A \setminus X^i : f^A(x) \cap X^i \neq \varnothing$ then remove these result elements from X^{i+1}, i.e.,
   $X^{i+1} = X^i \setminus \bigcup_{f \in \Sigma} f^A(A \setminus X^i)$
3) $X^\omega = \bigcap_{i \in \omega} X^i$

More explicitly, in point 2) we remove from X^i the elements which are reachable from outside of X^i, i.e., $X^{i+1} = X^i \setminus \bigcup_{x \in A \setminus X^i \wedge f^A(x) \cap X^i \neq \varnothing} f^A(x)$ as f ranges over all operation symbols in Σ.

We define Σ structure A^X on X^ω by letting, for all $x \in X^\omega$ and every operation f from the signature: $f^{A^X}(x) = f^A(x) \cap X^\omega$. This makes A^X obviously closed under pre-images of all operations.

The inclusion $\iota : X^\omega \hookrightarrow A$ is OT. We have $\iota^-(Y) = Y \cap X^\omega$, and have to check that $f^{A^X}(\iota^-(a)) = \iota^-(f^A(a)) = f^A(a) \cap X^\omega$. Now if $f^A(a) \cap X^\omega \neq \varnothing$ then, by 2., $a \in X^\omega$ and we have $f^{A^X}(\iota^-(a)) = f^A(a) \cap X^\omega$, i.e., the required equality holds.

If, on the other hand, $f^A(a) \cap X^\omega = \varnothing$, then either $a \notin X^\omega$ and so $f^{A^X}(\iota^-(a)) = \varnothing$, or else $a \in X^\omega$ and then $f^{A^X}(a) = f^A(a) \cap X^\omega = \varnothing$. So the equality holds also in this case.

A^X is in fact the largest subalgebra of A contained in X. For adding any element from $A \setminus A^X$, would require adding it either to X or else among elements removed in step 2). In the former case, the result would not be contained in X, while in the latter would not be a subalgebra of A (inclusion would not be an OT-homomorphism). □

For instance, for A from example 2.30, $A^{\{7\}} = A^{\{3\}} = \varnothing$. We can easily see that $A^X = \varnothing$ if the set X has no downward closed subset, i.e., whenever $\forall x \in X \exists y \in A \setminus X : x \in f^A(y)$.

Utilising fact 2.23, we can reformulate the constructions of A_X and A^X. Let $Cl(\overline{X})$ be the supremum (in the respective lattice, mentioned after fact 2.28) of all subsets of A closed under pre-images of A-operations and not intersecting X, i.e.,

$$Cl(\overline{X}) = \bigsqcup_i X_i : X_i \cap X = \varnothing \wedge (x \in X_i \wedge y \in f^A(x) \Rightarrow y \in X_i).$$

On the other hand, let $cl(X)$ be the infimum of all $X_i \subseteq A$ which are closed under pre-images of A-operations and whose complement is contained in X ($A \setminus X_i \subseteq X$ or, equivalently, $X_i \cup X = A$), i.e.,

$$cl(X) = \sqcap_i X_i : A \setminus X_i \subseteq X \wedge (x \in X_i \wedge y \in f^A(x) \Rightarrow y \in X_i).$$

We then have alternative formulations of the two facts:

2.29. $A_X = A \setminus Cl(\overline{X})$.

2.31. $A^X = A \setminus cl(X)$.

Finally, we have the expected relations between homomorphic images and subalgebras.

Lemma 2.32. *Let $\phi : A \to B$ be a homomorphism:*

1) The image $\phi[A] \sqsubseteq B$ is a subalgebra of B.

2) For any $B' \sqsubseteq B : \phi^-[B'] \sqsubseteq A$.

3) For any $A' \sqsubseteq A : \phi[A'] \sqsubseteq B$.

PROOF:

1) By fact 2.23, it is enough to show that $\phi[A]$ is closed under pre-images of B-operations. If $b' \in \phi[A]$ and $b' \in f^B(b)$ then, since ϕ is OT, $\varnothing \neq \phi^-(b') \subseteq \phi^-(f^B(b)) = f^A(\phi^-(b))$. But this implies that $f^A(\phi^-(b)) \neq \varnothing$, i.e., $b \in \phi[A]$.

2) By fact 2.23, it is enough to show that $\phi^-[B']$ is closed under pre-images of A-operations. If $a' \in \phi^-[B']$ then $\phi(a') \in B'$, and if $a' \in f^A(a)$ then also $\phi(a') \in \phi(f^A(a)) \subseteq f^B(\phi(a))$, since OT are also weak. By assumption, B' is closed under pre-images of B-operations, so the last inclusion impilies $\phi(a) \in B'$, i.e., $a \in \phi^-[B']$.

3) Follows directly from 1, since the restriction of ϕ to A' (pre-composition with the inclusion $A' \subseteq A$) is a homomorphism.

□

Point 1 gives immediately epi-mono factorisation of homomorphisms: any $\phi : A \to B$ can be factored as $\phi = e; m$ where $e : A \to \phi[A]$ is epi and $m : \phi[A] \to B$ is mono. We will address this factorisation in the context of congruencess below (lemma 2.42).

As we will see, $\mathsf{MAlg}_{OT}(\Sigma)$ may fail to have final objects and products. We will identify a class of its subcategories which are complete and cocomplete, namely, the categories of κ-bounded multialgebras. We register their definition now, as it is based on the concept of subalgebra, but it will become of relevance first in Section 5.. (See, e.g., [38, 17], for the corresponding definitions for coalgebras.)

Definition 2.33. *For an infinite cardinal κ, a multialgebra A is κ-bounded if for every $x \in A : |A_{\{x\}}| < \kappa$. $\mathsf{MAlg}^{\kappa}_{OT}(\Sigma)$ is the subcategory of $\mathsf{MAlg}_{OT}(\Sigma)$ containing all κ-bounded algebras.*

One observes easily that in a κ-bounded multialgebra, pre-image of every operation for an arbitrary element must have cardinality less than κ.

2.3. OT-congruences

In order for the quotient construction performed on a carrier of a (classical) Σ-algebra to yield a (quotient) Σ-algebra, the equivalence must be a Σ-congruence. However, for any (classical) algebra A and any equivalence $\sim$ on its carrier, the quotient $A/_\sim$, with operations collecting the possibly non-congruent results (i.e., defined by $R^{A/\sim}([a]) = \{[n] \mid n \in R^A(a'),\ a' \in [a]\}$), is a multialgebra, and the construction works in the same way if we start with a multialgebra, and not only classical algebra, A. Defining the mapping $q : A \to A/_\sim$ by $q(a) = [a]$, the operations are obtained as $R^{A/\sim} = q^-; R^A; q$. In general, this mapping is only a weak homomorphism, just like the kernel of a weak homomorphism is, in general, only an equivalence. (This correspondence is perhaps the clearest expression of the weakness of this homomorphism notion.) OT-homomorphisms come along with a much stronger notion of congruence.

Definition 2.34. *An equivalence $\sim$ on A is an OT-congruence iff:* $\sim; R^A; \sim = \sim; R^A$.

More explicitly, the inclusion $\subseteq$ says that

$$\forall a'', a', b, b' : a'' \sim a' R^A b' \sim b \Rightarrow \exists a : a'' \sim a R^A b, \tag{2.35}$$

which, when $\sim$ is equivalence, is equivalent to

$$\forall a', b, b' : a' R^A b' \sim b \Rightarrow \exists a : a' \sim a R^A b. \tag{2.36}$$

((2.36) is a special case of (2.35) whenever $\sim$ is reflexive, while transitivity (and symmetry) of $\sim$ yields the opposite implication.) Any equivalence satisfying this last condition is OT, since the opposite inclusion $\sim; R^A; \sim \supseteq \sim; R^A$ holds trivially for any reflexive $\sim$.

This characterisation of OT-congruence can be viewed as a converse (bi)simulation.[2] (Bi)simulation requires propagation of $\sim$ forward, while OT-congruence backward. Let us call a relation satisfying two symmetric conditions (for each $R \in \Sigma$):

$$\begin{array}{rcl} \forall b, b'\ \forall a' : b \sim b' \wedge a' R^A b' & \Rightarrow & \exists a : a \sim a' \ \wedge\ a R^A b \\ \&\ \forall b, b'\ \forall a\ : b \sim b' \wedge\ a R^A b & \Rightarrow & \exists a' : a \sim a' \wedge a' R^A b' \end{array} \tag{2.37}$$

"bireachability" – OT-congruence is then an equivalence which is also bireachability or, simply, equivalence satisfying (2.36) (since symmetry makes (2.36) imply (2.37)).

(2.38)

[2]We are not addressing any details concerning bisimulations. For the sake of analogy, since OT-congruences are equivalences, it is most convenient to think of bisimulation defined as a symmetric simulation, rather than merely as a simulation with converse being also a simulation. Exact duality obtains between our bireachability and the equivalences satisfying the condition that for every $R : \sim; R^A; \sim = R^A; \sim$. This characterizes the bisimulation in (2.38) and is the same as the congruence induced by the coalgebraic model of binary relations, referred to in remark 1.13. In [7] such equivalences were said to "preserve the arguments" (in contradistinction to congruences which "preserve the values"). In [19], the relation dual to mere simulation, without the requirement of equivalence, was called "opsimulation," but the name "biopsimulation" does not seem very appealling.

We can describe bireachability/OT-congruence in the following terms dual to the classical congruence. Classical congruence requires propagation of the relation: if two elements are related, $a_1 \sim a_2$, then also their results are, $R(a_1) \sim R(a_2)$. Bireachability requires propagation of distinctions, albeit in a special way. Given a binary relation $\sim$ on elements, define its (Egli-Milner) extension to sets by

$$P_1 \sim P_2 \iff \begin{array}{l} \forall p_1 \in P_1 \exists p_2 \in P_2 : p_1 \sim p_2 \wedge \\ \forall p_2 \in P_2 \exists p_1 \in P_1 : p_2 \sim p_1. \end{array} \tag{2.39}$$

Propagation of distinctions amounts to the requirement on an OT-congruence $\sim$ that whenever $R^-(b_1) \not\sim R^-(b_2)$ then also $b_1 \not\sim b_2$.

Fact 2.40. *If $\phi : A \to B$ is OT then so is its kernel $\sim_\phi = ker(\phi) = \phi; \phi^-$.*

PROOF:
$$\begin{array}{rl} \phi^-; R^A = & R^B; \phi^- \quad (\phi \; is \; OT) \\ \phi; \phi^-; R^A = & \phi; R^B; \phi^- \\ \sim_\phi; R^A = & \phi; R^B; \phi^-. \end{array}$$

On the other hand, we also have:

$$\begin{array}{rll} \phi^-; R^A & = R^B; \phi^- & (\phi \; is \; OT) \\ \phi; \phi^-; R^A; \phi; \phi^- & = \phi; R^B; \phi^-; \phi; \phi^- & \\ \sim_\phi; R^A; \sim_\phi & = \phi; R^B; \phi^- & (since \; \phi^-; \phi; \phi^- = \phi^-) \end{array}$$

which gives the conclusion when combined with the above. □

The inverse does not hold generally; even if $ker(\phi)$ is OT, ϕ itself may be not, even if it is surjective. (The mapping 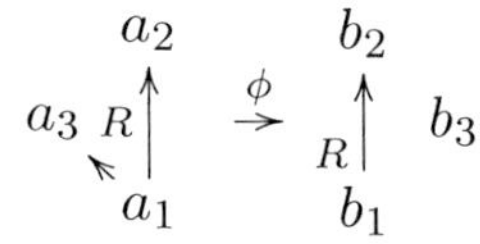 defined as $\phi(a_i) = b_i$ has the kernel id_A, which is OT, but ϕ is not an OT-homomorphism.) We have a slightly weaker claim.

Fact 2.41. *If $\sim$ is an OT-congruence then the mapping $q : A \to Q = A/_\sim$, $q(a) = [a]$, is an OT-homomorphism.*

PROOF: (The operations in Q are defined by $R^Q = q^-; R^A; q$.)

$$\begin{array}{rll} q; q^-; R^A; q; q^- & = q; q^-; R^A & assumption, \; since \; \sim = \sim_q = q; q^- \\ q; R^Q; q^- & = q; q^-; R^A & def. \; of \; Q \\ q^-; q; R^Q; q^- & = \quad q^-; R^A & \\ id_Q; R^Q; q^- & = \quad q^-; R^A & q \; is \; surjective \end{array}$$ □

This gives epi-mono factorisation of morphisms in $\mathsf{MAlg}_{OT}(\Sigma)$.

Lemma 2.42. *For every homomorphism $h : A \to B$ there is a (regular) epi $e : A \to Q$ and mono $m : Q \to B$ such that $h = e; m$.*

PROOF: We let $\sim$ denote the kernel of h and choose $Q = A/_\sim$. By Fact 2.41 and Proposition 2.13, $e : A \to Q$ defined by $e(a) = [a]$, is an epi in $\mathsf{MAlg}_{OT}(\Sigma)$. (It is regular by Fact 2.55.) We verify that m, defined by $m([a]) = h(a)$ is OT. (It is trivially injective, and hence mono by 2.13, and makes $h = e; m$ by definition.) Let $b \in B$ and assume first that $m^-(b) = \{[a]\} \neq \varnothing$:

$$
\begin{array}{rcll}
f^Q(m^-(b)) & = & f^Q([a]) & \text{definition of } m \\
& = & \{[c] \mid c \in f^A(a) : h(a) = b\} & \text{definition of } Q \text{ with } a : h(a) = b \\
& = & \{[c] \mid c \in f^A(h^-(b))\} & \\
& = & \{[c] \mid c \in h^-(f^B(b))\} & h \text{ is OT} \\
& = & e(h^-(f^B(b))) & \text{definition of } e \\
& = & e(e^-(m^-(f^B(b)))) & \text{since } h^-(x) = e^-(m^-(x)) \\
& = & m^-(f^B(b)) & \text{since } e^-; e = id_Q
\end{array}
$$

The same argument applies also when $m^-(b) = \varnothing$, since this implies that $h^-(b) = \varnothing$. □

Corollary 2.43. *1) For an epi $\phi : A \to B$ with kernel $\sim$, $A/_\sim \simeq B$.*

2) If $e_i : A \to B_i$, $i \in \{1, 2\}$, are epis with equal kernels, $\sim_1 = \sim_2$, then $B_1 \simeq B_2$.

PROOF:

1) By 2.42, we have an epi-mono factorisation of $\phi = e; m$. But since ϕ is epi, so is m. As m is also mono, it is bijective and thus iso by proposition 2.13.

2) By 1, we have $A/_{\sim_1} \simeq B_1$ and $A/_{\sim_2} \simeq B_2$. But $A/_{\sim_1} = A/_{\sim_2}$. □

Hence the epi-mono facorization from 2.42 coincides with the factorisation mentioned after lemma 2.32, in the sense that $A/_\sim \simeq \phi[A]$.

Remark 2.44. *Recall remark 2.8 in which topology on a multialgebra reflected the possible observations of its elements by means of the results of the operations. In the present context, bireachability can be seen as topological indistinguishability – albeit, not as in the topological tradition, of topological spaces or features invariant under homeomorphisms, but of actual elements of a given topological space.*

As an immediate corollary of the fact that the quotient morphism is OT and that such homomorphisms are continuous, remark 2.8, we obtain that, for instance, pre-image of an Q-open is A-open, i.e., that $q^-(f^Q([x]))$ can be written as (possibly union of intersections, and possibly of different symbols but, as it turns out, simply as) $\bigcup_{x \in [x]} f^A(x)$. (This can be verified directly, for $f^Q([x]) = \{[y] \mid y \in f^A([x])\}$, i.e., its pre-image $q^-(f^Q([x])) = \{y' \mid \exists y \sim y' : y \in \bigcup_{x \in [x]} f^A(x)$ which, by OT, is equal to $\bigcup_{x \in [x]} f^A(x)$.)

However, the topology obtained by our quotient construction according to remark 2.8, is not exactly the same as the standard quotient topology on the quotient space, i.e., one according to which $Y \subseteq Q$ is open iff $q^-(Y)$ is A-open. For instance:

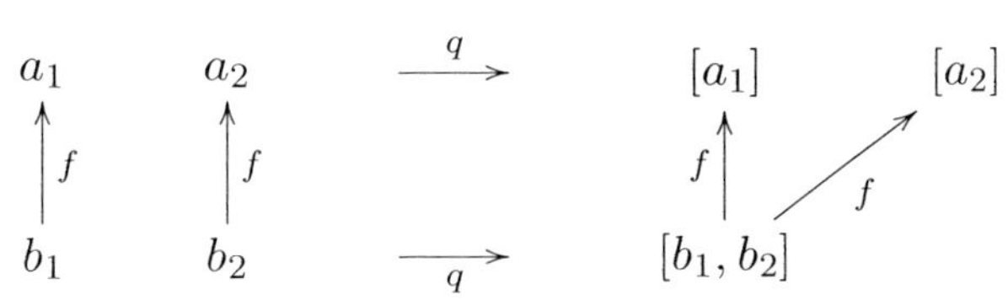

The pre-image $q^-([a_1]) = \{a_1\} = f^A(b_1)$ and hence is open, but $[a_1]$ is not since the only open set in Q (besides $\varnothing$) is the whole carrier of the a-sort $\{[a_1], [a_2]\} = f^Q([b_1, b_2])$.

2.3.1. The Complete Lattice of OT-congruences on an Algebra

The condition (2.37) is trivially preserved by taking unions of bireachabilities and so, for any algebra, there is the maximal (with respect to $\subseteq$) bireachability, namely, the union of all bireachabilities. We address now the more specific question of the existence of maximal OT-congruence.

Given a collection $C = \{\sim_i \mid i \in I\}$ of equivalences (on a set/algebra A), one obtains their supremum $\sim = \bigvee_i \sim_i$ as the transitive closure of their union, i.e., $\bigvee_i \sim_i = (\bigcup_i \sim_i)^*$. Explicitly, one lets $a \sim a'$ iff there exists a finite sequence $a = a_0 a_1 ... a_n = a'$ and a respective sequence of the equivalences from C, $\sim_1 \sim_2 \ldots \sim_n$, such that $a_i \sim_{i+1} a_{i+1}$ for all $0 \leq i < n$. As all members of C are equivalences, then so is the transitive closure of their union by the standard argument (e.g., [15], §5, th.2). The construction applies also to OT-congruences.

Lemma 2.45. *Given a collection $C = \{\sim_i \mid i \in I\}$ of OT-congruences on a multialgebra A, then $\sim = \bigvee_{i \in I} \sim_i$ is an OT-congruence.*

PROOF: Assume that for each $i : \sim_i ; R^A ; \sim_i = \sim_i ; R^A$. We have to show that then $\sim ; R^A ; \sim = \sim ; R^A$. The inclusion $\sim ; R^A ; \sim \supseteq \sim ; R^A$ is trivial, so we show the opposite. Assume $\langle a, b \rangle \in \sim ; R^A ; \sim$, i.e., there are the respective sequences such that $a \sim_{a1} a_1 \sim_{a2} a_2 ... \sim_{an} a_n R^A b_0 \sim_1 b_1 \sim_2 b_2 ... \sim_m b$. By induction on m we show that then also $\exists a' : a \sim a' R^A b$ which will establish the claim. The basis for $m = 0$ is trivial, so assume IH

$$
\begin{array}{ll}
IH \ \forall a, a_0, b_0, ..., b_m : & a \sim a_0 R^A b_0 \sim_1 b_1 ... \sim_m b_m \ \Rightarrow \ \exists a' : a \sim a' R^A b_m, \\
& \qquad\qquad\qquad and \\
& a \sim a_0 R^A b_0 \sim_1 b_1 ... \sim_m b_m \sim_{m+1} b_{m+1}
\end{array}
$$

From the latter we obtain, by IH, $a \sim a' R^A b_m$, and $b_m \sim_{m+1} b_{m+1}$. Since $\sim_{m+1}$ is OT, there is an $a'' \sim_{m+1} a'$ such that $a'' R^A b_{m+1}$. But then we can just extend the chain $a \sim a' \sim_{m+1} a''$ obtaining $a \sim a'' R^A b_{m+1}$. □

In particular, performing this construction on the collection of *all* OT-congruences on a given multialgebra A yields the maximal OT-congruence on A. Notice, however, that it need not be the standard universal relation. For instance, for the algebra $\begin{array}{cc} b_1 & b_2 \\ {\scriptstyle R}\uparrow & \\ a_1 & \end{array}$ the elements b_1 and b_2 cannot be related by any OT-congruence, since it would violate the condition (2.37).

One verifies easily that the construction yields, in fact, the least upper bound – with respect to subset relation – of the argument congruences. Thus, the collection of all OT-congruences on a multialgebra is a complete upper semilattice – with respect to the subset relation – with identity being the least element. By the standard result (e.g., [16], p.24), we obtain the useful fact.

Fact 2.46. *The collection of all OT-congruences on an algebra is a complete lattice.*

Infima are not, however, obtained as mere intersections. In the following algebra:

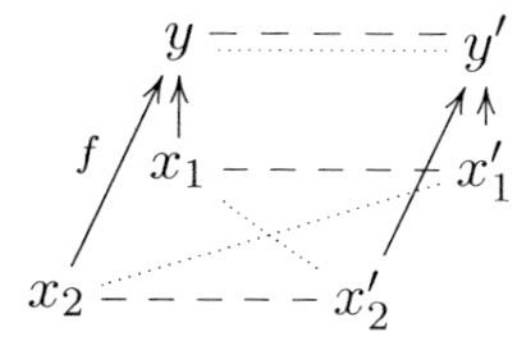

both relations:

$$\overline{\sim} \quad = \quad id \cup \{\langle y, y'\rangle, \langle y', y\rangle, \langle x_1, x_1'\rangle, \langle x_1', x_1\rangle, \langle x_2, x_2'\rangle, \langle x_2', x_2\rangle\} \quad \text{marked with the dashed line}$$
$$\dot{\sim} \quad = \quad id \cup \{\langle y, y'\rangle, \langle y', y\rangle, \langle x_1, x_2'\rangle, \langle x_2', x_1\rangle, \langle x_2, x_1'\rangle, \langle x_1', x_2\rangle\} \quad \text{marked with the dotted lines}$$

are OT-congruences. Their intersection, however, $id \cup \{\langle y, y'\rangle, \langle y', y\rangle\}$, is not an OT-congruence. In fact, the infimum of the two will be identity.

Fact 2.47. *Given two OT-congruences,* $\sim_a, \sim_b$*, on an algebra* A*, their infimum* $\sim\, = \,\sim_a \wedge \sim_b$ *can be constructed by "propagating the distinctions" (cf. the remark following (2.38)) as follows:*

1. $\sim_0 \quad = \quad \sim_a \cap \sim_b$
2. $\sim_{i+1} \quad = \quad \sim_i \setminus \{\langle y_1, y_2\rangle, \langle y_2, y_1\rangle \in \sim_i \mid \exists f : f^-(y_1) \not\sim_i f^-(y_2)\}$
3. $\sim_\lambda \quad = \quad \bigcap_{i \in \lambda} \sim_i,\ for\ limit\ ordinal\ \lambda$
4. $\sim \quad = \quad \sim_{|A|}$

PROOF: As $\sim_0$ is an equivalence relation, so each $\sim_i$, and hence also $\sim$, is obviously reflexive and symmetric. To see that it is transitive, we show that each $\sim_{i+1}$ is transitive, which will establish the claim as intersection of transitive relations is transitive. $\sim_0$ is transitive, so assume $\sim_i$ be transitive and let $y_1 \sim_{i+1} y_2 \sim_{i+1} y_3$. (Hence also $y_1 \sim_i y_2 \sim_i y_3$ and, since $\sim_i$ is transitive, so $y_1 \sim_i y_3$.) Then $\forall x_1 \in f^-(y_1)\ \exists x_2 \in f^-(y_2) : x_1 \sim_i x_2$, and likewise $\forall x_2 \in f^-(y_2)\ \exists x_3 \in f^-(y_3) : x_2 \sim_i x_3$. But since $\sim_i$ is transitive, this implies that also $\forall x_1 \in f^-(y_1)\ \exists x_3 \in f^-(y_3) : x_1 \sim_i x_3$ (and vice versa), i.e., $y_1 \sim_{i+1} y_3$. The condition in step 2 amounts to removing all pairs which violate the bireachability requirement (2.37). That is, any OT-congruence contained in $\sim_0$ must not contain any of these pairs. On the other hand, the resulting $\sim$ is indeed an OT-congruence. By the above argument, it is transitive and hence an equivalence. Moreover, whenever $y_1 \sim y_2$, then the negation of condition 2 holds, i.e., $\forall x_1 \in f^-(y_1)\ \exists x_2 \in f^-(y_2) : x_1 \sim x_2$ (and vice versa). Thus, indeed, $\sim\, = \,\sim_a \wedge \sim_b$. (Infimum of a set of congruences $\{\sim_i \mid i \in I\}$ is constructed in the same way, only starting with $\bigcap_{i \in I} \sim_i$.) □

The construction is given by ordinal induction and the cardinal $|A|$ appearing in the last point shall be understood as: for some ordinal of cardinality $|A|$. It must stop for some ordinal with cardinality $|A|$, since then all possible ways of reaching every element have been checked for possible inequivalent pre-images. In many cases, the above construction will reach a fixpoint after ω steps but, in general, one may need to continue the process as illustrated in the following example.

Example 2.48. *Let M have a unary operation f, being the transitive closure of the following:*

That is, the operation is defined by

$$f(x) = \begin{cases} \{y \mid x \leq y\} & for\ x = 0 \\ \{y \mid x \leq y\} \cup \{0\} & for\ x = 1 \\ \{y \mid x < y\} & for\ x > 1 \end{cases}$$

Consider the following two OT-congruences

$$\sim_a = \{\langle i, j\rangle \mid i, j \geq 1\} \cup \{\langle 0, 0\rangle\}$$
$$\sim_b = \{\langle 0, i\rangle, \langle 0, i\rangle, \langle i, j\rangle \mid i, j \geq 2\} \cup \{\langle 0, 0\rangle, \langle 1, 1\rangle\}$$

We obtain:

$$\sim_0 = id_M \cup \{\langle i, j\rangle \mid i, j \geq 2\}$$
$$\sim_1 = id_M \cup \{\langle i, j\rangle \mid i, j \geq 3\}$$
$$\sim_2 = id_M \cup \{\langle i, j\rangle \mid i, j \geq 4\}$$

etc., where the distinction of a new element in each step, e.g., in $2 \not\sim_1 3$, results from the fact that $f^-(2) = \{0, 1\} \not\sim_0 \{0, 1, 2\} = f^-(3)$, since neither $0 \sim_0 2$ nor $1 \sim_0 2$. Then

$$\sim_\omega = id_M \cup \{\langle i, j\rangle \mid i, j \geq \omega\}$$

and in the next step we still have to make $\omega \not\sim_{\omega+1} \omega + 1$ for the analogous reason that $f^-(\omega) = \omega \not\sim_\omega \omega \cup \{\omega\} = f^-(\omega + 1)$ while for all $n \in \omega : n \not\sim_\omega \omega$. In short, $\sim_a \wedge \sim_b = id$, but this relation is not obtained by our construction after ω steps but first after $\omega + \omega$. In general, we might have arbitrary sequence of such ω sequences, so that number of iterations needed is limited by the cardinality κ of M (which in the example is ω) not in the sense of the least ordinal with cardinality κ but of some ordinal with this cardinality (one might want to say, by the largest possible ordinal of cardinality κ).

Proposition 2.49. *If M is κ-bounded, the result of the construction from Fact 2.47 is obtained after κ steps, i.e., $\sim = \sim_\kappa$.*

PROOF: If $y_1 \not\sim y_2$, they are split at some stage $i + 1$ due to non-congruence $f^-(y_1) \not\sim_i f^-(y_2)$. Since M is κ-bounded, $|M_{\{y_i\}}| < \kappa$, so y_i is reachable from at most κ elements. We reach a fix-point, after which $\sim_i = \sim_j$ for all $j \geq i$, once $(M_{\{y_1\}} \times M_{\{y_2\}}) \cap \sim_i = (M_{\{y_1\}} \times M_{\{y_2\}}) \cap \sim_{i+1}$. But the cardinality of these relations is bounded by $M_{\{y_1\}} \times M_{\{y_2\}} \leq \kappa \cdot \kappa = \kappa$, so that all required splittings of pre-images (of pre-images of pre-images...) of y_i's will happen within κ steps. (Example 2.48 illustrates the worst case of chains for an arbitrary ordinal of cardinality κ.) □

Let now $\approx_A$ denote the maximal OT-congruence and $\sim_A$ the maximal bireachability (i.e., union of all bireachabilities) on A.

Proposition 2.50. *The maximal bireachability on A is an equivalence, in fact: $\approx_A = \sim_A$.*

PROOF: Since OT-congruence is bireachability, we obviously have $\approx_A \subseteq \sim_A$. The opposite inclusion follows because every bireachability is included in some OT-congruence. Namely, given a bireachability $\sim$, its converse $\sim^-$ is also bireachability, which follows trivially by inspecting the definition (2.37). Likewise, union of bireachabilities is a bireachability, in particular, the reflexive, symmetric closure of $\sim$, i.e., $\simeq = \sim \cup \sim^{-} \cup id_A$ is a bireachability. One also verifies easily that transitive closure of a bireachability is a bireachability:

$$\begin{aligned} b \sim b_1 \sim b_2 \quad &\Rightarrow \quad \forall aRb \quad \exists a_1 : a \sim a_1 \wedge a_1 R b_1 \\ &\Rightarrow \quad \forall aRb \quad \exists a_1 : a \sim a_1 \wedge a_1 R b_1 \wedge \exists a_2 : a_1 \sim a_2 \wedge a_2 R b_2 \\ &\Rightarrow \quad \forall aRb \quad \exists a_1, a_2 : a \sim a_1 \sim a_2 \wedge a_2 R b_2 \end{aligned}$$

Consequently, the equivalence closure $\simeq_A^*$ of $\sim_A$ is OT-congruence, and so: $\sim_A \subseteq \simeq_A^* \subseteq \approx_A$. □

Fact 2.51. *Let $B \sqsubseteq A$, $\sim_A$ be an OT-congruence on A, and $\sim_B \subseteq \sim_A$ be restriction of $\sim_A$ to the carrier of B, i.e., $\sim_A \cap B \times B$. Then*

1) $\sim_B$ is OT-congruence on B and

2) $\sim_B \cup id_A$ is OT-congruence on A.

PROOF: 1. Let $a, a_1, b_1, b \in B$ be such that $a \sim_B a_1 R^B b_1 \sim_B b$. Then also $a \sim_A a_1 R^A b_1 \sim_A b$ and since $\sim_A$ is OT-congruence on A, so $\exists a_0 \in A : a \sim_A a_0 R^A b$. Since $B \sqsubseteq A$, B is closed under pre-images of A-operations, so $b \in B$ implies $a_0 \in B$, and then $a \sim_B a_0 R^B b$.

2. Let us write $\sim_B$ for the union $\sim_B \cup id_A$. To show that $\sim_B; R^A; \sim_B \subseteq \sim_B; R^A$, consider the cases of $a_0 \sim_B a_1 R^A a_2 \sim_B a_3$:

– when all $a_i \in B$, there exists an $a' : a_0 \sim_B a' R^A a_3$ since $\sim_B$ is bireachability on B;

– if $a_0 \notin B$ while $a_1 \in B$, then $a_0 = a_1$ and the result follows when $a_2, a_3 \in B$;

– if $a_2 \notin B$ or $a_3 \notin B$, then $a_2 = a_3$ and the result follows trivially;

– if $a_1 \notin B$ then also $a_2 \notin B$ since $B \sqsubseteq A$ (i.e., inclusion is OT), and so $a_0 = a_1$ and $a_3 = a_2$. □

As an example of quotienting an algebra by a (maximal) OT-congruence, we can consider a kind of minimization of a nondeterministic automaton.

Example 2.52. *The automaton (multialgebra) A from example 2.30, quotiented by the largest OT-congruence yields the automaton (multialgebra) $B = A/_{\sim}$:*

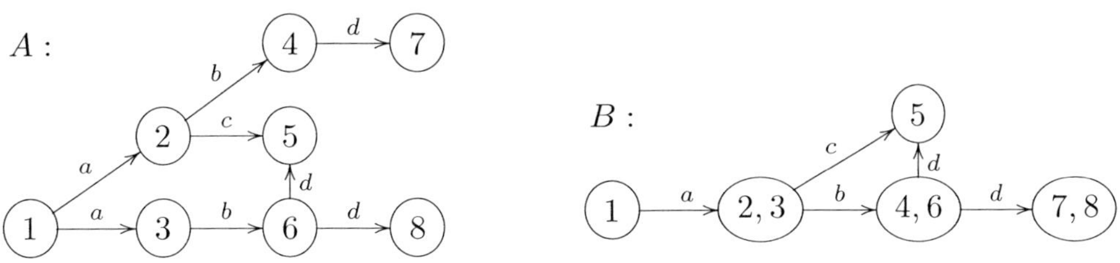

We cannot have $5 \sim 8$ because, although both can be reached by d from 6, i.e., $5, 8 \in d^A(6)$, so $5 \in c^A(2)$ while $8 \notin c^A(2)$ and $8 \notin c^A(3)$ and there are no more states $s \sim 2$.

To model accepting states, we introduce additional constant ac. (Likewise, we can introduce a constant st for identifying the initial state.) If we let only 7 in A be the accepting *state, the picture will be modified accordingly:*

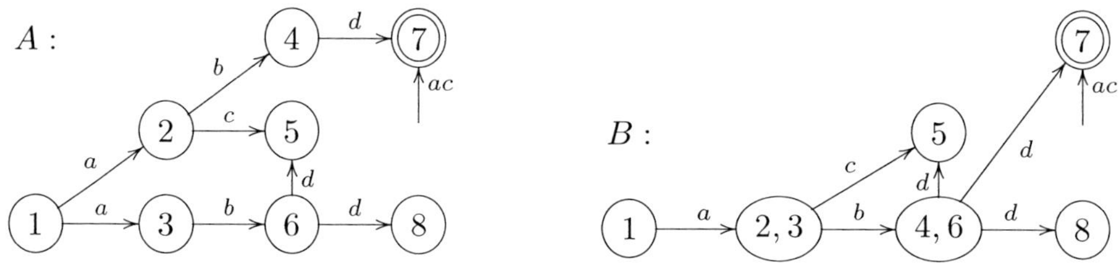

Obviously, with respect to the accepted language, the obtained automaton is not minimal (we could, for instance, safely remove states 8 *and* 5*). It remains to determine what – if any – known or useful construction on automata is represented by the quotient by OT-congruence.*

Example 2.53. *A more refined notion of OT-congruence on automata can be obtained by an alternative model in which an automaton is represented as one operation* $tr : S \times Alph \to S$*, taking a state and an alphabet symbol and returning the set of possible resulting states. In this case, we can, in addition, consider also various bireachabilities on the alphabet symbols. When it is identity, we obtain the same result as in the previous example. On the other hand, if it is the total relation (no operations returning* $Alph$*-elements leaves us full freedom in determining OT-congruence on this sort),* $Alph^A \times Alph^A$*, the maximal OT-congruence identifies states* s, t *iff for each number of steps in which* s *can be reached from some state* s'*,* t *can be reached in the same number of steps from a state* t' *which is bireachable with* s'*, and vice versa.*

Thus, for instance, if we represent the search space by a multialgebra A *with the subset* $X \subseteq A$ *of goals, the subalgebra* A_X *represents, as at the end of example 2.30, the states from which some goal in* X *is reachable, and then, quotient by the maximal OT-congruence (identifying all symbols), will yield, roughly, a collection of paths (possibly with loops and common nodes) leading to* X *and having distinct lengths.*

2.3.2. Σ-structure of OT-congruence

Just like classical Σ-congruence has algebraic Σ-structure, so OT-congruence on a Σ-multialgebra has itself a multialgebraic Σ-structure. In fact, we define such a structure for an arbitrary bireachability and all the results apply to OT-congruences as special cases.

Definition 2.54. *For a bireachability* $\sim$ *on* $A \in \mathsf{MAlg}_{OT}(\Sigma)$*, we define* $A^\sim \in \mathsf{MAlg}_{OT}(\Sigma)$*:*

- $A^\sim = \{\langle a_1, a_2\rangle \mid a_1, a_2 \in A \wedge a_1 \sim a_2\}$*, and*
- $f^{A^\sim}(\langle a_1, b_1\rangle ... \langle a_n, b_n\rangle) = \{\langle x, y\rangle \mid x \in f^A(a_1...a_n) \wedge y \in f^A(b_1...b_n) \wedge x \sim y\}$*, i.e., for constants* $c^{A^\sim} = \{\langle x, y\rangle \mid x, y \in c^A \wedge x \sim y\}$.

Fact 2.55. *Given a bireachability* $\sim$ *on* A.

1) *The projections* $\pi_1, \pi_2 : A^\sim \to A$*,* $\pi_i(\langle a_1, a_2\rangle) = a_i$ *are OT.*
2) $A/_\sim$ *with the quotient homomorphism* $q : A \to A/_\sim$ *is their coequalizer.*

PROOF: 1. We verify that π_1 is OT. $\pi_1^-(a) = \{\langle a, x\rangle : x \sim a\}$, and thus:

(i) $\pi_1^-(f^A(a)) = \{\langle b, y\rangle \mid b \in f^A(a), y \sim b\}$, while

(ii) $f^{A^\sim}(\pi_1^-(a)) = f^{A^\sim}(\{\langle a, x\rangle \mid x \sim a\}) = \{\langle b, y\rangle \mid b \in f^A(a), y \sim b, y \in f^A(x), x \sim a\}$

Obviously (ii) $\subseteq$ (i). The opposite inclusion holds because $\sim$ is bireachability: if $b \in f^A(a)$ and $y \sim b$ then, by (2.37), $\exists x \sim a : y \in f^A(x)$. But this is exactly the restriction in (ii).

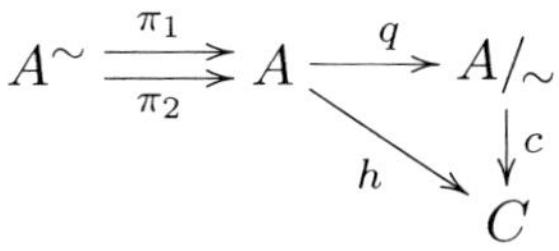

2. For every $\langle a_1, a_2\rangle \in A^\sim$, we have $q(a_1) = q(a_2)$, so $\pi_1; q = \pi_2; q$. Assume some other $h : A \to C$ with $\pi_1; h = \pi_2; h$. Define $c : A/_\sim \to C$ by $c([a]) = h(a)$. It is well defined, for if $a \sim a'$, i.e., $\langle a, a'\rangle \in A^\sim$, then $h(a) = h(a')$ by assumption. Obviously $q; c = h$ and this equality forces also its uniqueness.

To see that c is OT, consider:

(i) $f^{A/\sim}(c^-(c_1)...c^-(c_n)) = f^{A/\sim}(q(h^-(c_1))...q(h^-(c_n)))$ since $c^-(c_i) = q(h^-(c_i))$ and

(ii) $c^-(f^C(c_1...c_n)) = q(h^-(f^C(c_1...c_n))) = q(f^A(h^-(c_1)...h^-(c_n)))$ since h is OT.

To see that (i)=(ii), we observe that the h pre-image of any $c_i \in C$ consists of one or more $\sim$-equivalence classes: (*) $h^- = h^-; q; q^-$, simply because $h^- = c^-; q^-$ and $c^- = h^-; q$. So, since q is OT, we have the first equality, and since $q^-; q = id_{A/\sim}$ and h is OT, the last one:

$$\begin{aligned}
q^-\big(f^{A/\sim}(q(h^-(c_1))...q(h^-(c_n)))\big) &= f^A\big(q^-(q(h^-(c_1)))...q^-(q(h^-(c_n)))\big)\\
(*) &= f^A\big(h^-(c_1)...h^-(c_n)\big)\\
q\big(q^-\big(f^{A/\sim}(q(h^-(c_1))...q(h^-(c_n)))\big)\big) &= q\big(f^A\big(h^-(c_1)...h^-(c_n)\big)\big)\\
(i) = f^{A/\sim}\big(q(h^-(c_1))...q(h^-(c_n))\big) &= q\big(h^-(f^C(c_1...c_n))\big) = (ii)
\end{aligned}$$

□

Corollary 2.56. *All epis in* $\mathsf{MAlg}_{OT}(\Sigma)$ *are regular.*

PROOF: Given an epi $e : A \to B$ with kernel $\sim$, we have by corollary 2.43 an isomorphism $i : A/_\sim \simeq B$ and such that $q; i = e$ where $q : A \to A/_\sim$. But since q is coequalizing, so is e. □

Strictly speaking, congruence on A is a (special kind of morphism) $i : R \to A \times A$. But we will not verify the existence of products in our category until section 5., and so we abbreviate the respective $i; \pi_i$ as the span $r_1, r_2 : R \to A$. In the standard way, given any relation $p_1, p_2 : P \to A$, its congruence closure is the equalizer of $p_1; q$ and $p_2; q : A \to A/_P$, where $(A/_P, q)$ is coequalizer of p_1 and p_2. Assuming that all such equalizers and coequalizers exist (which will be shown first in proposition 3.12), we also obtain the following standard result.

Fact 2.57. *Given OT-congruences P, R on $A : P \subseteq R \Rightarrow \exists h : A/_P \to A/_R$ with $q_P; h = q_R$.*

PROOF: We consider the diagram:

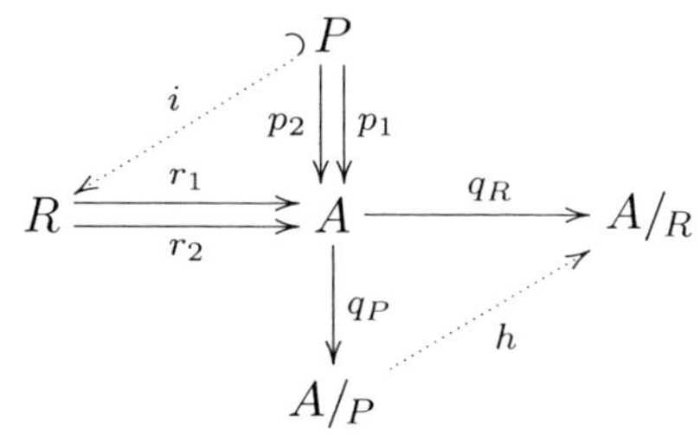

As P, R are congruences on A, so $(A/_R, q_R)$, resp. $(A/_P, q_P)$, coequalize r_1, r_2, resp., p_1, p_2.
Assume $P \subseteq R$, i.e., for $k \in \{1, 2\} : p_k = i; r_k$, where i is the inclusion. First, since q_R coequalizes r_1 and r_2, we obtain that also $i; r_1; q_R = i; r_2; q_R$, i.e., $p_1; q_R = p_2; q_R$. But as $(A/_P, q_P)$ is coequalizer of p_1, p_2, we obtain a unique $h : A/_P \to A/_R$ making $q_P; h = q_R$. □

2.3.3. Bireachabilities between algebras

The notion (2.37) of bireachability on an algebra is a special case of the following notion of bireachability *between* algebras.

Definition 2.58. *Bireachability* between *two algebras A and B is a subset $\sim \subseteq A \times B$ satisfying the following bireachability condition:*

$$\begin{array}{rl} \forall a, b, a_1 : & a \sim b \wedge a \in f^A(a_1) \Rightarrow \exists b_1 \in B : b \in f^B(b_1) \wedge a_1 \sim b_1 \\ \& \ \forall a, b, b_1 : & a \sim b \wedge b \in f^B(b_1) \Rightarrow \exists a_1 \in A : a \in f^A(a_1) \wedge a_1 \sim b_1 \end{array}$$

Relation $\sim$ is a bireachability on A according to (2.37) iff it is a bireachability between A and A according to the above definition.

A bireachability $\sim$ between A and B can be given a natural Σ-structure, generalising definition 2.54, as follows

$$f^{\sim}(\langle a_1, b_1\rangle ... \langle a_n, b_n\rangle) = f^A(a_1...a_n) \times f^B(b_1...b_n) \cap \sim . \tag{2.59}$$

When addressing algebra structure of some bireachability we will always mean the above condition unless explicitly stated otherwise. An equivalent formulation of $\sim$ being a bireachability is then as follows.

Lemma 2.60. $\sim \subseteq A_1 \times A_2$ *(with the Σ-structure given by (2.59)) is a bireachability iff the projections $\pi_i : \sim \to A_i$, $\pi_i(\langle a_1, a_2\rangle) = a_i$, are homomorphisms.*

PROOF: $\Rightarrow$) We verify that $f^{\sim}(\pi_1^-(a_1)) = \pi_1^-(f^{A_1}(a_1))$. If $\langle a, b\rangle \in \pi_1^-(f^{A_1}(a_1))$ then $a \in f^{A_1}(a_1)$ and $a \sim b$ so, by 2.58, $\exists b_1 : a_1 \sim b_1$ and $b \in f^{A_2}(b_1)$. But then $\langle a_1, b_1\rangle \in \pi_1^-(a_1)$ and by (2.59) $\langle a, b\rangle \in f^{\sim}(\langle a_1, b_1\rangle)$.

Conversely, if $\langle a, b\rangle \in f^{\sim}(\pi_1^{-}(a_1))$ then, by (2.59), $a \in f^{A_1}(a_1)$. But then obviously $\langle a, b\rangle \in \pi_1^{-}(f^{A_1}(a_1))$.

$\Leftarrow$) Assume both π_i are OT and let $a \in f^{A_1}(a_1)$ and $a \sim b$. Since π_1 is OT we have $\pi_1^{-}(f^{A_1}(a_1)) = f^{\sim}(\pi_1^{-}(a_1))$ and since $\langle a, b\rangle \in \pi_1^{-}(a) \subseteq \pi_1^{-}(f^{A_1}(a_1))$ so also $\langle a, b\rangle \in f^{\sim}(\pi_1^{-}(a_1))$, i.e., $\exists b_1 \in A_2 : \langle a, b\rangle \in f^{\sim}(\langle a_1, b_1\rangle)$. But by (2.59) this last fact means that $\exists b_1 \in A_2 : b \in f^{A_2}(b_1)$ and $a_1 \sim b_1$. □

As a special case, and in analogy to the case of coalgebras whose homomorphisms are functional bisimulations, the OT-homomorphisms are functional bireachabilities.

Fact 2.61. *A function $\phi : A \to B$ is OT-homomorphism iff its graph $Gr(\phi) = \{\langle a, \phi(a)\rangle : a \in A\}$ is a bireachability between A and B.*

PROOF: Denote the projections by $\pi_A, \pi_B : Gr(\phi) \to A, B$, i.e., $\pi_i(\langle x_1, x_2\rangle) = x_i$. We have that $\pi_A; \phi = \pi_B$ and π_A is a bijection.

$\Leftarrow$) If π_i's are OT then, π_A being iso, so is its converse π_A^{-}. But since $\phi = \pi_A^{-}; \pi_B$, so ϕ is OT.

$\Rightarrow$) Assume ϕ to be OT, and define Σ-structure on $Gr(\phi)$ by letting $f^{Gr}(\langle a, b\rangle) = \{\langle a', b'\rangle \in Gr(\phi) \mid a' \in f^A(a)\}$. Since $\pi_B = \pi_A; \phi$, it sufficies to verify that π_A is OT. $f^{Gr}(\pi_A^{-}(a)) = f^{Gr}(\langle a, b\rangle) = \{\langle a', b'\rangle \in Gr(\phi) \mid a' \in f^A(a)\} = \pi_A^{-}(f^A(a))$. □

Finally, we can also generalise lemma 2.60 as follows.

Lemma 2.62. *An arbitrary span $A_1 \overset{\phi_1}{\leftarrow} B \overset{\phi_2}{\to} A_2$, induces a bireachability between A_1 and A_2 given by $\sim = \{\langle \phi_1(b), \phi_2(b)\rangle \mid b \in B\}$.*

PROOF: We verify that the bireachability condition is satisfied. Assume $a_1 \sim a_2$, i.e., for some $b : \langle \phi_1(b), \phi_2(b)\rangle = \langle a_1, a_2\rangle$ and $a_1 \in f^{A_1}(x_1)$. Since ϕ_1 is OT, we then have $x_1 \in \phi_1[B]$, i.e., for some $y \in B : \phi_1(y) = x_1$ and $b \in f^B(y)$. But then, since ϕ_2 is OT (and hence also weak), $\phi_2(f^B(y)) \subseteq f^{A_2}(\phi_2(y))$, i.e., $a_2 = \phi_2(b) \in f^{A_2}(\phi_2(y))$ and we have the required witness $x_2 = \phi_2(y)$ with $x_1 \sim x_2$. □

Thus, any bireachability is a span (according to lemma 2.60) and, conversely, any span induces a bireachability according to the above lemma.

An unpleasant fact is that, given a bireachability $\sim$ induced by a span as above in lemma 2.62, with the algebra structure given by the equation (2.59), there need not be any homomorphism $B \to \sim$. We will address this problem in section 4. considering products.

Example 2.63. *Consider two isomorphic algebras over $\Sigma = \langle\{s_1, s_2\}, \{f : s_1 \to s_2\}\rangle$:*

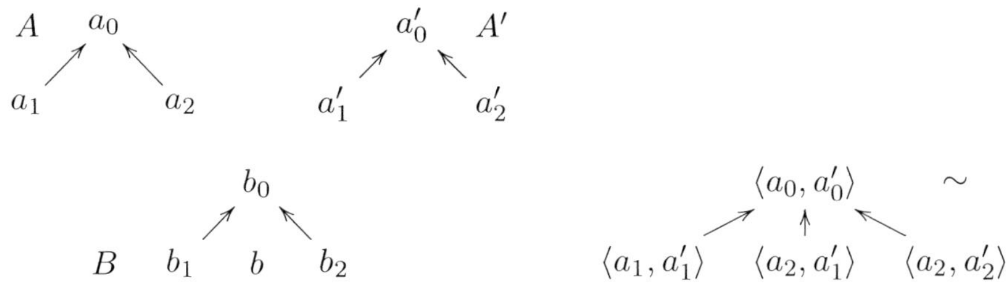

and two homomorphisms:

- $p : B \rightarrow A$, *given by* $p(b_i) = a_i$ *and* $p(b) = a_2$, *and*
- $p' : B \rightarrow A'$, *given by* $p'(b_i) = a_i'$ *and* $p'(b) = a_1'$.

The induced bireachability $\sim$, *with its algebraic structure, is shown to the right. There is no homomorphism* $\phi : B \rightarrow \sim$ *since sending* $\phi(b_0) = \langle a_0, a_0' \rangle$ *requires all the three arguments to be in the image of* ϕ, *in which case the OT-property of* ϕ *fails for* $x = \phi(b)$, *i.e.,* $f^B(\phi^-(x)) = f^B(b) = \varnothing \neq \{b_0\} = \phi^-(f^\sim(x))$.

It is easy to see that the following fact holds.

Fact 2.64. *The condition from definition 2.58 is preserved by unions.*

Consequently, for any two algebras, there is always the maximal (with respect to $\subseteq$) bireachability between them, namely, the union of all bireachabilities. In case this maximal bireachability is empty, we will say that the algebras are not bireachable.

The following examples illustrate further the duality of bireachability and bisimilarity.

Example 2.65. *Assume three operations* $a, b, c : s \rightarrow s$ *and consider the following standard example from process theory:*

A and B are not bisimilar but are both trace equivalent and bireachable. In fact, A is a quotient of B by the bireachability $1 \sim 1'$. *As might be expected, we have a dual situation: bisimulation distinguishes states with respect to differences which 'come after' while bireachability with respect to what 'comes before'. The following two algebras are trace equivalent and bisimilar but not bireachable (as any bireachability on B containing* $\langle 1, 1' \rangle$ *must also contain* $\langle 2, 3 \rangle$*):*

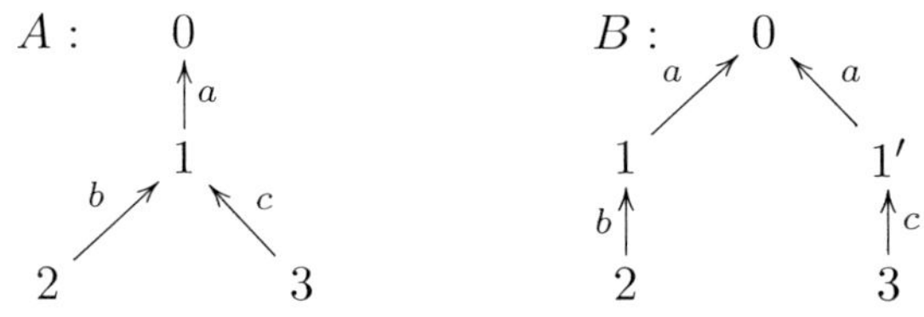

Example 2.66. *The duality of 'after' and 'before' – and at least occasional naturality of the latter – can be illustrated by the following. Let now* $0, a, b, c, d :\rightarrow s$ *be constants, and let the arrow represent the only operation* $tr : s \rightarrow s$. *(Subscripts serve only reference purposes.)*

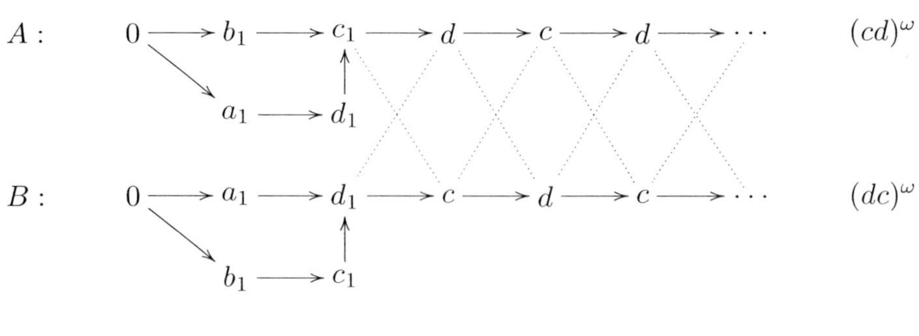

A bisimilarity between A and B is given by the pairs $\langle i_1, i_1\rangle$, for $i \in \{a, b, c, d\}$ and those indicated by the dotted lines. One might feel a bit uneasy about this bisimilarity since A satisfies the formula: "the first d_1 occurs before the first c_1" (or else: "the first c_1 is reachable from the first d_1") while B does not.

Unlike bisimilarity reflecting the relation of 'coming after', bireachability is exactly the relation of 'coming before'. The greatest bireachability $\sim \subseteq A \times B$ is simply the relation $\{\langle 0, 0\rangle, \langle a_1, a_1\rangle, \langle b_1, b_1\rangle\}$. We can not possibly get $c_1 \sim c_1$ as this would require $d_1 \sim b_1$ (since in $A : c_1 \in tr^A(b_1) \cap tr^A(d_1)$ while in B we only have $c_1 \in tr^B(b_1)$). But $d_1 \sim b_1$ is impossible as it, in turn, would require $a_1 \sim 0$ which cannot obtain because while $a_1 \in tr^A(0)$ there is no $b \in B : 0 \in tr^B(b)$. (Two states can be bireachable here if they have the same label and are reachable in the same number of steps from states with the same labels – compare Example 2.53.)

Example 2.67. *The following two structures are modally indistinguishable but not bisimilar:*

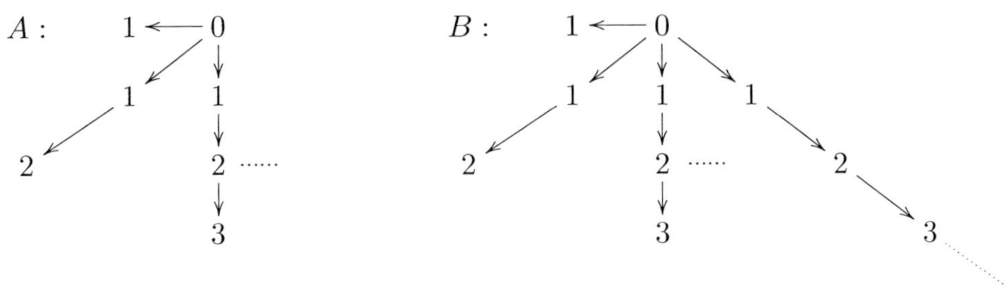

The natural attempt would be to relate all nodes reachable in the equal number of steps, i.e., $\sim = \{\langle n^A, n^B\rangle \mid n^A = n^B\}$. This does not work for the well-known reason that, attempting to set any node n^B on the infinite path of B bisimilar to some n^A on a finite branch of A of length $m > n$, leads to the impossibility of relating the last element m^A to the m-th element on the infinite path of B, since from the latter there is a further transition to $(m + 1)^B$.

The above relation yields, however, a bireachability since it involves only elements from which any element on the infinite path is reachable and not what elements lie ahead of it. Thus, even taking only the one infinite branch of B, yields the structure bireachable with A.

Example 2.68. *The dual character of bismilarity and bireachability is well summarized by looking at the following structures:*

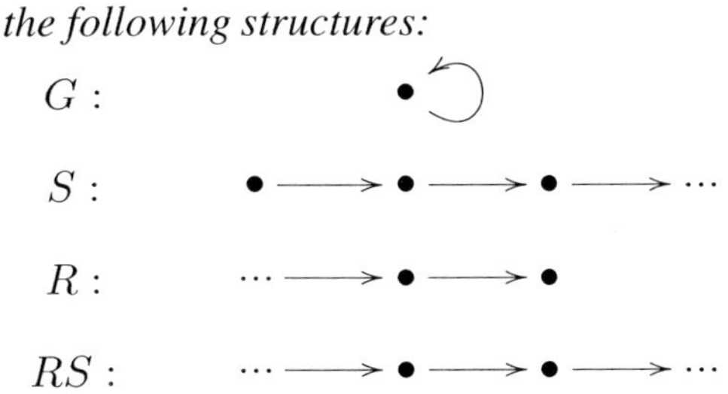

G and S are bisimilar but not bireachable, G and R are bireachable but not bisimilar, and G and RS are both bisimilar and bireachable.

Recall from remark 2.9 that a coalgebra $\alpha : A \to \Sigma(A)$ over a polynomial functor Σ can be represented as a multialgebra $\alpha^- : \Sigma(A) \to \mathcal{P}(A)$ with the special property that for all $a_1 \neq a_2 : \alpha^-(a_1) \cap \alpha^-(a_2) = \varnothing$. Denote the coalgebras by A, B and the corresponding multialgebras by A^-, B^-.

Fact 2.69. *$\sim \subseteq A^- \times B^-$ is a bireachability between A^- and B^- iff $\sim$ is a bisimilarity between A and B.*

PROOF: Follows trivially since each operation in A^- is converse of the respective function in A, while the bireachability condition from 2.58 is just the converse of the bisimilarity condition (as illustrated already in (2.38)). □

The bireachability remains, however, a wider notion as it applies to all multialgebras, also those which do not represent any coalgebra.

2.4. Final objects in $\mathsf{MAlg}_{OT}(\Sigma)$

In general, final objects do not exist in $\mathsf{MAlg}_{OT}(\Sigma)$ due to the usual cardinality reasons. Consider a signature with one sort and operation $f : s \to s$. In a multialgebra Z this requires $f^Z : s^Z \to \mathcal{P}(s^Z)$ (essentially a coalgebra for power-set functor) and, when Z is to be final, moreover isomorphism $s^Z \simeq \mathcal{P}(s^Z)$.

In this subsection we show one special case guaranteeing existence of final objects, mainly to illustrate their interesting features. The required extension of the category ensuring completeness is given in the following section 3.. Completeness of some subcategories of $\mathsf{MAlg}_{OT}(\Sigma)$ is then shown in section 5..

Example 2.70. *Let $\Sigma = \langle \{s_1, s_2\}, \{c :\to s_1; f : s_1 \to s_2\}\rangle$. The final object Z in $\mathsf{MAlg}_{OT}(\Sigma)$ can be described as follows. (Expressions like "$\varnothing_1$" or "$fc\varnothing$" are simple names – mnemonic devices – not any sets or function applications.)*

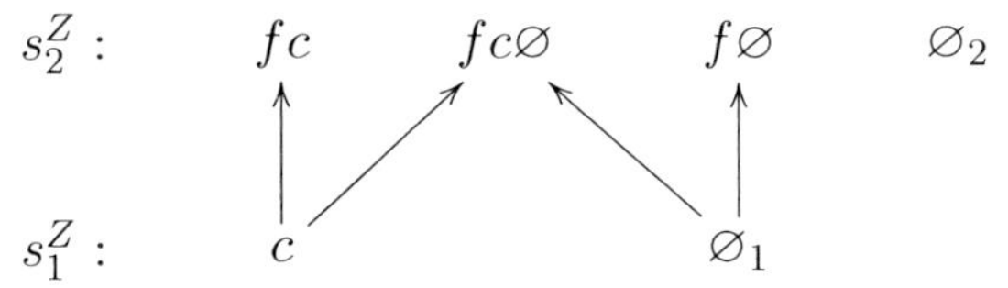

In words, each sort contains only elements needed to distinguish any combination of operations returning the elements of this sort. In s_1^Z it is enough with one element to interpret the constant, $c^Z = \{c\}$. In addition, there is always an element not belonging to the result of any operation, $\varnothing_1$. s_2^Z contains one such element, $\varnothing_2$, one element characteristic for $f^Z(c) \ni fc$, one for $f^Z(\varnothing_1) \ni f\varnothing$ and one for $f^Z(c) \cap f^Z(\varnothing_1) \ni fc\varnothing$.

If we had two constants of sort s_1, we would obtain corresponding collection $\{c, d, cd, \varnothing_1\}$ in s_1^Z, while s_2^Z would now contain characteristic element for every possible $f^Z(x)$ when $x \in s_1^Z$, as well as for every intersection $\bigcap_{x \in X} f^Z(x)$ for every possible $X \subseteq s_1^Z$.

Viewing results of an operation as possible (or nondeterministic) observations of its arguments, the construction amounts to providing the minimum needed for every series and every (possible intersection of a) set of observations to have its unique characteristic result. Recalling the topology we defined on (an arbitrary) multialgebra in remark 2.8, in case of the final multialgebra, it will amount to each set S of the basis (obtained as arbitrary intersections of the subbasis sets, i.e., sets of the form $f^Z(\overline{x})$) having a unique characteristic element z_S. Alternatively, we can say that the only bireachability on a final algebra is identity and just like final morphisms of coalgebras identify bisimilar states, so here final morphisms will identify bireachable elements.

One special case when this construction can be performed is when the signature does not contain any "loops". Call a signature "acyclic" if there is no derived operator t with target sort occurring also among the argument sorts. More precisely, we can define an ordering on sort symbols by taking the transitive closure of the relation: $s_1 < s_2$ iff $\exists f : \ldots s_1 \ldots \to s_2$. Σ is *acyclic* if there are no two (possibly the same) sort symbols such that $s_1 < s_2$ and $s_2 < s_1$. We then have a well-founded partial ordering of all sort symbols with the minimal elements MIN for which there are at most some constants.

Proposition 2.71. *If Σ is acyclic then $\mathsf{MAlg}_{OT}(\Sigma)$ has final objects.*

PROOF: Constructions and arguments will depend heavily on the ordering $<$ of sort symbols. We define the carriers of the final algebra Z in this way. $\mathcal{T}(\Sigma)$ denotes all ground Σ-terms, $\mathcal{T}(\Sigma)_s$ all ground terms of sort s, and $\mathcal{T}(\Sigma, X)_s$ all ground terms of sort s relative to a set of additional constants X.

1) For each sort $s \in MIN : s^Z = \mathcal{P}(\mathcal{T}(\Sigma)_s)$ – notice that $\mathcal{T}(\Sigma)_s$ will contain in this case at most some constants.

2) For each sort $s \notin MIN$, let F be the set of all non-constant operations with s as the target sort. For each such $f \in F$, $f : s_1 \ldots s_n \to s$, we have, by induction, constructed s_i^Z for all argument sorts. Let X be the (disjoint) union of all elements from all the argument sorts for all operations from F. We then consider all terms relative to this set, $\mathcal{T}(\Sigma, X)_s$, and define $s^Z = \mathcal{P}(\mathcal{T}(\Sigma, X)_s)$.

Notice that for each sort s, we will obtain the element $\varnothing_s$ – this will represent the element(s) of the respective sort which are "absolute junk", i.e., not in the image of any operation (for any choice of arguments). An element (a set) $p \in s^Z$ is intended to represent the unique point which belongs to the intersection of all terms $t \in p$. The operations in Z are defined as:

3) $p \in c^Z \iff c \in p$

4) $p \in f^Z(p_1 \ldots p_n) \iff f(p_1 \ldots p_n) \in p$

and the definition is extended pointwise to the sets of p's. Notice that, in the last point, the argument p_i's are all from lower levels, i.e., from sorts $s_i < s$, where s is the target sort of f.

Given any Σ-algebra A, we define a homomorphism $\phi_A : A \to Z$ by induction on sort ordering:

5) $s \in MIN : a \in s^A : \phi_A(a) = \{c \mid a \in c^A\}$

6) $s \notin MIN : a \in s^A : \phi_A(a) = \{c \mid a \in c^A\} \cup \{f(p) \mid \exists x\, p = \phi_A(x) \wedge a \in f^A(x)\}$

It is an OT homomorphism:

$$\begin{array}{rrcl} \text{for constants:} & \phi_A^-(c^Z) & = & \phi_A^-(\{p \mid c \in p\}) \\ & & = & \{a \mid c \in \phi_A(a)\} \\ & 5)\ 6) & = & \{a \mid a \in c^A\} \\ & & = & c^A \\ \text{and for operations:} & a \in \phi_A^-(f^Z(p)) & \iff & \phi_A(a) \in f^Z(p) \\ & 4) & \iff & f(p) \in \phi_A(a) \\ & 6) & \iff & \exists x : p = \phi_A(x) \wedge a \in f^A(x) \\ & & \iff & a \in f^A(\phi_A^-(p)) \end{array}$$

Finally, assume another $\psi : A \to Z$, where for some $a \in A : \phi_A(a) \neq \psi(a)$. We show that then ψ cannot be an OT-homomorphism, by induction on the sort ordering:

- $s \in MIN, a \in s^A$ and $\{c \mid a \in c^A\} = \phi_A(a) \neq \psi(a) \Rightarrow \exists c$ such that either

  i) $a \in c^A \wedge c \notin \psi(a)$ – then $a \notin \psi^-(c^Z)$, so ψ wouldn't be OT; or else

  ii) $a \notin c^A \wedge c \in \psi(a)$ – then $a \in \psi^-(c^Z)$ so, again, ψ wouldn't be OT

- $s \notin MIN, a \in s^A$ and $\phi_A(a) \neq \psi(a)$. If the difference from definition 6) concerns some constant c, the argument is the same as above. So assume that it concerns some f, p, i.e., $\exists f \in \Sigma\ p \in Z$ such that either

  iii) $f(p) \in \phi_A(a) \wedge f(p) \notin \psi(a)$; or else

  iv) $f(p) \notin \phi_A(a) \wedge f(p) \in \psi(a)$

  By IH, for any $x : \phi_A(x) = p$ we also have $\psi(x) = p$ since given such an f, the sort of x must be $<$ then the sort of a. Thus also $\phi_A^-(p) = \psi^-(p)$. Then we have:

  $$a \in \psi^-(f^Z(p)) \overset{OT}{\iff} a \in f^A(\psi^-(p)) \overset{IH}{\iff} a \in f^A(\phi_A^-(p)) \overset{6)}{\iff} f(p) \in \phi_A(a)$$

  so neither iii) nor iv) can be the case if ψ is OT.

□

If Σ is cyclic, we simply can not stop in point 2) but have to keep constructing new power-sets *ad infinitum*. The construction can terminate for arbitrary Σ if we impose some limitations on the power-set functor. Similarly to the case of coalgebras we need a restriction on the size of one-generated subalgebras, namely, to κ-bounded multialgebras. We will not prove it at this point, but extend first the category $\mathsf{MAlg}_{OT}(\Sigma)$ to allow for the existence of final objects without any cardinality limits nor restrictions on the signature. As in the case of coalgebras, we have to leave the set-based categories and allow algebras with carriers being classes. The constructions of colimits and equalizers to be given in the following section, can be applied also in $\mathsf{MAlg}_{OT}(\Sigma)$. All constructions can be applied (sometimes with minor modifications) in $\mathsf{MAlg}^{\kappa}_{OT}(\Sigma)$ and so, in section 5., we will obtain its (co)completeness as a consequence of the constructions for $\mathsf{MAlg}^{*}_{OT}(\Sigma)$.

3. The Category Outer-Tight with classes, $\mathsf{MAlg}^*_{OT}(\Sigma)$

Given a Σ with sort symbols $\{s_1...s_n\}$, we allow algebras where carrier of each sort is a class. Constants can denote proper classes and so can operations applied to single elements return proper classes, i.e., the power-set used in definition 1.2, denotes the collection of all subcollections (also proper subclasses) of the argument collection. [3] But we have to require here one restriction. We will need a form of representability of large algebras by small ones, essentially, that any algebra can be obtained as a colimit of its small subalgebras. This, however, may in general be impossible. Assume that $X \subseteq A$ is a proper class and that, for some operation $f : f^A(X) = \{x\}$. Whenever $\phi : B \to A$ is an OT-homomrphism, with $x \in \phi(B)$, B can not be small since it has to be surjective (at least) on the whole class X (this follows from outer-tightness; it is condition 2) from figure 2.1). We therefore limit our category to only special kind of algebras with carriers being proper classes.

Definition 3.1. *A Σ-multialgebra A is set-reflecting iff for every $a \in A$ and every (relevant) $f \in \Sigma$, there exists at most a set $X \subseteq A$ such that $a \in \bigcap_{x\in X} f^A(x)$.*

Put differently, for every f and a, a's pre-image $(f^A)^{\text{-}}(a) = \{x \mid a \in f^A(x)\}$ is a set. (This is not to be confused with the "set-based" functors from [2], even though both restrictions serve the same purpose.) The definition implies – and derives the name from the fact – that if $f^A(X)$ is a set, so is X, i.e., no function collapses a class to a set. (If $Z = f^A(X)$ is a set then, for every $z \in Z$, there is at most a set X_z, such that $z \in \bigcap_{x\in X_z} f^A(x)$. Then also $X_Z = \bigcup_{z\in Z} X_z$ is a set – but $X \subseteq X_Z$.)

$\mathsf{MAlg}^*_{OT}(\Sigma)$ considered in the following is the category of all set-reflecting multialgebras with OT-homomorphisms. Saying algebra we mean from now on a set-reflecting multialgebra.

3.1. Set-reflecting algebras are colimits of small subalgebras

The apparent "inversion" of the condition in definition 3.1 (one might expect it to require $f^A(X)$ to be a set, whenever X is) reflects the inverted direction of bireachability with respect to bisimulation, (2.38). It is crucial in the point 2) of the proof of the following result which extends fact 2.29 to the present category.

Lemma 3.2. *For every (set-reflecting) $A \in \mathsf{MAlg}^*_{OT}(\Sigma)$ and every subset $sX \subseteq A$, there is a small subalgebra $sA \sqsubseteq A$ with $sX \subseteq sA$.*

Moreover, there exists a smallest such sA, namely, such that for every other subalgebra $B \sqsubseteq A$ with $sX \subseteq B$, we have $sA \subseteq B$.

PROOF: sX is sorted, and the construction extends in each step each sort (if at all):

1) $X_0 = sX$

[3] This might cause some foundational worries since functions returning classes, and hence also indexed families of classes, are not legal objects in NBG. This signals that we must rather work with Grothendieck's hierarchy of universes, in which set-algebras reside at the first level, $\mathcal{U}_1$, while all our objects at the second one, $\mathcal{U}_2$. (As will be commented in the appendix 7., we actually end up in $\mathcal{U}_3$.) We will use the words "small"/"set" and "large"/"class" in the sense of being a member of the lowest level $\mathcal{U}_1$ versus of any higher level $\mathcal{U}_i \setminus \mathcal{U}_1$ (for $i \geq 2$), respectively.

2) For all $x \in A$, if $f^A(x) \cap X_i \neq \varnothing$ then include into X_{i+1} also all such x.

3) $X_\omega = \bigcup_{i \in \omega} X_i$

The argument showing that the construction indeed yields a smallest subalgebra containing sX is exactly as in fact 2.29. The only additional observation to be made is that, since X_0 is a set then so is every X_i. For, given in step 2) a set X_i, $f^A(x) \cap X_i$ is a set, and so is $\bigcup_{x \in A} f^A(x) \cap X_i$. Hence, since A is set-reflecting, the elements added to X_{i+1} will form at most a set. Iterating this extension ω times yields X_ω which is indeed a set. □

In particular, given an OT-homomorphism $\phi : A \to B$ and a small subalgebra $sA \sqsubseteq A$, there is also a small subalgebra $sB \sqsubseteq B$ such that the restriction $\phi|_{sA}$ of ϕ to sA is an OT-homorphism $\phi|_{sA} : sA \to sB$.

By the above lemma, each set-reflecting algebra with carrier being a proper class has small subalgebras, and it is used to show:

Lemma 3.3. *Every (set-reflecting) algebra in* $\mathsf{MAlg}^*_{OT}(\Sigma)$ *is a colimit of its small subalgebras.*

PROOF: Given an A, take all its small subalgebras and form the diagram with all the inclusions $\iota_{ij} : A_i \hookrightarrow A_j$ between these subalgebras. (By fact 2.22, these inclusions are OT-monomorphisms.) A is colimit of this diagram with the inclusions $\iota_i : A_i \hookrightarrow A$. Since all morphisms are inclusions, the commutativity condition is trivially satisfied. Assume that there is another algebra B with $\beta_i : A_i \to B$ such that $\beta_i = \iota_{ij}; \beta_j$ whenever this composition is defined (i.e., whenever there exists ι_{ij}). We define the unique $u : A \to B$ using the fact that $\forall a \in A\ \exists A_i : a \in A_i$ (by lemma 3.2) – $u(a) := \beta_i(a)$. It is well-defined because the collection of all small subalgebras is directed. If $a \in A_j$ for some other small $A_j \sqsubseteq A$, then there is also a small $A_k \sqsubseteq A$ with $A_i \cup A_j \subseteq A_k$, and since $\beta_i = \iota_{ik}; \beta_k$ and $\beta_j = \iota_{jk}; \beta_k$ we have, in particular, that $\beta_i(a) = \beta_k(\iota_{ik}(a)) = \beta_k(a) = \beta_k(\iota_{jk}(a)) = \beta_j(a)$.
• $\beta_i = \iota_i; u$: for every $a \in A_i$ we have, by definition of u and the above argument, that $u(a) = \beta_i(a)$, which verifies this claim.
• u is unique: for if some $u' : A \to B$ makes $\iota_i; u' = \beta_i$ for all i then, for every $a \in A$ and A_i such that $a \in A_i$, we must have $u'(a) = \beta_i(a) = u(a)$.
• u is OT: Assume not, i.e., for some f and $b \in B : f^A(u^-(b)) \neq u^-(f^B(b))$. There are two cases. 1) $a \in f^A(u^-(b)) \setminus u^-(f^B(b))$: Let A_i be small subalgebra containing a and $u^-(b)$. Since β_i is OT, we have that $a \in f^{A_i}(\beta_i^-(b)) = \beta_i^-(f^B(b))$ and substituting $\iota_i; u$ for $\beta_i : a \in f^{A_i}(\iota_i^-(u^-(b))) = \iota_i^-(u^-(f^B(b))))$. But then also $a \in \iota(\iota^-(u^-(b))) \subseteq u^-(b)$.
2) $a \in u^-(f^B(b)) \setminus f^A(u^-(b))$. Let A_i be as above. Since $\beta_i = \iota_i; u$ is OT, we have $a \in \iota_i^-(u^-(f^B(b))) = f^{A_i}(\iota_i^-(u^-(b)))$, and since ι_i is OT, $f^{A_i}(\iota_i^-(u^-(b))) = \iota_i^-(f^A(u^-(b)))$. But then $a \in \iota_i^-(f^A(u^-(b)))$ implies that also $a \in f^A(u^-(b))$. □

Notice, however, that the diagram can be large, as $\mathsf{MAlg}^*_{OT}(\Sigma)$ is not well-powered. (An A with s^A being a class and $f^A : s^A \to s^A$ an identity, has a proper class of subobjects – one for each subset, and subclass, of s^A.)

We also have the opposite fact.

Fact 3.4. *If A is colimit of small algebras then A is set-reflecting.*

PROOF: Let the components of the colimit be $\iota_i : A_i \to A$, with all A_i small, and consider an arbitrary $a \in A$ and operation f from the signature. We have to show that $(f^A)^{\neg}(a)$ is a set. As the collection of ι_i's is jointly epi, i.e., surjective (fact 2.13.2), there is some small A_i with $a \in \iota_i[A_i]$. Let $a^- = \iota_i^-(a)$. Since $\iota_i : A_i \to A$ is OT, so $\forall b \in (f^A)^{\neg}(a)\ \exists b_i \in (f^{A_i})^{\neg}(a^-)$. But as A_i is small so a^- as well as $(f^{A_i})^{\neg}(a^-)$ is a set, and hence also $(f^A)^{\neg}(a)$ must be a set. □

3.1.1. Congruences and quotients

Concerning the OT-congruences, we make first the following observation.

Fact 3.5. *Given a bireachability $\sim$ on a set-reflecting $A \in \mathsf{MAlg}^*_{OT}(\Sigma)$, the corresponding congruence-algebra $A^\sim$, as defined in 2.54, is also set-reflecting.*

PROOF: Let double-letters symbols, like XY, denote sets of (some) pairs $\langle x, y\rangle$ where $x \in X, y \in Y$, i.e., $XY \subseteq X \times Y$.
Let XY be the pre-image under f of some element $\langle z, u\rangle$, i.e., $XY = (f^{A^\sim})^{\neg}(\langle z, u\rangle)$. By definition 2.54 of $A^\sim$, $f^{A^\sim}(XY) = \{\langle z_k, u_k\rangle \mid \langle x, y\rangle \in XY \wedge z_k \in f^A(x) \wedge u_k \in f^A(y) \wedge z_k \sim x_k\}$, so that $XY \subseteq (f^A)^{\neg}(z) \times (f^A)^{\neg}(u)$. But both these pre-images are sets since A is set-reflecting, and so XY is a set, too. □

Lemma 2.45 applies unchanged when the collection is a proper class of small OT-congruences. Performing the same standard construction on the collection of *all small* OT-congruences on a given multialgebra yields the following lemma.

Lemma 3.6. *On every $A \in \mathsf{MAlg}^*_{OT}(\Sigma)$ there exists a (unique) maximal OT-congruence $\sim_A$.*

PROOF: Let $C = \{\sim_i \mid i \in I\}$ be the class of all small OT-congruences on A, then $\sim_A = \bigvee_i \sim_i$ is an OT-congurence, by lemma 2.45. It is, in fact, the maximal such.
Suppose that $\approx$ is an OT-congruence, i.e., $\approx; R^A; \approx\, = \,\approx; R^A$. For any $a_1 \approx a_2$, there is, by Lemma 3.2, a small subalgebra $sA \sqsubseteq A$, with $a_1, a_2 \in sA$. Consider the restriction of $\approx$ to sA, i..e., let $\sim_s = \approx \cap (sA \times sA)$. By Fact 2.51, $\sim_s$ is an OT-congruence and thus, any two elements related by $\approx$, are related already by some small OT-congruence in C. Hence $\approx \subseteq \sim_A$. □

The following easy technicality will be needed it in the proof of the next lemma.

Fact 3.7. *Let $\{A_i \mid i \in I\}$ be the class of small subalgebras of A (A being their colimit), R be the maximal OT-congruence on A and R_i the respective resitriction of R to A_i. Then $\{r_i : R_i \to R \mid i \in I\}$ is jointly epi and, for every $c : A \to C$, if $\forall i \in I : \pi_{i1}; \iota_i; c = \pi_{i2}; \iota_i; c$ then $\pi_1; c = \pi_2; c$.*

PROOF: We have the following diagram

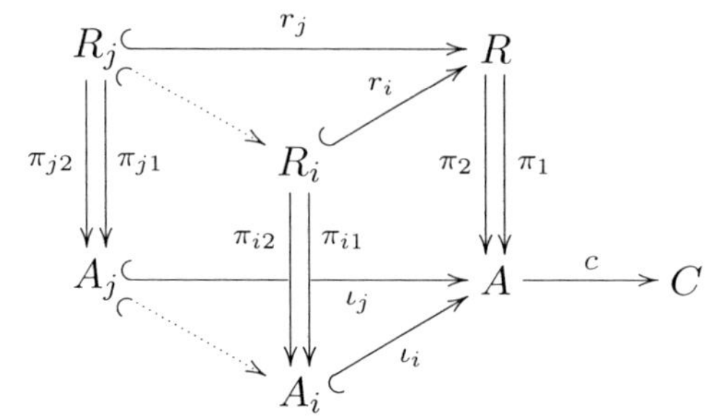

A, with inclusions ι_i, is colimit of the diagram containing all A_i's which is indicated by the dotted arrow. Also various R_i's are related by inclusions, which is indicated by the corresponding dotted arrow. All ι_i and r_i are inclusions.

That all r_i's are jointly epi follows from the proof of the previous lemma. If $\langle a_1, a_2\rangle \in R$ then there is a small subalgebra $A_i \sqsubseteq A$ containing a_1, a_2, and so $\langle a_1, a_2\rangle \in R_i = R \cap A_i \times A_i$.

Assume that $\pi_1; c \neq \pi_2; c$, i.e., for some $\langle a_1, a_2\rangle \in R : c(\pi_1(\langle a_1, a_2\rangle)) = c(a_1) \neq c(a_2) = c(\pi_2(\langle a_1, a_2\rangle))$. Let R_i be one such that $\langle a_1, a_2\rangle \in R_i$. By definition of R_i, for each $i \in I : r_i; \pi_k = \pi_{ik}; \iota_i$, for $k \in \{1, 2\}$. Thus we would obtain $c(\iota_i(\pi_{i1}(\langle a_1, a_2\rangle))) = c(a_1) \neq c(a_2) = c(\iota_i(\pi_{i2}(\langle a_1, a_2\rangle)))$, i.e., $\pi_{i1}\iota_i; c \neq \pi_{i2}\iota_i; c$. □

Lemma 3.8. *Given an $A \in \mathsf{MAlg}^*_{OT}(\Sigma)$ and an OT-congruence R on A, the quotient $A/_R$ is a colimit of small algebras, and hence $A/_R \in \mathsf{MAlg}^*_{OT}(\Sigma)$.*

PROOF: We consider the following (schema of the) diagram:

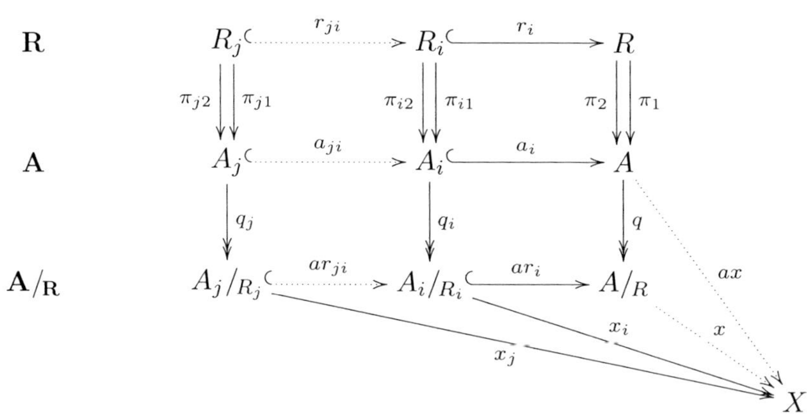

A, resp. **R**, stand for the whole diagrams consisting of the respective small subalgebras A_i of A and $R_i = R \cap A_i \times A_i$ (by fact 3.5, R and all $R_i \in \mathsf{MAlg}^*_{OT}(\Sigma)$, while by fact 2.51, $R_i \sqsubseteq R$) with the inclusion arrows a_{ji}, resp. r_{ji}. A with inclusions a_i is colimit of **A**. The collection of all r_i's, resp., all a_i's is jointly epi. All q_i's are epi.

The diagram $\mathbf{A}/_\mathbf{R}$ contains all quotient algebras $A_i/_{R_i}$ and monos (inclusion arrows) between them. Since each A_i is small, so is each $A_i/_{R_i}$, by Fact 2.55. Since for each $i : R_i = R \cap A_i \times A_i$, we have an inclusion $a_{ji} : A_j \hookrightarrow A_i$ iff $r_{ji} : R_j \hookrightarrow R_i$. But then, this implies the existence of a mono $ar_{ji} : A_j/_{R_j} \hookrightarrow A_i/_{R_i}$. For each $A_i/_{R_i}$, we can obtain an isomorphic algebra by replacing every element $[a]^{R_i}$ by $[a]^R$.

We want to show that $A/_R$ with all ar_i is colimit of $\mathbf{A}/_{\mathbf{R}}$. Obviosuly, for each (existing) ar_{ji} we have that $ar_j = ar_{ji}; ar_i$, since each $(A_i/_{R_i}, q_i)$ is coequalizer of the respective π_{i1}, π_{i2}, Fact 2.55. So assume an X with arrows $x_i : A_i/_{R_i} \to X$ such that $x_j = ar_{ji}; x_i$ for all (relevant) i, j.

1. Since $q_j; ar_{ji} = a_{ji}; q_j$, we obtain that for all (relevant) $j, i : x_j = ar_{ji}; x_i \Rightarrow q_j; x_j = q_j; ar_{ji}; x_i = a_{ji}; q_i; x_i$. That is, X with $q_i; x_i$ is a commutative cocone over $\mathbf{A}$. Since A is colimit of $\mathbf{A}$, we obtain a unique arrow $ax : A \to X$ such that for all $i : q_i; x_i = a_i; ax$.

2. For every i, since $\pi_{i1}; q_i = \pi_{i2}; q_i$, so also $\pi_{i1}; q_i; x_i = \pi_{i2}; q_i; x_i$ and by 1, $\pi_{i1}; a_i; ax = \pi_{i2}; a_i; ax$. By Fact 3.7, we thus have $\pi_1; ax = \pi_2; ax$.

3. By Fact 2.55, $(A/_R, q)$ is coequalizer of π_1, π_2, and thus we obtain a unique arrow $x : A/_R \to X$ making $q; x = ax$. This is the arrow we are looking for:

4. Commutativity: $q_i; ar_i; x = a_i; q; x \stackrel{3.}{=} a_i; ax \stackrel{1.}{=} q_i; x_i$. But q_i is epi and so $ar_i; x = x_i$.

5. Uniqueness: assume another arrow $y : A/_R \to X$ with $ar_i; y = x_i$ for all i. Then also, $q_i; x_i = q_i; ar_i; y = a_i; q; y$ and thus, for every $i : a_i; q; y = a_i; q; x$. Since a_i are jointly epi, this means that $q; y = q; x$ and now, since q is epi, $x = y$.

Since $A/_R$ is a colimit of small algebras, it is set-reflecting, i.e., $A/_R \in \mathsf{MAlg}^*_{OT}(\Sigma)$, by fact 3.4. □

3.2. Co-completeness

Given two functors, $F, G : \mathsf{Set} \to \mathsf{Set}$, one forms dialgebras $\delta : F(X) \to G(X)$ as suggested in section 1., p.28, obtaining the category Set^F_G. Theorem 13 in [41] states that the forgetful functor $\mathsf{Set}^F_G \to \mathsf{Set}$ creates and preserves all kinds of colimits that are preserved by F. (In case of coalgebras, $F = id_{\mathsf{Set}}$, and so creation of colimits (e.g., theorem 4.5 in [38]) follows immediately.) Although we have moved from Set to CLASS, we might be tempted to retain this theorem and apply it to our case, where F is the (polynomial) signature functor. But, of course, this is not possible because we are working with different homomorphisms than those induced by the definition of dialgebras. Nevertheless, although the theorem does not apply to our case, its conclusion does: colimits in $\mathsf{MAlg}^*_{OT}(\Sigma)$ are indeed created by the forgetful functor. The following results apply also to $\mathsf{MAlg}_{OT}(\Sigma)$ and these are given in square brackets.

Proposition 3.9. $\mathsf{MAlg}^*_{OT}(\Sigma)$ *[and* $\mathsf{MAlg}_{OT}(\Sigma)$*] has initial objects and all coproducts [of small diagrams].*

PROOF: Empty algebra is trivially an initial object.

Consider first a class $\{A_i \mid i \in I\}$ of small algebras. We define their coproduct $\coprod_{i\in I} A_i$ to be the algebra CP whose carrier is the disjoint union of the carriers of all A_i, i.e., the class $\biguplus_i A_i = \{\langle a, i\rangle \mid i \in I,\ a \in A_i\}$, with the operations defined as follows:

$$f^{CP}(\langle a_1, i_1\rangle ... \langle a_n, i_n\rangle) = \begin{cases} f^{A_i}(a_1...a_n) \times \{i\} & \text{if } i_1 = ... = i_n = i \\ \emptyset & otherwise \end{cases} \tag{3.10}$$

and constants as: $c^{CP} = \biguplus_i c^{A_i}$.

The injections $\iota_i : A_i \hookrightarrow CP$ are obviously OT-homomorphisms.

Assume an object X with arrows $\psi_i : A_i \to X$, for every $i \in I$, with the OT-arrows, i.e., satisfying for every f:

$$f^{A_i}(\psi_i^{-}(x)) = \psi_i^{-}(f^X(x)) \tag{3.11}$$

The mediating arrow $u : CP \to X$ defined by $u(\langle a, i\rangle) = \psi_i(a)$ trivially satisfies $\iota_i; u = \psi_i$ for every i. We show that u is an OT-homomorphism: $f^{CP}(u^{-}(x)) = u^{-}(f^X(x))$.

$$\begin{array}{rcll} f^{CP}(u^{-}(x)) & = & f^{CP}(\biguplus_i \psi_i^{-}(x)) & \text{def. of } u \\ & = & \biguplus_i f^{A_i}(\psi_i^{-}(x)) & \text{by (3.10)} \\ & = & \biguplus_i \psi_i^{-}(f^X(x)) & \text{by (3.11)} \\ & = & u^{-}(f^X(x)) & \text{def. of } u \end{array}$$

u is unique: Assume $u \neq u_2 : CP \to X$, which also satisfies: $\iota_i; u_2 = \psi_i$ for all i. Then there is a $\langle c, i\rangle \in CP$ such that $u(\langle c, i\rangle) \neq u_2(\langle c, i\rangle)$. But then $\iota_i; u_2(\langle c, i\rangle) \neq \psi_i(c)$.

CP is trivially set-reflecting by the definition of operations in (3.10), as all A_i are small.

If now class $\{A_i \mid i \in I\}$ contains arbitrary set-reflecting algebras, the construction and verification of universality proceed in the same way as above, and we only check that the resulting CP is still set-reflecting. It is, in fact, colimit of small subalgebras. (Just replace each large A_i (in the discrete coproduct diagram) by the diagram of its small subalgebras (or isomorphic ones, with the elements of CP). CP, with the arrows $a_{ik} : A_{ik} \hookrightarrow A_i$ (for each large A_i and all small $A_{ik} \sqsubseteq A_i$) replaced by the respective compositions $a_{ik}; \iota_i$, is colimit of this expanded diagram.) Hence CP is set-reflecting by fact 3.4.

[It is clear that the construction works for small diagrams in the category $\mathsf{MAlg}_{OT}(\Sigma)$, as well as in $\mathsf{MAlg}^{\kappa}_{OT}(\Sigma)$.] □

Proposition 3.12. $\mathsf{MAlg}^{*}_{OT}(\Sigma)$ *[and* $\mathsf{MAlg}_{OT}(\Sigma)$*] has all coequalizers.*

PROOF: Given two arrows $\phi_1, \phi_2 : A \to B$, we start as usual by considering the equivalence closure $\sim$ on B of the relation $E = \{\langle \phi_1(a), \phi_2(a)\rangle \mid a \in A\}$.[4] Equivalence classes induced by this relation are denoted $B_1, B_2 \ldots$. Assuming the global axiom of choice, we can choose the representatives $b_i \in B_i$, and the carrier of the coequalizer object CE is the collection of such representatives. We may occasionally write $[b_i]$ for B_i.[5] Operations are defined by:

$$b_2 \in f^{CE}(b_1) \iff B_2 \subseteq f^B(B_1) \tag{3.13}$$

which for constants specializes to: $b_i \in c^{CE} \iff B_i \subseteq c^B$. The arrow $ce : B \to CE$ is the usual $\forall x \in B_i : ce(x) = b_i$. By the definition of $\sim$, it makes $\phi_1; ce = \phi_2; ce$. It is also

[4] If this relation is a class, we can perform the needded closure even if we worked in NBG, as their definitions do not require any quantification over classes. E.g., $ref(E) = E \cup \{\langle a, a\rangle \mid a \in A\}$, $sym(E) = E \cup \{\langle a, b\rangle \mid \langle b, a\rangle \in E\}$, $X; E = \{\langle a, b\rangle \mid \exists c : aXc \wedge cEb\}$, and the last operation can be iterated ω times startig with $X = id$.

[5] In case some of B_i's are proper classes, we have to follow the trick of Dana Scott (quoted in [1], Appendix B) in order to obtain the quotient, i.e., to consider as B_i only its subset of the elements having the least possible rank in the cumulative hierarchy.

OT. Let $b_2' \sim b_2$:

$$\begin{array}{rcl} b_2' \in ce^-(f^{CE}(b_1)) & \Rightarrow & b_2 \in f^{CE}(b_1) \\ (3.13) & \Longleftrightarrow & B_2 \subseteq f^B(B_1) \\ ce^-(b_1) = B_1 & \Rightarrow & b_2' \in f^B(ce^-(b_1)) \\ \text{and other way:} & & \\ b_2' \in f^B(ce^-(b_1)) & \Rightarrow & b_2' \in f^B(B_1) \\ (3.15) & \Rightarrow & B_2 \subseteq f^B(B_1) \\ (3.13) & \Longleftrightarrow & b_2 \in f^{CE}(b_1) \\ ce^-(b_2) = B_2 & \Rightarrow & B_2 \subseteq ce^-(f^{CE}(b_1)) \\ b_2' \in B_2 & \Rightarrow & b_2' \in ce^-(f^{CE}(b_1)) \end{array} \tag{3.14}$$

The transition marked (3.15) needs a more involved justification. The claim we are making is even stronger, namely, (we write now b_2 instead of b_2' since this choice does not matter here):[6]

$$b_2 \in f^B(b_1) \Rightarrow B_2 \subseteq f^B(B_1) \tag{3.15}$$

So assume that (3.15) does not hold, i.e.,

a. $b_2 \in f^B(b_1)$ but

b. $\exists b_2' \in B_2 : \forall b_1' \in B_1 : b_2' \notin f^B(b_1')$.

Then, certainly, $b_2' \neq b_2$ and since these two elements end up in the same equivalence class, they both must be in the image of either ϕ_1 or ϕ_2. Moreover, a. and b. mean that we can divide B_2 into two non-empty subclasses: $Y = B_2 \cap f^B(B_1)$ and $N = B_2 \setminus Y$ (with $b_2 \in Y$ and $b_2' \in N$). Since $B_2 = N \cup Y$ so, by definition of $\sim$, there must exist an $a \in A : \phi_1(a) \in N \wedge \phi_2(a) \in Y$. Let us, without loss of generality, call these elements $\phi_1(a) = b_2' \in N$ and $\phi_2(a) = b_2 \in Y$ (ambiguously, since these need not be the same as b_2, b_2' used so far). We now have:

$$\begin{array}{ccc} b_2' \notin f^B(B_1) & \text{and} & b_2 \in f^B(B_1) \\ \Downarrow & & \Downarrow \\ \phi_1(a) \notin f^B(B_1) & & \phi_2(a) \in f^B(B_1) \\ \Downarrow & & \Downarrow \\ a \notin \phi_1^-(f^B(B_1)) & & a \in \phi_2^-(f^B(B_1)) \\ \Downarrow & \text{since } \phi_i \text{ are } OT & \Downarrow \\ a \notin f^A(\phi_1^-(B_1)) & & a \in f^A(\phi_2^-(B_1)) \\ \Downarrow & \phi_1^-(B_1) = X = \phi_2^-(B_1) & \Downarrow \\ a \notin f^A(X) & \text{and} & a \in f^A(X) \end{array}$$

The equality $\phi_1^-(B_i) = \phi_2^-(B_i)$ holds for all equivalence classes B_i by definition of $\sim$. This contradiction establishes (3.15) and hence the equality (3.14), so ce is OT-homomorphism.

To show universality, assume a $\psi : B \to X$ with $\phi_1;\psi = \phi_2;\psi$. We define the mediating arrow $u : CE \to X$ in the standard way: $u([b]) = \psi(b)$. By the standard argument (since ψ coequalizes ϕ_1, ϕ_2), we have that $[b] \subseteq [b]^\psi$ (where $[b]^\psi = \{b' \in B \mid \psi(b') = \psi(b)\} = \psi^-(\psi(b))$) which, in turn, implies that u is well defined and unique making $\psi = ce; u$. (We

[6]This, as a matter of fact, is a general property implied by outer-tightness.

use the notation $[b]$ ambiguously: whenever followed by $[b] \in ...$ it stands for the chosen representative, while in $[b] \subseteq ...$ it stands for the whole class.)
We show that u is OT-homomorphism. First the inclusion $f^{CE}(u^-(x)) \supseteq u^-(f^X(x))$:

$$\begin{array}{rcl} [b] \in u^-(f^X(x)) & \Rightarrow & u([b]) \in f^X(x) \\ \text{def. of } u & \Rightarrow & \psi(b) \in f^X(x) \\ & \Rightarrow & \psi^-(\psi(b)) \subseteq \psi^-(f^X(x)) \\ \psi \text{ is } OT & \Rightarrow & [b]^\psi \subseteq f^B(\psi^-(x)) \\ [b] \subseteq [b]^\psi & \Rightarrow & [b] \subseteq f^B(\psi^-(x)) \\ & \Rightarrow & ? \end{array}$$

What we want now is that $[b] \in f^{CE}(u^-(x))$ but this requires a more involved argument. We have that $\exists b' : \psi^-(x) = [b']^\psi$ and also that $[b']^\psi = \bigcup_{[b_i] \in u^-(x)} [b_i]$ by definition of u (i.e., $[b]^\psi$ may comprise several distinct $[b_i]$.) Rewriting the conclusion of the above implications, we thus have

$$[b] \subseteq f^B(\bigcup_{[b_i] \in u^-(x)} [b_i]) = \bigcup_{[b_i] \in u^-(x)} f^B([b_i]). \tag{3.16}$$

We want to show that $[b]$ is actually included in $f^B([b_i])$ for some particular $[b_i] \in u^-(x)$. Now, from (3.16) we certainly have then that $\exists [b_i] \in u^-(x) : b \in f^B([b_i])$. The desired fact, namely, $\exists [b_i] \in u^-(x) : [b] \subseteq f^B([b_i])$, follows now by outer-tightness of ce or, more specifically, by (3.15). The overall conclusion, that $[b] \in f^{CE}(u^-(x))$, follows now by (3.13).
We show the other inclusion $f^{CE}(u^-(x)) \subseteq u^-(f^X(x))$:

$$\begin{array}{rcl} [b] \in f^{CE}(u^-(x)) & \Rightarrow & [b] \subseteq ce^-(f^{CE}(u^-(x))) \\ ce \text{ is } OT & \Rightarrow & [b] \subseteq f^B(ce^-(u^-(x))) \\ \psi^- = u^-; ce^- & \Rightarrow & [b] \subseteq f^B(\psi^-(x)) \\ \psi \text{ is } OT & \Rightarrow & [b] \subseteq \psi^-(f^X(x)) \\ \psi^- = u^-; ce^- & \Rightarrow & [b] \subseteq ce^-(u^-(f^X(x))) \\ & \Rightarrow & [b] \in u^-(f^X(x)) \end{array}$$

So, CE is a coequalizer object with the OT-homomorphism ce.
The equivalence $\sim$ we have started with is the kernel of ce and so, since ce is OT, $\sim$ is OT-congruence by fact 2.40. Thus CE, being a quotient of $B \in \mathsf{MAlg}^*_{OT}(\Sigma)$ by this congruence, is set-reflecting, i.e., $CE \in \mathsf{MAlg}^*_{OT}(\Sigma)$, by lemma 3.8.
[It is clear that the construction for small algebras can be applied to obtain coequalizers in $\mathsf{MAlg}_{OT}(\Sigma)$, as well as in $\mathsf{MAlg}^\kappa_{OT}(\Sigma)$.] □

This fact shows why we must admit operations in multialgebras returning proper classes, and not only sets. Let A have sorts s^A and t^A, both proper classes, and a function $f^A : s^A \to t^A$ which is bijective. The relation $\sim$ given by $s^A \times s^A$ and id_{t^A} is OT-congruence on A, and a coequalizer of the (projection) arrows from the congruence algebra $A^\sim$ to A, is C with $t^C = t^A$ and $s^C = \{\bullet\}$, and with $f^C(\bullet) = t^C$.

As existence of all colimits is equivalent to the existence of initial objects, coequalizers and coproducts, we obtain

Theorem 3.17. $\mathsf{MAlg}^*_{OT}(\Sigma)$ *[and* $\mathsf{MAlg}_{OT}(\Sigma)$*] is cocomplete.*

This strengthens the initial lemmata 3.3-3.4 which only showed equivalence of being set-reflecting and being colimit of small subalgebras without either claiming nor demonstrating the actual existence of all such colimits.

3.3. Completeness

Theorem 9 from [41], corresponding to the one quoted at the beginning of the previous subsection, states that the forgetful functor $\mathsf{Set}^F_G \to \mathsf{Set}$ creates and preserves all kinds of limits that are preserved by G. (In case of algebras, $G = id_{\mathsf{Set}}$, and so completeness follows from this general statement.) In our case, G is the power-set functor which preserves weak pullbacks (and hence intersections) or pullbacks with at least one arrow being injective but, unfortunately, neither products nor equalizers. Thus, even if applicable, the theorem would not yield any positive result. As we will show, constructions of limits are challenging and novel and offer new insights into the structure of our category. In particular, in case of final objects and products, we will see close and intricate relationships to the notion of bireachability.

Proposition 3.18. $\mathsf{MAlg}^*_{OT}(\Sigma)$ *[and* $\mathsf{MAlg}_{OT}(\Sigma)$*] has all equalizers.*

PROOF: We show first the claim only for small algebras, namely, the existence of an equalizer object E and arrow $e : E \to A$ for a pair of arrows $\phi_1, \phi_2 : A \to B$, where A is small. It is constructed in the more or less standard way.

We let $E_0 = \{a \in A \mid \phi_1(a) = \phi_2(a)\}$ and let E be the largest subalgebra of A contained in E_0. I.e., following the construction from fact 2.31, given E_i, we obtain E_{i+1} by removing all elements $e \in E_i$ such that for some $a_0 \in A \setminus E_i : e \in f^A(a', a_0, a)$. $E = \bigcap_{i\in\omega} E_i$. The operations are defined by $f^E(x) = f^A(x) \cap E$ for all $x \in E$, and the arrow $e : E \to A$ is inclusion (which is OT, by fact 2.31).

We verify the universal property. Assume $\psi : X \to A$ with $\psi; \phi_1 = \psi; \phi_2$. We define the arrow $u : X \to E$ by $u(x) = \psi(x)$. This will do the job (yielding unique u such that $u; e = \psi$) whenever $\psi(x) \in E$, so we have to show that this will be the case for all $x \in X$, i.e., that $\psi[X] \subseteq E$. Since ψ equalizes ϕ_1, ϕ_2, we certainly have $\psi[X] \subseteq E_0$. So assume, as the induction hypothesis, $\psi[X] \subseteq E_i$. For any $x \in X$ we obtain $f^{A-}(\psi(x)) = \psi(f^{X-}(x)) \subseteq \psi[X] \subseteq E_i$, where the equality holds since ψ is OT. By definition of E_{i+1} this means that $\psi(x) \in E_{i+1}$ and so $\psi[X] \subseteq E_i \Rightarrow \psi[X] \subseteq E_{i+1}$. Hence, eventually, $\psi[X] \subseteq E$.

In the general case, when A is set-reflecting, it is colimit of its small subalgebras, $\{A_k \mid k \in I\}$, over some diagram D. Take equalizer (E_k, e_k) of each pair $\iota_k; \phi_1$ and $\iota_k; \phi_2$ and then the colimit E of the diagram D with each A_k replaced by E_k (Colimit exists since $\mathsf{MAlg}^*_{OT}(\Sigma)$ is cocomplete, and the shape of D remains the same since, if for some $k, l : A_l \sqsubseteq A_k$, then both $E_l, E_k \sqsubseteq A_k$ and thus, by fact 2.22, also $E_l \sqsubseteq E_k$.) Denote the arrows from E_k to E by i_k (since, for each $k : i_k; e = e_k; \iota_k$ and both latter arrows are inclusions, each i_k must be injective.) The arrows $e_k; \iota_k : E_k \to A$ imply the existence of unique universal arrow

$e : E \to A$, and we show that (E, e) is equalizer of ϕ_1, ϕ_2.

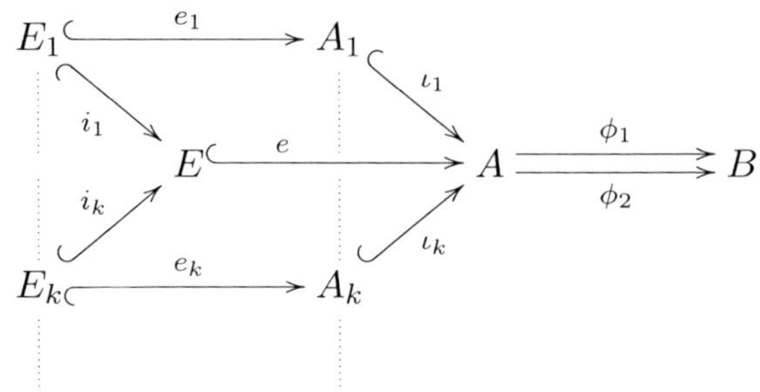

Since $e_k; \iota_k = i_k; e$ for every k, and each $e_k; \iota_k$ equalizes ϕ_1, ϕ_2, we also have $i_k; e; \phi_1 = i_k; e; \phi_2$. Let $x \in E$ be arbitrary. If for some k and $x' \in E_k : x = i_k(x')$, we obtain that $\phi_1(e(x)) = \phi_2(e(x))$. But since E is colimit of all E_k, all $x \in E$ must satisfy this condition (i.e., by the construction of coproducts and coequalizers, $\forall x \in E\ \exists E_k, x' \in E_k : x = i_k(x')$), and so $e; \phi_1 = e; \phi_2$.

We verify the universal property. Given an X with an arrow $\psi : X \to A$ such that $\psi; \phi_1 = \psi; \phi_2$. If X is small, the arrow ψ can be factored through some small subalgebra $\psi : X \stackrel{\psi_k}{\to} A_k \stackrel{\iota_k}{\to} A$, and since E_k is an equalizer with respect to $\iota_k; \phi_1$ and $\iota_k; \phi_2$, we obtain a unique arrow $u_k : X \to E_k$ with $u_k; e_k = \psi_k$, yielding also $u_k; e_k; \iota_k = \psi$ and hence also (since i_k is mono) a unique $u_k; i_k = u : X \to E$ with $u; e = \psi$. If X is not small (but set-reflecting) it is a colimit of its small subalgebras and the above construction follows for each such $X_k \sqsubseteq X$. We obtain the collection of (unique) arrows $u_k; i_k : X_k \to E$ which, by the colimit property of X, give a unique arrow $u : X \to E$. Chasing the diagram yields the required fact that $u; e = \psi$.

Since E is colimit of its small subalgebras, it is set-reflecting, i.e., $E \in \mathsf{MAlg}^*_{OT}(\Sigma)$, by fact 3.4.

[It is clear that the construction for small algebras will yield equalizers also in $\mathsf{MAlg}_{OT}(\Sigma)$, as well as in $\mathsf{MAlg}^{\kappa}_{OT}(\Sigma)$.] □

To show the existence of final objects, reported in [42], we first state a simple lemma.

Lemma 3.19. *For a multialgebra A, let $\sim_A$ be the maximal OT-congruence on A (existing by Lemma 3.6). For any algebra B there is at most one OT-homomorphism $B \to A/_{\sim_A}$.*

PROOF: By the construction of coequalizers in $\mathsf{MAlg}^*_{OT}(\Sigma)$, Fact 3.12. If there were two distinct $\phi_1, \phi_2 : B \to A/_{\sim_A}$, there would be a non-trivial coequalizing arrow $ce : A/_{\sim_A} \to CE$, making $\phi_1; ce = \phi_2; ce$. Its non-triviality means that its kernel $\sim_{ce} \neq id_{A/_{\sim_A}}$ and, since ce is OT so, by Fact 2.40, $\sim_{q;ce}$ is an OT-congruence, where q is the quotient homomorphism $q : A \to A/_{\sim_A}$. But then we can use $\sim_{q;ce}$ to obtain a larger OT-congruence on A than $\sim_A$, contradicting the assumption that $\sim_A$ was the largest such. □

Theorem 3.20. $\mathsf{MAlg}^*_{OT}(\Sigma)$ *has final objects.*

PROOF: Let CP be a coproduct of all (non-isomorphic) small algebras in $\mathsf{MAlg}^*_{OT}(\Sigma)$ (which exists and is set-reflecting by Fact 3.9). Let $\sim_{CP}$ be the maximal OT-congruence on CP (existing by Lemma 3.6), and let $Z = CP/_{\sim_{CP}}$. (By Lemma 3.8, Z is set-reflecting and so $Z \in \mathsf{MAlg}^*_{OT}(\Sigma)$.)

For every small algebra $A \in \mathsf{MAlg}^*_{OT}(\Sigma)$, there is (at least one) morphism $A \to CP$ and then, composing it with the quotient morphism $CP \to Z$, exactly one (by lemma 3.19) morphism $a : A \to Z$.

Any other (large) $A \in \mathsf{MAlg}^*_{OT}(\Sigma)$ is colimit of its small subalgebras, with the inclusions $\iota_i : A_i \to A$. Since there is also (exactly) one morphism $a_i : A_i \to Z$ for each small subalgebra $A_i \sqsubseteq A$, the colimit property yields a (unique) morphism $u : A \to Z$ (making $\iota_i; u = a_i$). But then, since there is such a morphism $A \to Z$ so, by lemma 3.19, it is unique. □

Construction of products is a more complicated task and we devote to it the next Section.

4. Construction of Products

We comment first on the relationship between product and (maximal) bireachability between algebras in order to signal potential complications. The actual construction and proofs are given in the three subsections. The following section 5. shows that this construction can be utilized also in the categories $\mathsf{MAlg}^{\kappa}_{OT}(\Sigma)$ of κ-bounded multialgebras.

In the case of coalgebras, preservation of mono-sources (by the signature functor) is equivalent with the coincidence of product and maximal bisimulation (theorem 8.6 in [17]). Thus, by the duality from remark 2.9 and that between bisimilarity and bireachability, if we considered only the subcategory of multialgebras obtained from coalgebras (over a given polynomial functor), we could conclude the existence of products, namely, of maximal bireachabilities between the arguments (with the algebraic structure defined in (2.59)). However, our case is more general and also more complicated since, in a given $\mathsf{MAlg}_{OT}(\Sigma)/\mathsf{MAlg}^*_{OT}(\Sigma)$, there are multialgebras which are not converses of coalgebras over (the respective) polynomial functor Σ. The problems and counterexamples will be provided exactly by such multialgebras. (The category of coalgebras for power-set functor is isomorphic to $\mathsf{MAlg}_{OT}(\Sigma)$ for a Σ with a single operation $S \to \mathcal{P}(S)$. But power-set functor does not preserve mono-sources, and so, by the just quoted theorem, products do not coincide with maximal bisimulations. Our results will yield also a construction of products for coalgebras over power-set functor.)

Recall the definition 2.58 of bireachability between two algebras as a subset $C \subseteq A_1 \times A_2$ satisfying the bireachbility condition:

$$\begin{array}{ll} \forall a, b, a_1 : & C(a,b) \wedge a \in f^{A_1}(a_1) \Rightarrow \exists b_1 \in A_2 : b \in f^{A_2}(b_1) \wedge C(a_1, b_1) \\ \& \ \forall a, b, b_1 : & C(a,b) \wedge b \in f^{A_2}(b_1) \Rightarrow \exists a_1 \in A_1 : a \in f^{A_1}(a_1) \wedge C(a_1, b_1) \end{array} \qquad (2.58)$$

As noted earlier, this condition is preserved under arbitrary unions and thus, collecting all small bireachabilities between two algebras A and B, we obtain the counterpart of lemma 3.6. We also register the counterpart of fact 3.5 (with essentially the same proof.)

Fact 4.1. *For every $A, B \in \mathsf{MAlg}^*_{OT}(\Sigma)$ there exists a (unique) maximal bireachability between A and B. Moreover, any bireachability between A, B (with operations defined according to (2.59)) is set-reflecting.*

This maximal bireachability need not, however, be the product of A, B.

Example 4.2. *Consider two algebras over* $\Sigma = \langle\{s_1, s_2\}, \{f : s_1 \to s_2\}\rangle$ *(as in example 2.63):*

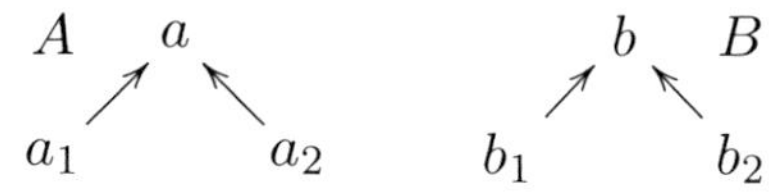

Following are examples of bireachabilities between A *and* B*:*

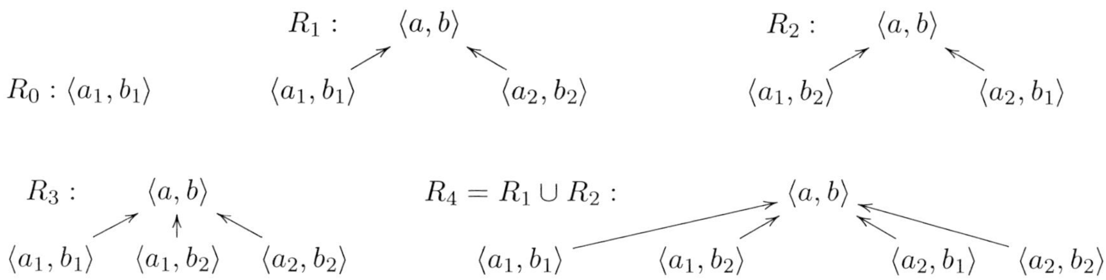

R_4 *is the maximal bireachability between* A *and* B *– every other bireachability is a subset of it. However, only* $R_0 \sqsubseteq R_4$*, while niether* R_1, R_2 *nor* R_3 *is a subalgebra of* R_4*: the inclusions are not OT-homomorphisms. Consequently,* R_4 *can not possibly be the product of* A*,* B*, as the projections from, say,* R_2 *would not factor through it.*

We will conduct the proof for the binary products only, but it will be easy to see that all the constructions and results generalize to products of arbitrary sets of objects.

Our category $\mathsf{MAlg}^*_{OT}(\Sigma)$ has all colimits and, given A_1, A_2, we proceed as follows:

4.1. show that it has epi-monosource factorisation, namely, proposition 4.7; moreover, that the monosource is a quotient of the domain of the span by a unique congruence

4.2. take colimit $\mathbf{P}$ of the diagram $\mathcal{D}$ of all non-isomorphic monosources for A_1, A_2 with arrows commuting with the span arrows (uniqe monos)

4.3. show that $\mathbf{P}$ is a monosource and hence (since it is colimit of monosources) any span has a uniqe factorisation through $\mathbf{P}$.

For the rest of this section, we fix some A_1, A_2. All considerations are relative to these two objects, in particular, all spans and monosources have them as their codomain.

Definition 4.3. *1. A (binary) monosource is a span* $A_1 \xleftarrow{m_1} M \xrightarrow{m_2} A_2$ *such that for any* $\phi, \psi : X \to M$ *we have:* $(\forall i : \phi; m_i = \psi; m_i) \Rightarrow \phi = \psi$ *(we also say,* m_1, m_2 *are jointly mono.)*

2. A morphism between monosources (M, m_i) *and* (N, n_i) *with the same codomain is a morphism* $h : M \to N$ *such that* $m_i = h; n_i$*.*

3. Monosources (M, m_i) *and* (N, n_i) *are isomorphic iff there exists an isomorphism* $h : M \simeq N$ *which is monosource morphism.*

Non-isomorphic monosources can still have isomorphic domains. Obviously, if (M, m_i) is a monosource and $N \sqsubseteq M$ (with mono $\iota : N \to M$), then also $(N, \iota; m_i)$ is a monosource. (We will often skip ι in the notation for monosources/spans from subobjects, i.e., we will usually write simply (N, m_i).) Given two objects $A_1, A_2 \in \mathsf{MAlg}^*_{OT}(\Sigma)$, we obtain the category $\mathsf{MS}(A_1, A_2)$ with all monosources with the codomain A_1, A_2 as objects and monosource morphisms as morphisms.

Fact 4.4. *1. Given a span* $A_1 \xleftarrow{n_1} N \xrightarrow{n_2} A_2$ *and a morphism* $h : M \to N$*, if* $(M, h; n_i)$ *is a monosource, then* h *is mono.*

2. For any monosource morphism $h : (M, m_i) \to (N, n_i)$*,* $h : M \to N$ *is mono.*

PROOF: 1. If for two morphisms $f, g : X \to M$ we have $f; h = g; h$ then also $f; h; n_i = g; h; n_i$, and so $f = g$ since $(M, h; n_i)$ is a monosource.
2. follows from 1. since $(M, m_i) = (N, h; n_i)$. □

The following fact helps in establishing some uniqueness results.

Fact 4.5. *Given a span* (M, m_i)*, let* $\sim_i$ *be the kernel of* m_i*.* (M, m_i) *is a monosource iff the greatest lower bound* $\sim_1 \wedge \sim_2 = id_M$*.*

PROOF: $\Rightarrow$) Let $\sim\ = \ \sim_1 \wedge \sim_2$ denote the greatest lower bound of m_is' kernels and $M^\sim$ be as in definition 2.54. By fact 2.55, there is a coequalizer diagram: $M^\sim \underset{\pi_2}{\overset{\pi_1}{\rightrightarrows}} M \xrightarrow{n} M/_\sim$. Now $\sim \subseteq \sim_i$ ensures the existence of a unique $n_i : M/_\sim \to A_i$ such that $n; n_i = m_i$.

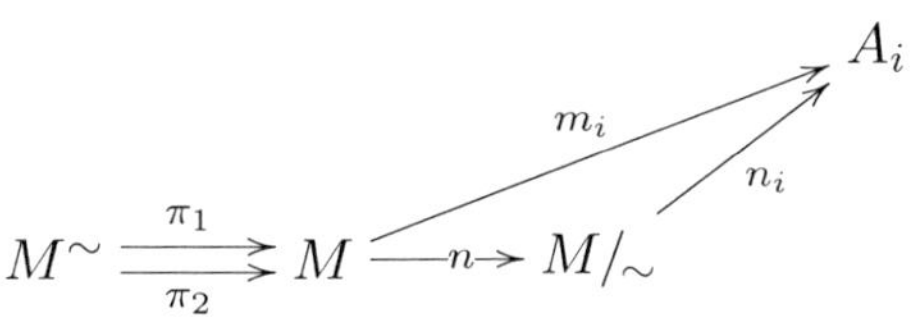

This entails $\pi_1; m_i = \pi_1; n; n_i = \pi_2; n; n_i = \pi_2; m_i$ and so $\pi_1 = \pi_2$ since (M, m_i) is a monosource. Hence $\sim \subseteq id_M$ with the opposite inclusion following trivially since $\sim$ is a congruence.

$\Leftarrow$) Conversely, assume $\sim_1 \wedge \sim_2 = id_M$, and let (*) $\pi_1; m_i = \pi_2; m_i$ for some $\pi_i : M^\sim \to M$ as in the diagram above. Let $n : M \to M/_\sim$ be their coequalizer. By assumption (*), the coequalizer property gives then unique $n_i : M/_\sim \to A_i$ such that $n; n_i = m_i$. This means that $ker(n; n_i) = \sim_i$ which, in particular, implies that $id_M \subseteq \sim \subseteq ker(n) \subseteq \sim_1 \wedge \sim_2 = id_M$, since $\sim$ is an equivalence. $ker(n) = id_M$, however, means that $\pi_1 = \pi_2$ due to the construction of coequalizers. □

Example 4.6. *Note that monosource need not have domain which is a subset of the cartesian product of the codomains. E.g.:*

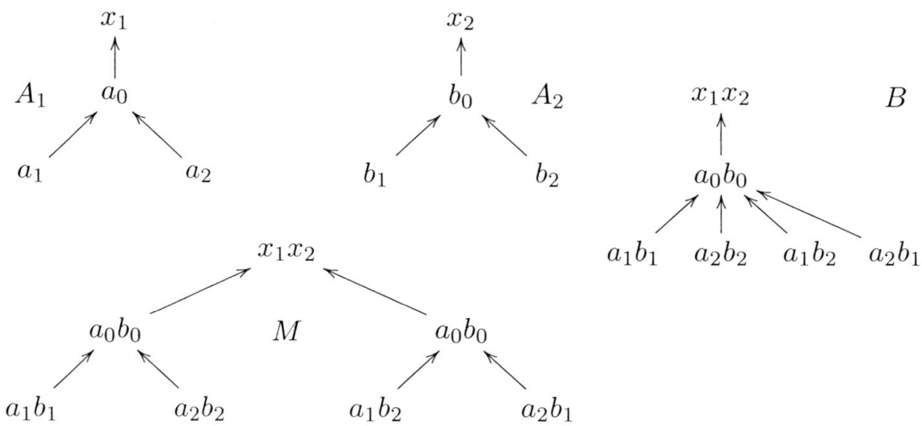

The names of M elements identify the images under $m_i : M \to A_i$. B is the bireachability induced between A_1 and A_2 by this span. (It is also the maximal bireachability between them.) Using the criterion from the above fact, it is easy to convince oneself that M is a monosource. In particular, the obvious mapping $M \to B$ is not a homomorphism (i.e., the relation relating (only) the two copies of a_0b_0 is not a congruence on M.) B, with the indicatedd projections, is also a monosource.

4.1. Epi-monosource Factorisation

The first main partial result is:

Lemma 4.7. *For any span $A_1 \xleftarrow{\phi_1} C \xrightarrow{\phi_2} A_2$ there is a monosource $A_1 \xleftarrow{m_1} M \xrightarrow{m_2} A_2$ and an epi $e_M : C \to M = C/_\sim$ such that $\phi_i = e_M; m_i$ and $ker(e_M) = ker(\phi_1) \wedge ker(\phi_2)$.*

PROOF: Let $\sim_i$ denote the kernel of ϕ_i and $\sim = \sim_1 \wedge \sim_2$ their greatest lower bound (which exists by fact 2.46). We show first that we have m_i making $M \simeq C/_\sim$ a monosource. Since $\sim \subseteq \sim_i$, we obtain by the coequalizer property of $e_M : C \to C/_\sim$, unique $m_i : C/_\sim \to A_i$ such that $\phi_i = e_M; m_i$:

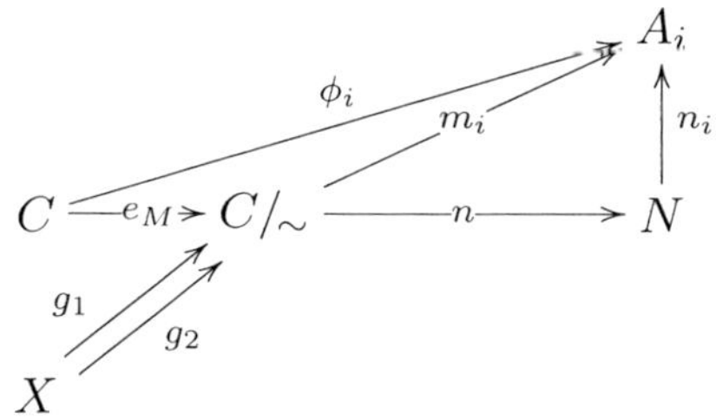

To show that (M, m_i) is a monosource, assume given $g_1, g_2 : X \to M$ with $g_1; m_i = g_2; m_i$. Let $n : C/_\sim \to N$ be their coequalizer. As coequalizer arrow (*) n is epi and, moreover, $\sim = ker(e_M) \subseteq ker(e_M; n)$.

By coequalizer property, there exist unique $n_i : N \to A_i$ making $n; n_i = m_i$. Then, since $e_M; n; n_i = e_M; m_i = \phi_i$, so $ker(e_M; n) \subseteq ker(e_M; n; n_i) = \sim_i$ and thus $ker(e_M; n) \subseteq \sim$. Together with (*) we obtain $\sim = ker(e_M; n)$ which implies that n is injective. Since n is also epi, it is iso by proposition 2.13. But then $g_1 = g_1; n; n^- = g_2; n; n^- = g_2$. □

We strengthen the above lemma showing that $C/_\sim$ is the unique monosource satisfying the conditions. To do this, we first verify that our category has the diagonal fill-in property.

Lemma 4.8. *Given a span $g_i : G \to A_i$, an epi $e : C \to G$, a monosource (N, n_i) and an $f : C \to N$ such that $e; g_i = f; n_i$, there exists a unique $k : G \to N$ such that $e; k = f$ and $k; n_i = g_i$.*

PROOF: By corollary 2.56, e is reqular, so let $\pi_i : X \to C$ be coequalized by e.

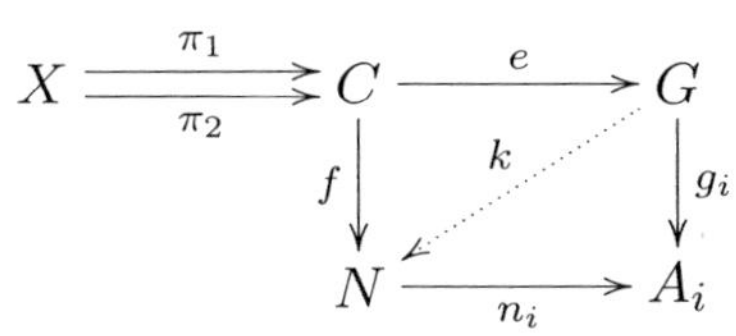

By assumption, $\pi_1; f; n_i = \pi_1; e; g_i = \pi_2; e; g_i = \pi_2; f; n_i$ and thus $\pi_1; f = \pi_2; f$ since N is a monosource. Since $e : C \to G$ is a coqualizer of π_is, we obtain a unique $k : G \to N$ with $e; k = f$. Now, $e; k; n_i = f; n_i = e; g_i$ and so $k; n_i = g_i$ since e is epi. □

Corollary 4.9. *$(C/_\sim, m_i)$ in lemma 4.7 is unique (up to monosource isomorphism).*

PROOF: Consider a span $A_1 \xleftarrow{\phi_1} C \xrightarrow{\phi_2} A_2$, and let (M, m_i), (N, n_i) be two monosource factorisations of this span.
By lemma 4.8 there exists a unique $k : M \to N$ such that $e_M; k = e_N$ and $m_i = k; n_i$ and, dually, a uniqe $g : N \to M$ with the respective $e_N; g = e_M$ and $n_i = g; m_i$. Then $k; g; m_i = k; n_i = m_i = id_M; m_i$ and, since (M, m_i) is a monosource, $k; g = id_M$. Analogously, we get $g; k = id_N$. □

4.2. Colimit of Monosources...

Given a pair $A_1, A_2 \in \mathsf{MAlg}^*_{OT}(\Sigma)$, we obtain the category $\mathsf{MS}(A_1, A_2)$ of monosources with the codomain A_1, A_2 and with monosource morphisms. We let $\mathcal{D}$ be its skeleton. As $\mathsf{MAlg}^*_{OT}(\Sigma)$ has all colimits, consider the colimit $\mathbf{P}$ of the "base" of the diagram $\mathcal{D}$, namely $(\mathbf{P}, \{\iota_{(M,m_i)} : M \to \mathbf{P} \mid (M, m_i) \in \mathcal{D}\})$. (We will skip the morphisms in the notation, i.e., will write ι_M rather than $\iota_{(M,m_i)}$.) According to fact 4.4.1, each ι_M is a mono. For any $g : (M, m_i) \to (N, n_i)$ in $\mathcal{D}$, we have $m_i = g; n_i$ and so the colimit property provides a unique "mediating" span $\pi_i : \mathbf{P} \to A_i$ such that $m_i = \iota_M; \pi_i$ for every $(M, m_i) \in \mathcal{D}$.

(Typically, given a subobject $S \sqsubseteq \mathbf{P}$, we will identify in the notation the arrows $\pi_i : \mathbf{P} \to A_i$ and $\pi_i : S \to A_i$.)

4.3. ... Is a Product

To show that $(\mathbf{P}, \pi_i)$ is a product, we show first some auxiliary results.

Fact 4.10. *1. For every monosource* $(M, m_i) \in \mathcal{D}$*, the restriction* $\iota_M : M \to \iota_M[M]$ *gives a (monosource) isomorphism* $(M, m_i) \simeq (\iota_M[M], \pi_i)$*.*

2. For every monosource $(N, n_i) \in \mathsf{MS}(A_1, A_2)$ *there is a subalgebra* $P_N \sqsubseteq \mathbf{P}$ *such that* $\iota_N : (N, n_i) \to (P_N, \pi_i)$ *is a monosource isomorphism.*

PROOF: 1. $\iota_M[M] \sqsubseteq \mathbf{P}$ so ι_M is actually a span morphism $\iota_M : (M, m_i) \to (\iota_M[M], \pi_i)$. It is surjective and, by fact 4.4.1, mono so, by 2.13 it is iso. Hence $(\iota_M[M], \pi_i)$ is a monosource, and so ι_M is a monosource iso.

2. By definition, for every monosource $(N, n_i) \in \mathsf{MS}(A_1, A_2)$ there is a unique $(M, m_i) \in \mathcal{D}$ with a monosource iso $j_N : (N, n_i) \to (M, m_i)$. By 1, we can choose $P_N = \iota_M[M]$ and let $\iota_N = j_N; \iota_M$. □

Lemma 4.11. *Let* $(M, m_i) \in \mathcal{D}$ *and assume given* $f : N \to M$ *and* $g : N \to \mathbf{P}$ *such that* $(N, g; \pi_i)$ *is a monosource and* f *is a monosource morphism* $(N, g; \pi_i) \to (M, m_i)$*. Then* $g = f; \iota_M$*.*

PROOF: We consider the following diagram

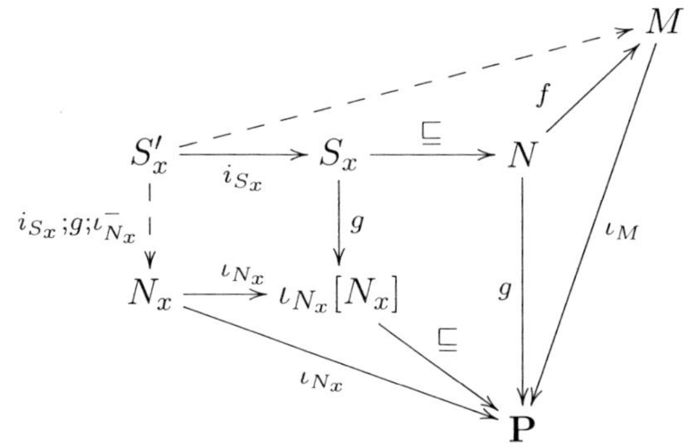

(4.12)

Since colimit arrows are jointly epi, for any $x \in N$ there exists a monosource $(N_x, n_i) \in \mathcal{D}$ such that $g(x) \in \iota_{N_x}[N_x] \sqsubseteq \mathbf{P}$. By lemma 2.32.2, $S_x = g^-[\iota_{N_x}[N_x]] \sqsubseteq N$. By assumption, $(N, g; \pi_i)$ is a monosource and so is $(S_x, \sqsubseteq; g; \pi_i)$ since $\sqsubseteq : S_x \to N$ is mono. By definition of $\mathcal{D}$ there exists a monosource $(S'_x, s_i) \in \mathcal{D}$ with a monosource isomorphism $i_{S_x} : (S'_x, s_i) \to (S_x, \sqsubseteq; g; \pi_i)$. Since the restriction ι_{N_x} is a monosource isomorphism by fact 4.10.1, so we have a monosource morphism $i_{S_x}; g; \iota^-_{N_x} : (S'_x, s_i) \to (N_x, n_i)$ in $\mathcal{D}$ (marked with the dashed arrow). On the other hand, we also have in $\mathcal{D}$ a monosource morphism $i_{S_x}; \sqsubseteq; f : (S'_x, s_i) \to (M, m_i)$. The colimit property entails then $i_{S_x}; g; \iota^-_{N_x}; \iota_{N_x} = \iota_{S_x}; \sqsubseteq; f; \iota_M$ which, according to the definition of S_x, implies $i_{S_x}; g; \sqsubseteq = i_{S_x}; \sqsubseteq; f; \iota_M$. We have $g; \sqsubseteq = \sqsubseteq; g$, so we obtain $i_{S_x}; \sqsubseteq; g = i_{S_x}; \sqsubseteq; f; \iota_M$ from which it follows that $\sqsubseteq; g = \sqsubseteq; f; \iota_M$ since i_{S_x} is iso. Since $x \in S_x$, this proves $g(x) = \iota_M(f(x))$.

□

Corollary 4.13. *1. Given $k : N \to K$, $g : N \to \mathbf{P}$, $h : K \to \mathbf{P}$ such that $(N; g; \pi_i)$, $(K, h; \pi_i)$ are monosources and k is monosource morphism between them – then $k; h = g$.*

2. For every monosource (M, m_i) there is exactly one monosource $M' \sqsubseteq \mathbf{P}$ such that (M, m_i) and (M', π_i) are isomorphic (as monosources).

PROOF: 1. By definition of $\mathcal{D}$ there is an isomorphism $i : (K, h; \pi_i) \to (M, m_i)$, for some $(M, m_i) \in \mathcal{D}$.

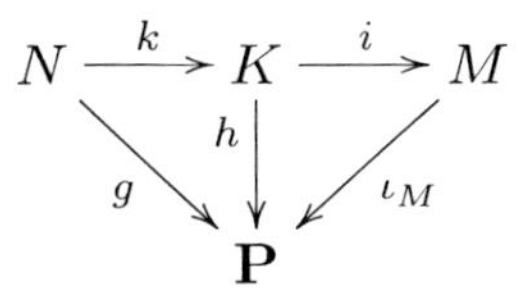

By 4.11, we obtain $k; i; \iota_M = g$ and $i; \iota_M = h$ so $k; h = g$.

2. The existence of such an M' is given in fact 4.10.1. As to uniqueness, assume two isomorphic subobjects $N, K \sqsubseteq \mathbf{P}$ with an isomorphism $k : N \to K$. In the diagram above, h, g are then inclusions. By 1. $k; \sqsubseteq = \sqsubseteq$, which means that k itself is an inclusion, and likewise is k^-. □

The proof of the following lemma follows the same argument as the proof of lemma 4.11.

Lemma 4.14. *Given some $g : C \to \mathbf{P}$, let $(e_g : C \to g[C]; \sqsubseteq: g[C] \to \mathbf{P})$ be epi-mono factorisation of g (existing by lemma 2.42). Furthermore, let (M, m_i) and $e : C \to M$ be epi-monosource factorisation of the span $(C, g; \pi_i)$ (existing by lemma 4.7). Then $e; \iota_M = g$ is also epi-mono factorisation of g.*

PROOF: By assumption $g; \pi_i = e_g; \sqsubseteq; \pi_i = e; m_i$

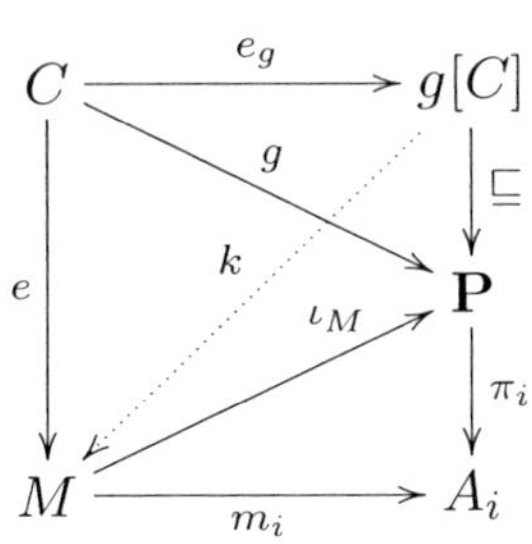

Thus, by lemma 4.8, there exists a (unique) $k : g[C] \to M$ such that (*) $e_g; k = e$ and $k; m_i = \sqsubseteq; \pi_i$. That is, k is a span morphism $k : (g[C], \sqsubseteq; \pi_i) \to (M, m_i) = (M, \iota_M; \pi_i)$. Showing that $k; \iota_M = \sqsubseteq$ will yield the claim.

We refer to the diagram (4.12) where we substitute $g[C]$ for N and k for f. We annotate some inclusions to ease the references.

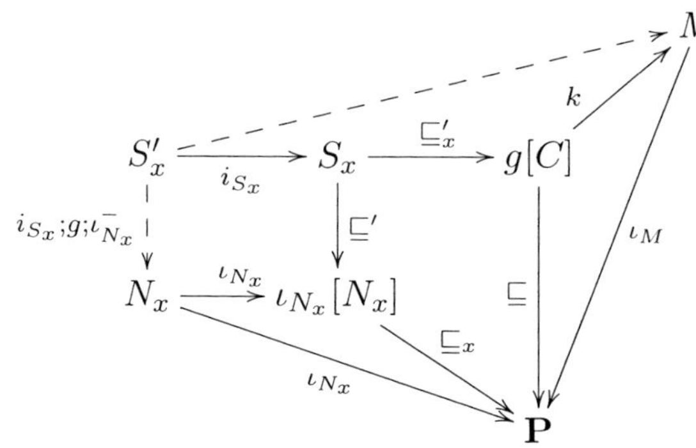

As in the proof of 4.11, for any $x \in g[C]$ there is a monosource $(N_x, n_i) \in \mathcal{D}$ with $x \in \iota_{N_x}[N_x]$. Then, by fact 2.25, also $g[C] \cap \iota_{N_x}[N_x] = S_x$ is a subalgebra of $g[C]$ and of $\iota_{N_x}[N_x]$. By fact 4.10.1, $(\iota_{N_x}[N_x], \sqsubseteq_x; \pi_i)$ is a monosource, and hence $(S_x, \sqsubseteq'; \sqsubseteq_x; \pi_i) = (S_x, \sqsubseteq'_x; \sqsubseteq; \pi_i)$ is a monosource, since $\sqsubseteq'$ is mono.

By definition of $\mathcal{D}$, there is a monosource $(S'_x, s_i) \in \mathcal{D}$ with the isomorphism $i_{S_x} : (S'_x, s_i) \to (S_x, \sqsubseteq'_x; \sqsubseteq; \pi_i)$. As in the proof of 4.11, we can conclude $i_{S_x}; \sqsubseteq'; \iota^-_{N_x}; \iota_{N_x} = i_{S_x}; \sqsubseteq'; k; \iota_M$, i.e., $i_{S_x}; \sqsubseteq'; \sqsubseteq_x = i_{S_x}; \sqsubseteq'_x; \sqsubseteq = i_{S_x}; \sqsubseteq'; k; \iota_M$. Since i_{S_x} is iso, this implies $\sqsubseteq'_x; \sqsubseteq = \sqsubseteq'; k; \iota_M$, and as $x \in S_x$, this shows that $x = \iota_M(k(x))$ and thus (**) $\sqsubseteq = k; \iota_M$ since x was arbitrary.

We now obtain $g = e_g; \sqsubseteq \overset{(**)}{=} e_g; k; \iota_M \overset{(*)}{=} e; \iota_M$. □

Corollary 4.15. *1.* $(\mathbf{P}, \pi_i)$ *is a monosource and 2. every subobject* $C \sqsubseteq \mathbf{P}$ *is a monosource* $(C, \sqsubseteq; \pi_i)$.

PROOF: 2. follows from 1. since composition of a mono with a monosource is a monosource. To show 1, assume $f, g : C \to \mathbf{P}$ with $f; \pi_i = g; \pi_i$. Let (F, f_i) with $e_f : C \to F$ be epi-monosource factorisation of f, and similarly (G, g_i) with $e_g : C \to G$ for g.

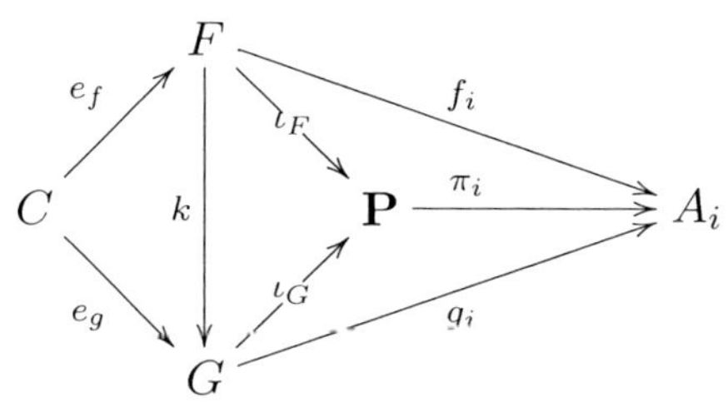

By lemma 4.8, there is a unique $k : F \to G$ such that (*) $e_f; k = e_g$ and $k; g_i = f_i$. This latter equality means that $k : (F, f_i) \to (G, g_i)$ is a monosource morphism. By fact 4.10.2, we also have a monosource morphism $\iota_F : (F, f_i) \to (\mathbf{P}, \pi_i)$, hence $(F, f_i) = (F, \iota_F; \pi_i)$ and likewise for $(G, g_i) = (G, \iota_G; \pi_i)$. So k is a monosource morphism $k : (F, \iota_F; \pi_i) \to (G, \iota_G; \pi_i)$. By corollary 4.13.1, we then have $\iota_F = k; \iota_G$, which gives the second of the following equalities, with the first and the last one following from lemma 4.14: $f = e_f; \iota_F = e_f; k; \iota_G \overset{(*)}{=} e_g; \iota_G = g$. □

Theorem 4.16. *Colimit* $\mathbf{P}$ *of the diagram* $\mathcal{D}$ *– a skeleton of* $\mathsf{MS}(A_1, A_2)$ *– with the projections* π_i *as defined in Subsection 4.2., is a product* $A_1 \times A_2$.

PROOF: Let $\phi_i : C \to A_i$ be a span. By lemma 4.7, there is a morphism $e : C \to M$ into a monosource (M, m_i) such that $\phi_i = e; m_i$. Composed with $\iota_M : M \to \mathbf{P}$ (which commutes with the projections, i.e., $m_i = \iota_M; \pi_i$), this gives an $u = e; \iota_M$ such that $\phi_i = u; \pi_i$. We thus obtain an arrow $u : C \to \mathbf{P}$ which, by corollary 4.15, is unique.
Since $\mathbf{P}$ is colimit object of a diagram over $\mathsf{MAlg}^*_{OT}(\Sigma)$, it is set-reflecting by cocompleteness of the category, i.e., $\mathbf{P} \in \mathsf{MAlg}^*_{OT}(\Sigma)$. □

Extension to products of arbitrary sets of objects, $\prod_{i \in I} A_i$, is straightforward. (The only changes of some significance are to consider I-indexed monosources and taking greatest lower bound of I kernels, in 4.1., which is possible since collection of congruences on a given algebra is a complete lattice.)

Theorem 4.17. *For any set* I *and collection of objects* $\{A_i \in \mathsf{MAlg}^*_{OT}(\Sigma) \mid i \in I\}$, *the colimit of the diagram of all non-isomorphic monosources* $(M, m_i : M \to A_i)$ *is the product* $\prod_{i \in I} A_i$.

Notice that we do not obtain products for all class-indexed families. Extending the proof might, for instance, require showing that not only any set but also any class of congruences on an algebra has an infimum. This limitation follows directly from the fact that a category that has all, also class-indexed, products is thin (e.g., theorem 10.32 in [3]), while our category obviously is not thin.

5. The Categories $\mathsf{MAlg}^{\kappa}_{OT}(\Sigma)$

Thus, category $\mathsf{MAlg}^*_{OT}(\Sigma)$ is complete and cocomplete, but $\mathsf{MAlg}_{OT}(\Sigma)$, although cocomplete and possessing equalizers, can fail to have final objects as well as products. The former failure was discussed in 2.4. and the latter is illustrated by the following example, adapted (and corrected) from [17].

Example 5.1. *Consider the signature with one unary operation* $f : S \to S$ *and the following two algebras* A *and* B:

$A :$ 

In B, f *is the transitive closure of the following graph:*

$B :$ 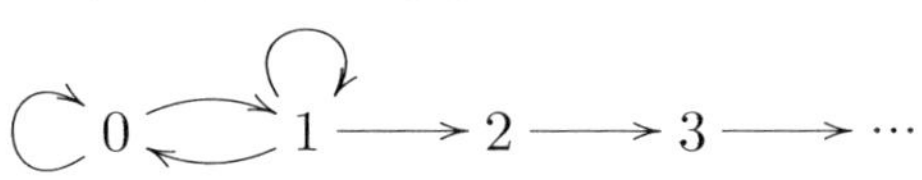

Looking for the product $A \times A$, *consider two homomorphisms* $B \to A$ *given by:*
$\phi_a(0) = 0$ *and* $\phi_a(x) = 1$ *for* $x > 0$,
$\phi_b(1) = 1$ *and* $\phi_b(y) = 0$ *for* $y \neq 1$.
Their respective kernels are $\sim_a$ *and* $\sim_b$ *as shown in Example 2.48, with* $\sim_a \wedge \sim_b = id_B$. *I.e.,* (B, ϕ_a, ϕ_b) *is a monosource and hence its mediating morphism into* $A \times A$ *must be injective. The same applies to* B *extended with any further chain of elements for an arbitrary ordinal. Hence, there is no cardinality limit on the product* $A \times A$ *in* $\mathsf{MAlg}_{OT}(\Sigma)$, *and one concludes that this product does not exists in* $\mathsf{MAlg}_{OT}(\Sigma)$.

We therefore consider now the category $\mathsf{MAlg}^{\kappa}_{OT}(\Sigma)$, for some infinite cardinal κ. Inspecting the constructions of coproducts and coequalizers, one concludes easily that

Fact 5.2. $\mathsf{MAlg}^{\kappa}_{OT}(\Sigma)$ *is cocomplete.*

Equalizers exists by essentially the same construction as in Proposition 3.18. The proof of the existence of final objects, Theorem 3.20, does not extend directly to the category $\mathsf{MAlg}^{\kappa}_{OT}(\Sigma)$, since the collection of all non-isomorphic κ-bounded algebras can be a proper class. But it can be adapted in the standard way (e.g., [5], I:4.5, [38], 10). κ-boundedness implies that the category $\mathsf{MAlg}^{\kappa}_{OT}(\Sigma)$ has a set of generators, namely, the collection of all (non-isomorphic) algebras generated by a single element. (It is a set due to the cardinality limit κ on every such algebra.) Due to cocompleteness, one can take a coproduct of all generators, and its quotient by the maximal OT-congruence yields a final object.

Finally, the construction and proofs for products apply without any changes to the category $\mathsf{MAlg}^{\kappa}_{OT}(\Sigma)$, provided that, given a pair/set of such algebras, the diagram $\mathcal{D}$ is small. This is ensured by the following lemma. $\mathsf{MS}^{\kappa}(A_1, A_2)$ denotes the category of κ-bounded monosources with κ-bounded codomain A_1, A_2.

Lemma 5.3. *Given an infinite cardinal κ, there is a function $f : \mathsf{Card} \times \mathsf{Card} \to \mathsf{Card}$ such that for any $A_1, A_2 \in \mathsf{MAlg}^{\kappa}_{OT}(\Sigma)$ and any $(M, m_i) \in \mathsf{MS}^{\kappa}(A_1, A_2)$, $|M| \leq f(|A_1|, |A_2|)$.*

PROOF: Let $\alpha_i = |A_i|$ be the cardinalities of A_i's and $\alpha = \alpha_1 * \alpha_2 = |A_1 \times A_2|$. Assume $(M, m_i) \in \mathsf{MS}^{\kappa}(A_1, A_2)$ and let $\simeq_i = ker(m_i)$. We show that there is a cardinal number limiting from above the possible size of M. We use fact 4.5 and show that if cardinality of M is too large then $\simeq_1 \wedge \simeq_2 \neq id_M$. To do this, we apply the construction of infimum of two congruences as given in Fact 2.47, adapting it so that in each step we determine a limit on the possible number of obtained equivalence classes.

1. The first step gives $x \sim_0 x' \iff x \simeq_1 x' \wedge x \simeq_2 x'$, i.e., each equivalence class is associated with a unique pair $\langle a_1, a_2 \rangle \in A_1 \times A_2$, namely such that $m_1([x]^{\sim_0}) = a_1$ and $m_2([x]^{\sim_0}) = a_2$. Hence, the number of these classes $\gamma_0 \leq \alpha$.
2. The inductive step amounts to propagation of the existing distinctions, i.e., splitting of the equivalence classes obtained so far. A class $[y_1]^{\sim_i}$ is split by removing the pairs $\langle y_1, y_2 \rangle \in \sim_i$ for which there exist noncongruent pre-images, i.e., such pairs that (*) $\exists x_1 \in f^-(y_1)\ \forall x_2 \in f^-(y_2) : \langle x_1, x_2 \rangle \notin \sim_i$ for some $f \in \Sigma$.[7] Now, for any y_1 and f, the pre-image $f^-(y_1)$ determines a subset of $\sim_i$-equivalence classes, namely $[f^-(y_1)]^{\sim_i} = \{[x]^{\sim_i} \mid [x]^{\sim_i} \cap f^-(y_i) \neq \varnothing\}$. If y_1, y_2 satisfy (*), i.e., are split in the step $i + 1$, then also $[f^-(y_1)]^{\sim_i} \neq [f^-(y_2)]^{\sim_i}$. There are 2^{γ_i} such subsets, i.e., there are no more than 2^{γ_i} possible splittings of every one of γ_i equivalence classes at step $i + 1$. So we obtain $\gamma_{i+1} \leq \gamma_i * 2^{\gamma_i}$. (We have ignored some finite constants which do not increase this estimate when γ_i's are infinite, namely, the number of operations in the signature (which is finite), as well as the arity of the operations (which is finite).)
3. Due to κ-boundedness, the construction terminates in at most κ steps by Proposition 2.49. Hence we obtain $f(\alpha_1, \alpha_2) = \gamma \leq \bigcup_{i \in \kappa} \gamma_i$, which gives the upper bound on the number of equivalence classes for the congruence $\sim = \simeq_1 \wedge \simeq_2$.

[7] We write $f^-(y)$ for $(f^M)^-(y)$.

So if $|M| > \gamma$, the congruence $\sim$ will yield some equivalence class with more than 1 element, i.e., $\sim \neq id_M$. But then, by fact 4.5, (M, m_i) will not be a monosource. □

Proposition 5.4. *For any set I and collection of objects $\{A_i \in \mathsf{MAlg}^{\kappa}_{OT}(\Sigma) \mid i \in I\}$, the diagram $\mathcal{D}$ of all non-isomorphic monosources $(M, m_i : M \to A_i)$ is small and its colimit is a product $\prod_{i\in I} A_i$.*

PROOF: By the above lemma 5.3, the size of monosources is limited by (a function of) the size of the codomain objects, and so there is at most a set of non-isomorphic monosources with codomain $\{A_i \mid i \in I\}$. Since $\mathsf{MAlg}^{\kappa}_{OT}(\Sigma)$ is cocomplete, a colimit of $\mathcal{D}$ exists in $\mathsf{MAlg}^{\kappa}_{OT}(\Sigma)$. The rest of the proof is exactly the same as the proof of theorem 4.16. □

The expansion given in Table 5.5, of the respective row from Table 1.12, summarizes our results on the variants of the OT-categories.

Table 5.5. Limits and colimits in the OT-categories of multialgebras

	initial	co-prod.	co-equal.	final	prod.	equal.
$\mathsf{MAlg}^{\kappa}_{OT}(\Sigma)$	+	+	+	+	+	+
$\mathsf{MAlg}_{OT}(\Sigma)$	+	+	+	+/−	−	+
$\mathsf{MAlg}^{*}_{OT}(\Sigma)$	+	+	+	+	+	+

Recalling the remark 2.12, the category of coalgebras for the (direct image) power-set functor is isomorphic to $\mathsf{MAlg}_{OT}(\Sigma)$ for Σ containing one sort and operation symbol $f : S \to S$. This isomorphism obtains also between $\mathsf{MAlg}^{\kappa}_{OT}(\Sigma)$ and the category of coalgebras for κ-bounded power-set functor. Hence, all our constructions give the respective constructions for this particular category of colagebras.

Corollary 5.6. *The construction from section 4. yields products of coalgebras for κ-boundend power-set functor.*

6. Conclusion

Multialgebras lie at the intersection of several research topics. They

- represent relational structures and, generally, Boolean algebras with operators, [25, 26];
- generalise traditional – both total and partial – algebras;
- provide a fundamental instance of power structures;
- provide an example of dialgebras, [18], by combining the general algebraic and specific coalgebraic aspect in the signature (arbitrary products in arguments, only power-set in the result);

- can represent categories of coalgebras for polynomial functors, as well as for power-set functor;
- can represent (nondeterministic) automata, Kripke-frames, topological spaces...

The fact that multialgebras have attracted only limited attention might be the result of the poor algebraic structure obtained with the apparently most natural choice of weak homomorphisms. Although the category $\mathsf{MAlg}_W(\Sigma)$ is complete and cocomplete, the congruence associated with weak homomorphism is simply equivalence. On the other hand, the multiplicity of choices in defining most of the standard notions, including that of homomorphism, leaves too much freedom for a systematic study of multialgebras.

We have shown that, as far as the notion of homomorphism is concerned, the number of choices is limited to 9, and that most of these do not appear very attractive. (Of course, we do not mean that they can not possibly find applications which depend on the specific context. Also, limiting the objects of the category, e.g., to only deterministic or partial algebras, may yield several alternatives which do not obtain in the general situation investigated here.) The structural properties as well as most other choices are heavily conditioned by this notion. We have shown that choosing outer-tight homomorphisms (which imply weakness and, in the case of standard deterministic algebras, the classical notion), multialgebras and their category obtain strong algebraic structure: the associated notion of congruence – bireachability – can be seen as dual of the traditional notion of congruence (and of bisimilarity), requiring propagation of the congruence to the pre-images (e.g., subalgebras are closed under pre-images and not, as in the classical case, under images of the operations) or, equivalently, propagation of the distinctions to the images. The category $\mathsf{MAlg}_{OT}(\Sigma)$ of all Σ-multialgebras is cocomplete and has interesting final objects reflecting the maximal bireachability relation in the way analogous to final coalgebras reflecting maximal bimsimilarity. However, to ensure the existence of final objects and products in general, we have to extend the category to $\mathsf{MAlg}^*_{OT}(\Sigma)$ by allowing algebras with carriers being proper classes. We have characterized its objects as set-reflecting algebras which condition is equivalent to every algebra being colimit of small algebras. The category is complete and cocomplete. We have then shown that (minor modifications of) the constructions in $\mathsf{MAlg}^*_{OT}(\Sigma)$ can be also applied to κ-bounded multialgebras and that $\mathsf{MAlg}^{\kappa}_{OT}(\Sigma)$ is complete and cocomplete.

We have not addressed here the issue of logic and reasoning. However, sound and strongly complete logics for various variants of multialgebras have been designed [27, 21, 44, 45], the most recent one in [29]. Its primitives contain set-inclusion and deterministic equality which holds when both sides are not merely equal but equal one-element sets. (A different approach, based on membership relation, is developed and studied in [9, 10].) Its main specificity is the lack of substitutitivity property (as variables range only over individuals while terms denote arbitrary sets). This can be seen as a serious drawback (precluding the possibility of algebraization of the logic) or as a feature interesting in itself – representing not so unusual situations when, for some reason, variables range only over a subset of semantic objects (as is also the case, for instance, with partial algebras) or when allowed substitutions are restricted for other reasons (as in first-order logic where one has to avoid variable capture).

The natural next step will be to study the preservation properties of the OT-homomorphisms which may lead to adjustments in the primitive predicates of the logics used so far. Then one would like to investigate the possibilities of lifting the current results on the existence of (co)limits to the axiomatic classes.

7. Appendix: Assumptions in the Treatment of Classes

We use Grothendieck universes (after [34], 12.1) each satisfying the following axioms (for Zermelo universe):

ax1) $x \in \mathcal{U} \Rightarrow x \subseteq \mathcal{U}$ – $\mathcal{U}$ is transitive;

ax2) $x, y \in \mathcal{U} \Rightarrow \{x, y\}, \langle x, y \rangle \in \mathcal{U}$ – finite sets and pairs of members of $\mathcal{U}$ belong to $\mathcal{U}$;

ax3) $x \in \mathcal{U} \Rightarrow \mathcal{P}(x) \in \mathcal{U} \wedge \bigcup x \in \mathcal{U}$ – collection of all subcollections and unions of members of $\mathcal{U}$ belong to $\mathcal{U}$;

ax4) $\omega \in \mathcal{U}$ natural numbers/finite ordinals belong to $\mathcal{U}$;

ax5) $x \in \mathcal{U}, y \subset \mathcal{U}, f : x \twoheadrightarrow y \Rightarrow y \in \mathcal{U}$ – image of a member of $\mathcal{U}$ under surjection belongs to $\mathcal{U}$.

In addition, one postulates Grothendieck axiom:

ax6) every set/class belongs to some universe,

and obtains thus the hierarchy $\mathcal{U}_1 \in \mathcal{U}_2 \in \mathcal{U}_3 \in \ldots$ which, by transitivity, **ax1**), is cumulative (i.e., $\in$ can be repalced by $\subseteq$). $\mathcal{U}_{i+1}$ can be thought of as $\mathcal{P}(\mathcal{U}_i)$ where $\mathcal{P}(\_)$ forms not only subsets (not only $\mathcal{U}_i$-objects), but all subcollections (also subclasses, i.e., $\mathcal{U}_{i+1}$-objects) of the argument $\mathcal{U}_i$.

For instance, the following facts used at some places, are implied:

- $K \in \mathcal{U}_i, s_k \in \mathcal{U}_i \Rightarrow \bigcup_{k \in K} s_k \in \mathcal{U}_i$ – in particular, set-indexed union of sets is a set,
- $c \in \mathcal{U}_{i+1}, s \in \mathcal{U}_i \Rightarrow c \cap s \in \mathcal{U}_i$ – in particular, intersection with a set is a set,

which are among the axioms of NBG. But we are not working in NBG, for the reasons expressed after fact 3.12 – we need allow in multialgebras operations retuning proper classes. We thus have the following picture:

1) Usual algebras, $A = \langle \{s_1 ... s_n\}; f_k \subseteq s_{ik} \times ... \times s_{rk}; ... \rangle$ belong all to $\mathcal{U}_1$.

2) When the collections are proper classes, i.e, $s_i \in \mathcal{U}_2$, then:

   - $\langle s_1 ... s_n \rangle \in \mathcal{U}_2$ and $s_{ik} \times ... \times s_{rk} \in \mathcal{U}_2$ by **ax2**)
   - $f_k : s_{ik} \times ... \times s_{jk} \rightarrow \mathcal{P}(s_{rk})$, from definition 1.2 is thus generalised to an operation with the result $\mathcal{P}(s_{rk}) \in \mathcal{U}_2$ – and $f_k \subseteq s_{ik} \times ... \times s_{rk} \in \mathcal{U}_2$ by **ax3**) and **ax1**)

   and so class-algebras, with carriers being proper classes and operations returning proper classes, are also in $\mathcal{U}_2$.

3) Our constructions from section 3. apply thus to $\mathcal{U}_2$-objects; in particular, the diagrams (of limits, colimits) referred to by the word "all" are all $\mathcal{U}_2$ diagrams, but they work in the same way if we were to move higher up in the hierarchy.

4) This, in fact, we have to do. Consider an operation $s \rightarrow \mathcal{P}(s)$ and the isomorphism $s \simeq \mathcal{P}(s)$ required by finality. The proof from [2] obtains this bijection by letting s range over classes – objects of $\mathcal{U}_2$ – while $\mathcal{P}(\_)$ constructing only sub*sets*, i.e., objects of $\mathcal{U}_1$. Let us write (confusedly) $\mathcal{U}_i$ also for the cardinality of $\mathcal{U}_i$ (or the i-th (strongly) inaccessible cardinal, if one prefers), and denote by $\mathcal{U}_0$ – $\aleph_0$, by $\mathcal{U}_1$ – the (cardinality of the) class of all sets, by $\mathcal{U}_2$ – the collection of all classes, etc. Just like we have the bijection $\mathbf{N} \simeq \bigcup_{\lambda<\mathcal{U}_0} \mathcal{P}^\lambda(\mathbf{N})$, where $\mathcal{P}^\lambda(X)$ denotes the collection of subclasses of X of cardinality λ, so in [2] we obtain:

$$s_2 \simeq \bigcup_{\lambda<\mathcal{U}_1} \mathcal{P}^\lambda(s_2) \quad \text{for some } s_2 \in \mathcal{U}_2 \text{ with } s_2 \geq \mathcal{U}_1 \tag{7.1}$$

which is but another instance of the general fact (e.g., [13], 10.2, p.119), according to which for a (strongly) inaccessible cardinal υ:

$$\upsilon = \sum_{\lambda<\upsilon} \upsilon^\lambda \;\; = |\bigcup_{\lambda<\upsilon} \mathcal{P}^\lambda(\upsilon)|.$$

Accidentaly, it seems that the bijection (7.1) could be obtained working in NBG with the limitation of size, as choosing s_2 to be a class, i.e., V, the collection of its subsets (with or without subclasses) has the same cardinality being, too, a class.

In our case, we start with $s \subseteq \mathcal{U}_1$, i.e., $s \in \mathcal{U}_2$, and then also $\mathcal{P}(s) \in \mathcal{U}_2$, which might suggest that everything happens at the same level as in (7.1). However, $\mathcal{P}(s)$ forms now not only $\mathcal{U}_1$-objects but, as pointed out at the beginning of section 3. and after fact 3.12, also proper subclasses of s, i.e., $\mathcal{U}_2$-objects, and so, for every $s \in \mathcal{U}_2 : |s| < |\mathcal{P}(s)|$. The desired isomorphism is possible first at the next level, i.e., we must allow carriers at the level $\mathcal{U}_3$:

$$s_3 \simeq \bigcup_{\lambda<\mathcal{U}_2} \mathcal{P}^\lambda(s_3) \quad \text{for some } s_3 \in \mathcal{U}_3 \text{ with } s_3 \geq \mathcal{U}_2.$$

According to theorem 3.20, a final object (which satisfies this isomorphism, for a signature with an $f : s \rightarrow s$) is set-reflecting and hence is a colimit of small subalgebras – a colimit, as mentioned above in 3, possibly over a diagram of size $\mathcal{U}_2 \in \mathcal{U}_3$.

In addition to the above axioms, we have also used (in the proof of fact 3.12) the global axiom of choice $\exists C : \mathcal{U} \rightarrow \mathcal{U} \; \forall x : x \neq \varnothing \Rightarrow C(x) \in x$, or rather its equivalent:

ax7) Every equivalence relation on a class has a system of representatives.

Acknowledgments

Norwegian Research Council, NFR, provided financial support for parts of this work under the project SHIP.

We also express our thanks to our earlier students, Kristen Naley and Adis Hodzic, who had worked on various aspects of some problems discussed here.

References

[1] Peter Aczel. Non-well-founded sets. Technical Report 14, CSLI, 1988.

[2] Peter Aczel and Nax Mendler. A final coalgebra theorem. In G. Goos and J. Hartmanis, editors, *Category Theory and Computer Science*, volume 389 of *LNCS*, pages 357–365. Springer, 1989.

[3] Jiří Adámek, Horst Herrlich, and George Strecker. *Abstract and Concrete Categories*. John Wiley & Sons, Inc., 1990.

[4] Patrick Blackburn, Maarten de Rijke, and Yde Venema. *Modal Logic*. Cambridge University Press, 2001.

[5] F. Borceux. *Handbook of Categorical Algebra*. Cambridge, 1994.

[6] Ivica Bošnjak and Rozália Madarász. On power structures. *Algebra and Discrete Mathematics*, **2**:14–35, 2003.

[7] Chris Brink. Power structures. *Algebra Universalis*, **30**:177–216, 1993.

[8] Peter Burmeister. *A Model Theoretic Oriented Approach to Partial Algebras*. Akademie-Verlag, Berlin, 1986.

[9] Janis Cīrulis. A logical system admitting vacuous and plural temrs. *Zeitschrift fü Mathematische Logik und Grundlagen der Mathematik*, **31**, 1985.

[10] Janis Cīrulis. Multialgebras from the viewpoint of algebraic logic. *Algebra and Discrete Mathematics*, **2**:20–31, 2003.

[11] Paul M. Cohn. *Universal Algebra*, volume 6 of *Mathematics and Its Applications*. D.Reidel Publishing Company, 1965.

[12] Willem-Paul de Roever and Kai Engelhardt. *Data Refinement: Model-Oriented Proof Methods and their Comparison*. Cambridge University Press, 1998.

[13] Keith J. Devlin. *Foundamentals of Contemporary Set Theory*. Springer, 1979.

[14] George Grätzer. A representation theorem for multialgebras. *Arch. Math.*, **13**, 1962.

[15] George Grätzer. *Universal Algebra*. Springer, 1968.

[16] George Grätzer. *General Lattice Theory*. Birkhäuser, Basel, 1978.

[17] H. Peter Gumm and Tobias Schröder. Products of coalgebras. *Algebra Universalis*, **46**:163–185, 2001.

[18] Tatsuya Hagino. *A Categorical Programming Language*. PhD thesis, Department of Computer Science, University of Edinburgh, 1987.

[19] Claudio Hermida. A categorical outlook on relational modalities and simulations. In Michael Mendler, Rajeev P. Goré, and Valeria de Paiva, editors, *Intuitionistic Modal Logic and Aplications*, volume 02-15 of *DIKU technical reports*, pages 17–34, July 26 2002.

[20] Wim H. Hesselink. A mathematical approach to nondeterminism in data types. *ACM ToPLaS*, **10**, 1988.

[21] Heinrich Hußmann. Nondeterministic algebraic specifications and nonconfluent term rewriting. In *Algebraic and Logic Programming*. *LNCS* vol. 343, Springer, 1988.

[22] Heinrich Hußmann. *Nondeterministic algebraic specifications*. PhD thesis, Fak. f. Mathematik und Informatik, Universitat Passau, 1990.

[23] Heinrich Hußmann. *Nondeterminism in Algebraic Specifications and Algebraic Programs*. Birkhäuser, 1993. [revised version of [22]].

[24] Bjarni Jónsson. The theory of binary relations. In H. Andéka, J.D.Monk, and I.Németi, editors, *Colloquia Mathematica Societas János Bolyai, 54. Algebraic Logic*, pages 245–291. North-Holland, 1988.

[25] Bjarni Jónsson and Alfred Tarski. Boolean algebras with operators i. *American J. Mathematics*, **73**:891–939, 1951.

[26] Bjarni Jónsson and Alfred Tarski. Boolean algebras with operators ii. *American J. Mathematics*, **74**:127–162, 1952.

[27] B. Konikowska and M. Białasik. Reasoning with nondeterministic specifications. *Acta Informatica*, **36**(5):375–403, 1999.

[28] Yngve Lamo. *The institution of multialgebras – a general framework for algebraic software development*. PhD thesis, Department of Informatics, University of Bergen, 2002.

[29] Yngve Lamo and Michał Walicki. Quantifier-free logic for multialgebraic theories. *Theoretical Computer Science*, **355**:215–227, 2006.

[30] Rozália Madarász. Remarks on power structures. *Algebra Universalis*, **34**(2):179–184, 1995.

[31] J. C. C. McKinsey and Alfred Tarski. The algebra of topology. *The Annals of Mathematics*, **45**(1):141–191, 1944.

[32] J. C. C. McKinsey and Alfred Tarski. On closed elements in closure algebras. *The Annals of Mathematics*, **47**(1):126–162, 1946.

[33] J. C. C. McKinsey and Alfred Tarski. Some theorems about the sentential calculi of lewis and heyting. *The Journal of Symbolic Logic*, **13**(1):1–15, 1948.

[34] Colin McLarty. *Elementary Categories, Elementary Toposes*. Oxford Science Publications, 1991.

[35] José Meseguer. Membership algebra as a logical framework for equational specification. In *In 12th International Workshop on Recent Trends in Algebraic Development Techniques (WADT'97)*, volume 1376 of *LNCS*, pages 18–61. Springer, 1998.

[36] Günter Pickert. Bemerkungen zum homomorphie-begriff. *Mathematische Zeitschrift*, **53**, 1950.

[37] H.E. Pickett. Homomorphisms and subalgebras of multialgebras. *Pacific J. of Mathematics*, **21**:327–342, 1967.

[38] Jan J.M.M Rutten. Universal coalgebra: a theory of systems. *Theoretical Computer Science*, **249**:3–80, 2000.

[39] Dietmar Schweigert. Congruence relations on multialgebras. *Discrete Mathematics*, **53**:249–253, 1985.

[40] Steven Vickers. *Topology via Logic*. Cambridge University Press, 1989.

[41] George Voutsadakis. Universal bialgebra: unifying universal algebra and coalgebra. Technical report, New Mexico State University, 2000.

[42] Michal Walicki. Bireachability and final multialgebras. In J. L. Fiadeiro, N. Harman, M. Roggenbach, and J. Rutten, editors, *Algebra and Coalgebra in Computer Science*, volume 3629 of *LNCS*, pages 408–423. Springer, 2005.

[43] Michał Walicki, Adis Hodzic, and Sigurd Meldal. Compositional homomorphisms of relational structures. In R. Freivalds, editor, *Fundamentals of Computation Theory*, volume 2138 of *LNCS*. Springer, 2001.

[44] Michał Walicki and Sigurd Meldal. A complete calculus for the multialgebraic and functional semantics of nondeterminism. *ACM ToPLaS*, **17**(2), 1995.

[45] Michał Walicki and Sigurd Meldal. Multialgebras, power algebras and complete calculi of identities and inclusions. In *Recent Trends in Data Type Specifications*, volume 906 of *LNCS*. Springer, 1995.

[46] Michał Walicki and Sigurd Meldal. Algebraic approaches to nondeterminism – an overview. *ACM Computing Surveys*, **29**(1), March 1997.

[47] Michał Walicki and Sigurd Meldal. Singular and plural nondeterministic parameters. *SIAM J. Computing*, **26**(3), 1997.

In: New Topics in Theoretical Computer Science
Editors: Oleg N. Terikhovsky *et al.*, pp. 95-118
ISBN: 978-1-60456-100-5

Chapter 3

A Model Transformation and Refinement Approach to MDA*

Jifeng He [**] ***and Jing Liu*** [***]
Software Engineering Institute, East China Normal University, Shanghai, China

Abstract

Model transformation and refinement are playing a key role in Model Driven Development, or MDA. Although well-established standards for creating meta-models such as the Meta-Object Facility exist, there is currently no mature foundation for specifying transformation and refinement among models. Recently we have developed a refinement calculus of object system rCOS which can support model translation and refinement. Mathematical characterization of object-oriented concepts is presented by defining observation oriented semantics of rCOS with a rich variety of features including subtypes, visibility, inheritance, type casting, dynamic binding and polymorphism.

rCOS is class-based and the refinement is about making correct changes to the structure, methods of classes and the main program. The logic of rCOS is a conservative extension of standard predicate logic. In our model, both commands and class declarations are identified as predicates whose alphabets include logic variables representing the initial and final values of program variables, as well as those variables representing the contextual information of classes and their links. A variable of a built-in primitive type, such as the type Int of integers, stores data of the corresponding type whereas a variable of an object type holds the identity or reference and the current type information of an object as its value. We define the traditional programming constructs, such as conditional, sequential composition and recursion, in exactly the same way as their counterparts in an imperative programming language without reference types. This makes the approach more accessible to users who are already familiar with the existing imperative languages. All the laws about imperative commands remain valid without the need of reproving. rCOS has been proven to provide formal support to software design and program refactoring. All these features together show that rCOS can be used as a formal

* Supported by the National High Tech Research 863 Program of China under Grant No.2006AA01Z165; National Grand Fundamental Research 973 Program of China under Grant Nos.2002CB312001, 2005CB321904; the National Natural Science Foundation of China under Grant No.60673114, 60603037; the Natural Science Foundation of Shanghai of China under Grant No.05ZR14052; 211 Project
** E-mail address: jifeng@sei.ecnu.edu.cn. Phn:+86-21-62232971 (Corresponding author)
*** E-mail address: jliu@sei.ecnu.edu.cn, ggpu@sei.ecnu.edu.cn

framework for the model based development. With rCOS, we can construct models according to the object-orient design principles and use patterns as refinement laws.

As UML is now used as a standard modeling language, we reinforce the ability of UML in modeling software architecture by defining a generic model of component and software architecture, and integrate the model with UML class model and interaction model to unify software development process. In UML, software development is modeled in different views. With formal semantics, designer can keep consistency among these views. We demonstrate how to use the method to construct software and how to keep the consistency among different models.

Keywords: Model transformation, UML, UTP, semantics

1. Introduction

The Model Driven Architecture (MDA) [OMG04], an Object Management Group initiative, promotes the separation of concerns between two modeling dimensions: one focusing on the business functionality (resulting in *Platform Independent Models – PIMs*), and another one focusing on the implementation of that functionality on a specific middleware platform (resulting in *Platform Specific Models – PSMs*). While model transformations [OMG02] should be used to refine PIMs into PSMs, code generators are supposed to map PSMs to concrete implementations, providing thus an elegant approach to adapt PIMs to the peculiarities of the new infrastructures that do not cease to appear. Besides reducing development costs and improving software quality, MDA provides the basis for facilitating integration, evolution, and migration of software solutions, hence contributing to the limitation of maintenance costs for distributed applications.

Software architecture is an aspect of software engineering directed at developing large, complex applications in a manner that reduces development costs, increases the potential for commonality among different members of a closely related product family, and facilitates evolution, possibly at system runtime [GS94]. The primary focus of architecture-based software development is shifted from lines-of-code to coarser-grained architectural elements, their high-level interactions, and their overall interconnection structure. This enables developers to abstract away unnecessary details and focus on the “big picture”—system structure, high-level communication protocols, assignment of software components and connectors to hosts, development process, and so on [GS94, Kru95, LV95, PW92, SNH95, Tay96]. The basic promise of software architecture research is that better software systems can result from modeling their important architectural aspects throughout, and especially early in, the development lifecycle.

A large number of architecture description languages (ADLs) have been proposed [AG97, LV95, Ves93]. Each ADL embodies a particular approach to the specification and evolution of architecture. But ADLs can only support software architecture modeling, not include others, so we can’t model the whole software development process in ADL.

The Unified Modeling Language (UML) is a family of design notations that is rapidly becoming a de facto standard software modeling language. It has also been selected as standard language for architectural description by OMG [Rat04]. Now UML has been selected as a standard language for architectural description [Rat04], as it provides a large, useful, and extensible set of predefined constructs, is semi-formally defined, has the potential for substantial tool support, and is based on experience with mainstream development methods. However, there is no directly mapping from architecture description to UML description [MRR02]. Furthermore, UML admittedly does not have a rigorous (neither static nor dynamic) semantics. On the other hand, to be liberal and accommodate, UML gives a lot of freedom such that a non-experienced user is often disconcerted among the possible modeling choices. These problems, as a consequence, cause the consistencies, correctness issues and the like. Formal specifications provide a more precise definition of the functionality supplied by the software, and its well-defined syntax and semantics enable the automation of their processing. Formal methods enable applying the notion of refinement, demonstrating that lower levels of abstraction satisfy higher levels. There are several methods for specifying components. However, their work focuses on the specification technique with little concern for modeling different software development phases.

We have undertaken some work attempting at proposing a more stringent method, which we are in part experimenting. For example, in [HLL02, HLL05, LHL05] we have presented a refinement calculus of component and object system, in [LLLH04] we have constructed a formal requirement model and in [LLHL04] we have investigated the link between the requirement model and the design model. In [LMG02] we have given a specification-based software construction framework.

Our approach is expressed in a rigorous multiview, use case driven and UML-based way. At first, the choice of a restricted subset of the UML constructs has been guided by a formal semantic analysis of those constructs. The general approach to addressing the semantic problems of UML, together with references to our work on more specific aspects, can be found in [LHLL04]. Essentially, it shows how the refinement calculus of component and object system rCOS can be taken as a basis for defining UML systems as formal semantic models. We describe the static properties of software system with class model and dynamic properties with interaction diagram. Furthermore, the consistency between different models is checked. Our aim is to provide abstract modeling constructs that relate well to programming constructs of component infrastructure technology to support smooth transitioning between different software development phases and system descriptions. Formal specifications are used to construct software in a stepwise fashion, adding more details in each step of refinement.

2. Overview of the Approach

Software development process usually can be divided into four steps. In the first step, they analyze user's requirement and then construct a requirement model. In the second step, system is divided into several interconnected modules or high-level components. The components are organized in some architectural style. In the third step developers design every module respectively. In the fourth step they compose the modules, and a system is constructed. These activities are interdependent

The development process can be implemented as stepwise model refinement. Firstly, we construct a conceptual architecture model, then refine the model and got a concrete one, as shown in Figure 2.1.

Given a specification *SP*, we need to construct a program *P* that is a correct realization of *SP*. In a stepwise fashion, we can gradually enrich the original specification with more and more detail, incorporating more and more design and implementation decisions. Such decisions include choosing between the different alternative behaviors left open by the specification, such as data representation, function implementations, etc. Each decision is recorded separately, as a different step consisting of a local modification to the specification. With this approach, developing a program from its specification proceeds via a sequence of such small, easily understandable and verifiable steps:

$$SP_0 \sqsubseteq SP_1 \sqsubseteq \ldots \sqsubseteq SP_n$$

In this chain, SP_0 is the original requirement specification and $SP_1 \sqsubseteq SP_i$ for any $i = 1, \ldots, n$ is an individual refinement step. The aim is to reach a specification, in this case SP_n, that is an exact description of the program in full detail, one that incorporates all design decisions and that is a correct realization of SP.

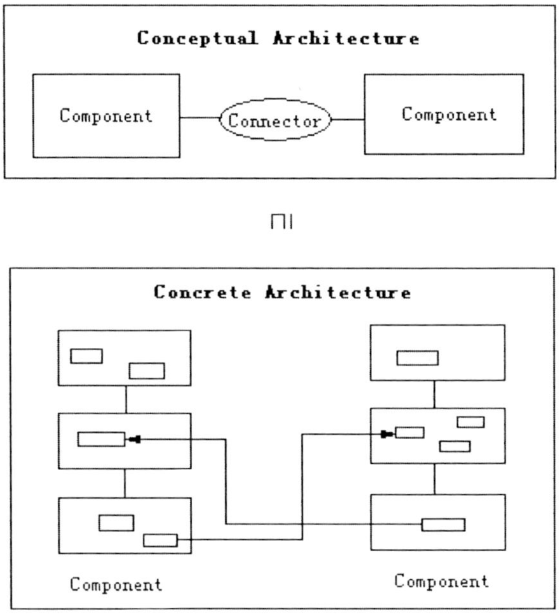

Figure 2.1. Refinement of Software System.

Let S_1 and S_2 be object programs that have the same set of global variables *glb*. S_1 is a refinement S_2, denoted by $S_1 \sqsubseteq_{sys} S_2$, if its behavior is more controllable and predictable than that of S_2:

$$\forall \underline{x}, \underline{x}', ok, ok' \cdot (S_1 \Rightarrow S_2)$$

where $\underline{x}$ are the variables in glb.

This means the external behavior of S_1, that is, the pairs of pre-global and post-global states, is a subset of that of S_2. To prove one program S_1 refines another S_2, we require that they have the same set of global variables and there exists a refinement mapping from the variables of S_1 to those of S_2 that is identical on global variables.

3. Models in Object Oriented Design

- UML provides constructs for modeling software components, their interfaces, and their deployment on hosts. The minimum set of requirements [MRR02] for objectively evaluation UML's ability to represent object oriented development effectively are as follows:
- UML should be well suited to model the *structural* concerns (i.e., the configuration or topology [MT00]) of a system. This requirement is also advocated in a study of modeling the structural aspects of architecture in UML by Garlan et al. [GK00].
- UML should be able to capture a variety of *stylistic* issues addressed both explicitly and implicitly by ADLs. These issues include a standard design vocabulary, recurring topologies, and, possibly, generic system behavior.
- UML should be able to model the different *behavioral* aspects of a system.
- UML should be able to support modeling of a wide range of component *interaction* paradigms (whether specific to or independent of a particular style). This requirement stems from one of the key contributions of software architecture research—the focus on component interactions (i.e., software *connectors*) as first-class system modeling concerns [Meh00, Sha01].
- Finally, a requirement derived from the ones above is that UML should be able to capture any *constraints* arising from a system's structure, behavior, interactions, and style(s).

However, UML built-in constructs are not suitable for describing architecture-level components because they assume both too much and too little. Components in UML are assumed to be concrete, executable artifacts that consume machine resources such as memory. In contrast, architectural components are conceptual artifacts that decompose the system's state and behavior. Although instances of architectural components in a given system may be implemented by concrete UML component instances, the architectural components are not themselves concrete. Furthermore, components in UML may have any number of interfaces and any internal structure, whereas architectural components must satisfy the rules or constraints imposed on them. For these reasons, we regard architectural components as a module concept. A component has module-like properties (i.e., package-like properties in the UML) in that it represents a namespace, has contents and provides services to other components. In this sense a component is more like a UML subsystem than a UML component.

We construct a generic architectural model and use refinement calculus of component and object system (rCOS) to formalize the related UML models. In UML the approach to identifying system requirements is based on use case diagrams representing the different ways an actor uses the system. Starting from the use case model of the system, we derive the "abstract" components (the conceptual components) modeling how a specific use case is organized. Analyzing the sequence of actions, beginning when an actor sends some form of message, we can model the sequences of interactions with interaction diagrams. The correctness and consistency of models can be checked according to the semantics and well-foundness conditions.

3.1. Structural Model

In general, structural model can be described by a class diagram and a (set of) state assertion. A class diagram shows a number of classes, their attributes, their methods and their associations. An association is undirected in a requirement model, but directed in a design model. The definition for a class diagram can be given below.

Class Diagram A class diagram is a tuple

$\mathcal{R} = < CN, Att, Ass, \Leftarrow, Op >$

where CN is a set of class names, Att assigns each class C in CN a set $\{T_1\ a_1, \ldots, T_n\ a_n\}$ of attributes, Ass is a subset of $CN \times AN \times CN$ such that each triple $< C, A, D >$ represents an association with a name A between class C and class D. Op is the operation of the class. In low-level design, it is the method of the class which is the mapping from C to a set of methods of the form $m(paras)\{c\}$ where $paras$ is a list of typed parameters, and $\Leftarrow \subseteq CN \times CN$ is the direct generalization relation between classes. We leave the specification of multiplicities of associations in the state assertion of a class model, though syntax could be given to them as well (see [LHLC03]).

Then class diagram can be formalized as a class declaration section in RCOS:

- For each class N in CN, if M is a direct super class of N, then

```
Class N extends M {
    T a;                //* for each attribute T a in Att(N)
    Method m1(paras1){c1}; //* for each m in Meth(N)
        ...
        mi(parasi){ci};
}
```

- For each undirected association $< C, A, D >$, we declare a class

```
    Class A{
C c; // the role C of A
D d; // the role D of A
    }
```

Such a class is also represented as a product of $C \times D$.

- For each directed association $< C, A, D >$, we declare A as an attribute in C, in addition to the primitive attributes of C. The type of A is the power set of D if the multiplicity of D in A is more than one, otherwise of type D only

```
    Class C extends M { //*M is the direct super Class of C;
        T a;  // for each T a in Att(C)
        ℙD A; // or D A depending on multiplicity
}
```

In general, a **class model** is a pair $CM = \langle \nabla, \Phi \rangle$ where ∇ is a class diagram and Φ is a state constraint on the classes and associations.

A state property $\wp$ of a class model can be reasoned about by showing that $\theta \wedge \Phi \rightarrow \wp$, meaning that $\wp$ can be proven from θ and Φ in the relational calculus, where θ is a given property. We denote by $CM \models \wp$ that CM satisfies $\wp$. It also allows us to define transformations between conceptual diagrams that preserve a state constraint.

3.2. Interactive Model

Interactive model can be described by sequence diagrams which consist of objects and messages describing how the objects communicate. An interaction occurs when one object interact with the others.

Message Assume a set with a partial order Ω. A **message** is a tuple
$Msg = \langle \underline{s: N}, action, \underline{t: M}, sord, rord \rangle$
Where

- $\underline{s: N}$ is an object s of class N called source of the message and can be denoted by *source*(*Msg*).
- $\underline{t: M}$ represents the target object t of the message and its type M, can be denoted by *target*(*Msg*).
- *action*, denoted by *Action*(*Msg*), is a guarded method call of the form $g \rightarrow act$, where g is a Boolean expression of attributes of *source*(*Msg*) and possibly public variables, and *act* is either a command without method calls (an internal action) or a method call *target*(*Msg*).*m*(*paras*).
- *sord* and *rord* are elements from Ω, denoted by *Sord*(*Msg*) and *Rord*(*Msg*) respectively, representing the orders of the message invocations and returns in the sequence diagram. We require that $sord > rord$.

A guarded command $g \rightarrow act$ is equal to false, i.e. magic, when the guard g is *false*. We require that if *Action*(*Msg*) is a guarded command without a method call then *source*(*Msg*) = *target*(*Msg*), i.e. interactions between objects can only be carried out via method invocation.

Sequence Diagram A sequence diagram is a tuple:
$SD = \langle \underline{s: S}, MSG \rangle$
where

- $\underline{s: S}$ is the initiating (often an actor) object that calls the message *Start*. *Start* is the starting message such that *target*(*Start*) = s: S. We say that message Msg_2 *directly follows* message Msg_1 if they are from the same source object and $Rord(Msg_1) < Sord(Msg_2)$, but there is not a message *Msg* in the diagram such that $Rord(Msg_1) < Sord(Msg) < Sord(Msg_2)$. We say that Msg_1 *directly invokes* Msg_2 if $target(Msg_1) = source(Msg_2)$, $Sord(Msg_1) < Sord(Msg_2)$ and $Rord(Msg_1) > Rord(Msg_2)$, but there is not a message *Msg* in the diagram such that $Sord(Msg_1) < Sord(Msg) < Sord(Msg_2)$.

- *MSG* is a set of messages that contains *Start*, *Sord*(*Start*) < *Sord*(*Msg*) for any other message in *MSG*, and for every message *Msg* other than *Start*, there is one and only one message Msg^- such that Msg^- directly invokes *Msg*.

Often, the target object in the starting message is a use case handler and the operation is a method (i.e. a system operation in [LHLC03]) of the handler.

Notice that our definition for a sequence diagram is a bit more general than that in UML and we allow internal actions of objects. This is necessary when we want to relate a model of design to some required use cases.

For simplicity, we do not deal with loops in a sequence diagram, by assuming the design ensures the termination of a loop, or reference to another sequence diagram proposed in UML2.0 [Obj03].

We formalize a sequence diagram in our rCOS as follows. For each object $\underline{o : N}$ and each message *Msg* such that *target*(*Msg*) = $\underline{o: N}$ and *Action*(*Msg*) is a guarded method $g \rightarrow o.m(paras)$, let *MS*(*Msg*) be the set of all sequences of messages $Sm = Msg_1, \ldots, Msg_k$ such that

- Msg_1 is directly invoked by *Msg*,
- Msg_{i+1} directly follows Msg_i,
- there is no message in the sequence diagram directly follows Msg_k.

Notice that there may be more than one sequence of messages starting from the same message.

Let $Act(Sm) = Action(Msg_1); \cdots ; Action(Msg_k)$

We can then define a method *m*(*paras*) in class *N*:

Class *N* :: *m*(*paras*){

$\sqcap_{Sm \in MS(Msg)} Act(Sm)$

}

The *semantics* of a *sequence diagram Sd* is defined to be the definitions of all the methods whose signatures appear in *Sd*.

Even though without loops, the above definition of sequence diagrams covers very complicated graphic representations which describe nested conditional choices and sequential composition. It is in practice not possible to draw such complicated diagrams. This indicates a limitation of a graphic notation. However, there are a number of ways to use simple diagrams to represent non-trivial designs:

1. Use a family of sequence diagrams, each representing one sequence of messages of a complicated sequence diagram, and then combines their semantics by using the non-deterministic choice operator.
2. Draw a diagram which only represents the starting message *m*(*paras*), the messages it directly invokes, and their following messages from the target of *m*. This is enough to define method *m* in the class of its target object.

3. Combine 1 and 2 to simplify construction of sequence diagrams even further and to make the method more effective.

However, it should be noted that UML only allows specification of the messages received (corresponding to the operations provided) by a class, but not messages sent by the class, *call actions* can be used in a state diagram associated with the class to invoke required operations in another class, but the call actions are not explicitly declared as elements of the invoking class. We see this as a major shortcoming of UML, and we solve the problem by defining a message $Msg = \langle \underline{s: N}, action, \underline{t: M}, sord, rord \rangle$ with the source of a message.

4. Model Construction and Refinement

Based on structural model and interactive model, we can define component model and connect model, and thus construct software architecture. We use component and connector as system construction elements, as Mary Shaw's model [GS94] is adopted by OMG as the architecture frame of UML 2.0. Software system is built on components and connectors and constrains on them. Component is described by interface and the core of implementation.

4.1. Component Model

We regard components as a module and defined as follows.

Component Component is a turple:

$$Component = \langle Intf, M, A, MImpl, Init \rangle$$

where

- $Intf$ is the set of all interfaces including internal interfaces and external interfaces,
- M is design class model,
- A is a set of fields whose types are all declared in M,
- $MImpl$ maps each operation declared in $Intf$ to a pair (α, Q), where Q is a command written in the above RCOS, and α is the alphabet obtained from A and the input and output parameters of the operations in $Intf$.

The set of interface $Intf$ can be described as: $Intf = \langle intf_1, intf_2, \ldots, intf_n \rangle$, and each interface $intf_i$ is a tuple

$$intf_i = \langle ID, Publ_i, Exte_i, Priv_i, Beha_i, Msgs_i, Cons_i, Nonf_i \rangle$$

ID is the identity of a component,

$Publ_i$ is a set of function that provided by the interface i to other components,

$Exte_i$ is a set of function that provided by other components to interface i,

$Priv_i$ is a set of private attribute of interface i,

$Beha_i$ is the description of the behavior of interface i,

$Msgs_i$ is a set of message of interface i,

$Cons_i$ is the constrain over interface i, including initial states, pre/post conditions of the component usually,

$Nonf_i$ is non-functional description of interface i, including the description of security and reliability of the component.

The implementation part comprises the design class model and interaction diagram of the component.

In the definition of component, interface gives out the formal description of a component and defines the general framework of a type of components. For convenience, *ID* is used to represent a set of elements of component *ID*. For example, *Publ(C)* denotes a set of *Publ* elements of each interface *intf* of component *C*.

Refinement Suppose A and B are two components, if A and B meet the following conditions, then B is a refinement of A, denoted as $B \sqsubseteq A$.

(1) $Dom(A) = Dom(B)$
(2) $Publ(A) \subseteq Publ(B)$
(3) $Exte(B) \subseteq Exte(A)$
(4) $Priv(B) \subseteq Priv(A)$
(5) $Beha(B) \Rightarrow Beha(A)$
(6) $Msgs(B) = Msgs(A)$
(7) $(Cons(B) = Cons(A))$ or $(Cons(B) \Rightarrow Cons(A))$
(8) $(Nonf(B) = Nonf(A))$ or $(Nonf(B) \Rightarrow Nonf(A))$

Definition of component and the refinement relation reflect the property of reusability and refinement ability of a component. Moreover, components also have the ability of interoperation. So we need to analysis the typical components interoperation.

Interoperation Suppose A and B are two components, if $\exists x \in Publ(A) \wedge \exists y \in Extn(B)$ such that $(x \Rightarrow y) \wedge (pre\text{-}cons(B))$. In that condition, component A invokes $Publ(B)$ of component B by sending a message 'invocation [TMAD96]', then an 'invocation' calculation is executed, denoted as $Inv(A, B)$ or $A \otimes B$.

For example, the mechanism of connection between components in CORBA is 'invocation'. Component A and B are independent when the mechanism of 'invocation' is used.

A and B are still components, they have the following properties:

(1) $Dom(A \otimes B) = Dom(A) \cup Dom(B)$
(2) $Publ(A \otimes B) \supseteq Publ(A) \cup Publ(B)$
(3) $Exte(A \otimes B) \subseteq Exte(A) \cup Exte(B)$
(4) $Priv(A \otimes B) \subseteq Priv(A) \cup Priv(B)$
(5) $Beha(A \otimes B) \Leftrightarrow Beha(A) \wedge Beha(B)$
(6) $Msgs(A \otimes B) = Msgs(A) \cup Msgs(B)$
(7) $Cons(A \otimes B) \Leftrightarrow Cons(A) \wedge Cons(B)$
(8) $Nonf(A \otimes B) \Leftrightarrow Nonf(A) \wedge Nonf(B)$

Equivalence Suppose A and B are two components, if A and B meet the following conditions, then A is equal to B, denoted as $A=B$.

(1) $Dom(A) = Dom(B)$
(2) $Publ(A) = Publ(B)$
(3) $Exte(A) = Exte(B)$
(4) $Priv(A) = Priv(B)$
(5) $Beha(A) \Leftrightarrow Beha(B)$
(6) $Msgs(A) = Msgs(B)$
(7) $Cons(A) \Leftrightarrow Cons(B)$
(8) $Nonf(A) = Nonf(B)$

4.2. Connector Model

Connector is an element of architecture, it connects components by modeling the rules of interaction between components. Not like component, connector need not compile. Connector usually includes Client/Server protocols, pipe, procedure call etc..

Nenad Medvidovic indicates that a connector has six characters. They are interface, type, semantics, constrains, evolvement and nonfunctional property [Med97]. The six characters usually need to be cut partly out according to the context.

To date, the representative points of view to connector are as follows:

- Allen R. thought connector type can be defined by a set of roles and the specification of glue. Role describes local behavior of expect interoperate components. The specification of glue describes cooperation of the role of clients and server [OT98].
- Marry Shaw took connector as cooperation relation between components. It act as an mediator of components, and can be atomic or compositional [SG96].
- J. L. Fiadeiro etc. thought that connection can be defined as a tuple with channel, glue, connect role and category [FL97].
- Nenad Medvidovic took connector as a architectural element, which is a model of interoperation of components, as well as the rules to control the interoperation [Med97].
- Hirsch etc. thought connector is an important element of architecture. It can be used to compose components [HDU99].
- Y.Yu etc. took connector as conceptual unit of describing cooperation of components [YKK99].
- D.Balek etc. thought connector is an element of architecture. It reflects some characters of interaction of components in the system [BP00].
- Nikunj R.Mehta thought that connector describes the interaction of components and support the communication, harmonize and transformation [Meh00].

Based on the research result about and our experience, we describe connector in the aspect of behavior, role, message, constrain and nonfunctional property.

Connector Connector is a tuple

$Connector = <ID, Role, Beha, Msgs, Cons, Nfun>$

Where:

- *ID* is identification of connector;
- *Role* is a set of interaction points that connector and component interact in. Each element role in set *Role* is described as *role*= <*Id, Action, Event, Lconstrains*>, where, *Id* is the identity of role; *Action* is a set of activities of role, each action is the interconnection of events; *Event* is a set of events produced by *Role*; *Lconstrains* is a set of constrains of *Role*. We discuss *Role* separately, so that to emphasize the polymorphism of connector, or one connector can connect with a couple of components.
- *Beha* is semantic description of the behave of connector;
- *Msgs* is a set of message produced by the events of each role in the set *Role*;
- *Cons* is a set of constrains of a connector, including initial state and pre/post conditions;
- *Nfun* is non-function description of connector, including the security and reliability, etc..

Connector plays an important part in improve the adaptability of software architecture [BP00]. As we said above, the connection need to be changed when functional or structural requirement is changed. Connector divides functional requirement and connectional requirement, so it insulates the change of environment and component. It can also change connection relationship by adjusting component, to make connector modification and architecture dynamic configuration easier, so as to improve the adaptability of software architecture.

4.3. System Framework

A software system, even if a small one, is very complicate, so it is impossible for us to put all of the construction elements in one layer and keep the correctness of the system. So we divide the system into different layers and construct each layer from its lower one. When one layer is correct with respect to the hypothesis, the higher layers are correct, if the transition is correct in that context. In that manner, the problems are separated, so that we can concentrate on a couple of problems in certain design phase.

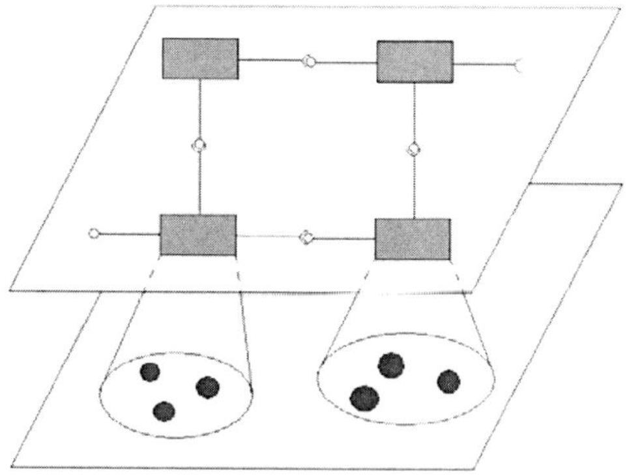

Figure 4.1. Layered generic software construction framework.

Components are integration of objects, whereas objects are instance of class. If the *require* interface of one component is match with the *provide* interface of another one, then the two components can be connected. Components can be organized in some software architecture styles, as shown in Figure 4-1.

Software architecture includes the description of all kinds of elements (component and connector), interaction between elements and paradigm of construction [GK00]. In that direction, we define architecture as elements and related rules.

Software architecture Software architecture is a tuple:

$SA = \langle Unit, \Pi \rangle$

- *Unit* denotes the set of elements, which includes component and connector.
- denotes the set of elements operation, including elements composition constrains and paradigm.

Where, component and connector are architecture; the composition of components and connector is also an architecture.

An architecture has the following properties, according to the definition of software architecture,

- envelopment: When a component composes with a component, a component composes with an architecture or an architecture composes with an architecture, the result is also an architecture.
- hierarchy: an architecture can built from components, and large architecture can build from smaller one.
- expansibility: an qualified new component can join an architecture by connection.

5. Modeling Object Oriented Development Process

The software development process is usually start from user requirement analyze and follows the requirement model, then design model, and end with executable codes. For developing a large scale software system, project manager often divide the whole system into several interconnected parts, or components, then compose the component together in some kind of topology or software architecture. The components in software architecture model are high level components. They are integration of concrete, executable components or objects in UML. The objects are instance of class.

5.1. Requirement

Architecture model in the phase is a sketch plan, without details. In UML, requirements are captured and described by a conceptual class model and some use cases.

In fact, requirement analysis is not usually concerned about what an object does or how it behaves. Therefore, a class that models a domain concept does not have methods, and the associations among conceptual classes are undirected. A class model *CM* is called a conceptual class model if all the classes do not have any method and all the associations are undirected.

The functional requirements are described by use cases and each use-case is represented by a sequence diagram *Sd*, called a *system sequence diagram*, which satisfies the following conditions:

- there exists one and only one object $\underline{h : UH}$, called the *use-case handler*, such that for each message *Msg* if *source*(*Msg*) = $\underline{h : UH}$, then *target*(*Msg*) = $\underline{h : UH}$ and *Action*(*Msg*) is method call,
- for any object $\underline{o : M}$ which differs from $\underline{h : UH}$, there does not exist *Msg* in *Sd* such that *target*(*Msg*) = $\underline{o : M}$

The first condition means that the methods of a use-case handler are to realize the system operations of the use case that are to be called by actors. In fact, at the highest level of specification of the requirements, we only need to specify the guarded commands in terms of framed designs by their pre- and post-conditions. The second condition indicates that we are only interested in effect of system operations on the system itself, i.e. what state changes they make, not their effect on the environment.

A model of requirements *RM* = <*CM, SSD*>, where *CM* is a conceptual class model and *SSD* is a family of *system sequence diagrams*, one for each use case. The formalization of a conceptual class model *CM* is simple and given in Section 4. However, to obtain a full specification of a model of requirements we need that the class declaration section of *CM* includes for each use case a use-case handler class declaration of:

Class *UH*{
Method $op_1(paras_1)\{c_1\}$;
...
$op_n(paras_n)\{c_n\}$;
}

where $op_i(paras_i)\{c_i\}$, $i= 1, \ldots, n$, are all the methods of the messages from actors to *UH h*, and c_i is the command directly invoked by message op_i. Let us denote such a class declaration as *Spec*(*UH*) for a use case. We also assume that *UH* can have access to all the classes of the conceptual class diagram.

5.2. Design

In design phase, project manager must give a system architecture diagram in detail. In that diagram, modules and the interaction between the modules should be displayed. The function of every component and the structure of each connector, as well as the signature of the ports should be clearly represented. The system architecture diagram of design is a refinement of that of the requirement.

We can choose the extended UML design class model *DC* to represent the static property of the system architecture diagram and a family of sequence diagrams *SD* to represent the dynamic property. Therefore, the model of design *DM* can be constructed from *DC* and *SD*: *DM* = <*DC*, *SD*>. Classes in this class model now have methods and a method of a class may call methods of other classes. The semantics of <*DC, SD*> is defined to be the declaration section obtained from the formalization of *DC* by defining the methods method *DC*(*N*) for each class *N* in *DC* with all the method definitions for *N* in the formalization of *SD*, i.e.

$$\text{method}_{DC}(N) =_{\text{df}} \{m(paras)\{c\} | \textbf{Class } N :: m(paras)\{c\} \text{ is defined in } SD\}$$

In next section, we use an example to show the process.

5.3. Consistency Checking

A requirement model *RM* = <*CM, SSD*> is consistent, i.e. the class model and the use-case model are consistent, if

- the following class declaration section is well defined in RCOS:

$$CM; Spec(UH_1); \ldots ; Spec(UH_k)$$

where all of the $Spec(UH_i)$ are the use-case handler classes for all the sequence diagrams in *SSD*, and

- each c_i in a method body is well-defined, i.e., all types and variables used in the command are declared in *CM* and expressions and commands are built following the syntax rules too, and more generally,
- the framed design for each c_i should not equal to *chaos*.

Notice that to fix any inconsistency is to refine the declaration section [HLL02]. Checking inconsistency could be carried out to provide information about the cause of the inconsistency rather than deciding whether a command is chaos or not. In fact, the static consistency of the conceptual model and a family of system sequence diagrams can be checked just as if to compile the class declaration section that formalizes them.

A design model <*DC, SD*> is *consistent* if its formalization is a well-defined class declaration section, no methods of the class will violate the state constraint of *CM*, and all commands and expressions are well formed. Therefore, the treatment of the static consistency can be done in a similar way that a compiler compiles the class declaration section. In particular, if *CD* and *SD* are consistent, we must have

- If *Action* is $g \rightarrow o.m$ in a message $Msg = < \underline{s : N}, Action, \underline{t : M}, sord, rord >$ in *SD*, then $o : M$ is declared as an attribute of the class *N* of source object $s : N$.
- If *Action*(*Msg*) is $g \rightarrow o.m$ and *m* is a method name then *m* is a defined method in the class of *target*(*Msg*), and the body of this method in the class model agrees with the definition given in the formalization of *Msg* at the end of Section 4, i.e. the former refines the later.
- The corresponding class declaration section obtained from *CD* is well-defined.
- No methods in the class model violates the state constraint of the model.

Therefore, the consistency covers both static and semantic consistency, and the static consistency can be checked in a way like compiling the formalization of the model of the design. Further work will be useful to give practical classifications of inconsistencies and to develop tools for checking these inconsistencies.

The correctness of the design model <*DC, SD*> w.r.t a model <*CM, SSD*> of requirements is defined by the refinement relation [HLL02]

$$<CM, SSD> \sqsubseteq <DC, SD>$$

Also refinement between designs is defined and reasoned about in this way. The refinement calculus in [HLL02] supports class declaration refinement, i.e. structural refinement and refactoring [Fow99]. In the refinement calculus, each of the following transformations of a declaration section is a refinement.

6. Case Study

Now consider a simple store management system. There are various kinds of products in the store and each kind of product has some items. When customers order some kind of products, the store will deliver those products to the customers.

We can divide the system into three parts, or high level components, namely *Customer*, *Store* and *Order*, as shown in figure 6-1. The architecture style of the system is pipeline.

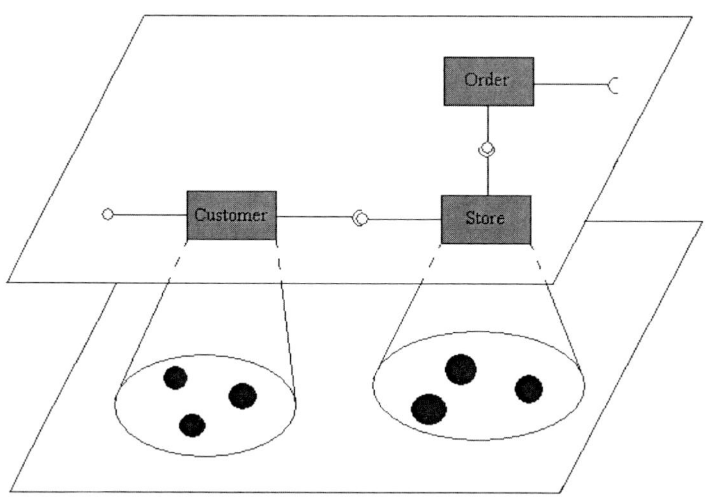

Figure 6.1. A simple store management system.

Then developers can design each component separately and project manager or team leader compose the components together after the individual components are done. To obtain a component, developer designs various kinds of classes first and then instantiate the classes. We use the component store to illustrate the process.

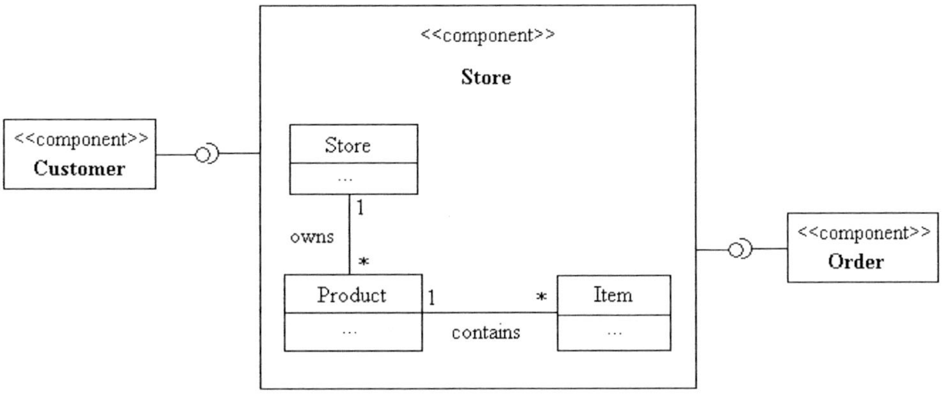

Figure 6.2. The components of the system.

Conceptual model We consider the component *Store*, use case *RecordItem* is taken into account, which records items of some products to the store, as shown in Figure 6-3.

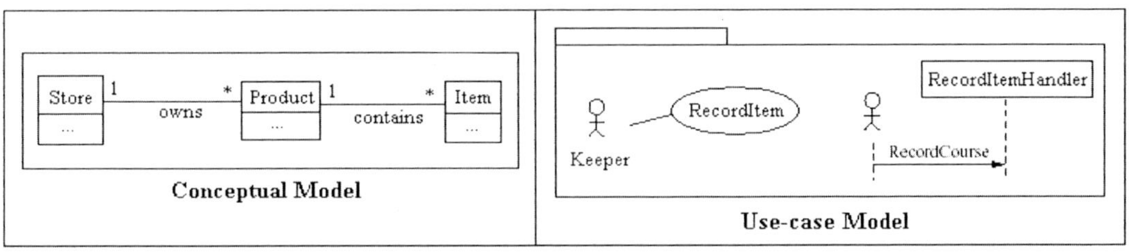

Figure 6.3. Rquirement model.

Class *Store*{ *String name, String address, String id*};
Class *Product*{ *String name, String id*};
Class *Item*{ *String name, String id*};
Class *Owns*{ *Store s, Product p*};// **Association Classes**
Class *Contains*{ *Product p, Item i*};// **Association Classes**

We assume the system initial state is: $\mathbb{P}$*Store Sto*= *{s}*; $\mathbb{P}$*Product Pro* = ∅, $\mathbb{P}$*Item It* = ∅, $\mathbb{P}$*Owns Ow* = ∅, and $\mathbb{P}$*Contains Co* = ∅.

Use case model An identification of the use case is important for the creation of the conceptual model. However, the formal specification of the use cases depends on the specification of the conceptual model. We provide a *canonical form* of a use case specification by introducing a class of use-case handler, which encapsulates the conceptual model. Considering the use case *RecordItem* that adds a new item of an *existing* product to the library. We specify this use case by introducing a class *RecordItemHandler*:

CM; *// import the conceptual model*
Class *RecordItemHandler* {
  Method *RecordItem*(**val**(*String iid, String pid*)){**var** *Item i*

$\exists p \in Pro \bullet p.id = pid \vdash$
i : = **New** *Item*(*iid*);
It : = *It*$\cup$$\{i\}$; *Co* : = *Co*$\cup$$\{<p, i>\}$; **end** *i, p*}};

Use Case *RecordItem* :: {
var *RecordItemHandler h, String iid, String pid*;
h = **New** *RecordItemHandler( )*;
read (*iid, pid*) ;
h.RecordC (*iid, pid*); **end** *h, iid, pid}*;

The **main** method is then specified as:
main( ){**var** *Bool stop*, *Services s*, *stop* : = *false;*
while $\neg$*stop* **do** {*read*(*s*);
if {(*s* = "*RecordItem*") $\rightarrow$ *RecordItem*;} **fi**;
read(*stop*)}; **end** *stop*, *s*}

where the type *Services* denotes the services that the store management system will provide. Note that a UML conceptual model also determines some state invariants, such as there is only one *Store* instance. The use cases need to be checked to preserve these invariants [LLHL04].

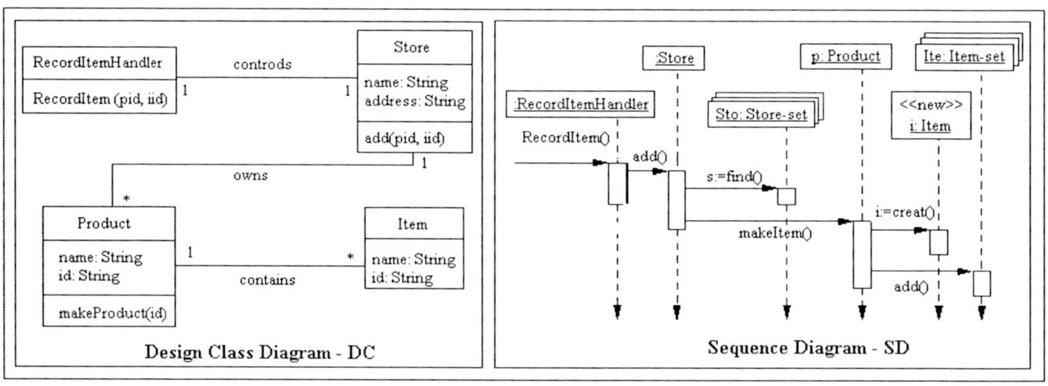

Figure 6.4. Design Model.

Design model Assume for each type $\mathbb{P}C$, methods *add*( ) , *delete*( ), and *find*( ) are declared for adding, deleting and finding an object of *C* in a set. The object sequence diagram and its corresponding design class diagram in Figure 6-4 are specified by the following program. Assume classes *Pro* and *It* have declared these three methods. The design model $\mathbf{DM_1}$ is constructed as:

Class *Store*{*String name, String address;*
$\mathbb{P}$*Product Pro; // newly added*
Method *add*(**val** (*String cid, String pid*)) {
var *Product p;*
p = *Pro.find(pid); p. makeItem(iid);* **end** *p*}}

Class *Publication { String id, String title, String manufacture, Item-Set It;*
Method *makeItem (***val** *String id) {*
var *Item i; i* : = **New** *Item(id); It* : = *It.add(i)* ; **end** *i}}*
Class *Item {String id }*
Class *RecordItemHandler { Product-Set Pro, Item-Set It, Contain-Set Co;*
Method *RecordItem*(**val** (*String iid, String pid*)){

Lib . add (*iid, pid*) } }

Let *StringL* be the type of the list of strings of the attributes of Store. In design phase, **main**( ) program is almost the same as that in the conceptual model.

$$StringL\ storeattr \equiv \{String\ name \times String\ address\}$$

main( ){**var** *Bool stop* = *false, Services s, StringL storeattr, RecordItemHandler h,Univ univ*;
h := *RecordItemHandler* **New**(); *store* := *Store* **New**(*storeattr*);
while ¬*stop* **do** {*read*(*s*); **if** {(*s* = "*RecordItem*") → *RecordItem*} **fi**;

read(*stop*)}; **end** *stop, s, rch}*

The other components can be handled in the same way. We then can construct the system.

7. Conclusion & Discussion

7.1. Conclusion

This work is towards a formal foundation for component and object systems development. Specifications are better than programming language in some way because they can express the essentials ignoring irrelevances. We integrate our models with UML to describe component-based development process. A generic architecture model and formal UML class model, as well as sequence diagram, are defined with a formal OO notation rCOS described in [HLL02, HLL04]. We extend the UML modeling ability in software architecture description and construct unified UML models of different phases, from requirement analysis to design. The consistency between model is guaranteed by constrains and well-formedness conditions. This formalization is a step towards using UML as a programming language [Fow03]. To this end, the semantics is the base for compiling or interpreting UML diagrams into programs. This approach is useful not only in the process of component development, but also in evaluating the semantics of the integrated system.

The stepwise refinement of UML models within the development process supports the maintenance of consistency during model transformation and evolution. This has taken the initiative of developing UML as a formal modeling language an essential step forward. It also provides fundamental support to UML based model driven development.UML represents maturation in the development of object-oriented design notations. It offers a diverse collection of notations for capturing many aspects of the software development lifecycle, including not only traditional design concerns (such as functional decomposition), but also aspects of requirements analysis (particularly domain modeling), implementation, and testing (particularly scenario-based functional testing). Our paper has described approaches to overcoming two major weaknesses of UML, its lack of adequate formal semantics and support for modeling software architectural concerns. Current semantics of UML are quite loose. It needs to be made precise in order to provide more useful semantic information of the applications.

7.2. Discussion

To date, the specifications of components used in practices are still limited primarily to syntactic specifications, such as the specification of logical components (e.g. business components, process components) and physical components (e.g. EJB components, CORBA components, COM+ and .NET components, WSDL components, etc.). The information that can be obtained from a component specification is limited to what operations the component provides and the number and types of their parameters. There is no information about the effect of invoking the operations. So these kinds of specification can only be used to check the type of the code. Finding appropriate formal approaches for specifying the semantics of components, refinement strategies and the architectures for composing them is critical.

In this paper, we take some informal views of [BPP99, HC01] that a component both provides services to and requires services from other components. However our models are built on services and there is a standard calculus for reason about and refine at different levels of abstraction. It will facilitate model checking and verification which is included in our future work.

There are several ongoing initiatives for making UML precise, e.g., the ones by the OMG, with a RFP in process called "Action semantics for UML" that tries to move UML beyond first order (declarative) semantics into second order (imperative) semantics. The work of the precise UML consortium (see *www.puml.org*) use a transformational approach to transform certain UML models into existing formalisms such as Z, VDM, B, CSP, etc. Our work focuses on modeling a system in multiple views and keep consistency among the views. Further more our formal language provides built-in facilities to naturally capture the object-oriented features of UML, rather than using an existing formalism which was not designed for object-oriented systems to derive the definitions of classes, objects, inheritance, etc.

A model expressed in an ADL essentially provides a single view of an architecture, which is typically formal. In contrast, the views constructed in multiple-view approaches are often informal or semiformal. Two representative examples of work with multiple views are provided by Kruchten [Kru95] and Soni et al. [Son95]. Kruchten [Kru95] presented the 4+1 view model of software architectures. The four main views are the *conceptual*, *static*, *dynamic*, and *physical* views. Together, these views capture a software system's architecture. Kruchten [Kru95] provides system usage scenarios, similar to UML's use cases, as the fifth view to relate the other four. Similarly, Soni et al. [Son95] identified four structural categories of software architectures—*conceptual*, *module interconnection*, *execution*, and *code*. The module interconnection view is a refinement of the conceptual view, it provides a functional and layered decomposition of the system. Our model is also multiple-view model, we construct it in dynamic and static views.

Garlan and Kompanek [Gar00] also conducted a study whose goal was to enumerate and evaluate different options an architect has in selecting UML modeling constructs to represent architectural structure (i.e., components, connectors, systems, and styles). Unlike our choice of UML classes to represent architectural elements, Garlan and Kompanek [Gar00] investigated five possibilities: UML classes as architectural types and objects as their instances; UML stereotypes as types and classes as instances; UML classes as both types and instances; UML components; and UML subsystems (stereotyped UML packages). Their study shows that, while each of the five choices has its merits, none of them is an ideal fit for the needs of software architectures in terms of semantic match, understandability, or completeness.

The creators of UML have developed a process model, the Unified Software Process, for applying UML in object-oriented analysis and design [JBR99, Kru00]. The Unified Software Process is oriented toward early development of an architecture from use cases. It is worth noting that the

Unified Software Process is supported by a UML profile comprising a number of UML stereotypes and tagged values—much like the approach described in this paper—but also requires additional graphical notation beyond what UML provides. In the Unified Software Process, the *architecture description* of a system is a cross-section of the "architecturally significant" elements of the models in the *architecture baseline*. The architecture baseline comprises early versions of the use-case model, analysis model, and design model developed as part of the *elaboration phase* [JBR99]. The architecture description is developed iteratively and is considered to be fundamentally important for analyzing and understanding the structure, behavior, performance, and other global characteristics of a software system under construction. Hence, the architecture description achieves the level of importance advocated by the software architecture research community. However, the fact that the Unified Software Process considers the architecture to be an implicit attribute of existing UML models rather than an explicit model in its own right.

7.3. Future Work

We intend to expend the work in several directions, including providing tool support for using UML precisely in modeling system architecture, refinement and maintaining trace ability. We also intend to draw upon our experience to date to suggest specific extensions needed in the UML meta model to better support object oriented development.

References

[AG97] Allen, R. and Garlan, D. A Formal basis for architectural connection. *ACM Trans. Softw. Eng. Methodol.* **6**, 3 (July), 213–249, 1997.

[BP00] Balek D, Plasi F. A *Hierarchical Model of Software Connectors.* Prague Tech. Report No. 2000/2, Dept. of SW Engineering, Charles University, 2000

[BPP99] Back R J R, Petre L, and Paltor I P. *Formalizing UML use cases in the refinement calculus.* Technical Report 279, Turku Centre for Computer Science, Turku, Finland, May 1999.

[FL97] Fiadeiro J L. Lopes A. Semantics of Architectural Connectors. In *Proc. of TAPSOFT'97, LNCS* **1214**, Springer-Verlag, 1997: 505-519

[Gar00] Garlan, D. and Kompanek, A. Reconciling the needs of architectural description with objectmodeling notations. In *Proceedings of the Third International Conference on the Unified Modeling Language* (UML 2000, York, UK, October), Springer-Verlag, Berlin, Germany, 2000.

[GBS04] Holger Giese, Sven Burmester, Wilhelm Schäfer, and Oliver Oberschelp, 'Modular Design and Verification of Component-Based Mechatronic Systems with Online-Reconfiguration', in *Proc. of 12th ACM SIGSOFT Foundations of Software Engineering* 2004 (FSE 2004), Newport Beach, USA, pp. 179--188, ACM Press, November 2004.

[GK00] D. Garlan and A. Kompanek, 2000, Reconciling the needs of architectural description with object modeling notations. In *Proceedings of the Third International Conference on the Unified Modeling Language*, Springer-Verlag, Berlin, Germany.

[GS94] Garlan, D., Shaw, M. *An introduction to software architecture.* Technique Report, CMU/SEI-94-TR-21, Carnegie Mellon University, 1994

[HC01] Heineman G T and Councill W T, *Component-Based Software Engineering*, Putting the Pieces Together. Addison-Wesley, 2001.

[HDU99] Hirsch, Dan, Uchitel, et al. Towards a Periodic Table of Connectors. *Proc. of Coordination'99*, Amsterdam, Holanda. Lecture Notes in Computer Science, 1999

[HLL02] J. He, Z. Liu, and X. Li. Towards a refinement calculus for object-oriented systems (invited talk). In *Proc. ICCI02,* Alberta, Canada. IEEE Computer Society, 2002.

[HLL05] He J, Li X and Liu Z, Component-Based Software Engineering. In Dang Hung, Martin Wirsing, *Proc. of International Colloquium on Theoretical Aspects of Computer* (ICTAC 2005), Lecture Notes in Computer Science 3722, 2005, 70—95

[JBR99] Jacobson, I., Booch, G., and Rumbaugh, J. *The Unified Software Development Process.* Addison-Wesley, Reading, MA. 1999.

[Kru95] Kruchten, P. B. The 4+1 view model of architecture. *IEEE Software*, **12**, 6 (Nov.), 42–50. 1995.

[Kru00] P. Kruchten, 2000, *The Rational Unified Process – An Introduction.* Addison-Wesley

[LHL05] Liu Z, He J and Li X, rCOS: refinement of component and object systems, Proc. 3rd International Symposium on Formal Methods for Components and Objects, *Lecture Notes in Computer Science* **3657**, Springer, 2005, 183-221

[LHLC03]Z. Liu, J. He, X. Li, and Y. Chen. A relational model for formal object-oriented requirement analysis in UML. In Proc. ICFEM03, *Lecture Notes in Computer Science* **2885**. Springer, 2003.

[LHLL04]Zhiming Liu, Jifeng He, Jing Liu and Xiaoshan Li, Unifing Views of UML, *Electronic Notes in Computer Science.* 2004

[LLHL04]Jing Liu, Zhiming Liu, Jifeng He and Xiaoshan Li , Linking UML Models of Design and Requirement, *Proc. Australian Software Engineering Conference,* Melboune, Australia, pp.329-338, IEEE Computer Society Press. 2004

[LLLH04] Jing Liu, Zhiming Liu, Xiaoshan Li and Jifeng He, Formal Support to Incremental Development, *Proc. of the 14th Information Resources Management Association International Conference*, New Orleans, USA, IGP Press. 2004

[LMG02] Jing Liu, Huaikou Miao and Xiaolei Gao, A Specification-Based Software Construction Framework for Reuse, *Lecture Notes in Computer Science*, *LNCS* **2495**, Springer. 2002

[LV95] Luckham, D. C. and Vera, J. An event-based architecture definition language. *IEEE Trans. Softw. Eng.* **21**, 9 (Sept.), 717–734, 1995.

[Med97] Medvidovic N. A Classification and Comparison Framework for Software Architecture Description Languages. Technical Report UCIICS-9702, Department of Information and Computer Science, University of California, Irvine, 1997

[Meh00] Mehta N R, Towards a Taxonomy of Software Connectors. Limerick, Ireland: In *Proceedings of the 22th International Conference on Software Engineering*(ICSE 2000), 2000

[MRR02] N. Medvidovic, D. S. Rosenblum, D. F. Redmiles and J.E. Robbins, Modeling Software Architectures in the Unified Modeling Language, *ACM Transactions on Software Engineering and Methodology*, Vol. 11, January 2002, pages 2-57.

[MT00] N. Medvidovic, and R. N. Tayloy, A Classification and Comparison Framework for Software Architecture Description Language. *IEEE Trans. On Software Engineering* **26**, 1(Jan.), 70-93, 2000.

[Obj03] Object Management Group. Unified Modeling Language Specification, ver 2.0. Object Management Group, Inc., Needham Ma, http://www.omg/technology/documents/, 2003.

[OMG02] Object Management Group, Inc. MOF 2.0 Query/Views/Transformations RFP. Document ad/02-04-10, April 2002.

[OMG04] Object Management Group, Inc. Model Driven Architecture. http://www.omg.org/mda/, August 2004.

[OT98] Oreizy P. Taylor R N. On the Role of Software Architectures in Runtime System Recofuguration. Maryland: ICCDS 4, 1998

[PW92] Perry, D. E. and Wolf, A. L. 1992. Foundations for the study of software architectures. ACM SIGSOFT *Softw. Eng. Notes* **17**, 4 (Oct.), 40–52.

[Rat04] Rational, Reusable Asset Specification – Architectural Description Standard: [Technique Report]. From http://www.Rational.com/publications

[SG96] Shaw, M. And Garlan, D., Software architecture: perspectives on an emerging discipline. Prentice Hall, 1996.

[Sha01] Shaw M. The coming-of-age of software architecture research. In: *Proceedings of the 23rd International Conference on Software Engineeting*, IEEE Computer Society, 2001.

[SNH95] Soni, D., Nord, R., and Hofmeister, C. Software architecture in industrial applications. In *Proceedings of the 17th International Conference on Software Engineering* (ICSE 17, Seattle,WA, Apr.). ACM Press, New York, NY, 1995.

[Tay96] Taylor, R. N., Medvidovic, N., Anderson, K. M., Whitehead, JR., E. J., Robbins, J. E., Nies, K. A., Oreizy, P., and Dubrow, D. L. A component- and message-based architectural style for GUI software. *IEEE Trans. Softw. Eng.* **22**, 6 (June), 390–406. 1996.

[TMAD96] Taylor R. N., Medvidovic N., Anderson K. M., Dubrow D. L., A component and message-based architectural style for GUI software, *IEEE Trans Software Engineeting*, 1996

[Ves93] Vestal, S. *A cursory overview and comparison of four architecture description language*. Honeywell Technology Center Technical Report, 1993, http://www-ast.tds-gn.lmco.com/arch/four-adl.ps

[YKK99] Yu Y, Kim S, Kin D., *Connector Modeling Method for Component Extraction*. Takamatsu, Japan: Sixth Asia Pacific Software Engineering Conference, 1999

In: New Topics in Theoretical Computer Science
Editors: Oleg N. Terikhovsky *et al.*, pp. 119-141
ISBN 978-1-60456-100-5

Chapter 4

THE MAXIMUM AGREEMENT OF TWO NESTED PHYLOGENETIC NETWORKS*

Jesper Jansson[1,2†] ***and Wing-Kin Sung***[2,3‡]
[1]INRIA Lille - Nord Europe, Equipe SEQUOIA, Villeneuve d'Ascq, France
[2]School of Computing, National University of Singapore, Singapore
[3]Genome Institute of Singapore, Genome, Singapore

Abstract

Given a set $\mathcal{N}$ of phylogenetic networks, the maximum agreement phylogenetic subnetwork problem (MASN) asks for a subnetwork embedded in every $N_i \in \mathcal{N}$ with as many leaves as possible. MASN can be used to identify shared branching structure among phylogenetic networks or to measure their similarity. In this chapter, we prove that the general case of MASN is NP-hard already for two phylogenetic networks (in fact, even if one of the two input networks is a binary tree), but that the problem can be solved efficiently if each of the two input phylogenetic networks exhibits a nested structure. For this purpose, we introduce the concept of a nested phylogenetic network and study some of its underlying fundamental combinatorial properties. We first show that the total number of nodes $|V(N)|$ in any nested phylogenetic network N with n leaves and nesting depth d is $O(n(d+1))$. We then describe a simple algorithm for testing if a given phylogenetic network is nested, and if so, determining its nesting depth in $O(|V(N)| \cdot (d+1))$ time. Next, we present a polynomial-time algorithm for MASN for two nested phylogenetic networks N_1, N_2. Its running time is $O(|V(N_1)| \cdot |V(N_2)| \cdot (d_1+1) \cdot (d_2+1))$, where d_1 and d_2 denote the nesting depths of N_1 and N_2, respectively. In contrast, the previously fastest algorithm for this problem runs in $O(|V(N_1)| \cdot |V(N_2)| \cdot 2^{f_1+f_2})$ time, where $f_1 \geq d_1$ and $f_2 \geq d_2$. Finally, we prove that if the nodes are allowed to have outdegree greater than 2 then the problem becomes NP-hard even if restricted to two phylogenetic networks with nesting depth 1.

---

*A preliminary version of this chapter has appeared in *Proceedings of the 15* th*Annual International Symposium on Algorithms and Computation* (ISAAC 2004), volume 3341 of *Lecture Notes in Computer Science*, pages 581–593, Springer-Verlag, 2004.

†E-mail address: Jesper.Jansson@lifl.fr

‡E-mail address: ksung@comp.nus.edu.sg

1. Introduction

Phylogenetic trees are commonly used to describe evolutionary relationships among a set of objects (e.g., biological species, proteins, nucleic acids, viruses, or languages) believed to have been produced by an evolutionary process, and can help scientists to understand the mechanisms of evolution as well as to classify the objects being studied and to organize information [2, 20, 25, 26]. However, evolutionary events such as horizontal gene transfer or hybrid speciation (often referred to as *recombination events*) which suggest convergence between objects cannot be adequately represented in a single tree structure [12, 13, 21, 22, 23, 24, 28]. Phylogenetic *networks* solve this shortcoming by allowing internal nodes to have more than one parent, thereby making it easier for scientists to describe more complex evolutionary relationships. Phylogenetic networks can also be used to visualize several conflicting phylogenetic trees at the same time in order to represent ambiguity [4, 15, 16].

Various methods for constructing and comparing phylogenetic networks have been proposed recently [4, 6, 12, 16, 17, 21, 22, 23, 24, 28]. Phylogenetic network *comparison* has many uses; one application described in [22] is to assess the topological accuracy of different phylogenetic network construction methods [1]. Another application for phylogenetic network comparison is to identify a subnetwork with as many leaves as possible which is contained in all of the networks in a given set (obtained, for example, by employing different phylogenetic network construction methods or by using the same method on alternative data sets) to determine which ancestral relationships are present in all networks. Moreover, the size of such a subnetwork provides a measure of how similar the networks in a given set are. This problem was formalized as a computational problem called *the maximum agreement phylogenetic subnetwork problem* (MASN) and initially studied in [6].

The general case of MASN is NP-hard for three or more phylogenetic networks [6]. Actually, it is NP-hard even for just *two* networks, as we shall prove in Section 4.1.. On the other hand, in the special case of no recombination events at all, MASN for two networks (i.e., rooted, leaf-labeled binary trees) can be solved very efficiently [2]. Fortunately, in nature, recombination events usually do not occur in an unrestricted manner [12, 28]. It is therefore important to establish what structural restrictions on the input networks make the problem efficiently solvable. In this chapter, we investigate the computational complexity of MASN for two phylogenetic networks whose merge paths are *nested*, which is a natural generalization of rooted, leaf-labeled, binary trees and so called galled-trees previously studied in [12, 17, 23, 28] (see below for definitions), and prove that this case can be solved by a polynomial-time algorithm. The decomposition technique for nested phylogenetic networks that we develop here may also be applicable to other computational and combinatorial problems related to phylogenetic network construction and comparison.

[1]To evaluate a construction method $\mathcal{M}$, the following steps are performed a number of times. First, a phylogenetic network N is randomly generated and a sequence is evolved down the edges of N according to some chosen model of evolution, then a phylogenetic network N' for the resulting set of sequences is reconstructed using $\mathcal{M}$, and finally the similarity between N' and N is measured.

[2]See the comments about *the maximum agreement subtree problem* (MAST) in Section 1.3..

1.1. Problem Definition

A *phylogenetic network* is a connected, rooted, simple, directed acyclic graph in which: (1) each node has outdegree at most 2; (2) each node has indegree 1 or 2, except the root node which has indegree 0; (3) no node has both indegree 1 and outdegree 1; and (4) all nodes with outdegree 0 are labeled by elements from a finite set L in such a way that no two nodes are assigned the same label. From here on, nodes of outdegree 0 are referred to as *leaves* and identified with their corresponding elements in L. We denote the set of all nodes and the set of leaves in a phylogenetic network N by $V(N)$ and $\Lambda(N)$, respectively.

Given a phylogenetic network N and a set L', *the topological restriction* of N to L', denoted by $N \mid L'$, is defined as the phylogenetic network obtained by first deleting all nodes which are not on any directed path from the root to a leaf in L' along with their incident edges, and then, for every node with outdegree 1 and indegree less than 2, contracting its outgoing edge (any resulting set of multiple edges between two nodes is replaced by a single edge).

Given a set $\mathcal{N} = \{N_1, N_2, \ldots, N_k\}$ of phylogenetic networks, an *agreement subnetwork of* $\mathcal{N}$ is a phylogenetic network A such that $\Lambda(A) \subseteq \bigcap_{N_i \in \mathcal{N}} \Lambda(N_i)$ and for every $N_i \in \mathcal{N}$, it holds that A is isomorphic to a graph obtained from $N_i \mid \Lambda(A)$ by deleting zero or more edges and contracting each outgoing edge from a node with resulting outde-

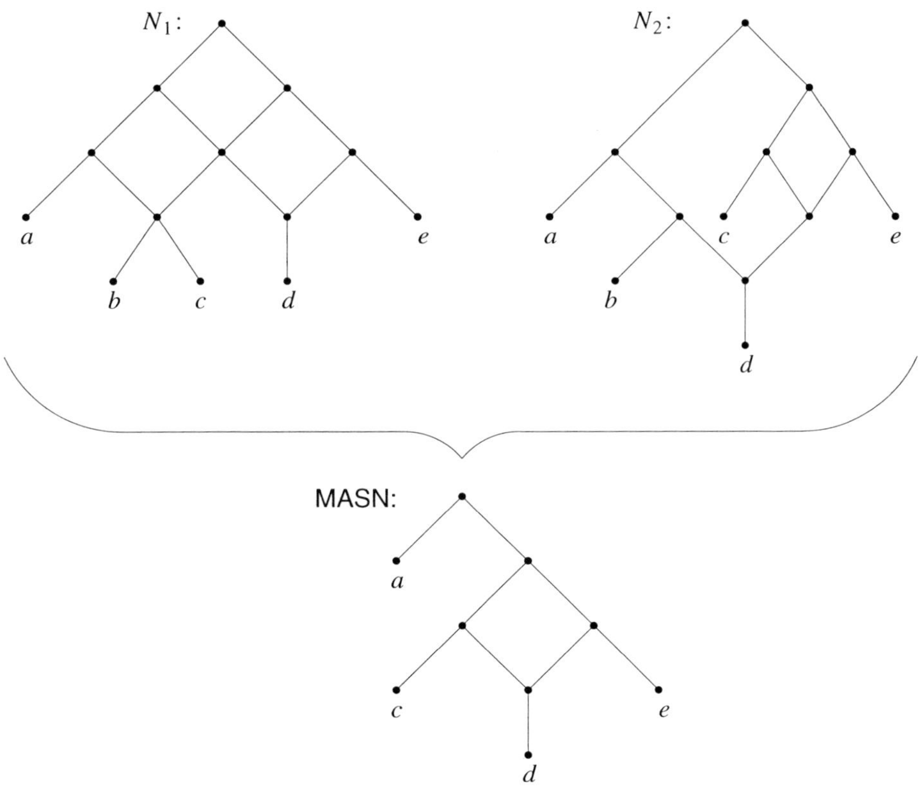

Figure 1. A maximum agreement subnetwork of two given phylogenetic networks N_1 and N_2. Another maximum agreement subnetwork of N_1 and N_2 (not shown here) has leaf set $\{a, b, d, e\}$.

gree 1 and indegree less than 2. A *maximum agreement subnetwork of* $\mathcal{N}$ is an agreement subnetwork of $\mathcal{N}$ with the maximum possible number of leaves. *The maximum agreement phylogenetic subnetwork problem* (MASN) is: Given a set $\mathcal{N} = \{N_1, N_2, \ldots, N_k\}$ of phylogenetic networks, find a maximum agreement subnetwork of $\mathcal{N}$. See Figure 1 for an example. A leaf can appear in a maximum agreement subnetwork of $\mathcal{N}$ only if it is present in every network in $\mathcal{N}$, so we assume without loss of generality that $\Lambda(N_1) = \Lambda(N_2) = \ldots = \Lambda(N_k)$ and call this leaf set L. Throughout this chapter, we let n denote the number of different leaves and k the number of input networks, i.e., $n = |L|$ and $k = |\mathcal{N}|$ in the problem definition above.

1.2. Terminology

Let N be a phylogenetic network. Recall that nodes in N with outdegree 0 are called *leaves*. We refer to nodes with indegree 2 as *hybrid nodes*. For any hybrid node h, every ancestor s of h such that h can be reached using two disjoint directed paths starting at the children of s is termed a *split node of* h. If s is a split node of h then any path starting at s and ending at h is called a *merge path of* h, and any path starting at a child of s and ending at a parent of h is called a *clipped merge path of* h.

We say that N is a *nested phylogenetic network* if for each pair of hybrid nodes h_1, h_2 and each merge path P_1 of h_1 and merge path P_2 of h_2, one of the following three conditions holds: (1) P_1 and P_2 are disjoint; (2) one of P_1 and P_2 is a subpath of the other; or (3) the intersection of P_1 and P_2 equals either h_1 and the first node on P_1, or h_2 and the first node on P_2. For example, in Figure 1, the phylogenetic network N_2 and the displayed maximum agreement subnetwork are nested, but N_1 is not.

For each node u in a nested phylogenetic network N, define the *nesting depth of* u, $d(u)$, as the number of hybrid nodes in N that have a clipped merge path passing through u. Figure 3 contains an example of a nested phylogenetic network where the nesting depths of some nodes are shown. The *nesting depth of* N, denoted by $d(N)$, is the maximum value of $d(u)$ over all $u \in V(N)$. Observe that $d(N) = 0$ if and only if N is a binary tree. Gusfield *et al.* [12] defined a *galled-tree* (also referred to in the literature as a *gt-network* [23] or a *topology with independent recombination events* [28]) as a phylogenetic network in which all clipped merge paths are disjoint. For a discussion on the biological significance of galled-trees, see [12]. Clearly, $d(N) \leq 1$ if and only if N is a galled-tree. Thus, nested phylogenetic networks naturally extend the notion of rooted, leaf-labeled, binary trees and galled-trees.

Finally, given any phylogenetic network N, let $\mathcal{U}(N)$ be the undirected graph obtained from N by replacing each directed edge by an undirected edge. For every biconnected component B in $\mathcal{U}(N)$, the *level of* B is the number of nodes it contains which are hybrid nodes in N. N is said to be a *level-*f phylogenetic network if the maximum level of all biconnected components in $\mathcal{U}(N)$ is equal to f. To illustrate, N_1 and N_2 in Figure 1 are level-3 and level-2 phylogenetic networks, respectively, and the shown maximum agreement subnetwork of N_1 and N_2 is a level-1 phylogenetic network. If N is a nested phylogenetic network with nesting depth d then $f \geq d$ because any node in N that has nesting depth d must belong to the same biconnected component in $\mathcal{U}(N)$ as at least d different hybrid nodes. Also, $f = 0$ if and only if $d = 0$, and $f = 1$ if and only if $d = 1$.

1.3. Previous Results

Median-joining, split decomposition (SplitsTree), PYRAMIDS, statistical parsimony (TCS), molecular-variance parsimony (Arlequin), reticulogram (T-REX), and netting are some of the existing general methods for *constructing* phylogenetic networks (see [21] and [24] for a survey). More recently presented methods include Neighbor-Net [4] and the Z-closure method [16]. Algorithms for some reconstruction problems with additional constraints on the networks were given in [5, 12, 17, 23, 28]; in particular, these papers considered problems involving constructing a phylogenetic network with nesting depth 1.

As for *comparing* two given phylogenetic networks, one method based on the Robinson-Foulds (RF) measure for phylogenetic trees was proposed in [22]. MASN was introduced in [6], where it was shown to be NP-hard if restricted to $k = 3$ and an $O(n^2)$-time algorithm for the special case of two level-1 phylogenetic networks (i.e., having nesting depth 1) was presented. [6] also showed that MASN for a level-f_1 phylogenetic network N_1 and a level-f_2 phylogenetic network N_2 can be solved in $O(|V(N_1)| \cdot |V(N_2)| \cdot 2^{f_1+f_2})$ time.

MASN extends a well-studied problem known as *the maximum agreement subtree problem* (MAST)[3] (see, e.g., [1, 3, 7, 9, 11, 14, 18, 19, 27] and the numerous references therein) in which the input is a set of distinctly leaf-labeled trees and the goal is to compute a tree embedded in all of the input trees with the maximum possible number of labeled leaves. The fastest known algorithm for MAST for two trees runs in $O(\sqrt{D}\, n \log(2n/D))$ time, where n is the number of leaves and D is the maximum degree of the two input trees [18]. Note that this is $O(n \log n)$ for two trees with D bounded by a constant and $O(n^{1.5})$ for two trees with unbounded D. MAST is NP-hard for three trees with unbounded degrees [1], and solvable in $O(kn^3 + n^\delta)$ time for $k \geq 3$ trees, where δ is an upper bound on at least one of the input trees' degrees [3, 9] (for $\delta = 2$, even faster algorithms exist [19]). The inapproximability of MAST has been studied in [11] and [14], in terms of how the heights and degrees of the input trees as well as the number of input trees affect the polynomial-time approximability of MAST.

1.4. Our Results and Organization of Chapter

In this chapter, we focus on MASN for two nested phylogenetic networks.

In Section 2., we derive some useful combinatorial properties of nested phylogenetic networks. We first prove that $|V(N)| = O(n(d+1))$ for any nested phylogenetic network N with n leaves and nesting depth d and then show how to test whether a given phylogenetic network is nested, and if so, determine its nesting depth in $O(|V(N)| \cdot (d+1))$ time. In Section 3., we present a fast dynamic programming-based algorithm for solving MASN for two nested phylogenetic networks N_1 and N_2 running in $O(|V(N_1)| \cdot |V(N_2)| \cdot (d_1+1) \cdot (d_2+1))$ time, where d_1 and d_2 are the nesting depths of N_1 and N_2, respectively, which generalizes the algorithm from [6]. (The algorithm given in [6] could be applied here directly but its running time is $O(|V(N_1)| \cdot |V(N_2)| \cdot 2^{f_1+f_2})$, where $f_1 \geq d_1$ and $f_2 \geq d_2$.) For the special case $d_1 = 1$, $d_2 = 1$, i.e., two galled trees/level-1 networks, the running

[3]MAST is also known in the literature as *the maximum homeomorphic subtree problem* (MHT).

time of our new algorithm coincides with the running time of $O(n^2)$ of the algorithm in [6]. Next, in Section 4.1., we strengthen the NP-hardness result of [6] by proving that MASN is NP-hard already for *two* phylogenetic networks, even when one of the networks is required to be a binary tree[4]. In Section 4.2., we consider a new variant of MASN in which the definition of a phylogenetic network is relaxed to allow nodes to have outdegree greater than 2 and prove that with this modification, the problem becomes NP-hard even if restricted to two nested phylogenetic networks with nesting depth 1 (i.e., two galled-trees/level-1 networks). Finally, we discuss possible extensions of our techniques in Section 5..

2. Preliminaries

We first investigate some basic properties of nested phylogenetic networks.

Lemma 1. *If N is a nested phylogenetic network then: (1) each split node in N is a split node of exactly one hybrid node, and (2) each hybrid node in N has exactly one split node.*

Proof. Let s be any split node in N and denote the two children of s by c and d. Suppose, for the sake of contradiction, that there exist two hybrid nodes h_1 and h_2 such that s is a split node of both h_1 and h_2. For $i \in \{1, 2\}$, let C_i and D_i be two disjoint clipped merge paths of h_i starting at c and d, respectively, and ending at the two parents of h_i, and let C'_i and D'_i be the corresponding (non-clipped) merge paths. Since the intersection of C'_1 and C'_2 contains c, one must be a subpath of the other by the definition of a nested phylogenetic network, and similarly for D'_1 and D'_2. Now, if C'_1 is a subpath of C'_2 then D'_1 must be a subpath of D'_2 (otherwise, there would exist a directed path from h_1 to h_2 and from h_2 to h_1, contradicting that a phylogenetic network has no cycles), but then C_2 and D_2 are not disjoint because both pass through h_1. Contradiction. The case where C'_2 is a subpath of C'_1 is analogous. (1) follows.

To prove (2), suppose some hybrid node h has two split nodes s_1 and s_2. Denote the parents of h by p and q. For $i \in \{1, 2\}$, let P_i and Q_i be two disjoint clipped merge paths of h starting at the two children of s_i and ending at p and q, respectively, and let P'_i and Q'_i be the corresponding (non-clipped) merge paths. Let h_p be the node in the intersection of P'_1 and P'_2 closest to the root, let h_q be the node in the intersection of Q'_1 and Q'_2 closest to the root, and let s be the lowest common ancestor of s_1 and $_2$. If $s \neq s_1$ and $s \neq s_2$ then s is a split node of three hybrid nodes (h, h_p, and h_q), and if $s = s_1$ or $s = s_2$ then s is a split node of two hybrid nodes (h and either h_p or h_q). In both cases, we have a contradiction with (1). □

Because of Lemma 1, each hybrid node in a nested phylogenetic network corresponds to a unique split node. For any such hybrid node h and split node s, s is called *the split node of h* and h is called *the hybrid node of s*.

[4]The reduction in [1] for proving the NP-hardness of MAST restricted to three trees with unbounded degrees cannot be used directly for MASN with $k = 2$ because it constructs *three* trees and because here we require all nodes to have outdegree at most two. It is interesting to note that MAST for two binary trees is solvable in $O(n \log n)$ time [7, 18].

Lemma 2. *Let h be a hybrid node in a nested phylogenetic network and let s be the split node of h. Then $d(h) = d(s)$.*

Proof. Suppose $d(h) < d(s)$. Then there exists some clipped merge path P containing s but not h. Let P' be the corresponding (non-clipped) merge path. Since s has outdegree 2, P' must contain one of the outgoing edges from s. Let Q be the merge path of h which also uses this edge. Now, P' and Q are not disjoint and one is not a subpath of the other, yet their intersection contains at least two nodes, contradicting the definition of a nested phylogenetic network. The case $d(h) > d(s)$ can be disproved in the same way. □

We now derive an upper bound on the total number of nodes in a nested phylogenetic network. The next two lemmas generalize Lemmas 2 and 3 in [6].

Lemma 3. *If N is a nested phylogenetic network with n leaves and nesting depth d then the number of hybrid nodes in N is at most $(n-1) \cdot d$.*

Proof. Let $T_N(d)$ be the phylogenetic network N. Then, for $i \in \{0, 1, \ldots, d-1\}$, define $T_N(i)$ as the rooted directed graph constructed from $T_N(i+1)$ as follows. For every hybrid node h in $T_N(i+1)$ with $d(h) = i$, remove h's two incoming edges, contract the split node of h and all nodes on the two clipped merge paths of h to a single node s, and add a directed edge from s to h. (Note that the obtained $T_N(i)$ may contain nodes with outdegree greater than 2.) $T_N(0)$ is a tree because every node with indegree 2 in N has indegree 1 in $T_N(0)$ and no contraction increases the indegree of any node. Furthermore, $T_N(0)$ contains n leaves. Thus, the number of internal nodes in $T_N(0)$ with outdegree > 1 is at most $n-1$. Next, observe that at most d split nodes in N correspond to each internal node in $T_N(0)$ with outdegree > 1 and that the number of hybrid nodes in N equals the number of split nodes in N since N is nested. □

Lemma 4. *If N is a phylogenetic network with n leaves and H hybrid nodes then the total number of nodes in N is at most $2(n+H)-1$.*

Proof. Let z_{ij} denote the number of nodes in N which have i incoming edges and j outgoing edges. By the definition of a phylogenetic network, the total number of nodes in N is $|V(N)| = z_{02} + z_{10} + z_{12} + z_{20} + z_{21} + z_{22}$. For every $u \in V(N)$, let $in(u)$ and $out(u)$ denote the number of incoming and outgoing edges incident to u. Since

$$\begin{cases} \sum_{u \in V(N)} in(u) = z_{02} \cdot 0 + (z_{10} + z_{12}) \cdot 1 + (z_{20} + z_{21} + z_{22}) \cdot 2 \\ \sum_{u \in V(N)} out(u) = (z_{10} + z_{20}) \cdot 0 + z_{21} \cdot 1 + (z_{02} + z_{12} + z_{22}) \cdot 2 \end{cases}$$

and $\sum_{u \in V(N)} in(u) = \sum_{u \in V(N)} out(u)$, we have $z_{12} = z_{10} + 2z_{20} + z_{21} - 2z_{02}$.

Next, $H = z_{20} + z_{21} + z_{22}$, $n = z_{10} + z_{20}$, and $z_{02} = 1$ give us $z_{12} \leq n + H - 2$. Hence, $|V(N)| \leq 1 + n + (n + H - 2) + H = 2n + 2H - 1$. □

For an example showing that the bounds given above are tight, refer to Figure 2. By combining Lemmas 3 and 4, we get:

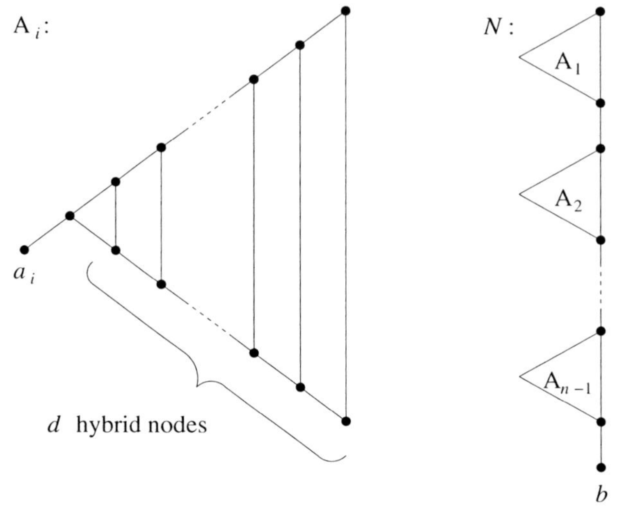

Figure 2. An example of a nested phylogenetic network N with nesting depth d and n leaves for which the upper bounds given in Lemmas 3 and 4 are tight. N (shown on the right) consists of $n-1$ copies of A_i (shown on the left) and is distinctly leaf-labeled by $\{a_1, a_2, \ldots, a_{n-1}, b\}$. The number of hybrid nodes H in N equals $(n-1)\cdot d$ and $|V(N)| = (2d+2)\cdot(n-1)+1 = 2H+2n-1$.

Theorem 5. *If N is a nested phylogenetic network with n leaves and nesting depth d then $|V(N)| \leq 2dn + 2n - 2d - 1$, i.e., $|V(N)| = O(n(d+1))$.*

We also have the following.

Theorem 6. *Let N be a phylogenetic network with n leaves and H hybrid nodes. We can test whether N is nested in $O(|V(N)| \cdot (H+1))$ time; if N is nested, the test takes only $O(|V(N)|\cdot(d(N)+1))$ time and its nesting depth can be determined in the same asymptotic time bound.*

Proof. Use the following method to construct a list $L(u)$ for every $u \in V(N)$ consisting of all hybrid nodes which have a clipped merge path passing through u, plus u itself if u is a hybrid node. Associate an initially empty list $L(u)$ to each $u \in V(N)$, and define $L(\emptyset) = \emptyset$. Visit the nodes of N according to a reverse topological ordering of N. Whenever a non-leaf node u is visited, examine $L(u_L)$ and $L(u_R)$, where u_L and u_R are the children of u (if u only has one child then let u_R equal $\emptyset$). If $L(u_L)$ is empty then let $L(u) := L(u_R)$; else if $L(u_R)$ is empty then let $L(u) := L(u_L)$. Otherwise, check whether $L(u_L)$ equals $L(u_R)$. If no then N is not nested, and the algorithm terminates; if yes then let $L(u) := L(u_L)$ and remove the last element ℓ from $L(u)$ (in this case, u is the split node for the hybrid node ℓ). Finally, if u is a hybrid node then insert u at the end of $L(u)$. Note that a node may be both a split node and a hybrid node. The length of any $L(u)$ can never exceed the number of hybrid nodes in N. Moreover, when the algorithm is finished, if N is a nested phylogenetic network then its nesting depth $d(N)$ equals the maximum length of $L(u)$ over all $u \in V(N)$ since $d(u) = |L(u)|$ for each non-hybrid node u.

The time taken at each node in N is bounded by $O(1 + \max_{u \in V(N)} |L(u)|)$. □

3. An Algorithm for MASN for Two Nested Phylogenetic Networks

In this section, we show how to solve MASN for two nested phylogenetic networks N_1, N_2 with n leaves in $O(|V(N_1)| \cdot |V(N_2)| \cdot (d_1 + 1) \cdot (d_2 + 1))$ time, where d_1 and d_2 are the nesting depths of N_1 and N_2, respectively. We first introduce some additional notation.

Let N be any nested phylogenetic network. From this point onward, assume that some arbitrary left-to-right ordering of the children of every node has been fixed. If $u \in V(N)$ has two children then let u_L and u_R denote the left and right child of u, respectively, and if u only has one child c then set $u_L = c$ and $u_R = \emptyset$. For every $u \in V(N)$, $N[u]$ is the subnetwork of N rooted at u, i.e., the minimal subgraph of N which includes all nodes and directed edges of N reachable from u. $N[\emptyset]$ refers to the empty network with no nodes or edges.

Each $u \in V(N)$ belongs to $d(u)$ different clipped merge paths. Since N is nested, the $d(u)$ different hybrid nodes corresponding to these clipped merge paths have nesting depths $0, 1, \ldots, d(u) - 1$. For $i \in \{1, \ldots, d(u)\}$, we define $h^i(u)$ as the hybrid node h which has a clipped merge path passing through u and which satisfies $d(h) = i - 1$. Next, for $i \in \{1, \ldots, d(u)\}$, let $N^i[u]$ be the subgraph of $N[u]$ where $N[h^i(u)]$ and $h^i(u)$'s incoming edge have been removed, and let $N^0[u]$ be $N[u]$. Define $N^i[u]$ for $i > d(u)$ as $N^0[u]$ if u is not a hybrid node, and as $N[\emptyset]$ if u is a hybrid node. See Figure 3. Intuitively,

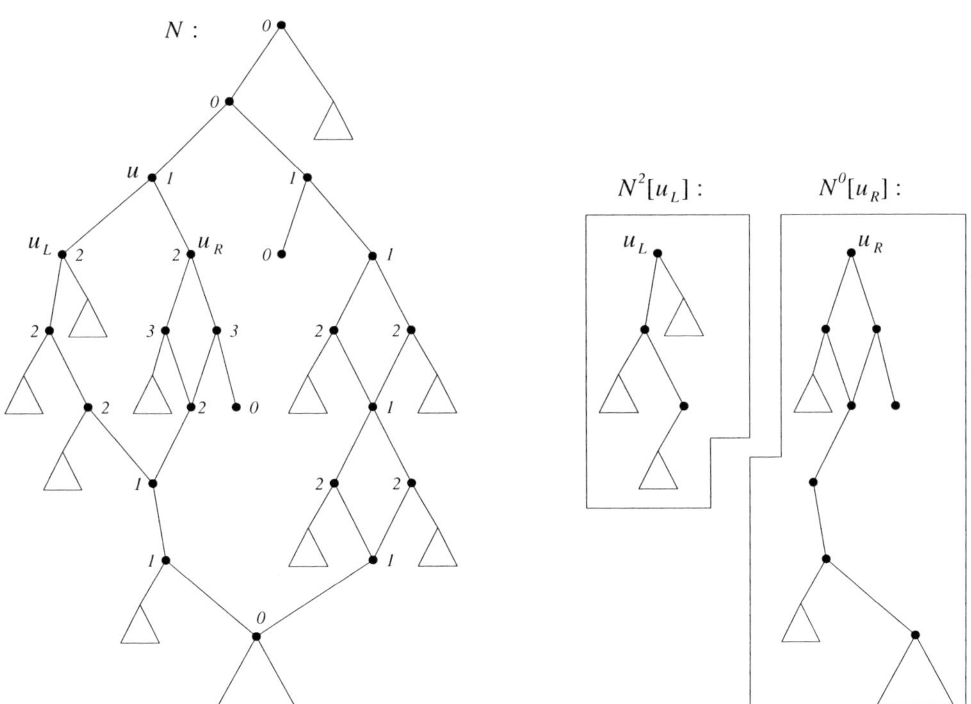

Figure 3. N is a nested phylogenetic network with nesting depth 3 and u is a split node in N. The numbers shown next to the nodes of N are their respective nesting depths. $N^2[u_L]$ and $N^0[u_R]$ are the subgraphs of N displayed on the right.

the parameter i informs us at which descendant hybrid node of u to cut $N[u]$ to obtain $N^i[u]$.

Lemma 7. *For any nested phylogenetic network N, $u \in V(N)$, and $0 \leq j < i \leq d(u)$, it holds that $N^i[u]$ is a proper subgraph of $N^j[u]$.*

Proof. If $j = 0$ then $N^i[u]$ is trivially a proper subgraph of $N^j[u]$ $(= N^0[u] = N[u])$. If $j > 0$, the node $h^j(u)$ is a descendant of $h^i(u)$ since $j < i$, so $N[h^j(u)]$ is a proper subgraph of $N[h^i(u)]$, and therefore $N^i[u]$ is a proper subgraph of $N^j[u]$. □

Lemma 8. *Let N be a nested phylogenetic network. For any $u \in V(N)$ and $i \in \{0, 1, \ldots, d(u)\}$, it holds that: (1) $N^i[u_L]$ and $N^x[u_R]$ are disjoint, and (2) $N^x[u_L]$ and $N^i[u_R]$ are disjoint, where $x = d(u) + 1$ if u is a split node and $x = i$ otherwise.*

Proof. If u is a split node then let h be the hybrid node of u. By Lemma 2, $d(h) = d(u)$. Let c_1 be a child of u with $c_1 \neq h$ and let c_2 be the other child of u, possibly with $c_2 = h$. We have $h^x(c_1) = h^{d(u)+1}(c_1) = h$, which means that $N^x[c_1]$ does not contain any nodes in $N[h]$; hence, $N^x[c_1]$ and $N^0[c_2]$ are disjoint, and Lemma 7 then implies that $N^x[c_1]$ and $N^i[c_2]$ are disjoint. Similarly, $N^i[c_1]$ and $N^x[c_2]$ are disjoint (if $c_2 \neq h$ then $h^x(c_2) = h^{d(u)+1}(c_2) = h$ so $N^x[c_2]$ contains no nodes in $N[h]$ and thus no nodes in $N^i[c_1]$; if $c_2 = h$ then $N^x[c_2] = N^{d(u)+1}[h] = N^{d(h)+1}[h] = N[\emptyset]$).

If u is not a split node then $N[u_L]$ $(= N^0[u_L])$ and $N[u_R]$ $(= N^0[u_R])$ are always disjoint. By Lemma 7, $N^i[u_L]$ and $N^i[u_R]$ are disjoint. □

For any two phylogenetic networks N_1, N_2, define $Masn(N_1, N_2)$ as the number of leaves in a maximum agreement subnetwork. If N_1 or N_2 is an empty network then $Masn(N_1, N_2)$ is equal to 0. Otherwise, $Masn(N_1, N_2)$ for two nested phylogenetic networks can be expressed recursively using the following lemma which is a generalization of the main lemma in [27] for MAST. In the $Match$ case, when trying to match two subnetworks $N_1^i[u_L]$ and $N_1^x[u_R]$ to two subnetworks $N_2^k[v_L]$ and $N_2^y[v_R]$, Lemma 8 ensures that the set of nodes in the intersection of $V(N_1[u_L])$ and $V(N_1[u_R])$ is matched to only one of $N_2^k[v_L]$ and $N_2^y[v_R]$, and vice versa.

Lemma 9. *Let N_1 and N_2 be two nested phylogenetic networks. For every $(u, v) \in V(N_1) \times V(N_2)$ and $0 \leq i \leq d(u)$, $0 \leq k \leq d(v)$,*

$$Masn(N_1^i[u], N_2^k[v]) = \begin{cases} |\Lambda(N_1^i[u]) \cap \Lambda(N_2^k[v])|, & \text{if at least one of } u \text{ and } v \text{ is a leaf} \\ \max\{Diag(N_1^i[u], N_2^k[v]),\ Match(N_1^i[u], N_2^k[v])\}, & \text{otherwise} \end{cases}$$

where

$$\begin{aligned} Diag(N_1^i[u], N_2^k[v]) = \max\{&Masn(N_1^i[u], N_2^k[v_L]),\ Masn(N_1^i[u], N_2^k[v_R]), \\ &Masn(N_1^i[u_L], N_2^k[v]),\ Masn(N_1^i[u_R], N_2^k[v])\} \end{aligned}$$

and

$$\begin{aligned} Match(N_1^i[u], N_2^k[v]) = \max\{&Masn(N_1^i[u_L],\ N_2^k[v_L]) + Masn(N_1^x[u_R],\ N_2^y[v_R]), \\ &Masn(N_1^i[u_L],\ N_2^y[v_L]) + Masn(N_1^x[u_R],\ N_2^k[v_R]), \\ &Masn(N_1^i[u_L],\ N_2^k[v_R]) + Masn(N_1^x[u_R],\ N_2^y[v_L]), \\ &Masn(N_1^i[u_L],\ N_2^y[v_R]) + Masn(N_1^x[u_R],\ N_2^k[v_L]), \end{aligned}$$

$$Masn(N_1^x[u_L], N_2^k[v_L]) + Masn(N_1^i[u_R], N_2^y[v_R]),$$
$$Masn(N_1^x[u_L], N_2^y[v_L]) + Masn(N_1^i[u_R], N_2^k[v_R]),$$
$$Masn(N_1^x[u_L], N_2^k[v_R]) + Masn(N_1^i[u_R], N_2^y[v_L]),$$
$$Masn(N_1^x[u_L], N_2^y[v_R]) + Masn(N_1^i[u_R], N_2^k[v_L])\},$$

$$\textit{where } x = \begin{cases} d(u)+1, & \text{if } u \text{ is a split node} \\ i, & \text{otherwise} \end{cases}$$

$$y = \begin{cases} d(v)+1, & \text{if } v \text{ is a split node} \\ k, & \text{otherwise} \end{cases}$$

Proof. [Generalization of [27]] If at least one of u and v is a leaf ℓ then the size of a maximum agreement subnetwork of $N_1^i[u]$ and $N_2^k[v]$ is either 0 or 1, depending on whether or not ℓ occurs in the other subnetwork, i.e., $Masn$ is equal to $|\Lambda(N_1^i[u]) \cap \Lambda(N_2^k[v])|$.

If neither of u and v are leaves then let A be any maximum agreement subnetwork of $N_1^i[u]$ and $N_2^k[v]$ which is a tree (such an A must exist because for any agreement subnetwork B which is not a tree, if one parent edge of each hybrid node in B is deleted and edge contractions are performed, we get an agreement subnetwork A with $\Lambda(A) = \Lambda(B)$ which is a tree). Write $M = \Lambda(A)$ so that $|M| = Masn(N_1^i[u], N_2^k[v])$. Let a_1 and a_2 be the lowest common ancestor in $N_1^i[u]$ and $N_2^k[v]$, respectively, of the leaves in M. There are two main cases:

1. $a_1 \neq u$ or $a_2 \neq v$ (the $Diag$ case).
   Here, A is also a maximum agreement subnetwork of each pair of networks $(N_1^i[x], N_2^k[y])$ where x belongs to any path from u to a_1 and y belongs to any path from v to a_2. Hence, $Masn(N_1^i[u], N_2^k[v])$ is equal to $Masn(N_1^i[w_1], N_2^k[w_2])$ for some $(w_1, w_2) \in \{(u, v_L), (u, v_R), (u_L, v), (u_R, v)\}$.

2. $a_1 = u$ and $a_2 = v$ (the $Match$ case).
   The elements in M are descendants of both of u's children and also of both of v's children. Let A_a and A_b be the two subtrees of A rooted at the children of the root of A.

   By Lemma 8, $N_1^i[u_L]$ and $N_1^x[u_R]$ are disjoint; furthermore, every $v \in V(N_1^i[u]) \setminus \{u\}$ belongs to exactly one of $N_1^i[u_L]$ and $N_1^x[u_R]$. The same holds for $N_1^x[u_L]$ and $N_1^i[u_R]$ (observe that if u is not a split node then $x = i$ and these two cases coincide), and there are no other ways to divide $N_1^i[u]$ into two disjoint subnetworks rooted at u_L and u_R. Similarly, $N_2^k[v]$ can be divided into two disjoint subnetworks rooted at v_L and v_R in at most two ways. A_a is therefore a maximum agreement subnetwork of $N_1^{p_1}[u_a]$ and $N_2^{p_2}[v_a]$, and A_b is a maximum agreement subnetwork of $N_1^{q_1}[u_b]$ and $N_2^{q_2}[v_b]$ for some $u_a, u_b \in \{u_L, u_R\}$ with $u_a \neq u_b$ and some $v_a, v_b \in \{v_L, v_R\}$ with $v_a \neq v_b$, and where $p_1 = i$ and $q_1 = x$, or $p_1 = x$ and $q_1 = i$, and where $p_2 = k$ and $q_2 = y$, or $p_2 = y$ and $q_2 = k$. Now, $Masn(N_1^i[u], N_2^k[v]) = |M| = |\Lambda(A)| = |\Lambda(A_a)| + |\Lambda(A_b)|$ is given by one of the eight cases in the equation for $Match$.

Finally, note that in the $Diag$ case, the value of $Match$ is at most $|M|$, and in the $Match$ case, the value of $Diag$ is at most $|M|$. Taking the maximum of $Diag$ and $Match$ thus gives us the size of a maximum agreement subnetwork. □

Now, given two nested phylogenetic networks N_1 and N_2, we can use Lemma 9 to compute $Masn(N_1^i[u], N_2^k[v])$ for all $0 \leq i \leq d(u)$ and $0 \leq k \leq d(v)$ by applying dynamic programming in a bottom-up manner, e.g., by evaluating all pairs in $V(N_1) \times V(N_2)$ in increasing order in the lexicographic ordering $\mathcal{O}$ of $V(N_1) \times V(N_2)$ where the nodes in each $V(N_i)$ are ordered according to a reverse topological ordering of N_i. The resulting algorithm (Algorithm *NestedMasn*) is listed in Figure 4.

Algorithm *NestedMasn*
Input: Two nested phylogenetic networks N_1 and N_2.
Output: The number of leaves in a maximum agreement subnetwork of $\{N_1, N_2\}$.

1 Compute and store $d(u)$ and $h^i(u)$ for all $u \in V(N_1) \cup V(N_2)$, $i \in \{1, \ldots, d(u)\}$.
2 Let $\mathcal{O}$ be the lexicographic ordering of $V(N_1) \times V(N_2)$ where the nodes in each $V(N_i)$ are ordered according to a reverse topological ordering of N_i.
3 **for** each $(u, v) \in V(N_1) \times V(N_2)$ in increasing order in $\mathcal{O}$ **do**
  Compute $Masn(N_1^i[u], N_2^k[v])$ for all $0 \leq i \leq d(u)$, $0 \leq k \leq d(v)$ by using the expression in Lemma 9.
endfor
4 **return** $Masn(N_1^0[r_1], N_2^0[r_2])$, where r_i is the root of N_i for $i \in \{1, 2\}$.
End *NestedMasn*

Figure 4. A dynamic programming algorithm for computing all values of $Masn$.

Lemma 10. *NestedMasn runs in* $O(|V(N_1)| \cdot |V(N_2)| \cdot (d(N_1) + 1) \cdot (d(N_2) + 1))$ *time.*

Proof. In Step 1 of Algorithm *NestedMasn*, we may compute $d(u)$ and $h^i(u)$ for all $u \in V(N), i \in \{1, \ldots, d(u)\}$ for a given nested phylogenetic network N in a way similar to the algorithm in the proof of Theorem 6 by traversing the nodes of N in bottom-up order. (For every leaf u, $d(u) = 0$; when a non-leaf node u is reached, compute $h^i(u)$ for all valid i by using $d(u_L)$, $d(u_R)$, $h^i(u_L)$, and $h^i(u_R)$ and checking if any of u_L and u_R is a hybrid node, and then assign $d(u)$.) This takes $O(|V(N)| \cdot (d(N) + 1))$ time.

Next, the algorithm evaluates $O(|V(N_1)| \cdot |V(N_2)|)$ pairs of nodes. For any such pair (u, v), if neither u nor v is a leaf then it takes constant time to compute each one of the $O((d(N_1) + 1) \cdot (d(N_2) + 1))$ different $Masn(N_1^i[u], N_2^k[v])$-values from previously computed values. If u is a leaf then the value of each $|\Lambda(N_1^i[u]) \cap \Lambda(N_2^k[v])|$ can be obtained in constant time as follows. Associate a binary vector $L(w)$ of length n to each $w \in V(N_1) \cup V(N_2)$, where the ith bit of $L(w)$ is set to 1 if and only if leaf i is a descendant of w (note that all $L(w)$-vectors can be computed in advance in $O((|V(N_1)| + |V(N_2)|) \cdot n)$ time by traversing each of N_1 and N_2 according to a reverse topological ordering). Then to determine whether $u \in \Lambda(N_2^0[v])$, check if bit u in $L(v)$ equals 1; for $k \geq 1$, the condition $u \in \Lambda(N_2^k[v])$ is equivalent to $u \in \Lambda(N_2^0[v])$ and $u \notin \Lambda(N_2^0[h^k(v)])$. The case where v is a leaf is analogous. □

Algorithm *NestedMasn* can be modified to compute the set of leaves in a maximum agreement subnetwork without increasing the asymptotic running time by also recording information about how each $Masn$-value is attained as it is computed, e.g., by saving pointers. To construct an actual maximum agreement subnetwork from such a set L', we may use a standard traceback technique to obtain a tree with leaf set L' which is an agreement subnetwork. This yields:

Theorem 11. *Given two nested phylogenetic networks N_1 and N_2 with nesting depths d_1 and d_2, respectively, a maximum agreement subnetwork can be computed in $O(|V(N_1)| \cdot |V(N_2)| \cdot (d_1+1) \cdot (d_2+1))$ time.*

4. New NP-hardness Results

Below, we first show that MASN is NP-hard already for $k = 2$. We then show that if our definition of a phylogenetic network is relaxed so that the outdegrees of the nodes are unbounded, then the problem becomes NP-hard even if restricted to two nested phylogenetic networks with nesting depth 1.

4.1. MASN with $k = 2$ is NP-hard

To prove the NP-hardness of MASN for every fixed $k \geq 2$, we provide a polynomial-time reduction from the following problem.

Three-Dimensional Matching (3DM)

Instance: A set $M \subseteq X \times Y \times Z$, where X, Y, and Z are disjoint sets and $X = \{x_1, \ldots, x_q\}$, $Y = \{y_1, \ldots, y_q\}$, and $Z = \{z_1, \ldots, z_q\}$.

Question: Is there a subset M' of M with $|M'| = q$ such that M' is a matching, i.e., such that for every pair $e_1, e_2 \in M'$ it holds that e_1 and e_2 differ in all coordinates?

3DM is NP-complete (see, e.g., [10]). Given an arbitrary instance of 3DM, construct an instance of MASN with two phylogenetic networks N_1 and N_2 with a leaf set L as described next. (In fact, N_1 will be a leaf-labeled binary tree.) The elements of M are encoded in subtrees called S_{x_i,z_k} in N_1 and in subtrees called U_{y_j} in N_2. The purpose of the subtrees named A_{x_i}, B_{x_i,z_k}, and W_{z_k} is to make sure that for any two triples e and f in M, a maximum agreement subnetwork of N_1 and N_2 can contain both of the two leaves representing e and f if and only if e and f differ in all coordinates.

Let the leaf set L equal $M \cup A \cup B$, where A is a set of $q^6 \cdot (q+2)$ elements not in M and B is a set of q^6 elements not in M or A. Let $A_{x_0}, A_{x_1}, \ldots, A_{x_q}, A_{x_{q+1}}$ be $q+2$ binary trees with q^6 leaves each, distinctly labeled by A. For every $(x_i, z_k) \in X \times Z$, let B_{x_i,z_k} be a binary tree with q^4 leaves, distinctly labeled by B.

For every $(x_i, z_k) \in X \times Z$, define: (1) M_{x_i,z_k} as the subset of M containing all triples of the form (x_i, y, z_k) where $y \in Y$; and (2) S_{x_i,z_k} to be a tree obtained from a binary caterpillar tree with $|M_{x_i,z_k}| + 1$ leaves distinctly labeled by M_{x_i,z_k} and where one of the bottommost leaves has been replaced by the root of B_{x_i,z_k}. See Figure 5. For every $y_j \in Y$, define: (1) M_{y_j} as the subset of M containing all triples of the form (x, y_j, z) where $x \in X$ and $z \in Z$; and (2) U_{y_j} to be a binary caterpillar tree with $|M_{y_j}| + q$ leaves in which the $|M_{y_j}|$ leaves closest to the root are distinctly labeled by M_{y_j} and the rest are unlabeled nodes referred to as v_{y_j,z_k} for $1 \leq k \leq q$. Finally, for every $z_k \in Z$, define W_{z_k} to be a tree

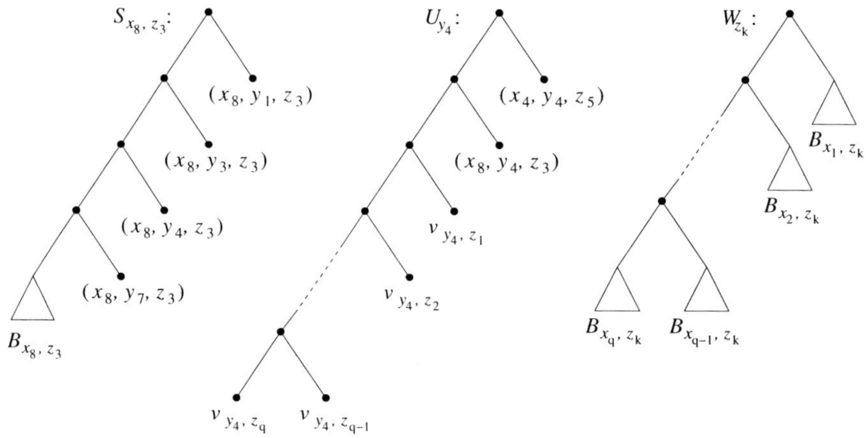

Figure 5. Assume $M_{x_8,z_3} = \{(x_8, y_1, z_3), (x_8, y_3, z_3), (x_8, y_4, z_3), (x_8, y_7, z_3)\}$ and $M_{y_4} = \{(x_4, y_4, z_5), (x_8, y_4, z_3)\}$. S_{x_8,z_3} and U_{y_4} are shown on the left and in the center, respectively. The structure of each W_{z_k} is shown on the right.

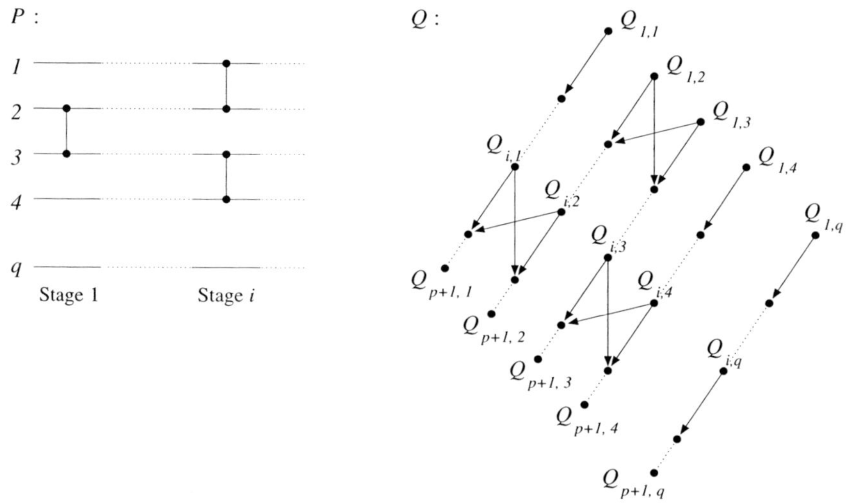

Figure 6. The sorting network P on the left yields a directed acyclic graph Q.

obtained from the binary caterpillar tree with q leaves by replacing the leaves with the roots of $B_{x_1,z_k}, \ldots, B_{x_q,z_k}$.

Next, let P be any sorting network (see, e.g., [8]) for q elements with a polynomial number p of comparator stages. Build a directed acyclic graph Q from P with $(p+1) \cdot q$ nodes $\{Q_{i,j} \mid 1 \le i \le p{+}1,\ 1 \le j \le q\}$ such that there is a directed edge $(Q_{i,j}, Q_{i+1,j})$ for every $1 \le i \le p$ and $1 \le j \le q$, and two directed edges $(Q_{i,j}, Q_{i+1,k})$ and $(Q_{i,k}, Q_{i+1,j})$ for every comparator (j, k) at stage i in P for $1 \le i \le p$, as illustrated in Figure 6. Furthermore, construct q directed paths $\{G_1, \ldots, G_q\}$ where each $G_k = (G_{1,k}, \ldots, G_{q,k})$.

Let N_1 be a phylogenetic network obtained by attaching to a directed path $(m_1, m_2, \ldots, m_{q^2+q+2})$, in order of non-decreasing distance from m_1, the roots of A_{x_0},

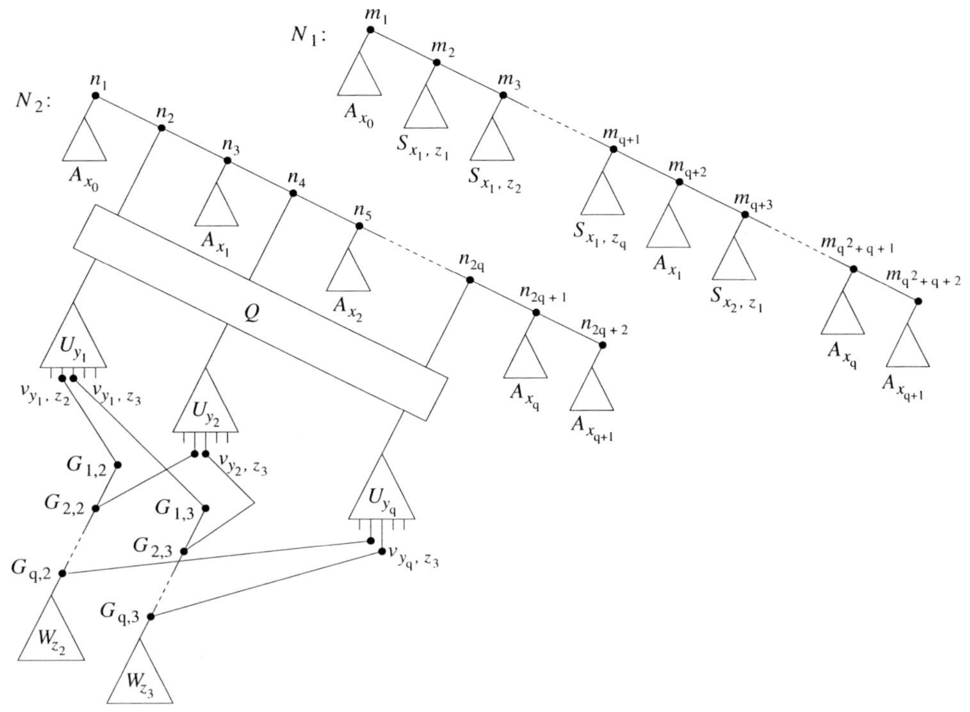

Figure 7. The phylogenetic networks N_1 and N_2.

S_{x_1,z_1}, S_{x_1,z_2}, ..., S_{x_1,z_q}, A_{x_1}, S_{x_2,z_1}, ..., S_{x_q,z_q}, A_{x_q}, and $A_{x_{q+1}}$, and letting m_1 be the root of N_1. (Note that N_1 is actually a binary tree.) See Figure 7. The phylogenetic network N_2 is obtained by first attaching to a directed path $(n_1, n_2, \ldots, n_{2q+2})$, in order of non-decreasing distance from n_1, the root of A_{x_0}, the node $Q_{1,1}$, the root of A_{x_1}, the node $Q_{1,2}$, the root of A_{x_2}, ..., the root of A_{x_q}, and the root of $A_{x_{q+1}}$, and letting n_1 be the root of N_2. Then, for $j \in \{1, \ldots, q\}$, let $Q_{p+1,j}$ coincide with the root of U_{y_j}, and for every $1 \leq j \leq q$ and $1 \leq k \leq q$ add a directed edge $(v_{y_j,z_k}, G_{j,k})$. Next, for every $1 \leq k \leq q$ add a directed edge from $G_{q,k}$ to the root of W_{z_k}. Again, see Figure 7. Finally, for every node in N_1 and N_2 having indegree 1 and outdegree 1, contract its outgoing edge.

Lemma 12. *If M has a matching of size q then there exists an agreement subnetwork of (N_1, N_2) with $q^7 + 2q^6 + q^5 + q$ leaves.*

Proof. Suppose M has a matching M' of size q. For every $(x_i, z_k) \in X \times Z$, denote by V_{x_i,z_k} the set of all leaves in B_{x_i,z_k}. Let $C = M' \cup \bigcup_{(x_i,y_j,z_k)\in M'} V_{x_i,z_k}$ and let T be $N_1 \mid (A \cup C)$. For each $x_i \in X$, there is precisely one triple (x_i, y_j, z_k) in M', so the path in T from the root of S_{x_i,z_k} to the root of B_{x_i,z_k} has one leaf (x_i, y_j, z_k) attached to it. Now consider the structure of $N_2 \mid (A \cup C)$. Since P is a sorting network, there are q disjoint paths in Q from $(Q_{1,\pi(1)}, Q_{1,\pi(2)}, \ldots, Q_{1,\pi(q)})$ to $(Q_{p+1,1}, Q_{p+1,2}, \ldots, Q_{p+1,q})$ for any given permutation π of $\{1, 2, \ldots, q\}$; in particular, this holds for the permutation π defined by the relation $\pi(j) = i$ for all $(x_i, y_j, z_k) \in M'$. Thus, for every (x_i, y_j, z_k) in M', there exists a path in N_2 from node n_{2i} to the root of B_{x_i,z_k} (passing through the root of U_{y_j} and the nodes v_{y_j,z_k} and $G_{q,k}$) along which the leaf (x_i, y_j, z_k) is attached. This implies that T is a subgraph of $N_2 \mid (A \cup C)$, i.e., T is an agreement subnetwork of (N_1, N_2) with $|A| + q \cdot (1 + q^4) = q^7 + 2q^6 + q^5 + q$ leaves. □

Lemma 13. *If there exists an agreement subnetwork of (N_1, N_2) with $q^7 + 2q^6 + q^5 + q$ leaves then M has a matching of size q.*

Proof. Suppose there exists an agreement subnetwork T' with a leaf set $L' \subseteq L$ such that $|L'| = q^7 + 2q^6 + q^5 + q$. Write $M' = L' \cap M$, $A' = L' \cap A$, and $B' = L' \cap B$. First observe that the number of elements in L' is strictly greater than the number of elements in $L \setminus \{a \mid a \text{ is a leaf of } A_{x_0}\}$, so at least one leaf from A_{x_0} must be included in L' by the pigeonhole principle. Hence, the root of T' corresponds to the roots of N_1 and N_2. Similarly, at least one leaf ℓ_i from A_{x_i} for every $x_i \in X$ and at least one leaf ℓ_{q+1} from $A_{x_{q+1}}$ must belong to L'. Also by the pigeonhole principle, a total of at least $|L'| - |M| - |A| \geq q^5 + q - q^3$ leaves from B must be included in L', and these leaves must in fact belong to at least q different subtrees of the form B_{x_i,z_k} (this is because $q - 1$ different subtrees of the form B_{x_i,z_k} can only contain $(q-1) \cdot q^4$ leaves and $(q-1) \cdot q^4 < q^5 + q - q^3$). However, L' cannot contain leaves from both $B_{x_{i_1},z_{k_1}}$ and $B_{x_{i_2},z_{k_2}}$ if $i_1 \neq i_2$ and $k_1 = k_2$ (if b_1 and b_2 are two such leaves then they appear in different S_{x_i,z_k} in N_1 but in the same W_{z_k} in N_2, so, e.g., $N_1 \mid \{b_1, b_2, \ell_{q+1}\}$ and $N_2 \mid \{b_1, b_2, \ell_{q+1}\}$ differ, which contradicts that $\{b_1, b_2, \ell_{q+1}\}$ are leaves in T'), or if $i_1 = i_2$ and $k_1 \neq k_2$ (if b_1 and b_2 were two such leaves then $N_1 \mid \{b_1, b_2, \ell_{i_1-1}, \ell_{i_1}\}$ and $N_2 \mid \{b_1, b_2, \ell_{i_1-1}, \ell_{i_1}\}$ would differ); thus B' consists of leaves from at most q (and hence, precisely q by the above) different subtrees of the form B_{x_i,z_k}, and we have $|B'| \leq q \cdot q^4$, yielding $|M'| = |L'| - |A'| - |B'| \geq |L'| - |A| - q^5 = q$.

We now show that for any two triples $e = (x_{i_1}, y_{j_1}, z_{k_1})$ and $f = (x_{i_2}, y_{j_2}, z_{k_2})$ in M, if e and f agree on at least one coordinate then they cannot both belong to L', i.e., M' is a matching of M. Using the same argument as above, if L' contains a leaf in $B_{x_{i_1},z_{k_1}}$ then L' cannot contain any triple $(x_{i_2}, y_{j_2}, z_{k_2})$ with $i_1 \neq i_2$ and $k_1 = k_2$, or with $i_1 = i_2$ and $k_1 \neq k_2$. Then for any $(x_{i_1}, y_{j_1}, z_{k_1}) \in L'$, L' must also contain a leaf from $B_{x_{i_1},z_{k_1}}$ since leaves from q different subtrees of the form B_{x_i,z_k} must be included in L', so e and f cannot both belong to L' if $i_1 \neq i_2$ and $k_1 = k_2$, or if $i_1 = i_2$ and $k_1 \neq k_2$. Next, if $i_1 \neq i_2$, $j_1 = j_2$, and $k_1 \neq k_2$ then $N_1 \mid \{e, f, \ell_{q+1}\}$ and $N_2 \mid \{e, f, \ell_{q+1}\}$ differ, implying that L' cannot contain both e and f. Finally, if $i_1 = i_2$, $j_1 \neq j_2$, and $k_1 = k_2$ and $e, f \in L'$ then the roots of $U_{y_{j_1}}$ and $U_{y_{j_2}}$ in N_2 both have to correspond to nodes located in the same subtree $S_{x_{i_1},z_{k_1}}$ in N_1 because e and f belong to $S_{x_{i_1},z_{k_1}}$, and then there are strictly less than $q - 1$ available U_{y_j}-roots for the remaining $q - 1$ subtrees of the form S_{x_i,z_k} with leaves in L', which is a contradiction. □

From the above, we obtain:

Theorem 14. *MASN is NP-hard even if restricted to $k = 2$, and even if one of the two input networks is a binary tree.*

4.2. MASN with Unrestricted Outdegrees is NP-hard

Here, we prove that MASN for two nested phylogenetic networks with nesting depth 1 (i.e., two galled trees/level-1 networks) is NP-hard if the nodes are allowed to have unrestricted outdegree. We give a polynomial-time reduction from the problem 3SAT, which is known to be NP-complete (see, e.g., [10]).

Three-Satisfiability (3SAT)

Instance: A set $U = \{u_1, ..., u_p\}$ of Boolean variables and a collection $C = \{c^1, ..., c^q\}$ of disjunctive clauses over U, each containing exactly 3 literals.

Question: Is there a truth assignment for U that makes every clause in C true?

For every $u_i \in U$, let $J(u_i)$ be the set $\{j : u_i \text{ occurs in clause } c^j\}$. Without loss of generality, assume that $|J(u_i)| \geq 2$. Let $J(u_i)_k$ be the kth smallest integer in $J(u_i)$ so that $J(u_i)_1 \leq J(u_i)_2 \leq ... \leq J(u_i)_{|J(u_i)|}$. Now, given an instance of 3SAT, construct an instance of MASN with two nested phylogenetic networks $\mathcal{N} = \{N_1, N_2\}$ (where the outdegrees of the nodes are unrestricted) having a leaf set L as follows.

For each $u_i \in U$, define a set of new elements $V(u_i) = \{v_i^j, \overline{v}_i^j, w_i^j, \overline{w}_i^j : j \in J(u_i)\}$. Similarly, for each $c^j \in C$, define a set of six new elements $D(c^j) = \{d^j[1], d^j[2], d^j[3], e^j[1], e^j[2], e^j[3]\}$. Let $L = \bigcup_{u_i \in U} V(u_i) \cup \bigcup_{c^j \in C} D(c^j)$. Note that for each $c^j \in C$, there are exactly 18 elements with the symbol j in their exponent, so $|L| = 18q$.

For any nonempty $L_1, L_2, L_3 \subseteq L$, define $S(L_1; L_2; L_3)$ to be a nested phylogenetic network with nesting depth 1 having a single hybrid node h where: (1) $|L_1|$ leaves distinctly labeled by L_1 are attached to a path of length $|L_1|$ starting at the left child of the root and ending at h; (2) $|L_2|$ leaves distinctly labeled by L_2 are attached to a path of length $|L_2|$ starting at the right child of the root and ending at h; and (3) h is the parent of $|L_3|$ leaves distinctly labeled by L_3. See Figure 8 for an example. For any $c^j \in C$, let $T(c^j)$ be a tree whose root has one child with three children x_1, x_2, x_3, and where for $k \in \{1, 2, 3\}$, x_k is the parent of two leaves labeled by $d^j[k]$ and $e^j[k]$.

We build the nested phylogenetic network N_1 as follows. First, for every $u_i \in U$, construct for all $k \in \{1, ..., |J(u_i)|\}$ the networks $S(\{v_i^{J(u_i)_k}\}; \{\overline{v}_i^{J(u_i)_{k+1}}\}; \{w_i^{J(u_i)_k}, \overline{w}_i^{J(u_i)_{k+1}}\})$, where $J(u_i)_{|J(u_i)|+1} \equiv J(u_i)_1$, and let all their roots coincide with the root of N_1. Then, construct $T(c^1), \ldots, T(c^q)$ and make all of their roots also coincide with the root of N_1. See Figure 9.

Next, for every $u_i \in U$ and all $j \in J(u_i)$, if u_i is the kth literal in c^j then define $R(u_i, j)$ as $S(\{v_i^j\}; \{\overline{v}_i^j, d^j[k], e^j[k]\}; \{w_i^j, \overline{w}_i^j\})$; otherwise, if $\overline{u}_i$ is the kth literal in c^j then let $R(u_i, j)$ be $S(\{v_i^j, d^j[k], e^j[k]\}; \{\overline{v}_i^j\}; \{w_i^j, \overline{w}_i^j\})$. Let N_2 be the nested phylogenetic network whose root node coincides with the roots of all $R(u_i, j)$, where $u_i \in U$ and $j \in J(u_i)$. See Figure 10.

Lemma 15. *If U has a truth assignment that makes every clause in C true then there exists an agreement subnetwork of (N_1, N_2) with $10q$ leaves.*

Proof. Suppose U has a truth assignment $A : U \to \{\text{true, false}\}$ that satisfies all clauses in C. For each $u_i \in U$, construct a set $L(u_i)$ as follows. If $A(u_i) = \text{true}$ then let $L(u_i) = \{v_i^j, w_i^j : j \in J(u_i)\}$ and define $\ell(u_i^j) = \overline{v}_i^j$ for all $j \in J(u_i)$, and if $A(u_i) = \text{false}$ then $L(u_i) = \{\overline{v}_i^j, \overline{w}_i^j : j \in J(u_i)\}$ and $\ell(u_i^j) = v_i^j$ for all $j \in J(u_i)$. Next, for every $j \in J(u_i)$, if u_i is the variable with the lowest index which makes c^j true then add $d^j[k]$

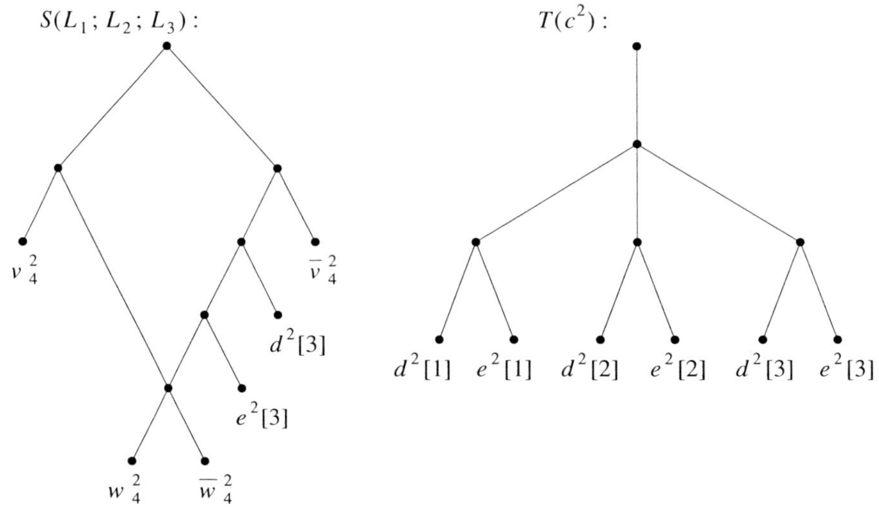

Figure 8. $S(L_1; L_2; L_3)$ with $L_1 = \{v_4^2\}$, $L_2 = \{\overline{v}_4^2,\ d^2[3],\ e^2[3]\}$, and $L_3 = \{w_4^2,\ \overline{w}_4^2\}$ is shown on the left. $T(c^2)$ is shown on the right.

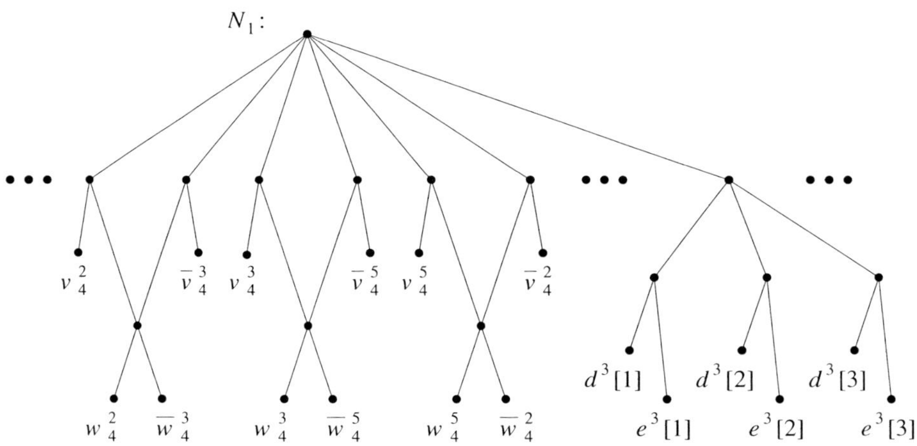

Figure 9. The phylogenetic network N_1. Assume that variable u_4 occurs in c^2, c^3, and c^5 in the given instance of 3SAT. Then the portion of N_1 that corresponds to u_4 has the structure shown above. Also shown is $T(c^3)$, the part corresponding to c^3.

and $e^j[k]$ to $L(u_i)$, where u_i is the kth variable in c^j; otherwise, if u_i is not the variable with the lowest index which makes c^j true then add $\ell(u_i^j)$ to $L(u_i)$. Let $L' = \bigcup_{u_i \in U} L(u_i)$.

Let T be the following tree, distinctly leaf-labeled by L'. For each $c^j \in C$, the root r of T has 6 children. Let u_i be the variable (the one with the lowest index, if there exists more than one) which makes c^j true when assigned the value $A(u_i)$, and denote the other two variables in c^j by u_x and u_y. Two of the children of r corresponding to c^j are leaves labeled by $\ell(u_x^j)$ and $\ell(u_y^j)$. Another one of the children of r is a node with two children labeled by $d^j[k]$ and $e^j[k]$, where u_i is the kth variable in c^j. The remaining three children of r corresponding to c^j are nodes with two children each, labeled by either v_z^j and w_z^j (if

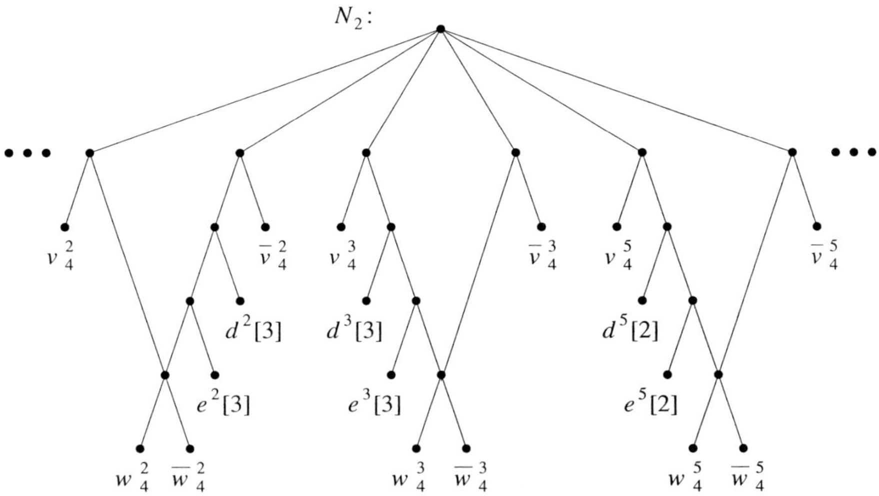

Figure 10. The phylogenetic network N_2. If $c^2 = (\ldots \vee \ldots \vee u_4)$, $c^3 = (\ldots \vee \ldots \vee \overline{u}_4)$, and $c^5 = (\ldots \vee \overline{u}_4 \vee \ldots)$ then the part corresponding to u_4 looks as above.

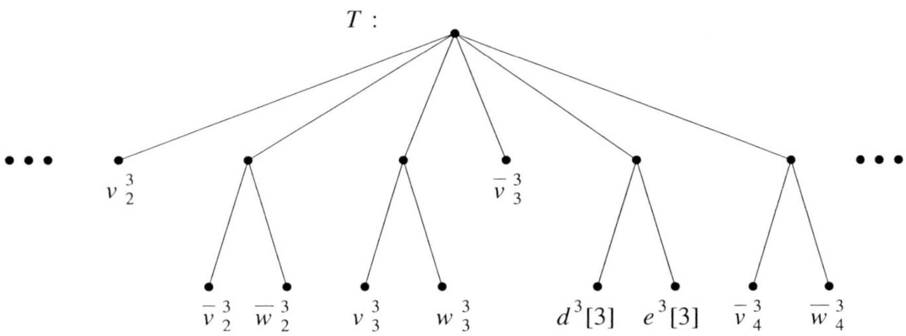

Figure 11. Assume $c^3 = (u_2 \vee \overline{u}_3 \vee \overline{u}_4)$, $A(u_2) = \text{false}$, $A(u_3) = \text{true}$, and $A(u_4) = \text{false}$. The part of T corresponding to c^3 is displayed. $d^3[3]$ and $e^3[3]$ belong to T since c^3 is satisfied because of u_4, i.e., the third variable in c^3.

$A(u_z) = \text{true}$) or $\overline{v}_z^j$ and $\overline{w}_z^j$ (if $A(u_z) = \text{false}$) for $z \in \{i, x, y\}$. See Figure 11. T has 10 leaves for each $c^j \in C$, and thus $10q$ leaves in total. It is easily verified that T is a subgraph of $N_1 \mid L'$ and also a subgraph of $N_2 \mid L'$, and hence an agreement subnetwork of (N_1, N_2). □

Lemma 16. *If there exists an agreement subnetwork of* (N_1, N_2) *with* $10q$ *leaves then* U *has a truth assignment that makes every clause in* C *true.*

Proof. Suppose there exists an agreement subnetwork T' with a leaf set $L' \subseteq L$ such that $|L'| = 10q$. For each $c^j \in C$, denote the set of all leaves in L' with the symbol j in their exponent as L_j. By the structure of N_1 and N_2, at most one of w_i^j and $\overline{w}_i^j$ for every $u_i \in U$ and $j \in J(u_i)$ may appear in L'. Also, for each $c^j \in C$, elements from at most one of the three pairs $(d^j[1], e^j[1])$, $(d^j[2], e^j[2])$, and $(d^j[3], e^j[3])$ can belong to L'. Furthermore, if some $d^j[k]$ or $e^j[k]$ is in L' then either v_i^j (if the kth literal of c^j is of the form u_i) or $\overline{v}_i^j$ (if the kth literal of c^j is of the form $\overline{u}_i$) cannot be in L'. Hence, for each $c^j \in C$, at most 10 leaves with the symbol j in their exponent belong to L'. Denote the three variables which are included in c^j by u_x, u_y, and u_z. Since $|L'| = 10q$ it follows that $|L_j| = 10$ and L_j must consist of: (1) $d^j[k]$ and $e^j[k]$ for some $k \in \{1, 2, 3\}$; (2) five of the six elements in $\{v_x^j, \overline{v}_x^j, v_y^j, \overline{v}_y^j, v_z^j, \overline{v}_z^j\}$; and (3) for each $t \in \{x, y, z\}$, either w_t^j or $\overline{w}_t^j$.

Next, for each $u_i \in U$, if $w_i^j \in L'$ for some $j \in J(u_i)$ then $w_i^k \in L'$ for every $k \in J(u_i)$ (and analogously if $\overline{w}_i^j \in L'$). This follows because $w_i^{J(u_i)_k} \in L'$ implies that $\overline{w}_i^{J(u_i)_{k+1}} \notin L'$ (they belong to the same S in N_1 but different S in N_2), where $J(u_i)_{|J(u_i)|+1} \equiv J(u_i)_1$, and by (3) above, $w_i^{J(u_i)_{k+1}} \in L'$. We can now define a truth assignment $A' : U \rightarrow \{$true, false$\}$ as follows. For each $u_i \in U$, if $w_i^k \in L'$ for every $k \in J(u_i)$ then set $A'(u_i) =$ true, and if $\overline{w}_i^k \in L'$ for every $k \in J(u_i)$ then set $A'(u_i) =$ false.

Finally, we show that each $c^j \in C$ is satisfied by A'. By the above, $d^j[k]$ and $e^j[k]$ for some $k \in \{1, 2, 3\}$ belong to L_j. Let ℓ be the kth literal in c^j. If ℓ is of the form u_i then $\overline{v}_i^j$ lies on the same side as $d^j[k]$ and $e^j[k]$ in $R(u_i, j)$ in N_2, and hence $\overline{v}_i^j \notin L'$ and $\overline{w}_i^j \notin L'$, giving us $w_i^j \in L'$ and $A'(u_i) =$ true. Otherwise, ℓ is of the form $\overline{u}_i$ and then v_i^j lies on the same side as $d^j[k]$ and $e^j[k]$ in $R(u_i, j)$ in N_2, and hence $v_i^j \notin L'$ and $w_i^j \notin L'$, giving us $\overline{w}_i^j \in L'$ and $A'(u_i) =$ false. In both cases, c^j is satisfied. □

Lemmas 15 and 16 give us the next theorem.

Theorem 17. *If the restriction on the outdegrees of the nodes is removed then MASN is NP-hard even for two nested phylogenetic networks with nesting depth* 1 *(i.e., two galled-trees/level-*1 *networks).*

5. Conclusion

MASN with $k = 2$ is NP-hard (as proved in Section 4.1.), but efficiently solvable for some special types of phylogenetic networks. For example, if N_1 and N_2 are trees then the problem can be solved in $O(n \log n)$ time [7, 18], if N_1 and N_2 are level-1 phylogenetic networks (i.e., "galled-trees", using the terminology of [12]) then the problem is solvable in $O(n^2)$ time [6], and more generally, if N_1 and N_2 are level-f phylogenetic networks, where $f = O(\log(|V(N_1)| + |V(N_2)|))$, then the $O(|V(N_1)| \cdot |V(N_2)| \cdot 4^f)$-time algorithm in [6] runs in time which is polynomial in the input size. In this chapter, we have demonstrated that even when the parameter f is unrestricted, the problem can be solved in polynomial time if N_1 and N_2 are nested.

Does MASN for other types of structurally restricted phylogenetic networks admit efficient algorithms? In particular, is it possible to extend our method in Section 3. to two networks in which every hybrid node has exactly one split node? An example of such a network is shown in Figure 12. We would also like to know if MASN can be solved efficiently for an even more complex structure which we call a *planar phylogenetic network*, defined as follows: for any positive integers a, b, let $M(a, b)$ be a rooted, directed graph with node set $\{M_{i,j} \mid 1 \leq i \leq a,\ 1 \leq j \leq b\}$ such that there is one directed edge from $M_{i,j}$ to $M_{i-1,j}$ for every $2 \leq i \leq a$ and $1 \leq j \leq b$, and one directed edge from $M_{i,j}$ to $M_{i,j-1}$ for every

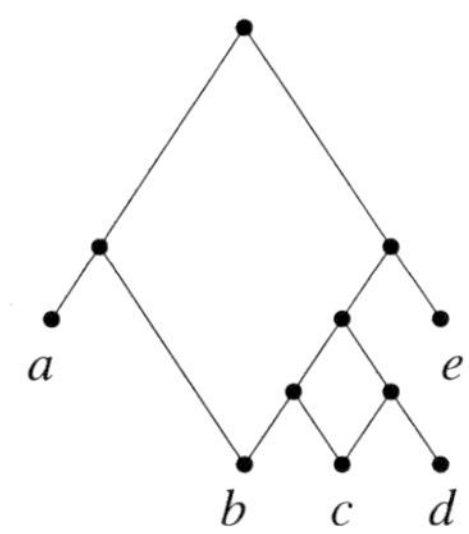

Figure 12. This phylogenetic network is not nested although every hybrid node has exactly one split node, and every split node has exactly one hybrid node. (Thus, the converse of Lemma 1 is not true.)

$1 \leq i \leq a$ and $2 \leq j \leq b$; we say that the network N is an (a, b)-*planar phylogenetic network* if each biconnected component in $\mathcal{U}(N)$ is isomorphic to a subgraph of $M(a, b)$.

We believe MASN for more than two nested phylogenetic networks can be solved in polynomial time when $k = O(1)$. It would also be interesting to investigate if any other computational problems which are hard to solve for unrestricted phylogenetic networks but known to be solvable in polynomial time for galled-trees can be solved efficiently for nested phylogenetic networks with unrestricted nesting depths. One example of such a problem might be *the perfect phylogenetic network with recombination problem* , which is NP-hard for unrestricted networks [28] but solvable in polynomial time for galled-trees [12].

The final open question is: can the running time of our algorithm for two nested phylogenetic networks be improved, e.g., by applying sparsification techniques?

References

[1] A. Amir and D. Keselman. Maximum agreement subtree in a set of evolutionary trees: Metrics and efficient algorithms. *SIAM Journal on Computing*, **26**(6):1656–1669, 1997.

[2] M. Bonet, C. Phillips, T. Warnow, and S. Yooseph. Constructing evolutionary trees in the presence of polymorphic characters. *SIAM Journal on Computing*, **29**(1):103–131, 1999.

[3] D. Bryant. *Building Trees, Hunting for Trees, and Comparing Trees: Theory and Methods in Phylogenetic Analysis*. PhD thesis, University of Canterbury, Christchurch, New Zealand, 1997.

[4] D. Bryant and V. Moulton. Neighbor-Net: An agglomerative method for the construction of phylogenetic networks. *Molecular Biology and Evolution*, **21**(2):255–265, 2004.

[5] H.-L. Chan, J. Jansson, T.-W. Lam, and S.-M. Yiu. Reconstructing an ultrametric galled phylogenetic network from a distance matrix. *Journal of Bioinformatics and Computational Biology*, **4**(4):807–832, 2006.

[6] C. Choy, J. Jansson, K. Sadakane, and W.-K. Sung. Computing the maximum agreement of phylogenetic networks. *Theoretical Computer Science*, **335**(1):93–107, 2005.

[7] R. Cole, M. Farach-Colton, R. Hariharan, T. Przytycka, and M. Thorup. An $O(n \log n)$ algorithm for the maximum agreement subtree problem for binary trees. *SIAM Journal on Computing*, **30**(5):1385–1404, 2000.

[8] T. Cormen, C. Leiserson, and R. Rivest. *Introduction to Algorithms*. The MIT Press, 1990.

[9] M. Farach, T. Przytycka, and M. Thorup. On the agreement of many trees. *Information Processing Letters*, **55**:297–301, 1995.

[10] M. Garey and D. Johnson. *Computers and Intractability – A Guide to the Theory of NP-Completeness*. W. H. Freeman and Company, New York, 1979.

[11] L. Gąsieniec, J. Jansson, A. Lingas, and A. Östlin. On the complexity of constructing evolutionary trees. *Journal of Combinatorial Optimization*, **3**(2–3):183–197, 1999.

[12] D. Gusfield, S. Eddhu, and C. Langley. Optimal, efficient reconstruction of phylogenetic networks with constrained recombination. *Journal of Bioinformatics and Computational Biology*, **2**(1):173–213, 2004.

[13] J. Hein. Reconstructing evolution of sequences subject to recombination using parsimony. *Mathematical Biosciences*, **98**(2):185–200, 1990.

[14] J. Hein, T. Jiang, L. Wang, and K. Zhang. On the complexity of comparing evolutionary trees. *Discrete Applied Mathematics*, **71**:153–169, 1996.

[15] B. Holland and V. Moulton. Consensus networks: A method for visualising incompatibilities in collections of trees. In *Proceedings of the 3rd Workshop on Algorithms in Bioinformatics* (WABI 2003), volume 2812 of *LNCS*, pages 165–176. Springer, 2003.

[16] D. H. Huson, T. Dezulian, T. Klöpper, and M. Steel. Phylogenetic super-networks from partial trees. *IEEE/ACM Transactions on Computational Biology and Bioinformatics*, **1**(4):151–158, 2004.

[17] J. Jansson, N. B. Nguyen, and W.-K. Sung. Algorithms for combining rooted triplets into a galled phylogenetic network. *SIAM Journal on Computing*, **35**(5):1098–1121, 2006.

[18] M.-Y. Kao, T.-W. Lam, W.-K. Sung, and H.-F. Ting. An even faster and more unifying algorithm for comparing trees via unbalanced bipartite matchings. *Journal of Algorithms*, **40**(2):212–233, 2001.

[19] C.-M. Lee, L.-J. Hung, M.-S. Chang, C.-B. Shen, and C.-Y. Tang. An improved algorithm for the maximum agreement subtree problem. *Information Processing Letters*, **94**(5):211–216, 2005.

[20] W.-H. Li. *Molecular Evolution*. Sinauer Associates, Inc., Sunderland, 1997.

[21] C. R. Linder, B. M. E. Moret, L. Nakhleh, and T. Warnow. Network (reticulate) evolution: Biology, models, and algorithms. Tutorial presented at *the 9thPacific Symposium on Biocomputing* (PSB 2004), 2004.

[22] L. Nakhleh, J. Sun, T. Warnow, C. R. Linder, B. M. E. Moret, and A. Tholse. Towards the development of computational tools for evaluating phylogenetic reconstruction methods. In *Proceedings of the 8th Pacific Symposium on Biocomputing* (PSB 2003), pages 315–326, 2003.

[23] L. Nakhleh, T. Warnow, C. R. Linder, and K. St. John. Reconstructing reticulate evolution in species – theory and practice. *Journal of Computational Biology*, **12**(6):796–811, 2005.

[24] D. Posada and K. A. Crandall. Intraspecific gene genealogies: trees grafting into networks. *TRENDS in Ecology & Evolution*, **16**(1):37–45, 2001.

[25] C. Semple and M. Steel. *Phylogenetics*, volume 24 of *Oxford Lecture Series in Mathematics and its Applications*. Oxford University Press, 2003.

[26] J. C. Setubal and J. Meidanis. *Introduction to Computational Molecular Biology*. PWS Publishing Company, Boston, 1997.

[27] M. Steel and T. Warnow. Kaikoura tree theorems: Computing the maximum agreement subtree. *Information Processing Letters*, **48**:77–82, 1993.

[28] L. Wang, K. Zhang, and L. Zhang. Perfect phylogenetic networks with recombination. *Journal of Computational Biology*, **8**(1):69–78, 2001.

In: New Topics in Theoretical Computer Science
Editors: Oleg N. Terikhovsky *et al.*, pp. 143-160
ISBN 978-1-60456-100-5

Chapter 5

AN INVESTIGATION OF HIERARCHICAL BIT VECTORS

***James Glenn*[*] *and David Binkley*[†]**
Loyola College in Maryland, MD, USA

Abstract

Hierarchical bit vectors represent sets of integers using a collection of bit vectors. At the top level, a single bit is set iff the set is non-empty. The bits of this next level summarize ranges of the elements. In the case of a binary hierarchical bit vector the two bits of the next level summarize two ranges: the lower half and the upper half of the possible elements. At the lowest level each bit records the membership of a particular integer.

Hierarchical bit vectors find application in information retrieval, bioinformatics, non-averaging sets, and the conversion of *NFA*s to *DFA*s. Competing data structures for such applications include simple bit vectors and tree-based structures such as skip-lists. A comparison of hierarchical bit vectors with two other representations (simple bit vectors and binary search trees) is presented. The comparison includes both analytical and empirical analysis of the hierarchical bit vectors.

The analytical results show that as the size of the set used increases, hierarchical bit vectors enjoy an advantage over tree-based structures and that as the sets used become sparser, hierarchical bit vectors perform better than standard bit vectors. The empirical results confirm that hierarchical bit vectors sit in between the other two. The empirical investigation also highlights the impact that the processor cache has on the break-even points.

1. Introduction

A *hierarchical bit vector* (*HBV*) is data structure for storing sets of integers in some fixed range $0, \cdots, N-1$. *HBV*s are useful as a compromise between standard bit vectors, which can perform set insertions and deletions in constant time, but are slower to enumerate

[*]E-mail address: jglenn@cs.loyola.edu
[†]E-mail address: binkley@cs.loyola.edu

the elements of a set, and tree related structures where insertions and deletions require logarithmic time, but enumeration is quick.

A *HBV* can be viewed as a sequence of bit vectors arranged in layers. At the lowest layer is a vector of N bits. Each bit at this level records the membership of a particular integer in the set – this is a standard bit vector. The next higher level is a bit vector of N/k bits, each bit of which summarizes a group of k consecutive bits of the level below. A bit at this level is set iff any of the summarized bits are set. Consecutive layers summarize groups of k bits from the next lower level until a layer of a single bit is produced. This bit records whether or not the set is empty. The value of k can differ on different levels.

For example, consider the *HBV* with $N = 8$ and $k = 2$ (the layered version is shown in the left of Figure 1). The bits of the lowest level represent the bit vector for the set that contains 2, 3, and 6. The bits of the second level (up from the bottom) summarize pairs of bits from the lowest level. Here the first bit in the second level records whether or not either of the values 0 or 1 is in the set (*i.e.*, if either of the first two bits is set in the bottom level). The second bit of the second level records whether or not either of the values 2 or 3 is in the set, and so on. The bit vector at the third level (from the bottom) summarizes pairs of bits from the second level (*i.e.*, groups of four integers from the underlying set). Working up, at the top level a single bit records whether or not the set is empty.

An *HBV* can also be viewed as a tree. For example, if $k = 2$ and N is a power of two, then the *HBV* can be thought of as a full binary tree with N leaves at the lowest level. Each of those leaves corresponds to a number from 0 to $N - 1$ and records whether or not that integer is in the set. Each internal node in the tree will contain a 1 if and only if one of its two children contains a 1. The tree view of an *HBV* with $N = 8$ and $k = 2$ is shown in the right of Figure 1. Relating the two views of a *HBV*, the nodes from a given level of the tree correspond to the bit vector at the same layer as seen in Figure 1.

This chapter introduces *HBV*s. It first considers several applications where the information in the upper-level bit vectors is used to speed up set operations. The chapter then presents a theoretical and an experimental analysis of *HBV*s. The theoretic analysis carefully bounds the constants of the *HBV*s operations. The empirical work compares the running time of the *HBV* with that of simple linked lists and binary search trees.

2. Applications

To provide a context for the investigation of *HBV*s, we first consider four applications. In each the *HBV* represents an alternative to simple bit vectors and tree-based structures such as binary search trees, skiplists [5], and other competing data structures [4, 9]. The applications require the following operations over sets of positive integers where the largest possible element is known *a priori*:

create()	make an empty set
insert(n)	add an element to the set
delete(n)	remove an element from the set
contains(n)	determine if an integer is in the set
min()	find the smallest element in the set
succ(n)	find the smallest element in the set that is greater than n

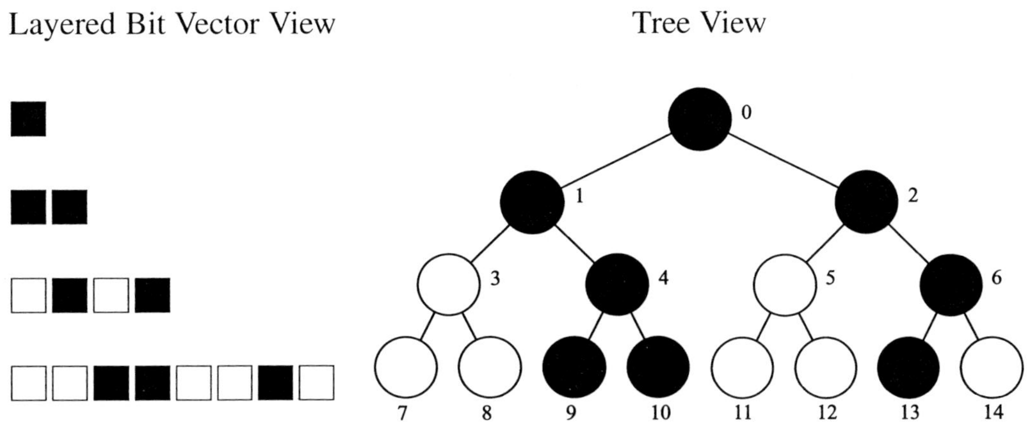

Figure 1. An *HBV* representing $\{2, 3, 6\}$.

The first of the four applications considered is the conversion of nondeterministic finite autotmata (*NFA*) to deterministic finite automata (*DFA*) [3]. The standard algorithm (see Algorithm 1), first assigns an arbitrary but unique integer label to each state of the *NFA* and then builds sets of states that represent which states the nondeterministic machine could be in. The operations this algorithm performs on the state sets are those given above. For example, min and succ are used to iterate through the state sets in sorted order to check if a state set is equal to a previously generated state set.

In the second application Putonti et al. consider the problem of testing for the presence of certain organisms (*e.g.*, Anthrax) while excluding all DNA subsequences that are present in a selected host (*e.g.*, a benign bacteria) or a background genome (*e.g.*, the human genome) [6]. This is done by identifying all the fixed-length DNA subsequences (k-mers) that occur in all of one set of genomes, but in none of another set of genomes.

The basic idea is to set in correspondence each of the 4^k k-mers and a particular element of a counting array, A, by converting each k-mer character sequence to an index of an element in A. As described by Putonti et al. the algorithm builds a bit vector of every possible k-mer (note that for k=12 there are 4^{12} possible 12-mers). (In contrast traditional blast-based approaches use approximation heuristics and thus may miss certain cases.) The approach then computes matches using a sequence of set unions and intersections. Based on the experiments presented in this chapter, the *HBV* would make a good choice for this identification.

The third application is to non-averaging sets. A non-averaging set is a set of integers that does not contain the average of any pair of its elements (this is equivalent to saying that the set does not contain all three elements of any arithmetic progression $x, x + d, x + 2d$; thus, non-averaging sets are sometimes called 3-free sets). Gasarch et al. survey and give empirical results from several methods of constructing large non-averaging subsets of a fixed range $0, \cdots, N - 1$ [2]. The best method (due to Behrend [1]) still does not produce sets of optimal density. Post-processing of the sets in order to add elements can be

Algorithm 1 *NFA* to *DFA* conversion

```
Require: M = (K, Σ, Δ, s, F) is an ε-free NFA.
Ensure: M' = (K', Σ, δ, {s}, F') is a DFA such that L(M') = L(M).
  Add {s} to K'.
  repeat
      Choose a state S in K' such that δ(S) is undetermined.
      D ← ∅
      for all σ ∈ Σ do                                  ▷ Determine δ(S, σ)
          for all s ∈ S do
              for all q such that (s, σ, q) ∈ Δ do
                  D ← D ∪ {q}                           ▷ Uses insert
              end for
          end for
      end for
      if D ∉ K' then                                    ▷ Can use min and succ
          K' ← K ∪ {D}
          if D ∩ F ≠ ∅ then
              F' ← F' ∪ {D}
          end if
      end if
      δ(S, σ) ← D                                       ▷ δ(S, σ) is now determined
  until All states in K' have δ determined
```

performed using the *HBV*'s operations. Furthermore, the maximum value and density of the resulting sets are within the range for which *HBV*s perform best relative to the alternatives.

The final application is in information retrieval (IR) and exploits a form of lazy allocation. The *HBV*'s bit vectors are usually initialized by setting all the bits to zero. For sparse sets, the initialization time can dominate the total time. Lazy initialization avoids allocating and zeroing tree nodes until they are needed. Thus, the first time a bit is set among a group of k siblings, we allocate the node and then initialize all the other bits in the group to zero. In exchange for this space and initialization-time savings, membership tests can no longer be performed by checking the corresponding bit in the lowest level. Instead, the algorithm must do a top-down traversal of the structure.

Lazy allocation is important for IR applications such as the building of a *concordance* [7, 8]. A concordance records, for a list of keywords $w_1, \cdots, w_n$, which documents in the collection $d_1, \cdots, d_n$ contain which keywords. A bit vector is a natural way to represent this data: for each keyword w_i store a bit vector b_i such that the jth bit of b_i is set if and only if document d_j contains w_i. As concordances are often stored on slow secondary storage units (hard drives or optical disks, for example), the reduced storage space can lead to time savings from the reduced number of I/O operations necessary to read the data.

Typically, the resulting bit vectors will be very sparse; thus, lazily initialized *HBV*s will naturally compress the data, as blocks of all zeros are never allocated. The remaining bits in the higher levels allow the complete structure to be recovered: anywhere a bit vector contains a zero, we know a group of zeros is in the vector at the next lowest level.

3. Hierarchical Bit Vectors

This section first considers the special case of a binary *HBV* (a *HBV* with $k = 2$) before generalizing to a k-ary *HBV*. The discussion of binary *HBV*s first considers two representation choices. It then looks at the definition and complexity of the six *HBV* operations: create, contains, insert, delete, min, and succ. The key to an efficient implementation is the function that determines the next bit to visit as part of the succ operation; thus, careful consideration is given to this function.

3.1. Binary Hierarchical Bit Vectors

Two representations for a binary *HBV* are considered. The first stores the data in a single bit vector. Viewing this bit vector as a tree, the root of the tree is stored in bit zero. The left child of an internal node stored in bit i is stored in bit $2i + 1$; its right child is stored in bit $2i + 2$. The parent of bit i is bit $\lfloor (i - 1)/2 \rfloor$.

As an alternative, the structure can be stored in an array of bit vectors having length N, $N/2$, $N/4$, $\cdots$. In the subsequent discussion it is convenient to number the bottom layer as Level 0 and the remaining levels in increasing order as we go up the layers towards the root. Again viewed as a tree, the children of bit i at layer l are then bits $2i$ and $2i + 1$ in layer $i - 1$ (not $2i + 1$ and $2i + 2$ as in the single bit vector case). The parent of bit i of layer l is bit $\lfloor i/2 \rfloor$ at layer $l + 1$. The empirical study presented in Section 4. uses this method because of the simplicity of implementation.

The size of the single bit vector is no more than $3N$. In the case where N is a power of two, it is $2N - 1$. Otherwise, there are wasted bits. For example, the lowest level can include at most $N - 1$ unused (wasted) bits (at N unused bits, the height of the tree can simply be reduced by 1). At higher levels, bits that summarize only unused bits are also wasted bits. Using layers of bit vectors obviates the need to allocate space for unused bits as they always occur at the end of the vector. However, it has to allocate the array to hold the levels, which has size $O(\log_2 N)$.

Algorithm 2 Inserting an integer in a *HBV*

Require: $0 \leq x < N$.
Ensure: $x \in HBV$

```
l ← 0
b ← x
while level l is not higher than the highest level do
    if bit b at level l is set then                    ▷ (*)
        STOP
    else
        Set bit b in level l                           ▷ (**)
        l ← l + 1
        b ← b div 2
    end if
end while
```

We now analyze the complexity of the six *HBV* operations: create, contains, insert, delete, min, and succ. The *HBV* create operation takes $O(N)$ time for a set capable of holding the integers $0, \cdots, N-1$. The contains(n) operation can be performed in $O(1)$ time by simply examining the appropriate bit at the bottom of the tree. The insert operation in a *HBV* is shown in Algorithm 2. In essence, this algorithm first finds the appropriate bit in the vector at the bottom layer. If the bit is not set, it sets it and moves to the next level up. We continue upwards through the layers setting bits until we find a bit that is already set or we come to the root of the tree. Using this algorithm, we can perform an insertion in worst-case $O(\log_2 N)$ time. As the time for insert depends on the number of previous insertions, we note that the total time over a sequence of insertions with no intervening deletions is proportional to the number of bits which must be set, which is $O(N)$ since each bit can be set at most once. The delete operation starts on the lowest level where it clears the selected bit. This bit is part of a pair summarized at the second to last level. The delete operation must check the other summarized bit. If this bit is zero, then the process is recursively repeated up one level until the root of the tree is reached. Thus, deletion is worst-case $O(\log_2 N)$ time.

The min and succ operations are used to determine if two *HBV*s represent the same set. This is done by enumerating the two in sorted order. Our goal is to enumerate the elements faster than can be done with a standard bit vector. The bit vector's weakness is that it has to examine each bit in turn; thus, for small sets with large ranges, it must examine long stretches of 0's. We can overcome this by using the additional data stored in the *HBV*. Once we have found one integer in the set, we can use the information in the next-to-last level of the *HBV* to answer the question "is either of the next two integers in the set?" If the answer is no, we use the next level up to answer the question "are any of the next four integers in the set?" Continuing in this way, we can leap over long expanses of emptiness in a few bounds. Once the answer to one of our questions is 'yes', we can go down the identified subtree to find which integer is next.

It is easier to describe the min and succ operations using the tree view of a *HBV*. It is also convenient to define a new operation min(n) that finds the minimum element contained in the subtree rooted at node n. Thus, min() is equivalent to min(root). The succ operation, described below, also uses the min(n) operation.

To perform the min(n) operation on a *HBV* we begin at node n. If there is a zero stored in that bit then the (sub)set is empty and we report that fact. If there is a one, we test the left child. If the left child is one, we visit that node, otherwise we visit the right child. In either case we proceed recursively. The complete algorithm is given as Algorithm 3. This operation clearly takes time proportional to the number of layers, which is $O(\log_2 N)$.

Finally, the succ(x) operation, Algorithm 4, makes use of one more auxiliary function, next(x), which denotes the next bit to consider after considering bit x. Thus, when searching for the next element of a set, the succ operation considers first next(x), then next(next(x)), and so forth until a bit that is set is encountered or the search falls off the side of the tree, in which case x was the largest element in the set. In the following paragraphs several different candidate next functions are considered. Some candidates may return an interior node, n, from the tree. In this case, the successor is the smallest element in the tree rooted at n (*i.e.*, min(n)).

Algorithm 3 The min operation for a *HBV*

Require: n is a node in the *HBV*

Ensure: The algorithm terminates with min equal to the index of the leftmost set bit at the bottom of the subtree rooted at n, or -1 if and only if n is not set.

```
if n is not set then
    min ← −1
    STOP
end if
while n is not a leaf do
    n ← left(n)
    if n is not set then
        n ← sibling(n)
    end if
end while
min ← the index of node n
```

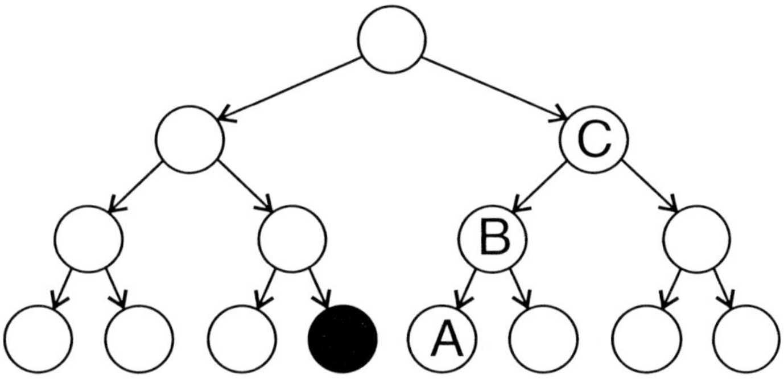

Figure 2. From the black node we can go to A, B, or C.

The definition of next(x) has a significant impact on the performance of the algorithm. Three possibilities are considered. First, if next(x) = x+1 then we are always checking along the bottom of the tree; this corresponds to how we would search in a normal bit vector. A better choice for sparse sets is to move up one or more levels for right children. The second options move up a fixed single level:

$$\text{next(x)} = \begin{cases} \text{x} + 1 & \text{if x is a left child,} \\ \text{parent(x)} + 1 & \text{if x is a right child.} \end{cases}$$

Finally, the third choice allows succ to find the ideal level. Initially we define next(x) as the node on the right branch from the last (lowest) node from which the path from the root to x went left; this will visit nodes in the same order as a pre-order recursive traversal that skips the children of nodes where the bit is not set. Note that for a left child this is x + 1 as it was for Option 2. After some analysis a *cap* will be placed on just how far up the structure to go.

All three next functions result in different answers to the question "when we reach the right edge of a subtree, how far up in the tree do we resume searching?" In the first case,

Algorithm 4 The succ operation for a *HBV*

Require: $0 \le x < N$

Ensure: The algorithm terminates with $succ$ equal to the smallest element of the set greater than x, or -1 is there is no such element.

```
n ← the node containing bit x
while n is not null and is not set do
    n ← next(n)
end while
if n is null then
    succ ← −1
else if n is a leaf then
    succ ← the index of node n
else
    succ ← min(n)
end if
```

we always look at the same level and hence never get out of the bottom level. In the second case we look up at most one level. In the third case we look up as far as possible. Starting from the black node, Figure 2 illustrates these three: going across the bottom (choice A) works well when the set is dense. Going as far up the tree as possible works well when the set is sparse (choice C). Going one level up (choice B) works well for in-between cases.

The remainder of this section demonstrates that the best definition of next is one that dynamically determines which of the latter two options works best for a particular set. Consider the choice of going to a node at level l versus going to its left child at level $l - 1$. For example, from the black node in Figure 2, this is the choice of going to node C or node B. If we expect the bit at C to be 0 then we should visit it next; doing so will skip its two children altogether. However, if our expectation is incorrect, then upon finding that the node was 1 we will have to visit B next – we would have been better off going directly to B.

To simplify the following analysis, we assume that the elements of the set are chosen randomly and uniformly. Let p denote the probability that an integer is included in the set and $q = 1 - p$ the probability that an integer is not in the set. Thus, for example, the size of the set, n, is expected to be pN. As a further simplification, assume that $N = 2^h$ for some natural number h.

In general, if the node at level l is 0 then we save one visit by going directly to it; that happens with probability q^{2^l}. If that node is 1 we visited one extra node; that happens with probability $1 - q^{2^l}$. Thus, we want to go to the node at level l when that move will, on average, save us work, or when $q^{2^l} \ge 1 - q^{2^l}$. This leads to the sequence of equivalent inequalities

$$\begin{aligned} q^{2^l} &\ge 1 - q^{2^l} \\ q^{2^l} &\ge \frac{1}{2} \\ 2^l \cdot \log_2 q &\ge -1 \\ 2^l &\le -\frac{1}{\log_2 q} \end{aligned}$$

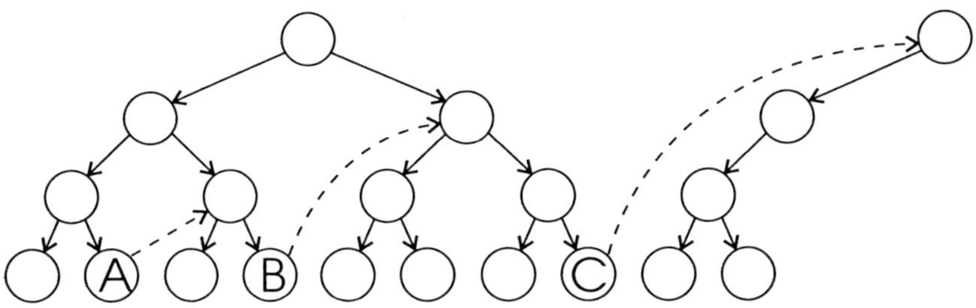

Figure 3. Maximum possible levels to move up in a binary *HBV*.

$$l \leq -\log_2(-\log_2 q). \tag{1}$$

If l satisfies the last inequality then it is to our advantage to go to level l instead of level $l-1$; the optimal l is the greatest level l that satisfies that inequality: $l_{opt} = \min(\lfloor -\log_2(-\log_2 q)\rfloor, h)$. Alternately, we can find the densities for which a given level is better than the one beneath it by rewriting the above inequalities as

$$q \geq \left(\frac{1}{2}\right)^{\frac{1}{2^l}}$$

and evaluating for different values of l. For example, for $l=1$ we get $q \geq \sqrt{\frac{1}{2}}$ and for $l=2$ we get $q \geq \sqrt[4]{\frac{1}{2}}$.

As we build a set, q will start at 1 and decrease. As q decreases, l_{opt} decreases. To simplify keeping track of l_{opt} (by which we mean keeping down the number of floating point operations needed to compute l_{opt}), we can first solve for d_{h-1}, the highest density for which traversing level $h-1$ is better than traversing level h. This can be done by taking the original inequality and solving for q when $l = h-1$ and yields $d_{h-1} = 1 - (\frac{1}{2})^{\frac{1}{2^h}}$. When that density is reached, we compute d_{h-2}, which is just $1-(1-d_{h-1})^2$.

Based on the proceeding analysis we update Option 3 for the function next such that next(x) determines k, the maximum number of levels it can move up from x. For example, in Figure 3, the values of k for nodes A, B, and C are 1, 2, and 3 respectively. If moving up k levels results in a move above the optimal level l, it moves only as high as level l. Otherwise, it moves up all k levels. This cap on how far up the tree to go complicates the computation of next(x) for right children (for left children we still have next(x) $= x+1$). Note that it is not the case that every time we move up a level we move to the optimal level: we only move to the optimal level from the rightmost child of a subtree rooted at that level. For example, if the optimal level is Level 2 then from node A we cannot move to the optimal level, but nodes B and C will move to the optimal level (from C we do not move as high as possible because such a move would not be optimal).

When each level is kept in a separate vector, the location of the least significant zero in the binary representation of $x+1$ gives k. We can then 'shift compute' next(x) by shifting x right by k bits to find the index of x's ancestor within the desired level. In the case where a single bit vector is used for all of the levels, similar bit-level computations can be used. Note that in both cases a lookup table can be used to compute the location of the least significant zero on machines for which there is no appropriate hardware instruction to perform that calculation.

Having explained the three options used for the function next, we now analyze the running time to enumerate a set using the succ operation. Some intermediate values will be convenient in the ensuing computations: let $C(l)$ denote the expected number of nodes visited in a subtree rooted at level l given that we enter it at its root and let $C'(l)$ denote the expected number of nodes visited in a subtree entered at its level-l root given that the root's parent was 1. Then $C(0) = C'(0) = 1$ and

$$C'(l) = 1 + \frac{1 - q^{2^l}}{1 - q^{2^{l+1}}} \cdot 2C'(l-1) \tag{2}$$

for $l > 0$. In other words, $C'(l)$ is the work done to visit the root plus the probability that the root is non-zero times the work that must be done to visit the children, given that their parent was non-zero. $C(l)$ needs to account for the work done at the root and the work that is done for its two children in the case that the root is non-zero:

$$C(l) = 1 + (1 - q^{2^l}) \cdot 2C'(l-1). \tag{3}$$

If l is the optimal level next should skip to, then an enumeration will visit *every* node at level l. The total work done for a traversal done at level l, denoted by $T(l)$, is therefore the number of nodes at level l times the amount of work done to traverse each level's subtree:

$$T(l) = \frac{N}{2^l} \cdot C(l) = N \cdot \frac{C(l)}{2^l} \tag{4}$$

where $\frac{C(l)}{2^l}$ is the constant of proportionality hidden by the $O(N)$ from before.

To bound $C(l)$ we first bound the q^{2^l} term that appears in both Equations 2 and 3. From Equation 1 we can derive

$$\sqrt{\frac{1}{2}} \geq q^{2^l} \geq \frac{1}{2}$$

for the optimal value of l, where the minimum value is achieved when $-\log_2(-\log_2 q)$ is an integer. We also have

$$\frac{1 - q^{2^l}}{1 - q^{2^{l+1}}} \leq \frac{2}{3},$$

which can be used to find an upper bound on $C'(l)$: substitution into Equation 2 gives

$$\begin{aligned} C'(l) &\leq 1 + \frac{2}{3} \cdot 2C'(l-1) \\ &= 1 + \frac{4}{3}C'(l-1) \\ &= \sum_{i=0}^{l} \left(\frac{4}{3}\right)^i \\ &= 3\left[\left(\frac{4}{3}\right)^{l+1} - 1\right]. \end{aligned}$$

In addition, we have $(1 - q^{2^l}) \leq \frac{1}{2}$, and so we can refine Equation 3:

$$\begin{aligned} C(l) &= 1 + (1 - q^{2^l}) \cdot 2C'(l-1) \\ &\leq 1 + C'(l-1) \\ &\leq 1 + 3\left[\left(\frac{4}{3}\right)^{l+1} - 1\right] \\ &= 3\left(\frac{4}{3}\right)^{l+1} - 2 \end{aligned}$$

.

The constant of proportionality in Equation 4, $\frac{C(l)}{2^l}$, can then also be bounded above by substitution:

$$\begin{aligned} \frac{C(l)}{2^l} &\leq \frac{\left[3\left(\frac{4}{3}\right)^{l+1} - 2\right]}{2^l} \\ &= 3 \cdot \left(\frac{2}{3}\right)^l - \frac{2}{2^l} \\ &= 3 \cdot (2^l)^{\log_2 \frac{2}{3}} - \frac{2}{2^l} \\ &\leq 3 \cdot \left(-\frac{1}{\log_2 q}\right)^{\log_2 \frac{2}{3}} - \frac{2}{-\frac{1}{\log_2 q}} \\ &= 3(-\log_2 q)^{log_2 \frac{3}{2}} + 2\log_2 q. \end{aligned} \tag{5}$$

The first term in this expression is the dominant one.

The following table gives values for the number of nodes visited enumerating the set in sorted order. The first line shows the number when the level used by next is capped based on Equation 5. The values when there is no cap on how high up in the tree the next function goes are listed on the second line for comparison. These figures can be compared with the work done by an ordinary bit vector, which is always $1.00\,N$. Note that because the fraction of nodes tends to zero along with p, there must be a density below which the running time to enumerate the set in sorted order is lower for a *HBV* than for a standard bit vector.

$p =$	0.000135	0.00540	0.0214	0.0830	0.293
cap	$0.0165N$	$0.0772N$	$0.223N$	$0.555N$	$1.000N$
no cap	$0.0311N$	$0.0929N$	$0.251N$	$0.583N$	$1.077N$

As illustrated above, for low density sets, *HBV*s outperform standard bit vectors because they can enumerate a set in sorted order faster. For higher density sets, *HBV*s are better than tree structures because they can perform a collection of inserts faster. The time taken for all insertions (assuming no intervening deletes) is proportional to the number of times the two marked lines of Algorithm 2 are executed. The total number of times those lines are executed is equal to the number of bits that are set in *HBV* plus the number of times the insert operation is used. Each of the 2^h leaves of the tree is set with probability $p = 1 - q$. Each of the 2^{h-1} nodes at the second level from the bottom is set with probability $1 - q^2$.

	p (the probability that an integer is included in the set)				
$N(=2^h)$	p =0.0020	p =0.0078	p =0.0312	p =0.1250	p =0.5000
2	3.00	3.00	2.98	2.94	2.75
4	3.99	3.98	3.94	3.77	3.22
8	4.99	4.96	4.84	4.42	3.47
16	5.97	5.90	5.63	4.86	3.59
32	6.94	6.79	6.27	5.11	3.66
64	7.89	7.58	6.70	5.23	3.69
128	8.77	8.21	6.95	5.30	3.70
256	9.56	8.64	7.08	5.33	3.71
512	10.2	8.89	7.14	5.34	3.71
1024	10.6	9.02	7.17	5.35	3.72
2048	10.9	9.08	7.18	5.36	3.72
4096	11.0	9.11	7.19	5.36	3.72
8192	11.1	9.12	7.20	5.36	3.72
16384	11.1	9.13	7.20	5.36	3.72
32768	11.1	9.14	7.20	5.36	3.72
65536	11.1	9.14	7.20	5.36	3.72
131072	11.1	9.14	7.20	5.36	3.72
262144	11.1	9.14	7.20	5.36	3.72
524288	11.1	9.14	7.20	5.36	3.72

Figure 4. Insertion Cost

Proceeding in this manner, we can compute $I(h)$, the expected number of bits that are set in a tree of height h:

$$I(h) = \sum_{i=0}^{h} 2^{h-i}(1 - q^{2^i}).$$

This is the number of times the line in Algorithm 2 marked with (**) is executed. The line marked (*) is executed once for each insertion; if all the insertions are unique then (*) is executed $n = pN = (1-q)N$ times. The total $I(h)+n$ is a measure of the work done by *all* insertions together; the cost per insertion is $\frac{I(h)}{n} + 1$. A table of this value for different combinations of N and p is given in Figure 4.

Note that for a fixed density p, the average work per insertion approaches a constant and so the total work for n insertions is $O(n)$. Also under this assumption, the work to enumerate the set in sorted order is $O(N) = O(\frac{n}{p}) = O(n)$. Therefore, for fixed p, an *HBV* performs n distinct insertions followed by a enumeration in $O(n)$ time. On the other hand, a binary search tree will perform $O(n \log_2 n)$ work to do n distinct insertions followed by $O(n)$ work to enumerate the set in order for a total of $O(n \log_2 n)$. Therefore, for a fixed density, there is always an N large enough so that an *HBV* will outperform a binary search tree or similar structure. For example, the empirical data presented in Section 4. show that the break-even point for $p = \frac{1}{1024}$ is around $N = 2^{26}$. Larger p yield lower break-even points: for $p = \frac{1}{4}$ it is around $N = 1024$.

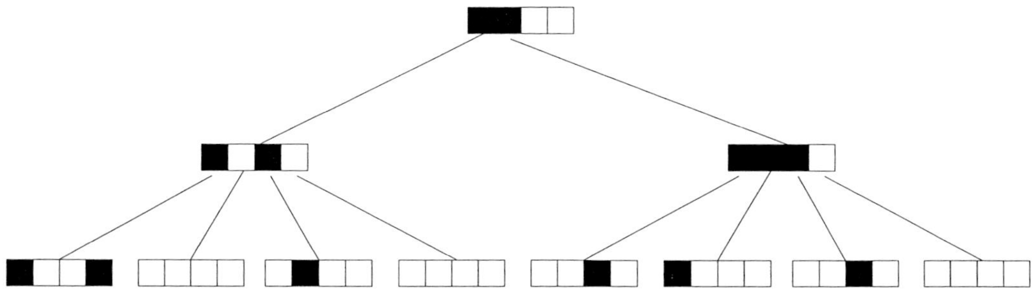

Figure 5. An *4*-HBV representing $\{0, 3, 9, 18, 20, 26\}$.

However, as p increases, the advantage the *HBV* has over the bit vector gets smaller and smaller until it disappears completely. Tests have shown that for $p \leq \frac{1}{65536}$ the *HBV* outperforms an ordinary bit vector. However, for such sparse sets the range must be extremely high for the *HBV* to outperform a binary tree.

3.2. k-ary Hierarchical Bit Vectors

This section generalizes the 2-ary *HBV*s from the previous section to values of k other than 2. The high performance of the ordinary bit vector comes from the fact that no processor works one bit at a time. If we want to list the elements stored in a bit vector in order using a 32-bit processor, we can break the vector into words of 32 bits each and examine each word using one instruction. If a word is zero then we can ignore it. Only if it is non-zero do we have to slow down and check it bit by bit. We use the same strategy to speed up the *HBV*.

A k-ary *HBV* (k-*HBV* for short) is similar to a binary *HBV*, but each node in the tree has k children all stored in the same k-bit word. Insertions and membership tests can be done in much the same way as in the binary *HBV*. The next operation can be reworked to take advantage of the power of microprocessors to examine more than one bit at a time: when finding the next integer in the set after m, we first examine the rest of the bits in m's word. If one is non-zero, we find the first non-zero bit, often using a single CPU instruction, for example BSR ("bit scan reverse") on the x86 family of processors. If all the other bits were zero, we choose a word in a higher level (the sibling of an ancestor of m's word) and examine it, continuing in this manner until we find a non-zero bit. Once found, we can go down the tree to find the smallest non-zero descendant.

For example, in the 4-ary *HBV* shown in Figure 5, to find succ(0) we would mask the most significant bit of the first word at the bottom level to get the bit pattern 0001. The BSR instruction tells us that the first non-zero bit is bit number 3, so we know that succ$(0) = 3$. To compute succ(3), we first notice that 3 was the last bit of its word, so we go directly to that word's parent, the first word of the middle layer of the figure. We have already examined that word's leftmost child, so we again mask off the most significant bit to get 0010. BSR tells us that the first non-zero bit is number 2, so we next examine the third child where we find the bit pattern 0100. BSR now tells us that the first bit set is bit number 1, so succ$(3) = 1 + 2 * 4 = 9$, for bit number 1 in word number 2 at the lowest level.

With the k-*HBV* we face the same choice of the highest level used to traverse the structure during a sorted enumeration as we did for the binary *HBV*. In Figure 5, if we traverse at the middle level we will examine the first word at the middle level and discover that its first bit is set, forcing us to examine the first word on the second level; we discover that its first bit is set and then examine the last three bits, finding that the last is set; at that point we return to the middle level and check the remaining three bits of the first word. By continuing in that manner we will examine 17 words or parts of words. By simply going along the bottom layer we would have examined only 13. In this case the set is dense enough that a standard bit vector would outperform a *HBV*.

In general, whenever we probe a word at any level of a k-*HBV*, we will examine the entire word once and will examine parts of the word for each one we find in bits 0 through $k-2$. So if we examine a word at level l that has m non-zero children among its first $k-1$ children, we should expect to examine that word $m+1$ times. We will also have to examine those non-zero children but we will not examine the children with all zero bits. On the other hand, if we bypass the level-l word and instead examine all of its children, we will do the same work that we did before for its non-zero children plus one examination each for the children with all zero bits.

The expected benefit of traversing level l instead of $l-1$ is then the expected number of zero words at level $l-1$ minus the expected number of non-zero words among the first $k-1$ children minus 1. The probability that a word at level $l-1$ is zero is $(1-p)^{k^l}$ so the expected number of empty children is $k \cdot (1-p)^{k^l}$. The probability that a word at level $l-1$ is non-zero is $1-(1-p)^{k^l}$, so the expected number of those among the first $k-1$ children is $(k-1)\cdot(1-(1-p)^{k^l})$. The expected benefit is then

$$k \cdot (1-p)^{k^l} - (k-1)\cdot(1-(1-p)^{k^l}) - 1.$$

As long as the above value is non-negative it is better (or at least just as good) to traverse level l instead of level $l-1$. After some algebra, we conclude that traversing level l is better than traversing level $l-1$ when

$$(1-p)^{k^l} \geq \frac{k}{2k-1}.$$

By plugging in values for k and l, we can find the densities that are good for traversing at any level. For $k = 32$ and $l = 1$, we find that $p \leq 1 - \sqrt[32]{\frac{32}{63}} \approx \frac{1}{48}$, which means Option 2 for the function next is preferred over Option 1 as traversing level 1 we examine fewer words than an ordinary bit vector (Option 1) for sets that are less than $\frac{1}{48}$ full. For $k = 32$ and $l = 2$ we have $p \leq 1 - \sqrt[1024]{\frac{32}{63}} \approx \frac{1}{1512}$ and for $k = 32$ and $l = 3$ we get $p \leq 1 - \sqrt[32768]{\frac{32}{63}} \approx \frac{1}{48374}$; however, at this point the binary search trees has a decided advantage for commonly used values of N.

4. Empirical Analysis

The three data structures: bit vectors, *HBV*s, and binary search trees were each implemented and used in an empirical evaluation. This complements the analysis from the previous section, which counted the number of words examined to enumerate a set in sorted order, but ignored the associated constants and the work that has to be done for other operations. The experiments confirm that tree structures are superior for small sparse sets, bit vectors are superior for dense sets, and *HBV*s are the best choice for large but sparse sets.

We ran the three implementations using randomly generated sets with various values of N and p on an AMD Athlon 64. Each test consists of constructing an empty set, inserting each integer with probability p (so the expected number of elements in the set is pN), and finally outputting the elements of the set in sorted order. The order of the insertions is randomized to avoid the worst-case $O(n)$ behavior of the binary search tree for this operation. Each test run is intended to reflect the usage pattern of *NFA* determinization, where state sets are created, populated, and then output in sorted order to allow comparisons to other sets. We include only one enumeration because in the determinization algorithm, the insertions are all performed before any enumerations; thus, the result from the the first can be stored and used for subsequent operations. A model of the sequence of operations for post-processing non-averaging sets would be similar but would include contains and delete operations as well.

Three *HBV* design decisions warrant mention. First, given the hardware we used, an appropriate value for k was 32. Second, to save initialization time the *HBV* implementation only initialized the top layer (to zero). The first time a bit is set (at internal nodes and leaves) among a group of k siblings, we initialize the other bits in its group to zero. Testing whether we are setting the first bit in a group of k siblings can be determined by checking whether we have just changed the parent from 0 to 1. The sorted-order enumeration algorithm does not need to be changed because it will never check bits that have not been initialized. Membership tests can not be performed by checking the corresponding bit in the lower lever, however. Instead, we must do a top-down traversal of the structure.

The third design decision follows from the theoretical result that levels above the bottom three would only be useful for very sparse sets ($p < \frac{1}{48374}$) where binary search trees have a decided advantage. This is because above this level we do not expect to encounter many zero bits; thus, the function next should never choose to traverse the tree above this level. Retaining at most the bottom three levels pragmatically means either retaining 3 or just 2 (as retaining just 1 would find the *HBV* degenerate into a simple bit vector). For the experiment, rather than create one structure that adapts to different densities, we chose a fixed cutoff. Making the structures non-adaptive significantly reduces the overhead of the operations.

Two different fixed cutoff values were experimented with: a 2-layer 32-ary *HBV* (essentially implementing Option 2 for the function next) and a 3-layer 32-ary *HBV* (essentially implementing a limited version of Option 3). The 2-layer version maintains only the bottom two levels; thus, it assumes that all bits at higher levels are always 1. The 3-layer version maintains the bottom 3 levels. Both choose the topmost retained layer as the optimal layer for the purposes of the next operation.

Comparing the simple bit vector and the two *HBV* implementations empirically (see Figure 6), the data reveal that the 2-level 32-ary *HBV* can enumerate in sorted order in less time than an ordinary bit vector for sets sparser than $p = 2^{-9}$ and the 3-layer 32-ary *HBV* enumerates in sorted order in less time than the 2-layer 32-ary *HBV* for sets sparser than $p = 2^{-14}$. However, over the range of values for N we used during our experiment, densities

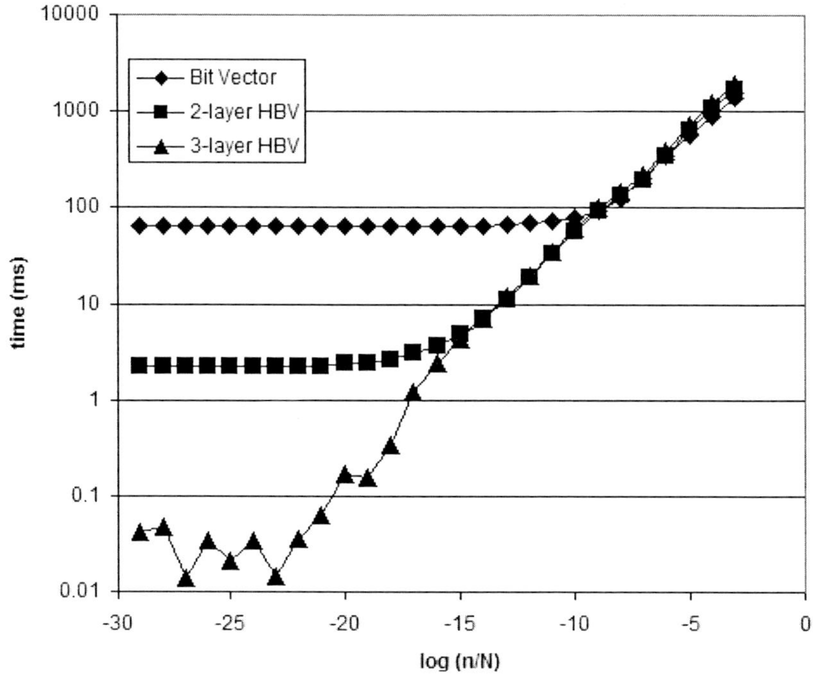

Figure 6. Time to enumerate in sorted order versus density.

lower than $p = 2^{-14}$ give a clear advantage to tree structures. Thus, in the remainder of this section only the $2\text{-}layer\ 32\text{-}ary$ *HBV* is considered.

The results of the experiment are summarized graphically in Figure 7. The x-axis of the figure shows the range of values while the y-axis shows the number of elements inserted. Both use a logarithmic scale. The three bands in the figure follow the prediction of the analysis done in Section 3. with the binary search tree being fastest for small sparse sets, the bit vector being fastest for dense sets, and the *HBV* being fastest in the middle range.

As evident in the figure, the boundaries are not straight lines, but show two anomalies (regions where the results appear to 'backtrack'). The first anomaly occurs at $(N, n) = (2^{17}, 2^5)$ where the *HBV* is faster even though the binary search tree is faster for both $N = 2^{16}$ and $N = 2^{18}$. The second anomaly occurs at $n = 2^{17}$ where bit vectors perform better for $N = 2^{22}$ and $N = 2^{25}$ but not $N = 2^{23}$, $N = 2^{24}$, or $N = 2^{26}$. Both appear to be cache effects. For example, at $N = 2^{22}$ the bit vector would occupy all of the AMD's 512KB L2 cache, yet layer 1 of the *HBV* will fit in the 64KB L1 cache for $N \leq 2^{24}$.

To investigate this hypothesis, the experiment was repeated using an Intel Core 2, which has a larger L2 cache, but a smaller L1 cache. The data, shown in Figure 8, supports the hypothesis: the first anomaly moves to the left along with the decrease in the Core 2's L1 cache size, while the second anomaly moves to the right along with the increase in the L2 cache size.

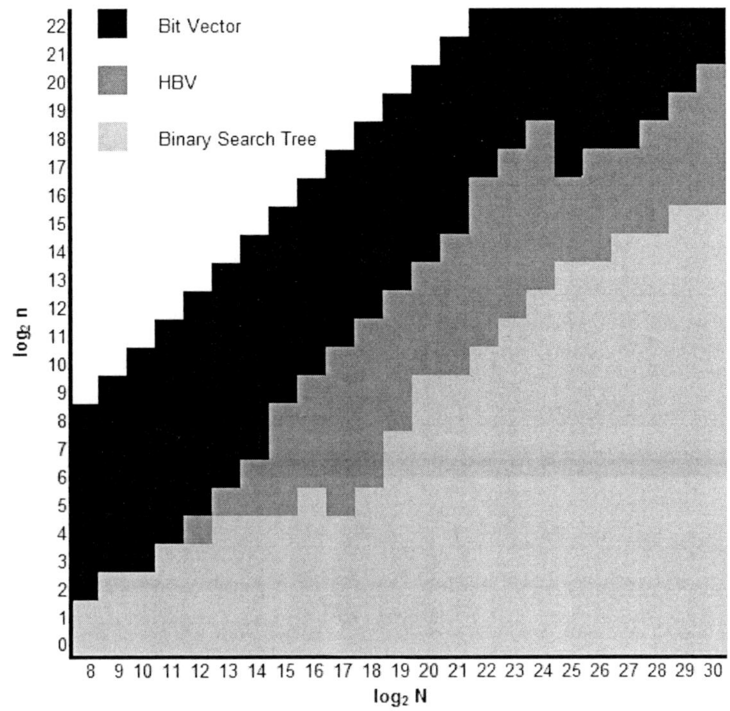

Figure 7. Comparison of three data structures (AMD Athlon 64 Architecture).

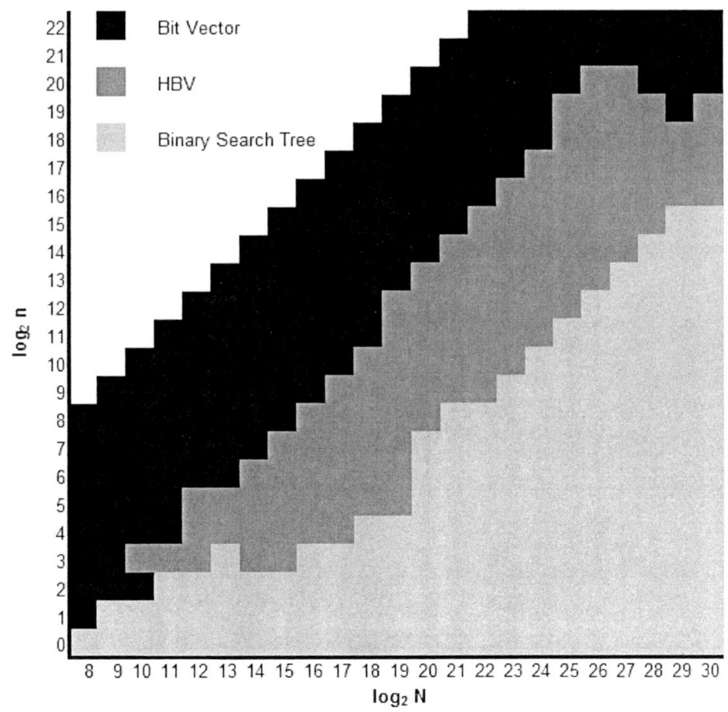

Figure 8. Comparison of three data structures (Intel Core 2 Architecture).

5. Conclusion

If it is known ahead of time that an application will make use of sparse sets and will have to perform the succ operation on those sets, then the 32-ary *HBV* can be put to good use. The more times the succ operation is used, the greater the *HBV*'s advantage is over the standard bit vector. The larger the set or the more times the contains operation is used, the greater the *HBV*'s advantage over the binary search tree. Applications such as non-averaging set post-processing where it is possible to determine the density of the sets used, the *HBV* supports a more time-efficient implementation.

References

[1] F. Behrend. On sets of integers which contain no three in arithmetic progression. *Proc. of the National Academy of Science (USA)*, **23**:331–332, 1946.

[2] W. Gasarch, J. Glenn, and C. Kruskal. Finding large 3-free sets I: the small n case. *Journal of Computer and System Sciences*, (to appear).

[3] James Glenn and William I. Gasarch. Implementing ws1s via finite automata: Performance issues. In Derick Wood and Sheng Yu, editors, *Workshop on Implementing Automata*, volume 1436 of *Lecture Notes in Computer Science*, pages 75–86. Springer, 1997.

[4] M. Korda and R. Raman. An experimental evaluation of hybrid data structures for searching. In *Proceedings of the 3rd International Workshop in Algorithm Engineering* , Lecture Notes in Computer Science 1668, pages 213–227. Springer Verlag, 1999.

[5] W. Pugh. Skip lists: A probabilistic alternative to balanced trees. *Commun. ACM*, **33**(6):668–676, 1990.

[6] C. Putonti, S. Chumakov, R. Mitra, G. Fox, R. Willso, and Y. Fofanov. Human-blind probes and primers for dengue virus identification – exhaustive analysis of subsequences present in the human and 83 dengue genome sequences. *Federation of European Biochemical Societies (FEBS)*, **273**, Feb 2006.

[7] O. Vallarino. On the use of bit-maps for multiple key retrieval. *SIGPLAN Notices, Special Issue*, **II**:108–114, 1976.

[8] H. Wedekind and T. Härder. *Datenbanksysteme II.* B.-I. Wissenschaftsverlag, 1976.

[9] D. E. Willard. New trie data structures which support very fast search operations. *Journal of Computer and System Sciences*, **28**(3):279–294, 1984.

In: New Topics in Theoretical Computer Science
Editors: Oleg N. Terikhovsky *et al.*, pp. 161-187
ISBN 978-1-60456-100-5

Chapter 6

Real-World Evolutionary Designs: Secure Evolvable Hardware for Public-Key Cryptosystems

***Nadia Nedjah*[*] *and Luiza de Macedo Mourelle*[†]**
Department of System Engineering and Computation, Engineering Faculty,
State University of Rio de Janeiro, Rua São Francisco Xavier, 524,
Sala 5022-D, Maracanã, Rio de Janeiro, Brazil

Abstract

In this chapter, we propose a methodology based on genetic programming to automatically generate data-flow based specifications for hardware designs of combinational digital circuits. We aim at allowing automatic generation of balanced hardware specifications for a given input/output behaviour. It minimises space while maintaining reasonable response time. We show that the evolved designs are efficient and creative. We do so comparing the obtained circuits of some benchmarks against those that were produced by human designers as well as to other evolutionary ones.

To emphasize the applicability of the methodology to real-world problems, we use genetic programming as an alternative methodology to automatically generate secure and minimal hardware designs of public-key cryptosystems such as RSA encryption system. We evolve optimal hardware circuits for modular exponentiation, which a cornerstone operation in almost every cryptographic system. The evolved circuits minimize both space (i.e. required gate number) and time (i.e. encryption and decryption time). The evolved designs are shielded against side-channel leakage and hence secure. The structure of the cryptographic circuit is random and so the private key cannot be deduced using known attacks. We compare our results against existing well-known designs, which were produced by human designers based on the binary method.

[*]E-mail address: nadia@eng.uerj.br, www.eng.uerj.br
[†]E-mail address: ldmm@eng.uerj.br

1. Introduction

Designing a hardware that fulfils a given function consists of deriving from specific input/output behaviour, an architecture that is operational (i.e. produces all the expected outputs from the given inputs) within a specified set of constraints. Besides the input/output behaviour of the hardware, conventional designs are essentially based on knowledge and creativity. These are two human characteristics too hard to be automated.

The problem of interest consists of designing efficient and creative circuits that implement a given input/output behaviour without much designing effort. The obtained circuits are expected to be minimal both in terms of space and time requirements: The circuits must be compact i.e. use a reduced number of gates and efficient, i.e. produce the output in a short response time. The response time of a circuit depends on the number and the complexity of the gates forming the longest path in it. The complexity of a gate depends solely on the number of its inputs. Furthermore, the design should take advantage of the all the kind of gates available on reconfigurable chip of field programmable gate array (FPGAs).

The three most popular are minimisation techniques are: algebraic method, Karnaugh map [10] and Quine-McCluskey procedure [8]. The algebraic method consists of applying some known algebraic theorems and postulates. This method depends heavily on the designer ability, as it does not offer general rules to assist her/him in recognising the theorem to apply. The Karnaugh map [10] is a matrix-based representation of logical functions and allows minimisation of up to 5-input functions. McCluskey procedure [8] is a tabular method and allows one to minimise functions of any number of inputs. Both Karnaugh map and McCluskey procedure produce a minimal sum of products. A combinational circuit based on this minimal form offers the shortest response time, but not at all the smallest size. However, in some cases, the designer great concern is the minimisation of the number of gates of the circuit as well as the signal propagation delay. Moreover, the McCluskey procedure needs an execution time that grows exponentially with the number of input signals. Furthermore, Karnaugh map and McCluskey procedure produces design that only use AND, OR and NOT gates and ignores all the rest of gates. So the designer needs to perform further refinement on the circuit yield by these methods in order to introduce other kind of gates such as XOR gates [20].

Evolutionary hardware is a hardware that is yield using simulated evolution as an alternative to conventional-based electronic circuit design. Genetic evolution [7] is a process that evolves a set of individuals, which constitutes the population, producing a new population. Here, individuals are hardware designs. The more the design obeys the constraints, the more it is used in the reproduction process. The design constraints could be expressed in terms of hardware area and/or response time requirements. The freshly produced population is yield using some genetic operators such as crossover and mutation that attempt to simulate the natural breeding process in the hope of generating new design that are fitter i.e. respect more the design constraints. Genetic evolution is usually implemented using genetic algorithms.

In this work, we design innovative and efficient evolutionary digital circuits. Circuit evaluation is based on their possible implementation using CMOS technology [5], [18], [21]. The produced circuits are balanced i.e. use a reduced number of gate equivalent and propagate result signals in a reduced response time such that the factor area×performance is minimised. We do so using genetic programming.

The remainder of this chapter is divided in five sections. In Section 2, we describe the principles of genetic programming. In Section 3, we describe the methodology we employ to evolve new compact and fast hardware for a given input/output behaviour. In Section 4, we compare the discovered hardware against existing most popular ones. Finally, we draw some conclusions.

2. Genetic Programming

Genetic programming [9] is an extension of genetic algorithms. The chromosomes are computer programs and the genes are instructions. In general, genetic programming offers a mechanism to get a computer to provide a solution of problem without being told exactly how to do it. In short, it allows one to automatically create a program. It does so based on a high level statement of the constraints the yielded program should obey to. The input/output behaviour of the expected program is generally considered as an omnipresent constraint. Furthermore, the generated program should use a minimal number of instructions and have an optimal execution time.

Starting form random set of computer programs, which is generally called initial population, genetic programming breeds a population of programs through a series of steps, called generations, using the Darwinian principle of natural selection, recombination also called crossover, and mutation. Individuals are selected based on how much they adhere to the specified constraints. Each program is assigned a value, generally called its fitness, which mirrors how good it is in solving the program. Genetic programming [9] proceeds by first, randomly creating an initial population of computer programs; then, iteratively performing a generation, which consists of going through two main steps, as far as the constraints are not met. The first step in a generation assigns for each computer program in the current population a fitness value that measures its adherence to the constraints while the second step creates a new population by applying the three genetic operators, which are reproduction, crossover and mutation to some selected individuals. Selection is done with on the basis of the individual fitness. The fitter the program is, the more probable it is selected to contribute to the formation of the new generation. Reproduction simply copies the selected individual from the current population to the new one. Crossover recombines two chosen computer programs to create two new programs using single-point crossover as shown in Figure 1(a) or two-points crossover as shown in Figure 1(b). Mutation yields a new individual by changing some randomly chosen instruction in the selected computer program. The number of genes to be mutated is called mutation degree and how many individuals should suffer mutation is called mutation rate.

3. Evolving Hardware for Combinational Digital Circuits

There three main aspects in implementation of genetic programming [9], [13]: *(i)* program encoding; *(ii)* crossover and mutation of programs; *(iii)* program fitness. In this section, we explain how we treat these three aspects in our implementation.

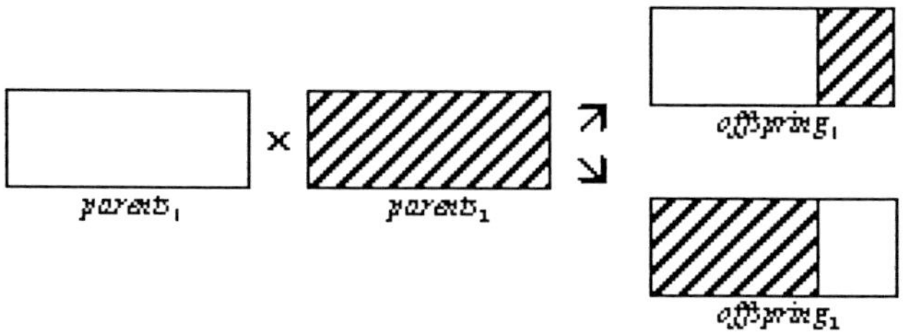

(a) single-point crossover

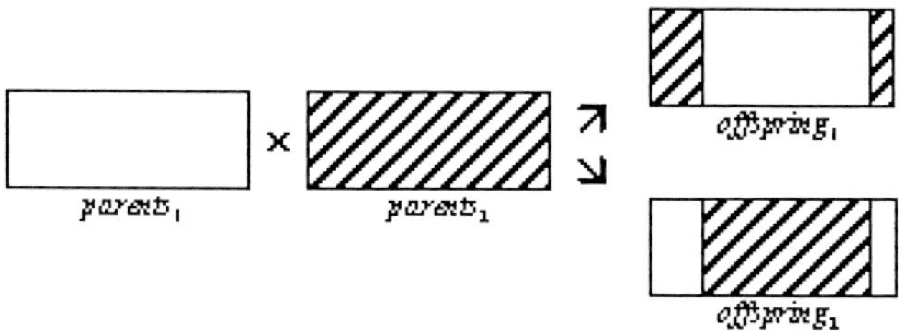

(b) double-point crossover

Figure 1. Types of crossover genetic operator

3.1. Circuit Specification Encoding

Encoding of individuals is one of the implementation decisions one has to take in order to use evolutionary computation. It depends highly on the nature of the problem to be solved. There are several representations that have been used with success: *binary encoding* which is the most common mainly because it was used in the first works on genetic algorithms, represents an individual as a string of bits; *permutation encoding* mainly used in ordering problem, encodes an individual as a sequence of integer; *value encoding* represents an individual as a sequence of values that are some evaluation of some aspect of the problem; and *tree encoding* represents an individual as tree. Generally, the tree coincides with the concrete tree as opposed to abstract tree [1] of the computer program, considering the grammar of the programming language used.

Here a design is specified using register transfer level equations. Each instruction in the specification is an output signal assignment. A signal is assigned the result of an expression wherein the operators are those that represent basic gates in CMOS technology of VLSI circuit implementation and the operands are the input signals of the design. The allowed operators are shown in Table 1. Note that all gates introduce a minimal propagation delay as the number of input signal is minimal, which is 2.

A NOT gate inverts the input signal, an and-gate propagates a 1-signal when both input signals are 1 and 0-signal otherwise and an or-gate propagates a 0-signal when both input signals are 0 and 1-signal otherwise. An AND gate inverts the signal propagated by a NAND

Table 1. Node operators

Name	Symbol	Name	Symbol
NOT	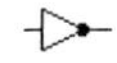	NAND	
AND	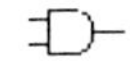	NOR	
OR		XNOR	
XOR		MUX	

gate while an OR gate inverts that propagated by a NOR gate. Note that, in CMOS technology, an and-gate is a NAND gate coupled with a NOT gate and an OR gate is a NOR gate followed by a NOT gate and not the inverse [5]. The XOR gate is a CMOS basic gate that has the behaviour of sum of products $x\bar{y} + \bar{x}y$ wherein x and y are the input signals. However, a XOR gate is not implemented using 2 AND gates, 2 NOT gates and an OR gate. A 2to1-multipliexer MUX is also a CMOS basic gate and implements the sum of products $x\bar{s} + ys$ wherein x and y are the first and the second input signals and s is the control signal. It is clear that a XOR and MUX gates are of the same complexity [5], [18].

For instance, a 2-bit multiplier has 4-bit result signal so an evolved register transfer level specification is as follows, wherein the input operands are $X = \langle x_1x_0\rangle$ and $Y = \langle y_1y_0\rangle$ and the output is the product $P = \langle p_3p_2p_1p_0\rangle$. The schematic of the digital circuit implementing the above specification is given in Figure 2.

$$\begin{array}{lcl} p_3 & \Longleftarrow & (x_0 \text{ AND } y_0) \text{ AND } (x_1 \text{ AND } y_1) \\ p_2 & \Longleftarrow & (x_0 \text{ NAND } y_0) \text{ AND } (x_1 \text{ AND } y_1) \\ p_1 & \Longleftarrow & (x_1 \text{ NAND } y_0) \text{ XOR } (x_0 \text{ NAND } y_1) \\ p_0 & \Longleftarrow & (y_0 \text{ AND } x_0) \text{ OR } y_0 \end{array} \tag{1}$$

We encode specifications using an array of concrete trees corresponding to its signal assignments. The ith tree represents the evaluation tree of the expression on the left-hand side of the ith signal assignment. Leaf nodes are labelled with a literal representing a single bit of an input signal while the others are labelled with an operand. The individual corresponding to above specification is shown in Figure 3.

3.2. Circuit Specification Reproduction

Crossover of circuit specification is implemented using a double-point crossover as described in Figure 1. One of the important and complicated operators for genetic programming is the mutation. It consists of changing a gene of a selected individual. The number of individuals that should suffer *mutation* is defined by the *mutation rate* while how many genes should be altered within a chosen individual is given by the *mutation degree*.

Here, a gene is the tree of the expression on the left hand side of a signal assignment. Altering an expression can be done in two different ways depending the node that was randomised and so must be mutated. A node represents either an operand or operator. In the former case, the operand, which is a literal representing a bit in the input signal, is

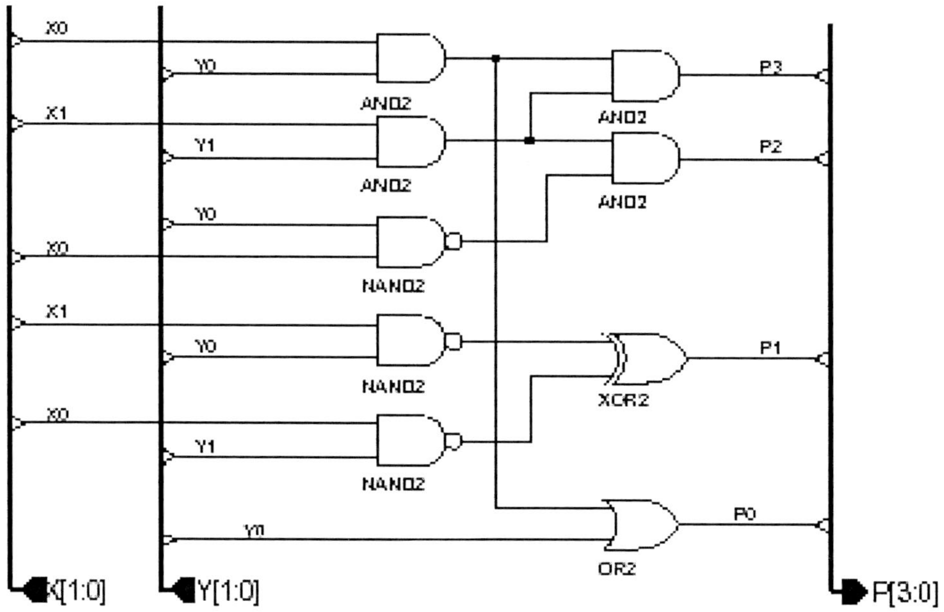

Figure 2. Evolved 2-bit multiplier

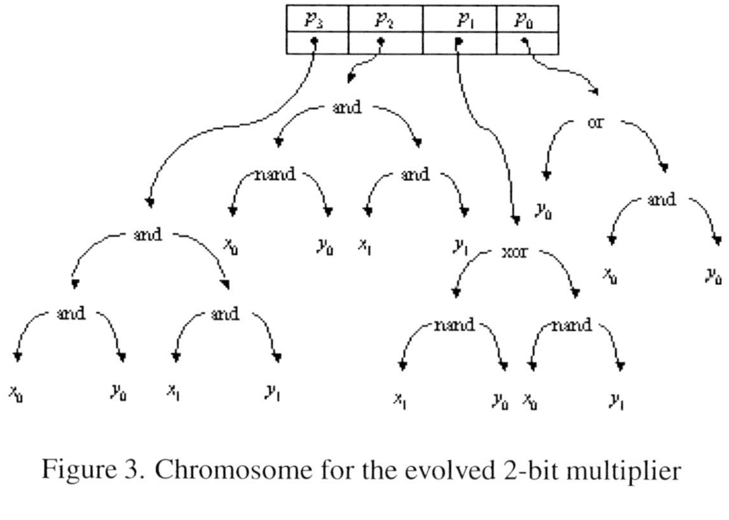

Figure 3. Chromosome for the evolved 2-bit multiplier

substituted with either a literal or simple expression. The decision is random. In the case in which the operand has to be changed by another operand, the literal representing the bit of lesser significance in the binary notation of the input signal or that representing its most significant bit is used. This is performed as indicated by function mutate1 below, wherein $X = \langle x_{n-1}x_{n-2}\ldots x_1x_0\rangle$ is the signal obtained by the concatenation of all input signals:

$$mutate_1(x_i) = \begin{cases} x_{n-1} & i = 0 \\ x_{i-1} & \text{otherwise} \end{cases} \tag{2}$$

In the case of mutating an operand node to an operator node, we proceed as follows: First let x_i be the operand being mutated. We choose randomly an operator among those available. Let OP be this operator. Its first operand is x_i. So if the chosen operator is NOT then the operand node is mutated to NOT x_i. When the selected operator is binary, a new literal is generated using $mutate_1(x_i)$. Thus, in this case, x_i is mutated to either x_iOP$mutate_1(x_i)$, wherein OP is an available binary operator. If the chosen operator is MUX, then a third operand is generated using $mutate_1(mutate_1(x_i))$. Last but not least, when the selected operator is quaternary a fourth literal is generated in the same way, i.e. using $mutate_1(mutate_1(mutate_1(x_i)))$. This mutation procedure is implemented by function $mutate_2$ below wherein the notation $mutate_1^{[i]}$ represents the i times application of $mutate_1$ and #OP represents the arity of operator OP:

$$mutate_2(x_i) = \begin{cases} \text{NOT } x_i & \#\text{OP} = 0 \\ x_i \text{ OP } mutate_1^{[1]} & \#\text{OP} = 1 \\ x_i \text{ OP } mutate_1^{[1]} mutate_1^{[2]} & \#\text{OP} = 2 \\ x_i \text{ OP } mutate_1^{[1]} mutate_1^{[2]} mutate_1^{[3]} & \#\text{OP} = 3 \end{cases} \tag{3}$$

So far we explained how an operand node is mutated. Now, we describe the mutation process of an operator node. Let OP be the operator being changed. An operator node can be mutated to another operator node or to an operand node. In the latter case, a literal is randomised and used to substitute the operator node. In the former case, however, things become a little more complicated depending on the relation between the arity OP and that of the operator selected to substitute it, say OP′. So we mutate OP to OP′. When #OP = #OP′ we leave the operands unchanged. Note that this case happens only for binary operators. When #OP ¿ #OP′, we use only a random subset of OPs operands. Finally, i.e. when #OP ¡ #OP′, we generate a random set of literals using function $mutate_1$repetitively as in function $mutate_2$ above.

3.3. Circuit Specification Evaluation

Another important aspect of genetic programming is to provide a way to evaluate the adherence of evolved computer programs to the imposed constraints. In our case, these constraints are of three kinds. First of all, the evolved specification must obey the input/output behaviour, which is given in a tabular form of expected results given the inputs. This is the truth table of the expected circuit. Second, the circuit must have a reduced size. This constraint allows us to yield compact digital circuits. Thirdly, the circuit must also reduce the signal propagation delay. This allows us to reduce the response time and so discover

Table 2. Gate equivalent and propagation delays

Name	Gate equiv.	Delay (ns)
NOT	1	0.0625
AND	2	0.209
OR	2	0.216
XOR	3	0.212
NAND	1	0.13
NOR	1	0.156
XNOR	3	0.211
MUX	3	0.212

efficient circuits. In order to take into account both area and response time, we evaluate circuits using the $area \times performance$ factor. We evolve balanced digital circuits that implement a given behaviour that require a reduced hardware area and produce the result in a reduced time such that $area \times performance$ factor is minimal.

We estimate the necessary area for a given circuit using the concept of gate equivalent. This is the basic unit of measure for digital circuit complexity [5], [18]. It is based upon the number of logic gates that should be interconnected to perform the same input/output behaviour. This measure is more accurate that the simple number of gates [5].

When the input to an electronic gate changes, there is a finite time delay before the change in input is seen at the output terminal. This is called the propagation delay of the gate and it differs from one gate to another. Of primary concern is the path from input to output with the highest total propagation delay. We estimate the performance of a given circuit using the worst-case delay path. The number of gate equivalent and an average propagation delay for each kind of gate are given in Table 2. The data were taken form [5].

Let C be a digital circuit that uses a subset (or the complete set) of the gates given in Table 2. Let $Gates(C)$ be a function that returns the set of all gates of circuit C and $Levels(C)$ be a function that returns the set of all the gates of C grouped by level. For instance, applied to the circuit of Figure 2, it returns the set of sets $\{\{$AND, AND, NAND, NAND, NAND$\}$, $\{$AND, AND, XOR, OR$\}\}$. Notice that the number of levels of a circuit coincides with the cardinality of the set expected from function $Levels$. On the other hand, let $Value(T)$ be the Boolean value that the considered circuit C propagates for the input Boolean vector T assuming that the size of T coincides with the number of input signals required for circuit C. The fitness function, which allows us to determine how much an evolved circuit adheres to the specified constraints, is given as follows, wherein I represents the input values of the input signals while O represents the expected output values of the output signals of circuit C, n denotes the number of output signals that circuit C has and function $Delay$ returns the propagation delay of a given gate as shown in Table 2. For each difference between the evolved circuit output values and the expected output signals, penalty ψ is accumulated. Note that for a correct circuit the first term in the definition of function $Fitness$ is zero and so the value returned by this function is the factor $area \times performance$ of the evaluated circuit.

Table 3. Truth table of the example of circuit fitness evaluation

x_1	x_0	y_1	y_0	Z_2	Z_1	Z_0
0	0	0	0	0/0	0/0	0/1
0	0	0	1	0/0	0/0	0/1
0	0	1	0	0/0	0/0	0/1
0	0	1	1	0/0	0/0	0/1
0	1	0	0	0/0	0/0	0/1
0	1	0	1	0/0	0/0	0/1
0	1	1	0	0/0	0/0	1/0
0	1	1	1	0/0	0/0	1/0
1	0	0	0	0/0	0/0	0/1
1	0	0	1	0/0	0/0	1/0
1	0	1	0	0/0	1/1	1/1
1	0	1	1	0/0	1/1	1/0
1	1	0	0	0/0	0/0	0/1
1	1	0	1	0/0	0/0	1/0
1	1	1	0	0/0	1/1	1/0
1	1	1	1	1/1	0/0	0/0

$$
\begin{aligned}
Fitness(C) = {} & \sum_{j=0}^{n} \left(\sum_{i \mid Value(x_i) \neq y_{i,j}} \psi \right) \\
& + \sum_{g \in Gates(C)} GateEquiv(g) \times \sum_{l \in Levels(C)} \max_{g \in l} Delay(g)
\end{aligned} \tag{4}
$$

For instance, consider the evolved circuit of Figure 4. It should propagate the output signals of Table 3 that appear first (i.e. before symbol /) but it actually propagates the output signals that appear last (i.e. those after symbol /). Observe that signals Z_1 and Z_2 are correct for every possible input combination of the input signals. However, signal Z_0 is correct only for the combinations 1010 and 1111 of the input signals and so for the remaining 14 combinations, Z_0 has a wrong value and so the circuit should be penalised 14 times. Applying function $Gates$ to this circuit should return 5 AND gates and 3 NAND gates while function $Levels$ should return $\{\{$ AND, AND, NAND, NAND, NAND $\}, \{$ AND, AND, AND$\}\}$. If ψ is set to 10 then, function $Fitness$ should return $140+(5\times2+3\times1)+(0.209+0.209)$. This fitness sums up to 153.418.

In order to speed up the computation of the evolved circuit fitness, we take advantage of the parallelism of the central processing unit. This technique was first used by Poli in [16]. Instead of obtaining the output signal values one by one, one can compute them i.e. for all possible input signal combinations, in parallel. For instance, to compute the values of output signal $Z_2 \Longleftarrow (x_0$ AND $y_0)$ AND $(x_1$ AND $y_1)$ considering the circuit of Figure 4

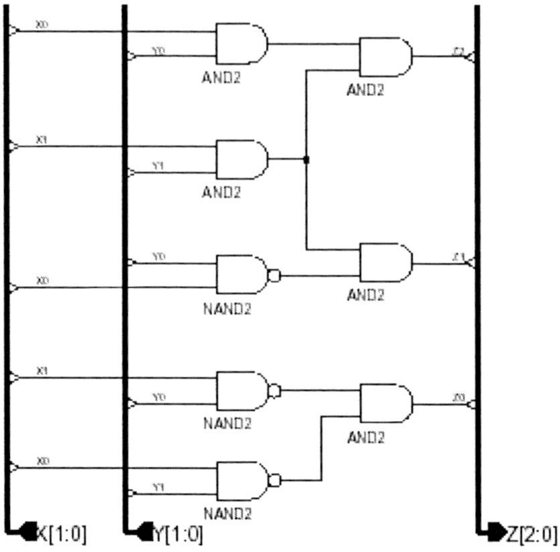

Figure 4. Evolved circuits for the input/output behavior of Table 3

and the values of Table 3, we proceed as follows:

1. Convert 0000111100001111, which is the content of column x_0 to integer value 3849 and 0101010101010101, which is the content of column y_0 to integer value 21849;

2. Compute the bitwise operation 3849 & 21849 = 2569;

3. Convert 0000000011111111, which is the content of column x_1 to integer value 255 and 0011001100110011, which is the content of column y_1 to integer value 51;

4. Compute the bitwise operation 256 & 21849 = 51;

5. Compute the bitwise operation 169 & 2569 = 1;

6. Convert 1 to its 16-bit binary representation 000000000000001, which is exactly the content of column Z_2.

The use of this technique to compute the first term of fitness of an evolved circuit speeds up the process to an order of magnitude of 10. Note that for circuits of more than 6 input signals, the bitwise operations need to be split out in several 16, 32 or 64-bit operations depending on the size of the memory word.

4. Evolutionary vs. Conventional Designs

In this section, we compare the evolutionary circuits yield by our genetic programming based evolution to those designed by a human as well as to those evolved by Coello's genetic algorithm [4].

The truth table of the first benchmark is given in Table 4. It has three-bits input signal $X = \langle x_2 x_1 x_0 \rangle$ and propagates a single-bit output signal Y.

Table 4. Truth table of the first benchmark

x_2	x_1	x_0	Y
0	0	0	0
0	0	1	0
0	1	0	0
0	1	1	1
1	0	0	0
1	0	1	1
1	1	0	1
1	1	1	0

For this circuit specified in Table 4, a human designer came with a digital circuit that uses 2 AND gates, 1 OR gate and 2 XOR gates. The output signal is computed as in signal assignment of Equation 5. The Coello's genetic algorithm evolved the circuit specified in signal assignment of Equation 6. It uses 1 XOR gate less than the human designed circuit.

$$Y \Longleftarrow x_0 \text{ AND } (x_2 \text{ XOR } x_1) \text{ OR } x_1 \text{ AND } (x_2 \text{ XOR } x_0) \tag{5}$$

$$Y \Longleftarrow x_0 \text{ AND } (x_2 \text{ OR } x_1) \text{ XOR } (x_2 \text{ AND } x_1) \tag{6}$$

Our genetic programming-based evolutionary computation yields two different circuits for the first benchmark. Both of them use 1 AND gate, 1 XOR gate and 1 MUX gate. The specifications of theses two circuits are given in signal assignment of Equation 7 and Equation 8 respectively:

$$Y \Longleftarrow \text{MUX } ((x_0 \text{ AND } x_1), (x_0 \text{ XOR } x_1), x_2) \tag{7}$$

$$Y \Longleftarrow \text{MUX } ((x_0 \text{ AND } x_2), (x_0 \text{ XOR } x_2), x_1) \tag{8}$$

The schematics of these two circuits are given in Figure 5. The circuit, we evolved needs less hardware area, propagates the output signal faster and so the factor area $\times$performance is minimised. The numerical figures are given in Table 6 at the end of this section.

Both the second and third benchmarks need a 4-bit input signal $X = \langle x_3 x_2 x_1 x_0 \rangle$ and yield a single-bit output signal Y. The fourth and fifth benchmarks also requires a 4-bit input signal X but the respective circuits propagate a 4-bit and 3-bit output signal respectively. The truth tables of the four benchmarks are summarised in Table 5 below. Note that the fourth benchmark is a simple 2-bit multiplier of $X = \langle x_3 x_2 \rangle$ times $Y = \langle x_1 x_0 \rangle$. (The notation of the input signals is purely for space sake!)

For the second example, a human designer came with a circuit that requires 4 AND gates, 1 OR gate, 2 XOR gates and 4 NOT gates. The specification of the signal assignments as follows:

$$Y \Longleftarrow ((\overline{x}_3 \text{ AND } x_1) \text{ XOR } (\overline{x}_0 \text{ AND } \overline{x}_2)) \text{ OR } ((\overline{x}_2 \text{ AND } x_0) \text{ AND } (x_3 \text{ XOR } \overline{x}_2)) \tag{9}$$

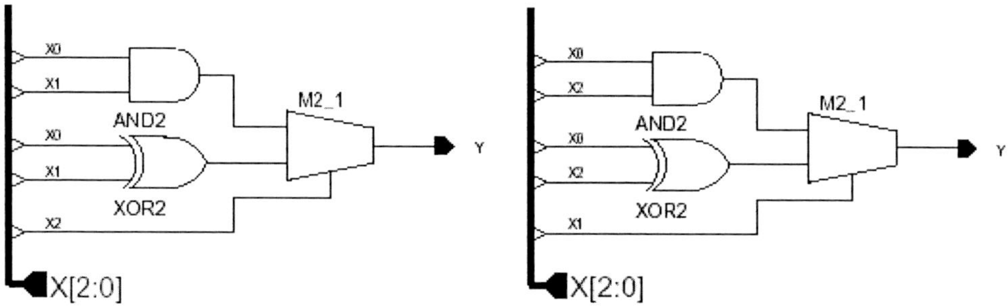

(a) First circuit (b) Second circuit

Figure 5. Schematics of the evolved circuits for the first benchmark

Table 5. Truth tables of second, third, fourth and fifth benchmarks respectively

Input				2nd	3rd	4th Benchmark				5th Benchmark		
x_3	x_2	x_1	x_0	Y	Y	p_3	p_2	p_1	p_0	y_2	y_1	y_0
0	0	0	0	1	1	0	0	0	0	1	0	0
0	0	0	1	1	0	0	0	0	0	0	1	0
0	0	1	0	0	1	0	0	0	0	0	1	0
0	0	1	1	1	0	0	0	0	0	0	1	0
0	1	0	0	0	1	0	0	0	0	0	0	1
0	1	0	1	0	0	0	0	0	1	1	0	0
0	1	1	0	1	1	0	0	1	0	0	1	0
0	1	1	1	1	1	0	0	1	1	0	1	0
1	0	0	0	1	1	0	0	0	0	0	0	1
1	0	0	1	0	1	0	1	0	0	0	0	1
1	1	1	0	1	1	0	1	1	0	1	0	0
1	0	1	1	0	0	0	1	1	0	0	1	0
1	0	0	0	0	0	0	0	0	0	0	0	1
1	1	0	1	1	1	0	0	1	1	0	0	1
1	1	1	0	0	1	0	1	1	0	0	0	1
1	1	1	1	0	1	1	0	0	1	1	0	0

For the second benchmark, the Coello's genetic algorithm evolved the circuit specified in signal assignment of Equation 10. It uses 1 AND gate, 3 OR gates, 3 XOR gates and 1 NOT gate.

$$Y \Longleftarrow ((x_3 \text{ XOR } ((x_2 \text{ XOR } x_0) \text{ OR } (x_1 \text{ AND } x_0)) \text{ XOR } (\text{ NOT } ((x_3 \text{ OR } (x_1 \text{ OR } x_0))) \quad (10)$$

The schematics of the circuit we evolved are given in Figure 6. It needs less hardware area, but propagates the output signal a little bit slower than Coello's evolved circuit. However, the factor $area \times performance$ is the smallest. Again, the numerical figures are given in Table 6.

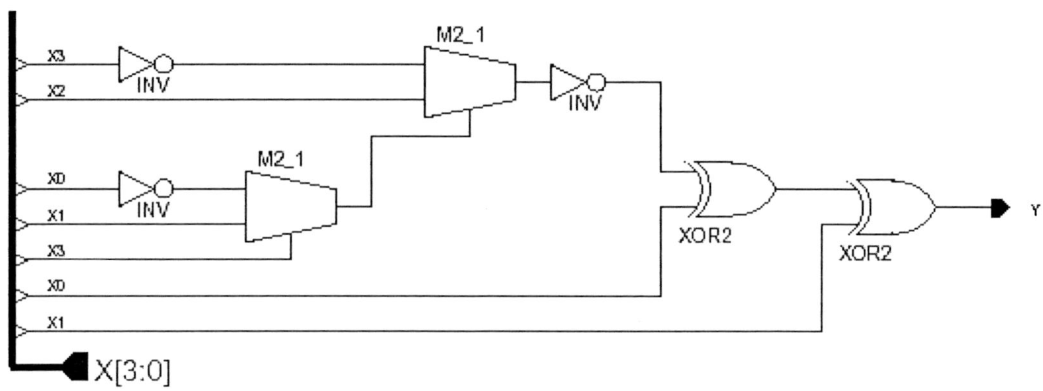

Figure 6. Evolved circuit for the second benchmark

For the third benchmark, a human designer obtained a circuit that requires a total of 20 gates equivalent: 5 AND gates, 3 OR gates and 4 NOT gates. The specification of the signal assignment (11) is as follows:

$$Y \Longleftarrow ((\overline{x}_3 \text{ AND } \overline{x}_0) \text{ OR } (\overline{x}_3 \text{ AND } \overline{x}_2)) \text{ OR } ((x_2 \text{ AND } x_1) \text{ OR } (x_3 \text{ AND } \overline{x}_1 \text{ AND } x_0)) \quad (11)$$

For the third benchmark, the Coello's genetic algorithm evolved the circuit specified in signal assignment of Equation 12. It requires 2 AND gates, 2 OR gates, 2 XOR gates and 1 NOT gate.

$$Y \Longleftarrow \text{ NOT } (((x_2 \text{ AND } x_1) \text{ XOR } (x_2 \text{ OR } x_0)) \text{ AND } (x_1 \text{ OR } (x_3 \text{ XOR } x_0))) \quad (12)$$

The schematics of the circuit we evolved are given in Figure 7. The circuit, we evolved needs less hardware area, propagates the output signal faster than both circuits i.e. Coello's and the one designed by the human, and so the factor $area \times performance$ is minimised. Once more, the numerical figures about gate equivalent, delay and $area \times performance$ factor are shown in Table 6.

Another circuit was obtained for that benchmark. Its schematics are given in Figure 8 below. The circuit of is less efficient than that shown in Figure 7. However, it is more

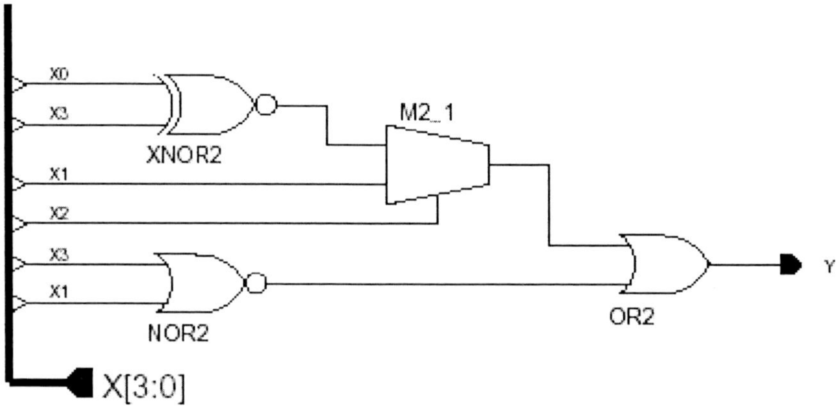

Figure 7. Evolved circuits for the third benchmark

compact that the circuits obtained by the human designer and that evolved by Coello's genetic algorithm as it requires only 11 gates equivalent compared to 20 for the circuit designed by the human and 15 for Coello's evolved circuit. Moreover, the circuit of Figure 8 has a smaller propagation delay of 0.853ns compared to the 0.912ns required by the human designed circuit. The circuit presents a $area \times performance$ factor of 9.383.

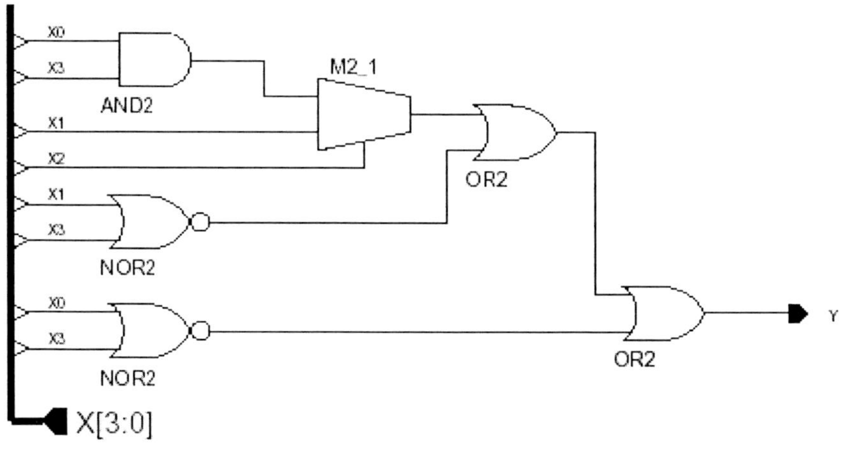

Figure 8. Less efficient evolved circuits for the third benchmark

For the fourth benchmark, a human designer obtained a circuit that requires a total of 24 gates equivalent: 8 AND gates, 2 OR gates, 1 XOR gate and 1 NOT gate. The specification of the signal assignments is as follows (Equation 13), wherein $y_1 = x_3$ and $y_0 = x_2$ when Table 5 is used.

$$\begin{aligned} p_0 &\Longleftarrow (x_0 \text{ AND } y_0) \\ p_1 &\Longleftarrow (x_1 \text{ OR } x_0) \text{ AND } (y_1 \text{ OR } y_0) \text{ AND } ((x_1 \text{ AND } x_0) \text{ XOR } (y_1 \text{ AND } y_0)) \\ p_2 &\Longleftarrow (x_1 \text{ AND } y_1) \text{ AND } \text{ NOT } ((x_0 \text{ AND } y_0)) \\ p_3 &\Longleftarrow (x_1 \text{ AND } y_1) \text{ AND } (x_0 \text{ AND } y_0) \end{aligned} \tag{13}$$

For the fourth benchmark, the Coello's genetic algorithm evolved the circuit specified in the output signal assignments of Equation 14. It requires an area of 16 gates equivalent. That is 5 AND gates and 2 XOR gates.

$$\begin{aligned}
p_0 &\Longleftarrow (x_0 \text{ AND } y_0) \\
p_1 &\Longleftarrow (x_0 \text{ AND } y_1) \text{ XOR } (x_1 \text{ AND } y_0) \\
p_2 &\Longleftarrow (x_1 \text{ AND } y_1) \text{ XOR } ((x_0 \text{ AND } y_0) \text{ AND } (x_1 \text{ AND } y_1)) \\
p_3 &\Longleftarrow (x_1 \text{ AND } y_1) \text{ AND } (x_0 \text{ AND } y_0)
\end{aligned} \tag{14}$$

The schematics of the circuit we evolved are given in Figure 9. The circuit we evolved needs the same hardware area as Coello's evolved circuit but it propagates the output signal faster than both circuits i.e. Coello's and the one designed by the human, and so the factor $area \times performance$ is minimised. The comparison of the numerical figures such as gate equivalent numbers, propagation delays and $area \times performance$ factors is detailed in Table 6.

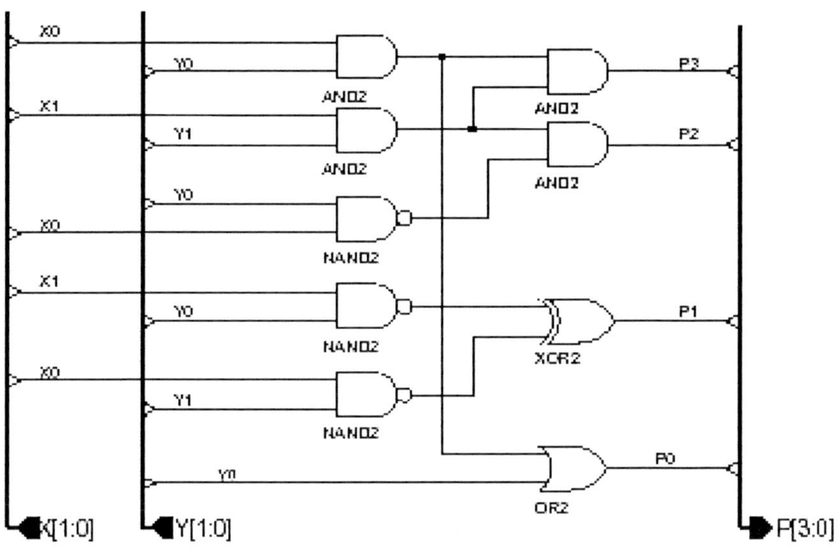

Figure 9. Evolved circuits for the fourth benchmark

Finally for the fifth benchmark, a human designer engineered a circuit that requires a total of 34 gates equivalent, i.e. 7 AND gates, 4 OR gates, 2 XOR gate and 6 NOT gates. The specification of the signal assignments of Equation 15, wherein $y_1 = x_3$ and $y_0 = x_2$ when Table 5 is used.

$$\begin{aligned}
y_0 &\Longleftarrow \text{NOT } (x_3 \text{ XOR } x_1) \text{ AND } \text{ NOT } (x_2 \text{ XOR } x_0) \\
y_1 &\Longleftarrow (\overline{x}_2 \text{ AND } x_0) \text{ AND } (\overline{x}_3 \text{ OR } x_1) \text{ OR } (x_3 \text{ AND } x_1) \\
y_2 &\Longleftarrow (\overline{x}_0 \text{ AND } x_2) \text{ AND } (\overline{x}_1 \text{ OR } x_3) \text{ OR } (\overline{x}_1 \text{ AND } x_3)
\end{aligned} \tag{15}$$

For the same example, the Coelho's genetic algorithm evolved the circuit specified in the output signal assignments of Equation 16. It requires an area of 22 gates equivalent, which consist of 2 AND gates, 3 OR gate, 3 XOR gates and 3 NOT gates.

$$
\begin{array}{lcl}
y_0 & \Longleftarrow & \text{NOT } ((x_3 \text{ XOR } x_1) \text{ AND } (x_2 \text{ XOR } x_0)) \\
y_1 & \Longleftarrow & (temp \text{ AND} \\
 & & \text{NOT } (((x_3 \text{ XOR } x_1) \text{ AND } x_3 \text{ XOR } (x_0 \text{ OR } (x_3 \text{ XOR } x_1))) \text{ OR } temp)) \\
y_2 & \Longleftarrow & \text{NOT } (((x_3 \text{ XOR } x_1) \text{ AND } x_3 \text{ XOR } ((x_0 \text{ OR } (x_3 \text{ XOR } x_1)) \\
 & & \text{OR NOT } temp) \\
temp & \Longleftarrow & (x_2 \text{ XOR } x_0) \text{ OR } (x_3 \text{ XOR } x_1)
\end{array}
\quad (16)
$$

The schematics of the circuit that our genetic algorithm evolved are given in Figure 10. This circuit requires one gate equivalent more than Coello's evolved circuit but our circuit propagates the output signal much faster. Compared with the human designed circuit, our circuit has the same response time but needs a much smaller area. Furthermore, the factor $area \times performance$ for our circuit is minimal compared with the other two. The numerical figures such as gate equivalent numbers, propagation delays and $area \times performance$ factors are given in Table 6.

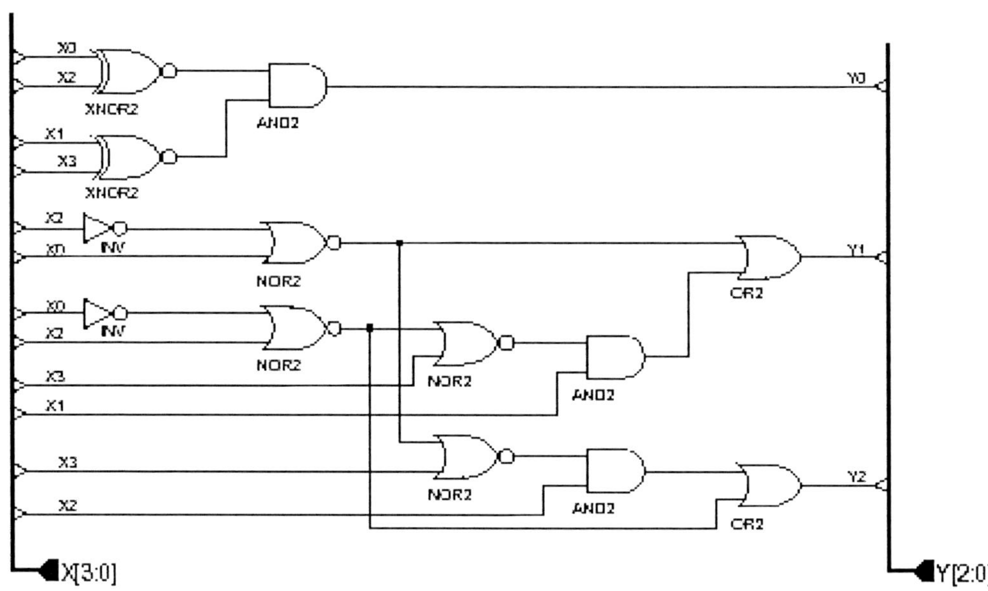

Figure 10. Evolved circuits for the fifth benchmark

The convergence graphs of our evolutionary process for the benchmarks are shown in Figure 11. The best circuits for the 1st, 2nd, 3rd, 4th and 5th examples were obtained in 100, 280, 320, 370 and 540 generations.

In order to evolve the circuits for the proposed behaviours (see Table 5) and for all of the examples we used a population of 100 individuals. The double-point crossover was used with mutation rate of 0.5 and a mutation degree of 1.

Table 6 shows a comparison between the fittest circuits engineered by a human designer, Coello's genetic algorithm and our genetic algorithm, which is based on genetic programming. For each benchmark, the required hardware area, the necessary propagation delay and the product $area \times performance$ are detailed. The graphical representation of these

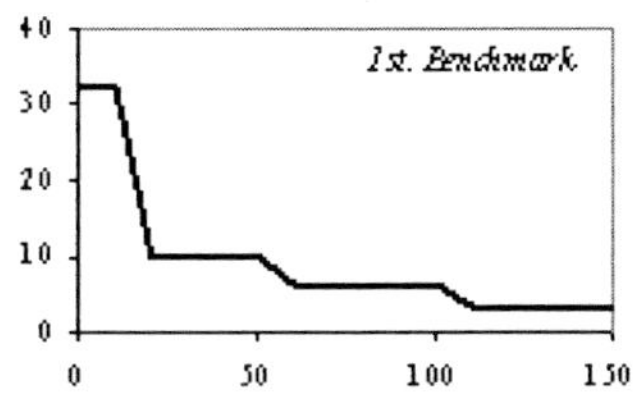

(a) First benchmark

(b) Second benchmark

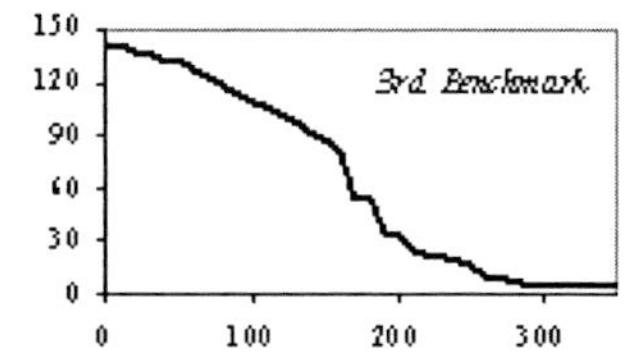

(c) Third benchmark

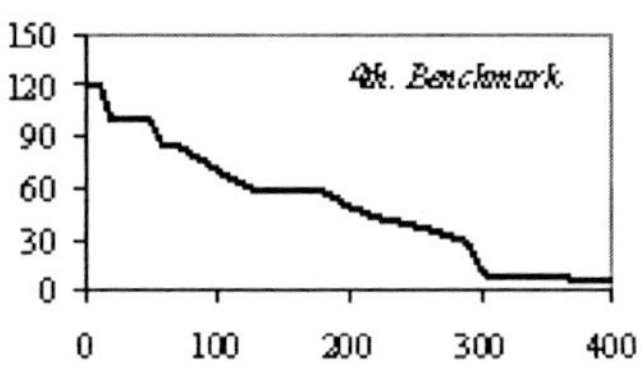

(d) Fourth benchmark

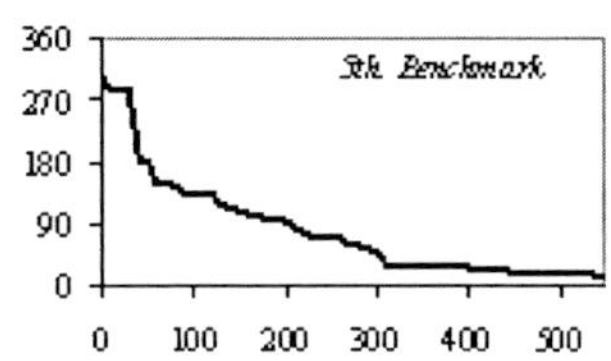

(e) Fifth benchmark

Figure 11. Convergence graphs for the evolution of the circuits of the benchmarks

figures is shown in the chart of Figure 12.

5. RSA-Based Cryptosystems

Cryptography is the science of keeping secrets secret. Its main task is to provide confidentiality by encryption methods. The original message, which can be some text, numerical data or any other kind of information, is usually called plaintext and the encrypted plaintext is called ciphertext. Information transmission between two parties through public channels occurs after plaintext T is encrypted into ciphertext C so that an eventual adversary third party in possession of c cannot derive any information about T. Cryptosystems must provide an encryption and a decryption algorithm. Existing cryptosystems can be classi-

Table 6. Numerical comparison of the three methods

	area			delay			factor		
	Our	Coello	Human	Our	Coello	Human	Our	Coello	Human
1st	8	9	12	0.424	0.637	0.637	3.392	5.733	7.644
2nd	15	16	20	0.973	0.918	0.702	14.595	14.696	14.050
3rd	9	15	20	0.639	0.699	0.912	5.751	10.492	18.250
4th	16	16	24	0.425	0.842	0.853	6.800	13.472	20.472
5th	22	21	34	0.799	1.065	0.703	17.589	22.365	23.919

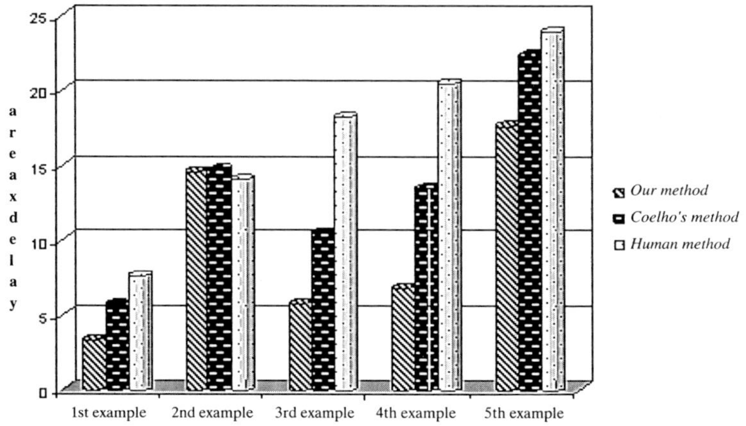

Figure 12. Graphical comparison of the $area \times delay$ factor for the three methods

Table 7. Conventional vs. evolutionary designs for the RSA-based cryptosystems

Design	Size	Time (ns)
Sequential Binary	524	7.321
Parallel Binary	992	4.992
Evolved circuit	24	1.313

fied into symmetric and asymmetric systems. Both encryption and decryption processes in symmetric cryptosystems depend on the same secret key while in asymmetric ones there exist a public key on which depends the encryption algorithm and another private key used by the decryption process.

A Rivest-Shamir-Adleman or simply RSA-based cryptosystem [17] is asymmetric. It consists of triple $\langle M, e, d \rangle$, which consists of the *modulus*, *public* and *private key* respectively. The modulus and the public key of the system are made public while the private key is kept secret. To build an RSA-based cryptosystem, one needs to:

1. Create two primes p and q;
2. Compute $M = p \times q$;
3. Calculate the value of *Euler totient* function defined for M as $N = \Phi(M) = (p - 1)(q - 1)$;
4. Choose e, such that the greatest common divisor of N and e is 1—$gcd(e, N) = 1$, with $e \neq 1$ and $e \neq N$;
5. Compute d such that $e \times d \equiv 1 \bmod N$. (This can be done using the extended Euclidean algorithm [11].)

Note the public and private keys of a given cryptosystem are non-negative integer smaller than its modulus, i.e. for the system defined by $\langle M, e, d \rangle$, we have $0 \leq e, d \leq$

$M - 1$. With modulus of reasonable length, i.e. about 1024 bits, solving the factoring problem i.e. discovering p and q, which will lead to discovering the private key is impossible considering the computation power and the factoring algorithms one disposes of nowadays.

Both the encryption and decryption algorithms in RSA-based cryptosystems are implemented using the same algorithm: modular exponentiation. That is, the *ciphertext* C is obtained from *plaintext* T by $C = T^e \bmod M$ and T is obtained from C by $T = C^d \bmod M$. This characteristic is very attractive and so it increased the popularity of RSA-based cryptosystems. Note that the plaintext and its corresponding ciphertext in a given RSA-based cryptosystem are non-negative integers smaller than the modulus.

The practicality of cryptosystem depends heavily on how fast the encryption and essentially decryption process can be done. Therefore, the practicality of RSA-based cryptosystems depends essentially on how fast modular exponentiation of large integers can be performed.

Clearly, modular exponentiation is the cornerstone operation in RSA-based cryptosystem. It consists of several successive modular multiplications. Modular multiplication is time consuming for large operands. Engineering fast public-key cryptography hardware needs either optimising the time consumed by a single modular multiplication or reducing the total number of modular multiplication performed or both of them [14], [3], [2], [19]. The so far engineered hardware designs using modular exponentiation as encryption process suffer from a very serious drawback that is called *side-channel leakage*. As the designs for modular exponentiation are regular and repetitive one can trace the data transfers between operations, which usually reveal the beginning of every long integer operation very clearly [12]. This allows one with an extra little effort to discover the private key of the cryptosystem. Here, we use evolutionary computation to discover new efficient, creative and above all secure hardware for RSA-based cryptosystems.

6. Evolutionary vs. Conventional Cryptographic Hardware

Several efficient designs for RSA-based cryptosystems were developed [14], [3], [2]. In the following, we compare two conventional designs: one sequential and the other parallel to the evolutionary design obtained.

First of all, we describe an sequential design based on the binary exponentiation method [6] we presented in earlier research work [14], [15]. Subsequently, we present the parallel design based on the same method.

The sequential straightforward binary exponentiation algorithm is given hereafter (Algorithm 1, wherein m is the number of digits in exponent e. Observe that the multiplication of line 5 of the algorithm depends on the result of the squaring of line 4.

The hardware architecture of Figure 13 includes two Montgomery modular systolic multipliers, i.e. MULTIPLIER_1 and MULTIPLIER_2.

The parallel algorithm of binary exponentiation is given in Algorithm 2 and the parallel architecture in Figure 14.

To illustrate the obtained results, we evolved a specification for two different modulus and keys, which are $M = 11$, $e = 5$ and $M = 13$, $e = 11$. The specification of the evolved RSA-based cryptographic hardware for the first case is given below, wherein the signals t_0

Algorithm 1 Sequential binary modular exponentiation

Input. Plaintext/ciphertext T, private/public key e and modulus M
Output. Ciphertext/palintext R

```
int R := 1;
if e_{k-1} = 1 then R := T;
for i := m - 2 downto 0
    R := R × R mod M;
    if e_i = 1 then R = R × T mod M;
return R; end.
```

Algorithm 2 Parallel binary modular exponentiation

Input. Plaintext/ciphertext T, private/public key e and modulus M
Output. Ciphertext/palintext R

```
int R^(0) := 1, P^(0) := T;
for i := 0 to m - 1
    P^(i+1) = P^(i) × P^(i) mod M;
    if e_i = 1 then R^(i+1) := R^(i) × P^(i) mod M
    else R^(i+1) := R^(i)
return R;
end.
```

to t_3 are the bits constituting the plaintext from the less to most significant bit. For the sake of clarity, we use the expression prefix notation.

$$
\begin{array}{lll}
c_3 & \Longleftarrow & \text{AND}\ (\ \text{OR}\ (t_3,\ \text{NOR}\ (\ \text{NOR}\ (\bar{t}_0, t_2), \bar{t}_1)),\ \text{NAND}\ (\ \text{NOR}\ (\bar{t}_0, t_2), \bar{t}_2)) \\
c_2 & \Longleftarrow & \text{NOR}\ (\bar{t}_0, t_0) \\
c_1 & \Longleftarrow & \text{AND}\ (\ \text{NAND}\ (\ \text{NOR}\ (\bar{t}_0, t_2), \bar{t}_2),\ \text{OR}\ (t_3,\ \text{NOR}\ (\ \text{NOR}\ (\bar{t}_0, t_2), \bar{t}_1))) \\
c_0 & \Longleftarrow & \text{MUX}\ (\bar{t}_1,\ \text{NOR}\ (\bar{t}_0, t_2), \bar{t}_2)
\end{array}
\tag{17}
$$

The specification of the evolved RSA-based cryptographic hardware for the second case, i.e. $M = 13$, $e = 11$ is given below, wherein NUX stands for NOT MUX.

$$
\begin{array}{lll}
c_3 & \Longleftarrow & \text{NUX}\ (\ \text{AND}\ (\ \text{NAND}\ (t_2, \bar{t}_0),\ \text{NAND}\ (\bar{t}_1, t_2)), \\
 & & \text{NOR}\ (\ \text{NOR}\ (\ \text{NOR}\ (\bar{t}_0, \bar{t}_2), \bar{t}_0),\ \text{AND}\ (\ \text{NAND}\ (t_2, \bar{t}_0), \bar{t}_1)), \\
 & & \text{NOR}\ (\ \text{MUX}\ (\bar{t}_3, \bar{t}_1,\ \text{NOR}\ (\ \text{NOR}\ (\bar{t}_0, \bar{t}_2), \bar{t}_0)), t_3)) \\
c_2 & \Longleftarrow & \text{NUX}\ (\ \text{NOR}\ (\ \text{MUX}(\bar{t}_3, 6,\ \text{NOR}\ (\ \text{NOR}\ (\bar{t}_0, \bar{t}_2), \bar{t}_0)), t_3), \\
 & & \text{MUX}\ (\bar{t}_3, \bar{t}_1,\ \text{NOR}\ (\ \text{NOR}\ (\bar{t}_0, \bar{t}_2), \bar{t}_0)),\ \text{NAND}\ (\bar{t}_2, t_1)) \\
c_1 & \Longleftarrow & \text{MUX}\ (\ \text{NOR}\ (\ \text{NOR}\ (\bar{t}_0, \bar{t}_2), \bar{t}_0),\ \text{NOR}\ (\ \text{NOR}\ (\ \text{NOR}\ (\bar{t}_0, \bar{t}_2), \bar{t}_0), \\
 & & \text{AND}\ (\ \text{NAND}\ (t_2, \bar{t}_0), \bar{t}_1)), \bar{t}_3) \\
c_0 & \Longleftarrow & \text{AND}\ (\ \text{NAND}\ (\bar{t}_1, t_2),\ \text{MUX}\ (\ \text{NOR}\ (\ \text{NOR}\ (\bar{t}_3, \bar{t}_1), \\
 & & \text{NOR}\ (\bar{t}_0, \bar{t}_2)), t_3,\ \text{NOR}\ (t_0, t_1)))
\end{array}
\tag{18}
$$

The schematics of the evolved circuit with the above given specification were generated automatically using the XILINX^{TM} Project Manager [22] and are shown in Figure 16. The

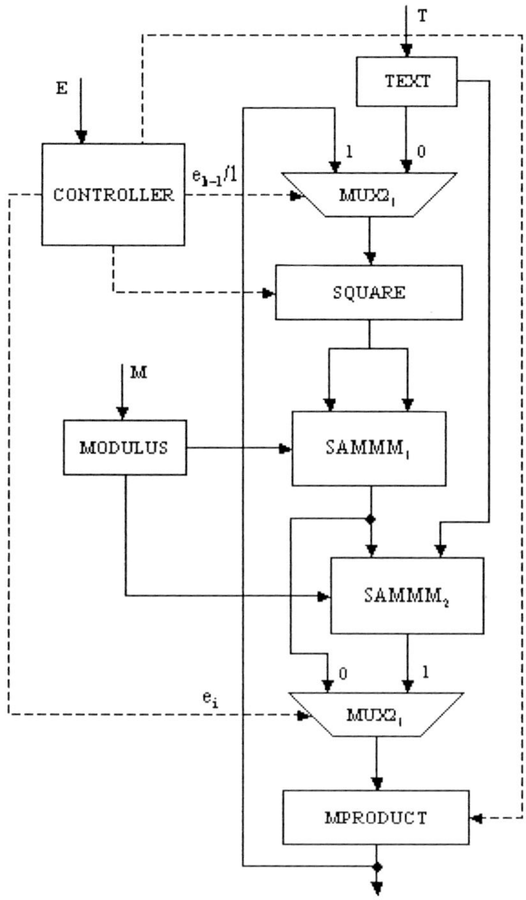

Figure 13. Sequential architecture for modular exponentiation

simulation waveform of the yielded circuit is depicted in Figure 15. The ciphertext for all possible values of the plaintext are considered.

We also generated automatically from the XILINX^{TM} Project Manager [22] the evolved circuit schematics using look-up tables. The basic unit is a four inputs and one output look-up table. The circuit requires 4 look-up tables as shown in Figure 17. We obtained and compared the size and response time for the evolved circuit with those corresponding to the sequential and parallel binary exponentiation implementations whose architectures are depicted in Figure 6 and Figure 14. Table 7 lists the collected data for $M = 13$ and $e = 11$.

The size of the circuits is expressed in terms of gate equivalent and the response time is nano-seconds. The data provide in this table show clearly that the evolved circuit is far better than the conventional designs: It requires much less hardware area and encrypts/decrypts much faster. Furthermore, it is shielded against side-channel leakage as it has no repetitive behaviour, as it is the case for conventional designs. However, the evolved circuit is not scalable. When a new cryptosystem with new modulus and/or key, a new design need be evolved from scratch.

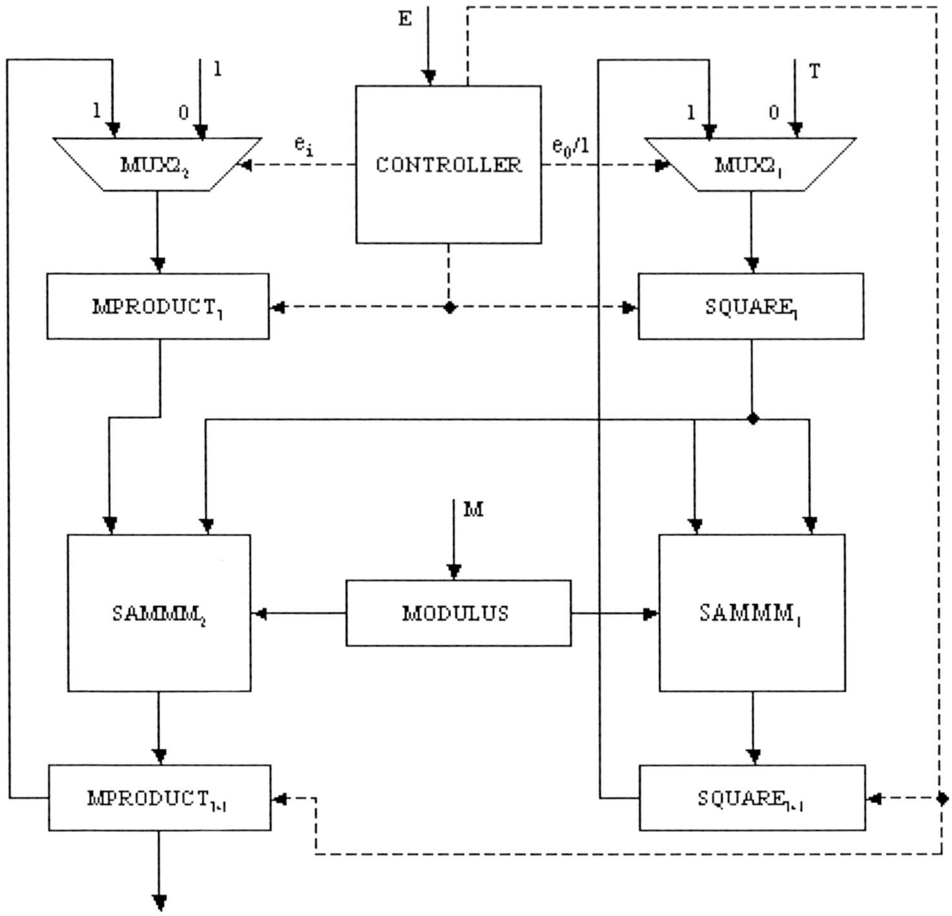

Figure 14. Parallel architecture for modular exponentiation

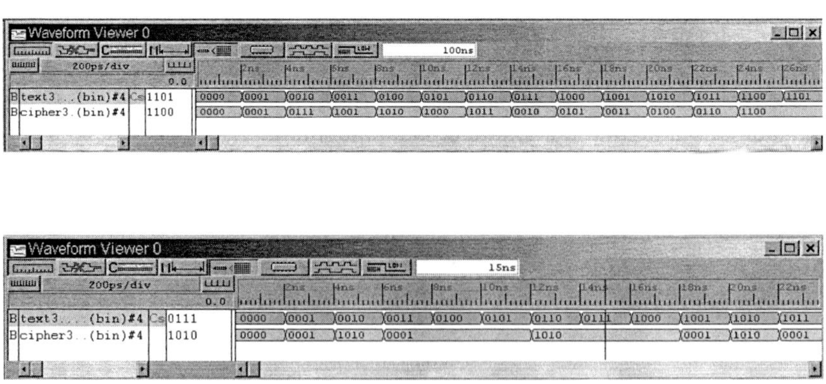

Figure 15. Simulation result of the evolved circuit behaviour

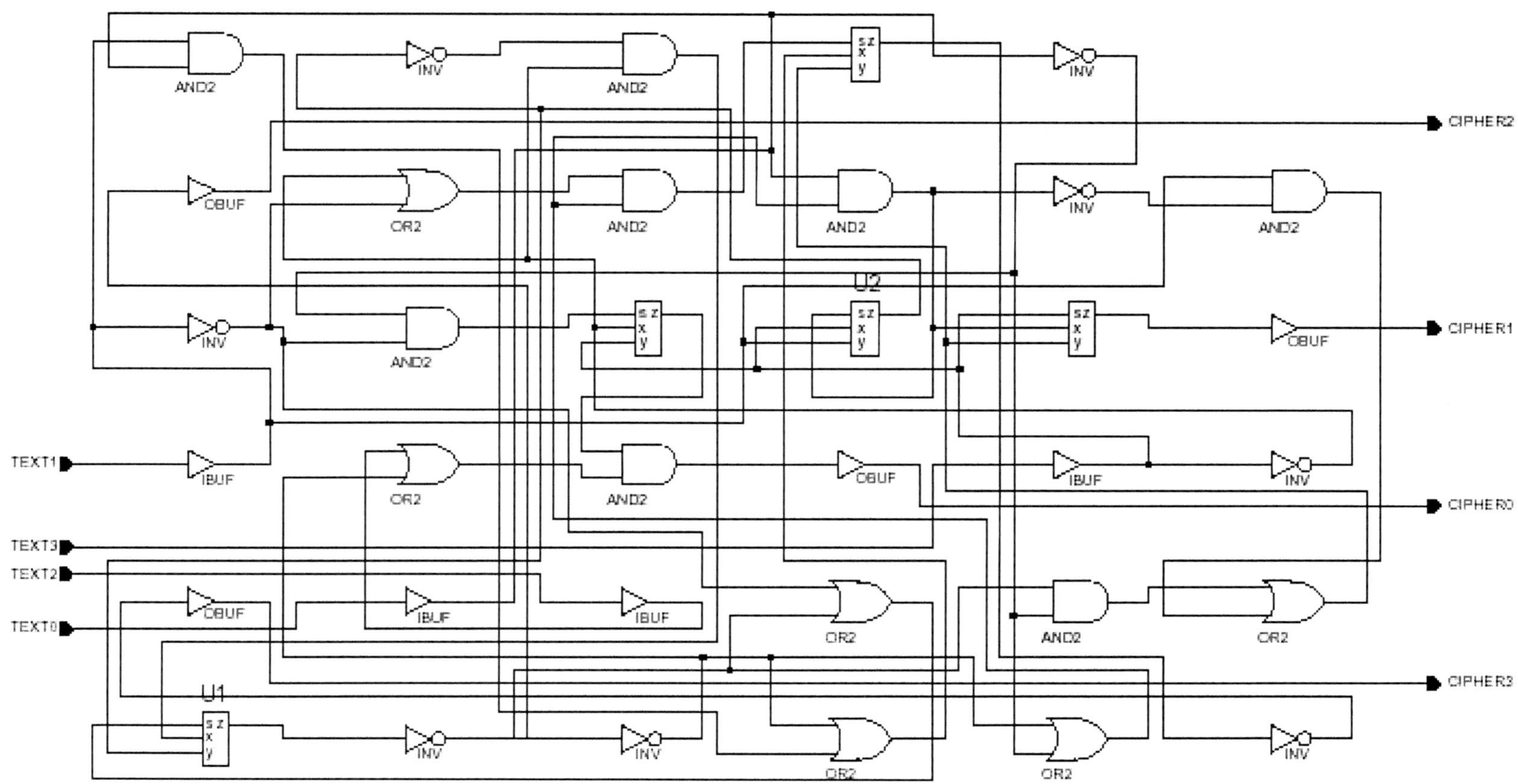

Figure 16. Schematics of the evolved RSA-based cryptographic hardware for M=13 and E=11

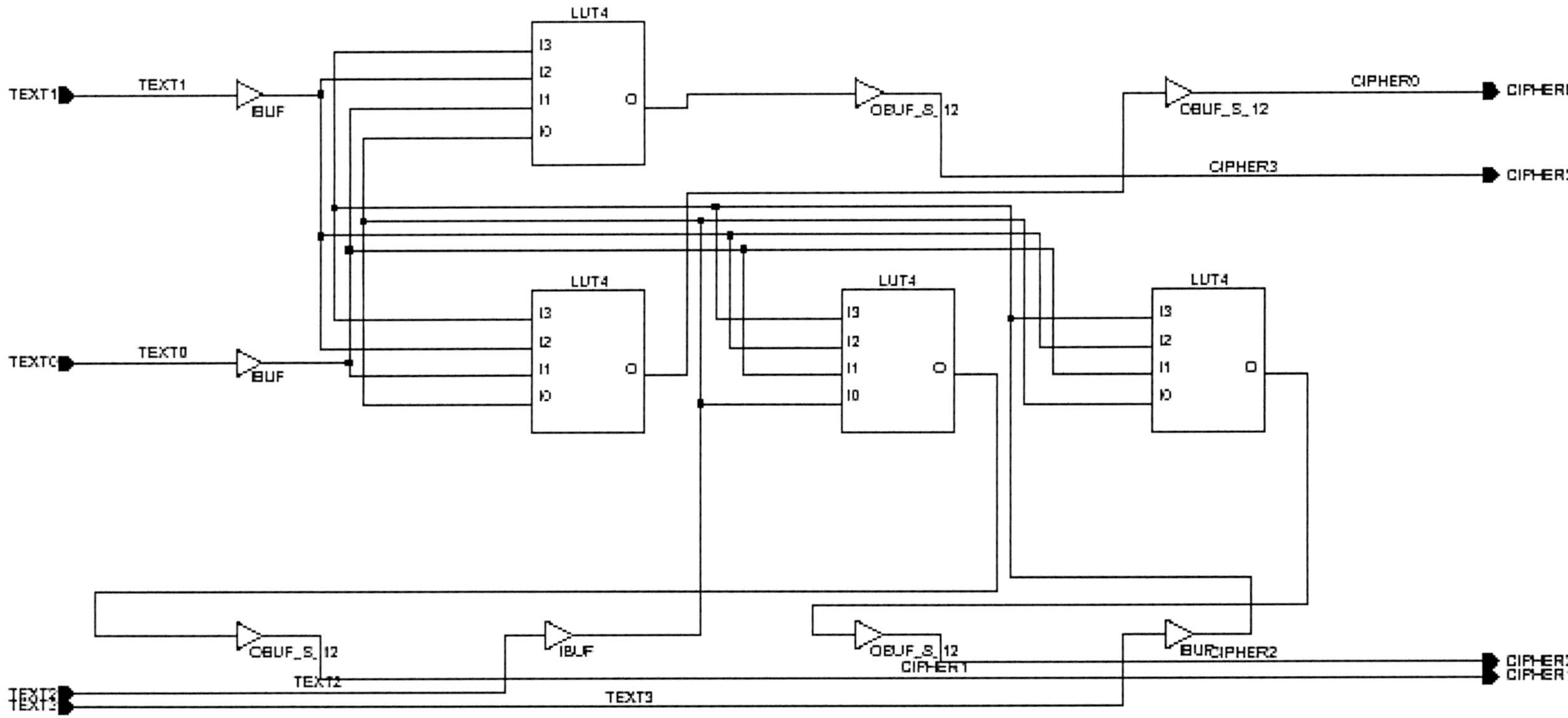

Figure 17. Circuit schematics using look-up tables generated by the Xilinx^{TM} project manager for the evolved circuit

7. Summary

In this chapter, we described an evolutionary technique to engineer compact, efficient and creative digital combinational circuit given the expected input/output behaviour. We explored the use of genetic programming and changing from the binary representation of circuits to a tree representation. We showed how to improve the evolution process by taking advantage of the central processing unit parallelism. An advantage of using genetic programming consists of the readability of the evolved circuit for synthesis using one of the available synthesis tools [15].

Our evolutionary process is multi-objective as it allows one to yield balanced i.e. compact and efficient digital circuits. The proposed fitness function evaluates a given circuit with respect to correctness, required hardware area and necessary propagation delay of output signals. It does so using the well-agreed-upon factor $area \times performance$ as a measure to appreciate the complexity of a digital circuit.

We evolved a better circuit for every example used by Coello et al. [12] compared to both human designs and evolved circuit that only consider the number of required gates to evaluate an evolved solution. On one hand, this proves that the fitness function we engineered is far more realistic than that of used by Coello et al. On the other hand, it also proves that evolutionary hardware can offer an alternative way to human design techniques to design efficient digital circuit. We showed how the evaluation of circuit fitness can be computed efficiently taking advantage of the inherent parallelism of the central processing units of the computers.

Using the evolutionary process described earlier, we automatically generate data-flow based specifications for hardware designs of public-key cryptosystems such as RSA-based encryption system. We focussed on evolving minimal hardware specifications, i.e. hardware that minimises both space (i.e. required gate number) and time (i.e. encryption and decryption time), for modular exponentiation. Modular exponentiation is the cornerstone operation of most public-key cryptosystems. The advantage of such evolved cryptosystems are shielded against side-channel leakage. However, the designs are not scalable, i.e. for new modulus or keys, one needs to evolve a new design. We compared our results against existing and well-known designs, which are based on the binary modular exponentiation method. The evolved is far more efficient in both required hardware area and encryption/decryption throughput.

References

[1] Aho, A.V., Ravi, S. and Ullman, J.D., *Compilers: principles, techniques and tools*, Addison-Wesley, 1986.

[2] Blum, T. and Paar, C. Montgomery modular exponentiation on reconfigurable hardware, *Proceedings of the 14th. IEEE Symposium on Computer Arithmetic*, Australia, 1999.

[3] Brickell, E.F., A survey of hardware implementation of RSA, In G. Brassard, ed., Advances in Cryptology, *Proceedings of CRYPTO'98*, *Lecture Notes in Computer Science* **435**:368-370, Springer-Verlag, 1989.13:39 3/6/2004

[4] Coello, C.A.C., Christiansen, A.D. and Aguirre, A.H., Towards Automated Evolutionary Design of Combinational Circuits, *Comput. Electr. Eng.*, **27**, pp. 1-28, 2001

[5] Ercegovac, M.D., Lang, T. and Moreno, J.H., *Introduction to digital systems*, John Wiley, 1999.

[6] Gordon, D.M., A survey of Fast exponentiation methods, *Journal of Algorithms* **27**, pp. 129-146, 1998.

[7] Haupt, R.L. and Haupt, S.E., *Practical genetic algorithms*, John Wiley and Sons, 1998.

[8] Karnaugh, M., A map method for synthesis of combinational logic circuits, Transactions of the AIEE, *Communications and Electronics*, **72**(I):593-599, November 1953.

[9] Koza, J.R., *Genetic Programming*. MIT Press, 1992.

[10] McCluskey, E.J., Minimisation of Boolean functions, *Bell Systems Technical Journal*, **35**(5):1417-1444, November 1956.

[11] Menezes, A.J., Van Oorschot, P.C., and Scott A. Vanstone. *Handbook of Applied Cryptography*. CRC Press, 1996.

[12] Dabbish, E.A. and Sloan, R.H., Power analysis attacks of modular exponentiation in smartcards, Proc. Cryptographic Hardware and Embedded Systems, *Lecture Notes in Computer Science*, vol. 1717, pp. 144-157, 1999.

[13] Miller, J.F. and Job, D., *Principles in the evolutionary design of digital circuits*

[14] Nedjah, N., Mourelle, L.M., Two hardware implementations for the Montgomery multiplication: sequential vs. parallel, *Proceedings of the 15th. Symposium on Integrated Circuits and Systems Design*, Porto Alegre, RS, Brazil, R. Reis and Calazans, N. (Eds.), IEEE Computer Society Press, pp. 3-8, 2002.

[15] Nedjah, N., Mourelle, L.M., Reconfigurable hardware implementation of Montgomery modular multiplication and parallel binary exponentiation, *Proceedings of the Euromicro Symposium on Digital System Design*, Dortmund, Germany, IEEE Computer Society Press, pp. 226-235, 2002.

[16] Poli, R., Efficient evolution of parallel binary multipliers and continuous symbolic regression expressions with sub-machine code GP, *Technical Report CSRP-9819*, University of Birmingham, School of Computer Science, December 1998.

[17] Rivest, R., Shamir, A. and Adleman, L., A method for obtaining digital signature and public-key cryptosystems, *Communications of the ACM*, **21**:120-126, 1978.

[18] Rhyne, V.T., *Fundamentals of digital systems design*, F.F. Kuo Ed. Prentice-Hall Electrical Engineering Series, 1973.

[19] Tiountchik, A., Systolic modular exponenti13:38 3/6/2004ation via Montgomery algorithm, *Electronic Letters*, **34**(9):874-875, 1998.

[20] Turton, B.C.H., Extending Quine-McCluskey for exclusive-or logic synthesis, *IEEE Transactions on Education*, **39**(1):81-85, February 1996.

[21] Thompson, A., Layzel, P. and Zebelum, R.S., Explorations in design space: unconventional design through artificial evolution, *IEEE Transactions on Evolutionary Computations*, **3**(3):81-85, February 1996.

[22] XILINX^{TM}, Inc., Foundation Series Software, http://www.xilinx.com, 2002.

In: New Topics in Theoretical Computer Science
Editors: Oleg N. Terikhovsky *et al.*, pp. 189-212
ISBN 978-1-60456-100-5

Chapter 7

PERFORMANCE OF DIRECTIONAL COLLISION AVOIDANCE IN MULTIHOP WIRELESS NETWORKS*

J. J. Garcia-Luna-Aceves[1,2†] ***and Yu Wang***[1‡]
[1]Department of Computer Engineering, University of California at Santa Cruz, Santa Cruz, CA 95064, U.S.A.
[2]Palo Alto Research Center, 3333 Coyote Hill Road Palo Alto, CA 94304, U.S.A.

Abstract

This chapter analyzes the performance of directional collision avoidance schemes, in which antenna systems are used to direct the transmission and reception of control and data packets in channel access protocols based on four-way handshakes to try to avoid collisions. The first analytical model to consider directional reception and the possible difference in gain between omni-directional and directional transmissions is presented. Analytical results show that, when the directional collision avoidance scheme in which all transmissions are directional is augmented with directional receiving, one-hop throughput does not decrease due to the increased spatial reuse, even when the number of competing nodes within a region increases. It is also shown that, as expected, the performance of directional collision avoidance schemes degrades when directional transmissions have much higher gain than omni-directional transmissions. However, this degradation is relatively small. Simulations of the IEEE 802.11 protocol and its directional variants validate the results predicted in the analysis. The simulation results also show that the presence of broadcast traffic does not degrade the performance of the all-directional collision avoidance scheme significantly, even for relatively large percentages of broadcast traffic. The performance results of this study indicate that the most attractive collision avoidance approach consists of using directional transmissions of control and data packets, together with the directional reception of packets whenever a node is expecting a particular packet. Given the high tolerance to broadcast traffic of directional collision avoidance schemes, it is argued

*This work was supported in part by the Defense Advanced Research Projects Agency (DARPA) under Grant No. DAAD19-01-C-0026, the US Air Force/OSR under Grant No. F49620-00-1-0330 and the Jack Baskin Chair of Computer Engineering at UCSC.

†E-mail address: jj@cse.ucsc.edu
‡E-mail address: ywang@cse.ucsc.edu

that the periodic transmission of beacons omni-directionally suffices to provide such schemes with the relative location of neighboring nodes.

Keywords: Collision avoidance, MAC, ad hoc networks, IEEE 802.11, directional antennas, spatial reuse

1 Introduction

Collision avoidance is very important in ad hoc networks to combat the "hidden terminal" problem that can degrade throughput significantly. The usual four-way collision avoidance handshake, as deployed in the popular IEEE 802.11 MAC protocol [1] and some other protocols, requires a pair of sending and receiving nodes to exchange short request-to-send (RTS) and clear-to-send (CTS) packets before the actual transmissions of data and acknowledgment (ACK) packets. Other nodes that overhear RTS or CTS packets need to defer their access to the shared channel to avoid collisions. Though these collision avoidance schemes perform much better than the simple carrier sense multiple access (CSMA) protocols in ad hoc networks, their performance still degrades rapidly when the number of nodes competing for a shared channel increases moderately. This is because those nodes within the range of a pair of sending and receiving nodes are refrained from both initiating and returning a handshake during the time, and nodes two hops away from either the sender or the receiver can be affected and this greatly reduces the possible spatial reuse.

Hence, limiting the size of the area that the handshake between sending and receiving nodes can influence is very desirable, and can be achieved with space division. Consequently, several schemes based on directional antennas have been proposed recently to enhance the performance of existing omni-directional collision-avoidance schemes [2–6]. In these schemes, which we call *directional collision avoidance* protocols, RTS and CTS packets are transmitted either omni-directionally or directionally depending on the design tradeoff between spatial reuse and collision avoidance, and data and ACK packets are transmitted directionally to reduce the interference to neighboring nodes.

The majority of the performance analysis of directional collision avoidance schemes has been done via simulations and experimental systems [2–7], and there is little prior work on the analytical modeling of directional collision-avoidance protocols. Wang and Garcia-Luna-Aceves [8] extended the model by Takagi and Kleinrock [9] to analyze three directional collision-avoidance schemes based on omni-directional packet reception, together with omni-directional and directional transmissions. The limitation of that work is that it assumes that the gain for omni-directional transmissions is the same as that for directional transmissions, and that all packet reception is omni-directional. In current systems, it is possible to have directional packet reception, and the range of directional transmissions can be longer than the range of omni-directional transmissions.

Section 2 reviews recent work on directional collision avoidance schemes, and Section 3 outlines the directional collision avoidance schemes that we study analytically and by simulation. The schemes we address consider that nodes communicate directly only with neighboring nodes within their omni-directional transmission range. The rationale for this approach is that, as our study shows, allowing nodes to obtain information about the relative location of neighboring nodes can be easily done with broadcast transmissions, without degrading the system performance considerably.

Section 4 presents the first analytical study of directional collision avoidance in ad hoc networks that considers (a) the effect of directional transmitting and receiving on spatial reuse and collision avoidance, and (b) the effect of the differences in gains between omni-directional and directional transmissions. Our model generalizes the analytical model adopted in [8]. To attain a tractable analytical model, we assume that interference due to side lobes and outside the transmission beamwidth are negligible. Although this is not the case with real directional antennas, our model does provide a good approximation for ad hoc networks in which any node communicates with only those other nodes that reside within its omni-directional transmission range. The results of the analysis show that the scheme that uses both narrow-beam directional transmissions and receptions throughout the collision-avoidance handshake can achieve the best performance among all the schemes investigated, and that one-hop throughput does not degrade by increasing the number of competing nodes within a neighborhood because of the increased spatial reuse. It is also shown that, as expected, the performance of directional collision avoidance schemes degrades when directional transmissions have much higher gain than omni-directional transmissions, because of the increased interference range and reduced spatial reuse.

The analytical model we use assumes a priori knowledge of the position of neighbors around a node. Section 5 presents the results of simulations carried out to validate the results from the analytical model, as well as to analyze the effect of using broadcast beacons to communicate relative node location information among neighboring nodes. The IEEE 802.11 MAC protocol and its variants that implement directional collision avoidance are investigated.

The results obtained via simulations validate the results predicted by our analytical model. It is further shown that directional reception helps to cancel out almost all the adverse effects of hidden terminals, and achieves very low data packet collision ratio. The simulation results also show that the presence of broadcast traffic does not degrade the performance of the all-directional scheme more than the other schemes that combine directional and omni-directional transmissions, and that the degradation in throughput is small even for large percentages of broadcast traffic. This indicates that a practical and efficient implementation of directional collision avoidance consists of nodes broadcasting beacons of their presence and location periodically, listening omni-directionally while not transmitting or expecting to receive directional packet, and transmitting and listening directionally otherwise.

Section 6 summarizes our results and outlines directions for future work.

2 Related Work

There have been many proposals to modify the existing omni-directional IEEE 802.11 MAC protocol to take advantage of directional antennas in the recent past.

Ko et al. [2] proposed two schemes. One scheme consists of nodes using directional transmission of RTS packets and omni-directional transmission of CTS packets in collision avoidance, and then using directional transmissions of data and ACK packets after successful exchange of RTS and CTS packets. The other scheme consists of nodes using both directional and omni-directional transmissions of RTS packets alternately when nodes' locations are not always known. These two schemes show the tradeoff between increased possibility of simultaneous transmissions by neighboring nodes (scheme one) and reduced possibility of collisions of control packets (scheme two).

Nasipuri et al. [3] proposed a MAC protocol similar to those summarized above, but used a different model. The authors also assumed that directional reception capability is available. However, the authors do not consider the effects of possible difference in gain between omni-directional and directional transmissions and the simulations are limited to rather regular network topologies.

Ramanathan [4] studied the performance of beamforming antennas in ad hoc networks when RTS and CTS packets are transmitted omni-directionally with the same range as directional transmissions while data and ACK packets are transmitted directionally. The author also addressed some interesting problems arising from directional transmissions, such as link power control and directional neighbor discovery. In the follow-up work Ramanathan et al. [7] described the DARPA UDAAN (Utilizing Directional Antennas for Ad hoc Networks) project in detail and showed the superior performance of using directional antennas.

In the work done by Takai et al. [5] and Choudhury et al. [6], direction information is included in the network allocation vector (NAV), which is used by nodes in IEEE 802.11 to notify other nodes how long they should defer their access to the shared channel. With detailed direction information, a node receiving NAV from one direction can still transmit in other directions. Choudhury et al. [6] also proposed a multi-hop RTS scheme to take advantage of the higher gain in directional transmissions. The authors also show the importance of considering the different ranges of omni-directional and directional transmissions as the results may be quite different from those when omni-directional and directional transmissions are assumed to have similar ranges.

In addition to the recent surge of simulation-based study of directional collision avoidance schemes in ad hoc networks (e.g., [10, 11]), some researchers have also begun to use analytical models to evaluate the performance of directional collision avoidance protocols. Wang and Garcia-Luna-Aceves [8] used a simple model to analyze three MAC schemes that use omni-directional packet reception together with omni-directional transmissions, directional transmissions, or a combination of both. This model was first used by Takagi and Kleinrock [9] to derive the optimal transmission range of a node in a multihop network, and was used subsequently by Wu and Varshney [12] and Wang and Garcia-Luna-Aceves [13] to derive the throughput of non-persistent CSMA, some variants of busy tone multiple access (BTMA) protocols [14] and the traditional omni-directional RTS/CTS based collision avoidance scheme in multi-hop ad hoc networks, respectively. As we have stated, the limitation of the analytical work presented in [8] is that the authors assume that omni-directional and directional transmissions have the same range, and consider only the case of omni-directional packet reception.

3 Directional Collision Avoidance Schemes

In the omni-directional MAC scheme, all packet transmissions and receptions are omni-directional. The IEEE 802.11 MAC protocol is an example of a protocol based on this scheme. We call this scheme *OTOR* (for "omni-directional transmission and omni-directional reception").

We consider two directional collision-avoidance schemes in our analytical study. In both schemes, RTS, CTS, data packets and ACK are transmitted directionally. When a node is transmitting in one direction, it appears "deaf" to other directions and cannot sense any channel activity at all. In these schemes, spatial reuse is maximized as nodes limit their transmission to as small area as possible. They differ in whether directional receiving is used or not.

One scheme uses omni-directional receiving mode whenever it is not transmitting; we call such a scheme *DTOR*, which is short for "directional transmission and omni-directional reception." In the other scheme, which we call *DTDR* (for "directional transmission and directional reception"), a node directs its antenna to the neighbor from which it expects to receive a packet, such as a CTS, a data packet, or an ACK, and appears "deaf" to transmissions from other directions. A node that is not expecting a packet from a neighbor listens to the channel omni-directionally. If a node does not receive an expected packet within its due time, the node returns to omni-directional receiving mode.

It is also possible to establish schemes that combine both omni-directional and directional transmissions and receptions. For example, in one scheme, only CTS packets are transmitted omni-directionally, while all the other types of packets are transmitted directionally. The purpose of the omni-directional transmission of CTS packets would be to try to silence the neighbors of a receiver and to prepare a clear *floor* for the sending node. Omni-directional or directional reception can be applied to this approach. However, directional reception is intuitively more attractive, and results in the *MTDR* scheme (short for "mixed-directional transmission and directional reception").

To implement any of the directional collision avoidance schemes, nodes have to know the relative locations of their neighbors. In practice, exact locations of nodes' neighbors are not required for directional collision avoidance schemes to function. Generally speaking, the angle of arrival (AoA) information reported by the radio can be cached and used later to direct antenna orientation.

In this chapter, we assume that broadcast beacons are used by nodes to determine who their neighbors are and their relative locations. Hence, even though a node can transmit and receive directionally, it communicates directly only with nodes within its omni-directional transmission range. The rationale for this approach derives from the results obtained in our analysis. Our analytical model studies the case in which location information is already known, and computer simulations are used to verify the results from this model and to show that even a crude and simple beaconing mechanism in which nodes let their neighbors know about their existence (and relative location) using periodic broadcast transmissions suffices to support directional collision avoidance schemes without a significant impact on performance.

4 Approximate Analysis

In this section, we present the analysis of the *DTOR* and *DTDR* schemes and compare their performance with the existing omni-directional *OTOR* scheme. The *MTDR* scheme can be analyzed using the approach presented here, but its analysis is omitted for brevity. However, it is still compared with the other schemes later in simulations.

4.1 Assumptions

For ease of explanation, we assume that directional transmissions and receptions have equal beamwidth, though it is trivial to extend the analysis to the case when their beamwidths are unequal.

Most of the assumptions made in our analysis of directional collision avoidance schemes have been used successfully in the performance evaluation of several MAC protocols [8, 9, 12, 13, 15] to obtain tractable analytical models.

As we have stated, to make the analysis of a multi-hop network tractable, we follow the line of modeling first used by Takagi and Kleinrock [9]. In this network model, the nodes are two dimensionally Poisson distributed with density λ, i.e., the probability $p(i, S)$ of finding i nodes in an area of S is given by:

$$p(i, S) = \frac{(\lambda S)^i}{i!} e^{-\lambda S}.$$

Varying λ has the effect of changing the congestion level within a region, as well as the number of hidden terminals.

The range of an omni-directional transmission is R, and the range of a directional transmission is $R' = \gamma R$, where $\gamma \geq 1$. Suppose N is the average number of nodes within a circular region of radius R; therefore, we have $N = \lambda \pi R^2$. Similarly we have $N' = \lambda \pi R'^2 = \gamma^2 N$.

We assume that nodes operate in time-slotted mode, with time slots of length equal to a propagation delay τ, which is much smaller than the length of any packet. Given that τ is very small, the performance of the time-slotted protocol is very close to the performance of the asynchronous version of the protocol, because the time-slotted version of the protocol delays the transmission of a packet by only a propagation delay that tends to 0. However, the analysis of the time-slotted version of the protocol is far simpler than the analysis of the pure protocol.

The transmission times of RTS, CTS, data, and ACK packets are normalized with regard to τ and are denoted by l_{rts}, l_{cts}, l_{data}, and l_{ack}, respectively. For the sake of simplicity, we also assume that all packet lengths are multiples of the length of a time-slot.

We derive the throughput of directional collision avoidance schemes based on a heavy-traffic assumption (i.e., a node always has a packet to be sent) which is reasonable given that nodes in ad hoc networks are busy sending both data and network-level signaling packets. We also assume that a silent node begins transmission with probability p at each time slot. Obviously, p cannot be 1 due to the way in which collision avoidance operates, such as deferring and backing off. Thus, p is a protocol-specific parameter but is slot independent.

In the analysis done in [12, 13], it is assumed that a node becomes ready independently with probability p_0 at the beginning of each time slot. It is also assumed that a node initiates a successful handshake with any other node with probability p_s. Obviously, relationship between these quantities is that $p_s < p < p_0$. To be specific, $p = p_0 \cdot$ Prob.{Channel is sensed idle in a slot}. In [12, 13], two Markov chains are used to

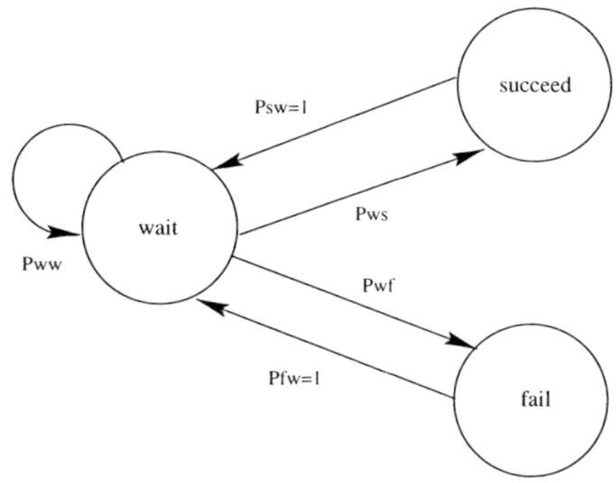

Figure 1: Markov chain model for a node

analyze the performance of CSMA, BTMA, and RTS/CTS based collision avoidance with omni-directional antennas. A Markov chain of the shared channel is used to derive the rough relationship between p and p_0, and a Markov chain is used to model the state of a node to derive the throughput. It is shown that the throughput is largely decided by p.

For any collision avoidance scheme to operate properly, p must be kept very small. Accordingly, as advocated in [8], rather than trying to derive a relationship between p and p_0, we simply assume that p takes on a range of values and then derive the throughput using the node model only. Given that the key objective of the model is to provide a comparative analysis of collision-avoidance strategies, and that the probability of successful handshakes by any one node in an ad hoc network cannot be very large, this approximation is very sensible, and is validated subsequently in our simulation analysis.

The node model is a three-state Markov chain shown in Fig. 1(from Fig. 1 in [8]), where *wait* is the state when the node defers for other nodes or backs off, *succeed* is the state when the node can complete a successful four-way handshake with other nodes, and *fail* is the state when the node initiates a handshake that is unsuccessful or cannot be completed due to collisions.

PwwP_{ww} PwsP_{ws} PwfP_{wf} Pfw=1$P_{fw} = 1$ Psw=1$P_{sw} = 1$

When a node transmits directionally, its transmissions can have longer range than its omni-directional transmissions. The effect of this is that a receiver can have more interfering sources than the nodes within an omni-directional transmission range. In our analysis and simulations, we assume that a node communicates directly only with other nodes that are within its omni-directional transmission range R, and communicate only indirectly with nodes outside R and inside its directional transmission range R', even though it can still be an interfering source for these nodes. The rationale for this assumption is twofold. First, in any directional collision avoidance scheme, a node needs to find the location of the nodes around it to direct its packet transmissions and receptions, and a simple way to accomplish this is by means of omni-directional beacons, especially in ad hoc networks in which nodes can be mobile. Second, it is possible to reduce the transmission power of directional transmissions to attain transmission ranges similar to those of omni-directional transmissions [11], in which case omni-directional and directional transmissions have the same range.

4.2 Throughput

The throughput Th of each directional collision avoidance scheme can be calculated by the proportion of time that a node spends transmitting data packets successfully in the average. With some simplifications, all the directional collision avoidance schemes we address in this chapter can be analyzed using the same node model of Fig. 1, and differ only in the duration of certain states and the transition probabilities among these states. Let π_s, π_w and π_f denote the steady-state probability of state *succeed*, *wait* and *fail* respectively. From the node model of Fig. 1 we have:

$$Th = \frac{\pi_s \cdot l_{data}}{\pi_w T_w + \pi_s T_s + \pi_f T_f}. \tag{1}$$

where T_s, T_f and T_w are the duration of states *succeed*, *fail* and *wait*, respectively.

We first derive those steady-state probabilities, transition probabilities and times spent at different states that are common to *DTOR* and *DTDR*, and then derive the results that are particular to each scheme.

For the sake of simplicity, we regard *succeed* and *fail* as the states when two different kinds of *virtual* packets are transmitted.

In all the directional collision avoidance schemes, the duration in time slots of a node in the *succeed* state is

$$\begin{aligned} T_s &= (l_{rts} + 1) + (l_{cts} + 1) + (l_{data} + 1) + (l_{ack} + 1) \\ &= l_{rts} + l_{cts} + l_{data} + l_{ack} + 4. \end{aligned}$$

Because by assumption collision avoidance is enforced at each node in all the schemes we consider, no node is allowed to transmit data packets continuously; therefore, as shown in Fig. 1, the transition probabilities from *succeed* to *wait* and from *fail* to *wait* are both one, and the transition probabilities from *succeed* to *succeed* and from *fail* to *fail* are both zero.

Given that a node in the *wait* state listens omni-directionally, the transition probability P_{ww} that node x continues to stay in *wait* state in a slot equals the probability that it does not initiate any transmission and there is no node around it initiating a transmission in the direction towards node x. Because this two events are independent, we have that

$$P_{ww} = (1 - p)e^{-p'N'}. \tag{2}$$

From Fig. 1, we have that the steady-state probability of the *wait* state equals

$$\pi_w = \pi_w P_{ww} + \pi_s P_{sw} + \pi_f P_{fw} \tag{3}$$

Noting that $\pi_s + \pi_f = 1 - \pi_w$, and substituting the results presented above for P_{sw},

P_{fw} and P_{ww} in Eq. (3), we obtain

$$\begin{aligned}
\pi_w &= \pi_w P_{ww} + \pi_s P_{sw} + \pi_f P_{fw} = \pi_w P_{ww} + \pi_s + \pi_f \\
\pi_w &= \pi_w P_{ww} + 1 - \pi_w \\
\pi_w &= \frac{1}{2 - P_{ww}} \\
&= \frac{1}{2 - (1-p)e^{-p'N}}.
\end{aligned} \tag{4}$$

The steady-state probability of *succeed* state π_s can be calculated by $\pi_s = \pi_w P_{ws} + \pi_s P_{ss}$. Given that $P_{ss} = 0$, we can use Eq. (4) to express π_s as a function of P_{ws} as follows:

$$\pi_s = \pi_w P_{ws} = \frac{P_{ws}}{2 - (1-p)e^{-p'N}}.$$

To derive the transition probability P_{ws} from *wait* to *succeed*, we need to calculate the probability $P_{ws}(r)$ that node x successfully initiates a four-way handshake with node y at a given time slot when the two nodes are at a distance r apart. The configuration is shown in Fig. 2, where θ is the beamwidth of transmissions and receptions. In Fig. 2, solid circles indicate omni-directional transmission ranges of nodes, while dashed circles indicate directional transmission ranges.

It is important to note that this analytical model assumes complete attenuation of the transmitted signal outside the range of the transmission beamwidth, and does not consider the effect of side lobes present in directional transmission and reception which is the subject of future work. The rationale for this simplification, which makes the model much more tractable, derives from the fact that nodes are required to communicate directly only with nodes within their omni-directional transmission range. Accordingly, the likelihood that a receiver y in the *wait* state engages in a handshake that is disrupted by either the main transmission beamwidth or a side lobe from neighboring node z within a directional reception side lobe of y is very small. If the transmission beamwidth of x is wide, node z is likely to listen to the transmission from node x when y does; if the beamwidths of nodes x and y are narrow, node z is unlikely to affect node y, unless it is almost collocated with y and this event has a very small probability according to the Poisson deployment of nodes on the plane.

xthetayθ

The success of the handshake between nodes x and y depends on the nodes for which y is within their omni-directional transmission range and those nodes for which y is within their directional transmission range. Fig. 2 indicates in dashed lines the area around nodes x and y that may contain nodes whose directional transmissions can reach x or y. To simplify our computation of throughput, we assume that there are, in effect, N' nodes around a node's omni-directional transmission range, though no node is assumed to communicate directly with any other node that is only reachable from directional transmissions. In fact, this simplifying assumption avoids the complexity of calculating interference directly from those nodes that are between the solid and dashed circles and instead such interference is taken into account by increasing the number of nodes within omni-directional range from N to N'.

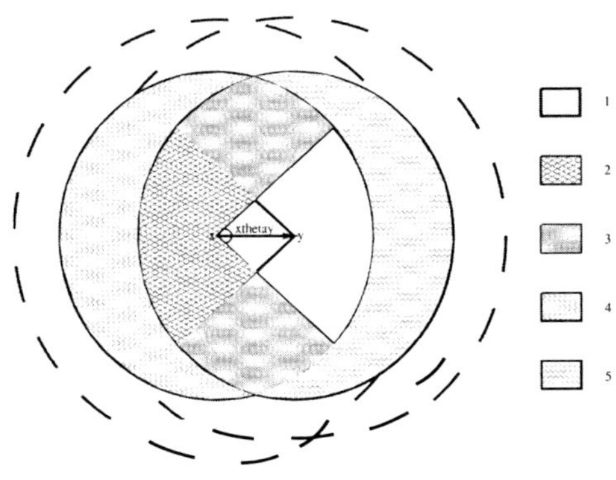

Figure 2: *DTOR* scheme

From Fig. 2, we can see that the region around nodes x and y can be divided into five areas. Denote by S_i the size of Area i, the size of each of the five areas are:

$$\begin{aligned} S_1 &= \theta/(2\pi) \\ S_2 &= \theta/(2\pi) - r^2\tan(\theta/2)/(2\pi) \\ S_3 &= 2q(r/2)/\pi - \theta/\pi + r^2\tan(\theta/2)/(2\pi) \\ S_4 &= 1 - 2q(r/2)/\pi \\ S_5 &= 1 - 2q(r/2)/\pi \end{aligned} \tag{5}$$

where we have normalized r with regard to R by setting $R = 1$ and S_i with regard to πR^2, and $q(t) = \arccos(t) - t\sqrt{1-t^2}$. The calculation of these areas is straightforward and omitted here.

With the above definitions, $P_{ws}(r)$ equals the probability that x does not transmit in a given time slot, y does not transmit in the same time slot, and none of the nodes in the five areas defined above interfere with the handshake between x and y. Given that transmissions are independent, we have:

$$P_{ws}(r) = p_x \cdot p_y \cdot \prod_{i=1}^{5} p_i$$

where

$$\begin{aligned} p_x &= \text{Prob.}\{x \text{ transmits in the time slot}\} = p, \\ p_y &= \text{Prob.}\{y \text{ does not transmit in the time slot}\} = 1 - p, \\ p_i &= \text{Prob.}\{\text{none of the nodes within Area } i \text{ interfere} \\ &\qquad \text{with the handshake between } x \text{ and } y\}. \end{aligned}$$

Computing the various probabilities p_i requires us to compute the probability P that no node transmits in a time slot within a planar area of size S in which nodes are randomly placed according to a two-dimensional Poisson distribution. This probability equals

$$
\begin{aligned}
P &= \sum_{i=0}^{\infty}(1-p)^i \frac{(\lambda S)^i}{i!} e^{-\lambda S} \\
&= \sum_{i=0}^{\infty} \frac{[(1-p)\lambda S]^i}{i!} e^{-(1-p)\lambda S} \cdot e^{-p\lambda S} \\
&= e^{-p\lambda S} = e^{-pS\lambda\pi R^2/(\pi R^2)} \\
&= e^{-pNS/(\pi R^2)}.
\end{aligned}
\tag{6}
$$

The next two subsections compute the remaining periods and probabilities needed to compute the throughput of the *DTOR* and *DTDR* schemes.

4.3 DTOR

Because the *DTOR* scheme cannot prevent interference from neighboring nodes, the handshake between any pair of sending and receiving nodes may be interrupted at any time. Consequently, the failed period T_f can last from $T_1 = l_{rts}+1$ to $T_2 = l_{rts}+l_{cts}+l_{data}+l_{ack}+4$.

Given that transmissions start at slot boundaries, we assume that the length of the failed period follows a truncated geometric distribution with parameter p, with a lower bound T_1 and an upper bound T_2. We can then consider T_f to be the mean value of the truncated geometric distribution, which is [8]:

$$T_f = \frac{1-p}{1-p^{T_2-T_1+1}} \sum_{i=0}^{T_2-T_1} p^i(T_1+i). \tag{7}$$

Obviously, the duration of a node in *wait* state T_w is 1.

In the following, we use the definitions of Areas 1 to 5 to compute the probability that there is no interference from nodes in each of those areas using Eq. (6).

The probability that no node in Area 1 interferes with the handshake between nodes x and y equals the probability that no node in the area transmits in the same time slot as node x does, which equals

$$p_1 = e^{-pS_1N'}.$$

For no interference to exist from nodes in Area 2, it must be true that no node transmits in $2l_{rts}$ slots in the direction of node y and does not transmit in the slot when the transmission of node y arrives at them. Therefore,

$$p_2 = e^{-p'S_2N'(2l_{rts})} \cdot e^{-pS_2N'}$$

where $p' = p\theta/(2\pi)$.

In Area 3, no interference exists if no node transmits in the direction to nodes x and y during the whole handshake between the two nodes, and the span angle of the direction θ' is $\theta+\phi$, where ϕ is the angle formed by the two lines joining a node in Area 3 with nodes x and y if ϕ is less than θ; otherwise, θ' is just 2θ. When nodes x and y are very close to each other, $\theta' \approx \theta$. Though the range of θ' is between θ and 2θ, for simplicity, we use $\theta' = \theta$.

Therefore,

$$p_3 = e^{-p'' S_3 N' (l_{rts}+l_{rts}+1+l_{cts}+1+l_{data}+1+l_{ack}+1)}$$
$$= e^{-p'' S_3 N' (2l_{rts}+l_{cts}+l_{data}+l_{ack}+4)}$$

where $p'' = p\theta'/(2\pi) = p\theta/(2\pi)$.

No interference to x and y exists from nodes in Area 4 if no node in that area transmits in node x's direction when node y is transmitting. Therefore, there are two such periods. One is the time when node y transmits a CTS packet to node x and the other is the time when node y transmits an ACK packet to node x. The durations of these two periods in the number of time slots are approximately $l_{rts} + l_{cts} + 1$ and $l_{rts} + l_{ack} + 1$ respectively which follows the assumption that nodes transmit in each time slot independently with probability p. Accordingly, the probability p_4 that no interference takes place from nodes in Area 4 is

$$p_4 = e^{-p' S_4 N' (l_{rts}+l_{cts}+1)} \cdot e^{-p' S_4 N' (l_{rts}+l_{ack}+1)}$$
$$= e^{-p' S_4 N' (l_{rts}+l_{cts}+1+l_{rts}+l_{ack}+1)}$$
$$= e^{-p' S_4 N' (2l_{rts}+l_{cts}+l_{ack}+2)}.$$

No interference exists from nodes in Area 5 if no node transmits in node y's direction when node x is transmitting. Similar to the previous case, there are two such periods. One is the time when node x transmits an RTS packet to node y and the other is the time when node x transmits a data packet to node y. The durations of these two periods in the number of time slots are approximately $l_{rts} + l_{rts} + 1$ and $l_{rts} + l_{data} + 1$ respectively. Therefore, the probability p_5 that no interference from nodes in Area 5 takes place is

$$p_5 = e^{-p' S_5 N' (l_{rts}+l_{rts}+1)} \cdot e^{-p' S_5 N' (l_{rts}+l_{data}+1)}$$
$$= e^{-p' S_5 N' (l_{rts}+l_{rts}+1+l_{rts}+l_{data}+1)}$$
$$= e^{-p' S_5 N' (3l_{rts}+l_{data}+2)}.$$

Because each sending node chooses any one of its neighbors with equal probability and the average number of nodes within a region of radius r is proportional to r^2, the probability density function of the distance r between nodes x and y is

$$f(r) = 2r, \quad 0 < r < 1$$

where we have normalized r with respect to R by setting $R = 1$.

Therefore, P_{ws} equals

$$P_{ws} = \int_0^1 2r P_{ws}(r) dr$$
$$= \int_0^1 2r \left(p \cdot (1-p) \cdot p_1 \cdot p_2 \cdot p_3 \cdot p_4 \cdot p_5\right) dr.$$

4.4 DTDR

Referring to Fig. 2, it is clear that, for the *DTDR* scheme, only nodes in Areas 1 and 2 can interfere with the handshake between nodes x and y. However, in the *DTDR* scheme, nodes are more vulnerable to the transmissions from nodes in these areas than they are in the *DTOR* scheme, because they receive omni-directionally only if they are in the *wait* state. To take the higher vulnerability into account, we use $l_{rts} + l_{cts} + 2$ as the lower bound for the distribution of T_f.

On the other hand, because nodes x and y are immune to the transmissions from nodes in Areas 3, 4, and 5, and because concurrent transmissions can go on unobstructed in these areas, we introduce a spatial reuse factor $\gamma(r)$ for this scheme in the calculation of $P_{ws}(r)$. The parameter $\gamma(r)$ is defined to be the number of possible concurrent transmissions in the combined region covered by nodes x and y, i.e.,

$$\gamma(r) = \min(\gamma_1(r), \gamma_2(r))$$

In the above expression, $\gamma_1(r)$ is the ratio between the total region covered nominally by nodes x and y and the actual region covered by the handshake between nodes x and y. If there is one handshake in Areas 1 and 2, then in theory there can be possibly $\gamma_1(r)$ concurrent handshakes in the total area of Areas 1 to 5. Hence,

$$\gamma_1(r) = (S_1 + S_2 + S_3 + S_4 + S_5)/(S_1 + S_2).$$

On the other hand, $\gamma_2(r)$ can be explained as follows: There are on average $N \cdot (S_3 + S_4 + S_5)$ nodes in the area of Areas 3 to 5 and in theory they can form a maximum of $\gamma_2(r) = N \cdot (S_3 + S_4 + S_5)/2$ pairs of concurrent handshakes. To be conservative, we take the smaller value of $\gamma_1(r)$ and $\gamma_2(r)$ to estimate the spatial reuse benefit enabled by the *DTDR* scheme.

The above is a very crude estimation of the gain in spatial reuse for the *DTDR* scheme, because the area unaffected by the handshake between nodes x and y cannot be used fully by their neighbors. Still, for this scheme, P_{ws} can be adjusted as follows:

$$P_{ws} = \int_0^1 2r\gamma(r)P_{ws}(r)dr.$$

The other quantities needed to derive the throughput are the same as those for the *DTOR* scheme.

4.5 Analytical Results

We compare the performance of the *OTOR*, *DTOR* and *DTDR* schemes. For the *OTOR* scheme, we use the results reported by Wang and Garcia-Luna-Aceves [8], who assume that correct collision avoidance is enforced, i.e., once a node starts sending a CTS packet in reply to an RTS destined to it, the following handshake can go on unobstructed. The performance of *OTOR* with this assumption constitutes an upper bound of the performance that can be attained with IEEE 802.11 MAC protocol, in which data packets may collide with other packets due to the additional imperfect collision avoidance.

We present the results of two typical configurations for the three schemes; similar results can be readily obtained for other configurations. In these configurations, τ denotes the duration of one slot and RTS, CTS, and ACK packets last 5τ, while a data packet lasts 100τ. In configuration one, both omni-directional and directional transmissions have the same

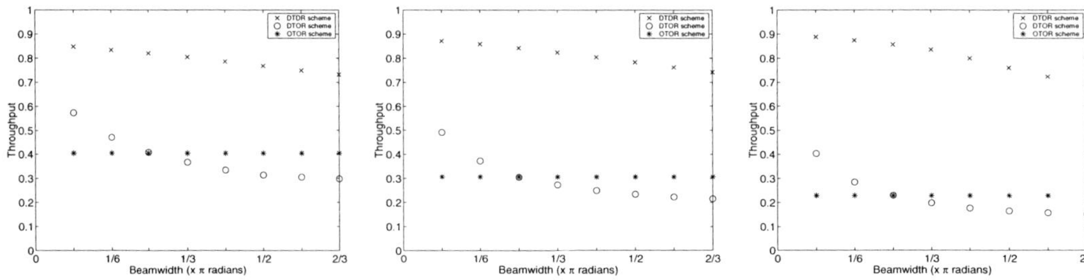

(a) Throughput (N=3) (b) Throughput (N=5) (c) Throughput (N=8)

Figure 3: Throughput comparison when omni-directional and directional transmissions have equal gain ($l_{rts} = l_{cts} = l_{ack} = 5\tau, l_{data} = 100\tau, \gamma = 1$).

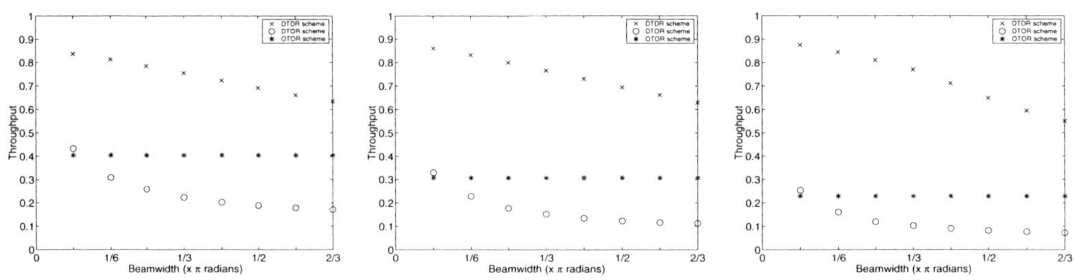

(a) Throughput (N=3) (b) Throughput (N=5) (c) Throughput (N=8)

Figure 4: Throughput comparison when the gain of directional transmissions equals one and a half times the gain of omni-directional transmissions ($l_{rts} = l_{cts} = l_{ack} = 5\tau, l_{data} = 100\tau, \gamma = 1.5$).

gain and thus we have $N' = N$. In configuration two, directional transmissions have higher gain than omni-directional transmissions and $\gamma = 1.5$. In this case, $N' = 1.5^2 N = 2.25N$.

For each configuration, we derive the maximum achievable throughput when the antenna beamwidth changes from $\theta = 15°(\frac{\pi}{12})$ to $\theta = 120°(2\pi/3)$ in increment of $\theta = 15°(\frac{\pi}{12})$. The results for configurations one and two are shown in Figs. 3 and 4, respectively.

Figs. 3 and 4 clearly show that the *DTDR* scheme maintains the highest throughput among the three schemes, even with the increase of transmission and receiving beamwidth. Two factors contribute to the superiority of the *DTDR* scheme. One is the significant increase in spatial reuse, because only a small area is covered by the transmissions between two nodes engaged in a handshake according to the analysis. The other is the much reduced interference from those nodes that are not aware of the handshake because of directional receiving.

Even though the *DTDR* scheme does not ensure perfect collision avoidance, the directional reception capability makes the receiving node immune to the transmissions from many other nodes in Areas 3, 4, and 5 after it transmits a CTS packet. Hence, in terms of avoiding collisions, the *DTDR* scheme is as good as or even better than the *OTOR* scheme, which silences all the neighbors around both a sender and a receiver.

Another significant advantage of the *DTDR* scheme is that its performance does not degrade with the increase of competing nodes within a neighborhood when antenna beamwidth is narrow. Instead, it even has a slight increase in throughput. This can be explained as follows: When the number of nodes is small, spatial reuse may be not utilized to its full advantage because some nodes may have to stay idle when all of their neighbors are engaged. This is not due to collision avoidance, but due to the scarcity of nodes. Hence, when more nodes are around, the effect of spatial reuse is more conspicuous and one-hop throughput increases accordingly.

The results in Figs. 3 and 4 also show that, as expected, the performance of the *DTOR* and *DTDR* schemes degrades when directional transmissions have higher gain than omni-directional transmissions. This is a direct consequence of the fact that the higher gain of directional transmissions leads to more interference at nodes receiving in omni-directional mode. However, it is clear that the *DTDR* scheme is superior to the *OTOR* scheme in all cases, and the same conclusion can be derived from the results of simulation experiments described in the next section. This helps to justify our approach of having each node consider as its neighbors those nodes that it hears through their omni-directional beacon transmissions.

5 Simulation Results

This section describes the results of computer simulations used to investigate the performance of the popular IEEE 802.11 DFWMAC protocol, which is labeled as *OTOR* in this section, and its variants corresponding to three directional collision avoidance schemes. The directional schemes considered are the *DTOR*, *MTDR* and *DTDR* schemes.

We use GloMoSim 2.0 [16] as the network simulator and implement the directional collision avoidance schemes under the assumption that there is a neighbor protocol that maintains a list of neighbors as well as their locations by means of beacons transmitted omni-directionally and periodically.

Given that we assume that location information is refreshed periodically by means of broadcast transmissions, it is important to investigate the impact of broadcast traffic on directional collision avoidance schemes. Accordingly, our simulations include two parts. We first present the performance of directional collision avoidance schemes when only unicast traffic is present in the network, which corresponds to the case in which location information is always known a priori. We then present the performance of the same schemes with different degrees of broadcast traffic, which results from beaconing location information with different degrees of persistence.

5.1 Performance Evaluation for Unicast Traffic

Direct sequence spread spectrum (DSSS) parameters are used throughout the simulations, which are shown in Table 1. The raw channel bit rate is 2Mbps. We use a uniform distribution to approximate the Poisson distribution used in our network model, which is mainly

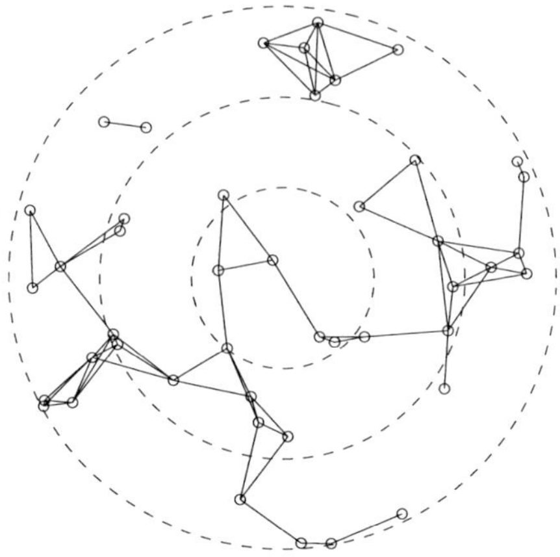

Figure 5: A sample network topology when $N = 5$

used to facilitate our derivation of analytical results. Even though the network model follows a uniform distribution, nodes in this model are distributed much less regularly than the grid model used in prior work, because nodes can have different number of one-hop neighbors and two-hop neighbors in different directions. In this network model, we place nodes in concentric circles or rings. That is, given that a node's transmitting and receiving range is R and that there are on average N nodes within this circular region, we place N nodes in a circle of radius R, subject to a uniform distribution. Because there are on average 2^2N nodes within a circle of radius $2R$, we place $2^2N - N = 3N$ nodes outside the previous circle of radius R but inside the concentric circle of radius $2R$, i.e., the ring with radii R and $2R$, subject to the same uniform distribution. Then $3^2N - 2^2N = 5N$ nodes can be placed in an outer ring with radii $2R$ and $3R$.

Because we cannot generate an infinite network model, we just focus our attention on the performance of the innermost N nodes. According to our experiments, conclusions drawn from a circular network of radius of more than $3R$ will not affect the conclusion to be drawn in this section, i.e., boundary effects can be safely ignored when the circular network's radius is $3R$. Therefore, we present only the results for a circular network of radius $3R$. To avoid some extreme cases, we only use network topologies that satisfy the following requirements:

- For the inner N nodes, each node should have at least 2 neighbors and at most $2N-2$ neighbors.

- For the intermediate outer $3N$ nodes, each node should have at least 1 neighbor and at most $2N - 1$ neighbors.

Fig. 5 illustrates a sample network topology used in our simulations when $N = 5$.

In our simulation, each node has a constant-bit-rate (CBR) traffic generator with data packet size of 1460 bytes, and one of its neighbors is randomly chosen as the destination for each packet generated. All nodes are always backloged. We run simulation programs with N = 3, 5, and 8, and for each choice of N we use beamwidth values of $\theta = 30°$, $90°$, and $150°$. The same beamwidth is used for directional transmissions and receptions.

Table 1: IEEE 802.11 protocol configuration parameters

RTS	CTS	data	ACK	DIFS	SIFS
20-byte	14-byte	1460-byte	14-byte	50μsec	10μsec

contention window	slot time	sync. time	prop. delay
31–1023	20μsec	192μsec	1μsec

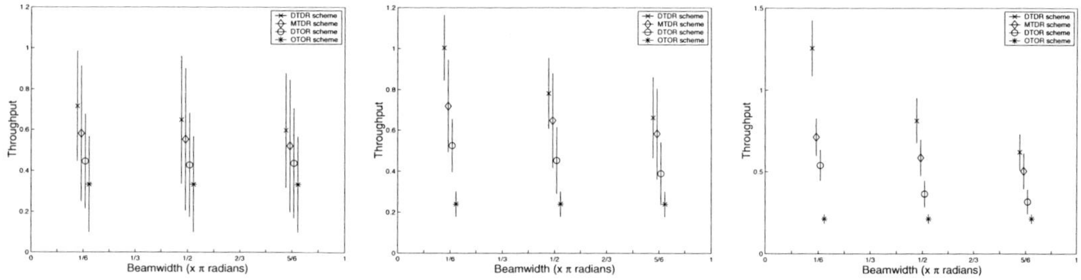

(a) N=3 (b) N=5 (c) N=8

Figure 6: Throughput Comparison – Equal Gain

It may be noted that both beamwidth and gain may not be adjusted independently in some current antenna systems. However, computer simulations do not need to be constrained by the capability of existing systems and it is expected that simulation results can provide insight or motivation for the design of more suitable antenna systems which we will show later.

Fifty random topologies were generated that satisfy the uniform distribution and the averages of the throughput and delay for the N nodes in the innermost circle of radius R were computed for each configuration.

The results for the case in which omni-directional and directional transmissions have equal gain are shown in Figs. 6 and 7. The results for the case in which directional transmissions have higher gain than omni-directional transmissions and $\gamma = 1.5$ are shown in Figs. 8 and 9.

In Figs. 6–9, the vertical lines show the range of throughput/delay achieved by each scheme, i.e., *mean* $\pm$ *standard variance*. The lines are shifted a bit for clarity. The *DTDR* scheme performs the best among all these schemes and its performance does not degrade even for large values of N as predicted in the analysis. The results also show that the *MTDR* scheme outperforms the *DTOR* scheme, which indicates that the directional receiving capability can boost performance significantly.

Without directional receiving, a scheme with mixed transmissions (*MT* scheme) performs worse than a scheme with only directional transmissions (*DT* scheme). This is because omni-directionally transmitted CTS packets make almost all the nodes around the receiver defer their access to the shared channel or interfere with the ongoing handshake around the nodes that transmit CTS packets. Such conservative collision avoidance can largely nullify the benefits of spatial reuse and an all-directional scheme such as *DT* is

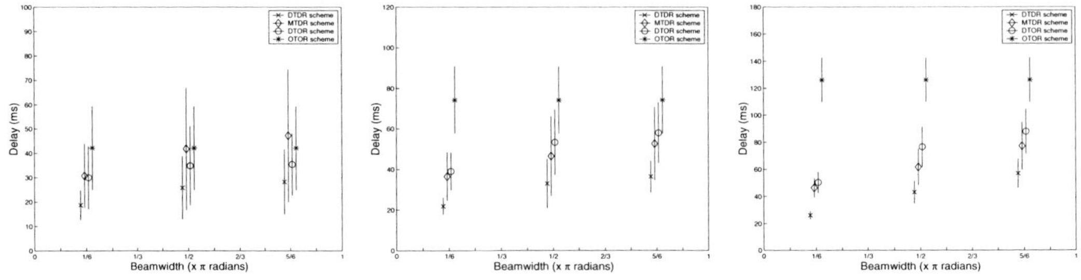

(a) N=3 (b) N=5 (c) N=8

Figure 7: Delay Comparison – Equal Gain

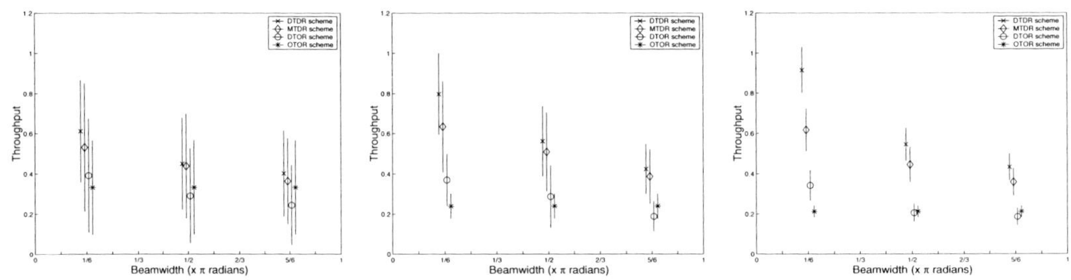

(a) N=3 (b) N=5 (c) N=8

Figure 8: Throughput Comparison – Higher Gain ($\gamma = 1.5$)

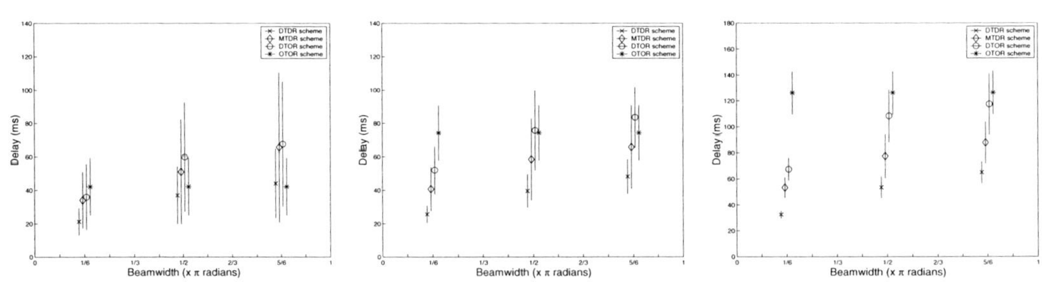

(a) N=3 (b) N=5 (c) N=8

Figure 9: Delay Comparison – Higher Gain ($\gamma = 1.5$)

Table 2: Comparison of percentage of ACK timeouts in different schemes ($\gamma = 1$)

	DTDR			*MTDR*		
	30°	90°	150°	30°	90°	150°
N = 3	0.04±0.02	0.06±0.05	0.06±0.04	0.03±0.02	0.04±0.04	0.06±0.06
N = 5	0.05±0.01	0.08±0.03	0.11±0.05	0.04±0.01	0.08±0.04	0.13±0.07
N = 8	0.07±0.01	0.14±0.02	0.19±0.04	0.07±0.02	0.15±0.03	0.22±0.05

	DTOR			*OTOR*
	30°	90°	150°	N/A
N = 3	0.38±0.17	0.35±0.19	0.33±0.18	0.29±0.21
N = 5	0.46±0.07	0.45±0.11	0.44±0.12	0.39±0.10
N = 8	0.55±0.03	0.58±0.04	0.57±0.05	0.46±0.05

shown to perform much better than *MT* when both schemes use only directional transmission capability of antenna systems.

However, when directional receiving is used, even though CTS is transmitted omnidirectionally, the handshakes of those nodes that have turned their receiving to other directions are not affected. Hence, the *MTDR* scheme can outperform the *DTOR* scheme in this case, although its performance is still inferior to the *DTDR* scheme because of the reduced spatial reuse.

It is also clear that, when beamwidth becomes wider, the performance of the *DTDR* scheme degrades faster when N becomes larger. This shows that when networks are dense, the performance of a directional scheme is more influenced by the transmission/reception beamwidth.

It should be noted again that, because correct collision avoidance is not enforced in the IEEE 802.11 MAC protocol, collisions of data packets can still occur and hence the *OTOR* scheme cannot achieve the same performance predicted in the analysis, which assumes correct collision avoidance. It is for this reason that the *DTOR* scheme performs better than the *OTOR* scheme, even when wider beamwidths are used.

When comparing the results shown in Figs. 6 and 7 with those in Figs. 8 and 9, it is clear that higher directional transmission gains can have negative effects on both throughput and delay. This is because a node's directional transmissions interfere with more nodes, which translates into a reduction in spatial reuse, given that more nodes spend more time in the wait state after perceiving the channel busy.

We also collected statistics about the number of transmitted RTS packets that lead to ACK timeouts due to collisions of data packets, as well as the total number of transmitted RTS packets that can lead to either an incomplete RTS-CTS-data handshake or a successful four-way handshake. Then we calculate the ratio of these two numbers which in fact shows the effectiveness of collision avoidance. The larger the ratio is, the worse the performance of the collision avoidance scheme becomes. The results are shown in Tables 2 and 3.

The results in Tables 2 and 3. show that directional collision avoidance schemes that do not employ directional receiving, such as the *DTOR* scheme, do have higher collision occurrences than the *OTOR* scheme. The reason for this result is that such directional schemes

Table 3: Comparison of percentage of ACK timeouts in different schemes ($\gamma = 1.5$)

	DTDR			*MTDR*		
	30°	90°	150°	30°	90°	150°
N = 3	0.06±0.03	0.09±0.05	0.11±0.07	0.06±0.04	0.14±0.11	0.21±0.13
N = 5	0.08±0.02	0.13±0.05	0.17±0.06	0.10±0.04	0.20±0.09	0.30±0.10
N = 8	0.11±0.01	0.19±0.02	0.23±0.04	0.14±0.03	0.32±0.05	0.40±0.05

	DTOR		
	30°	90°	150°
N = 3	0.42±0.20	0.39±0.21	0.40±0.18
N = 5	0.51±0.11	0.51±0.15	0.51±0.15
N = 8	0.63±0.03	0.65±0.05	0.60±0.06

are more aggressive in achieving spatial reuse, but are unable to force all the neighbors around the sending and receiving nodes to defer access to the shared channel. However, the adverse effects of hidden terminals are still conspicuous even for the *OTOR* scheme according to the high collision ratio shown in the table. It is also clear that, in addition to high spatial reuse, the schemes with narrow receiving beamwidth have far smaller collision ratios than the schemes without directional receiving. Hence, with directional receiving, the adverse effects of hidden terminals are almost completely canceled, leading to much higher throughput. It can also be noted that higher directional transmission gain leads to higher data collision ratio due to the increased interference it introduces. Therefore, directional antenna systems that are able to transmit and receive with narrow beamwidth while having the capability to reduce the power of directional transmissions are much more desirable than other variants.

5.2 Impact of Broadcast Traffic

In this set of simulation experiments we use the same network topologies discussed for the unicast experiments. Each node is a constant bit rate (CBR) generator that continuously generates unicast data packets and broadcast data packets alternately. For unicast packets, the destination node is chosen randomly from the node's neighbors. The size of a unicast data packet is 1460-byte and the size of a broadcast data packet is 500-byte, about one third the size of a unicast data packet, which is sensible given that the main use for broadcast packets is the beaconing of the nodes' presence and location.

We use r to denote the ratio between the number of broadcast data packets generated and the total number of data packets generated. We vary the number (N) of nodes in the innermost circular region of radius R as well as r to obtain the unicast throughput which is the aggregate throughput contributed by the innermost N nodes sending unicast data packets that are acknowledged. We show the results in Figs. 10–12. In the directional schemes (*DT* and *MT*), directional receiving is not used, because the results with directional receiving are similar and are not presented here for brevity.

Figs. 10–12 show that the throughput of the three schemes degrades very slowly even

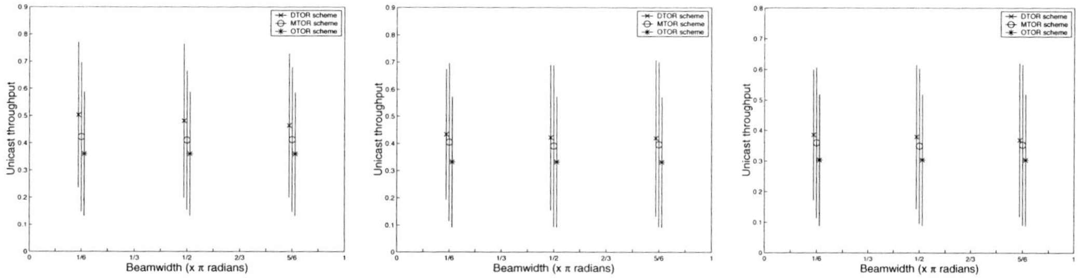

(a) $r = 0.0$ (b) $r = 0.1$ (c) $r = 0.3$

Figure 10: Unicast throughput with broadcast traffic ($N = 3$)

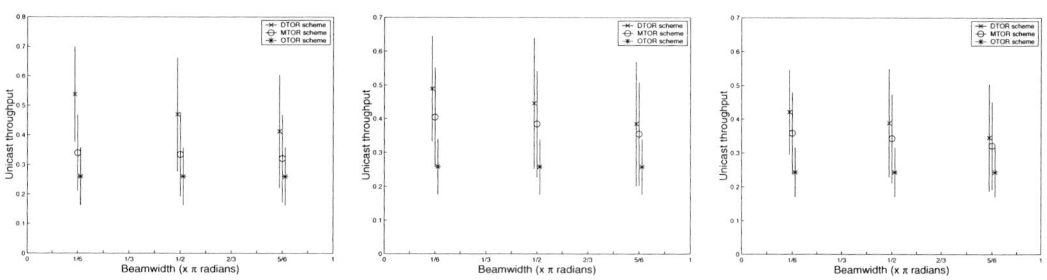

(a) $r = 0.0$ (b) $r = 0.1$ (c) $r = 0.3$

Figure 11: Unicast throughput with broadcast traffic ($N = 5$)

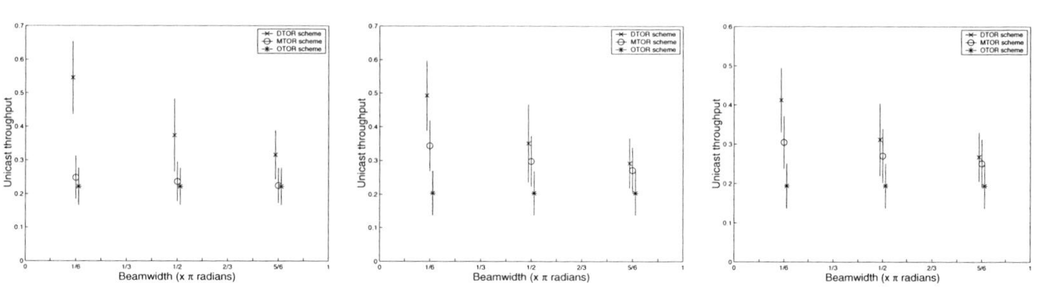

(a) $r = 0.0$ (b) $r = 0.1$ (c) $r = 0.3$

Figure 12: Unicast throughput with broadcast traffic ($N = 8$)

in the case in which 30% of each node's traffic is broadcast.

The only exception to the general behavior pattern observed for all schemes is that the throughput of the *MTDR* scheme increases slightly for $N = 5$ and 8 when r increases from 0 to 0.1. It seems that in these cases a small percentage of broadcast traffic helps to interrupt some nodes' long waiting time for collision avoidance and thus nodes are more aggressive in access to the shared channel. For all other cases, broadcast traffic can degrade unicast throughput gradually, but not dramatically. In addition, for small values of N (such as 3), the three directional schemes perform almost the same, considering both mean and standard variance.

When N increases, the *DTOR* scheme with small beamwidth θ performs indisputably much better than the other two schemes. This can be explained as follows. When the network becomes more congested, it is very difficult for a pair of sending and receiving nodes to get coordinated with their one-hop and two-hop neighbors in the *OTOR* scheme. If coordination is not achieved, then their handshake may be disrupted with high probability by the omni-directional transmissions of neighboring nodes. Even if coordination is achieved, all their one-hop and two-hop neighbors are prohibited from transmitting and spatial reuse is greatly reduced. The same reason applies to *MTOR* scheme due to the omni-directional transmission of CTS packets. In the *DTOR* scheme, transmissions are confined to much smaller regions and multiple flows may coexist at the same time. Hence the *DTDR* scheme performs the best in dense networks with larger N. When the network is less congested, the tradeoff between collision avoidance and spatial reuse is much more balanced and all schemes work similarly.

It should also be noted that the performance metrics can vary considerably even when the same uniform distribution is used throughout the simulation experiments, especially when N is small. This helps to emphasize the importance of using an analytical model and many network topologies in simulations, before meaningful conclusions can be drawn.

6 Conclusion

We have presented the first analytical model of directional collision avoidance schemes that takes into account directional transmission and reception capabilities and the possibility of having different gains in omni-directional and directional transmissions. The analytical results show that the scheme in which all transmitting and receiving are done directionally can achieve much higher throughput than any other scheme that combines directional and omni-directional transmissions or receptions. The all-directional scheme maintains high spatial reuse and largely cancels the interference from hidden terminals due to imperfect collision avoidance. Furthermore, the one-hop throughput of the all-directional scheme does not degrade with the increase of competing nodes within a region, which shows that the all-directional scheme is also much more scalable in dense ad hoc networks. It is also shown that higher directional transmission gain can have negative effects on the performance of directional collision avoidance schemes due to the increased interference range and reduced spatial reuse.

Extensive simulations of the popular IEEE 802.11 MAC protocol and its directional variants validate the analytical results. The very low ratio of data packet collisions in the schemes with directional receiving confirms that directional receiving can cancel out almost all the adverse effects of hidden terminals which seem to be the throughput bottleneck even for conservative collision avoidance scheme as exemplified in the IEEE 802.11 MAC protocol.

Simulation results also show that even a large fraction of broadcast traffic (e.g., 30%) does not degrade much the performance of directional collision avoidance schemes. Together with the analytical and the rest of the simulation results, this shows that an all-directional scheme is very attractive and practical for ad hoc networks. It attains much better throughput and delay than the other schemes, and the neighbor protocol that it needs to obtain location information of neighboring nodes can be implemented using very simple methods, without degrading its performance significantly.

In practice, some form of power control to achieve similar gains for both omni-directional and directional transmissions is desirable to take full advantage of the antenna systems. It is also possible to use power control to reduce both interference and energy consumption. Interesting areas of future research include analyzing the impact of side lobes in the performance of the protocols and eliminating omni-directional transmissions and receptions altogether by means of a directional beaconing mechanism, and comparing the performance of such a scheme against schemes that rely on omni-directional beaconing.

References

[1] IEEE Computer Society LAN MAN Standards Committee, ed., *IEEE Standard for Wireless LAN Medium Access Control (MAC) and Physical Layer (PHY) Specifications*. IEEE Std 802.11-1997, The Institute of Electrical and Electronics Engineers, New York, 1997.

[2] Y.-B. Ko, V. Shankarkumar, and N. H. Vaidya, "Medium Access Control Protocols Using Directional Antennas in Ad Hoc Networks," in *IEEE INFOCOM 2000*, Mar. 2000.

[3] A. Nasipuri, S. Ye, J. You, and R. E. Hiromoto, "A MAC Protocol for Mobile Ad Hoc Networks Using Directional Antennas," in *Proc. of the IEEE Wireless Comm. and Networking Conf. (WCNC) 2000*, (Chicago, IL, USA), Sept. 2000.

[4] R. Ramanathan, "On the Performance of Ad Hoc Networks with Beamforming Antennas," in *ACM MobiHoc '01*, (Long Beach, CA, U.S.A.), Oct. 2001.

[5] M. Takai, J. Martin, A. Ren, and R. Bagrodia, "Directional Virtual Carrier Sensing for Directional Antennas in Mobile Ad Hoc Networks," in *ACM MobiHoc '02*, (Lausanne, Switzerland), June 2002.

[6] R. R. Choudhury, X. Yang, R. Ramanathan, and N. Vaidya, "Medium Access Control in Ad Hoc Networks Using Directional Antennas," in *ACM MobiCom '02*, (Atlanta, GA, USA), Sept. 2002.

[7] R. Ramanathan, J. Redi, C. Santivanez, D. Wiggins, and S. Polit, "Ad Hoc Networking With Directional Antennas: A Complete System Solution," *IEEE Journal on Selected Areas in Communications*, vol. 23, pp. 496–506, Mar. 2005.

[8] Y. Wang and J. J. Garcia-Luna-Aceves, "Collision Avoidance in Single-Channel Ad Hoc Networks Using Directional Antennas," in *Proc. of IEEE Intl. Conf. on Distributed Computing Systems (ICDCS '03)*, (Providence, Rhode Island, U.S.A.), May 2003.

[9] H. Takagi and L. Kleinrock, "Optimal Transmission Range for Randomly Distributed Packet Radio Terminals," *IEEE Transactions on Communications*, vol. 32, no. 3, pp. 246–57, 1984.

[10] Z. Huang and C.-C. Shen, "A Comparison Study of Omnidirectional and Directional MAC Protocols for Ad Hoc Networks," in *IEEE Globecom 2002*, (Taipei, Taiwan), Nov. 2002.

[11] A. Nasipuri, K. Li, and U. R. Sappidi, "Power Consumption and Throughput in Mobile Ad Hoc Networks using Directional Antennas," in *Proc. of the IEEE Intl. Conf. on Computer Comm. and Networks (ICCCN)*, (Miami, Florida, USA), Oct. 2002.

[12] L. Wu and P. Varshney, "Performance Analysis of CSMA and BTMA Protocols in Multihop Networks (I). Single Channel Case," *Information Sciences, Elsevier Sciences Inc.*, vol. 120, pp. 159–77, 1999.

[13] Y. Wang and J. J. Garcia-Luna-Aceves, "Collision Avoidance in Multi-Hop Ad Hoc Networks," in *Proc. of IEEE/ACM Intl. Symposium on Modeling, Analysis and Simulation of Computer and Telecommunications Systems (MASCOTS '02)*, (Forth Worth, TX, U.S.A.), Oct. 2002.

[14] F. A. Tobagi and L. Kleinrock, "Packet Switching in Radio Channels: Part II - the Hidden Terminal Problem in Carrier Sense Multiple-access Modes and the Busy-tone Solution," *IEEE Trans. on Communications*, vol. 23, no. 12, pp. 1417–1433, 1975.

[15] F. Cali, M. Conti, and E. Gregori, "Dynamic Tuning of the IEEE 802.11 Protocol to Achieve a Theoretical Throughput Limit," *IEEE/ACM Transactions on Networking*, vol. 8, pp. 785–799, Dec. 2000.

[16] X. Zeng, R. Bagrodia, and M. Gerla, "GloMoSim: a Library for Parallel Simulation of Large-scale Wireless Networks," in *Proc. of the 12th Workshop on Parallel and Distributed Simulations*, May 1998.

In: New Topics in Theoretical Computer Science
Editors: Oleg N. Terikhovsky *et al.*, pp. 213-251
ISBN 978-1-60456-100-5

Chapter 8

Overlay Networks for Wireless Systems

Christian Scheideler*
Lehrstuhl für Effiziente Algorithmen, Institut für Informatik,
Technische Universität Mnchen, Boltzmannstr, Garching

Abstract

Radio networks are widely used today. People access voice and data services via mobile phones, Bluetooth technology replaces unhandy cables by wireless links, and wireless networking is possible via IEEE 802.11 compatible network equipment. Nodes in such networks exchange their data packets usually with fixed base stations that connect them with a wired backbone. However, in applications such as search and rescue missions or environmental monitoring, no explicit communication infrastructure may be available. In this case, the wireless hosts have to organize in a so-called wireless ad hoc network. As long as all of the hosts are within transmission range of each other, the problem of exchanging information in such a network basically boils down to designing suitable medium access control protocols, but if not all hosts can directly communicate with each other, we also need suitable routing algorithms. Designing routing algorithms for wireless ad hoc networks is an extremely challenging task and still research in progress. In this chapter, we mostly focus on the simpler question of how to maintain an overlay network of wireless links between the hosts so that, as long as this is in principle possible,

1. every node is reachable from every other node, i.e. the graph formed by the links is connected,
2. or better, for every pair of nodes (v, w) there is a route from v to w with a close to minimum possible hop distance or energy consumption,
3. and ideally, good routes to any destination can be discovered locally (i.e., without involving a global search operation), as long as the position of the destination is known.

The graph formed by the wireless links should also have a low degree to ensure a low maintenance cost, it should allow to find routes for the messages that have a low congestion, and it should be easy to update in case of arrivals or departures of nodes or changes in their positions. This chapter will present various local-control algorithms for reaching these goals.

*E-mail address: scheideler@in.tum.de

1 Introduction

The problem of designing overlay networks for wireless ad hoc networks has recently attracted a lot of attention. A basic requirement for these overlay network designs is that they maintain connectivity among the hosts, as long as this is possible. The most straightforward approach to achieve connectivity is to maintain a link between every pair of wireless hosts that are within their transmission range. However, this may require a high maintenance and update cost since the corresponding overlay network may have a high degree. Also, some links may have a high energy cost, and so a natural question would be whether these can be dropped without endangering connectivity.

An alternative approach would be to maintain connections only to the k nearest neighbors. However, Figure 1 demonstrates that it is easy to come up with examples in which the graph formed by the links would not be connected. So this approach does not work in general. As was shown by Xue and Kumar [46], it only works in specific cases. For example, if n hosts are distributed uniformly at random in a unit square and every host connects to more than $5.1774 \log n$ of its nearest neighbors, then the network formed by these links is connected with a probability that tends to 1 as n increases. But connecting to less than $0.074 \log n$ nearest neighbors results in almost sure disconnectivity.

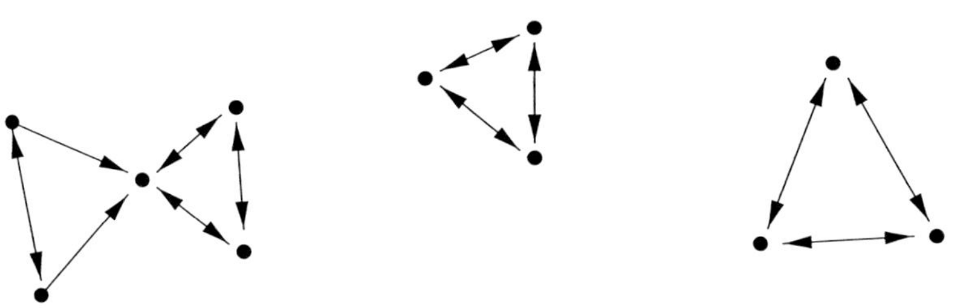

Figure 1: A counterexample for the naive approach with $k = 2$.

Another possible approach is that every host maintains connections to k hosts chosen uniformly at random among all hosts within its transmission range. This also does not guarantee connectivity in general but works well in certain cases. For example, Dubhashi et al. [12] recently showed that if every node has at least $\Theta(\log n)$ nodes within its transmission range, then choosing just 2 random nodes to connect to will establish connectivity almost surely.

In this chapter, we are only focusing on approaches that *guarantee* connectivity no matter how the hosts are distributed, as long as this is in principle possible. Most of these approaches are based on so-called *spanners*, which are properly selected subgraphs of the graph of all possible connections between the wireless hosts so that the hosts are not only connected but their (hop or Euclidean) distance in that graph is closely related to their minimum (hop or Euclidean) distance when considering all possible connections. Spanners first appeared in computational geometry [14, 47], were then discovered as an interesting tool for approximating NP-hard problems [42], and have recently attracted a lot of attention in the context of routing and topology control in wireless ad hoc networks [1, 17, 19, 3, 41].

In the following, the wireless hosts are simply called *nodes*. To simplify our presentation, we assume that the nodes are distributed in a perfect 2-dimensional Euclidean space, or formally, the nodes represent a set of points $V \subset \mathbb{R}^2$, but all of the approaches presented here can also be extended to higher dimensions. Given any pair of nodes $u = (u_x, u_y), v = (v_x, v_y) \in \mathbb{R}^2$,

$$||uv|| = \sqrt{(u_x - v_x)^2 + (u_y - v_y)^2}$$

denotes the *Euclidean distance* between u and v, and given any sequence of nodes $s = (u_1, u_2, \ldots, u_k)$ and any $\delta \geq 0$,

$$||s||^\delta = \sum_{i=1}^{k-1} ||u_i u_{i+1}||^\delta$$

denotes the *δ-cost* of s. For any graph $G = (V, E)$, a node sequence $s = (u_1, u_2, \ldots, u_k)$ is called a *path* in G if $(u_i, u_{i+1}) \in E$ for all $1 \leq i < k$.

Given any directed graph $G = (V, E)$ and any two nodes $u, v \in V$, the *δ-distance* $d^\delta_G(u, v)$ of u and v in G is the minimum δ-cost $||p||^\delta$ over all paths p from u to v in G. If $\delta = 0$, then $d^\delta_G(u, v)$ gives the *topological (or hop) distance* of u and v in G, and if $\delta = 1$, $d^\delta_G(u, v)$ gives the *Euclidean distance* of u and v in G. Also cases with $\delta > 1$ are interesting for us because the transmission of a packet over a distance of r usually has an energy consumption that scales with r^δ for some $\delta > 1$. In reality, δ is usually in the range $[2, 5]$, where it is closer to 2 outdoors and closer to 5 indoors.

We assume that every node has a maximum transmission range of 1, i.e., every node $u \in V$ can send messages only to nodes $v \in V$ with $||uv|| \leq 1$. From this assumption it follows that every overlay network connecting these nodes can only be a subgraph of the following graph.

Definition 1.1 *For any point set $V \subset \mathbb{R}^2$, the* unit disk graph *of V, called $UDG(V)$, is a directed graph that contains all edges (u, v) with $||uv|| \leq 1$.*

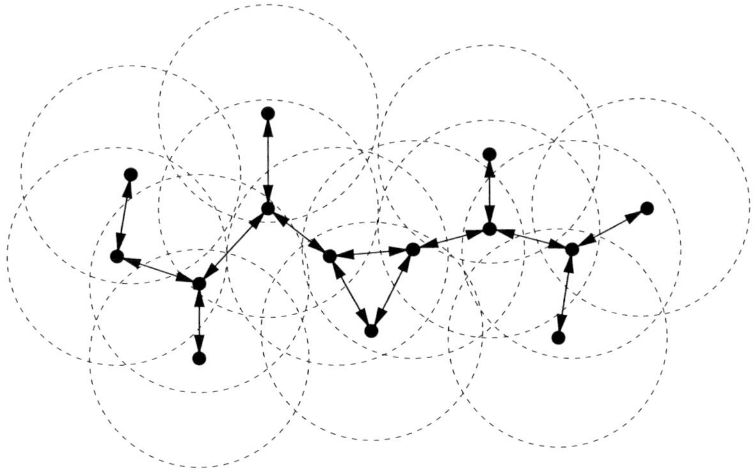

Figure 2: A connected unit disk graph.

In the following, we will always assume that V is chosen so that its UDG is connected and non-degenerate, i.e., there is a path in $UDG(V)$ between every pair of nodes and no two pairs of nodes have exactly the same Euclidean distance (see also Figure 2). The connectivity assumption is a prerequisite for our strategies below to establish a connected network among the nodes and the non-degenerateness property will simplify the proofs. When G is the UDG of V, we simply use $d^{\delta}(u, v)$ instead of $d_G^{\delta}(u, v)$.

The rest of this chapter is structured as follows. First, we define different kinds of geometric spanners and provide relationships between them (Section 3). Afterwards, we study a general class of graphs called *proximity graphs* that contain many of the spanner constructions proposed for ad hoc networks (Section 4). Among these spanner constructions are sector-based spanners and planar spanners. Various sector-based spanners are reviewed in Section 5, and various planar spanners are reviewed in Section 6. After that we focus on topological spanners, which are spanner constructions that aim at keeping the hop distance between any pair of nodes close to minimal. Besides showing how to construct the spanners in a distributed way, we also show how to route in them.

2 Spanners and Routers

First, we define spanners in which arbitrary pairs of nodes can, in principle, be connected by an edge (i.e., we do not limit the transmission range of nodes).

Definition 2.1 *Consider any finite set of nodes $V \subset \mathbb{R}^2$, and let $c \geq 1$ be any constant.*

- *A graph $G = (V, E)$ is called a* geometric c-spanner *of V if for all $u, v \in V$ there exists a path p from u to v in G with*

  $$||p|| \leq c \cdot ||uv|| \,.$$

  If G is a geometric c-spanner, c is called its stretch factor.

- *G is a (c, δ)*-power spanner *of V if for all $u, v \in V$ there is a path p from u to v in G with*

  $$||p||^{\delta} \leq c \cdot ||uv||^{\delta} \,.$$

  If for all $\delta \geq 2$ there exists a constant c so that G is a (c, δ)-power spanner, then we simply call G a power spanner.

- *G is a* weak c-spanner *of V if for all $u, v \in V$ there is a path p from u to v in G that is within a disk of diameter at most*

  $$c \cdot ||uv||$$

- *A graph $G = (V, E)$ is called a* constrained *(geometric, power, or weak) spanner of V if for every pair of nodes $u, v \in V$ there is a path p that, in addition to the specific requirement for the spanner type, also satisfies the condition that for every edge e in p,*

  $$||e|| \leq ||uv||$$

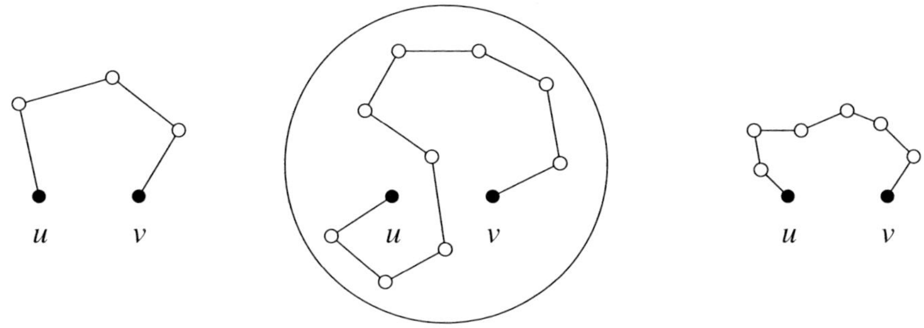

Figure 3: Examples of a spanner, weak spanner, and power spanner.

Since wireless nodes have a limited transmission range, the following spanner definitions are more relevant for ad hoc networks.

Definition 2.2 *Let $V \subset \mathbb{R}^2$ be any finite set of nodes with a connected UDG.*

- *A graph $G = (V, E)$ is called a* geometric c-spanner *of $UDG(V)$ if for all $u, v \in V$ there exists a path p from u to v in G with*

$$||p|| \leq c \cdot d(u, v) \ .$$

- *G is a (c, δ)-*power spanner *of $UDG(V)$ if for all $u, v \in V$ there is a path p from u to v in G with*

$$||p||^{\delta} \leq c \cdot d^{\delta}(u, v) \ .$$

- *G is a* weak c-spanner *of $UDG(V)$ if for all $u, v \in V$ there is a path p from u to v in G that is within a disk of diameter at most*

$$c \cdot d(u, v)$$

Interestingly, any constrained spanner of V in which all edges of length more than 1 are removed is also a spanner of the UDG of V, as shown in the next theorem.

Theorem 2.3 *Any constrained geometric c-spanner / (c, δ)-power spanner / weak c-spanner G of V restricted to edges of length at most 1 is also a geometric c-spanner / (c, δ)-power spanner / weak c-spanner of the UDG of V.*

Proof. Let U be the UDG of V. Suppose that G is a (c, δ)-power spanner of V for some $\delta \geq 0$. Then it holds for every pair of nodes $u, v \in V$ with $||uv|| \leq 1$ that there is a path p in $G \cap U$ with $||p||^{\delta} \leq c||uv||^{\delta}$. Now, consider an arbitrary pair $u, w \in V$, and let $p = (v_0, v_1, v_2, \ldots, v_k)$ be any path in U with $v_0 = u$ and $v_k = w$ that has a δ-cost of $d^{\delta}(u, w)$. Since $||v_i v_{i+1}|| \leq 1$ for all i, there is a path p_i from v_i to v_{i+1} in $G \cap U$ with $||p_i||^{\delta} \leq c||v_i v_{i+1}||^{\delta}$. Concatenating these paths, we end up with a path p' with

$$||p'||^{\delta} = \sum_{i=0}^{k-1} ||p_i||^{\delta} \leq \sum_{i=0}^{k-1} c||v_i v_{i+1}||^{\delta} = c \cdot d^{\delta}(u, w) \ .$$

Hence, $G \cap U$ is also a (c, δ)-power spanner of U. Since a geometric c-spanner is just a $(c, 1)$-power spanner, this also proves the theorem for constrained geometric spanners.

Finally, consider the case that G is a constrained weak c-spanner. Then it holds for every pair of nodes $u, v \in V$ with $||uv|| \leq 1$ that there is a path p in $G \cap U$ that is within a disk of diameter at most $c||uv||$. Consider now an arbitrary pair $u, w \in V$, and let $p = (v_0, v_1, v_2, \ldots, v_k)$ be any path in U with $v_0 = u$ and $v_k = w$ that has a Euclidean length of $d(u, w)$. Since $||v_i v_{i+1}|| \leq 1$ for all i, there is a path p_i from v_i to v_{i+1} in $G \cap U$ that is within a disk of diameter at most $c \cdot ||v_i v_{i+1}||$. Concatenating these paths, we end up with a path p' that is within a disk of diameter at most $c \cdot d(u, w)$. To prove this, we need the following straightforward fact.

Fact 2.4 *Any two disks of diameter d_1 and d_2 with a non-empty intersection are contained in a disk of diameter at most $d_1 + d_2$.*

Using this fact in an inductive manner on the length of p, it follows that when replacing the paths p_i in p' by their disks, p' is contained in a disk of radius at most

$$\sum_{i=0}^{k-1} c \cdot ||v_i v_{i+1}|| \leq c \cdot d(u, w)$$

□

Hence, it suffices to present and analyze algorithms for constrained spanners in order to obtain overlay networks that are also spanners of UDGs. However, just designing good overlay networks is not sufficient for wireless ad hoc networks. It is also important to have routing algorithms on top of these networks that can route messages from any source node to any destination node with a bounded amount of work. To study these routing algorithms, we introduce the following definitions.

Definition 2.5 *Let $V \subset \mathbb{R}^2$ be any finite set of nodes with a connected UDG.*

- *A graph $G \subseteq UDG(V)$ together with a routing algorithm A is called a* geometric c-router *if for all $s, t \in V$, A routes a packet from s to t along a path p in G with*

$$||p|| \leq c \cdot d(u, v) .$$

- *(G, A) is a* (c, δ)-power router *if for all $s, t \in V$, A routes a packet from s to t along a path p in G with*

$$||p||^{\delta} \leq c \cdot d^{\delta}(u, v) .$$

- *(G, A) is a* weak c-router *if for all $s, t \in V$, A routes a packet from s to t along a path p in G that is within a disk of diameter at most*

$$c \cdot d(u, v) .$$

We will see that not only good spanners can be designed in a distributed way but also good routers. Ideally, the protocols used for the design of spanners and routers should be self-stabilizing. Formally, a system or protocol is called *self-stabilizing* if for any initial configuration it will eventually reach a legal configuration. The definition of a legal configuration depends on the particular problem, but for an optimization problem this is usually any feasible solution of the problem. We are especially interested in protocols that are *locally* self-stabilizing, i.e., self-stabilization is achieved using only interactions with direct neighbors, and if the wireless network is static, the protocol should eventually arrive at a static solution.

3 Geometric Spanners, Power Spanners, and Weak Spanners

Next, we study general relationships between the different kinds of spanners. All of these relationships hold for general spanners as well as constrained spanners. However, to simplify the presentation, we only prove the statements for general spanners. The reader may verify that they also hold for constrained spanners.

Theorem 3.1 *Every graph $G = (V, E)$ that is a (constrained) geometric c-spanner is also a (constrained) weak c-spanner.*

Proof. Consider any pair of nodes $u, w \in V$. Since G is a geometric c-spanner, there is a path $p = (v_0, v_1, v_2, \ldots, v_k)$ with $v_0 = u$ and $v_k = w$ that has a length of at most $c \cdot ||uw||$. Replacing each edge (v_i, v_{i+1}) by the disk of diameter $||v_i v_{i+1}||$ containing v_i and v_{i+1} and using Fact 2.4 in an inductive manner implies that p is contained in a disk of diameter at most

$$\sum_{i=0}^{k-1} ||v_i v_{i+1}|| \leq c \cdot ||uw||$$

□

However, the theorem does not hold any more when considering power spanners [43].

Theorem 3.2 *For any $\delta > 1$ there is a family of (constrained) (c, δ)-power spanners which are not a (constrained) weak C-spanner for any constant C.*

Proof. Let $V = \{v_1, v_2, \ldots, v_n\}$ be a set of n nodes placed on a circle scaled so that $||v_1 v_n|| = 1$ and $||v_i v_{i+1}|| = 1/i$ for all $1 \leq i < n$. Now, consider the graph $G = (V, E)$ with edges (v_i, v_{i+1}) for all $1 \leq i < n$ (see also Figure 4). First, we show that G is not a weak C-spanner for any constant C, and then we show that G is a (c, δ)-power spanner for all $\delta > 1$.

It is easy to see that for every $n \geq 2$, the circumference of the circle through the n nodes is at least

$$\sum_{i=1}^{n-1} \frac{1}{i} \geq \int_{x=1}^{n} \frac{1}{x}\, dx = \ln n$$

which implies that its diameter is at least $(\ln n)/\pi$. Since the distance between v_1 and v_n is just 1 but any path from v_1 to v_n would have to traverse all nodes v_i along the circle, there cannot be a constant C so that G is a weak C-spanner.

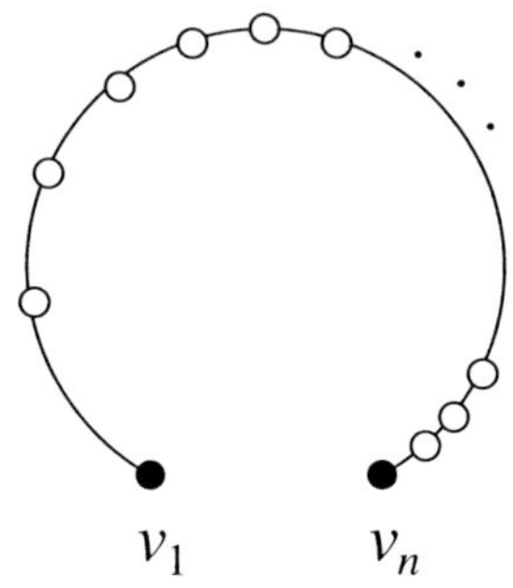

Figure 4: Example graph for Theorem 3.2.

On the other hand, if we look at the δ-cost of the unique path p from v_1 to v_n in G, we see that for $\delta = 1+\epsilon > 1$,

$$||p||^\delta = \sum_{i=1}^{n-1} \left(\frac{1}{i}\right)^\delta \leq 2\int_{x=1}^{n} -\frac{1}{\epsilon}\left(\frac{1}{x}\right)^\epsilon dx \leq \frac{2}{\epsilon} = \frac{2}{\delta-1} .$$

Since p uses all edges of G, this is an upper bound for the δ-cost of any path connecting any other pair of nodes (v_i, v_j) in G. Hence, for all pairs of nodes (v_i, v_j) with $||v_i v_j|| \geq 1$, the δ-cost is at most $2/(\delta-1)$. Moreover, it is not hard to check that every pair of nodes (v_i, v_j) with $||v_i v_j|| < 1$ has a path p from v_i to v_j of length at most $1 + O(1/\ln n)$ and therefore of δ-cost at most $(1+O(1/\ln n))^\delta$. Hence, G is a (c, δ)-power spanner for some constant c (depending on δ) for any constant $\delta > 1$. □

Also, the reverse direction of Theorem 3.1 is not true, i.e., the fact that a graph is a weak spanner does not imply in general that it is also a geometric spanner (see also [43]).

Theorem 3.3 *There exists a family of graphs $G = (V, E)$ with $V \subset \mathbb{R}^2$ all of which are (constrained) weak $2(\sqrt{2}+1)$-spanners but not a (constrained) geometric c-spanner for any constant c.*

Proof. Consider the snowflake structure in Figure 5. As can be seen from the picture (see the nodes v and w), the stretch factor of the snowflake structure is equal to

$$\frac{4}{2+\sqrt{2}} > 1.17$$

Recursively replacing each edge by a snowflake structure over d levels increases the stretch factor to at least 1.17^d. Suppose now that we have n nodes, where n is a multiple of 4. Then we can use them to construct a snowflake structure with $d = \log_4 n$ levels. This results in a stretch factor of at least

$$1.17^{\log_4 n} = n^{(\log_2 1.17)/(\log_2 4)} > n^{0.11} .$$

Next we show that the recursive snowflake structure is a weak spanner. Consider the dashed triangle through v and w in Figure 5. This triangle certainly contains all the other

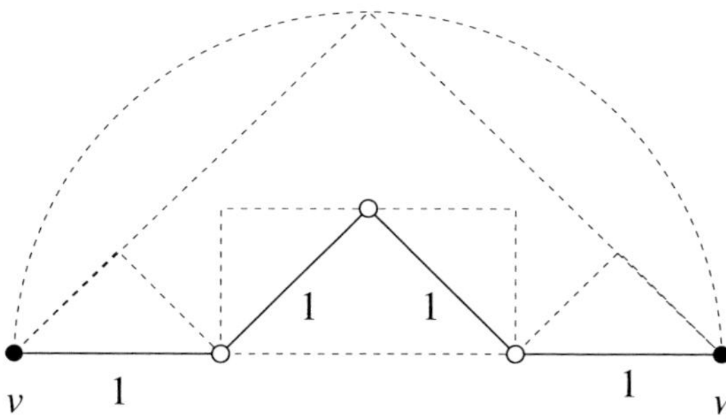

Figure 5: The basic snowflake structure.

triangles in the picture. Using this observation inductively, starting with the lowest level, it follows that for any recursion depth, the recursive snowflake structure with endpoints v and w is completely inside the triangle through v and w.

Now, let $G = (V, E)$ be any recursive snowflake structure of depth d. Consider any two nodes $v', w' \in V$. Let G' be the snowflake structure of largest depth within G that contains v' and w', and let S be the basic snowflake structure (i.e., we ignore further recursions) associated with G' and v and w be its endpoints (like in Figure 5). At this point we distinguish between two cases.

If v' and w' are associated with two non-adjacent edges in S, then it follows from the fact that any two points in non-adjacent triangles in Figure 5 have a distance of at least 1 that v' and w' must have a distance of at least 1. On the other hand, G' is completely contained in the disk of diameter $||vw||$ through v and w. Hence, G is a weak $2 + \sqrt{2}$-spanner for these (v', w') pairs.

If v' and w' are associated with two adjacent edges in S, then we recurse further on the snowflake structures of v' and w' until, for the first time, v' and w' are not associated with adjacent edges of adjacent snowflake structures, or we reached the lowest level. In this case, v' and w' are contained in triangles that are at least two edges away from each other. Going through all cases for these triangles, one can easily check that they must have a distance of at least $\sqrt{2}$ (relative to an edge length of 1 in the snowflake structures of v' and w') while the snowflake structures of v' and w' are contained in a disk of diameter $2(2 + \sqrt{2})$. Hence, G is a weak $2(\sqrt{2} + 1)$-spanner for these (v', w')-pairs.

Combining the two cases proves the theorem. □

The next theorem studies the relationship between geometric spanners and power spanners.

Theorem 3.4 *Every (constrained) geometric c-spanner is a (constrained) (c^δ, δ)-power spanner for every $\delta \geq 1$.*

Proof. Let $G = (V, E)$ be a geometric c-spanner. Then it holds that for every pair of nodes $u, w \in V$ there is a path $p = (v_0, v_1, \ldots, v_\ell)$ in G with $v_0 = u$ and $v_\ell = w$ and

$||p|| = \sum_{i=0}^{\ell-1} ||v_i v_{i+1}|| \le c \cdot ||uw||$. Hence, for every $\delta \ge 1$,

$$||p||^\delta = \sum_{i=0}^{\ell-1} ||v_i v_{i+1}||^\delta \le \left(\sum_{i=0}^{\ell-1} ||v_i v_{i+1}||\right)^\delta \le c^\delta \cdot ||uw||^\delta .$$

Therefore, G is also a power spanner for all $\delta \ge 1$, which proves the theorem. □

Hence, in order to prove that a graph is a power spanner, it suffices to prove that it is a geometric spanner. Interestingly, for $\delta \ge 2$, it even suffices to show that a graph is a weak spanner in order to prove that it is a power spanner. We only prove this fact for $\delta > 2$. The proof for $\delta = 2$ is involved and can be found (as well as the proof for $\delta > 2$) in [43].

Theorem 3.5 *Let $G = (V, E)$ be a (constrained) weak c-spanner. Then G is also a (constrained) (C, δ)-power spanner for $\delta > 2$ where $C = (4c+1)^2 \cdot \frac{c^\delta}{1-2^{2-\delta}}$.*

Proof. Consider any pair of nodes $v, w \in V$ and let p be any path from v to w that is in a disk $D(v, w)$ of diameter at most $c||vw||$. Suppose first there is no pair of nodes in p with a distance of at most $||vw||/2$. In this case, the disks of radius $||vw||/4$ around each of these nodes are disjoint. Since a disk of diameter d has a surface of $\pi(d/2)^2$, it follows that there can be at most

$$\frac{\pi((c+1/4)||vw||/2)^2}{\pi(||vw||/4)^2} \le (4c+1)^2$$

nodes in $D(v, w)$ that are used by p. Since the δ-cost of any edge in $D(v, w)$ is at most $(c||vw||)^\delta$, it follows that the δ-cost of p is at most $(4c+1)^2 c^\delta ||vw||^\delta$.

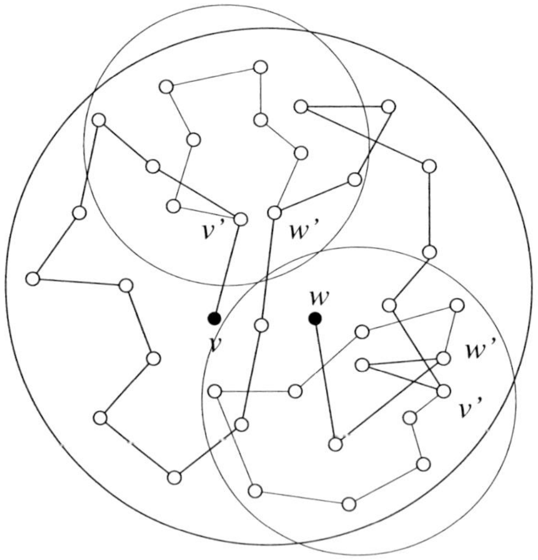

Figure 6: A possible path for the nodes v, w with two pairs v', w' that are too close.

Suppose now that there is a (not necessarily adjacent) pair of nodes in p with a distance of at most $||vw||/2$ (see Figure 6). Let v' be the first node reached when walking along p from v to w that has a node w' on p with $||v'w'|| \le ||vw||/2$. Then we replace the part of

p from v' to w' by the path p' from v' to w' that stays within a disk $D(v', w')$ of diameter at most $c||v'w'|| \leq c||vw||/2$. We continue walking along p at w' until we find the next node v' on p that has a node w' on p (*ignoring* the nodes in p') of distance at most $||vw||/2$. We do the same transformation for this pair and continue until the entire path p has been traversed.

After this transformation, all pairs of nodes (v', w') in p of distance at most $||vw||/2$ have been replaced by paths using edges of length at most $c||vw||/2$. Suppose that the nodes of these paths have a pairwise distance of more than $||vw||/4$. Since $D(v, w)$ can have at most $4(4c+1)^2$ such nodes and the δ-cost of any edge connecting these nodes is at most $(c||vw||/2)^\delta$, it follows that the δ-cost of all replaced parts of p is at most $4(4c+1)^2(c/2)^\delta||vw||^\delta$.

However, there may still be nodes in the new parts of p that have a pairwise distance of at most $||vw||/4$. Then we continue to reorganize the new parts of p as we did with the path p above. Each level i of reorganization creates an additional δ-cost of at most

$$2^{2i}(4c+1)^2(c/2^i)^\delta||vw||^\delta \ .$$

Since V is finite, and therefore the minimum distance between any two nodes is finite, this reorganization eventually terminates. At the end, the total δ-cost with $\delta > 2$ is at most

$$\sum_{i\geq 0}\left(\frac{2^2}{2^\delta}\right)^i(4c{+}1)^2c^\delta||vw||^\delta = (4c{+}1)^2c^\delta||vw||^\delta\sum_{i\geq 0}\frac{1}{2^{\delta-2}} = (4c{+}1)^2c^\delta||vw||^\delta\frac{1}{1-2^{2-\delta}}$$

□

However, a weak c-spanner may not be a (C, δ)-power spanner for any constant C if $\delta < 2$ [43].

Theorem 3.6 *For any $\delta < 2$ there exists a family of graphs $G = (V, E)$ with $V \subset \mathrm{IR}^2$ which are (constrained) weak c-spanners for a constant c but not a (constrained) (C, δ)-power spanner for any constant C.*

Summing up Theorems 3.1, 3.2, 3.3, 3.4, and 3.5, we obtain the following interesting relationship between the class of all geometric spanners, weak spanners, and power spanners with $\delta \geq 2$:

Geometric spanners $\subset$ Weak spanners $\subset$ Power spanners

4 Proximity Graphs

From our insights on spanners above it follows that it would often be sufficient to design protocols that guarantee a constrained weak c-spanner as long as this is possible because weak spanners are guaranteed to have energy-efficient paths. But how can such protocols be designed in a distributed way? Let us first focus on the weak spanner property. Consider the following definition:

Definition 4.1 *For any node set* $V \subset \mathbb{R}^2$*, the graph* $G = (V, E)$ *is called a* proximity graph *of* V *if and only if for all* $u, w \in V$ *it holds that*

- $(u, w) \in E$ *or*
- *there is a* $v \in V$ *with* $(u, v) \in E$ *and* $||vw|| < ||uw||$.

For an example of a node v satisfying the proximity conditions, see Figure 7. It is known that there are proximity graphs with a stretch factor as bad as $|V| - 1$ [4] but proximity graphs are always good weak spanners.

Theorem 4.2 *For any finite* $V \subset \mathbb{R}^2$*, every proximity graph of* V *is a weak 2-spanner.*

Proof. Let $G = (V, E)$ be any proximity graph of V. First we prove that G is connected. Certainly, a graph G is connected if and only if for every pair of nodes in G there is a path connecting these two nodes. So consider any pair of nodes $u, w \in V$. We distinguish between two cases:

1. $(u, w) \in E$: Then u and w are connected, and we are done.
2. There is a $v \in V$ with $(u, v) \in E$ and $||vw|| < ||uw||$: Then we use the edge (u, v) and get closer to w then we were before.

Since V is finite, we only have to apply case 2 a finite number of times until case 1 holds. Hence, G is connected.

Besides G being connected, it follows from the observation above that for any pair of nodes $u, w \in V$ there is a path p that monotonically converges against w. Hence, p is contained in a disk of diameter at most $2||uw||$, which proves the theorem. □

Hence, every proximity graph is also a power spanner of V for every $\delta \geq 2$. To make proximity graphs useful for ad hoc networks, we consider a constrained form of proximity graphs which are also known as relative neighborhood graphs [4].

Definition 4.3 *For any node set* $V \subset \mathbb{R}^2$*, the graph* $G = (V, E)$ *is called a* relative neighborhood graph *(RNG) of* V *if and only if for all* $u, w \in V$ *it holds that*

- $(u, w) \in E$ *or*
- *there is a* $v \in V$ *with* $(u, v) \in E$*,* $||uv|| < ||uw||$*, and* $||vw|| < ||uw||$.

It is easy to verify that relative neighborhood graphs satisfy the condition on constrained graphs we formulated for spanners in Definition 2.2. Hence, Theorems 2.3, 3.5, and 4.2 imply that relative neighborhood graphs are weak and power spanners of the UDG of V for every $\delta \geq 2$.

Figure 8 shows a simple distributed protocol for minimal relative neighborhood graphs. In this protocol we assume that every node $u \in V$ knows its neighborhood

$$N(u) = \{v \in V \mid ||uv|| \leq 1\}$$

and the current positions of the nodes in $N(u)$. Node u also keeps track of three sets:

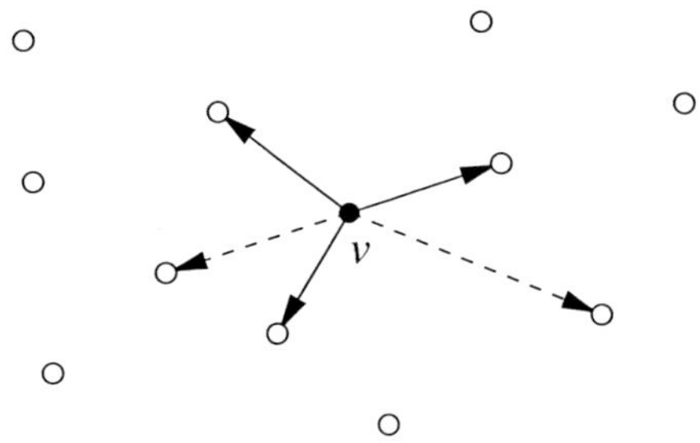

Figure 7: Connections satisfying the RNG condition for v. (Removing the dashed connections gives a minimum set of connections satisfying the RNG condition.)

- $E(u)$: set of edges that u currently has to nodes in $N(u)$.
- $B(u)$: set of nodes $w \in N(u) \setminus E(u)$ that have a node $v \in E(u)$ with $||uv|| < ||uw||$ and $||vw|| < ||uw||$.
- $U(u)$: nodes in $N(u)$ that are not in $E(u)$ or $B(u)$ (for example, nodes that newly entered $N(u)$).

Protocol RNG:

For every node $u \in V$ repeatedly do:
1) for every node $w \in E(u)$:
if there is a node $v \in E(u)$ with $||uv|| < ||uw||$ and $||vw|| < ||uw||$ then
move w to $B(u)$ (i.e., remove edge (u, w))
2) for every node $w \in B(u)$:
if there is no $v \in E(u)$ with $||uv|| < ||uw||$ and $||vw|| < ||uw||$ then
move w to $U(u)$
3) for every node $w \in U(u)$:
if there is a node $v \in E(u)$ with $||uv|| < ||uw||$ and $||vw|| < ||uw||$ then
move w to $B(u)$
else move w to $E(u)$

Figure 8: A self-stabilizing protocol for relative neighborhood graphs.

Theorem 4.4 *The RNG protocol self-stabilizes in at most 5 rounds. In the stable state, the outdegree of every node is at most 5.*

Proof. First we prove that the protocol self-stabilizes in at most 5 rounds. Suppose that node u is in an arbitrary state at the beginning of the first round. Only $N(u)$ and the positions of the nodes in $N(u)$ are assumed to be correct. Then it holds:

- After step 1) of round 1, $E(u)$ is minimal, and the nodes taken out of $E(u)$ were moved to $B(u)$.

- After step 2) of round 1, $B(u)$ is minimal, and the nodes taken out of $B(u)$ were moved to $U(u)$.

- After step 3) of round 1, $U(u)$ is empty and $E(u)$ and $B(u)$ satisfy the definitions of a RNG.

If $E(u)$ is minimal after step 3, $E(u)$ and $B(u)$ will not be changed in later rounds as long as $N(u)$ and the positions of the nodes do not change. Hence, in this case, the protocol has stabilized.

$E(u)$ may not be minimal after step 3 of the first round, but $E(u)$ is guaranteed to contain the node $v_1 \in N(u)$ of minimum distance to u, no matter whether initially $v_1 \in E(u)$ or $v_1 \neq E(u)$. Let

$$B_1(u) = \{w \in N(u) \mid ||uv_1|| < ||uw|| \text{ and } ||v_1w|| < ||uw||\}$$

and let $v_2 \in N(u) \setminus (\{v_1\} \cup B_1(u))$ be the remaining node of closest distance to u (if it exists). Notice that v_2 can only be prevented to join $E(u)$ if a node in $B_1(u)$ is in $E(u)$. Hence, it holds:

- After step 1) of round 2, $v_1 \in E(u)$ and $B_1(u) \subseteq B(u)$ and $v_2 \in E(u) \cup B(u)$.

- After step 2) of round 2, $v_1 \in E(u)$ and $B_1(u) \subseteq B(u)$ and $v_2 \in E(u) \cup U(u)$.

- After step 3) of round 2, $v_1, v_2 \in E(u)$ and $B_1(u) \subseteq B(u)$.

Now, let

$$B_2(u) = \{w \in N(u) \setminus B_1(u) \mid ||uv_1|| < ||uw|| \text{ and } ||v_1w|| < ||uw||\}$$

and $v_3 = N(u) \setminus (\{v_1, v_2\} \cup B_1(u) \cup B_2(u))$ be the remaining node of closest distance to u (if it exists). Following the arguments for v_2, it is guaranteed that $v_3 \in E(u)$ and $B_2(u) \subseteq B(u)$ after round 3. This is continued until there is no node v_i. At this point, $E(u)$ and $B(u)$ are stable.

It remains to bound the number of rounds the protocol needs to stabilize. For this we need the following lemma, which implies that in the final $E(u)$ there can be at most 5 nodes, and therefore the protocol needs at most 5 rounds to stabilize. In the following, $\angle(v, u, w)$ denotes the angle between the lines $\overline{uv}$ and $\overline{uw}$.

Lemma 4.5 *In a minimal set $E(u)$ there cannot be two nodes $v, w \in E(u)$ with $\angle(v, u, w) \leq \pi/3$.*

Proof. Suppose that there are two nodes $v, w \in E(u)$ with $\angle(v, u, w) \leq \pi/3$. Let v be the closer of the two nodes (which is unique because we only consider non-degenerate sets V). Then $||uv|| < ||uw||$ and also $||vw|| < ||uw||$ because of Lemma 5.4. □

If $|E(u)| \geq 6$, then there must be at least two nodes v and w in $E(u)$ with $\angle(v, u, w) \leq \pi/3$. But in this case, the lemma above implies that $E(u)$ cannot be minimal, which completes the proof of the theorem. □

Though relative neighborhood graphs may be good weak spanners, they may not be geometric spanners or power spanners with a low cost. Here, two basic approaches have been pursued in the literature to obtain geometric spanners and/or power spanners with low cost:

- The nodes cut the space around them into sectors of equal angle θ, where θ is sufficiently small. Such graphs are also known as θ-graphs or Yao graphs.
- The nodes triangulate the space to form Delaunay-like graphs.

We first consider Yao graphs and their variants, which we also call *sector-based spanners*, and afterwards we study Delaunay graphs and their variants, which we also call *planar spanners*.

5 Sector-Based Spanners

The basic idea underlying the Yao graphs is to cut the space around each node into sectors of equal angle θ and to connect each node to the nearest neighbor in each of its sectors (see Figure 9). As we will see, this will give a relative neighborhood graph if θ is sufficiently small. For any pair of nodes u, v, let $C_{u,v}$ denote the sector (or cone) of u containing v.

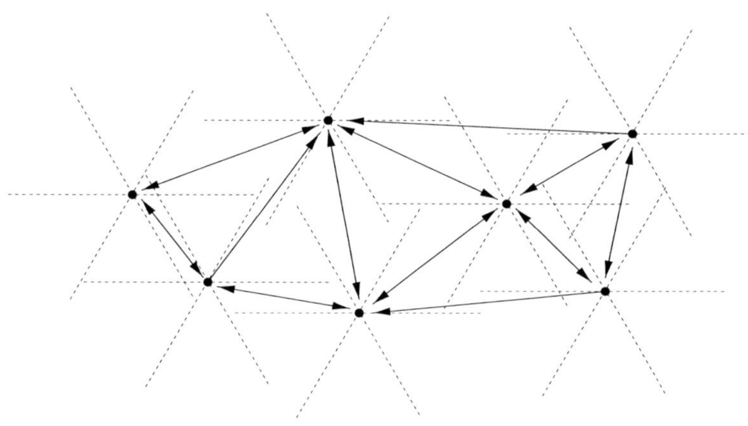

Figure 9: An example of a Yao graph.

Definition 5.1 *Consider any finite* $V \subset \mathbb{R}^2$ *and let* $k \in \mathbb{N}$. *Suppose that the space around every node* $v \in V$ *is cut into* k *sectors with angle* $\theta = 2\pi/k$. *Then the* Yao graph $YG_\theta(V)$ *of* V *consists of the following set of edges:*

$$E = \{(u,v) \mid u,v \in V \text{ and there is no } w \in V \text{ with } w \in C_{u,v} \text{ and } ||uw|| < ||uv||\}\ .$$

We start with a basic property of Yao graphs.

Theorem 5.2 *If* $\theta = 2\pi/k$ *with* $k > 6$, *then* $YG_\theta(V)$ *is a RNG.*

Proof. Follows immediately from Lemma 5.4. □

The theorem immediately implies that Yao graphs with $k > 6$ are weak spanners. But they are more than that, as shown in the next theorem.

Theorem 5.3 *If $\theta = 2\pi/k$ with $k > 6$, then $YG_\theta(V)$ is a geometric spanner with stretch factor at most*

$$\frac{1}{1 - 2\sin(\theta/2)} .$$

Proof. We first need a lemma.

Lemma 5.4 *Let $p \in \mathrm{IR}^2$ be a point and C be a sector originating at p. Furthermore, let q and r be two points in C with $||pq|| \leq ||pr||$. Then $||qr|| \leq ||pr|| - (1 - 2\sin(\theta/2))||pq||$.*

Proof.

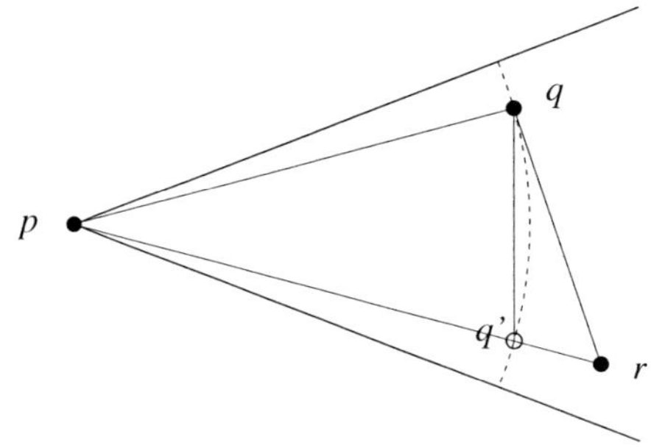

Figure 10: The sector of p that contains r.

Consider Figure 10. In this figure, q' represents the point on the line from p to r with the same distance to p as q. Applying the triangle inequality to q, q', and r, we get

$$||qr|| \leq ||qq'|| + ||q'r|| . \tag{1}$$

$||qq'||$ is certainly maximized if q and q' are on opposite sides of the sector. Hence,

$$||qq'|| \leq 2\sin(\theta/2) \cdot ||pq|| . \tag{2}$$

Moreover,

$$||q'r|| = ||pr|| - ||pq'|| = ||pr|| - ||pq|| . \tag{3}$$

Plugging (2) and (3) into (1) yields

$$\begin{aligned} ||qr|| &\leq 2\sin(\theta/2) \cdot ||pq|| + ||pr|| - ||pq|| \\ &= ||pr|| - (1 - 2\sin(\theta/2))||pq|| . \end{aligned}$$

□

Given a source-destination pair (s, t), consider the following strategy to get from s to t: Always take the edge whose other endpoint lies in the same sector as t.

Let the path obtained by this rule be $p = (s = v_0, v_1, \ldots, v_\ell = t)$. The path indeed ends at t, because for $k > 6$ we are guaranteed to have

$$||v_i t|| > ||v_{i+1} t||$$

for all i (see Figure 11).

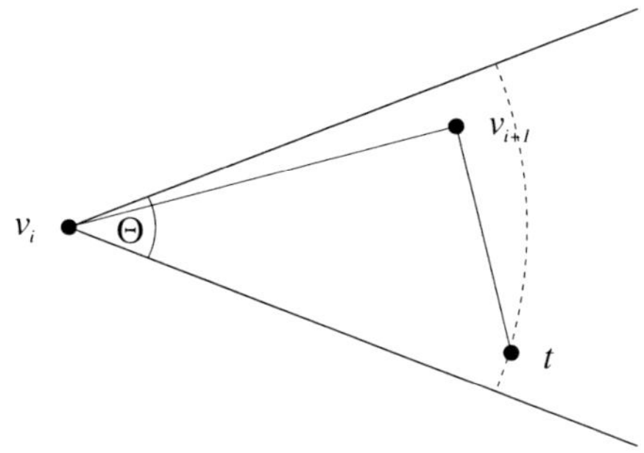

Figure 11: Figure illustrating that for $\theta < \pi/3$, v_{i+1} is closer to t than v_i.

Using Lemma 5.4, it holds that

$$\sum_{i=0}^{\ell-1} ||v_{i+1}t|| \leq \sum_{i=0}^{\ell-1} (||v_i t|| - (1 - 2\sin(\theta/2))||v_i v_{i+1}||) \ .$$

Rearranging the terms yields

$$\begin{aligned}\sum_{i=0}^{\ell-1} ||v_i v_{i+1}|| \ &\leq \ \frac{1}{1 - 2\sin(\theta/2)} \sum_{i=0}^{\ell-1} (||v_i t|| - ||v_{i+1} t||) \\ &= \ \frac{1}{1 - 2\sin(\theta/2)} \cdot ||st|| \ ,\end{aligned}$$

which proves the theorem. □

Combining this with Theorem 3.4 yields the following result.

Corollary 5.5 *If $\theta = 2\pi/k$ with $k > 6$, then $YG_\theta(V)$ is a (c, δ)-power spanner for every $\delta \geq 1$ with*

$$c \leq \left(\frac{1}{1 - 2\sin(\theta/2)}\right)^\delta \ .$$

A much better result was shown by Li et al. [34] for $\delta \geq 2$. We strengthen their result to any $\delta \geq 1$.

Theorem 5.6 *If $\theta = 2\pi/k$ with $k > 6$, then $YG_\theta(V)$ is a (c, δ)-power spanner for every $\delta \geq 1$ with*

$$c \leq \frac{1}{1 - (2\sin(\theta/2))^\delta} \ .$$

Proof. Let $c = \frac{1}{1-(2\sin(\theta/2))^\delta}$. We construct a path p from u to v. If $(u,v) \in YG_\theta(V)$ then we set p to (u,v). Otherwise, there must exist another node w in the same sector as v with $(u,w) \in YG_\theta(V)$. Then p is the concatenation of (u,w) and a path from w to v. Since $k > 6$, it follows from Lemma 5.4 that $||wv|| < ||uv||$. Hence, each node appears at most once in the path p. We prove by induction on the number of its edges that p has a cost of at most $c||uv||^\delta$.

If $(u,v) \in YG_\theta(V)$ then $||p||^\delta = ||uv||^\delta < c||uv||^\delta$. So assume that the claim is true for any path with ℓ edges. Then consider a path p from u to v with $\ell+1$ edges, which is the concatenation of an edge (u,w) and a path p' from w to v with ℓ edges. Let $\sigma = 2\sin(\theta/2)$ and $x \geq 0$ be chosen so that $||uv|| = (1+x)||uw||$. From the induction hypothesis it holds that $||p'||^\delta \leq c||wv||^\delta$. Hence,

$$\begin{aligned} ||p|| &\leq ||uw||^\delta + c||wv||^\delta \\ &\stackrel{\text{Lemma 1.20}}{\leq} ||uw||^\delta + \frac{1}{1-\sigma^\delta}(\sigma||uw|| + (||uv|| - ||uw||))^\delta \\ &= \left(1 + \frac{1}{1-\sigma^\delta}(\sigma+x)^\delta\right)||uw||^\delta \end{aligned}$$

To prove the theorem, we have to show that

$$||p|| \leq c||uv||^\delta = \frac{1}{1-\sigma^\delta}(1+x)^\delta||uw||^\delta$$

To show this, consider the function

$$f(x) = \frac{1}{1-\sigma^\delta}(1+x)^\delta - \frac{1}{1-\sigma^\delta}(\sigma+x)^\delta - 1\,.$$

It holds that

$$f'(x) = \frac{\delta}{1-\sigma^\delta}\left((1+x)^{\delta-1} - (\sigma+x)^{\delta-1}\right)$$

$f'(x)$ is obviously at least 0 for all $\sigma \leq 1$, $\delta \geq 1$, and $x \geq 0$. Hence, $f(x)$ attains its minimum at $x = 0$. Since

$$f(0) = \frac{1}{1-\sigma^\delta} - \frac{\sigma^\delta}{1-\sigma^\delta} - 1 = 0\,,$$

it follows that, indeed, $||p|| \leq c||uv||^\delta$ for all $\delta \geq 1$. □

There is also a simple distributed protocol for the Yao graph. Again, suppose that every node $u \in V$ knows its neighborhood $N(u)$ in the UDG and the current positions of the nodes in $N(u)$. Every node aims at maintaining a connection to the closest node in every sector. Let $E(u)$ be the current set of connections of node u. Then the protocol in Figure 12 can be used. This protocol has the following performance:

Theorem 5.7 *The Yao protocol self-stabilizes in one round. In the stable state, the outdegree of every node is at most k.*

Protocol Yao:

For every node $u \in V$ repeatedly do:
1) for every node $w \in E(u)$:
if there is a node $v \in N(u)$ in w's sector with $||uv|| < ||uw||$ then
remove w from $E(u)$
2) for every sector C of u:
if C has at least one node in $N(u)$ but no node in $E(u)$ then
add the node w in C of smallest distance to u to $E(u)$

Figure 12: A self-stabilizing protocol for Yao graphs.

Proof. Follows directly from the protocol. □

The drawback of the Yao graph is that, although its out-degree is at most k, its in-degree may be as high as $n-1$ (consider, for example, the disk in Figure 20 with one node in its center and all other nodes on its border). Various sub-graphs of the Yao graph have been suggested to remove this drawback. We will present two of them here.

Definition 5.8 *The* sparsified Yao graph $SpYG_\theta(V)$ *is a sub-graph of* $YG_\theta(V)$ *with edge set*

$$E = \{(u,v) \in E(YG_\theta(V)) \mid \textit{for all } w \in V \textit{ with } (w,v) \in E(YG_\theta(V)) \textit{ and } w \in C_{v,u}\text{: } ||vw|| > ||vu$$

In words, for every sector of every node v, the sparsified Yao graph only keeps the shortest of all edges into v. Hence, the sparsified Yao graph has an in-degree of at most k and an outdegree of at most k, and therefore a degree of at most $2k$.

Definition 5.9 *The* symmetric Yao graph $SyYG_\theta(V)$ *is a sub-graph of* $YG_\theta(V)$ *with edge set*

$$E = \{(u,v) \in E(YG_\theta(V)) \mid (v,u) \in E(YG_\theta(V))\} .$$

In words, the symmetric Yao graph only keeps an edge (u,v) if not only v is the nearest neighbor of u in $C_{u,v}$ but also u is the nearest neighbor of v in $C_{v,u}$. Hence, the symmetric Yao graph has a degree of at most k. Obviously,

$$SyYG_\theta(V) \subseteq SpYG_\theta(V) \subseteq YG_\theta(V)$$

and Figure 13 shows that there are cases in which the edge sets of the different graphs are proper subsets of each other. Thus, it suffices to prove connectivity for $SyYG_\theta(V)$ in order to prove connectivity for both variants of the Yao graph.

Theorem 5.10 ([17]) *For all non-degenerate node sets* V *and* $k > 6$, $SyYG_\theta(V)$ *is connected.*

Proof. We prove the theorem by induction over the distances between the pairs of nodes, starting with the pair of lowest distance, say (u,w). In this case, w must be the nearest

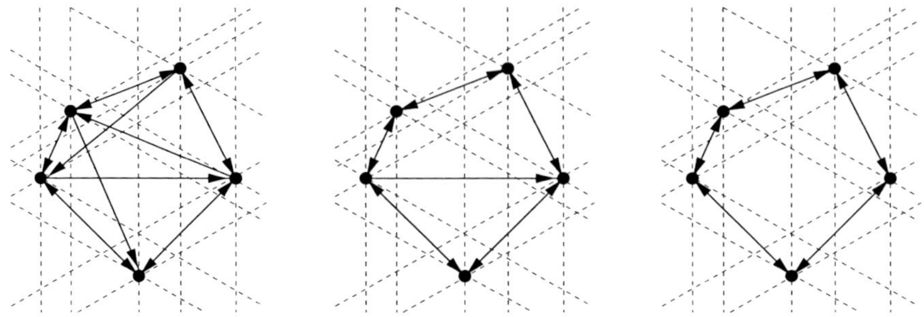

Figure 13: The Yao graph, the sparsified Yao graph, and the symmetric Yao graph of a point set.

neighbor in a sector of u and u must be the nearest neighbor in a sector of w. Hence, $(u, w) \in E(SyYG_{\theta}(V))$, and therefore u and w are connected.

Now, suppose that we already know for the k pairs with lowest distance that each of them is connected. Then let (u, w) be the next pair to be considered. We distinguish between three cases:

1. There is a node $v \in C_{u,w}$ that is closer to u then w: Since $k > 6$, it holds in this case that $||uv|| < ||uw||$ and $||vw|| < ||uw||$. Hence, according to our induction hypothesis, u and v and v and w must be connected. Thus, also u and w must be connected.

2. There is a node $v \in C_{w,u}$ that is closer to w then u: Using the same arguments as for the first case, it follows that also in this case u and w must be connected.

3. None of the two cases above hold: Then w must be the nearest neighbor of u in $C_{u,w}$ and u must be the nearest neighbor of w in $C_{w,u}$. Hence, $(u, w) \in E(SyYG_{\theta}(V))$, and therefore u and w are connected.

Thus, all pairs of nodes in V must be connected, and therefore $SyYG_{\theta}(V)$ must be connected. □

Unfortunately, the symmetric Yao graph is not a good power spanner for any $\delta \geq 1$, which implies that it is not even a good weak spanner.

Theorem 5.11 ([3]) *The symmetric Yao graph is not a (c, δ)-power spanner for any constant c and any $\delta \geq 1$.*

However, the sparsified Yao graph is a good weak spanner.

Theorem 5.12 ([3]) *If $k > 6$, then the sparsified Yao graph is a weak c-spanner with $c = \frac{2}{1-2\sin(\theta/2)}$.*

Proof. Let $G = (V, E)$ be the sparsified Yao graph and $G_Y = (V, E_Y)$ be the underlying Yao graph. Consider any two nodes $u, w \in V$. Our goal is to show that there is a path from u to w in G that is inside a disk with center u of radius $||uw||/(1-2\sin(\theta/2))$. For any sector, define the Yao-neighbor v of u as the (unique) node v in that sector with $(u,v) \in E_Y$. Then we know:

- if a node u has no directed edge in a sector, then either the sector is empty or there is a Yao-neighbor v incident to an edge $(u',v) \in E$ where u' is in another sector of u with $||u'v|| < ||uv||$. Furthermore, $||uu'|| < ||uv||$ because $\theta < \pi/3$.
- Every node u has at least one neighbor v because the sparsified Yao graph is connected.

We recursively construct the path $p(u,w)$ as follows: if $(u,w) \in E$ then $p(u,w) = (u,w)$. Suppose that w is not u's Yao-neighbor in $C_{u,w}$ but u has an edge to its Yao-neighbor, w_1, in $C_{u,w}$. Then $p(u,w)$ is defined as

$$p(u,w) = u \circ p(w_1,w)$$

where $u \circ p(w_1,w)$ is the concatenation of u with the node sequence for the path $p(w_1,w)$ from w_1 to w that still needs to be determined.

Suppose that u does not have a connection to its Yao-neighbor w_1 in $C_{u,w}$. Then we know that there exists an edge $(v_1,w_1) \in E$ where v_1 is in a sector adjacent to $C_{u,w}$ and $||uv_1|| < ||uw_1||$. Furthermore, we have $||uw_1|| \leq ||uw||$. Then we replace w by w_1 and repeat the arguments above. This iteration ends when u has a connection to a Yao-neighbor w_m or v_m. Because every node has at least one neighbor in E, this process terminates. If it terminates with w_m, then we define $p(u,w)$ as

$$p(u,w) = u \circ p(w_m,v_{m-1}) \circ p(w_{m-1},v_{m-2}) \circ \ldots \circ p(w_2,v_1) \circ p(w_1,w)$$

where $p(w_1,w)$ may just be equal to w if $w_1 = w$. Otherwise, we define $p(u,w)$ as

$$p(u,w) = u \circ v_m \circ p(w_m,v_{m-1}) \circ \ldots \circ p(w_2,v_1) \circ p(w_1,w)$$

Notice that all nodes v_i, w_i are inside the disk of radius $||uw||$ around u, and $||w_i,v_{i-1}|| \leq 2\sin(\theta/2)||uw||$ for all i due to Lemma 5.4. Hence, if we construct each path $p(w_i,v_{i-1})$ as we did for $p(u,w)$, then all nodes of these paths are within a disk of radius $||w_iv_{i-1}|| \leq 2\sin(\theta/2)||uw||$ and therefore within a disk of radius at most $(1+2\sin(\theta/2))||uw||$ around u. We then continue recursively with all the paths in the paths $p(w_i,v_{i-1})$.

Since V if finite and the distances between nodes for which we want to find paths shrink in each recursion, the construction eventually terminates. At the end, we get a path $p(u,w)$ that is within a disk of radius at most

$$\sum_{i\geq 0}(2\sin(\theta/2))^i||uw|| = \frac{1}{1-2\sin(\theta/2)} \cdot ||uw||$$

around u, which proves the theorem. □

Though the sparsified Yao graph is not a relative neighborhood graph like the original Yao graph, it is easy to check that when restricting to the UDG of V, the proof of Theorem 5.12 is still correct for all pairs u,w with $||uw|| \leq 1$. Hence, it follows from the proof of Theorem 2.3 that the sparsified Yao graph is also a weak c-spanner of the UDG of V. Thus, Theorem 3.5 implies that it is also a power spanner of the UDG of V for every $\delta \geq 2$ and therefore useful for wireless ad hoc networks.

Next, we present a distributed protocol for the sparsified Yao graph. Again, we assume that each node $u \in V$ knows its neighborhood $N(u)$ and the current positions of the nodes in $N(u)$. Node u also keeps track of the following sets:

- $E(u)$: set of edges that u currently has to nodes in $N(u)$.
- $R(u)$: set of nodes in $N(u)$ requesting a connection to u.

Then the nodes work as given in Figure 14.

```
Protocol SparseYao:
For every node u ∈ V repeatedly do:
  1) for every node w ∈ N(u):
     if w is the closest node in C_{u,w} and it is possible (from u's view) that (u, w) ∈ SpYG_θ(V) then
        u sends a connection request to w (causing w to add u to R(w))
     else remove w from E(u) if it is there
  2) for every node w ∈ R(u):
     if w is closest to u in w's sector among all nodes in R(u) then
        u sends w permission to connect (causing w to add u to E(w))
     else u notifies w that it gave permission to another node w' (s.t. w removes u from E(w))
```

Figure 14: A self-stabilizing protocol for the sparsified Yao graph.

Theorem 5.13 *The SparseYao protocol self-stabilizes in one round.*

Proof. Suppose that all neighbor sets are up-to-date. Then every node u knows the correct nodes w in step 1) that it has edges to in the Yao graph. Thus, at the end of step 1), every node w knows all the nodes v that have w as the closest node in one of their sectors. Hence, in step 2), every node u can select incoming edges according to the specifications of the sparsified Yao graph and will inform their starting points, which makes sure that at the end of step 2), all nodes w are added to $E(u)$ with (u, w) being an edge in $SpYG_\theta(V)$. On the other hand, $E(u)$ will contain only those nodes w with $(u, w) \in SpYG_\theta(V)$ because in step 1, all nodes w for which no request is sent are removed from $E(u)$, and in step 2, all nodes w that rejected the request are removed from $E(u)$. □

Routing

Next we show how to use the Yao graph and the sparsified Yao graph for routing. Consider any node set V that satisfies the following *density assumption*:

For every node u and every sector C of u it holds that if there is at least one neighbor in C then there is at least one neighbor v in C with $||uv|| \leq 1$.

Then the protocol given in Figure 15 correctly routes messages for every source-destination pair (s, t) if the position of t is known. In fact, the following theorem follows immediately from the proof of Theorem 5.3.

Theorem 5.14 *If the density assumption holds and* $\theta = 2\pi/k$ *with* $k > 6$*, then* $(YG_\theta(V), YaoRoute)$ *is a* $\frac{1}{1-2\sin(\theta/2)}$*-router.*

```
Protocol YaoRoute:
  For every node u ∈ V with a message to destination t:
    select the Yao edge (u, v) with v being in the sector of t
    forward the message to v
```

Figure 15: A routing protocol for the Yao graph.

For the sparsified Yao graph, the protocol is a bit more complicated because a node may not have an edge to a node in every sector, even if there are nodes in that sector. However, using the proof that the sparsified Yao graph is a weak spanner, we can still successfully route every message to its destination (see Figure 16). The protocol uses a technique for this also known as Multiprotocol Label Switching (or MPLS) [7, 10]. MPLS is being increasingly deployed by Internet service providers. In MPLS, each packet can have a stack of node labels, instead of just a single node label denoting its destination. Each node receiving the packet inspects the top label, and based on this label it decides where to send the packet next and may pop the top label from the stack or push other labels on top of the stack. From the proof of Theorem 5.12 it follows:

Theorem 5.15 *If the density assumption holds and* $\theta = 2\pi/k$ *with* $k > 6$*, then* $(SpYG_\theta(V), SpYaoRoute)$ *is a weak* $\frac{2}{1-2\sin(\theta/2)}$*-router.*

Combining this with the proof of Theorem 3.5, it follows that $(SpYG_\theta(V), SpYaoRoute)$ is also a good power router.

```
Protocol SpYaoRoute:
  For every node u ∈ V with a message m with a stack of labels s:
    w := pop(s)
    if (u, w) ∈ E then forward m to w
    else
      find nodes w_i, v_i as specified in Theorem 5.12
      if (u, w_m) ∈ E then
        p = (v_{m-1} w_{m-1} v_{m-2} ... v_1 w_1)
        push(p, s)
        forward m to w_m
      else
        p = (w_m v_{m-1} w_{m-1} ... v_1 w_1)
        push(p, s)
        forward m to v_m
```

Figure 16: A routing protocol for the sparsified Yao graph. Initially, s just contains the destination of the packet.

For the two routing protocols to work it is crucial that the density assumption above is satisfied. If not, then it is not clear how to provide robust routing protocols. As we will see, planar spanners can offer a solution here. However, this solution does not apply to the Yao graph and its variants since they may not be planar.

Mobility

Although the sparsified Yao graph has many nice properties such as having a constrained degree and being a power spanner, it has the drawback that it can cause a large amount of update work if the node set V changes (which may frequently happen in mobile ad hoc networks).

Theorem 5.16 ([17]) *There are node sets V where $\Theta(|V|)$ edges may have to be changed if an enter or leave operation happens in a Yao graph, sparsified Yao graph, or symmetric Yao graph.*

Proof. A bad situation for all Yao based graphs occurs, when two rows of nodes $U = \{u_1, \ldots, u_m\}$ and $V = \{v_1, \ldots, v_m\}$ are placed on two parallel lines so that the edge (u_i, v_i) is orthogonal to (u_1, u_n) and (v_1, v_n) and all nodes in U are in the same sector of a node in V and vice versa.

In this situation,we have $m = n/2$ edges for all Yao-based topologies, which all have to be erased if a node w pops up in the middle of the network. The inverse situation occurs if we remove this node. □

Ideally, we would like to have an overlay protocol that only requires a small amount of update work in case of any change in the network. We will see in Section 7 that this is easily possible by locally clustering the nodes. But first, we review results about planar spanners.

6 Planar spanners

The most well known class of planar spanners are the Delaunay graphs. The Delaunay graph of a set of points in $\mathbb{R}^2$ is equivalent to their Delaunay triangulation and the dual of their Voronoi diagram. Since the Delaunay triangulation of any point set in $\mathbb{R}^2$ is planar, the Delaunay graph is planar. In the following, let $\triangle(uvw)$ be the triangle formed by the nodes u, v, and w and $\bigcirc(uvw)$ be the unique circle through u, v, and w.

Definition 6.1 *For any $V \subset \mathbb{R}^2$, the* Delaunay graph *$Del(V)$ of V consists of all edges (u, v) that have a node $w \in V$ for which $\bigcirc(uvw)$ does not contain any other node of V.*

For an example of a Delaunay graph see Figure 17. It is known [11, 24] that the Delauney graph is a geometric c spanner with $c = \frac{2\pi}{3\cos(\pi/6)} \approx 2.42$, but the Delaunay graph is difficult to maintain locally. Therefore, several variants of it have been proposed. The most well-known variant is the Gabriel graph.

Definition 6.2 *For any $V \subset \mathbb{R}^2$, the* Gabriel graph *$GG(V)$ of V consists of all edges (u, w) with the property that there is no node $v \in V$ with*

$$||uv||^2 + ||vw||^2 < ||uw||^2$$

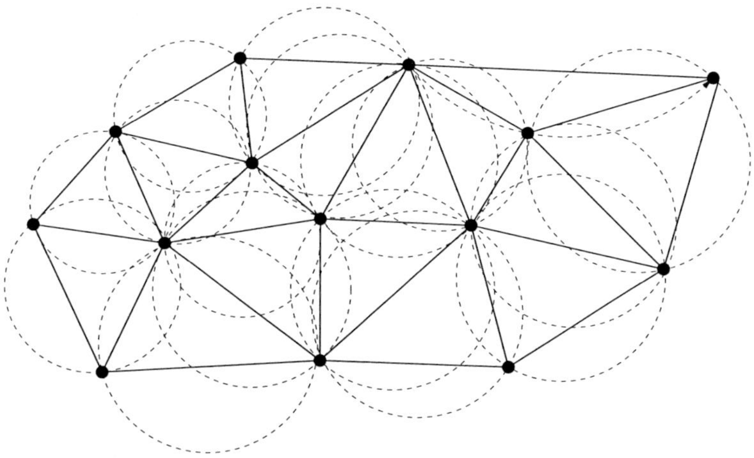

Figure 17: An example of a Delaunay graph.

In words, the Gabriel graph of V consists of all edges $\{u, w\}$ with the property that the open sphere through u and w with diameter $||uw||$ does not contain any other node in V. An example of a Gabriel graph is given in Figure 18. The Gabriel graph has the following interesting properties:

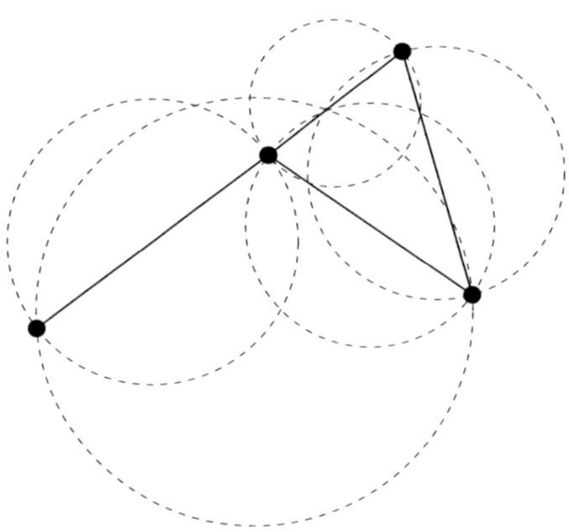

Figure 18: A Gabriel graph.

Theorem 6.3 *For any $V \subset \mathbb{R}^2$, the Gabriel graph of V is a relative neighborhood graph and a subgraph of the Delaunay graph of V.*

Proof. The Gabriel graph is a relative neighborhood graph because for all pairs (u, w) with $(u, w) \notin GG(V)$ there must be a node $v \in V$ with $||uv||^2 + ||vw||^2 < ||uw||^2$, which implies that $||uv|| < ||uw||$ and $||vw|| < ||uw||$.

It is also a subgraph of the Delaunay graph because for every edge (u, w) in $GG(V)$ it must hold that there is no node v in the open sphere of diameter $||uw||$ though u and w. If $|V| > 2$, we can then just extend the sphere into any direction until it hits a node v. In this case, there is no other node in $\bigcirc(uvw)$ which implies that (u, w) is also an edge in $Del(V)$. □

Unfortunately, Theorem 3.3 implies that the Gabriel graph is not a geometric spanner. With better techniques one can even create a counterexample with stretch factor $\Omega(\sqrt{n})$ [34]. But Theorem 4.2 implies that the Gabriel graph is a weak 2-spanner, and even more importantly, it is an optimal power spanner for every $\delta \geq 2$.

Theorem 6.4 ([34]) *For every $\delta \geq 2$, the Gabriel graph is an optimal power spanner.*

Proof. Consider any pair of nodes $u, w \in V$ and let p be their optimal energy path. Consider an arbitrary edge $\{x, y\}$ in p. Suppose that there is a node $v \in S_{x,y}$. Then, by the Theorem of Pythagoras, $||xv||^\delta + ||vy||^\delta < ||xy||^\delta$ for every $\delta \geq 2$. Hence, replacing the edge $\{x, y\}$ in p by $\{x, v\}$ and $\{v, y\}$ would reduce its energy, which would contradict our assumption that p is an optimal energy path. Hence, there cannot be a node in $S_{x,y}$, and therefore $\{x, y\}$ must be an edge in the Gabriel graph. Thus, p must be a path in the Gabriel graph, which proves the theorem. □

There is a simple protocol for the Gabriel graph. Again, suppose that every node $u \in V$ knows its neighborhood $N(u)$ in the UDG and the current positions of the nodes in $N(u)$. Let $E(u)$ be the current set of connections of node u. Then the protocol in Figure 19 can be used. It has the following performance:

Protocol Gabriel:

For every node $u \in V$ repeatedly do:
1) for every node $w \in E(u)$:
if there is a node $v \in N(u)$ with $||uv||^2 + ||vw||^2 < ||uw||$ then
remove w from $E(u)$
2) for every node $w \in N(u) \setminus E(u)$:
if there is no node $v \in N(u)$ with $||uv||^2 + ||vw||^2 < ||uw||$ then
add w to $E(u)$

Figure 19: A self-stabilizing protocol for Gabriel graphs.

Theorem 6.5 *The Gabriel protocol self-stabilizes in one round.*

Proof. Follows directly from the protocol. □

Unfortunately, the outdegree of a Gabriel graph can be as high as $n - 1$ (see Figure 20). Also, since the Gabriel graph is not a geometric spanner, one may ask whether there are locally constructible planar graphs that are geometric spanners. To investigate the latter issue, we define the following classes of graphs.

Definition 6.6 *A triangle $\triangle(uvw)$ satisfies the k-*localized Delaunay property *if the interior of the disk $\bigcirc(uvw)$ does not contain any node of V that is a k-neighbor of u, v, or w in $UDG(V)$ and $(u, v), (v, w), (w, u) \in UDG(V)$. Such a triangle is called a k-*localized Delaunay triangle.

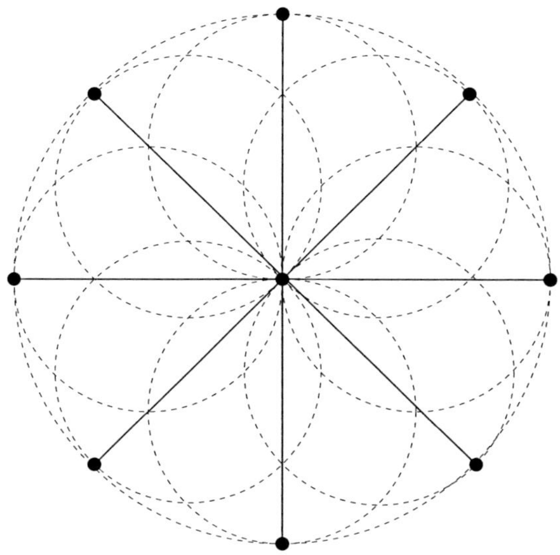

Figure 20: Gabriel graph for the unit disk with one node in its center and all other nodes on its border.

Definition 6.7 *The* k-localized Delaunay graph *over* V*, denoted by* $LDel^{(k)}(V)$*, has exactly all Gabriel edges and the edges of all* k*-localized Delaunay triangles.*

Let the *constrained Delaunay graph* of a point set V be defined as $UDel(V) = Del(V) \cap UDG(V)$. The following facts are known about k-localized Delaunay graphs (e.g., [33]).

Theorem 6.8 *Localized Delaunay graphs have the following properties:*

1. $UDel(V) \subseteq LDel^{(k)}(V)$ *for all* $k \geq 1$.
2. $LDel^{(k+1)}(V) \subseteq LDel^{(k)}(V)$ *for all* $k \geq 1$.
3. $LDel^{(2)}(V)$ *is a planar graph.*
4. $LDel^{(1)}(V)$ *is not always planar.*

Proof. The first two items follow immediately from the definition of localized Delaunay graphs.

Suppose that it is possible to choose some V so that $LDel^{(2)}(V)$ is not a planar graph. Then $LDel^{(2)}(V)$ must contain two edges that cross each other. Let these edges be (v, v') and (w, w'). Since $||vv'|| \leq 1$ and $||ww'|| \leq 1$ and the edges cross each other, there must be nodes $u \in \{v, v'\}$ and $u' \in \{w, w'\}$ so that $||uu'|| \leq 1$. But then $\{v, v', w, w'\} \subseteq N_2(u)$ and $\{v, v', w, w'\} \subseteq N_2(u')$ which implies that choosing (v, v') and (w, w') would violate the definition of $LDel^{(2)}(V)$. Hence, $LDel^{(2)}(V)$ is always planar.

It remains to show that there is a set V so that $LDel^{(1)}(V)$ is not planar. For this consider the example in Figure 21. In this example, $\bigcirc(u, v, w)$ does not contain any node

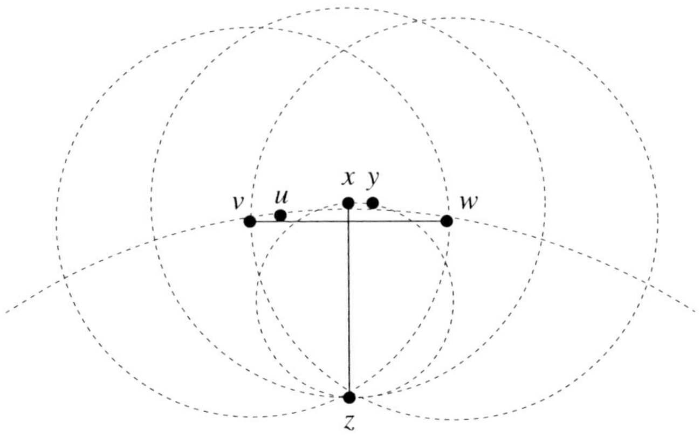

Figure 21: $LDel^{(1)}(V)$ is not planar.

in $N(u)$, $N(v)$, and $N(w)$, and $\bigcirc(x, y, z)$ does not contain any node in $N(x)$, $N(y)$, and $N(z)$. Hence, (v, w) and (x, z) are edges in $LDel^{(1)}(V)$, but they intersect.

□

Since $UDel(V)$ is a geometric c-spanner with $c \approx 2.42$ it follows that $LDel^{(2)}(V)$ is a geometric c-spanner with $c \approx 2.42$, and it is also planar. Also, $LDel^{(2)}(V)$ can be easily maintained locally. See Figure 22 for a self-stabilizing protocol. In this protocol we assume that every node $u \in V$ knows its 2-neighborhood

$$N^2(u) = \cup_{v \in N(u)} N(v)$$

and the current positions of the nodes in $N^2(u)$.

Protocol LDel2:
For every node $u \in V$ repeatedly do:
- 1) for every node $w \in E(u)$:
  - if $\{u, w\}$ is not a Gabriel edge and does not belong to a k-localized Delaunay triangle then remove w from $E(u)$
- 2) for every node $w \in N(u) \setminus E(u)$:
  - if $\{u, w\}$ is a Gabriel edge or belongs to a k-localized Delaunay triangle then add w to $E(u)$

Figure 22: A self-stabilizing protocol for the 2-localized Delaunay graph.

Theorem 6.9 *The LDel2 protocol self-stabilizes in one round.*

Proof. Follows directly from the protocol. □

However, as mentioned above, Gabriel graphs and therefore all graphs of the localized Delaunay graph family have the problem that the degree may be very high (see Figure 20). This problem can be solved by constraining a Delaunay graph in the same way Yao graphs are constrained to sparsified Yao graphs: cut the space around each node into $k > 6$ sectors of equal angle, and accept only the connection of the closest node with an incoming edge in the original graph. Similar to the proof of the sparsified Yao graph, this gives a sparsified Delaunay graph that is still a weak spanner. Other constructions have been proposed that can even maintain a Euclidean $O(1)$-spanner but at the cost of requiring an algorithm that may need a long time to stabilize at some solution [45].

Routing

Recall that for the routing strategies for Yao graphs to work properly we needed sufficiently dense distributions of wireless nodes. Such a distribution may not always be given, and if the distribution is not sufficiently dense, then our routing algorithms for the Yao graphs may not be able to deliver the message.

Interestingly, there are routing strategies for planar graphs that do not run into this problem. The main idea behind these routing strategies is that whenever a message cannot advance in a greedy fashion to get closer to its destination, it is forwarded along the face between it and the destination until a suitable node is found that allows the message to be sent closer to the destination.

This technique was first used in the *Face Routing* algorithm proposed in a seminal paper by Kranakis, Singh, and Urrutia [27] (in their short paper they actually call the algorithm *Compass Routing II*). For a detailed description of the Face Routing algorithm see Figure 23, and for a picture of how the algorithm works see Figure 24. In this algorithm, $\bar{st}$ denotes the line with endpoints s and t. The distance of an edge $e = u, v$ to a point t is the closest distance of a point on $\bar{uv}$ to t. It turns out that the Face Routing algorithm always terminates when used on a planar graph [27, 31].

Face Routing algorithm:

For every packet from s to t do:
  set $p := s$ and $v := s$
  repeat
    set $F :=$ face incident to p that is intersected by line $\bar{pt}$;
    1) run around F and remember the intersection point p' of $\bar{pt}$ on F closest to t
      until we are back to v or t has been reached
    2) go to any node w on the edge $e \in F$ containing p'
      set $p := p'$ and $v := w$
  until t has been reached

Figure 23: The Face Routing algorithm.

Theorem 6.10 *The Face Routing algorithm delivers the message to the destination t after traversing at most $O(n)$ edges where $n = |V|$.*

Proof. First we show that the algorithm terminates. By the choice of the faces F and the fact that the network is planar we see that there must always be a point on F that is

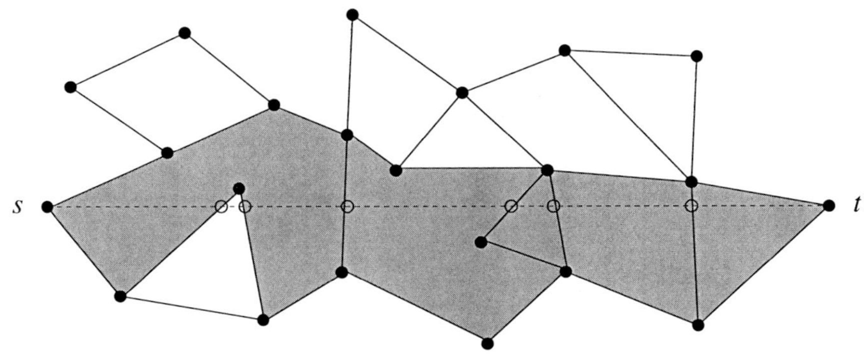

Figure 24: Faces visited by the Face Routing algorithm.

closer to t than the previously considered point. Hence, using this argument inductively, and combining it with the fact that $|V|$ is finite, the message must eventually reach t.

Notice that for the termination to work it is *crucial* that we consider closest *points* in the algorithm and not closest *nodes* because otherwise the face routing algorithm can get stuck in a local minimum.

For the performance analysis, we see that by always choosing an edge in F closest to t, we never traverse a face twice. Now, partition the edge set E into two subsets E_1 and E_2 where E_1 are the edges which are incident to only one face (the same face lies on both sides of the edge) and E_2 are the edges which are incident to two faces (the edge lies between two different faces). During the exploration of a face F in step 1, an edge of E_2 is traversed at most once and an edge of E_1 is traversed at most twice. The same holds for step 2. Since the edges of E_1 appear in only one face and the edges of E_2 appear in two faces, all edges of E are traversed at most four times during the whole algorithm. Each face in a planar connected graph (with at least 4 nodes) has at least three edges on its boundary. This together with the Euler polyhedral formula ($n - m + f = 2$) implies that the number of edges m is bounded by $m \leq 3n - 6$, which proves the theorem. □

Though the Face Routing algorithm guarantees delivery, the number of hops it takes to deliver a message to its destination cannot be bounded by the minimum number of hops it takes to deliver the message. To get rid of this disadvantage, we introduce the *Bounded Face Routing* (or short BFR) algorithm [31]. The main idea behind this algorithm is to use a restricted form of the Face Routing algorithm in which only nodes v are explored with

$$||sv|| + ||vt|| \leq d$$

where d is a fixed input parameter of the BFR algorithm. See Figure 25 for a detailed description of the algorithm.

Certainly, the BFR(d) algorithm only explores an area of size $O(d^2)$, and any path from s to t in the UDG with a node v outside of this area must have a length of more than d because of $||sv|| + ||vt|| > d$. Hence, if there is a path from s to t of length at most d, then it must be completely within the area explored by BFR(d), which means that the UDG restricted to the area containing all nodes v with $||sv|| + ||vt|| \leq d$ connects s and

BFR(d) algorithm:

For every packet from s to t do:
  set $p := s$ and $v := s$
  repeat
    set $F :=$ face incident to p that is intersected by line $\overline{pt}$;
    1) visit all nodes v on F with $||sv|| + ||vt|| \leq d$ and
      remember the intersection point p' of $\overline{pt}$ on F closest to t
    2) go to any node w on the edge $e \in F$ containing p'
      set $p := p'$ and $v := w$
  until t has been reached or no further progress can be made
  if no further progress can be made then
    set $t := s$ and reenter the repeat-loop (to send the packet back to the source)

Figure 25: The Bounded Face Routing algorithm.

t. Since BFR(d) works on this graph like the original Face Routing algorithm and the Face Routing algorithm is guaranteed to find a path from s to t if they are connected, we obtain the following result.

Theorem 6.11 *Let D be the unique ellipse containing all points v with $||sv|| + ||vt|| \leq d$. If $d \geq d_G(s,t)$ for the given network G, then the BFR(d) algorithm delivers the message to the destination t. If the BFR(d) algorithm fails to deliver the message, it manages to send it back to s. In any case, the BFR(d) algorithm visits every edge inside D at most a constant times.*

With the help of BFR(d), we can easily design now a routing algorithm that delivers every packet to its destination. This algorithm is known as *Adaptive Face Routing* (or short AFR). A detailed description of it is given in Figure 26, and an example can be found in Figure 25. The following theorem is immediate from Theorem 6.11.

AFR algorithm:

For every packet from s to t do:
  set $d := 2||st||$
  repeat
    execute BFR(d)
    if BFR(d) did not reach t, set $d := 2d$
  until t has been reached

Figure 26: The Bounded Face Routing algorithm.

Theorem 6.12 *For any planar graph $G \subseteq UDG(V)$ that is a weak c-spanner of V, (G, AFR) is a weak c-router of V. Moreover, if the minimum distance between any two nodes is a constant, then for any pair $s,t \in V$, AFR only performs $O((c||st||)^2)$ hops in G to send the packet to t*

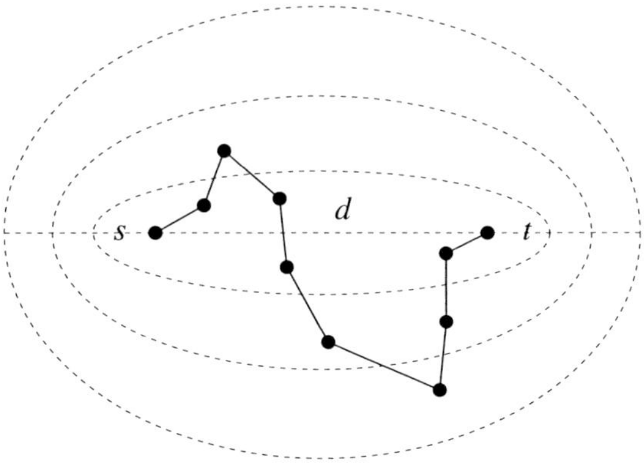

Figure 27: By successively increasing the d, the AFR algorithm will eventually find a near-shortest path from s to t.

It was shown in [31] that the hop bound in the theorem is worst-case optimal for any deterministic geometric ad hoc routing algorithm. Hence, in theory, AFR appears to be the best one can do in general. However, Face Routing and AFR are not applicable for practical purposes due to their strict employment of face traversal. Therefore, there have been recent proposals to combine greedy routing with face routing. However, the first [5, 9, 22] were without competitive worst-case guarantees. In [32] the first algorithm, called *GOAFR*, was suggested that combines greedy and face routing in a worst-case optimal way. The basic idea of GOAFR is to send the packet forward in a greedy fashion until a node is reached from which one cannot get closer to the destination. At this point, GOAFR switches to AFR to explore faces until a node v whose position on the current face is the closest point to t is reached. Then GOAFR switches back to greedy routing. A further improvement of GOAFR, GOAFR+, has recently been presented in [30].

Mobility

Like Yao graphs, also the Delaunay graphs can encounter a high update cost if there are many nodes within a unit disk. This update cost can easily be avoided when establishing local clusters, which is discussed next.

7 Topological Spanners

The problem with all of the constructions above is that they only minimize the Euclidean distance or energy but not the hop distance. Furthermore, the constructions rely on knowing the geometric coordinates of nodes in the network. This usually requires systems like the Geographic Positioning System (GPS). Another option is to compute a so-called *topological c-spanner*, i.e., a subgraph that preserves the hop distance.

In the following, the *length* of a path p, denoted by $|p|$, is the number of edges in p, and the *hop distance* of two nodes v, w in a graph G, denoted by $d_G(v, w)$, is the length of a shortest possible path in G from v to w. If G is the UDG of some set V, we simply write

$d(v, w)$ instead of $d_G(v, w)$.

Definition 7.1 *For any graph $G = (V, E)$, the subgraph $H = (V, E')$ is called a* (topological) c-spanner *of G if for all $v, w \in V$ it holds that*

$$d_H(v, w) \leq c \cdot d_G(v, w) + O(1)$$

Topological spanners have been introduced by Peleg and Ullman [40] where they used them to synchronize asynchronous networks. A survey of results and the constructibility of (sparse) spanners can be found in [39, 38]. The problem of finding a sparsest topological c-spanner was shown to be NP-complete [6] for most values of c. In the case $c = 2$ (i.e., the length of a shortest path in the spanner is at most twice the length of a shortest path in the original graph), an approximation algorithm to construct a 2-spanner was given by Kortsarz and Peleg [25]. However, 2-spanners cannot have a linear number of edges in general networks [25]. Hence, it appears to be more interesting for ad hoc networks to search for 3-spanners. In the following we show how such spanners can be constructed in a distributed way.

The basic idea behind all constructions of topological spanners for ad hoc networks is to select a group of leader nodes so that every node is either a leader node or has a leader node in its neighborhood. The leader nodes form a connected component with the help of gateway nodes. A message from a node v to a node w is sent by first sending it to a leader in the neighborhood of v and forwarding it along leaders with the help of gateway nodes until it reaches a leader in the neighborhood of w. At that point, the message is forwarded to w.

The problem of selecting proper leader nodes is related to the well-known dominating set problem, which we study next. Afterwards, we show how to connect the leaders via gateway nodes to obtain a 3-spanner. We start with a definition of dominating sets.

Definition 7.2 *Given any directed graph $G = (V, E)$, a subset $U \subseteq V$ is called a* dominating set *if all nodes $v \in V$ are either in U or have an edge to a node in U. A dominating set U is called* connected *if U forms a connected component in G. The* density *of a dominating set is the maximum over all nodes $v \in U$ of the number of neighbors that v has in U.*

The problem of finding a minimum dominating set is an important special case of the more general set cover problem. The minimum dominating set problem has been shown to be NP-complete in [16, 23]. If we take all nodes as the dominating set then this will be at most $(\Delta + 1)$ times the size of a minimum dominating set, where Δ is the maximum degree in the graph. So a $(\Delta + 1)$-approximation is trivial. A better strategy is to use a simple greedy algorithm that first takes a node with maximum degree and continues taking the node which covers the maximum number of uncovered nodes until every node is covered. This algorithm achieves a $(\log \Delta)$-approximation [21, 36, 44] and Feige [15] proved that the approximation ratio achieved by the greedy algorithm is best possible unless NP has $n^{O(\log \log n)}$ time deterministic algorithms.

Distributed algorithms for dominating sets have also been extensively studied. Liang and Haas [35] present a distributed implementation of the greedy algorithm. Jia et al. [20] extend this algorithm to a local randomized greedy algorithm. This algorithm is also a

$(\log \Delta)$-approximation algorithm which works in $O(\log n \log \Delta)$ time. Kuhn and Wattenhofer [29] proposed an algorithm based on LP relaxation techniques which achieves an $O(k\Delta^{2/k} \log \Delta)$-approximation in $O(k^2)$ time for any number k. Recently, Dubhashi et al. [13] presented a $(\log \Delta)$-approximation algorithm for the minimum connected dominating set problem which works in polylogarithmic time.

Alzoubi et al. [2] presented the first constant approximation algorithm for the minimum connected dominating set problem in unit-disk graphs with $O(n)$ and $O(n \log n)$ time and message complexity, respectively. Related results were also shown by Cheng et al. [8] and Huang et al. [18].

Recently, Kuhn et. al., [28] presented a distributed algorithm that computes a constant factor approximation of a minimum dominating set in unit disk graphs in $O(\log^2 n)$ time without needing any synchronization but it requires that nodes know an estimate of the total number of nodes in the network. In [37], Parthasarathy and Gandhi also present distributed algorithms to compute a dominating set. The running time of their algorithm depends on the amount of information available to the nodes, and nodes have to know an estimate of the size of the network. The results in both papers are also applicable to more general models than the unit disk model.

Consider now any unit disk graph of a node set V. The algorithm in Figure 28 constructs a constant density dominating set of V that is within a constant factor of the size of a minimum dominating set of V in $UDG(V)$. In this algorithm, we assume that all nodes are initially active and that the nodes proceed in synchronous rounds. We also assume that the nodes can perform physical carrier sensing and that a node can either send a signal or sense a signal at a time step but not both. Whenever a node u sends out a signal, we assume that all nodes v with $||uv|| \leq 1/2$ that listen to the wireless medium at that time can sense that, and all other nodes cannot sense that. Our assumptions are certainly over-simplifying the reality in wireless network, but they help to keep the algorithm simple. An algorithm for constant density dominating sets under much more realistic wireless network models has recently appeared in [26]. The results in [26] imply the following theorem.

```
CDS algorithm:
  For every node v ∈ V repeatedly do:
    if v is active then
      v sends out an ACTIVE signal
    else
      if v does not sense an ACTIVE signal then v becomes active
    if v is active then
      v sends out a LEADER signal with probability 1/2
      if v did not send a LEADER signal but sensed a LEADER signal then
        v becomes inactive
```

Figure 28: The Constant Dominating Set (CDS) algorithm.

Theorem 7.3 *The CDS algorithm is self-stabilizing and, from any state, requires at most $O(\log^4 n)$ rounds to arrive at a static constant density dominating set in which every inactive node has an active node within a disk of radius 1/2 around it and every active node has* *no other active node within a disk of radius 1/2 around it.*

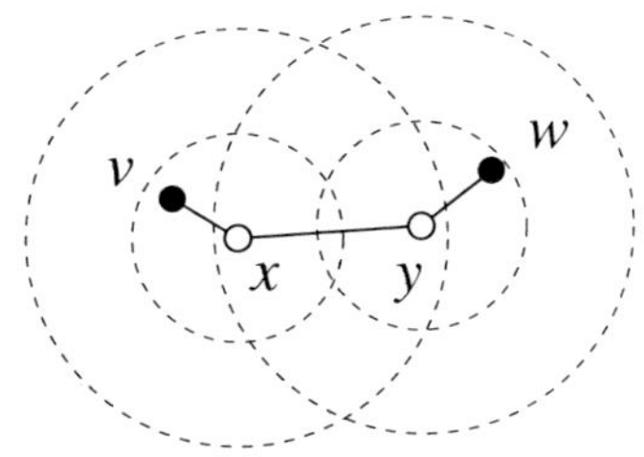

Figure 29: Active nodes have to connect via gateway nodes to form a connected dominating set. In the example, active nodes v and w have to connect via inactive nodes x and y.

Unfortunately, the CDS algorithm does not provide a connected dominating set because situations as shown in Figure 29 can occur. However, this can be achieved if the active nodes use some of the inactive nodes as gateway nodes in such a way that the following set of active node pairs is connected via gateways (A denotes the set of active nodes):

$$E = \{\{u, v\} \mid u, v \in A \text{ and there is an edge } \{x, y\} \in UDG(V) \text{ with } ||ux|| \leq 1/2 \text{ and } ||yv|| \leq 1/2\}$$

Since all pairs $\{u, v\} \in E$ satisfy $||uv|| \leq 2$ and it follows from Theorem 7.3 that, in the stable state, there can only be a constant number of active nodes v for any active node u with $||uv|| \leq 2$, the inactive nodes that we have to declare as gateway nodes also just have a constant density. Hence, altogether we get:

Theorem 7.4 *The network $CDS(V)$ of active nodes and gateway nodes making sure that all pairs $\{u, v\} \in E$ are connected is a constant density connected dominating set.*

Now, this set is also a topological 3-spanner:

Theorem 7.5 *For any V having a connected $UDG(V)$, $CDS(V)$ is a topological 3-spanner of V.*

Proof. Consider any pair of nodes $v, w \in V$ and let p be any path connecting them in $UDG(V)$ with $|p| = d(v, w)$. From the definition of E it follows that when using $CDS(V)$, any edge in p can be traversed by traversing at most 3 edges in $CDS(V)$. Hence, adding to this an edge from v to the nearest active node of v and an edge from w to the nearest active node of w in $CDS(V)$, we get

$$d_{CDS(V)}(v, w) \leq 3d(v, w) + 2$$

which proves that $CDS(V)$ is a topological 3-spanner. □

8 Sparse Topological $O(1)$-spanners

Instead of connecting *all* active node pairs in E via gateway nodes, one may also just connect those active node pairs so that the property of constrained sector-based graphs or Delaunay graphs presented earlier is satisfied. This allows us to significantly reduce the number of gateway connections active nodes have to maintain to other active nodes, which significantly reduces the maintenance overhead of the overlay network.

9 Conclusion

In this chapter we showed that there are local-control algorithms for wireless ad hoc networks that can establish sparse overlay networks between the nodes so that connectivity is guaranteed as long as this is in principle possible. Furthermore, these overlay networks even guarantee the existence of near-optimal paths between any pair of nodes. We also showed how to efficiently route packets in these overlay networks. However, many questions still remain open. For example, we only used very simple wireless network models in order to describe our algorithms. More sophisticated network models are still a topic of debate, and it is not clear whether there will ever be a clear favorite for the design of algorithms for wireless networks. Also, mobility issues and adversarial behavior are not yet well understood. So we expect further interesting research results in the area of overlay networks for wireless ad hoc networks in the future.

References

[1] K. Alzoubi, X.-Y. Li, Y. Wang, P. Wan, and O. Frieder. Geometric spanners for wireless ad hoc networks. *IEEE Transactions on Parallel and Distributed Systems* , **14**(4):408–421, 2003.

[2] K. Alzoubi, P.-J. Wan, and O. Frieder. New Distributed Algorithm for Connected Dominating Set in Wireless Ad Hoc Networks. In *Proceedings of the Thirty-Fourth Annual Hawaii International Conference on System Science (HICSS-35)* . IEEE Computer Society Press, 2002.

[3] F. M. auf der Heide, C. Schindelhauer, K. Volbert, and M. Grünewald. Energy, congestion and dilation in radio networks. In *Proc. of the 14th ACM Symp. on Parallel Algorithms and Architectures (SPAA)*, pages 230–237, 2002.

[4] P. Bose, L. Devroye, W. Evans, and D. Kirkpatrick. On the spanning ratio of Gabriel graphs and beta-skeletons. In *Proc. of Latin American Theoretical Informatics Conference (LATIN)*, 2002.

[5] P. Bose, P. Morin, I. Stojmenovic, and J. Urrutia. Routing with guaranteed delivery in ad hoc wireless networks. In *Proc. of 3rd Int. Workshop on Discrete Algorithms and Methods for Mobility (Dial-M)*, pages 48–55, 1999.

[6] L. Cai. NP-completeness of minimum spanner problems. *Discrete Applied Mathematics*, **48**:187–194, 1994.

[7] M. Charter. http://www.ietf.org/html.charters/mpls-charter.html.

[8] X. Cheng, D. Huang, W. Li, W. Wu, and D. Z. Du. A polynomial-time approximation scheme for the minimum-connected dominating set in ad hoc wireless networks. *NETWORKS: Networks: An International Journal*, **42**, 2003.

[9] S. Datta, I. Stojmenovic, and J. Wu. Internal node and shortcut based routing with guaranteed delivery in wireless networks. *Cluster Computing*, **5**:169–178, 2002.

[10] B. Davie and Y. Rekhter. *MPLS: Technology and Applications*. Morgan Kaufmann Publishers, 2000.

[11] D. Dobkin, S. Friedman, and K. Supowit. Delaunay graphs are almost as good as complete graphs. *Discrete Computational Geometry*, pages 399–407, 1990.

[12] D. Dubhashi, O. Häggström, A. Panconesi, and M. Sozio. Irrigating ad hoc networks in constant time. In *Proc. of the 17th ACM Symp. on Parallel Algorithms and Architectures (SPAA)*, pages 106–115, 2005.

[13] D. Dubhashi, A. Mei, A. Panconesi, J. Radhakrishnan, and A. Srinivasan. Fast distributed algorithms for (weakly) connected dominating sets and linear-size skeletons. In *Proceedings of the fourteenth Annual ACM-SIAM Symposium on Discrete Algorithms (SODA-03)*, pages 717–724, New York, Jan. 12–14 2003. ACM Press.

[14] D. Eppstein. *Handbook of Computational Geometry*, chapter Spanning trees and spanners, pages 425–461. Elsevier, 2000.

[15] U. Feige. A threshold of ln n for approximating set cover. *JACM: Journal of the ACM*, **45**, 1998.

[16] M. R. Garey and D. S. Johnson. *Computers and intractability; a guide to the theory of NP-completeness*. W.H. Freeman, 1979.

[17] M. Grünewald, T. Lukovszki, C. Schindelhauer, and K. Volbert. Distributed maintenance of resource efficient wireless network topologies. In *European Conference on Parallel Computing (EUROPAR)*, pages 935–946, 2002.

[18] H. Huang, A. W. Richa, and M. Segal. Approximation algorithms for the mobile piercing set problem with applications to clustering in ad-hoc networks. *ACM Baltzer Journal on Mobile Networks and Applications (MONET)*, pages 141–149, April 2004. A preliminary version of this paper appeared in the Proceedings of Sixth ACM Workshop on Discrete Algorithms and Methods for Communication (DIAL-M), 2002.

[19] L. Jia, R. Rajaraman, and C. Scheideler. On local algorithms for topology control and routing in ad hoc networks. In *Proc. of the 15th ACM Symp. on Parallel Algorithms and Architectures (SPAA)*, pages 220–229, 2003.

[20] L. Jia, R. Rajaraman, and R. Suel. An efficient distributed algorithm for constructing small dominating sets. In *PODC: 20th ACM SIGACT-SIGOPS Symposium on Principles of Distributed Computing*, 2001.

[21] D. S. Johnson. Approximation algorithms for combinatorial problems. *Journal of Computer and System Sciences*, **9**:256–278, 1974.

[22] B. Karp and H. Kung. GPSR: Greedy perimeter stateless routing for wireless networks. In *Proc. of 6th Int. Conference on Mobile Computing and Networking (MobiCom)*, pages 243–254, 2000.

[23] R. M. Karp. Reducibility among combinatorial problems. In R. E. Miller and J. W. Thatcher, editors, *Complexity of Computer Computations*, pages 85–103. Plenum Press, New York, 1975.

[24] J. Keil and C. Gutwin. Classes of graphs which approximate the complete Euclidean graph. *Discrete Computational Geometry*, **7**:13–28, 1992.

[25] G. Kortsarz and D. Peleg. Generating sparse 2-spanners. *Journal of Algorithms*, **17**:222–236, 1994.

[26] K. Kothapalli, M. Onus, A. Richa, and C. Scheideler. Constant density spanners for wireless ad-hoc networks. In *Proc. of the 17th ACM Symp. on Parallel Algorithms and Architectures (SPAA)*, pages 116–125, 2005.

[27] E. Kranakis, H. Singh, and J. Urrutia. Compass routing on geometric networks. In *Proc. of 11th Canadian Conference on Computational Geometry*, pages 51–54, 1999.

[28] F. Kuhn, T. Moscibroda, and R. Wattenhofer. Radio network clustering from scratch. In *European Symposium on Algorithms (ESA)*, 2004.

[29] F. Kuhn and R. Wattenhofer. Constant-time distributed dominating set approximation. In *Proceedings of the 22nd Annual ACM Symposium on Principles of Distributed Computing (PODC-03)*, pages 25–32, New York, July 13–16 2003. ACM Press.

[30] F. Kuhn, R. Wattenhofer, Y. Zhang, and A. Zollinger. Geometric ad-hoc routing: Of theory and practice. In *Proc. of the 22nd IEEE Symp. on Principles of Distributed Computing (PODC)*, 2003.

[31] F. Kuhn, R. Wattenhofer, and A. Zollinger. Asymptotically optimal geometric mobile ad-hoc routing. In *Proc. of 6th Int. Workshop on Discrete Algorithms and Methods for Mobility (Dial-M)*, pages 24–33, 2002.

[32] F. Kuhn, R. Wattenhofer, and A. Zollinger. Worst-case optimal and average-case efficient geometric ad-hoc routing. In *Proc. of 4th ACM Symposium on Mobile Ad-Hoc Networking and Computing (MobiHoc)*, 2003.

[33] X.-Y. Li, G. Calinescu, P.-J. Wan, and Y. Wang. Localized Delaunay triangulation with application in ad hoc wireless networks. *IEEE Transactions on Parallel and Distributed Systems*, **14**(10):1035–1047, 2003.

[34] X.-Y. Li, P.-J. Wan, and Y. Wang. Power efficient and sparse spanner for wireless ad hoc networks. In *Proc. of IEEE International Conference on Computer Communications and Networks (ICCCN)*, 2001.

[35] B. Liang and Z. J. Haas. Virtual backbone generation and maintenance in ad hoc network mobility management. In *Proceedings of the 2000 IEEE Computer and Communications Societies Conference on Computer Communications (INFOCOM-00)*, pages 1293–1302, Los Alamitos, Mar. 26–30 2000. IEEE.

[36] L. Lovasz. On the ratio of the optimal integral and fractional covers. *Discrete Mathematics*, **13**:383–390, 1975.

[37] S. Parthasarathy and R. Gandhi. Distributed algorithms for coloring and domination in wireless ad hoc networks. In *Proc. of FSTTCS*, 2004.

[38] D. Peleg. *Distributed Computing: A Locality-Sensitive Approach*. SIAM, 2000.

[39] D. Peleg and A. Schaffer. Graph spanners. *Journal of Graph Theory*, **13**:99–116, 1989.

[40] D. Peleg and J. Ullman. An optimal synchronizer for the hypercube. *SIAM Journal on Computing*, **18**:740–747, 1989.

[41] R. Rajaraman. Topology control and routing in ad hoc networks: a survey. *SIGACT News*, **33**(2):60–73, 2002.

[42] S. Rao and W. Smith. Approiximating geometrical graphs via spanners and banyans. In *Proc. of the 30th ACM Symp. on Theory of Computing (STOC)*, pages 540–550, 1998.

[43] C. Schindelhauer, K. Volbert, and M. Ziegler. Spanners, weak spanners, and power spanners for wireless networks. In *Proc. of 15th Annual International Symposium on Algorithms and Computation (ISAAC '04)*, pages 805–821, 2004.

[44] P. Slavik. A tight analysis of the greedy algorithm for set cover. In *Proceedings of the twenty-eighth annual ACM symposium on Theory of computing*, pages 435–441. ACM Press, 1996.

[45] Y. Wang and X.-Y. Li. Localized construction of bounded degree and planar spanner for wireless ad hoc networks. In *DIALM-POMC '03: Proceedings of the 2003 joint workshop on Foundations of mobile computing*, pages 59–68, 2003.

[46] F. Xue and P. Kumar. The number of neighbors needed for connectivity of wireless networks. *Wireless Networks*, **10**(2):169–181, 2004.

[47] A. C.-C. Yao. On constructing minimum spanning trees in k-dimensional space and related problems. *SIAM Journal on Computing*, **11**:721–736, 1982.

In: New Topics in Theoretical Computer Science
Editors: Oleg N. Terikhovsky *et al.*, pp. 253-274
ISBN 978-1-60456-100-5

Chapter 9

Flexible Scatternet-Wide Scheduling in Bluetooth Networks

Wensheng Zhang [*] ***and Guohong Cao*** [†]
Department of Computer Science and Engineering,
The Pennsylvania State University, University Park, PA, USA

Abstract

Bluetooth is a promising technology which enables the design of low-power, small-sized, low-cost radios that can be embedded in existing portable devices. Due to the limitation of a single channel capacity, scatternet techniques are proposed to increase the communication bandwidth. However, since a bridge may be shared by several piconets, simultaneously polling the bridge may result in bridge conflicts, and then seriously degrade the system performance. Thus, the potential of the scatternet may not be realized without a good scatternet-wide scheduling algorithm. In this chapter, we propose a dynamic scatternet-wide scheduling (DSS) scheme to address the problems associated with scatternet-wide traffic scheduling. The proposed scheme is based on a switch-table concept to avoid bridge conflicts. Further, the switch-table can be dynamically adjusted based on the traffic load to improve the system performance. Simulation results demonstrate that the DSS algorithm can significantly reduce the packet dropping rate and the transmission delay.

Index Terms: Bluetooth networks, scatternet, scheduling.

1 Introduction

Bluetooth [8, 9, 17] is a promising new technology which is aimed at supporting wireless connectivity among mobile devices such as cell phones, headsets, PDAs, digital cameras, laptop computers and their peripherals. The technology enables the design of low-power, small-sized, low-cost radios that can be embedded in existing portable devices. Initially,

[*] E-mail address: wezhang@cse.psu.edu
[†] E-mail address: gcao@cse.psu.edu

it will be used as a replacement for cables. Eventually, it will provide solutions for point-to-multipoint and multi-hop networking, and lead toward ubiquitous connectivity to truly connect everything to everything.

Due to the unpredictable interference of the existing 2.45 GHz ISM frequency band, Bluetooth relies on a pseudo-random frequency hopping mechanism. A set of 79 hop carriers have been defined with a 1 MHz spacing. Each hop sequence defines a Bluetooth channel, which can support 1Mbps. A group of devices sharing a common channel is called a *piconet* [2, 5], which has a master node and at most seven slave nodes. Within a piconet, the channel is shared using a slotted time division duplex (TDD) protocol where the master uses a polling style protocol to allocate time slots to slave nodes. Multiple piconets can co-exist in a common area because each piconet uses a different hopping sequence. Piconets can also be interconnected via bridge [4, 9, 14] nodes to form a bigger ad hoc network known as a *scatternet*. Bridge nodes are capable of timesharing between multiple piconets, receiving data from one piconet and forwarding it to another. A bridge can be a master in one piconet and slave in another (termed as M/S bridge) or a slave in all piconets (termed as S/S bridge).

To improve the performance of Bluetooth scatternet, two kinds of schedule are necessary: piconet and scatternet-wide schedule. Recent research on piconet schedule determines how the bandwidth capacity will be distributed among the slave nodes. As a simple solution, the master controls the traffic by means of polling the slaves according to a Round Robin scheme. As an improvement, Kalia *et al.* [13] proposed a dynamic weighted round-robin scheme in which the weights of the master-slave pairs depend on the queue status. Garg *et al.* [7] proposed schedule schemes to optimize the power. Johansson *et al.* [12] introduced an efficient fair exhaustive polling scheme to provide both high utilization and fair distribution of piconet capacity among the participating slaves.

At the scatternet level [10], the bridge node must schedule its presence in all the piconets of which it is a member. The main challenge for the scatternet-wide scheduling is to schedule the presence of the bridge node in its different piconets such that the traffic can flow within and between the piconets as efficiently as possible. Given that the bridge node is a single transceiver unit, it can only be active in one piconet at a time, and be blind in all other piconets. However, the master in a piconet always expects a slave to be present when it sends a data or (a poll) packet to it. If the slave is not present, the master may remove the slave from its piconet after some predefined timeout period. This is necessary since the slave may be out of range, in which case, polling the slave wastes bandwidth. However, in a scatternet, the slave may be a bridge node and it may be vising another piconet when the master sends it a packet. We call this phenomenon as *bridge conflict*. Thus, the main issue of scatternet-wide scheduling is to coordinate the simultaneous presence of bridge nodes and masters to avoid or reduce the bridge conflict, thus achieve higher performance in inter-piconet communication. Although many researchers have addressed the piconet scheduling problem, not much work [1, 11, 3] has been done on scatternet-wide schedule. These methods can not completely avoid bridge conflicts, since there is no explicit coordination between bridges and masters. Moreover, the current Bluetooth specification does not describe the algorithms or mechanisms to manage a scatternet due to a variety of unsolved issues. The research on scatternet formation [18, 19, 16], which is an important topic related to scatternet-wide scheduling, is also still in its nascent stage. These algorithms can only address the scenarios where nodes are within the communication range of each other.

In this chapter, we address the problem by proposing two scatternet-wide scheduling algorithms. First, we identify the *bridge conflict* problem, which occurs when two masters poll the same bridge at the same time. One simple solution is called *static scatternet-wide scheduling (SSS)*, in which a static reservation schedule (recorded in a *switch-table* [20]) is determined centrally when the scatternet is constructed. Since no knowledge about traffic patterns is known when the slot reservation schedule is determined, the number of slots reserved for each "master-bridge" link is calculated based on certain criteria such as fairness. This scheme has the advantage of simplicity and low cost. However, due to traffic pattern changes, using the statically determined reservation schedule may not be able to achieve high bandwidth utilization. To solve this problem, we propose a dynamic scatternet-wide scheduling (DSS) scheme, in which the switch-table can be dynamically adjusted based on the traffic pattern. Extensive experiments are conducted to evaluate the performance of the proposed methodology. Compared to the SSS scheme, the DSS scheme can significantly reduce the packet dropping rate and transmission delay.

The rest of the chapter is organized as follows. Section 2 presents preliminaries. The proposed scatternet-wide scheduling algorithms are described in section 3, which is followed by the performance evaluation presented in section 4. Section 5 concludes the chapter.

2 Preliminaries

In this section, we present a brief overview of the Bluetooth technology, and examine the challenges of scatternet-wide scheduling.

2.1 Bluetooth Overview

Bluetooth is a low-cost, low-power short range radio technology that uses the unlicensed 2.45 GHz ISM frequency band to support wireless communication in a person's operating space. To reduce the unpredictable interference of the ISM frequency band, Bluetooth relies on a pseudo-random frequency hopping mechanism. A set of 79 hop carriers are defined in a 1MHz spacing, and each hop sequence defines a Bluetooth channel which can support a nominal bandwidth of 1Mbps. Furthermore, the frequency hopping scheme is combined with fast automatic repeat request, CRC and forward error correction to achieve appropriate reliability on the wireless link.

Originally designed for supporting single hop connections, Bluetooth allows communication to occur only between a master and slave nodes belonging to a same piconet. Multiple piconets are allowed to co-exist in a common region since they have different frequency hopping patterns. Since a piconet can contain at most eight nodes, multiple piconets are allowed to be interconnected via bridge nodes to form a complicated topology called scatternet. A bridge node is a node belonging to two or more piconets. It can be a master in one piconet and a slave in other piconets, in which case it is called a M/S bridge. It can also be a slave in all piconets, in which case it is called a S/S bridge. Figure 1 illustrates these two kinds of topology.

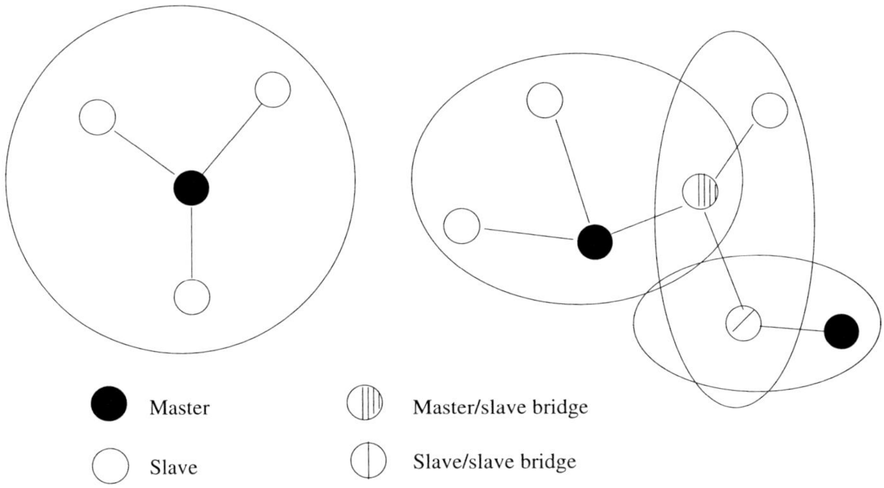

Figure 1: Illustration of a piconet (left picture) and a scatternet (right picture).

Within a piconet, the master defines the timing and the hop pattern. The frequency hopping pattern used in the piconet is derived from the master's device ID, and the slaves have to keep clock-synchronized to the master while participating in the piconet. The shared channel of a piconet is accessed using a slotted time division duplex (TDD) protocol. Using this protocol, the channel is divided into slots each has a length of $625\mu s$. The master may start to send a packet in even numbered slots only. The slave addressed by this packet is allowed to send in the odd numbered slot following the master's packet. To keep up with the alternation between even and odd slots, packets must occupy an odd number of slots. Thus, Bluetooth defines different packet types with a length of 1, 3 or 5 slots.

In default, a master assumes that its slaves are always present in the piconet. That is, whenever the master transmits to a slave, the slave must answer the packet unless the transmission fails. However, for the purpose of power saving, Bluetooth offers various modes which are used to reduce the duty cycle of devices: hold, park and sniff mode. Here, we only introduce the sniff mode which has often been proposed as the means to enable scatternet operations. In this mode, a slave arranges its presence in a piconet by negotiating specific slots which are called *sniff slots* with the master. Communication between the master and this slave may start at these sniff slots. If no communication takes place during these slots, both the nodes may spend the time freely until the next sniff slots. However, once the communication starts, it may be extended until one party quits the communication. Figure 2 illustrates the sniff mode. Here the master and the slave has negotiated a sniff period with T_{sniff}. At a sniff slot, they start to communicate and stay in this state until one party (the master) quits, and then the other party (the slave) quits after timeout.

2.2 Challenges in Scatternet-wide Scheduling

Even though the current Bluetooth specification defines scatternets, it focuses on operations within a piconet and does not describe the algorithms or mechanisms to form and manage a scatternet due to a variety of unsolved issues. In this subsection, we discuss some difficulties we face in addressing the scatternet-wide scheduling.

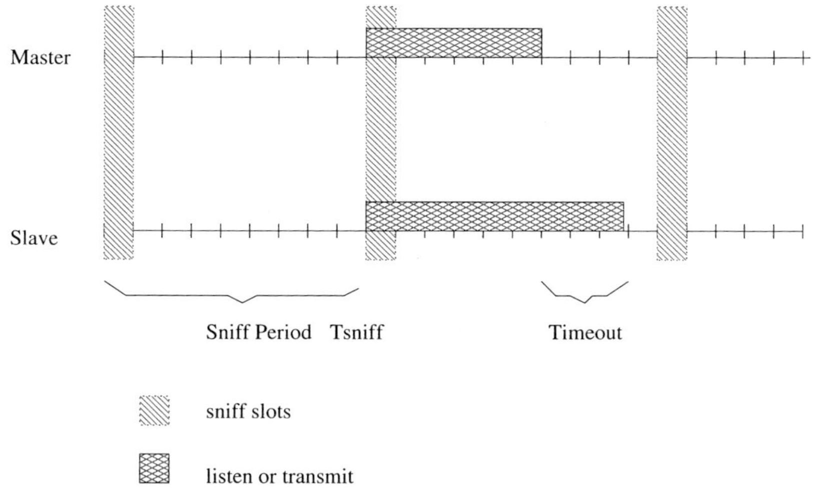

Figure 2: Illustration of sniff mode.

Bridge Conflicts

Piconets are interconnected via bridge nodes. We also assume that each node has only a single transceiver unit. Under such a model, a bridge node can switch between piconets to which it belongs, but can not be synchronized to two or more piconets simultaneously. If there is no coordination between these piconets, a bridge conflict occurs when two masters poll the same bridge at the same time, or when a master polls the bridge while the bridge shows up in another piconet. Figure 3 shows a bridge conflict scenario: when master M_2 polls a bridge, the bridge is synchronized to another piconet. Consequently, these polls are wasted. Bridge conflicts waste bandwidth. Scatternet-wide scheduling schemes should adopt some coordination to avoid or reduce bridge conflicts.

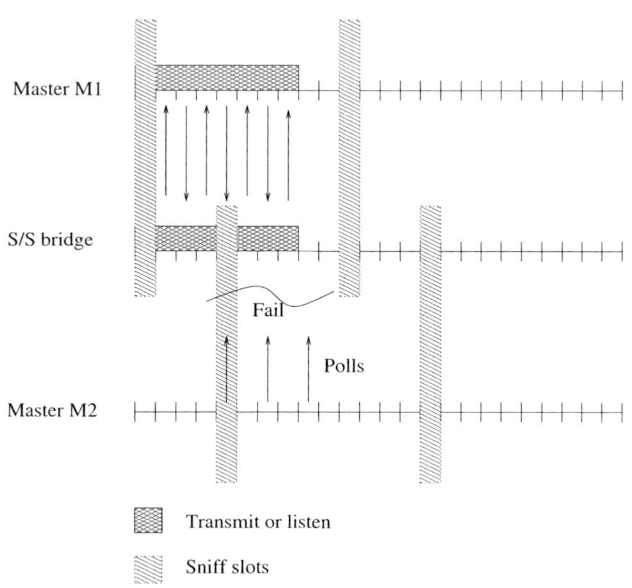

Figure 3: Illustration of bridge conflicts.

Bridge Switching Overhead

According to the Bluetooth specifications [8], the timing and frequency hopping pattern of a piconet are determined by the master node, and different piconet can not share a common master node. That is, the hop selection and timing of different piconets are typically independent of each other, unless certain inter-piconet timing synchronization mechanism is deployed. This may result in some bandwidth loss associated with the bridge node. An example of bandwidth loss due to bridge switching is shown in Figure 4. Considering this overhead, bridge nodes should not switch too frequently between piconets. However, low switching frequency may increase packet forwarding delays since packets have to wait longer before passing through a bridge node. Thus, there is a tradeoff between system throughput and delay.

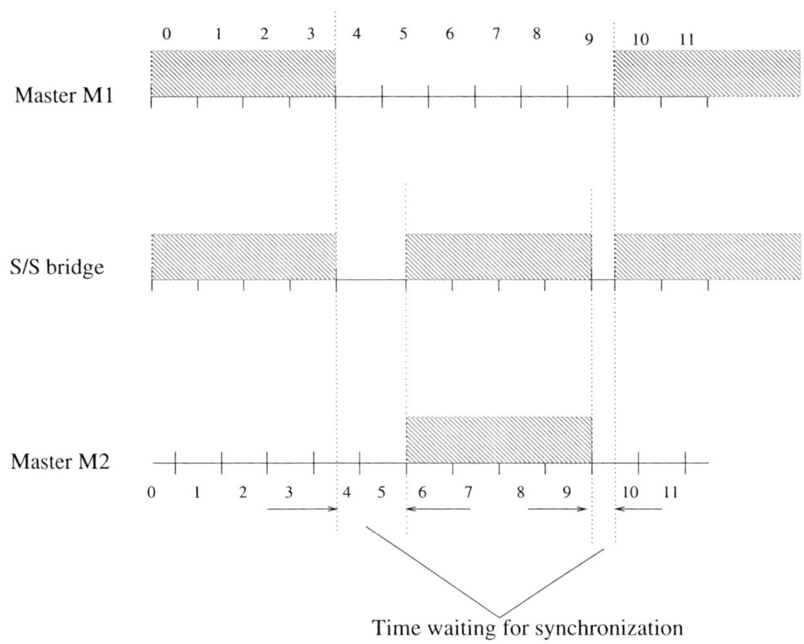

Figure 4: Illustration of bandwidth loss due to bridge switching.

Adaptive on Load Variation

Workload variation is common in a scatternet scenario. A scatternet-wide scheduling scheme should address bridge conflicts, and be adaptive to workload variations. Intuitively, a bridge node should be present more frequently in the piconet with higher inter-piconet traffic load.

3 The Proposed Scatternet-wide Scheduling Algorithm

In this section, we present the basic idea of the switch-table based scatternet-wide scheduling. We first present a simple solution called the static scatternet-wide scheduling (SSS) algorithm, and then enhance its performance by another algorithm called the dynamic scatternet-wide scheduling (DSS) algorithm.

3.1 The Basic Idea of Switch-table Based Scatternet-wide Scheduling

Piconets are interconnected via bridge nodes. A bridge node can be a M/S node or a S/S node. We only consider S/S bridge nodes in this chapter for simplicity, but we believe that the proposed technique can also be extended to M/S bridges. In fact, early work by Kalia *et al.* [15] has suggested that scatternets with only S/S bridge nodes have better performance. Figure 5(a) shows one scatternet example.

To avoid bridge conflicts, each bridge maintains a *switch-table*, which directs the bridge node how to switch between piconets, and notifies the master when it can poll the bridge node safely. Table 1 shows the switch-table of bridge B_4 corresponding to the topology of Figure 5(a). This switch table has four rows, each corresponds to one piconet. There are three parameters related to a piconet: the number of slots in each cycle, the start point and the end point of the slots when B_4 is synchronized to the piconet. Take the first row as an instance, three parameters together specify that B_4 is synchronized to piconet 0 during the slots from $26 * k$ to $26 * k + 5$, where k is a non-negative integer.

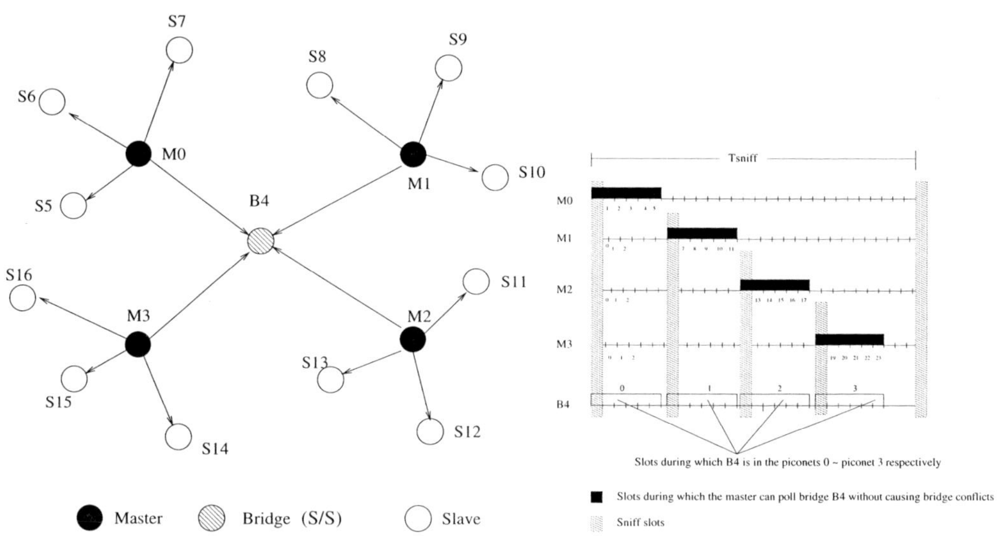

(a) An example scatternet topology (b) A possible scheduling process

Figure 5: Illustration of the proposed scatternet-wide scheduling algorithm

Table 1: Switch table for bridge B_4

Piconet#	Start slot	End slot	Cycle length (slots)
0	0	5	26
1	6	11	26
2	12	17	26
3	18	23	26

The switch-table directed bridge switching can be implemented via the sniff mode. In this implementation, the cycle length is mapped to the sniff period, and the start slots correspond to the sniff slots. As an example, Figure 5(b) shows the switching path of bridge B_4. At the start slot corresponds to piconet 0, B_4 switches to piconet 0. After that, it will stay in the piconet until another sniff slot (the start slot corresponds to piconet 1) approaches, at which point B_4 switches to piconet 1. A master should communicate with a bridge node only when the bridge is present in its piconet to avoid bridge conflicts. Figure 5(b) also shows the slots that each piconet can use to communicate with B_4 without causing bridge conflicts. Note that the switch-table directed bridge switching does not need any major change to the current specification, since it can be implemented using the sniff mode.

The switch-table of a scatternet can be constructed when the scatternet is formed. Taking the *Bluetooth Topology Construction Protocol (BTCP)* [18] as an example BTCP has two phases: first, a leader is elected with a complete knowledge of all nodes; second, this leader tells other nodes how a scatternet should be formed. The switch-table is constructed after the first phase since the leader has the complete knowledge of the scatternet at this time. The results will be sent to other nodes in the second phase. Note that the bridge node can modify the entry about itself after the switch-table has been constructed, but the master nodes can not modify it. To be consistent, whenever a bridge node modifies an entry, it should notify the corresponding masters to make necessary updates.

3.2 The Static Scatternet-wide Scheduling (SSS) Algorithm

In this subsection, we present the static scatternet-wide scheduling (SSS) algorithm, which solves the bridge conflict by using predefined switch-tables. The basic idea of the proposed algorithm is to let the master poll its slaves, including the bridge nodes, in a weighted round robin manner. For each frame, the master polls a bridge node only when the bridge node shows up in the piconet based on the switch-table, and the bridge node is polled according to its weight. This algorithm can solve the problem of bridge conflict, and can schedule traffic efficiently.

The weight of each slave is computed based on the estimated traffic load for each "master-slave" link. Hence, in each schedule cycle [13], only a subset of the slaves are polled. In order to decide the frequency for each slave to be polled, each slave has a polling weight which is represented by a tuple (P, R), where P indicates that the slave should be polled every P schedule cycles, and R represents the maximum times that the slave can be polled in a cycle if it is scheduled to be polled at the cycle. A master can dynamically change the polling weight of each slave based on its estimations of the traffic load carried by the link between itself and the slave. Note that a master can only directly monitor the length of the "master$\rightarrow$slave" queues. A master estimates each link's traffic based on the polling results. The rules for adjusting the slave's polling weight (P, R) are as follows: If a poll is wasted in the sense that both slots allocated for polling are not used, the value of P associated with the offending slave is increased until it reaches a certain upper threshold; otherwise, the polling period is decreased until it reaches one. If the current p value for a slave is already one, the value of R will be adjusted as follows: If a poll is wasted, the value of R is decreased until it reaches one, and in this case, the value of P is increased; If a poll is not wasted, the value of R is increased until it reaches an upper bound. A formal description of the algorithm is given in Figure 6.

For each master M_i, it maintains the following data structure:

- $(P_j, R_j)(0 \leq j \leq 6)$: the priority of each slave S_j of M_i. $P_j = k(k > 1)$ indicates that M_i should poll S_j once every k meta-frames; $P_j = 1 \wedge R_j = k(k \geq 1)$ indicates that M_i should poll S_j k times every metaframe. Initially $(P_j, R_j) = (1, 1)$. Note that a bridge node is also a slave.
- $poll\_q_i$: queues the dedicated slaves that should be polled during this metaframe. At the beginning of each metaframe, M_i's dedicated slaves that should be polled at the metaframe are put into this queue.
- P_{max}, R_{max}: The maximum P and the maximum R.

(A) At the beginning of each frame:

if (this frame is reserved as a synchronous connection oriented link between M_i and S_k)

then poll S_k;

else find a bridge B_j that has been polled the smallest times in the current metaframe and should be polled in the rest of the metaframe;

  if (found) **then** poll B_j;

  else if $(poll\_q_i \neq \emptyset)$ **then** poll dequeue($poll\_q_i$);

    else put the dedicated slaves that should be polled again in this metaframe into $poll\_q_i$;

      if $(poll\_q_i \neq \emptyset)$ **then** poll dequeue($poll\_q_i$);

      else M_i is idle in this frame;

(B) At the end of each frame, for each polled S_j (S_j is a bridge or a dedicated slave) :

if (the poll is wasted) **then** degrade_priority(S_j);

else raise_priority(S_j);

Procedure degrade_priority(S_j)

if $(R_j > 1)$ **then** $R_j = R_j - 1$;
else if $(P_j < P_{max})$ **then** $P_j = P_j + 1$;

Procedure raise_priority(j)

if $(P_j > 1)$ **then** $P_j = P_j - 1$;
else if $(R_j < R_{max})$ **then** $R_j = R_j + 1$;

Figure 6: The SSS Algorithm

3.3 The Dynamic Scatternet-wide Scheduling (DSS) Algorithm

In the SSS scheme, a static reservation schedule is determined centrally when the scatternet is constructed. Due to traffic pattern changes, using the statically determined reservation schedule may not be able to achieve high bandwidth utilization. In this section, we propose dynamic scatternet-wide scheduling (DSS) schemes to address this problem. In the DSS scheme, the switch-table can be dynamically adjusted based on the traffic pattern. Specifically, by monitoring the queue length, the bridge increases (decreases) the number of slots that a bridge appears in the piconet before it switches to another piconet if the traffic load between the master and the bridge is high (low). Similar to [6], we assume that the queues are maintained in the L2CAP layer. Since the information about queue length is very small, it can be piggy-backed in polling packets, instead of using extra packets, to save bandwidth.

The DSS algorithm contains two phases: First, the decision on how to adjust the switch-table is made by a bridge node. Second, the switch-table is updated through the coordination between bridge and master nodes.

Phase I: Decide how to adjust the switch-table

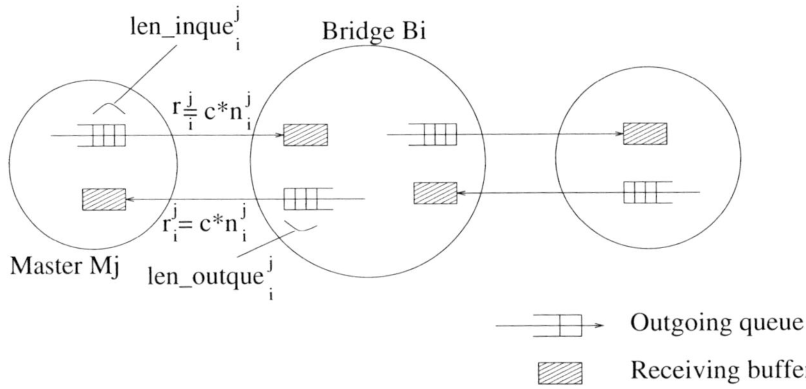

Figure 7: Illustration of the queue model

The traffic pattern change can be detected by monitoring the queue length. For this purpose, each master needs to notify the bridge about its queue length whenever it has a major change. At the bridge side, the bridge monitors the outgoing queue length and maintains the incoming queue length obtained from the master. Figure 7 shows the queue model considered in this chapter. Here, $len\_inque_i^j$ represents the length of the queue which queues packets from M_j to B_i, and $len\_outque_i^j$ represents the length of the queue which queues packets from B_i to M_j. Bridge B_i maintains the maximum value of the outgoing queue length and the incoming queue length (denoted as $len\_que_i^j = max\{len\_inque_i^j, len\_outque_i^j\}$). r_i^j and r_j^i represent the output rates of these two queues respectively, and they are in proportion to the number of slots assigned to the link in the switch-table, which is denoted as n_i^j. Obviously, the master-bridge link with long incoming or outgoing queue indicates a heavy traffic, and it should get more slots in the switch-table than those with relatively low queue length. Figure 8 shows the formal description of how to adjust the switch-table, which is further explained as follows.

First, the bridge checks the queue length every n_c cycles. The selection of this interval

Notations:

- n_c: check interval. That is, every n_c cycles the queue lengths are check to see if the switch-table should be adjusted.
- n_i^j, $len\_que_i^j$: defined before.
- $borrower\_que$: a priority queue queuing potential borrowers in the decreasing order of the number of slots they want to borrower.

  $lender\_que$: a priority queue queuing potential lenders in the decreasing order of the number of frames they can lend.

  Initially, $borrower\_que = lender\_que = NULL$.
- $r(j)$: indicate the number of slots M_j wants to borrow from or can lend to others.

The algorithm for deciding B_i's switch-table adjust scheme (Executed every n_c cycles)

$avg\_qlen = \sum_j len\_que_i^j / n_i^j$

for (each M_j)

  if $(len\_que_i^j > avg\_qlen * n_i^j)$ **then**

    $r(j) = \frac{len\_que_i^j - avg\_qlen * n_i^j}{n_c}$

    enque(borrower_que, M_j)

  else if $(len\_que_i^j < avg\_qlen * n_i^j)$ **then**

    $r(j) = \lfloor \frac{avg\_qlen * n_i^j - len\_que_i^j}{n_c} \rfloor$

    if $(r(j) > 0)$ **then** enque(lender_que, M_j)

if (!empty(borrower_que) and !empty(lender_que)) **then**

  Let deque(borrower_que) be the borrower and deque(lender_que) be the lender. Two slots will be transferred from the lender to the borrower.

Figure 8: The algorithm for deciding B_i's switch-table adjust scheme

has a significant impacts on the system performance. In order to adjust the switch-table promptly when the traffic pattern changes, the interval should not be too long. However, the interval should not be too short in order to avoid unnecessary adjustments and keep the frequency of adjustments within an affordable scope.

Second, the goal of an adjustment is to balance the queue lengths among all links in the bridge. For this purpose, a balanced queue length should be calculated for each link. A simple way to calculate the balanced queue length is to average all the queue lengths. However, links assigned different number of slots in the switch-table should have different balanced queue length. As shown in Figure 7, the number of slots assigned to a link $M_j - B_i$, is proportional to the service rate r_i^j of link $M_j - B_i$'s outgoing/incoming queue. For two queues that have the same length but different service rate, the delay for passing a packet through the queue with high service rate will be smaller than the one with low service rate. Considering the number of slots assigned, the desired balanced queue length for the link $M_j - B_i$ is calculated as: $n_i^j * \sum_k len\_que_i^k$.

Third, potential borrowers and lenders should be found. For link $M_j - B_i$, if its current queue length is larger than the desired balanced queue length, i.e., $len\_que_i^j > avg\_qlen * n_i^j$, it is beneficial for it to borrow slots from others. Conversely, if $len\_que_i^j < avg\_qlen * n_i^j$, the link can lend slots to others as long as its queue length is still less than the balanced queue length after lending. This condition is heuristically expressed as $\lfloor \frac{avg\_qlen * n_i^j - len\_que_i^j}{n_c} \rfloor > 0$, which means that the queue length is still less than the balanced value even if the number of packets transmitted each cycle is reduced by one. Finally, in order to keep the TDD protocol work, the number of slots transferred from the lender to the borrower should be even.

Phase II: Update the switch-table

When the sniff slot positions of the lender and the borrower are next to each other (as shown in Figure 9), the switch-table is updated by changing the sniff slot position of the borrower or lenders. The procedure can also be explained by Figure 10. In order to avoid bridge conflicts, the bridge cannot immediately notify them about the modification. Instead, the bridge has to notify the lender first. After the lender has acknowledged the modification, the borrower is notified. Thus, at least four messages are needed. However, when the sniff slot positions of the lender and the borrower are not next to each other (as shown in Figure 11), a series of changes in the sniff slot positions are needed.

4 Performance Evaluation

Extensive simulations are conducted to evaluate the performance of the proposed algorithms and the impacts of the system parameters. First, the performance of the SSS algorithm is evaluated and the impacts of the cycle length on the performance are studied. Second, we evaluate the performance of the DSS algorithm under the condition that traffic is changed frequently and study the impacts of n_c, the maximum queue length, and the the traffic change frequency on the system performance. Finally, the performance of the DSS algorithm and the SSS algorithm are compared under frequently changing traffic. We developed a packet level Bluetooth simulator to conduct the simulations. For simplicity, we assume a reliable communication channel. That is, no packet is lost or compromised during trans-

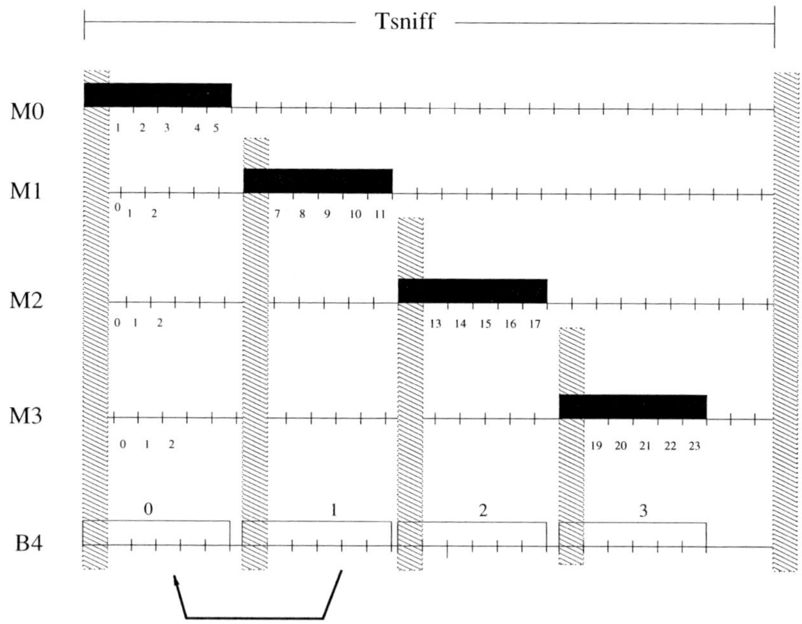

(a) (a) Before updating

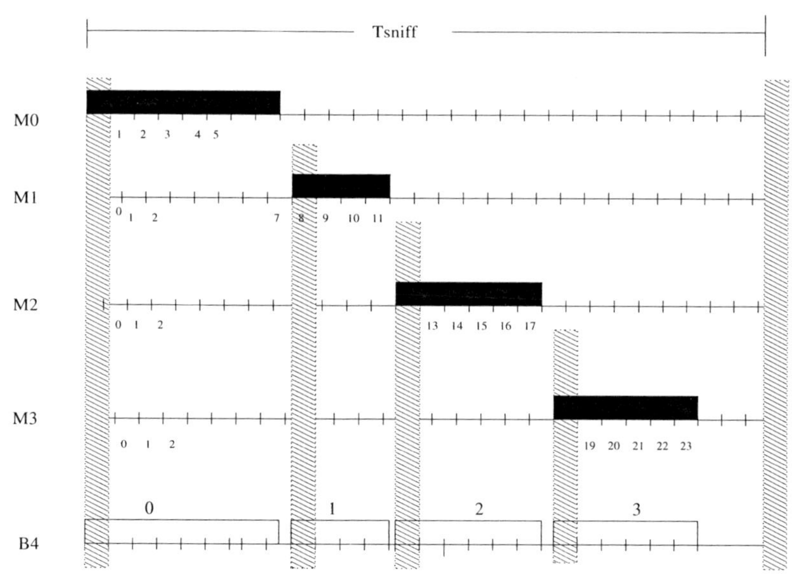

(b) (b) After updating

Figure 9: A simple switch-table updating process

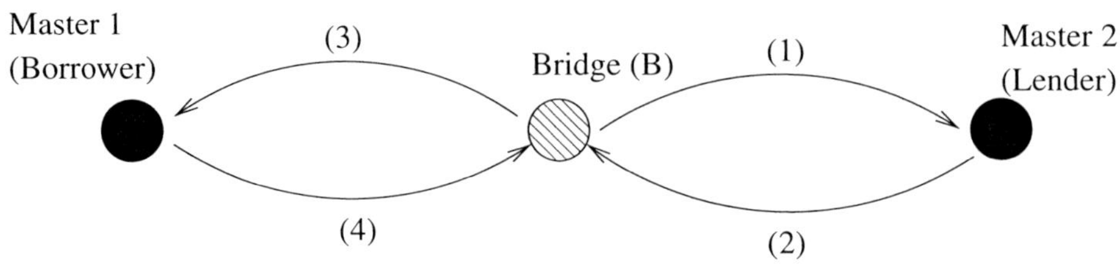

(1) B sends a $borrow\_request(slots)$ to $M_2(Lender)$;
(2) M_2 replies a confirm to B;
(3) B sends a $lend(slots)$ to $M_1(borrower)$;
(4) M_1 replies a $confirm$ to B.

Figure 10: Illustration of a switch-table updating process

mission, except for bridge conflict.

4.1 Evaluate the performance of the SSS algorithm

We simulate a simple scatternet system as shown in Figure 5(a). The system models a typical communication scenario where tens of mobile nodes form an ad-hoc network to exchange CBR traffic (e.g., voice or video) with each other. The traffic flows are listed in Table 2. Data are transmitted using DH1 packets. Note that each DH1 packet occupies one slot and there is no FEC in the payload.

Table 2: CBR traffic flows

Flow#	Source node	Destination node	Traffic rate (kbps)
0	S_5	S_9	34.6
1	S_8	S_{12}	34.6
2	S_{11}	S_{15}	34.6
3	S_{14}	S_6	34.6

The simulation results are shown in Figure 12. Since the traffic is evenly distributed to all master-bridge links and there is no variance in traffic load, the SSS algorithm, based on a predefined static switch-table which distributes the bandwidth evenly to all master-bridge links, can achieve good performance in terms of dropping rate and packet delay. The results also illustrate the impacts of the cycle length on the performance: when the cycle length increases, the dropping rate decreases while the delay increases, because the frequency for the bridge node to switch between piconets is decreased when the cycle length increases. Thus, the bandwidth loss due to clock variation between different piconets is reduced. On the other hand, the increase of the cycle length also increases the time a packet should wait before being forwarded, which increases the average packet transmission delay. We can also find that this trend is not affected by the maximum queue length, except that a large queue capacity can reduce the dropping rate and increase the transmission delay.

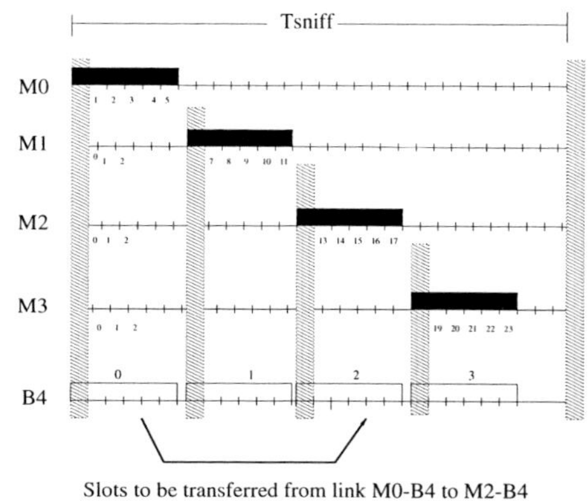

(a) (a) Before updating

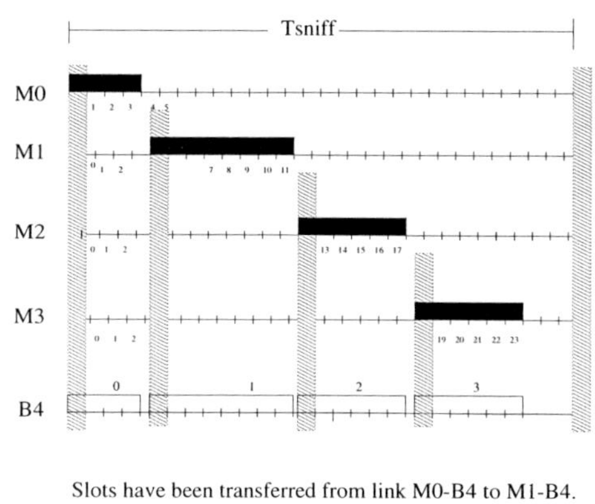

(b) (b) First step update

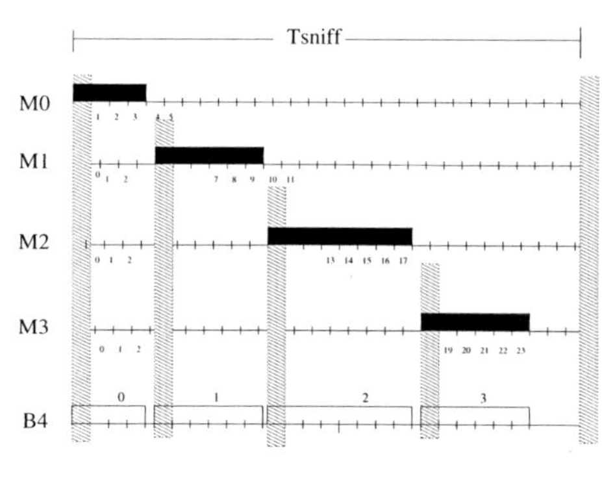

(c) (c) Second step update

Figure 11: A complicated switch-table updating process

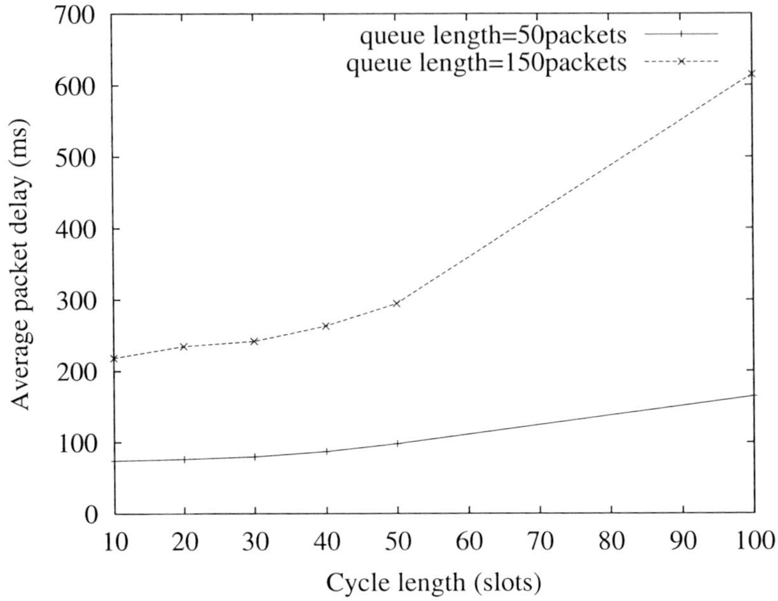

(a) (a) Average packet delay per hop

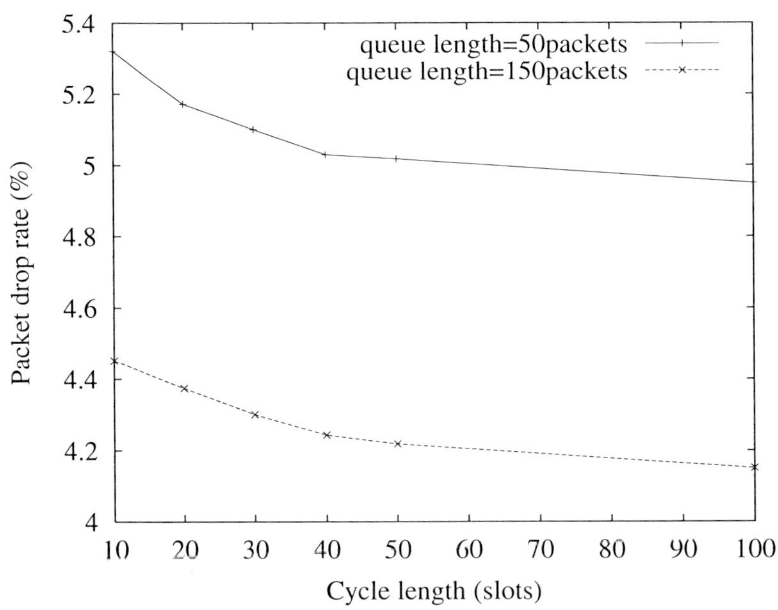

(b) (b) Drop rate

Figure 12: Evaluate the performance of the SSS algorithm under different cycle length (Simulation time: 50s)

4.2 Evaluate the Performance of the DSS Algorithm

To model frequent traffic changes, we simulate a small sensor network as follows. Node M_0 is a control center and all other nodes are sensors. Usually, each sensor reports to the control center at the rate of $1kbps$. In case of emergency, the report rate increases to $8kbps$. The arrival of the emergency events follows an exponential distribution with a mean of T_i. The lasting time of an emergency is also an exponentially distributed random variable, with a mean of $2 * T_i$. We assume that the packets are sent using DH1 format. The cycle length is 30 slots. The simulation results under various parameters are shown in Figure 13 and 14.

First, we study the impacts of n_c. As shown in Figure 13(a) and 14(a), when n_c decreases, the dropping rate decreases. This is due to the reason that, when the checking interval is small, the switch-table can be adjusted promptly based on the traffic pattern. However, when n_c is very small (i.e., less than $200ms$), the dropping rate increases since the cost of frequent adjustments outweighs the benefit. Figure 13(c) and 14(c) help explain this phenomenon: when n_c is very small, the number of adjustments becomes very large. This also explains the phenomenon shown in Figure 13(b) and 14(b): the average packet delay per hop decreases as n_c decreases in general. However, this trend reverses when n_c is very small; i.e., the average packet delay increases as T_c decreases.

Second, we study the impacts of the maximum queue length on the performance of the algorithm. As shown in Figure 13(a) and 14(a), when the queue is long, the dropping rate is low. This is due to the fact that a large queue can buffer more packets generated in bursty traffic than a small one. Note that the dropping rate increases sharply to more than 20% when the maximum queue length is 100 packets, and n_c is very large (i.e., larger than 1s). This is due to the fact that a small queue can not buffer many packets. If the adjustments are not done in time, most packets generated in bursty traffic are lost. Figure 13(b) and 14(b) also shows similar results.

Finally, we study the impacts of the traffic changing frequency. Comparing Figure 13(a)(b) and Figure 14(a)(b), we can see that the traffic changing frequency does not affect the performance too much. This demonstrates that the DSS algorithm can achieve good performance regardless of the traffic pattern. Comparing Figure 13(c) and Figure 14(c), we can see that the number of adjustments grows as the traffic changing frequency increases and drops as the traffic changing frequency decreases.

In general, this simulation results show that the DSS algorithm can achieve good performance when T_c is appropriate. The optimal value of T_c is between $200ms$ and $400ms$ in this scenario.

4.3 Compare the Performance of DSS and SSS

In this subsection, we compare DSS and SSS when the traffic pattern changes. We use the same simulation setting as that in Section 4.2, except that the checking interval of the DSS algorithm fixed at $300ms$. The simulation results are shown in Figure 15 and 16.

First, we study the impacts of the maximum queue length on the performance. As shown in Figure 15(a) and 16(a), the dropping rate of both algorithms decreases when the maximum queue length increases. Figure 15(b) and 16(b) show that the average packet delay increases when the maximum queue length increases, and the packet delay of the

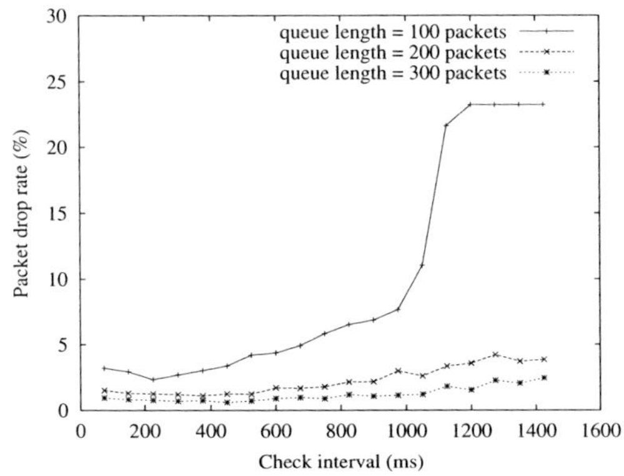

(a) (a) Drop rate

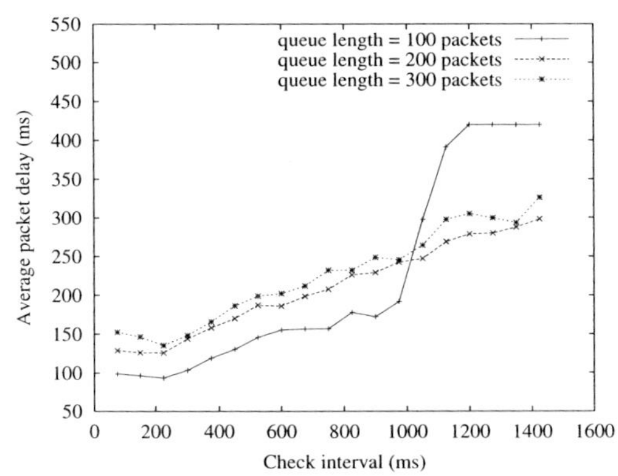

(b) (b) Average packet delay per hop

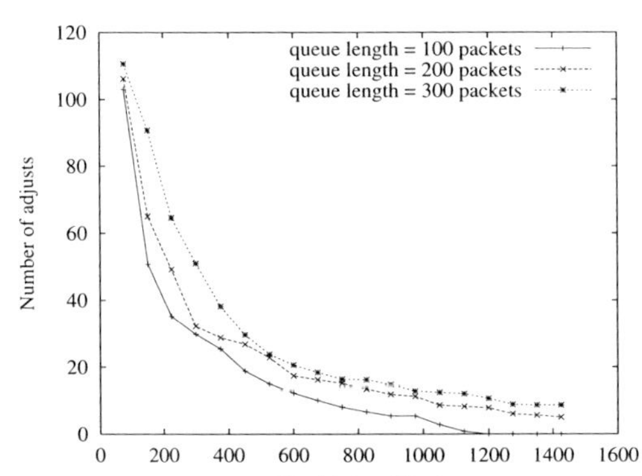

(c) (c) Average number of slot transfers

Figure 13: Evaluation of the DSS algorithm: $T_i = 1s$

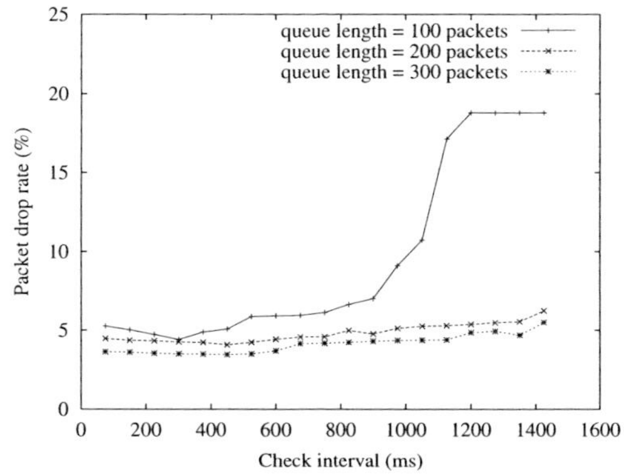

(a) (a) Drop rate

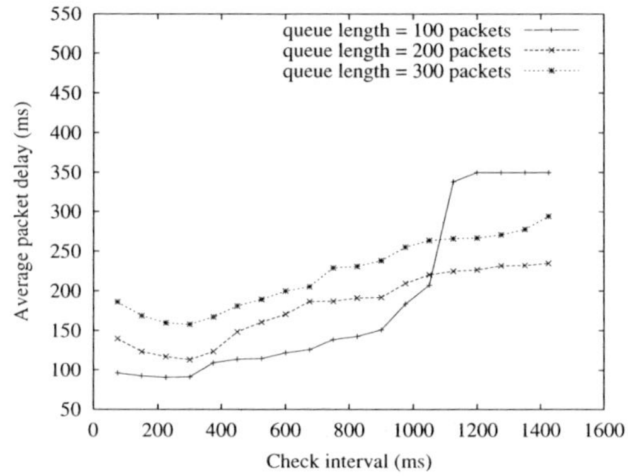

(b) (b) Average packet delay per hop

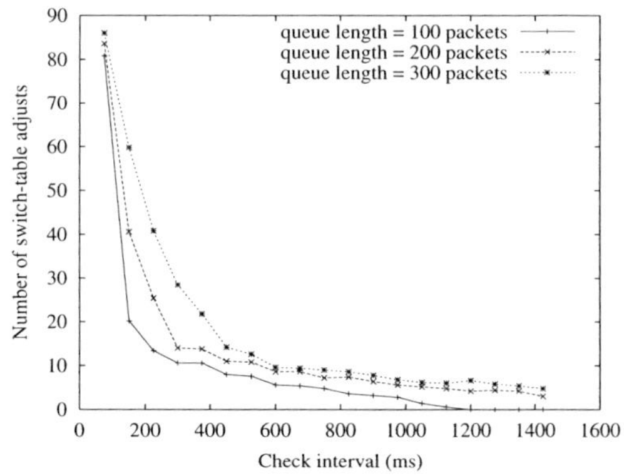

(c) (c) Average number of slot transfers

Figure 14: Evaluation of the DSS algorithm: $T_i = 5s$

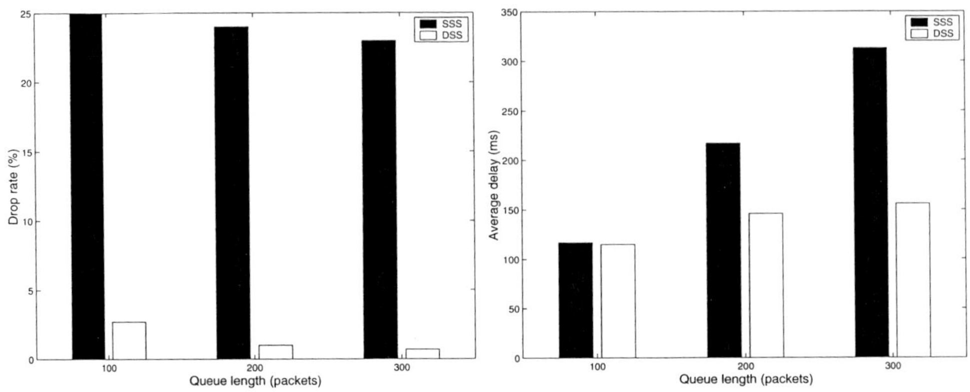

(a) Drop rate (b) Average packet delay per hop

Figure 15: Performance difference between DSS and SSS:$T_i = 1s$

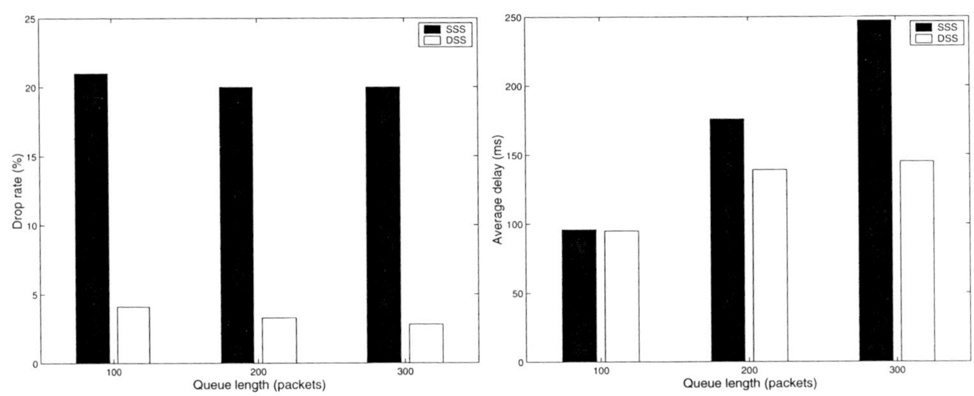

(a) Drop rate (b) Average packet delay per hop

Figure 16: Performance difference between DSS and SSS:$T_i = 5s$

SSS algorithm is more sensitive to the variation in maximum queue length than the DSS algorithm.

Second, we study the impacts of the traffic pattern changing frequency on the performance difference. Comparing Figure 15 and Figure 16, we can find that the difference becomes smaller as T_i increases. This is due to the fact that the SSS algorithm is suitable for the scenarios where the traffic does not change or changes infrequently, whereas the DSS algorithm is adaptive to traffic pattern variations.

5 Conclusion

Ubiquitous computing has created a strong demand for a low-power, low-cost, and small size wireless communication technology. This demand has led to the development of the Bluetooth technology. The basic communication structure in Bluetooth networks is piconet, which has limited communication capacity. In order to provide larger communication capacity and support efficient communication among a large number of devices, Bluetooth allows multiple piconets to form a larger, multi-hop network called scatternet. Due to the bridge conflict problem, scatternet-wide scheduling is essential. A reservation-based protocol can eliminate the bridge conflicts, but it can not achieve desirable bandwidth utilization when the traffic load changes. In this chapter, we addressed both the bridge conflict problem and the drawbacks associated with the reservation-based protocols by proposing a dynamic scatternet-wide scheduling scheme. Simulation results verified that the DSS scheme can significantly reduce the packet dropping rate and the transmission delay.

References

[1] F. Kubinszky A. Racz, G. Miklos and A. Valko, "A pseudo Random Coordinated Scheduling Aglrotihm for Bluetooth Scatternets," *MOBIHOC'01*, 2001.

[2] M. Albrecht, M. Frank, P. Martini, M. Schetelig, A. Vilavaara, and A. Wenzel, "IP Services over Bluetooth: Leading the Way to a New Mobility," *Proc. Conf. on Local Computer Networks (LCN'99)*, pp. 2–11, 1999.

[3] Simon Baatz, Matthias Frank, Carmen Kuhl, Peter Martini and Christoph Scholz, "Bluetooth Scatternets: An Enhanced Adaptive Scheduling Scheme," *IEEE INFOCOM'02*, 2002.

[4] P. Bhagwat and A. Segall, "A Routing Vector Method (RVM) for Routing in Bluetooth Scatternets," *The Sixth IEEE International Workshop on Mobile Multimedia Communications (MOMUC'99)*, 1999.

[5] J. Bray and C. Sturman, "Bluetooth: Connect Without Cables," *Prentice-Hall, Englewood Cliffs*, 2000.

[6] A. Das, A. Ghose, A. Razdan, H. Saran and R. Shorey, "Enhancing Performance of Asynchronous Data Traffic Over the Bluetooth Wireless Ad-hoc Network," *IEEE INFOCOM'01*, April 2001.

[7] S. Garg, M. Kalia, and R. Shorey, "MAC Scheduling Policies for Power Optimization in Bluetooth: A Master Driven TDD Wireless System," *IEEE VTC*, pp. 196–200, 2000.

[8] Bluetooth Special Interest Group, "Specification of the Bluetooth System, 1.1," *http://www.bluetooth.com*, Feb. 2001.

[9] J. Haartsen, "The Bluetooth Radio System," *IEEE Personal Communications*, vol. 7, no. 1, pp. 28–36, Feb. 2000.

[10] J. Haartsen, "Bluetooth: An Enabler for Personal Area Networking," *IEEE Network*, vol. 15, no. 5, Sep/Oct 2001.

[11] N. Johansson, F.Alriksson and U.Jonsson, "JUMP Mode - A Dynamic Window-based Scheduling Framework for Bluetooth Scatternets," *MobiHoc'01*, 2001.

[12] N. Johansson, U. Korner, and N. Johansson, "Performance Evaluation of Scheduling Algorithms for Bluetooth," *Broadband Communications: Convergence of Network Technologies, Kluwer*, pp. 139–150, 2000.

[13] M. Kalia, D. Bansal, and R. Shorey, "Data Scheduling and SAR for Bluetooth MAC," *IEEE VTC*, pp. 716–720, 2000.

[14] M. Kalia, S. Garg, and R. Shorey, "Efficient Policies for Increasing Capacity in Bluetooth: an Indoor Pico-Cellular Wireless System," *Proc. IEEE Vehicular Technology Conference (VTC 2000)*, pp. 907–911, 2000.

[15] M. Kalia, S. Garg, and R. Shorey, "Scatternet Structure and Inter-Piconet Communication in the Bluetooth System," *Technical Report, IBM India Research Lab*, 2000.

[16] C. Law and K. Siu, "A Bluetooth Scatternet Formation Algorithm," *GLOBECOM'01*, 2001.

[17] B Miller and C. Bisdikian, "Bluetooth Revealed," *Prentice Hall*, 2000.

[18] T. Salonidis, P. Bhagwat, L. Tassiulas, and R. LaMaire, "Distributed Topology Construction of Bluetooth Personal Area Networks," *IEEE INFOCOM'01*, April 2001.

[19] G. Zaruba,S. Basagni and I. Chlamtac, "Bluetrees - Scatternet Formation to Enable Bluetooth-based Ad Hoc Networks," *IEEE ICC'01*, 2001.

[20] W. Zhang and G. Cao, "A Flexible Scatternet-wide Scheduling Algorithm for Bluetooth Networks," *IEEE IPCCC'02*, 2002.

In: New Topics in Theoretical Computer Science
Editors: Oleg N. Terikhovsky *et al.*, pp. 275-296
ISBN: 978-1-60456-100-5

Chapter 10

INTRODUCTION TO PERFORMANCE ANALYSIS OF MOBILE AD HOC NETWORKS

***Chansu Yu*[†*] *and Chita R. Das*[‡**]**
[†]Department of Electrical and Computer Engineering, Cleveland State University, Cleveland, OH, USA
[‡]Department of Computer Science and Engineering, Pennsylvania State University, University Park, PA, USA

1 Introduction

Wireless communication technology together with the advancements in systems and network software helps us to remain connected and still be productive while on the road. Wireless LANs based on IEEE 802.11 standard [1], better known as *Wi-Fi hot spots*, are becoming ingreat popularity in public as well as in residential areas. They can be found in major airports, university campuses, shopping malls, coffee shops and more. *Wireless Personal Area Networks* (PANs) such as *Bluetooth* [8] are also on the rise to provide connectivity among portable devices in a small area. And, *wireless sensor networks* (WSNs) have a long-term potential in many interesting pervasive applications [9, 10]. However, they will bring us a new level of information accessibility and convenience of life once those independent hot spots, Bluetooth networks, and sensor networks are interconnected and interoperable. In the long run, this society will evolve into, so to speak, the *embarrassingly connected society* where every corner of the world is not left behind and one can always interact with the rest of the world as well as the surrounding environment wherever he or she is positioned.

Numerous efforts, planned or unplanned, already have been underway to connect the Wi-Fi hot spots to offer a better connectivity over a larger geographical area. For example, unplanned community networks cover a substantial part of downtown areas of major US cities such as New York [2], Seattle [3] and Boston [4]. A number of major industry players including Google have planned or studied for investment planned metropolitan area networks

[*] E-mail address: c.yu91@csuohio.edu
[**] E-mail address: das@cse.psu.edu

[5, 6]. In response to the ever increasing interest, IEEE 802.11 recently initiated a subcommittee called *802.11s ESS Mesh Network* [7] to develop the corresponding standard that conforms to existing 802.11 technology.

Those interconnected wireless networks require new ideas and new technologies. Among them, multi-hopping is one essential element because there may exist a corner that communication infrastructure does not or is costly to reach but can be reached via a few intermediate neighbors. While the field of mobile ad hoc networking attracts unprecedented attention from research community during the last decade, it still faces, we believe, fundamental challenges that demand new principles and mechanisms optimized for that particular type of mobile networks. For example, most of multihop research bases its study on Wi-Fi standard, officially called IEEE 802.11 PHY (physical layer) and MAC (Medium Access Control). However, it has not originally been designed or developed for multihop communication. Bluetooth version of multihop network, called *scatternet*, has been defined in the standard but no details were provided because multihop communication was not the primary focus.

Therefore, it is important to consider developing unique solutions suitable for multihop environment rather than developing multihop solutions based on single-hop technology. New wireless communication facilities such as *transmit power/rate control*, *variable beamwidth formation*, and *spectrum agility* must be integrated to create opportunities toward this end. Cross-layer optimization techniques that are against the legacy layered architecture must be seriously considered. And, in-depth understanding of the network is in desperate need: What is the maximum achievable capacity of a mobile ad hoc network without regard to MAC or network layer solutions used? How much can it be improved with new communication facilities such as directional antennas? How difficult is synchronization in mobile multihop environment? How does mobility affect the network performance? What does it take to establish and maintain connectivity between two end nodes and how long does it survive?

The motivation of this article is to provide a set of research work that discusses the above mentioned fundamental issues in the context of mobile ad hoc networks. We have been trying to include chapters that address those issues by way of mathematical analysis because they can give us the insights into the system internals and reveal tradeoffs. At the same time, we're interested in providing systematic way of performance analysis by asking questions like: What to measure, how to design experiments, how to model the network, traffic and mobility and how to summarize the results? We hope that the collection of research works presented in this book provide a groundwork for future research in the area of ad hoc networking. Before we present summary in Section 4, we overview IEEE 802.11 MAC and ad hoc routing algorithms in Sections 2 and 3, respectively, as they are basic building blocks that the text tries to measure up to or improve upon.

2 MAC Schemes in Mobile Ad Hoc Networks

A wireless network suffers from collisions and interference due to the broadcast nature of radio communication and thus requires a special MAC protocol. It is essentially a distributed scheduling algorithm that provides fair and efficient allocation of limited bandwidth in wireless networks. Two commonly used access principles in wireless networks are *fixed-assignment channel access* and *random access* methods [12]. In the former method, a pair of nodes is statically allocated a certain time slot (frequency band or spread spectrum code), as is the case for most of voice-oriented wireless networks. On the other hand, in random access MAC protocols, the sender dynamically competes for a time slot in a fully distributed way. This is a more flexible and efficient method of managing the channel, but suffers from collisions and interference. This section provides a general discussion on the random access MAC and then offers an in-depth discussion of *Distribution Coordination Function* (DCF) of IEEE 802.11, which is the most popular wireless LAN standard.

2.1 Random Access MAC

Random access MAC protocol in radio networks has long been an active research area. *Aloha* is a simple random access MAC algorithm with no collision avoidance mechanism. The throughput of Aloha and *carrier sensing* protocols has been analyzed with a wide range of system parameters such as propagation delay and offered load. A key factor in the analysis is *vulnerable period*, during which any other node must not start its own transmission in order to make the transmission of interest to be successful [13]. In the *pure Aloha* scheme, the vulnerable period is twice the packet transmission time as shown in Fig. 1(a). This is fairly large and cannot be ignored unless communication traffic is sufficiently light. It critically limits the maximum achievable channel utilization in Aloha, which is only 18% for pure Aloha and 36% for *slotted Aloha* [13].

Carrier sensing mechanisms reduce this period substantially by sensing the medium before attempting to transmit a packet. The chance of collisions is reduced to the case where a node does not sense the medium correctly due to the propagation delay, which is ignorable compared to the packet transmission time. Unfortunately, collisions are not completely avoidable in carrier sensing MAC protocols due to interference from "*hidden terminals*" [14]. A mobile node, which is located near the receiver but far from the sender, may be unaware of the on-going communication and causes collisions at the receiver by initiating its own data transmission. In Fig. 1(b), data transmission from S to R is hidden to N_R. In other words, N_R cannot sense S's transmission even though its signal is strong enough to corrupt the transmission at R. The shaded area shown in Fig. 1(b), where the hidden terminals can hide, is called the "*vulnerable region*" [11].

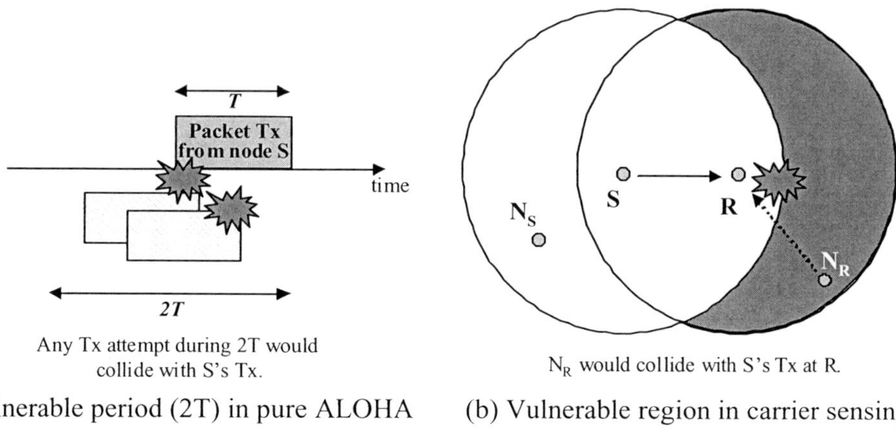

(a) Vulnerable period (2T) in pure ALOHA (b) Vulnerable region in carrier sensing MAC

Fig. 1: Vulnerable period and vulnerable region in random access MAC protocols.

A *busy tone* is one approach used to avoid the hidden terminal problem in a carrier sensing radio network [15]. Whenever any node detects a packet being transmitted, it starts to send a signal, called a busy tone, in a separate frequency channel. For example, when node S starts to send a packet to node R, node R as well as node N_S will start to send a busy tone. All the nodes that can hear the busy tone will not initiate their own transmission and thus node R will experience no collision. A critical problem with the use of busy tones is that too many nodes (all 2-hop neighbors of node S) will be inhibited from transmitting. The number of nodes affected will typically be about four times the number of nodes within the transmission range of the receiver. While this approach almost completely eliminates collisions, it is not a very promising approach from a throughput standpoint [15].

2.2 DCF of IEEE 802.11 MAC

Distributed coordination function (*DCF*) is the basic medium access method in IEEE 802.11 [1]. It supports best effort delivery of packets at the link layer and is described as the *Carrier Sense Multiple Access with Collision Avoidance* (*CSMA/CA*) protocol. Four key elements of DCF are *ACK*, *RTS/CTS*, *IFS* and *Backoff algorithm*.

ACK for Collision Detection

ACKnowledgement (*ACK*) packets enable a mobile node to determine whether its transmission was successful or not since it cannot otherwise detect a collision. The sender is made aware of the collision after it times out waiting for the corresponding ACK for the packet transmitted. If no ACK packet is received or an ACK is received in error, the sender will contend again for the medium to retransmit the data packet until the maximum allowed number of retransmissions has been tried. If all fail, the sender drops the packet. Note that this sort of link level ACKs are not usually used in wired networks because wired links are quite reliable and collisions are easily detectable.

RTS/CTS for Solving Hidden Terminal Problem

In DCF, collisions from the hidden nodes in the vulnerable region can be effectively avoided by using *four-way handshake* based on *Request-To-Send* (*RTS*) and *Clear-To-Send* (*CTS*) packets. By exchanging the two short control packets between a sender and a receiver, all neighboring nodes recognize the transmission and thus hold their own packets during the transmission time advertised along with the RTS and CTS packets. Using this information, each node maintains a *Network Allocation Vector* (*NAV*), which indicates the remaining time of the on-going communication. Fig. 2(a) shows the transmission range of RTS and CTS control packets. N_S and N_R would receive RTS or CTS, respectively, and set their NAVs accordingly. Fig. 2(b) shows the four-way handshake between S and R as well as IFS and contention window, which will be described shortly. In DCF, the use of RTS/CTS mechanism is optional and can be controlled by the *RTSTheshold* parameter that determines the payload size for which RTS/CTS should be used [16].

IFS for Prioritized Access to the Channel

Inter-Frame Spacing (*IFS*) is the time interval during which each node has to wait before transmitting any packet and is used to provide a prioritized access to the channel. For example, *Short IFS* (*SIFS*) is used after receiving a DATA packet and is the shortest to give the highest priority to an ACK packet. *DCF IFS* (*DIFS*) is longer than SIFS and is used when initiating a data transfer. When RTS/CTS is used, the RTS packet can be transmitted after waiting for DIFS duration of time. All other frames (CTS, DATA, and ACK) use SIFS before attempting to transmit. Fig. 2(b) shows the usage of DIFS and SIFS.

Another IFS is *Extended IFS* (*EIFS*). A node sets its NAV for the EIFS duration of time when it senses an on-going communication but does not know the duration of it because it cannot correctly decode the packet. EIFS is used in DCF to prevent collisions with ACK receptions at the sender, which is important because an ACK packet forms a vital piece of information as the last step of the four-way handshake. A loss of ACK results in retransmission of long DATA packet and thus significantly degrades the performance.

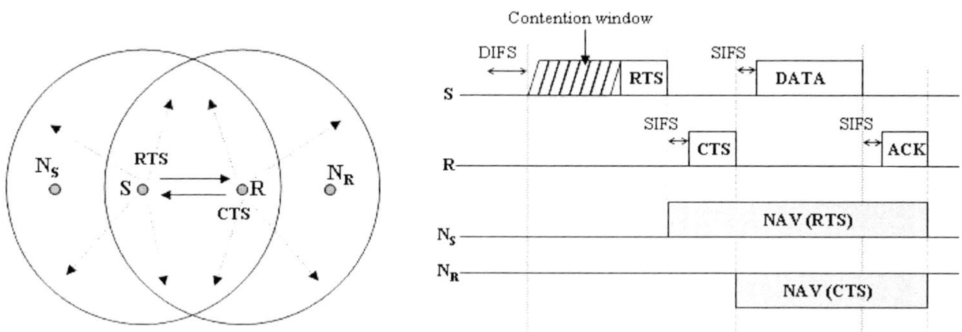

(a) RTS/CTS mechanism (b) IFS, RTS/CTS and NAV

Fig. 2: Collision avoidance mechanism of DCF.

Backoff Algorithm to Provide Fair Access with Congestion Control

The abovementioned IFS is followed by an additional waiting time defined by the backoff algorithm used in DCF. The main purpose of the backoff algorithm is to reduce the probability of collisions when contention is severe. After waiting for the IFS duration, each competing node waits for a backoff time, which is randomly chosen in the interval (0, *CW*), defined as *contention window*. During the first transmission of a packet, CW is set to its minimum preset value, CWmin. If the channel continues to be idle during the backoff time, it transmits (winner). Other waiting nodes (losers) become aware of the transmission, freeze their backoff time, and contend again in the next competition cycle after the current transmission completes. Now, the frozen backoff time plays an important role in ensuring fairness. Definition of fairness may differ, but in general all nodes entering the competition for the first time should have on an average equal chance of transmitting, and nodes that have lost in the previous competition cycle should have higher priority than newly arrived nodes. The losers are given a higher priority by using the remaining frozen backoff time thereby preserving the first-come, first-serve policy.

The aforementioned access scheme has problems under heavy or light loads. If CW is too small considering the number of competing nodes, it causes many collisions. On the other hand, if CW is too large, it causes unnecessary delay [14]. DCF adopts the *binary exponential backoff scheme* to allow an adaptive solution to this problem. When a node fails to receive an ACK in response to transmission of a DATA packet, CW is doubled after the collision until it reaches a preset limit, *CWmax*. It is noted that CW is restored to its minimum, *CWmin*, when a node successfully completes a data transmission. Fig. 3 shows the flow chart of the backoff algorithm used in DCF.

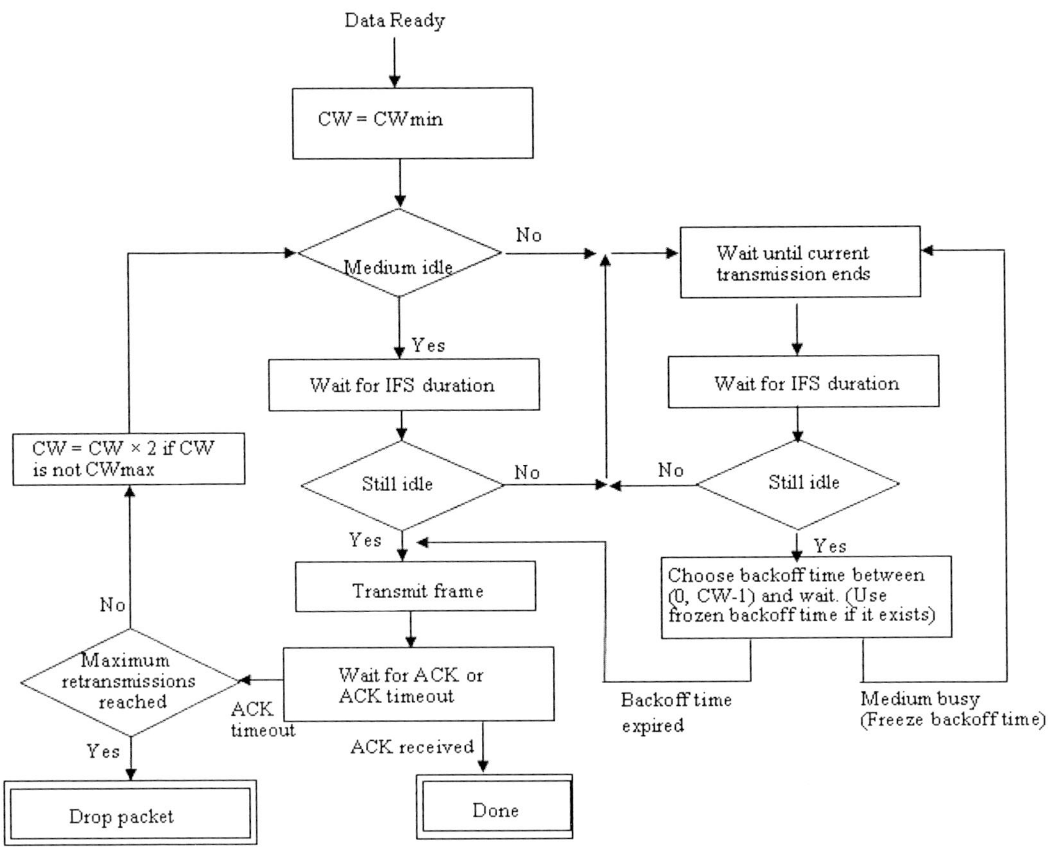

Fig. 3: Backoff algorithm used in DCF of IEEE 802.11 MAC.

2.3 Performance Limit of DCF and Channel Utilization Enhancing Techniques

There has been active research on estimating the performance of IEEE 802.11 MAC analytically as well as via simulation [16-20]. Among them, Cali *et al.* have provided a mathematical model for the maximum achievable throughput [18]. According to their results, the theoretical throughput is bounded by around 80% when the typical DCF parameters are used (propagation delay of 1 μsec and packet size of 50μsec~5msec). In reality, DCF operates very far from the theoretical limit due to collisions and control overhead associated with RTS/CTS and the backoff algorithm.

In a multihop MANET, the situation becomes even worse. Multi-hopping can potentially increase the channel utilization by allowing multiple simultaneous transmissions whenever they occur separated in space [8, 21]. However, it increases the total data traffic over the network by a factor of the number of hops. Moreover, it potentially causes self-generating collisions in addition to those from other data streams since each node acts as a router and uses a single network interface to receive a packet as well as to forward the previous packet of the same data stream to the next hop node.

Li *et al.* showed that the end-to-end throughput is at most 1/4 of the channel bandwidth even without any other interfering nodes [22]. In other words, when IEEE 802.11-based 2 Mbps wireless network interface is used, a source-destination pair in a MANET cannot support more than 500 kbps even though there is no additional traffic in the network. This is mainly due to collisions among intermediate forwarding nodes of the same data stream. In addition, the control overhead of DCF aggravates the situation and the maximum throughput is reduced to about 1/7 of the channel bandwidth [22]. When other data traffic exists, the throughput is reduced even further. For example, Xu and Saadawi reported that multiple simultaneous TCP sessions in a MANET result in unreasonably low aggregate throughput and suffers from severe unfairness [23].

Table 1: Enhancing temporal channel utilization.

Key elements	Parameter	Problem	Solution technique
RTS/CTS and NAV	RTSThreshold	Undetermined or fixed RTSThreshold	Adaptive adjustment based on - traffic and collision probability [24] - experienced collisions [16]
Backoff algorithm	CW restoration to CWmin	Many collisions or large delay	Multiplicative Increase and Linear Decrease (MILD) [25]
	Frozen backoff time	Staircase-like slot selection probability and more collisions	Offer later slots to new nodes and earlier slots to old and lost nodes [16]
	Backoff algorithm	CW is not optimal	Dynamic tuning with the estimation of the number of active nodes in its vicinity at run time [18]

The performance limitation is partly due to the limited capability of MAC protocols in a multihop communication environment. A key idea for improving DCF for MANET is *adaptivity*. For example, each node would be better off if it is able to behave adaptively depending on traffic intensity in its vicinity. Table 1 introduces adaptive mechanisms proposed in the literature that attempt to better schedule the channel along the time dimension by adjusting the DCF parameters such as RTSThreshold and the backoff algorithm. Table 2 summarizes the channel utilization enhancing techniques along the spatial dimension. While the temporal approaches can be applied to single-hop wireless LANs as well as multihop MANETs, the spatial approaches focus only on multihop MANETs and exploit the characteristics unique to the multihop communication environment.

Table 2: Enhancing spatial channel utilization.

Conventional facility	Problem	Additional facility	Solution technique
Single channel for data and control packet	Unnecessary space reservation around the sender by RTS (Exposed terminal problem)	Separate busy tone channel	Advertise the communication over the busy tone channel (DBTMA) [26]
Fixed carrier sense threshold	Unnecessary backoff due to lower (more sensitive) carrier sense threshold than necessary	Reduced or adjustable carrier sense threshold	Conservative CTS Reply (CCR) [64] Aggressive Virtual Carrier Sensing (AVCS) [65] Link layer salvaging (MASA) [63]
Single power model	Unnecessary interference and space reservation when the communicating distance is short	Transmission power control of radio transceiver	Advertise the tolerable noise level over the busy tone channel (PCMA) [27] Use low power for data packets [28] Periodic power adjustment when delivering data packets (PCM) [29]
Omni-directional antenna model	Unnecessary interference and space reservation since communication is omni-directional	Directional antenna	Omni-directional control packet transfer but directional data packet transfer [30] Directional RTS [31] Directional RTS and CTS [32] Multihop RTS to take into account the difference in antenna gain [33] Schedule-based directional MAC [34]

3 Routing Algorithms and Mobility Models

This section introduces routing algorithms proposed for MANET in the literature, discusses two important issues in the design of reactive routing protocols such as *Dynamic Source Routing* (DSR) [35] and *Ad-hoc On-demand Distance Vector* (AODV) [36], and overviews mobility models that affect the performance of routing algorithms the most.

3.1 Routing Algorithms and Issues

The routing protocols proposed for MANETs are generally categorized as *table-driven* and *on-demand driven* based on the timing of when the routes are updated. With table-driven routing protocols, each node tries to maintain consistent, up-to-date routing information to every other node in the network. This is done in response to changes in the network by having each node update its routing table and propagate the updates to its neighboring nodes. Thus, it is *proactive* in the sense that when a packet needs to be forwarded the route is already known and can be immediately used. Many routing protocols including *Destination-Sequenced Distance Vector (DSDV)* [37] and *Fisheye State Routing (FSR)* protocol [38] belong to this category. With on-demand driven routing, routes are discovered only when a source node desires them. When data traffic is light, on-demand routing significantly reduces the routing overhead. The following two subsections describe DSR and AODV, which are the most popular and highly efficient on-demand protocols.

DSR Routing Protocol [35]

When a node has a data packet to send but does not know the routing path to a destination, it initiates the *route discovery procedure* by broadcasting a control packet called RREQ (*route request packet*). When a RREQ reaches the destination, it prepares another control packet called RREP (*route reply packet*) and replies back to the source with complete route information. Upon receiving a RREP, the source begins transmitting data packets to the destination but at the same time it saves the route information in its *route cache* for later use. Since data transmission in wireless networks is broadcast in nature, intermediate relaying nodes as well as other nearby nodes also learn the path to the destination via overhearing. Therefore, the number of RREQ packets can be minimized because a node may have a learned path to a destination in its route cache. The number of RREQ packets can be reduced even further by allowing an intermediate node to reply to a RREQ if it has a path to the destination in its route cache. This prevents network-wide flooding of RREQ packets.

Since nodes move unpredictably in a MANET, link errors occur and the route information that includes a broken link becomes obsolete. When a node encounters a link error during its communication, it sends a control packet called RERR (*route error packet*) to the source and eliminates the stale route out of its route cache. On the way to the source, RERR informs nearby nodes about the erred link so that they can also eliminate the corresponding route. It is referred to as the *route maintenance mechanism*.

AODV Routing Protocol [36]

AODV uses the concept of route discovery and route maintenance mechanisms from DSR but uses the concept of sequence numbers, route table-based hop-by-hop routing and periodic beacons (i.e. *Hello* messages) from DSDV [37]. As in DSR, routes to the destination are discovered only when they are required and uses RREQ, RREP and RERR. A key differentiating feature of AODV apart from DSR is that it maintains *route table* instead of route cache, which means that AODV remembers the next hop node to reach each destination while DSR remembers the entire path information to each destination.

The route table of a node maintains entries for each destination the node is interacting with or forwarding packets to. The routing table has the following fields: *Destination IP address*, *Active neighbors*, *Number hops*, *Next hop*, *Destination Sequence Number*, and *Expiration time for the routing table entry*. They help a node to maintain the connectivity of the network. The expiration time associated with the route depends on the size of the ad-hoc network and indicates the time after which the route to the associated destination in the route table is to be removed. A node keeps the list of active neighbors that are the next hop to the destinations maintained in the route table, thus if a link to this active neighbor is broken the node can immediately transmits a RERR message.

AODV uses destination sequence number associated with each route entry, which is generated by the destination node, to ensure loop-free routing path and freshness of the route. And, in AODV, a node broadcasts Hello messages periodically at a default rate of one per second, to maintain connectivity. These messages contain the node's identity and sequence number to its neighbors so that its neighbors can update their local connectivity to the node that broadcasted the Hello message. A node can assume a link is broken when it has not heard for a specified period of time from the node that it considers a neighbor. It can then broadcast a RERR packet to its neighbors regarding the link failure.

Issues in On-demand Routing Algorithms

Although on-demand routing algorithms such as DSR and AODV are adopted in many experimental systems because they incur less control overhead, they still possess some undesirable characteristics such as stale route and load unbalance problem. For example, Marina and Das pointed out that link errors (or RERR) are not propagated "fast and wide" in DSR [39] and therefore, route caches often contain stale route information for an extended period of time. In addition, the erased stale routes are possibly un-erased due to in-flight data packets carrying the stale routes. When a node has an invalid route in its route cache or receives a RREP that contains an invalid route, it would attempt to transmit a number of data packets without success while consuming energy. Hu and Johnson studied design choices for route cache in DSR and concluded that there must be a mechanism, such as cache timeout, that efficiently evicts stale route information [40].

While the main cause of the stale route problem is node mobility, it is the route discovery mechanism itself together with unconditional overhearing that dramatically aggravates the problem. This is how it happens. DSR generates more than one RREP packets per route discovery to offer alternative routes. While the primary route is checked for its validity during data communication between the source and the destination, alternative routes may remain in route cache unchecked even after they become stale. This is the case not only for the nodes along the alternative routes, but also for all their neighbors because they become to know those routes via unconditional overhearing.

On-demand routing algorithms exhibit another undesirable characteristic, load unbalance. In a multihop mobile network, each node plays an important role as a router to forward packets on other nodes' behalf. In an ideal case, each mobile node takes equal responsibility of packet forwarding to others. However, it is observed that this is not usually the case primarily due to the "preferential attachment" [42] in the dynamics of route information construction in route caches, together with the expand ring search algorithm used in DSR and AODV. For example, suppose a node, say node *S*, has route information to a number of destination nodes. When a neighboring node, say node *T*, wishes to discover a route to one of those destinations, node *S* would supply the desired information to node *T*. Thus, node *S* becomes an intermediate node for the route from node *T* to the destination and node S will have an additional entry from *S* to node *T*. In other words, an overloaded node becomes more overloaded with time. Over-dependence of packet forwarding functionality on a few overloaded nodes [41] may cause several troubles. For example, overloaded nodes can exhaust their battery power much faster than other nodes and critically decrease the network lifetime.

3.2 Mobility Models

Performance of wireless ad hoc networks is greatly affected by the mobility of nodes as routing algorithms need to discover routes in the presence of frequent link changes. Simulation tools used in ad hoc network research try to mimic the distribution and movement pattern of nodes in real-life scenarios [43]. Recently researchers have concentrated on developing realistic mobility models for simulating mobile networks and providing consistent steady-state mobility parameters for correct and useful evaluations.

Before discussing steady-state mobility parameters in detail, this subsection overviews mobility models reported in the literature. *Random Walk* or *Brownian Motion* is used to model the erratic movement of various entities in nature and also used in wireless mobile networks [44]. *Random Waypoint Mobility Model* (RWP) has been proposed in [35]. It is similar to Random Walk with the exception of pause times. Each node pauses for a predefined amount time, moves toward a randomly selected waypoint with a random speed, and repeats the process. The model has been extensively used in ad-hoc network simulations and has become a reference model for other mobility models.

Mobility models such as *Manhattan Mobility Model* [45] and *Obstacle Mobility Model* [46] are a step forward towards realistic mobility model by including highways/roads and obstacles in their models, respectively. However, their applicability is limited to some particular applications and the selection of node destination and initial distribution is based on RWP. Another interesting area of adding practicality is group mobility, wherein a group of nodes share a common mobility pattern. Hong et al. proposed *Random Point Group Mobility Model* (RPGM) [47]. According to this model, each group has a logical center and the movement pattern of a logical center controls that of its member nodes including speed, direction, and acceleration, etc. In *Reference Velocity Group Mobility Model* (RVGM) [48], each mobility group is characterized by a common mean group velocity. Mean group velocity acts as the reference velocity for the nodes in a group. The RWP has been extended to incorporate the concept of group in [49]. *Virtual Track* (VT) is another group mobility model, which can simulate group dynamics such as group split and merge [50].

Steady-State Mobility Parameters

Now, let us consider the steady-state mobility parameters in RWP which is the most commonly used mobility model for simulating mobile ad hoc networks. Since simulation results are usually represented as time-averages, reaching the steady state is crucial as simulation runs for a fixed amount of time frame (e.g. 900 seconds). As explained earlier, in RWP, a node chooses a waypoint randomly within the simulation area and moves towards it at the randomly chosen speed. After reaching the waypoint the node pauses and then repeats the process till the end of the simulation. Since the node speed is chosen from a uniform distribution from [0, V_{max}], we expect that the average node speed is $V_{max}/2$ at steady-state. However, it has been discovered that the RWP fails to provide a steady state node speed during simulation [51-54]. In other words, average node speed reaches zero as simulation progresses because when a node selects a low speed between [0, V_{max}] it would continue to use the same speed without reaching the specified waypoint until the simulation ends. In the long run, more number of nodes gets stuck with such situation and thus, the average node speed diminishes. Therefore, the results obtained by averaging over time do not represent the true picture or performance of any protocol. A simple, although not perfect, solution is to use non-zero minimum speed. Nodes will select their speed from [V_{min}, V_{max}] and therefore, they do not get stuck with an extremely low speed.

It also has been discovered that RWP does not exhibit steady-state mobility parameters with respect to spatial, topological properties, either [55-58]. Royer et al. showed that average node connectivity does not reach a steady-state in RWP and nodes are more concentrated in the center of simulation area as time progresses [59]. This motivated them to propose *Random Direction Mobility Model* (RDIR), where a mobile node selects a random direction and speed and starts moving until it reaches the simulation boundary along that direction. Once the boundary is reached, the node pauses for a specified time, chooses another direction between (0 , π), and the process continues.

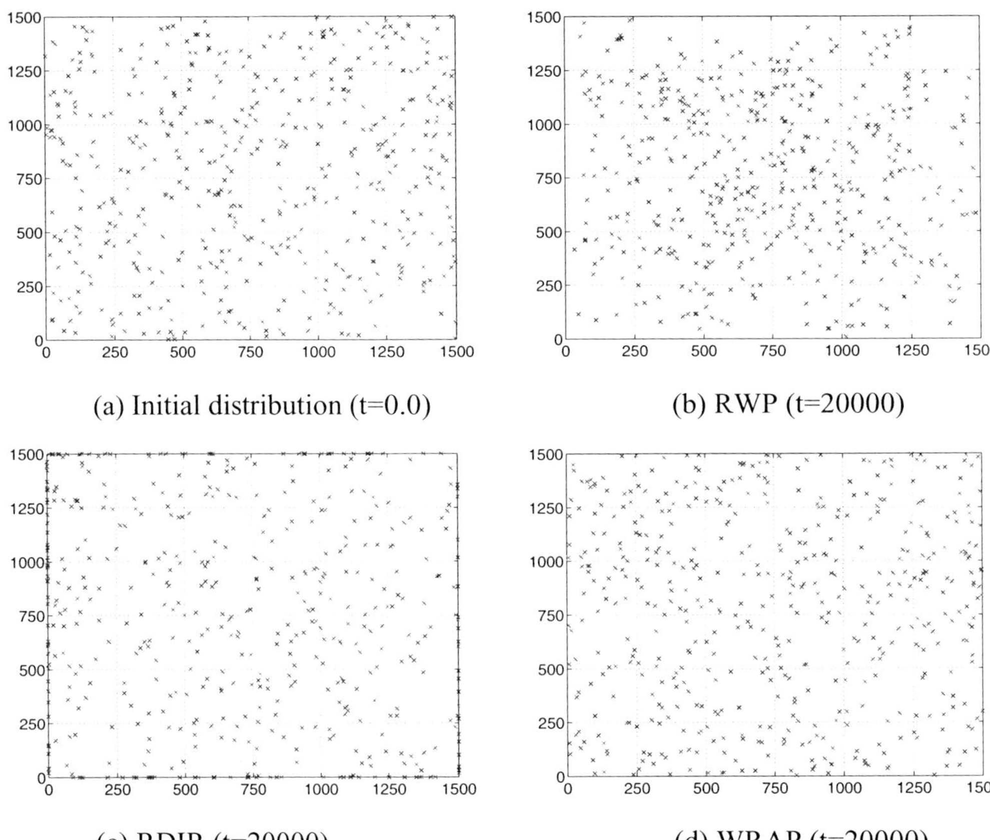

(a) Initial distribution (t=0.0) (b) RWP (t=20000)

(c) RDIR (t=20000) (d) WRAP (t=20000)

Fig. 4: Node distributions in RWP, RDIR, and WRAP models. (The number of nodes is 500, node speed is from [5, 20] m/sec, and pause time is 60 sec.)

However, many nodes following RDIR are located at boundaries while nodes following RWP tend to be cluttered at the center of the network [52], either of which is not realistic and not desirable. A simple modification can lead to a consistently a random node distribution even though it may not be realistic. *Random waypoint with wrap-around mobility model* (WRAP) follows the same movement as the RWP except that the network area is wrap-around, in which a node moves toward a waypoint in the shortest way [66]. Figure 4 compares RWP, RDIR, and WRAP with an example scenario of 500 nodes in a 1500×1500

m^2 network area. Pause time used is 60 seconds and node speed is selected randomly from [5, 20]. We used non-zero minimum node speed to reach steady-state node speed as discussed above. Figure 4(a) is the initial random distribution of nodes. Figures 4(b), (c) and (d) show the node distribution after 20,000 seconds of simulation with RWP, RIDR, and WRAP, respectively. As clearly shown in the figure, WRAP displays steady-state mobility parameters with respect to node positions which is not the case with RWP and RDIR.

Non-homogeneous Mobility Models

WRAP produces random locations of nodes where nodes are well balanced and scattered across the entire network area. Initial positions of mobile nodes are randomly and independently selected. When they move, their locations in the network area are also quite random because target waypoint is randomly and independently selected. Now, consider the spatial distribution of nodes in a network area based on WRAP. Assume that the entire area is divided into a number of equal-sized subareas. Each node is positioned in a particular subarea with independent probability p, which is the reciprocal of the number of subareas, S_{total}. The probability p_k that a subarea has exactly k nodes is given by the binomial distribution,

$$p_k = \binom{n}{k} p^k (1-p)^{n-k},$$

where n is the total number of nodes. As a limiting case, this probability becomes the well-known Poisson distribution

$$p_k = \frac{z^k e^{-z}}{k!},$$

where z is the mean number of nodes in a subarea, or n/S_{total}. Both binomial and Poisson distributions are strongly peaked about the mean z, and have a large-k tail that decays rapidly as a function of $1/k!$ [60]. In other words, with the random node locations, the majority of subareas have similar number of nodes and significant deviations from the average case, e.g., a subarea with a large fraction of nodes, is extremely rare.

However, it is sometimes desired to simulate a mobile network where nodes exhibit non-homogeneous node distribution in the network. In other words, the node distribution can be very different from the Poisson distribution. For example, Figure 5(a) shows an example of a disaster area where the infrastructure-less ad hoc network is well suited for supporting communication. Many rescue team members gather at three hub subareas, denoted as I, II and III in the figure, which may be a base camp or have many casualties. The three subareas out of 36 (S_{total} = 36) include about the half of the total rescue team members (66 out of 137). Figure 5(b) shows the node density distribution of the disaster area in Figure 5(a) as well as that of the random node locations that follows the Poisson distribution. It is clear from Figure 5(b) that WRAP does not model the node distribution of a real ad hoc network situation. Even in the presence of node mobility, node concentration would persist because, for example in Figure 5(a), a mobile node (i.e., a rescue team member) leaving a hub subarea is most likely to move to another hub subarea.

As evident in Figure 5(b), the corresponding node distribution contains a heavy tail unlike the Poisson distribution and can be modeled by a power-law distribution. In general, a power-law distribution is one for which $Pr\{K>k\} \sim k^{-\alpha}$, where $0<\alpha<2$. A smaller value of forms more concentrated clusters. If $\alpha<2$, the distribution has an infinite variance, and if $\alpha<1$, it has an infinite mean.

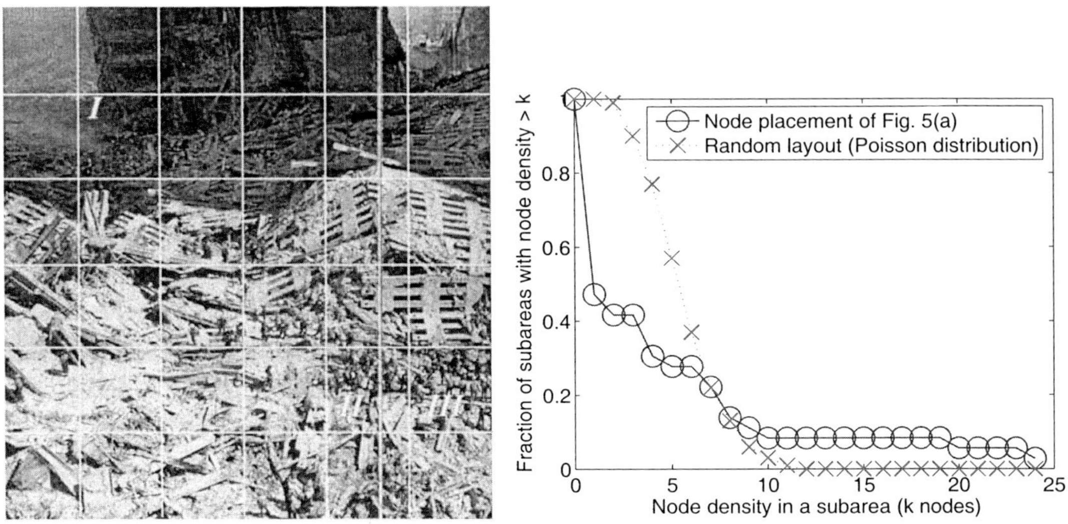

(a) Rescue team at Ground Zero [61] (b) Node density distribution

Fig. 5: Node distributions in an ad hoc network.

One important question in this area of research is therefore how to model such a non-uniform node distribution. Ingmar et al. explained a method to generate node clustering based on a binary multiplicative branching process [62]. It is an iterative process: At first, the total area is divided into four equal subareas. Two randomly chosen subareas get a fraction $(1+\beta)/4$ of the total number of nodes, and the rest two subareas get $(1-\beta)/4$ nodes. Here β is a constant less than one. In the second iteration each subarea is again divided into four subareas and non-uniformly redistributes its nodes into its four offspring subareas. This results in a multi-fractal or clustered distribution of nodes.

4 Summary of Chapters

With the background information on MAC and routing layer algorithms and issues provided in Sections 2 and 3, respectively, this section summarizes chapters in this book. We have tried to provide as many performance analysis aspects as possible such as network model, traffic model, performance metrics, evaluation techniques and simplifying assumptions in the study. This book consists of five parts each with three chapters except Part I. Three chapters in Part II deal with network capacity and link layer issues such as fairness. Part III discusses link layer management issues such as synchronization, power management and scheduling. Part IV includes three chapters that specifically look at the impact of node mobility on system performance such as path availability and routing efficiency. Chapters in Part V discuss end-to-end network performance such as broadcast efficiency, connectivity and network survivability.

4.1 Part II: Capacity and Link Layer Issues

Chapter 2 considers analytic models for capacity of mobile ad hoc networks and reveals fundamental capacity and delay tradeoff. Network capacity decreases as the number of nodes and the networks size increases mainly due to the increased hop count between two arbitrary end nodes. On the other hand, it was also shown that network capacity can be improved significantly by limiting the hop count, which is made possible by delaying packet transmission until the desired destination comes near to the source. It would increase the packet delay but enhance the network capacity, and therefore suggests a fundamental tradeoff between the two. Chapter 2 presents exact capacity and delay expressions to clearly show the tradeoff. It assumes a *cell partitioned network model*, a simple i.i.d. model for mobility and *Bernoulli* or *Poisson* processes for traffic model. Performance metrics used are delay and capacity versus the number of nodes (network size). The delay analysis uses reversibility of discrete B/B/1 queues. The capacity/delay tradeoff theorem uses stochastic technique coupling together with a novel technique for probabilistic conditioning. Simulation is also used to verify the analytical results.

Chapter 3 considers fair and efficient channel allocation at the MAC layer. While Chapter 2 addresses total network capacity, this chapter focuses on the per-node fairness in IEEE 802.11-based multihop ad hoc networks. In a multihop environment, unfair channel sharing among competing flows is an inherent problem of the IEEE 802.11 distributed medium access protocol, called DCF. This article shows how the DCF causes unfairness with three example scenarios (three-pair scenario, large-EIFS scenario and exposed node scenario) and proposes a distributed fair MAC protocol. As far as the network model is concerned, it uses the three network scenarios mentioned above plus grid model. No mobility is assumed, which is considered reasonable in case of evaluating link layer performance. Metrics are throughput and fairness. Since different nodes achieve different level of throughput, fairness is defined as the ratio of the maximum throughput over the minimum throughput. Evaluation is based on simulation.

Chapter 4 analyzes the network capacity with directional antennas and the corresponding directional collision avoidance MAC schemes. Directional communication based on directional antennas has potential to provide a fundamental breakthrough in ad hoc network capacity by avoiding unnecessary interference to other nodes and increasing the transmission range. This chapter analytically shows that the total network capacity can be increased as the number of nodes increases, which has been verified later via simulation. It uses one-hop network model for analysis but uses randomly distributed network for simulation. Mobility is not considered. Metrics are throughput and delay with respect to various input parameters such as the number of nodes, average transmission probability, directional transmission beamwidth, and the rate between directional transmission gain and omni-directional transmission gain. Markov chains are the major tool for analysis to model channel and node states and GloMoSim 2.0 has been used for simulation.

4.2 Part III: Synchronization and Scheduling

Chapter 5 discusses the issue of time synchronization in IEEE 802.11-based ad hoc networks. *Timing Synchronization Function* (TSF) specified in the standard allows neighboring nodes to synchronize to a leading transmitter. It is trivial in an infrastructure network with the help of a central control station called access point but it becomes difficult in ad hoc networks, particularly in large scale multihop networks. This chapter analyzes the root cause of the scalability problem and proposes solutions. It uses one-hop network model both for analysis and simulation and focuses on the synchronization issue with a different number of nodes. Mobility is not an issue because it is a one-hop network. A key metric is maximum clock difference among all nodes in the network with respect to the number of nodes and the number of beacon periods during which nodes compete to play a leading role in synchronizing the network.

Chapter 6 discusses the power save mode operation in IEEE 802.11-based ad hoc networks. Assuming that nodes are synchronized based on the TSF described above, nodes can save energy by entering into sleep mode during the periods they do not need to listen or transmit. A key observation made in this chapter is that nodes wake up a larger number of periods than necessary because network layer protocol such as *Dynamic Source Routing* (DSR) requires overhearing as many communications as possible to enhance the routing efficiency. Random waypoint model, which is the most commonly used mobility model, is used with different pause time to emulate different node mobility. Metrics are energy consumption, packet delay, packet delivery ratio, routing overhead and energy per bit (EPB) with respect to traffic intensity and the number of nodes. EPB is defined as the energy consumption used to successfully deliver a bit and can be considered a combined metric that shows the performance-energy tradeoff. Simulation based on ns-2 network simulator is the main evaluation technique used in this chapter.

Chapter 7 discusses the construction and operation of a multihop network using Bluetooth devices. Since Bluetooth uses *Frequency Hopping Spread Spectrum* (FHSS) technology, nodes in a communication group, called a *piconet*, must share a common frequency hopping sequence to use a common channel. In order for multiple piconets to communicate among themselves, it is necessary to have a good network-wide scheduler. Bridge nodes, who are the member of more than one piconets, should be able to timeshare between multiple piconets, receiving data from one piconet and forwarding to the other. The challenge is to schedule the presence of the bridge node in its different piconets such that the traffic can flow within and between the groups as efficiently as possible. This chapter overviews Bluetooth technology, introduces the bridge conflict problem that makes the network-wide scheduling hard, and proposes the switch-table based algorithm. As a network model, 17-node star network with five piconets is used. Four CBR traffic is considered. Performance metrics are packet delay and packet drop rate versus cycle length. Cycle length is an important parameter because a large cycle length makes the scheduling easy but incurs longer delay. Other parameters investigated are check interval and queue length. The schedule can be adjusted every check interval and queue length affects the performance particularly the packet drop rate. Simulation is the evaluation technique used in this chapter.

4.3 Part IV: Mobility Models

The key issue in Chapter 8 is mobility. In studying mobile ad hoc networks, synthetic mobility models that represent the behavior of a real mobile scenario plays an important role to evaluate proposed protocols. This chapter first of all summarizes the mobility models proposed and used in ad hoc network research. And the detailed description of its impact on network performance such as link and path bit error rate (BER), link and path stability, network capacity, MAC performance and routing performance has been provided.

Chapter 9 includes an analytical study on node mobility and its effect on path availability and power consumption, both of which are primary concerns in mobile ad hoc networks. Assuming that nodes move randomly and independently, it proves that node-to-node distance follows the *Rician* distribution. On the other hand, power consumption analysis is based on the assumption that the transmit power can be perfectly controlled such that the receive power at the receiver is always constant. With this, both path available time and power consumption are analyzed in terms of initial distance, mean node speed, speed variance and hop count. This chapter also considers the applicability of this analysis in cellular networks where multihoping can be used for communication between a base station and a far away node. With respect to network model, this chapter focuses on node-to-node relationship with a number of intermediate nodes instead of multi-node scenario. Traffic is not considered because the focus is on the end-to-end connectivity at the network layer. Performance metrics are path available time and power consumption as a function of initial node-to-node distance, mean node speed and hop count. Unique to this chapter is to combine the two performance measures to obtain the optimal operation parameters in cellular network environment.

In Chapter 10, node mobility is the main challenge as well as the ingredient in its location-based routing scheme. Assuming that each node has location information of its neighbors and a small number of database nodes, this chapter analytically solves the problem of finding routes that satisfy both the energy-efficiency and QoS constraints. In a large scale ad hoc network, location updates to its neighbors as well as to the database nodes can be costly. In the proposed routing algorithm, each node determines its optimal configuration in terms of location update thresholds that minimize the network-wide overhead. The solution is obtained by solving for location update cost and route discovery cost using the following node mobility and route request model: Random node mobility is assumed, which can be formulated as a *Rayleigh* distribution, and a heavy-tailed distribution is assumed for route request arrivals. Performance metric is routing overhead either in the number of packets or bits-per-second while maintaining high route-discovery success rate. Key parameters are mean-square speed, mean-square route-request interarrival time. Simulation is used to verify the analytical results.

4.4 Part V: End-to-End Performance

Chapter 11 studies broadcast service in mobile ad hoc networks. It is a fundamental service because most of routing algorithms are based on broadcast of their routing control packets. However, it easily overloads the network due to so many unnecessary rebroadcasts, which is known as broadcast storm problem. This chapter presents four efficient broadcast algorithms, the essential idea of which is for a node to rebroadcast to only a subset of its neighbors, called *geometric cover set*, such that the coverage area by the subset coincides that by all its neighbors. Each node comes up with the geometric cover set based on location information of its neighbors. Network model used in this study is a square network area (800×800m) with 40~100 nodes and the number of hop count is limited to five. Performance metrics observed are number of broadcast retransmissions and collision ratio (scalability), broadcast reachability (reliability) and propagation delay (latency) versus the number of nodes. Evaluation methodology is simulation using ns-2 network simulator.

Chapter 12 adopts graph theoretic approach to the issue of routing in ad hoc wireless networks. A key question in this chapter is how to construct an overlay network with a subset of wireless links so that connectivity as well as near-optimal path between any pair of nodes is guaranteed but maintenance and update cost is minimal. Reading this chapter requires familiarity with terminologies in graph theory such as *unit disk graph* (UDG), *relative neighborhood graph* (RNG) and *proximity graph*. It explains how to construct a *spanner* (sparse overlay network) at low cost that guarantees to offer energy-efficient paths. And, it shows the design of spanner-based distributed routing protocols. Two such approaches have been described in this chapter: *Sector-based spanner* (*Yao graph*) and *plannar spanner* (*Pelaunay graph*). The corresponding routing protocols are YaoRoute and SpYaoRoute for sector-based spanner and Face Routing algorithm, Bounded Face Routing algorithm and Adaptive Face Routing algorithm for plannar spanner. Lastly, this chapter introduces *Topological spanners* that aim at keeping the hop distance close to its minimal. Static network model is used with arbitrary set of nodes at arbitrary locations in a 2-dimensional Euclidian space. Traffic model is not considered because connectivity is the primary concern in this chapter. Performance metrics are overlay network size, path optimality, self-stability and routing efficiency.

Chapter 13 addresses network survivability which means continuous support of end-to-end connection in the presence of node/power/link failures in the intermediate system. To quantitatively characterize the survivability, this chapter shows the construction of the finite state machine in the form of *homogeneous continuous-time Markov chain* (CTMC). The CTMC model is solved for the steady-state probability for each state in the model. Then, the probabilities are used to derive steady-state availability of an end-to-end connection as well as failure frequency. Transient analysis is followed in order to account for transient traffic overload upon a communication failure. Network model used in this chapter is a simple ad hoc network with two cells, where two end nodes are located in different cells and a number of intermediate nodes are in the overlapping area between the two cells. System parameters are failure rate for each possible route, node/power/link fault probability, repair rate (switching to a different route), packet arrival rate, link speed, and buffer size. Performance metrics are *excess packet loss due to failures* (ELF) and *excess packet delay due to failures* (EDF). Queueing analysis is the evaluation methodology used in this chapter.

References

[1] IEEE Std 802.11-1999, *Local and Metropolitan Area Network, Part 11: Wireless LAN Medium Access Control and Physical Layer Specifications*, http://standards.ieee.org/getieee802/download/802.11-1999.pdf.
[2] http://NYCwireles.net
[3] http://SeattleWireless.net
[4] Rooftop@Media, http://rooftops.media.mit.edu/
[5] "Google Bids to Help San Francisco Go Wireless," *New York Times*, United States - Sep 30, 2005.

[6] Cheetah Wireless Technologies, Inc. (http://www.cwti.us/), BelAir Networks (http://www.belairnetworks.com/), Firetide (http://www.firetide.com/) and Tropos Networks (http://www.tropos.com/)

[7] IEEE 802.11s ESS Mesh Networks, http://grouper.ieee.org/groups/802/11/

[8] Frodigh, M., Johansson, P., and Larsson, P., "Wireless ad hoc networking – The art of networking without a network," *Ericsson Review*, No. **4**, pp. 248-263, 2000.

[9] Cerpa, A., Elson, J., Estrin, D., Girod, L., Hamilton, M., and Zhao, J. "Habitat Monitoring: Application Driver for Wireless Communications Technology," *The First ACM SIGCOMM Workshop on Data Communications in Latin America and the Caribbean*, December 2000.

[10] Schwiebert, L., Gupta, S. K. S. and Weinmann, J., "Research Challenges in Wireless Networks of Biomedical Sensors," *The seventh annual international conference on Mobile computing and networking* 2001, Pages 151-165.

[11] Yu, C., Shin, K. G. and Lee, B., "Power-Stepped Protocol: Enhancing Spatial Utilization in a Clustered Mobile Ad Hoc Network," *IEEE Journal on Selected Areas in Communications (J-SAC)*, Vol. 22, No. 7, pp. 1322-1334, Sep. 2004.

[12] Pahlavan, K., and Krishnamurthy, P., "Wireless Medium Access Alternatives," Ch. 4, *Principles of Wireless Networks*, Prentice Hall PTR, Upper Saddle River, New Jersey, 2002.

[13] Kleinrock, L., Tabagi, F. A., "Packet Switching in Radio Channels: Part I – Carrier Sense Multiple-Access Models and Their Throughput-Delay Characteristics," *IEEE Tr. Communications*, Vol. COM-23, No. 12, Dec. 1975.

[14] Schiller, J., "Wireless LAN," Ch. 7, Mobile Communications, Addison-Wesley, Harlow, UK, 2000.

[15] Bertsekas, D., and Gallager, R., "Multiaccess Communication," Ch. 4, Data Networks, 2nd Edition, Prentice Hall PTR, Upper Saddle River, New Jersey, 1992.

[16] Weinmiller, J., Woesner, H., Ebert, J.-P., Wolisz, A., "Analyzing and Tuning the Distributed Coordination Function in the IEEE 802.11 DFWMAC Draft Standard," MASCOT'96, 1996.

[17] Pahlavan, K., and Krishnamurthy, P., "Characteristics of Wireless Medium," Ch. 2, Principles of Wireless Networks, Prentice Hall PTR, Upper Saddle River, New Jersey, 2002.

[18] Cali, F., Conti, M., and Gregori, E., "Dynamic Tuning of the IEEE 802.11 Protocol to Achieve a Theoretical Throughput Limit," *IEEE/ACM Tr. Networking*, Vol. 8, No. 6, pp. 785-799, Dec. 2000.

[19] Bruno, R., Conti, M., Gregori, E., "Optimization of Efficiency and Energy Consumption in p-Persistent CSMA-Based Wireless LANs," *IEEE Tr. Mobile Computing*, Vol. 1, No. 1, pp. 10-31, Jan-Mar, 2002.

[20] Kwak, B.-J., Song, N.-O., and Miller, L. E., "Analysis of the Stability and Performance of Exponential Backoff," *IEEE WCNC*, 2003.

[21] Perkins, C., Ad Hoc Networking, Addison-Wesley Pub. Co., 2001.

[22] Li, J. *et al.*, "Capacity of Ad Hoc Wireless Networks," *ACM/IEEE MobiCom'01*, pp. 61-69, 2001.

[23] Xu, S., Saadawi, T., "Does the IEEE 802.11 MAC Protocol Work Well in Multihop Wireless Ad Hoc Networks?," *IEEE Communications Magazine*, pp. 130-137, Jun. 2001.

[24] Khurana, S., Kahol, A., Gupta, S. K. S. and Srimani, P. K., "Performance Evaluation of Distributed Co-Ordination Function for IEEE 802.11 Wireless LAN Protocol in Presence of Mobile and Hidden Terminals," *MASCOT'99*, pp. 40-47, 1999.

[25] Bharghavan, V., Demers, A., Shenker, S., and Zhang, L., "MACAW: A Media Access Protocol for Wireless LANs," *ACM SigComm*, pp. 212-225, 1994.

[26] Deng, J., and Haas, Z. J., "Dual Busy Tone Multiple Access (DBTMA): A New Medium Access Control for Packet Radio Networks," *IEEE ICUPC'98*, Florence, Italy, October 5-9, 1998.

[27] Monks, J. P., Bharaghavan, V., and Hwu, W. W., "A Power Controlled Multiple Access Protocol for Wireless Packet Networks," *IEEE Infocom*, 2001.

[28] Gomez, J., Campbell, A. T., Naghshineh, N., Bisdikian, C., "Conserving Transmission Power in Wireless Ad Hoc Networks," *ICNP'01*, 2001.

[29] Jung, E.-S., and Vaidya, N. H., "A Power Control MAC Protocol for Ad Hoc Networks," *ACM/IEEE MobiCom'02*, 2002.

[30] Nasipuri, A., Ye, S., You, J., Hiromoto, R. E., "A MAC Protocol for Mobile Ad Hoc Networks Using Directional Antennas," *IEEE WCNC*, 2002.

[31] Ko, Y.-B., Shankarkumar, V., Vaidya, N. H., "Medium Access Control Protocols Using Directional Antennas in Ad Hoc Networks," *IEEE Infocom*, 2000.

[32] Wang, Y., and Garcia-Luna-Aceves, J. J., " Spatial Reuse and Collision Avoidance in Ad Hoc Networks with Directional Antennas " *IEEE Globecom*, 2002.

[33] Choudhury, R. R., Yang, X., Ramanathan, R., and Vaidya, N. H., "Using Directional Antennas for Medium Access Control in Ad Hoc Networks," *ACM/IEEE MobiCom*, 2002.

[34] Bao, L., and Garcia-Luna-Aceves, J. J., "Transmission Scheduling in Ad Hoc Networks with Directional Antennas," *ACM/IEEE Mobicom*, 2002.

[35] D. B. Johnson and D. A. Maltz, "Dynamic Source Routing in Ad Hoc Wireless Networks," in *Mobile Computing*, Kluwer 1996, pp. 153–181.

[36] C. E. Perkins and E. Royer, "Ad-hoc On-Demand Distance Vector Routing," *IEEE Workshop on Mobile Computing Systems and Applications*, pp. 90-100, 1999.

[37] C. Perkins, P. Bhagwat, "Highly Dynamic Destination-Sequenced Distance-Vector Routing (DSDV) for Mobile Computers," *Computer Communications Review*, pp. 234-244, 1994.

[38] G. Pei, M. Gerla, T.-W. Chen, "Fisheye State Routing: A Routing Scheme for Ad Hoc Wireless Networks," *Proceedings of IEEE Int'l Conf. on Communications (ICC)*, pp. 70-74, 2000.

[39] M. K. Marina and S. R. Das. Performance of Route Caching Strategies in Dynamic Source Routing. In *Int'l Workshop on Wireless Networks and Mobile Computing (WNMC)*, pages 425–432, 2001.

[40] Y. Hu and D. B. Johnson. Caching Strategies in On-Demand Routing Protocols for Wireless Ad Hoc Networks. In *Proc. ACM MOBICOM*, pages 231–242, 2000.

[41] C. Yu, S.-M. Park, and H.-N. Kim. Every Node is Born Equal: Attacking Preferential Attachment in Peer-to-Peer Mobile Multihop Networks. In *Proc. IEEE PerCom Workshop on Mobile Peer-to-Peer Computing (MP2P'05)*, 2005.

[42] L. Barabasi. *Linked: The New Science of Networks*. Perseus Publishing, Cambridge, Massachusetts, 2002.

[43] T. Camp, J. Boleng, and V. Davies, "A Survey of Mobility Models for Ad Hoc Network Research," Wireless Communications Mobile Computing (WCMC): Special Issues on Mobile Ad Hoc Networking: Research, *Trends, and Application*s, vol. 2, no. 5, pp. 483–502, 2002.

[44] Bar-Noy, I. Kessler, and M. Sidi, "Mobile Users: To Update or Not To Update?" *Wireless Network*s, vol. 1, no. 2, pp. 175–185, 1995.

[45] USC Mobility Generator Tool, http://nile.usc.edu/important/software.htm

[46] Amit Jardosh, Elizabeth M. Belding-Royer, Kevin C. Almeroth, and SubhashSuri, "Towards realistic mobility models for mobile ad hoc networks," *International conference on Mobile computing and networking*, pages 217-229, 2003.

[47] K. Wang and B. Li, "Group Mobility and Partition Prediction in Wireless Ad-Hoc Networks," in *Proc. IEEE IC*C, 2002, pp. 1017–1021.

[48] K. H. Wang and B. Li, "Efficient and Guaranteed Service Coverage in Partitionable Mobile Ad-hoc Networks," in *Proc. IEEE INFOCO*M, 2002, pp. 1089–1098.

[49] Juan, M. Pietro, and S. Miguel, "Evaluating the Impact of Group Mobility on the Performance of Mobile Ad Hoc Networks," in *Proc.IEEE IC*C, 2004, pp. 4039–4043.

[50] Z. Biao, X. Kaixin, and G. Mario, "Group and Swarm Mobility Models for Ad Hoc Network Scenarios Using Virtual Tracks," in *Proc. IEEE Milco*m.

[51] Christian, H. Hannes, and C. Xavier, "Stochastic Properties of the Random Waypoint Mobility Model," *Wireless Network*s, vol. 10, no. 5, pp. 555–567, 2004.

[52] J. Yoon, M. Liu, and B. Noble, "Random Waypoint Considered Harmful," in *Proc. IEEE INFOCO*M, 2003, pp. 1312–1321.

[53] J. Amit, B. Elizabeth, A. Kevin, and S. Subhash, "Towards Realistic Mobility Models for Mobile Ad Hoc Networks," in *Proc. IEEE MOBICO*M, 2003, pp. 217–229.

[54] L. Guolong, N. Guevara, and R. Rajmohan, "Mobility Models for Ad Hoc Network Simulation," in *Proc. IEEE INFOCO*M, 2004, pp. 454–463.

[55] W. Navidi and T. Camp, "Stationary Distributions for the Random Waypoint Mobility Model," *IEEE Trans. on Mobile Computin*g, vol. 3, no. 1, pp. 99–108, 2004.

[56] Bettstetter, G. Resta, and P. Santi, "The Node Distribution of the Random Waypoint Mobility Model for Wireless Ad Hoc Newtorks," *IEEE Trans. on Mobile Computin*g, vol. 2, no. 3, pp. 257–269, 2003.

[57] M. Douglas, R. Giovanni, and S. Paolo, "A Statistical Analysis of the Long-run Node Spatial Distribution in Mobile Ad Hoc Networks," *Wireless Network*s, vol. 10, no. 5, pp. 543–554, 2004.

[58] Bai, N. Sadagopan, and A. Helmy, "The IMPORTANT Framework for Analyzing the Impact of Mobility on Performance of Routing for Ad Hoc Networks," *Ad Hoc Network Journa*l, vol. 4, pp. 383–403, 2003.

[59] M. Royer, P. M. Melliar-Smith, and L. E. Moser, "An Analysis of the Optimum Node Density for Ad Hoc Mobile Networks," in *Proc. IEEE IC*C, 2001, pp. 857–861.

[60] J. Watts and S. H. Strogatz, "Collective dynamics of 'small-world' networks," *Natur*e, no. 393, pp. 440–442, 1998.

[61] R. Sullivan, *One Nation: America Remembers September 11, 200*1. Time Warner Trade Publishing, 2001.

[62] Ingmar, K. Wolfram, S. Rudolf, and G. Martin, "Continuum Percolation of Wireless Ad Hoc Communication Networks," *Statistical Mechanics; Disordered Systems and Neural Networks, Journal-ref: Physica* A, vol. 325, pp. 577–600, 2003.

[63] C. Yu, K. G. Shin, and L. Song, "Link-Layer Salvaging for Making Routing Progress in Mobile Ad Hoc Networks," *The Sixth ACM International Symposium on Mobile Ad Hoc Networking and Computing* (MobiHoc 2005), pp.242-253, 2005.

[64] Xu, K., Gerla, M., and Bae, S. Effectiveness of RTS/CTS handshake in IEEE 802.11 based adhoc networks. *Ad Hoc Network Journal*, **1**(1), July 2003, 107-123.

[65] Ye, F., Yi, S., and Sikdar, B. Improving Spatial reuse of IEEE 802.11 Based Ad Hoc Networks. *IEEE GLOBECOM*, 2003.

[66] Lim, S., Yu, C., Das, C. R., "Topological Properties of Scale-Free Wireless Networks," Technical Report, Pennsylvania State University, 2005.

In: New Topics in Theoretical Computer Science
Editors: Oleg N. Terikhovsky *et al.*, pp. 297-315
ISBN: 978-1-60456-100-5

Chapter 11

IMPACT OF MOBILITY ON THE PERFORMANCE OF MOBILE AD HOC NETWORKS

Qing-An Zeng and Xiaolong Li
Department of ECECS, University of Cincinnati, Cincinnati, Ohio, USA

Abstract

Ad hoc networks are dynamically created and maintained by the individual nodes comprising the networks. They do not require a pre-existing architecture for communication and do not rely on any type of wired infrastructure. Thus, ad hoc networks have great flexibility and low cost of operation, which make them play an important role in future life. In recent years, many research works have been done to design and develop ad hoc networks, such as mobility modeling, MAC and routing protocol design and analysis, etc. The research works on the mobility is one of the most important research works in ad hoc networks. In this chapter, we summarize recent research works of mobility in ad hoc networks. Firstly, we summarize the mobility models used in ad hoc networks. Secondly, the detailed impact of mobility on the link and path BER, link and path stabilities, network capacity, MAC performance, and routing performance are provided. These summaries are very useful for researchers in ad hoc networks for reference.

1 Introduction

In recent years, there have been continuous advances in communication and networks and an ever-increasing demand for mobility of users. These have been fueling the interest in wireless communications. Mobility, installation speed, simplicity, scalability, and less vulnerability to point-of-break problem, make wireless local area networks (WLANs) a good candidate for providing wireless services. Depending on the architecture, the WLANs can be roughly classified into two categories: infrastructure network and infrastructureless network. The infrastructureless network is also called ad hoc network. In an infrastructure network, user communicates directly with access point (AP), which is responsible for controlling all transmissions and forwarding data to the intended user. Ad hoc networks are dynamically created and maintained by the individual nodes comprising the network. They do not require a pre-existing architecture for communication and do not rely on any type of wired infrastructure. In an ad hoc network, all communications occur through wireless medium. Unlike the infrastructure WLANs where there are fixed APs to route messages to and from mobile nodes (MN), ad hoc networks do not require the existence of a centralized message-passing device. Nodes temporarily form a network without the use of any preexisting network infrastructure or centralized administrator and forward/receive packets to/from each other. This adaptive scheme allows a network to be quickly formed even under the most adverse conditions.

Two different architectures exist for an ad hoc network: flat and hierarchical. Flat networks are the simplest because all mobile nodes (MNs) are considered to be equal. Flat networks require each MN to participate in the forwarding and receiving of packets depending on the implemented routing scheme. Hierarchical networks use a tiered approach and consist of two or more tiers. The bottom layer consists of MNs grouped into smaller networks. A single member from each of these groups acts as a gateway to the next higher level. Together, the gateway MNs create the next higher tier. When a MN wants to interact with another MN located in the same group, routing is the same as in a flat ad hoc network. However, if an MN in group A wants to communicate with another MN in group B, more advanced routing techniques incorporating the higher tiers must be implemented. In this chapter, we assume that ad hoc networks are flat networks.

In ad hoc networks, there are many factors such as node mobility, traffic pattern, network topology, radio interference and so on, which affect the performance of mobile ad hoc networks. In this chapter, we summarize recent research on the impact of mobility on the performance of mobile ad hoc networks. The rest of this chapter is organized as follows. Section 2 introduces mobility models used in mobile ad hoc networks. Section 3 presents the impact of mobility on performance in detail. Finally, Section 4 summarizes this chapter.

2 Mobility Models

The nodes in ad hoc networks are mobile and may move from one location to another. However, finding ways to model these movements is not obvious. Since a real movement pattern is difficult to obtain, a common approach is to use synthetic mobility models, which represent the behavior of a real mobile scenario. These mobility models are used to determine whether the proposed protocol will be useful when implemented. Therefore, the mobility models play a very important role while evaluating the performance of mobile ad hoc networks. The mobility model used in mobile ad hoc networks can be roughly divided into two categories: independent and group-based. The independent mobility models are used to describe the mobility of an individual node in which the movement of each node is modeled independently of any other nodes. The group mobility models are used to describe the aggregate pattern of all nodes where there is some relationship among the nodes and their movement.

2.1 Independent Mobility Models

In this subsection, we present several independent mobility models that have been proposed for performance evaluation of ad hoc network protocols.

Fluid flow model

The fluid flow model has been used to model the mobility of vehicles on highways and other similar situations with a constant flow of MNs. It requires a continuous movement without "stop-and-go" interruption.

Random walk model

The simplest mobility model used is known as the random walk mobility model, which is sometimes referred to as Brownian motion model. In this model, a MN moves from its current location to a new location by randomly choosing its moving speed and moving direction. The new moving speed and moving direction are both chosen from pre-determined ranges $[V_{\min}, V_{\max}]$ and $[0, 2\pi)$, respectively. Each movement in this model occurs in either a constant time interval or a constant distance, at the end of which a new moving speed and moving direction are generated.

The random walk model is memoryless since it does not use the past information when generating new moving speed and moving direction. This characteristic can generate sudden stops and sharp turns. Another characteristic of this mobility model is that it will not change the distribution of MNs if the initial distribution of MNs is uniform. Other models, such as the random waypoint model, which will be discussed in the following section, will change the distribution of MNs. In its use the model is sometimes modified. For example, the moving speed in [Mcdo99] is a random variable with mean μ_n and variance σ_n for MN n. MN n changes its moving speed and moving direction after an interval time t, where t is exponentially distributed with rate λ_n.

Random waypoint model

In mobile ad hoc network literature, the random waypoint model is probably the most widely used mobility model. In this model, a MN chooses uniformly a destination in the service area and travels toward the destination with a moving speed chosen uniformly in the range $[V_{\min}, V_{\max}]$. Once the mobile node reaches the destination, it will pause for a specified time period according to some random variable before starting the process again.

Recently, several studies of this model have revealed that the random waypoint model does not lead to a uniform distribution of mobile nodes if the MNs are initially distributed uniformly around the simulation area [Bett03]. It has a border effect which results in fewer nodes around the border. The border effect can be overcame by a boundless mobility model in which a node that reaches one side of the simulation area continues traveling and reappear on the opposite side of the simulation area [Haas97]. A recent study [Lin04] of random waypoint model also found that even though the speed of a mobile node is chosen uniformly at random from a given interval, the speed of a mobile node in steady state is not necessarily from the same distribution.

Gauss-Markov model

The Gauss-Markov mobility model was originally proposed in [Lian99] to adapt to different levels of randomness via one tuning parameter. In this model, an MN is initially assigned a moving speed and moving direction. The value of moving speed V_n and moving direction Θ_n of a MN at the time interval n are updated as follows:

$$V_n = \alpha V_{n-1} + (1-\alpha)\overline{V} + \sqrt{1-\alpha^2}\, X_{n-1} \tag{1}$$

and

$$\Theta_n = \alpha \Theta_{n-1} + (1-\alpha)\overline{\Theta} + \sqrt{1-\alpha^2}\, Y_{n-1}, \tag{2}$$

where α ($0 \leq \alpha \leq 1$) is the tuning parameter used to vary the randomness. $\overline{V}$ and $\overline{\Theta}$ are mean values of moving speed and moving direction when n approaches infinity. X_{n-1} and Y_{n-1} are random variables from Gaussian process with zero mean.

The Gauss-Markov model can eliminate the sudden stops and sharp turns encountered in the random walk mobility model by allowing past moving speeds and moving directions to influence future moving speeds and moving directions. The Gauss-Markov mobility model represents a wide range of mobility models, including the fluid flow model ($\alpha = 1$) and the random walk model ($\alpha = 0$).

Manhattan grid model

In this model, a grid is placed to model the streets. Each MN moves along the paths, changes its moving speed and moving direction with a certain probability at the intersections of grid.

A slight modification to the Manhattan grid model is the shortest path model [Abut97]. In this modified model, each MN will follow the shortest path from current position to the next position, which is chosen uniformly in the simulation area. At each intersection, the MN makes a decision to proceed to any of the neighboring paths such that the shortest distance assumption is maintained. This means that MN can only go straight or make a left or right turn at an intersection. Furthermore, a MN cannot make two consecutive left turns or right turns.

2.2 Group-Based Mobility Models

So far we have presented independent mobility models where MNs are completely independent of each other. However, in many situations such as conference seminar sessions, conventional events, military scenarios, the MNs are often involved in team activities and exhibit collaborative mobility. In order to model such situations, group-based mobility models are needed. Researchers have previously proposed several group-based mobility models [Berg96] [Hong99] for the purpose of simulating ad hoc networks with group-based movements.

Reference point group mobility model (RPGM)

The reference point group mobility (RPGM) model was developed by Hong in [Hong99] to represent the group mobility behavior of MNs. For each mobility group, the model defines a logical reference center whose movement is followed by all nodes within the group. First, the location $RP(t)$ of the group reference center is updated via a group motion vector, $\overrightarrow{GM}$.

Then each individual MN within a group updates its location by adding a random motion vector $\vec{RM}$ to the new reference location $RP(t)$. The vector $\vec{RM}$ has its length uniformly distributed within a certain radius centered at the reference point $RP(t)$ and its direction is uniformly distributed between 0 and 2π. This random vector $\vec{RM}$ is independent from the node's previous location.

The other group-based mobility models, such as column mobility model, nomadic community mobility model, and pursue mobility model, can be implemented as special cases of the RPGM model [Sanc05].

2.3 Other Mobility Parameters

While irrelevant to all mobility models, there are other factors that relate to the simulation of node mobility. Various parameters relating to the simulation area where nodes are moving may influence mobility. By applying constraints to the paths that nodes may follow, the simulation and analysis may be radically affected. For example, the obstacle mobility model in [Jard03] limits the nodes' movement due to the objects such as buildings and other structures.

Another consideration that affects the mobility model is the border of simulation area. In the real world, there may be no effective border effect or stay within a very big area (city, campus, etc.). However, in the synthetic model, the border effect has a significant impact on node distribution, such as can be seen in random waypoint model.

3 Impact of Mobility on the Performance of Mobile Ad Hoc Networks

In this section, we illustrate the impact of mobility on the performance of mobile ad hoc networks. The results presented show the importance of an appropriate mobility model for the performance evaluation of a given ad hoc network protocol.

The mobility of MNs causes frequent changes of network topology, which creates many challenging issues. Traditionally, research work has been centered on network connectivity, node distribution, and link and path availabilities. The impact of mobility on medium access control (MAC) protocols and routing protocols has also been studied. Lately, there is also some work on determining the statistical characteristic of link and path durations. The effect of mobility on network capacity and security are discussed recently. In this section, we summarized the past work in these areas.

3.1 Impact of Mobility on Link/Path BER

When researchers talk about the factors, which affect the bit error rate (BER) in wireless communications, they usually consider fading, signal to noise ratio (SNR), terrain conditions, etc. However, the mobility of nodes is also one of the most important factors that cause packet error. Due to node mobility during a packet transmission, the distance between the source and the destination nodes of a link changes and this results in a change in the SNR and hence the link BER. The end-to-end BER on a multi-hop route depends on the individual link BER. In [Ferr04], the authors proposed a simple approach to evaluate the impact of mobility on the BER performance of multi-hop ad hoc networks.

In a fixed ad hoc network, where M nodes are uniformly distributed at the vertices of a square grid in a circular area A and a multi-hop route is constituted by a sequence of minimum length hops, the BER of an average multi-hop route can be obtained as

$$\overline{BER} \approx 1-(1-P_L)^{\lfloor \sqrt{N/\pi} \rfloor}, \tag{3}$$

where $\lfloor \sqrt{N/\pi} \rfloor$ is the integer number of hops in an average multi-hop route and P_L is the BER of a link. The value of link BER depends on the SIR, modulation scheme, inter-node interference (INI). For example, assuming BPSK modulation, AWGN wireless channel with free-space loss, the BER of a link is

$$P_L = Q\left(\sqrt{2SNR}\right) = Q\left(\sqrt{\frac{2\beta P_t / d^2}{FkT_0 R_b + P_{INI}}}\right), \tag{4}$$

where β is Friis constant and is equal to $G_T G_R (c/4\pi f_c)^2$ [Rapp02]. G_T and G_R are the transmitter and receiver antenna gains; f_c is the center frequency of carrier; c is the speed of light; P_t is the transmission power (W); d is the distance between the transmitter and receiver; F is the noise figure, $k = 1.38 \times 10^{-23}\, Joule/K$ is the Boltzmann constant, T_0 is the noise temperature (K), and R_b is data rate. P_{INI} is the interference power and depends on the MAC protocol.

With node mobility, the distance d of a link changes during a packet transmission period. Figure 1 shows a simple scenario where the source N_s and destination N_d have constant moving speed and moving direction, indicated as (V_s, θ_s) and (V_d, θ_d) during the packet transmission period. In order to obtain the average performance analysis, the average link length is needed. To simplify the analysis, the authors assume that the inter-node distance d is uniformly distributed between $d_{original}$ and d_{new}. Therefore, the average link length $\overline{d}$ is

$$\overline{d} = \frac{d_{origina} + d_{new}}{2}. \tag{5}$$

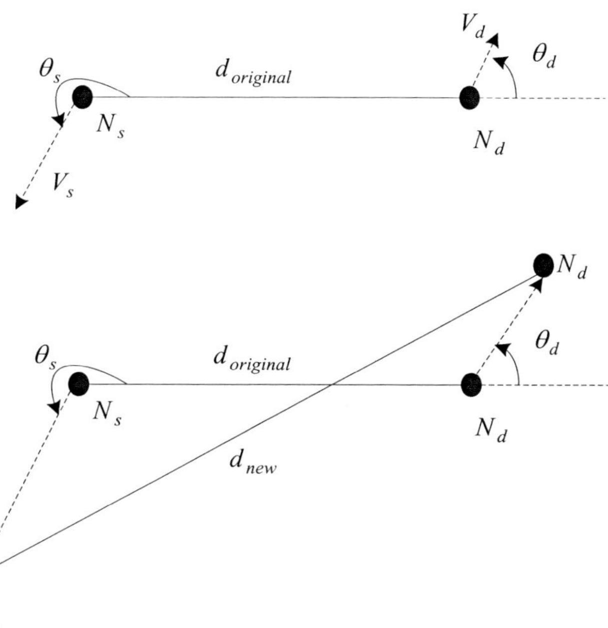

Figure 1. Distance evolution during a packet transmission

Substituting d with $\bar{d}$ in Equation (4), the average link BER during the transmission of a packet can be obtained. With this link BER, the BER of an average multi-hop route considering node mobility can be obtained by Equation (3). This model can be extended to include other mobility models, such as random walk-based model. [Mcdo99] proved that the distance d is approximately Rayleigh distributed. Thus the average distance $\bar{d}$ can be easily obtained with this Rayleigh distribution.

3.2 Impact of Mobility on Link/Path Stability

Communications between any two MNs in an ad hoc network requires routing over either single-hop (when these two MNs are neighbors) or multi-hop wireless paths. These wireless paths consist of wireless links whose endpoints (or MNs) are likely to be moving independently of one another. Consequently, the mobility of MNs creates the frequent failure and activation of wireless links. Several papers have discussed the link/path stability, which includes the link/path availability, average link/path durations, link/path breaking probability, etc. [Li04] [Sada03] [Mcdo99].

The link availability is defined as the probability that a link between two MNs exists at time t_0+t in case the link existed at the starting time t_0. Note that a link is considered to be available at time t_0+t even if the link may be torn down during one or more intervals (t_i,t_j); $t_0<t_i<t_j<t_0+t$. In [Mcdo99], the authors defined a random walk-based mobility model and got a close-form for the link availability. In this mobility model, let $<\lambda_n,\mu_n,\sigma_n>$

and $< \lambda_m, \mu_m, \sigma_m >$ be parameters of nodes n and m, respectively. Assuming that a link exists between nodes n and m at time t_0 and node m is located exactly at a uniform random point R from n, the link availability distribution ca be given according to the following expression.

$$A_{m,n}(t) = \frac{1}{2}\left(1 - I_0\left(\frac{-2R^2}{\gamma_{m,n}}\right)\exp\left(\frac{-2R^2}{\gamma_{m,n}}\right)\right), \tag{6}$$

where I_0 is a modified Bessel function of the first kind, and $\gamma_{m,n}$ is given by

$$\gamma_{m,n} = 2t\left(\frac{\sigma_m^2 + \mu_m^2}{\lambda_m} + \frac{\sigma_n^2 + \mu_n^2}{\lambda_n}\right) \tag{7}$$

The concept of link availability can be extended to an entire path. The path availability is defined as the probability that all links of a path are available at time $t_0 + t$ given that all links were available at time t_0. The path availability cannot easily be obtained since the consecutive links are not independent of each other. This is because they share a common MN. In order to simplify the study, we make an assumption that the links are independent of one another, which has been proved to be reasonable in [Yu03] [Sada03]. With this assumption, the availability of a path k is given by the following probability expression:

$$A_{m,n}^k = \prod_{(i,j)\in k} A_{i,j}(t). \tag{8}$$

Although the link/path availability can provide a metric for routing algorithm to favor more stable path, it does not ensure that the link always exists between the time t_0 and $t_0 + t$. In [Li04] [Sada03], the link and path durations are computed to better describe the link stability. For a given pair of MNs, the link duration is defined as the time during which the two MNs are within the radio transmission range of each other. The path duration is defined as the length of time that elapses from the moment the path is established until the time when one of the links along the path is torn down. A number of studies of link/path durations have shown that the distributions of link/path durations can be accurately approximated by exponential distributions, which are parameterized by the relative moving speed of MNs, radio transmission range, and the number of links in a path. In [Li04], close-forms have been presented to obtain the average link duration $1/\lambda_l$ and average path duration $1/\lambda_p$.

$$\frac{1}{\lambda_l} = \frac{\pi A}{E[V]L}, \tag{9}$$

and

$$\frac{1}{\lambda_p} = \frac{1}{k\lambda_l}, \tag{10}$$

where $E[V]$ is used to represent the average value of relative moving speed; the relative moving speed can be obtained by assuming that one MN is stationary while the other moves with a relative speed; A is the area of the radio transmission range and L is the perimeter of the area; k is the number of links in a path. Here, we show how to obtain the relative moving speed following the simple example in Figure 1 where the source N_s and destination N_d have constant moving speed and moving direction, indicated as $(V_s,\ \theta_s)$ and $(V_d,\ \theta_d)$. The moving speeds are random variables with a probability density function (pdf) $f_V(v)$ in the interval $[V_{\min},\ V_{\max}]$. The moving directions are chosen at random with a pdf $f_\Theta(\theta)$ in the interval $[0,\ 2\pi)$. The relative moving speed between N_s and N_d is

$$V = \sqrt{V_s^2 + V_d^2 - 2V_sV_d\cos(\theta_s - \theta_d)}\,. \tag{11}$$

The mean value of V is given by

$$E[V] = \int_{V_{\min}}^{V_{\max}}\int_{V_{\min}}^{V_{\max}}\int_0^{2\pi}\int_0^{2\pi}\sqrt{v_s^2 + v_d^2 - 2v_sv_d\cos(\theta_s - \theta_d)}\,f_{V_s,V_d,\Theta_s,\Theta_d}(v_s, v_d, \theta_s, \theta_d)d\theta_s d\theta_d dv_s dv_d\,, \tag{12}$$

where $f_{V_s,V_d,\Theta_s,\Theta_d}(v_s, v_d, \theta_s, \theta_d)$ is the joint pdf of the random variables V_s, θ_s, V_d, and θ_d. Since the moving speeds V_s and V_d and moving directions θ_s and θ_d are independent, Equation (12) can be simplified as

$$E[V] = \frac{1}{\pi^2}\int_{V_{\min}}^{V_{\max}}\int_{V_{\min}}^{V_{\max}}(v_s + v_d)F_e\left(\frac{2\sqrt{v_sv_d}}{v_s + v_d}\right)f_V(v_s)f_V(v_d)dv_s dv_d\,, \tag{13}$$

where $F_e(k) = \int_0^1\sqrt{\frac{1-k^2t^2}{1-t^2}}dt$ is a complete elliptic integral of the second kind.

Therefore, in the analysis, we can consider that source N_s is at rest, while the destination N_d is moving at a relative moving speed instead of the two nodes moving with their respective speed.

As one can see from the above results, the link availability and link duration only need to consider the mobility models and the radio transmission range. However, only the link availability and link duration are not enough to describe the link stability. In fact, routing protocol, MAC protocol and traffic characteristics affect the link stability too. The link breaking probability is an important statistical parameter to evaluate the link stability. The link breaking probability is defined as the ratio of the number of unsuccessful transmissions due to mobility to the total number of transmissions. The boundary crossing due to mobility while the virtual packet transmission is still in progress breaks the link. The virtual packet transmission time is defined as the time period from a packet generation to its successful transmission. Thus, the link breaking probability p_{lb} equals to the probability that the link duration T_d is less than the virtual packet transmission time T_v. Thus, we have

$$p_{lb} = \Pr\{T_d < T_v\}. \tag{14}$$

Since T_d and T_v are independent, we have

$$p_{lb} = \int_0^\infty \int_0^t f_{T_v}(t) f_{T_d}(u) du dt, \tag{15}$$

where $f_{T_v}(t)$ and $f_{T_d}(u)$ are the pdfs of virtual packet transmission time and link duration, respectively. As described above, the distribution of link duration can be approximated as an exponential distribution. Given the distribution of virtual packet transmission time, the link breaking probability can be easily obtained.

3.3 Impact of Mobility on Network Capacity

Concurrent wireless transmissions in an ad hoc network limit its throughput capacity, because they create mutual interference. In fact, Gupta and Kumar [Gupt00] have recently analyzed this capacity in an analytical model of fixed ad-hoc networks, where nodes are randomly located but are immobile. Each source node has a random destination to which it wants to communicate. Their main result shows that as the number of nodes M per unit area increases, the throughput per node decreases approximately by $1/\sqrt{M}$. This pessimistic result suggests that ad hoc networks with high node density are impractical.

On the other hand, wireless data services are expected to grow quickly over the next few years. Some of these services, such as electronic mail, paging, or database synchronization, possess very loose delay constraints (on the order of minutes to hours). In [Gros02], the authors show that such delay-tolerant applications can exploit node mobility to increase capacity through a new type of multiuser diversity. The strategy used in this paper is for each source node to distribute its packets to as many different nodes as possible. These nodes then serve as mobile relay nodes and whenever they get close to the final destination, they hand the packets off to the final destination. Using this strategy, this paper shows that the average long-term throughput per node can be kept constant even as the number of nodes M increases. This is in sharp contrast to the fixed network scenario, and the dramatic performance improvement is obtained by the exploitation of the time-variation of the users' channels due to mobility. However, the packets are temporarily buffered in the relay nodes until they are finally delivered to the final destination. Therefore, the delay experienced by the packet under this strategy was shown to be very large. This triggers some recent work [Mora04] [Neel04] to obtain the tradeoffs between capacity and delay. In [Mora04], the authors modified the strategy in [Gros02] by giving more than one copy of the packets from the source node to multiple nodes that are within the radio transmission range and are potential receivers. With this method, the delay of a packet can be decreased. After delivery, the destination node uses a side channel to broadcast a packet to notify its successful reception of this packet. Other nodes with the copy of this packet will drop it off when they receive this broadcast packet. In [Bans03], it is shown that for a network with mixture of stationary users and mobile relay nodes, delay can be decreased by exploiting velocity information and relaying packets to nodes moving in the direction of its destination.

3.4 Impact of Mobility on MAC Performance

In mobile ad hoc networks, the medium access control (MAC) protocol is the main element that determines the efficiency in sharing the limited communication bandwidth of the wireless channel. In the literature, researchers have proposed many MAC protocols to better support various applications. Among these protocols, the IEEE 802.11 has become the most widely used MAC protocol due to its compatibility with the IEEE 802 protocol suite. The IEEE 802.11 MAC protocol has two access methods: distributed coordination function (DCF) for asynchronous, contention-based, distributed access to the channel and point coordination function (PCF) for centralized, contention-free accesses. The IEEE 802.11 can operate both in DCF mode and PCF mode. Every IEEE 802.11 user should implement DCF mode, which is based on the carrier sense multiple access with collision avoidance (CSMA/CA) protocol. Unlike the DCF, the implementation of PCF is not mandatory in the standard. Much research work has been done to analyze the efficiency of the IEEE 802.11 MAC protocol. In this section, we summarize our research work on the performance analysis of CSMA/CA in stationary ad hoc networks and extend our work to include the impact of mobility.

In a fixed ad hoc network, a finite number M of nodes are uniformly distributed in a circular area with unit radius. The wireless channel in this network is assumed to be ideal, i.e., no fading. The time is slotted with a slot size α and the packets are allowed to transmit only at the beginning of a time slot. All packets are assumed to have the same length T_p. To simplify the analysis, we normalize the time by the packet length T_p. That is, the duration of the packet transmission time equals to unit time and is composed of $1/\alpha$ slots. The propagation delay among all nodes is assumed to be the same and equals to a time slot. At the end of each time slot, every node will be in either thinking state or backlogged state. In the thinking state, each node generates a new packet with probability g during a slot. If the transmission is successful, the node stays in the thinking state. A node is said to be in the backlogged state if its transmission is unsuccessful. No new packets are generated in the backlogged state. A backlogged terminal remains in the backlogged state unless it completes a successful transmission, at that time it switches to the thinking state. If we assume that the total traffic arrival process G is a Poisson process and g denotes a packet arrival process during a time slot, we have $Mg = G\alpha$ [Kim99]. Note that G equals to the number of total packets in the system during a normalized unit time period, while g equals to the number of packets of a node during a time slot.

We use the linear feedback model introduced by Tobagi and Kleinrock [Toba77] to compute the throughput for a finite number of nodes in a slotted CSMA/CA system. We assume that the channel state consists of a sequence of regeneration cycles composed of average idle period $\overline{I}$ and average busy period $\overline{B}$. Let $\overline{A}$ be the average time spent in useful transmission during a regeneration cycle. The throughput S is defined as the fraction of channel time occupied by a valid transmission and can be obtained by

$$S = \frac{\overline{A}}{\overline{B} + \overline{I}} \tag{16}$$

Let $X(t)$ be the number of nodes in the backlogged state. The random process $\{X(t) = i\}$ can be modeled by a homogeneous embedded Markov chain identified by the last slot of each idle period (see Figure 2). Since there are M nodes in the system, $X(t)$ can be 0, 1, 2,..., M. Thus the embedded Markov chain for $X(t)$ has $M + 1$ states as shown in Figure 3 where $P_{i,j}$ ($0 \le i \le M$, $0 \le j \le M$) is the probability of transition from state i to state j. Transition from state i to state j ($i \le j$) means that there are some thinking nodes entering the backlogged state. Similarly, transition from state $i+1$ to state i represents a successful packet transmission. It is assumed that each backlogged node has the same steady-state probability v_i to send a packet at the time slot t when $X(t)$ equals to i. It is also assumed that the acknowledgments are received perfectly. In order to determine the probability v_i, we need to know the collision probability. In [Tay01], an analytical model is developed to compute the collision probability $p_c(i)$ when $X(t)$ equals to i, which is given as

$$p_c(i) = 1 - \left\{1 - \frac{2[1 - 2p_c(i)]}{1 - p_c(i) - p_c(i)[2p_c(i)]^m} \frac{1}{W}\right\}^{i-1}, \quad i > 1, \tag{17}$$

where W is the minimum contention window and m is to determine the maximum contention window $W_{\max}$ and it satisfies $W_{\max} = 2^m W$. Note that the collision probability $p_c(i)$ is the probability that more than one backlogged nodes transmit at the same time slot. This yields to

$$p_c(i) = 1 - (1 - v_i)^{i-1}. \tag{18}$$

Then we can obtain the probability v_i ($i > 1$) from Equations (17) and (18). Obviously, $v_0 = 0$ and $v_1 = 1/W$.

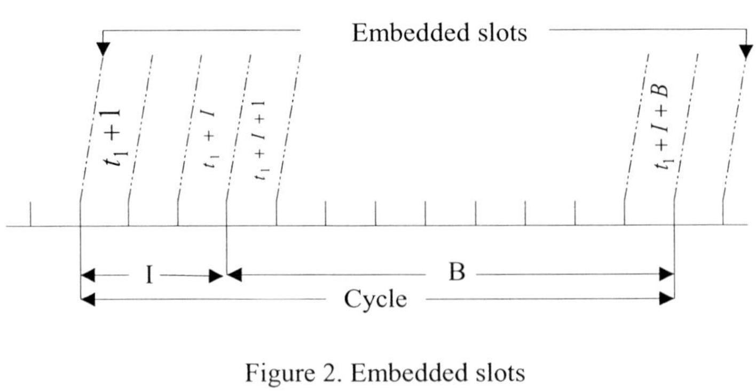

Figure 2. Embedded slots

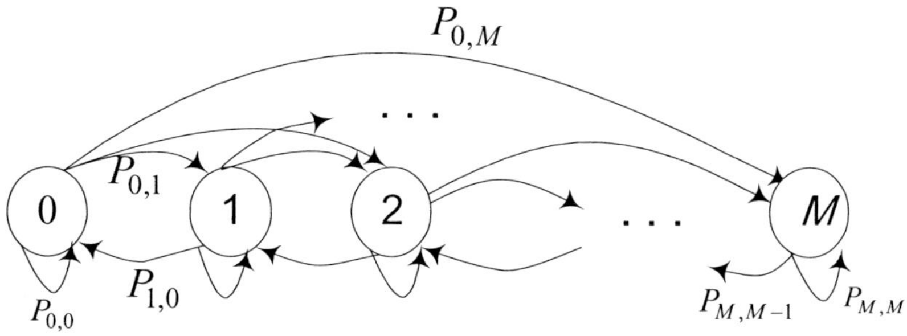

Figure 3. State transition diagram

Our goal is to obtain the stationary distribution of the Markov chain $\pi_i = \lim_{t\to\infty} \Pr\{x(t)=i\}$. For this purpose, we need to find the transition probability matrix *P*. Using the linear feedback model introduced in [Toba77], *P* is the product of several single slot transition matrices which we will define next. We denote the transition matrix by *R* for slot $t_1 + I$ and *Q* for all remaining slots of the busy period. Since the length of the busy period depends on the number of nodes, which become ready in time slot $t_1 + I$, we have *R*=*U*+*F*, where the (i,k)th element of *U* and *F* are defined as

$$u_{ik} = \Pr[x(t_1 + I + 1) = k \quad and \quad transmission \quad is \quad successful \mid x(t_1 + I)] = i \, . \tag{19}$$

and

$$f_{ik} = \Pr[x(t_1 + I + 1) = k \quad and \quad transmission \quad is \quad unsuccessful \mid x(t_1 + I)] = i \, . \tag{20}$$

Note that *U* means that there is only one node ready to transmit in time slot $t_1 + I$. *F* means that there are more than one node ready to transmit in the time slot $t_1 + I$. *Q* reflects the addition to the backlogged states from the $M - x(t)$ thinking nodes in any time slot t during a busy period. As we can see, if the transmission is successful, the busy period has length T; if it is unsuccessful, the busy period is C. The values of T and C depend on the MAC access methods. Such as, for basic CSMA/CA

$$\begin{cases} T = DIFS + T_p + SIFS + ACK + 2\alpha, \\ \quad C = DIFS + T_p + SIFS + \alpha. \end{cases} \tag{21}$$

and for CSMA/CA with RTS/CTS

$$\begin{cases} T = DIFS + RTS + CTS + T_p + 3SIFS + ACK + 4\alpha, \\ \qquad C = DIFS + RTS + \alpha. \end{cases} \tag{22}$$

According to [Toba77], the transmission matrix *P* is expressed as

$$P = UQ^{\mathrm{T}}J + FQ^{\mathrm{C}}, \tag{23}$$

where J represents the fact that a successful transmission decreases the number of backlogged nodes by 1 and the elements of matrices Q, J, U, and F are given by

$$q_{ik} = \begin{cases} 0, & k < i \\ \binom{M-i}{k-i}(1-g)^{M-k} g^{k-i}, & k \geq i+1 \end{cases} \tag{24}$$

$$j_{ik} = \begin{cases} 1, & k = i-1, \\ 0, & otherwise, \end{cases} \tag{25}$$

$$u_{ik} = \begin{cases} 0, & for \quad k < i, \\ \dfrac{(1-g)^{M-i}\left[i\nu_i(1-\nu_i)^{i-1}\right]}{1-(1-\nu_i)(1-g)^{M-i}}, & for \quad k = i, \\ \dfrac{(M-i)g(1-g)^{M-i-1}(1-\nu_i)^i}{1-(1-\nu_i)(1-g)^{M-i}}, & for \quad k = i+1, \\ 0, & for \quad k > i+1, \end{cases} \tag{26}$$

and

$$f_{ik} = \begin{cases} 0, & for \quad k < i, \\ \dfrac{(1-g)^{M-i}\left[1-(1-\nu_i)^i - i\nu_i(1-\nu_i)^{i-1}\right]}{1-(1-\nu_i)^i(1-g)^{M-i}}, & for \quad k = i, \\ \dfrac{(M-i)g(1-g)^{M-i-1}\left[1-(1-\nu_i)^i\right]}{1-(1-\nu_i)^i(1-g)^{M-i}}, & for \quad k = i+1, \\ \dfrac{\binom{M-i}{k-i}(1-g)^{M-k} g^{k-i}}{1-(1-\nu_i)^i(1-g)^{M-i}}, & for \quad k > i+1, \end{cases} \tag{27}$$

The steady-state probabilities of the Markov process are defined as a row vector $\pi = [\pi_1, \pi_2, ..., \pi_M]$, which can be determined by $\pi = \pi P$.

Since the idle period is geometrically distributed, its expectation is given by

$$\overline{I_i} = \frac{1}{1-(1-\nu_i)^i(1-g)^{M-i}}. \tag{28}$$

Let $p_s(i)$ be the probability of a successful transmission during a cycle when i nodes are in backlogged state. During this cycle, a transmission will be successful if and only if one of i backlogged nodes transmits or one of the $M-i$ thinking nodes transmits. Therefore, $p_s(i)$ can be obtained by

$$p_s(i) = \frac{(M-i)g(1-g)^{M-i-1}(1-v_i)^i + i v_i (1-v_i)^{i-1}(1-g)^{M-i}}{1-(1-v_i)^i(1-g)^{m-i}}. \tag{29}$$

Therefore, we have

$$S = \frac{\sum_{i=0}^{M} \pi_i p_s(i) T_p}{\sum_{i=0}^{M} \pi_i \left\{\overline{I_i} + 1 + p_s(i)T + [1-p_s(i)]C\right\}}. \tag{30}$$

With node mobility, the transmission fails if the link breaks before the transmission is completed. The link breaking probability can be obtained using Equation (15). In order to obtain the link breaking probability, we need to know the distributions of link duration and packet transmission time. As described above, the distribution of link duration can be obtained given the mobility model and radio transmission range. However, the exact distribution of virtual packet transmission is hard to obtain since it depends on the MAC protocol. The collision and exponential backoff make it harder to find the distribution of virtual packet transmission. In order to simplify the analysis, we assume that the virtual packet transmission time follows an exponential distribution with rate λ_v. Therefore, the link breaking probability is given by

$$p_{lb} = \frac{\lambda_l}{\lambda_l + \lambda_v}. \tag{31}$$

When nodes are mobile, performance degradation can be either due to packet collisions or link breaking. For this case, we only need to modify the above Equations (26), (27), and (29) to count to the factor of link breaking.

3.5 Impact of Mobility on Routing Performance

Routing is one of the most important issues in mobile ad hoc networks. The routing protocols for ad hoc networks can be divided into two categories based on how and when the route discovery process is being used: proactive (table-driven) and reactive (on-demand). In proactive routing protocols, consistent and up-to-date routing information is maintained at each node, whereas in reactive routing, the routes are created only when needed. Dynamic source routing (DSR) [John95], signal stability-based adaptive routing (SSA) [Dube97], ad hoc on-demand distance vector routing (AODV) [Perk00], and temporally ordered routing algorithm (TORA) [Park98] are reactive protocol and Destination Sequence Distance Vector Protocol (DSDV) [Perk94] is an example of a proactive routing protocol. Recently, a hybrid of proactive and reactive protocols, called the zone routing protocol (ZRP) [Hass98], has also been proposed.

Generally, a routing protocol needs to address three issues: route discovery, data forwarding, and route maintenance. When a source wants to deliver data to a destination, it has to find a route first. Then data packets can be delivered. The topology may change due to node mobility. This may deteriorate or even disconnect an existing route while data packets are being transmitted. The route maintenance takes responsibility of detecting broken links and repairing the corresponding routes. Recently, many researchers have done a lot of experiments to compare the routing performance with different mobility models. Using performance metrics packet delivery ratio and routing overhead, [Broc98] found that reactive protocols performed better than proactive protocols at high mobility rates, while proactive protocols performed quite well at low mobility. [Das00] performed a comparison study of two reactive protocols: DSR and AODV, using the packet delivery ratio and end-to-end delay metrics. They found that DSR outperforms AODV in light traffic, while AODV outperforms DSR at heavy traffic. The above results were obtained using the random waypoint mobility model. The authors in [Bai03] evaluated the performance of DSR, AODV and DSDV across RPGM, random waypoint, freeway and Manhattan mobility models. It was observed that DSR, DSDV, and AODV achieve a higher throughput and lower overhead for RPGM than for random waypoint model. At the same time, all protocols had a higher throughput and lower overhead for random waypoint model than for the freeway and Manhattan models. The reason behind these phenomena is that RPGM has the highest link duration, which results in the highest throughput and lowest overhead. This reason can be explained as follows: for a given mobility model, if nodes have a high degree of spatial dependence, an existing link is expected to remain stable for a longer period of time as the nodes are likely move together. Therefore, fewer packets will be dropped because of link breaking, which leads to higher throughput. At the same time, lower link breaking will cause lower overhead as little effort is needed to repair the seldom broken link.

4 Summary

In this chapter, we summarize the mobility models used in mobile ad hoc networks. The main focus is on the analysis of mobility models, the impact of mobility models on the BER, link stability, MAC and routing protocols. These help researchers to obtain an in depth understanding of the mobility models and realize their importance in the research of mobile ad hoc networks.

Most of the mobility models proposed so far are not realistic enough for performance analysis. More realistic models that can flexibly reflect different real world scenarios are needed. Furthermore, most of the proposed mobility models are independent mobility models where nodes move independently. The research on group mobility model is insufficient. More research on this area is desired.

References

[Abut97] A. Abutaleb and V. O. K. Li, "Location update optimization in personal communication systems," *Wireless Networks*, **3**, pp. 195-204, 1997.

[Bai03] F. Bai, N. Sadagopan, and A. Helmy, "IMPORTANT: A framework to systematically analyze the impact of mobility on performance of routing protocols for ad hoc networks," *The 22nd Annual Joint Conference of the IEEE Computer and Communication Societies*, March/April, 2003.

[Berg96] M. Bergamo, Hain R, K. Kasera, D. Li, R. Ramanathan, and M. Steenstrup, "System design specification for mobile multimedia wireless network (draft)," *Tech. Rep.*, DARPA project DAAB07-95-C-D156, October 1996.

[Bian00] G. Bianchi. 2000. "Performance Analysis of the IEEE 802.11 Distributed Coordination Function." *IEEE Journal on Selected Areas in Communications*, Vol. 18, pp. 535-547, 2000.

[Bett03] C. Bettstetter, G. Resta, and P. Santi, "The node distribution of the random waypoint mobility model for wireless ad hoc networks," *IEEE Transactions on mobile computing*, Vol. 2, NO. 3, pp. 257- 268, July-September 2003.

[Broc98] J. Broch, D. A. Maltz, D. B. Johnson, Y.-C. Hu, and J. Jetcheva, "A performance comparison of multi-hop wireless ad hoc network routing protocols," *In proceedings of the fourth annual ACM/IEEE international conference on mobile computing and networking*, ACM, October 1998.

[Chen03] Y. Chen, Q-A. Zeng, and D. P. Agrawal, "Performance of MAC Protocol in Ad Hoc Networks," *Proceedings of the Communication Networks and Distributed Systems Modeling and Simulation Conference (CNDS'03)*, Orlando, Florida, January 2003.

[Das00] S. R. Das, C. E. Perkins, and E. M. Royer, "Performance comparison of two on-demand routing protocols for ad hoc networks," *The 19th Annual Joint Conference of the IEEE Computer and Communication Societies*, March 2000.

[Dube97] R. Dube, C. D. Rais, K. Wang, and S. K. Tripathi, "Signal stability based adaptive routing (SSA) for ad hoc mobile networks," *IEEE Personal Communication*, Feb. 1997.

[Ferr04] G. Ferrari, O. K. Tonguz, S. Panichpapiboon, N. Wisitpongphan, and R. Chokshi, "Impact of mobility on the BER performance of multi-hop ad hoc wireless networks," *In Proceedings of Global Telecommunications of Conference (GLOBECOM'04)*, Vol. 2, pp. 882-886, 29 November – 2 December 2004.

[Gross02] M. Grossglauser and D. Tse, "Mobility increase the capacity of ad hoc wireless networks," *IEEE/ACM Transactions on Networking*, Vol. 10, No. 4, pp. 477-486, August 2002.

[Gupt00] P. Gupta and P. R. Kumar, "The capacity of wireless networks," *IEEE Transactions on Information Theory,* Vol. 46, No. 2, pp. 388-404, March 2000.

[Han04] Y. Han, R. J. La, and E. H. Abed, *Distribution of Path Durations in Mobile Ad Hoc Networks - Palm's Theorem at Work*, 16th ITC Specialist Seminar, Belgium, 2004.

[Hass97] Z. Hass, "A new routing protocol for reconfigurable wireless networks," *In proceedings of the IEEE International conference on universal personal communications (icupc)*, PP. 562-565, October 1997.

[Hass98] Z. Hass and M. Pearlman, "The performance of query control schemes for the zone routing protocol," in *ACM SIGCOMM*, 1998.

[Hong99] X. Hong, M. Gerla, G. Pei, and C. Chiang, "A group mobility model for ad hoc wireless networks," *In Proceedings of the 2nd ACM international workshop on modeling and simulation of wireless and mobile systems*, 1999.

[Jard03] A. Jardosh, E. M. Belding-Royer, K. C. Almeroth, and S. Suri, "Towards Realistic Mobility Models for Mobile Ad hoc Networks," *MobiCom'03*, September 2003.

[John95] D. B. Johnson and D. Maltz, "Dynamic source routing in ad hoc wireless networks," In *mobile computing*, edited by Tomasz Imielinski and Hank Korth, Kluwer Academic Publishers, 1995.

[Kim99] J. H. Kim and J. K. Lee, Throughput and Packet Delay Analysis of IEEE 802.11 MAC Protocol for Wireless LAN's, *Wireless Personal Communications*, Kluwer academic publishers, Vol. 11, No. 2, 1999.

[Li04] X. Li and Q-A. Zeng, "Modeling and analysis of link stability in mobile ad hoc networks," *ICWN04*, 2004.

[Li042] X. Li, D. P. Agrawal, and Q-A. Zeng, "Impact of mobility on the performance of wireless mobile ad hoc networks," *Proceedings of the 3rd IEEE Annual Wireless Telecommunications Symposium (WTS 2004)*, May 2004.

[Lian99] B. Liang and Z. Hass, "Predictive distance-based mobility management for PCS networks," *In Proceedings of the joint conference of the IEEE computer and communications societies (INFOCOM)*, March 1999.

[Lin04] G. Lin, G. Noubir, and R. Rajaraman, "Mobility models for ad hoc network simulation", *In proceedings of twenty-third annual joint conference of the IEEE computer and communication societies*, VOL. 1, pp. 454-463, March 2004.

[Mcdo99] A. B. McDonald and T. F. Znati, "A mobility-based framework for adaptive clustering in wireless ad hoc networks," *IEEE journal on selected areas in communications*, Vol. 17, NO. 8, August 1999.

[Mora04] R. Moraes, H. Sadjadpour, and J. J. Garcia-Luna-Aceves, "Reducing delay while maintaining capacity in mobile ad hoc networks using multiple random routes," *Asilomar Conference on Signals, Systems, and Computers*, Pacific Grove, CA, November 2004.

[Neel04] M. J. Neely and E. Modiano, "Capacity and delay tradeoffs for mobile ad hoc networks," *IEEE BroadNets 2004*, San Jose, CA, October, 2004.

[Park98] V. D. Park and M. S. Corson, "Temporally-ordered routing algorithm (TORA) version 1: Functional specification, internet-draft, draft-ietf-manet-tora-spec-01.txt," August 1998.

[Perk94] C. E. Perkins and P. Bhagwat, "Highly dynamic destination sequenced distance vector routing (DSDV) for mobile computers," in *ACM SIGCOMM*, pp. 234-244, 1994.

[Perk00] C. Perkins, "Ad hoc on demand distance vector (AODV) routing, internet draft, draft-ietf-manet-aodv-00.txt."

[Rapp02] T. S. Rappaport, *Wireless Communications: Principles & Practice*. Prentice Hall, second edition, 2002.

[Sanc05] M. Sanchez. Mobility models, http://www.disca.upv.es/misan/mobmodel.htm. Page accessed on April 13th, 2005.

[Sada03] N. Sadagopan, F. Bai, B. Krishnamachari, and A. Helmy, "PATHS: Analysis of PATH duration statistics and their impact on reactive MANET routing protocols," *MobiHoc03*, June 2003.

[Tay01] Y. C. Tay and K. C. Chua, "A Capacity Analysis for the IEEE 802.11MAC Protocol," *ACM/Baltzer wireless Networks*, Vol.7, pp.159-171, 2001.

[Toba77] F. Tobagi, and L. Kleinrock. 1977. "Packet Switching in Radio Channels: Part IV-Stability Considerations and Dynamic Control in Carrier Sense Multiple Access." *IEEE Transactions on Communications*, Vol. COM-25, pp. 1103-1120, 1977.

[Yu03] D. Yu and H. Li, "Lower bound on path availability in ad hoc network," *The 57th IEEE Semiannual Vehicular Technology Conference (VTC)*, Vol. 3, pp. 1758-1762, April 2003

INDEX

A

B

C

G

H

I

J

K

L

M

T